Panama

Regis St Louis

Scott Doggett

Contents

Highlights	6	Colón Province	248
Getting Started	13	Comarca de Kuna Yala	266
Itineraries	17	Darién Province	279
The Authors	23	Directory	292
Snapshot	24	Transportation	306
History	25	Health	316
The Culture	33	World Time Zones	323
Environment	41	Language	324
Panama Outdoors	53	Glossary	332
Food & Drink	63	Behind the Scenes	335
Panama City	70	Index	343
Panamá Province	115	Legend	348
Coclé Province	139		
Herrera Province	159		
Los Santos Province	171		
Veraguas Province	184		
Chiriquí Province	198		
Bocas del Toro Province	223		

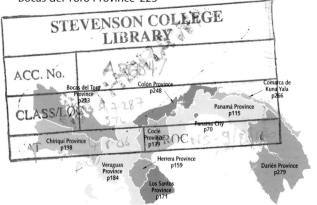

Destination Panama

Along the narrow isthmus bridging the Americas, the wildlife and terrain of two continents meld to form the striking contrasts of Panama. Ocean, forest, mountain and jungle set the stage for countless adventures.

Among Panama's 1500 islands you can go whale watching along the craggy Golfo de Chiriquí, snorkel coral reefs in the Caribbean or surf massive breaks off either coast. Island lovers revel in the white-sand beaches around the Comarca de Kuna Yala, while conservationists delight in the four species of sea turtle nesting on the country's beaches and wetlands.

Coursing along the spine of the isthmus, the mountains hold their own allure. You can kayak class-five rapids, hike through cloud forests and swim in crisp mountain streams. Adventurers trek up Volcán Barú, Panama's highest peak, for the view of both oceans at their feet.

Panama's jungles are some of the world's least explored areas. The villages of seven vibrant indigenous groups lie scattered among the country's 500 rivers and 22,000 sq km of rain forest, along with 940 bird species and 125 animal species found nowhere else in the world.

Panama's diversity doesn't end in the countryside. With immigrants from across the globe, Panama City is a 'melting pot'. You can sample French-Asian cuisine, then dance at clubs infused with salsa, merengue and Arabic-electronica. Charming highland towns, seaside fortresses and old-world festivals all lie within a day's travel. That Panama remains relatively undiscovered is just one of the country's many enticing features, and one that surely won't last forever.

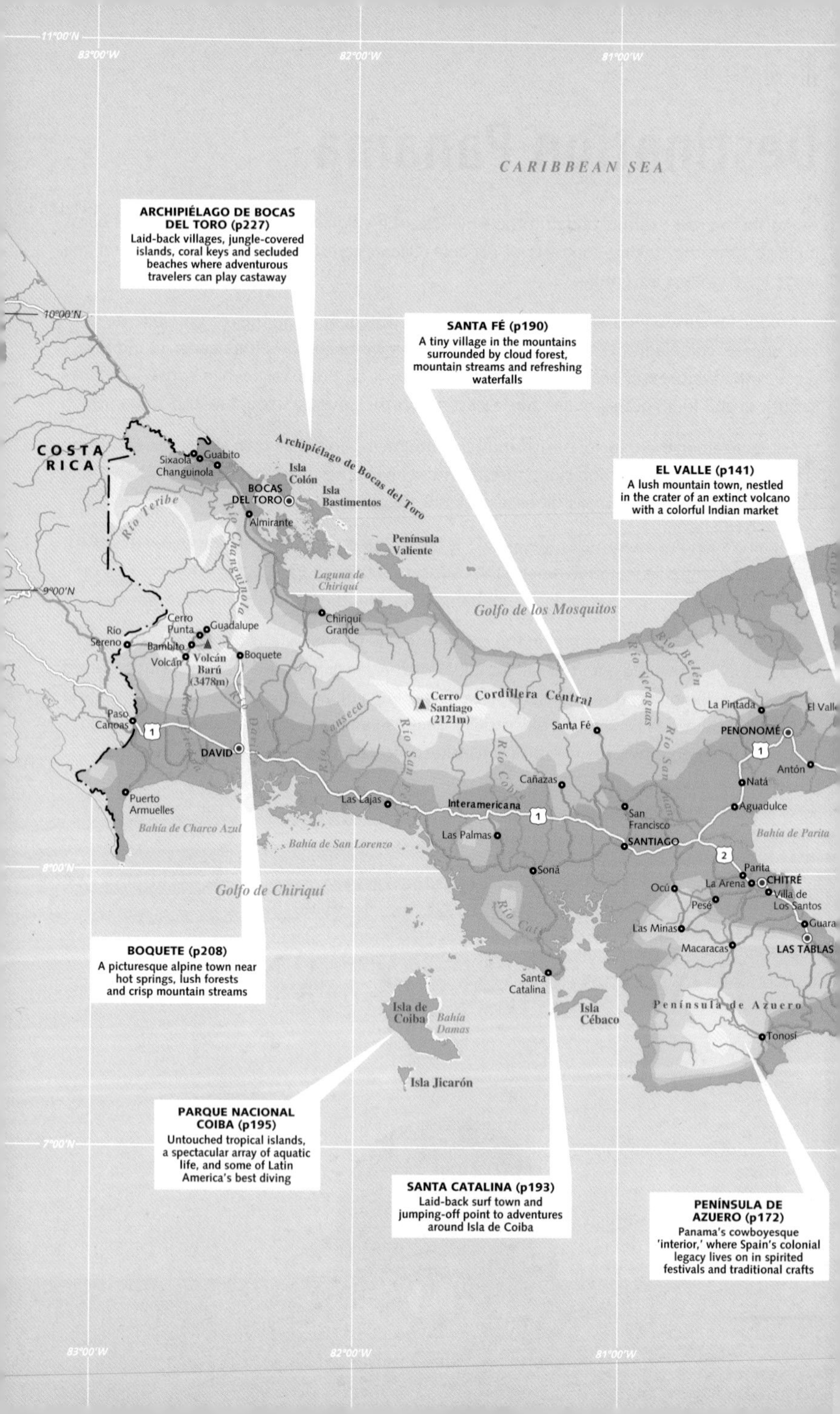

CARIBBEAN SEA

ARCHIPIÉLAGO DE BOCAS DEL TORO (p227)
Laid-back villages, jungle-covered islands, coral keys and secluded beaches where adventurous travelers can play castaway

SANTA FÉ (p190)
A tiny village in the mountains surrounded by cloud forest, mountain streams and refreshing waterfalls

EL VALLE (p141)
A lush mountain town, nestled in the crater of an extinct volcano with a colorful Indian market

COSTA RICA

Guabito
Sixaola
Changuinola
Isla Colón
BOCAS DEL TORO
Isla Bastimentos
Almirante
Río Teribe
Archipiélago de Bocas del Toro
Península Valiente
Río Changuinola
Laguna de Chiriquí
Chiriquí Grande
Golfo de los Mosquitos

Cerro Punta
Guadalupe
Río Sereno
Bambito
Volcán
Volcán Barú (3478m)
Boquete
Cerro Santiago (2121m)
Cordillera Central
Río Belén
La Pintada
El Valle
PENONOMÉ
Paso Canoas
DAVID
Río Chiriquí
Santa Fé
Río San Pablo
Río Santa María
Antón
Natá
Aguadulce
Puerto Armuelles
Las Lajas
Interamericana
Cañazas
San Francisco
SANTIAGO
Bahía de Parita
Bahía de Charco Azul
Bahía de San Lorenzo
Las Palmas
Soná
Ocú
Pesé
La Arena
CHITRÉ
Villa de Los Santos
Guara
Golfo de Chiriquí
Río Tabasará
Las Minas
Macaracas
LAS TABLAS
Santa Catalina
Isla de Coiba
Bahía Damas
Isla Cébaco
Península de Azuero
Isla Jicarón
Tonosí

BOQUETE (p208)
A picturesque alpine town near hot springs, lush forests and crisp mountain streams

PARQUE NACIONAL COIBA (p195)
Untouched tropical islands, a spectacular array of aquatic life, and some of Latin America's best diving

SANTA CATALINA (p193)
Laid-back surf town and jumping-off point to adventures around Isla de Coiba

PENÍNSULA DE AZUERO (p172)
Panama's cowboyesque 'interior,' where Spain's colonial legacy lives on in spirited festivals and traditional crafts

11°00'N
10°00'N
9°00'N
8°00'N
7°00'N
83°00'W
82°00'W
81°00'W

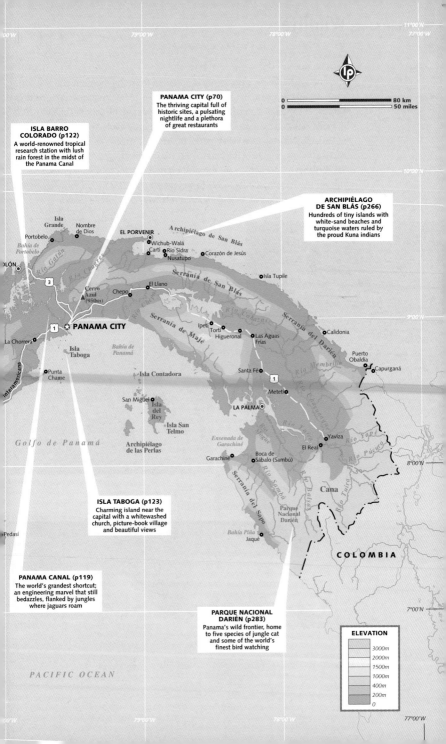

PANAMA CITY (p70)
The thriving capital full of historic sites, a pulsating nightlife and a plethora of great restaurants

ISLA BARRO COLORADO (p122)
A world-renowned tropical research station with lush rain forest in the midst of the Panama Canal

ARCHIPIÉLAGO DE SAN BLÁS (p266)
Hundreds of tiny islands with white-sand beaches and turquoise waters ruled by the proud Kuna indians

ISLA TABOGA (p123)
Charming island near the capital with a whitewashed church, picture-book village and beautiful views

PANAMA CANAL (p119)
The world's grandest shortcut; an engineering marvel that still bedazzles, flanked by jungles where jaguars roam

PARQUE NACIONAL DARIÉN (p283)
Panama's wild frontier, home to five species of jungle cat and some of the world's finest bird watching

80 km
50 miles

Isla Grande
Nombre de Dios
Portobelo
Bahía de Portobelo
Río Gatún
EL PORVENIR
Wichub-Walá
Cartí
Río Sidra
Nusatupo
Corazón de Jesús
Archipiélago de San Blás
COLÓN
Río Chagres
3
Cerro Azul (950m)
Chepo
El Llano
Serranía de San Blás
Isla Tupile
PANAMA CITY
1
Serranía de Majé
Ipetí
Tortí
Higueronal
Las Aguas Frías
Río Cabagra
Calidonia
Serranía del Darién
La Chorrera
Interamericana
Isla Taboga
Bahía de Panamá
Santa Fé
1
Río Membrillo
Puerto Obaldía
Capurganá
Punta Chame
Isla Contadora
Metetí
Río Chucunaque
San Miguel
Isla del Rey
Isla San Telmo
LA PALMA
Río Tuira
Yaviza
Río Yape
El Real
Río Pucro
Golfo de Panamá
Archipiélago de las Perlas
Ensenada de Garachiné
Boca de Sábalo (Sambú)
Cana
Río Tuira
Garachiné
Serranía del Sapo
Río Sambú
Parque Nacional Darién
Pedasí
Bahía Piña
Jaqué
COLOMBIA
PACIFIC OCEAN

ELEVATION
3000m
2000m
1500m
1000m
400m
200m
0

Panama's astounding biodiversity is apparent from the moment you leave the capital. You can go orchid-hunting near **Santa Fé** (p190), spot quetzals on **Volcán Barú** (p216) and sail alongside dolphins and whales in the **Golfo de Chiriquí** (p206). In **Punta Patiño** (p288), you'll find the majestic harpy eagle, the national symbol of Panama. Nearby, **Cana Valley** (p286) boasts four species of macaw and jungle cat. Turtle-lovers unite at **Isla Caña** (p182), **Isla Bastimentos** (p239) and **San-San Pond Sak Wetlands** (p246), which are the nesting grounds for four different species. A trip up the Panama Canal to **Isla Barro Colorado** (p122) is an opportunity to see a spectacular range of animal life on a relatively tiny jungle island.

Seek out toucans and other birds on your journey through the Darién (p280)

ALFREDO MAIQUEZ

TOM BOYDEN

Spot poison-dart frogs in the wetlands and rain forests of Panama (p41)

Discover some of Panama's 1200 orchid species (p44)

ALFREDO MA

With over 30% of its land set aside for conservation, the tiny land bridge of the Americas offers some dazzling beauty. The **Parque Nacional Coiba** (p195) is one of Panama's ecological treasures, and its rich aquatic life has earned comparisons to the Galapagos Islands. The nearby **Parque Nacional Marino Golfo de Chiriquí** (p206) has dozens of untouched islands ringed with white-sand beaches. For a view of both oceans, climb the peaks in **Parque Nacional Omar Torrijos** (p153), or wake at dawn in **Parque Nacional Volcán Barú** (p216), where you'll find Panama's highest point. For nature viewing at its finest visit the vast, remote **Parque Nacional Darién** (p283), or the **Parque Nacional Soberanía** (p121) along the Panama Canal.

Snorkel your way through the coral reefs of Parque Nacional Marino Isla Bastimentos (p242)

ALFREDO MAIQUEZ

Hike across the tranquil streams of the Pirre Mountain area in Parque Nacional Darién (p285)

ALFREDO MAIQUEZ

ALFREDO MAIQUEZ

Ascend to the summit of Volcán Barú (p216), Panama's highest point at 3478m

Among Panama's 1500 islands, there are plenty of opportunities to get in touch with your inner Robinson Crusoe. Once the sanctuary of pirates, the **Archipiélago de las Perlas** (p126) has dozens of white-sand beaches and deep blue seas. Closer in, the charming village of **Isla Taboga** (p123) may not be deserted, but its picturesque white-washed church and narrow streets once attracted the likes of Paul Gauguin. Surfers find their own sanctuary around **Playa Santa Catalina** (p193), around **Playa Venao** (p182), or on Isla Carenero, a spot near **Bocas town** (p227) where the waves can reach 4m. Bocas town itself offers a slice of laid-back Caribbean life with access to some lovely beaches on **Isla Bastimentos** (p239). Some of the Caribbean's loveliest islands are part of the **Comarca de Kuna Yala** (p266), where you'll find swaying palms and topaz seas.

EMILY RIDDELL

Doze to the sounds of waves lapping the white-sand shores of the Comarca de Kuna Yala islands (p271)

Soak up the laid-back vibe of the islands of Bocas del Toro (p241)

ALFREDO MAIQUEZ

Take a short boat ride from Panama City to picturesque Isla Taboga (p123)

ALFREDO MAI

History comes alive at **Panamá Viejo** (p83), site of Spain's capital in the New World before Henry Morgan sacked the city (p72). Nearby, fortified **Casco Viejo** (p81) still stands, and colonial ruins such as the **Iglesia y Convento de Santo Domingo** (p82) make for fine exploring among the cobbled streets. Fortresses on the Caribbean like **Fuerte San Lorenzo** (p255), **Fuerte San Jerónimo** and **Fuerte Santiago** (p258) allow you to spy over the old cannons and imagine the buccaneer ships appearing upon the horizon. Spain's legacy lives on in the traditional Península de Azuero. You'll find some of Panama's most colorful festivals in towns such as **Las Tablas** (p177), **Villa de Los Santos** (p173), **Guararé** (p176) and other parts of the peninsula.

LEE FOSTER

Spend a quiet moment in the ruins of Iglesia y Convento de Santo Domingo (p82)

ANDREW MARSHALL & LEANNE WALKER

Take yourself back to colonial times at the forts of Portobelo (p258)

Reflect upon the beauty of Casco Viejo (p81), with its mix of colonial architecture, cobblestone streets and ethnic diversity

ALFREDO MAIQUEZ

Panama's seven different indigenous groups are a vibrant part of the country's cultural diversity. The nearly 400 islands of the **Comarca de Kuna Yala** (p266) are ruled by a colorful tribe who welcome respectful visitors to their white-sand beaches and coral reefs. **Isla Tigre** (p276) is among the most traditional of the islands. A trip into the jungle-covered village of **Wetso** (p247) or **Las Delicias** (p246) allows a chance to visit the Naso. Those willing to brave the seas can visit the remote **Playa de Muerto** (p291), the only Emberá village on Darién's Pacific coast.

Learn about the rich cultural traditions of the Kuna people (p269)

ANDREW MARSHALL & LEANNE WALKER

LEE F

Shop for indigenous handicrafts as this Emberá woven basket (p2

Discover why the Emberá people (p281) stain their bodies with the juice of the *jagua* fruit

ERIC L WH

With mountains, jungles and beaches packed together along such a narrow isthmus, Panama has more than enough to satisfy mild-mannered (or die-hard) thrill seekers. The diving in and around the **Parque Nacional Coiba** (p195) has few equals, though many are lured by the possibility of finding sunken treasure off **Portobelo** (p257). You can snorkel with sea turtles off **Isla Contadora** (p128) or explore the coral near **Wreck Reef** (p275). You can kayak world-class rivers in **Chiriquí** (p214), and the next day go cave-crawling or surfing in **Isla Bastimentos** (p239). Bird watchers delight in the hundreds of species found along **Pipeline Road** (p121) and in **Cana Valley** (p286). Equestrians can head to the mountains for panoramic rides in **El Valle** (p141), **Santa Fé** (p190) or **Boquete** (p208). And sport fishermen who cast in **Bahía Piña** (p290) or the **Golfo de Chiriquí** (p206) are likely to leave Panama awestruck.

JOHN NEUBAUER

Bike or hike into Parque Nacional Soberanía (p121) for some of the world's best bird watching

Bathe in the saltwater tide pools of Las Piscinas (p157)

SCOTT DOGGETT

Throw yourself into white-water rafting on the Río Chiriquí (p210)

ALFREDO MAIQUEZ

Dinner and cocktails make a fine ending to a trip into the jungle. In the city by the sea, you can dine in historic **Casco Viejo** (p82), followed by jazz at **Restaurante Las Bóvedas** (p109) or **Take Five** (p109), then martinis at **Blu** (p106). Find your dance groove at **844** (p108) around the corner, or across town in nightlife-rich Bella Vista. Amid charming restaurants like **Bolero** (p102) and **Habibi's** (p107), you'll find nightclubs like **S6is** (p108), **Skap** (p109) and **Deep Room** (p109) – which doesn't get going until well after 2am. If you'd rather just enjoy the ocean breeze while nursing a cocktail, head to **Café Barko** (p101), **Moonlight** (p108) or **Traffic Island** (p107), all of which overlook the bay, with fine views of the city.

Indulge in ice cream on the Av Balboa beachfront (p75)

ALFREDO MAIQUEZ

ALFREDO M

Conclude your Panama adventure under the bright lights of the biggest city (p74)

Stroll through Panama City's old quarter, Casco Viejo (p81)

ALFREDO MAIQUEZ

Getting Started

Although Panama is a fine country for spontaneous adventuring, you'll get more out of your trip if you do some planning before you go. There are several destinations in particular that are quite popular, and it's unwise to show up without reservations. This is especially true in Bocas del Toro, which is currently the top destination in the country. If you plan to visit the Comarca de Kuna Yala, try to reserve your flight out to the islands as early as possible. Currently, Aeroperlas is the only carrier flying there, and demand far exceeds supply. (Hint: you can reserve online at www .aeroperlas.com.)

If you're planning on making a trip to one of Ancon's lodges in the Parque Nacional Darién (p283) – one of the world's great places to see wildlife – you'll need to book far in advance. That also holds true of Isla Barro Colorado, an outpost for the Smithsonian's Tropical Research Institute (STRI; p89).

See Climate Charts (p294) for more information.

Panama is a country for any budget. There is a plethora of budget accommodations around the country and many decent, inexpensive restaurants. At the other end of the scale, there are five-star lodges overlooking the sea and charming B&Bs tucked away in the mountains. The only thing limiting you on a trip to this vibrant country is your imagination.

WHEN TO GO

Panama's high tourist season corresponds with its Pacific-side dry season – from mid-December to mid-April. During these months, there is relatively little rain in Panama City and elsewhere south of the Continental Divide. North of the mountains, on the Caribbean side of Panama, it rains all year-round. However, it tends to rain less in February, March, September and October than it does the rest of the year.

The best time to visit Panama really depends on what you plan to do. If you intend to spend most of your time on the Pacific side, you might want to visit in December or January, when there's generally little rain and the weather is pleasant. Bear in mind, however, that hotel prices and airfares are generally higher from mid-December to mid-April. If you'll be doing any serious hiking, the dry season is the most comfortable time to do it.

DON'T LEAVE HOME WITHOUT...

- Learning at least a few basic phrases in Spanish
- A poncho for rainy days and wet boat trips
- A mosquito net for trips into the jungle – or a night's rest in well-ventilated quarters
- Decent insect repellent (30–50% DEET)
- A flashlight (torch)
- Binoculars, if you're planning to do any bird watching
- Sun protection – sunscreen, sunglasses, a hat
- Warm clothes for chilly nights in the mountains
- An ATM card or a Visa/MasterCard with (known) pin number
- An alarm clock for catching early-morning flights (to/from Comarca de Kuna Yala, for instance)
- An appetite for fresh seafood

For planning purposes, be aware that Panama's mountains can get very cold at night; if you're considering camping at altitude (in Boquete, El Valle or Cerro Punta, for example), be sure to bring warm clothing.

Some of Panama's colorful festivals draw large crowds. The Península de Azuero is very popular for its Carnaval (Mardi Gras) – the celebrations held on the four days leading up to Ash Wednesday. Panama City's Carnaval is also popular (and one of the world's largest). Hotel reservations during Carnaval are a must and should be made well in advance. Panama has a number of other festivals worth catching, especially on the Península de Azuero. See the Herrera Province (p160) and Los Santos Province (p172) chapters for details.

COSTS & MONEY

Prices in Panama tend to be slightly higher than in other parts of Central America. A hotel room that might cost only US$6 in Nicaragua or Guatemala might cost US$10 here. In Panama City you can get a very basic room for US$8 to US$12 a night; a modern room in a better area costs around US$15 to US$20. Away from Panama City, accommodations are less expensive; a modern room may cost around US$12. Die-hard shoestring travelers can still find a room almost anywhere in the country for around US$7. Good, inexpensive food isn't hard to come by. You can eat set meals *(comida corriente)* at Panamanian restaurants for about US$2.50 to US$3.50 no matter where you are in the country. Buses and taxis are also reasonable. A two-hour bus ride costs about US$3.50; a 15-minute cab ride in the capital costs around US$2. All in all, if you're traveling frugally, it's possible to get by on US$20 a day here.

Mid-range accommodations are reasonably priced in Panama and compared to other parts of Latin America, you tend to get a lot more for your money. You can eat at better restaurants for US$5 to US$10 a person and stay in decent quarters for US$20 and up a night. Add in a flight or two (Kuna Yala, Bocas), a few activities (national park fees, snorkeling, boat trips), a nightly cocktail or two and you can travel for US$50 to US$60.

You'll get more value for your money if you can split the costs with someone. At mid-range hotels, single rooms aren't much cheaper than doubles, and you'll save money on excursions – diving, snorkeling and wildlife watching – if there are more of you to share the cost.

At the top end, there are numerous ways to experience Panama's natural and cultural riches if you're looking to have a blow-out vacation. There are several excellent all-inclusive lodges in the Darién designed for both sport fishing and birding/wildlife watching. There are decadent restaurants throughout Panama, charming B&Bs in Bocas and a handful of luxury resorts scattered around the Pacific coast (the best being in the Pearl Islands).

TRAVEL LITERATURE

Anyone who doubts that Panama is still an overlooked country has only to take a look at its selection of travel literature. Unlike Guatemala, Peru or even Nicaragua, there are very few accounts of travel within the country. This is good news for would-be travel writers but bad news for anyone wanting to get something other than a historical look at the country. *Travelers' Tales Central America*, published in 2002, has only three stories about Panama, but they are interesting tales (one touches on life in Isla de Coiba's penal colony, while another provides an interesting account of shamanism and the Kuna). It's a decent book for those

TOP TENS
OUR FAVORITE FESTIVALS

The legacy of colonial Spain lives on in the many colorful celebrations that take place throughout Panama.

- Feria de las Flores y del Café, 10 days in January, Boquete (p212)
- Carnaval, four days prior to Ash Wednesday (February or March), Las Tablas (p178) and Panama City (p91)
- Feria de Azuero, late April or early May, Villa de Los Santos (p175)
- Corpus Christi, 40 days after Easter (May or June), Villa de Los Santos (p175)
- Nuestra Señora del Carmen, July 16, Isla Taboga (p124)
- Fiesta de Santa Librada and Festival of La Pollera, July 21, Las Tablas (p179)
- Festival del Manito Ocueño, third week of August, Ocú (p169)
- Feria de La Mejorana, September 23–27, Guararé (p177)
- Festival of Nogagope, October 10–12, followed by the Kuna Feria, October 13–16, Isla Tigre (p276)
- Black Christ Festival, October 21, Portobelo (p260)

BEST HISTORICAL READS

For such a small country, Panama has a voluminous history, as evidenced by the many books about the pirates, the visionaries and the demagogues who've all left their mark on the narrow isthmus.

- *Old Panama and Castilla Del Oro,* CLG Anderson
- *The Sack of Panama: Sir Henry Morgan's Adventures on the Spanish Main*, Peter Earle
- *Panama: Four Hundred Years of Dreams and Cruelty*, David Howarth
- *The Path Between the Seas: The Creation of the Panama Canal*, David McCullough
- *How Wall Street Created a Nation: JP Morgan, Teddy Roosevelt and the Panama Canal*, Ovidio Diaz Espino
- *Emperors in the Jungle: The Hidden History of the US in Panama,* John Lindsay-Poland
- *Panama: The Whole Story*, Kevin Buckley
- *The Noriega Mess: The Drugs, the Canal, and Why America Invaded*, Luis Murillo
- *America's Prisoner: The Memoirs of Manuel Noriega*, cowritten with Peter Eisner
- *A People Who Would Not Kneel: Panama, the United States, and the San Blás Kuna*, James Howe

THE FAMOUS & THE INFAMOUS

The lure of this lush country has been felt by some of history's most fascinating – and notorious – characters. Panama's most famous sojourners and residents include the following:

- Christopher Columbus, whose only attempt at founding a colony in the New World failed miserably in present-day Veraguas
- Francis Drake, who between raids on Spain's gold-filled warehouses in Nombre de Dios managed to find time to sail around the world
- Vasco Núñez de Balboa, who was the first European to lay eyes on the Pacific
- Ferdinand-Marie de Lesseps, who followed his success at Suez with the tragic failure of the Panama Canal endeavor
- Paul Gauguin, day laborer on the Panama Canal, and struggling artist
- Graham Greene, whose love affair with the country led to his invitation to attend the signing of the 1977 Carter–Torrijos treaty
- Frank Gehry, the highly acclaimed architect whose love of Panama will soon be manifest in the Biodiversity Museum
- Valentín Santana, who is king of the Teribe – the only group still governed by a monarch in all of the Americas
- Manuel Noriega, one of Florida's most infamous prisoners, who awaits his release
- Ruben Blades, a Grammy Award–winning, Harvard-educated lawyer and one-time presidential candidate (placing third)

interested in learning about other Central American countries; among the most notable contributions is Guatemalan Nobel-laureate Rigoberto Menchú's piece on indigenous village life in the highlands.

For a fictional look at one of Panama's spiciest cultures, read the work of short-story writer José María Sanchez. His work was first published in the 1940s but was re-released in an anthology titled *Cuentos de Bocas del Toro* (Tales of Bocas del Toro). Set in that beautiful province, where the author was born and raised, these fun stories – whose protagonists are driven by the sensuous, baroque excesses of the tropical jungle and sea – possess a language charged with powerful imagery.

Although *Panama*, by Carlos Ledson Miller, is a work of fiction, the story takes readers on a journey through the political turmoil of the country during the Noriega years. The author, who lived in Panama as a boy, also takes readers further back in history, giving snapshots of Balboa's arrival in 1514, Henry Morgan's sacking of Panama City in the 17th century and more recently the 1964 student riots that later led to the Torrijos–Carter treaty that returned the canal to Panamanian hands.

Getting to Know the General, by Graham Greene, is a biased but still fascinating portrait of General Omar Torrijos and the Panamanian political climate of the '60s and '70s, by one of England's finest 20th-century writers.

LONELY PLANET INDEX

Gallon (3.79L) of gas/ petrol: US$2.12

Liter of bottled water US$0.75

Bottle of Balboa beer US$1.25

Souvenir T-shirt US$8

Fresh *pipa* juice (coconut water) US$0.25

INTERNET RESOURCES

IPAT (www.ipat.gob.pa in Spanish) The official website of Panama's national tourism department.
Lanic (http://lanic.utexas.edu/la/ca/panama) Outstanding collection of links from the University of Texas Latin American Information Center.
Lonely Planet (www.lonelyplanet.com) The popular Thorn Tree bulletin board, travel news and links to other useful sites.
Panama Info (www.panamainfo.com) Panama's best Web-based travel resource, with lots of practical information as well as info on provinces and historical background.
Visit Panama (www.visitpanama.com) IPAT's English version of its website, with a small selection of practical and historical info, a few articles and links to other sites.

Itineraries

CLASSIC ROUTES

A TASTE OF PANAMA   12 Days

In **Panama City** (p70), the country's vibrant capital, start your journey at **Panamá Viejo** (p83), the ruins of Spain's first Pacific settlement. After its sacking by pirates, the settlement was moved to present-day **Casco Viejo** (p81), where you'll find colonial buildings, scenic plazas and 18th-century churches, as well as abundant nightlife amid the old quarters. The **Panama Canal** (p119) is a short trip away; you can visit the **Miraflores locks** (p119) here, sail through the canal or visit the wildlife-rich **Parque Nacional Soberanía** (p121) along its eastern shore. A train ride along the historic **Panama Railway** (p254) will take you along the canal to Colón. From there visit the forts guarding the bay in **Portobelo** (p257). Farther east lie the windswept beaches of **Isla Grande** (p261). Head back to Panama City for a quick flight out to **Bocas del Toro** (p223), where you can snorkel coral reefs, hike through rain forest and surf great breaks. Fly back to the capital then to the **Comarca de Kuna Yala** (p266), the indigenous-ruled region with hundreds of gorgeous islands.

At the end of your trip, return to Panama City for a bit of urban decadence in open-air **restaurants** (p98) and salsa-infused **nightclubs** (p108).

This well-traveled route, covering some 1200km including return flights, will take you to old Spanish forts, charming Caribbean towns and pristine, palm-covered islands.

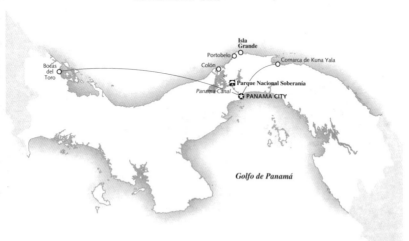

CARIBBEAN SEA

Isla Grande
Portobelo
Colón
Comarca de Kuna Yala
Bocas del Toro
Parque Nacional Soberanía
Panama Canal
PANAMA CITY

Golfo de Panamá

PACIFIC OCEAN

DRIVING THE INTERAMERICANA

Two Weeks

From Panama City, head along the Interamericana to the string of beaches along the Pacific coast. **Playa El Palmar** (p138) and **Playa Río Mar** (p138) get their share of surfers. A few kilometers west is the turnoff for **El Valle** (p141), which will lead you high up to a picturesque town surrounded by green peaks. The cool climate is ideal for horseback riding, cycling and hiking.

Forest-covered mountains, untouched beaches and towns alive with Spanish folklore set the stage for this meandering 1294km round-trip along the Interamericana, with detours along the way.

Continuing along the Interamericana, you'll reach **Santa Clara** (p147), with lovely beaches and charming places to stay. You can breeze through **Penonomé** (p149), known for its Panama hats, and **Natá** (p154) famous for its lovely cathedral. Visitors wanting a taste of the obscure can soak in the tidal pools of **Aguadulce** (p155). As you drive west, detour at Divisa to the picturesque town of **Villa de Los Santos** (p173), and check to see if any festivals (p175) are occurring on the Península de Azuero. These fantastic, colorful events shouldn't be missed. Back on the Interamericana, take the turnoff to **Santa Fé** (p190), a tiny mountain town amid sparkling rivers, green mountains and gorgeous waterfalls. On the way back is **San Francisco** (p189), a small village with a stunning 18th-century church.

The next stop is the beach of **Las Lajas** (p207). Get your fill of sun here, before heading via **David** (p202) into the crisp mountain town of **Boquete** (p208), one of Panama's top destinations. From here you can hike into nearby forests, lounge in the **Caldera hot springs** (p205) and fill up on mountain-grown coffee. Nearby lies the less-visited but equally picturesque town of **Cerro Punta** (p219); you'll also need to go via David to get here.

ROADS LESS TRAVELED

EXPLORING INDIGENOUS CULTURES   Three Weeks

Panama's seven indigenous groups are scattered throughout the country. From Panama City, head to **Changuinola** (p244), a transit point for nearby Naso (Teribe) villages. Then take a boat from El Silencio to **Wetso** (p247), a traditional village amid lush jungle. Near the Costa Rican border is **Las Delicias** (p246), another Naso village, set amid waterfalls, rivers and rain forest.

To visit Ngöbe-Buglé communities head out to Bastimentos. **Bahía Honda** (p239) lies near rain forest, caves and lovely swimming spots on Bastimentos; on the other side of the island is the Ngöbe-Buglé village of **Salt Creek** (p239). From Bocas, you can also arrange a boat trip out to **Península Valiente** (p61), home of white-sand beaches and several Ngöbe-Buglé villages.

Fly back to Panama City, then to the idyllic islands of the **Comarca de Kuna Yala** (p266) which are governed by one of the most autonomous tribes in the Americas. To see traditional Kuna villages, visit **Río Azúcar** (p275), **Isla Tigre** (p276) or **Mulatupo Sasardí** (p278).

Eastern Panama Province and the Darién are the best places to see Emberá and Wounaan villages. Take a bus from the capital to **Ipetí** (p133), where you'll find an Emberá village and a traditional Kuna village a few kilometers away. Dine on fresh seafood and take guided walks through the jungle at **Playa de Muerto** (p291), the only Emberá village on the Pacific coast. A trip up the **Río Sambú** (p289), best arranged in La Palma, provides opportunities to visit remote Emberá tribes.

This three-segment trip visits villages deep in rain forest or along island shores, and necessarily involves seeing some of the country's dazzling wildlife.

BIG JOURNEYS ACROSS THE ISTHMUS   Three Weeks

These various journeys visit parts of Panama's landscape that haven't changed much since Balboa and Bastidas first laid eyes on the Caribbean coast.

If you'd like to do some exploring along untraveled terrain, Panama has plenty of options. East of Panama City, you can turn off on a rutted road that leads into the **Nusagandi** (p132), an area inside the Área Silvestre de Narganá, or take any El Llano–bound bus from Panama City. The road eventually becomes impassable for any sort of vehicle, but you can hike along this road and eventually reach **Cartí** (p273) in the Comarca de Kuna Yala. Guides can be arranged in **Panama City** (p70).

In Veraguas Province, in **Santa Fé** (p190), reached by bus from Santiago, you can cross the Continental Divide to the Caribbean, ending up on empty beaches near the small village of Calovébora. Guides can be hired at the Hotel Santa Fé.

In Chiriquí Province, visitors can make a similar crossing, departing from Boquete, crossing over the Continental Divide, past rivers and through indigenous communities. After four days of hiking, you reach the coastal town of Punta Róbalo, an hour's drive from Almirante. See **Boquete** (p208) for guides.

Those who'd rather cross the isthmus on Panama's famous **canal** (p119) can do so by ship or by working their way through as a line handler.

TAILORED TRIPS

WORLD HERITAGE SITES

Panama's four Unesco World Heritage sites provide visitors with a chance to discover the well-preserved past, the country's rich wildlife and the indigenous cultures inside its borders.

The 576,000-hectare **Parque Nacional Darién** (p283) is Panama's crown jewel, with lush primary rain forest, an astounding variety of animal life and many indigenous villages scattered through remote jungle. Inside the park, **Cana Valley** (p286), with its hundreds of bird species, is a favorite of birders. A private lodge there is a fine base for seeing the wildlife. Hardy travelers can hike into **Pirre Station** (p285), where there's a rustic lodge and the park's best hiking trails.

Panama City has its own attractions, in the form of the many historical buildings of **Casco Viejo** (p81). The manicured **Plaza de la Independencia** (p83) is where Panamanian independence was declared. Nearby are striking churches like the **Iglesia de San Francisco** (p82) and the seaside overlook of **Paseo las Bóvedas** (p81). On the other side of town lie the ruins of **Panamá Viejo** (p83), the first European settlement on the Pacific.

Travel north of Panama City to reach the forts along the Caribbean. **Fuerte San Lorenzo** (p255) once guarded the Río Chagres. Further east, near Portobelo stand the equally impressive fortifications of **Fuerte San Jerónimo** (p259) and **Fuerte Santiago** (p259).

In the western part of the country, it's back into the rain forest at **Parque Internacional La Amistad** (p247), a national park shared with Costa Rica. Its lovely trails access waterfalls, lookouts and plenty of wildlife.

WILDLIFE WATCHING

Close to downtown Panama City, the **Parque Natural Metropolitano** (p89) is a good place to get a taste of the country's wildlife. For birding head east to the elfin forest on **Cerro Azul** (p122), then move on to the lush **Parque Nacional Soberanía** (p121). Nearby is the Smithsonian's Tropical Research Station on fauna-rich **Isla Barro Colorado** (p122). Little-visited **Parque Nacional Omar Torrijos** (p153) has amazing wildlife and excellent trails.

Turtle lovers shouldn't miss nesting season on **Isla de Cañas** (p182) or **Isla Iguana** (p181). **Parque Nacional Coiba** (p195) has macaws on its jungle-shrouded island, and whales and dolphins swimming along its shores. The reefs and islands in the **Golfo de Chiriquí** (p206) are also teeming with wildlife. In the mountains, **Parque Internacional La Amistad** (p247) and **Volcán Barú** (p216) have fine trails for seeking quetzals and *conejo pintado*. On the Caribbean coast, four species of turtle come to the **San-San Pond Sak Wetlands** (p246). The marine park of **Isla Bastimentos** (p239) is another great spot to see turtles and a wide variety of other marine life. Trips to **Punta Patiño** (p288) and **Parque Nacional Darién** (p283) will leave you awestruck.

ISLAND & BEACH HOPPING

A short flight from Panama City, **Isla Contadora** (p128) has a dozen fine beaches – and the country's only nude one. The charming island of **Isla Taboga** (p123) is closer in, with beaches, hiking trails and fine views. The windswept **Isla Grande** (p261) is a favorite of weekending urbanites, while the hundreds of islands of the **Comarca de Kuna Yala** (p266) are among Panama's loveliest – with white sands, palm trees and many coral reefs. Just west of the capital, lie half a dozen beaches – **El Palmar** (p138), **Río Mar** (p138), **Playa Coronado** (p137), **Santa Clara** (p147) and **Farallón** (p148). Drop into **Los Santos** (p171) for fine, untouched beaches on Isla Iguana and the picturesque surfing beach of **Playa Venao** (p182). Even better surf – and fantastic diving – is found in **Playa Santa Catalina** (p193). Local fishermen there can take you to all the hidden spots around **Isla de Coiba** (p195). Head to **Boca Brava** (p206) for a pure island getaway. Around Bocas are dozens of favorites: **Boca del Drago** (p231), **Isla Carenero** (p238), **Isla Solarte** (p241) and the gorgeous beaches of **Bastimentos** (p239).

CARIBBEAN SEA

Bocas del Toro

Isla Grande

Comarca de Kuna Yala

Isla Taboga

Pacific Beaches

Isla Contadora

Boca Brava

Playa Santa Catalina

Los Santos Province

Isla de Coiba

Playa Venao

PACIFIC OCEAN

The Authors

REGIS ST. LOUIS

Regis first explored Panama's islands, indigenous villages and lush forests on a six-month overland journey from Guatemala to the Darién. The country's biodiversity and cultural riches had a profound impact on him, and since then he's returned frequently. His travels constantly lead him in search of new haunts and undiscovered gems. Regis is also fascinated by Panama's rich and often savage history, and he has studied extensively the buccaneer conquests, the ill-fated colonies and the harrowing tales surrounding the world's greatest engineering feat, the Panama Canal. He lives in New York City.

My Favorite Trip

After flying into the capital, I like to spend a day or two in the Casco Viejo district (p81), soaking up the rhythms of this vibrant country. The lure of Comarca de Kuna Yala (p266) pulls me away from the city's distractions, and soon I'm out on the islands, absorbing the natural and cultural beauty of this indigenous community. Next I head to the jungle-covered mountains of Parque Nacional Omar Torrijos (p153), or perhaps embark on a trip to the waterfalls and mountain streams around Santa Fé (p190). The small village of Santa Catalina (p193) is the last stop. There I can find local fishermen to take me to secret spots in the gorgeous Parque Nacional Coiba (p195).

CONTRIBUTING AUTHOR

Dr David Goldberg MD wrote the Health chapter (p316). David completed his training in internal medicine and infectious diseases at Columbia-Presbyterian Medical Center in New York City, where he has also served as voluntary faculty. He is an infectious diseases specialist in Scarsdale, New York state, and the editor-in-chief of the website www.mdtravelhealth.com.

Snapshot

As Panama commemorated the 100-year anniversary of its independence in 2003, the country had a great deal on which to reflect. With the handover of the Panama Canal in 1999 and the closure of American military bases in the country, Panama was finally in charge of its own destiny. Manuel Noriega, who had harmed the country in many ways, was absent from the ceremonies. In his place was Mireya Moscoso, the country's first female president, who came to power in a fair election – a good sign for a country with a redoubtable history of corruption.

Unfortunately, the centennial was not a time for unbridled celebration. Although Panama proved successful at operating the canal safely and efficiently, it inherited an operation in need of costly improvements. The American pullout had happened rapidly – much too rapidly, cite critics – and the loss of US revenue had left a hole in the economy. The budget deficit was growing, unemployment was high, and social security verged on bankruptcy. Guerrilla incursions near the Colombian border were still occurring, and with greater frequency, though they remained little acknowledged by the government. In fact, many Panamanians blamed Moscoso for the country's ills and eagerly anticipated the 2004 elections.

As the elections neared, two candidates with deep connections to the past – Guillermo Endara and Martín Torrijos – brought the last three decades into focus. Endara had been elected president in 1989, but he had been pulled from power by Noriega. Many Panamanians still recall witnessing Endara getting beaten by Noriega's thugs on live television. After the American invasion that toppled Noriega, Endara assumed power, but he proved to be a lukewarm president. Torrijos is the son of former General Omar Torrijos, who ruled the country prior to Noriega. Although Torrijos had come to power when the Guardia Nacional deposed the elected president Arnulfo Arias, he had been a popular leader – particularly after signing the 1977 treaty putting the canal in Panamanian control. Martin Torrijos managed to connect to the popularity of his father, and he won the election, assuming power on September 1, 2004.

Panamanian politicians have a knack for confounding expectations, and as Martín Torrijos enters his presidency it's difficult to know what's in store for the country. His pro-business attitude pleases many investors, while his connection to his father (who was a socially minded leader), gives hope that he will carry out campaign promises to combat poverty, unemployment and even corruption – among Panama's biggest ills.

A major issue that didn't receive any lip service in the election was the destruction of the Darién. While the media focuses on Miss Universe pageants, the government continues to turn a blind eye to greedy loggers as they destroy one of the earth's most spectacular natural habitats.

The fate of tourism is another hot topic in Panama. Some approach Panama with dollar signs in their eyes and envision cruise-ship ports, giant resorts and American retirement communities. Others, notably nonprofit organizations, see Panama's tourism developing slowly and sustainably – and indeed, today there are many opportunities for visitors to put their money directly into struggling indigenous communities.

Meanwhile real growth is happening in the economy. With the increase of trade and the continued flow of foreign investment, Panama's future is looking brighter than ever – although the fate of its natural wonders is far from certain.

History

PRE-COLUMBIAN HISTORY

Archaeological evidence shows that people have been living in Panama for at least 11,000 years, and that agriculture arose here as early as 1500 BC. Panama's first peoples lived beside the Pacific Ocean and fished in mangrove swamps and estuaries, just as many of the country's Indians do today. Fishing was still the main occupation of the Indians in 1500 BC, and their ancient techniques have continued to be used to the present day. Given the tremendous importance that fish have had in the lives of Isthmians, it seems only fitting that the country's name means 'abundance of fish' in an Indian language.

Archaeologists divide pre-Columbian Panama into three distinct cultural zones – western, central and eastern. None of these zones was culturally isolated; there is evidence of trade taking place with cultures as far south as Peru and as far north as Mexico. In addition to trade and fishing, Panama's early societies engaged in extensive agriculture and hunting.

In western Panama on the slopes of the Barú volcano, Barriles is an important archaeological center where finds have included unusual life-size stone statues of human figures, as well as *metates* – stone platforms that were used for grinding corn. Archaeologists estimate that the early civilization in Barriles was established around the 4th or 5th century BC when settlers arrived from the west (now Costa Rica). This culture came to an abrupt end when Volcán Barú erupted violently in the 5th century AD. Later, the region was inhabited by two different groups whose archaeological remnants include a great variety of distinctive types of pottery.

Other important archaeological zones include Sitio Conte in Coclé, and Parque Arqueológico del Caño, Cerro Juan Díaz and Parque Nacional Sarigua all on the Península de Azuero.

Not as much is known about the early peoples of the eastern region of Panama, because the region hasn't been extensively studied. Most knowledge of the area's history and the hierarchical social structure of its people has been gleaned from accounts by the first Spanish explorers, who arrived in the Darién region during the 16th century.

Gold objects appeared in Panama suddenly, with a sophisticated and completely developed technology. Metallurgy was practiced in Peru as early as the 2nd century BC; by the 1st century AD it had arrived in Panama.

Colombia, Panamá and Costa Rica all became metallurgic provinces, and objects of gold and other metals were exchanged all the way from Mesoamerica to the Andes. Gold was made into ornaments and animal, human and other figures, and it was also used for ceremonial purposes; it probably did not connote wealth to the Indians in the same way that it did to the Spaniards.

Old Panama and Castilla Del Oro, by CLG Anderson, is a narrative history of the discovery, conquest and settlement of Panama by the Spaniards. This hard-to-find but impressive tome also reports on the search for a strait through to the New World and early efforts to build a canal.

SPANISH COLONIZATION

When Spaniards first arrived on the isthmus of Panama in the early 16th century, they found it inhabited by various indigenous peoples. The population may have been as large then as it is now, but it was rapidly decimated

TIMELINE	11,000 BC or earlier	1st Century BC
	First human occupation in Panama	Metallurgy arrives in Panama; trading of gold and other goods occurs from Mesoamerica to the Andes

by European diseases and Spanish swords. Several dozen Indian tribes lived in the region at the time of the Spaniards' arrival, but only seven of these exist today: the Kuna, the Ngöbe-Buglé, the Emberá, the Wounaan, the Bokatá, the Bribri and the Naso (also known as the Teribe).

The first Europeans in the area were led by the Spanish explorer Rodrigo de Bastidas, who sailed along Panama's Caribbean coast in 1501 with Vasco Núñez de Balboa and Juan de la Cosa as his first mates. The following year, Christopher Columbus sailed along the coast on his fourth and final New World voyage. His attempt to establish a colony at the mouth of the Río Belén in 1503 ended when he fled an imminent Indian attack.

In 1510 Diego de Nicuesa, attempting to do what Columbus couldn't, was also driven by Indians and hunger from the Río Belén. Leading a small fleet with 280 starving men aboard, the weary explorer looked upon a protected bay 23km east of what is now Portobelo and exclaimed: '¡Paremos aqui, en nombre de Dios!' ('Let us stop here, in the name of God!'). Thus was named the town of Nombre de Dios, one of the first Spanish settlements in the continental New World. It was soon abandoned, then was resettled in 1519. For many decades thereafter, the town was the main Caribbean port for commerce along the isthmus, as well as the beginning of the trail leading to the city of Panamá on the Pacific side. Nombre de Dios was finally abandoned in 1597 by order of King Félipe II of Spain.

When Balboa heard stories from Indians about a large sea and a wealthy, gold-producing civilization across the mountains of the isthmus – almost certainly referring to the Inca empire of Peru – he scaled the mountains and on September 26, 1513 became the first European to set eyes upon the Pacific Ocean, claiming it and the lands it touched for the king of Spain. He named the ocean the Mar del Sur (South Sea) because he had crossed Panama from north to south. The Caribbean was likewise known as the Mar del Norte (North Sea) for many years.

In 1519 a cruel and vindictive man named Pedro Arias de Ávila (or Pedrarias, as many of his contemporaries called him) founded the city of Panamá on the Pacific side, near where Panama City stands today. The governor is remembered for ordering the beheading of Balboa in 1517 on a trumped-up charge of treason; he's also remembered for ordering murderous attacks against Indians, whom he roasted alive or fed to dogs when opportunity permitted. Panamá became an important Spanish settlement, commercial center and base for further explorations, including the conquest of Peru and some expeditions north into Central America. The ruins of this old settlement, now known as Panamá Viejo (p83), can still be seen today.

Goods from Panamá and Peru were transported across the isthmus by foot to the town of Venta de Cruces, and then by boat from there to Nombre de Dios via the Río Chagres. This route was called the Sendero Las Cruces (Las Cruces Trail, also known as the Camino de Cruces), vestiges of which can still be found. Goods moved between the two ports until late in the 16th century, when Nombre de Dios was destroyed by the English pirate Sir Francis Drake. The small nearby bay of Portobelo then became the chief Caribbean connection. The Sendero Las Cruces continued to be used until the mid-19th century, when the Panama Railroad was completed.

Panama: Four Hundred Years of Dreams and Cruelty, by David A Howarth, is a readable history of the isthmus from Balboa's 1513 exploration through 1964. The best sections are those dealing with the conquistadors and buccaneers.

DID YOU KNOW?

Among those who made the famous crossing of the isthmus were 1000 Indian slaves and 190 Spaniards, including Francisco Pizarro, who later conquered Peru.

1501	1519
Spanish explorers Rodrigo de Bastidas and Vasco Núñez de Balboa sail along Panama's Caribbean coast	Pedrarias founds the city of Panama; it becomes a major transit point for gold plundered from Peru and taken to Spain

Also used to transport goods across the isthmus during the early Spanish days was the Camino Real (King's Highway), a series of trails that linked Panamá with Nombre de Dios and later Portobelo. Indeed, from the late 16th century until the arrival of the Americans in 1904, the Camino Real was the only semblance of a roadway across the isthmus. Peruvian gold and other natural products were brought to the two ports along the Camino Real by mule train from Panamá.

The Sack of Panamá: Sir Henry Morgan's Adventures on the Spanish Main, by Peter Earle, is a good read for those wanting an account of the Welsh pirate's looting of Panamá in 1671.

All this wealth concentrated in one small bay naturally attracted English, French, Dutch and other pirates who were plying the Caribbean at the time. The Spaniards built large stone fortresses to try to ward off attack; the ones at Portobelo and Fuerte San Lorenzo, at the mouth of the Río Chagres, can still be visited today.

These fortifications weren't enough, however. In 1671 the Welsh buccaneer Sir Henry Morgan overpowered Fuerte San Lorenzo, sailed up the Río Chagres and crossed the isthmus. His forces sacked the city of Panamá, made off with its entire treasure and arrived back on the Caribbean coast with 200 mules loaded with loot. The city burned down during the raid, but no one knows for certain whether it was his men or fleeing Spaniards who put the torch to it. The town was rebuilt a few years later on a cape several kilometers west of its original site, on the spot where the Casco Viejo (p81) district of Panama City is today.

DID YOU KNOW?

Scotland attempted to establish a colony on a rain-soaked peninsula in present-day Kuna Yala. This ended in horrendous tragedy as starvation and disease wiped out the settlers, and today New Edinburgh lies buried in the jungle.

In 1739 Portobelo was destroyed by British Admiral Edward Vernon, finally forcing Spain to abandon the Panamanian crossing in favor of sailing the long way around Cape Horn to the western coast of South America. Panama declined in importance and eventually became part of the viceroyalty of Nueva Andalucía, later called Nueva Granada and thereafter Colombia.

INDEPENDENCE

In 1821 Colombia, including Panama, gained its independence from Spanish rule. Panama joined Gran Colombia, which included Bolivia, Colombia, Ecuador, Peru and Venezuela, forming the united Latin American nation that had long been the dream of Simón Bolívar. Later Gran Colombia split up, but Panama remained a province of Colombia.

SALVAGING SUNKEN GALLEONS

During the period of colonization between the 16th and 18th centuries, Spanish galleons left home carrying goods to the colonies and returned loaded with gold and silver mined in Colombia, Peru and Mexico. Many of these ships sank in the Caribbean Sea, overcome by pirates or hurricanes. During these years, literally thousands of ships – not only Spanish but also English, French, Dutch, pirate and African slave ships – foundered in the green-blue waters of the Caribbean.

The frequency of shipwrecks spurred the Spaniards to organize operations to recover sunken cargo. By the 17th century, Spain maintained salvage flotillas in the ports of Portobelo, Havana and Veracruz. These fleets awaited news of shipwrecks and then proceeded immediately to the wreck sites, where the Spaniards used Caribbean and Bahamian divers, and later African slaves, to scour sunken vessels and the seafloor around them. On many occasions great storms wiped out entire fleets, resulting in a tremendous loss of lives and cargo.

1671	1739
Henry Morgan overpowers Fuerte San Lorenzo, then sacks the city of Panamá; a new walled city is later built a few kilometers away	Following numerous pirate attacks, Spain abandons the transisthmian route to sail around South America

PANAMA RAILROAD

From the moment that the world's major powers learned that the isthmus of Panama was the narrowest point between the Atlantic and Pacific Oceans, they focused their attention on the region.

In 1846 Colombia signed a treaty permitting the USA to construct a railway across the isthmus. The treaty guaranteed the USA free transit across the isthmus and the right to protect the railway with military force. This was a time of great political turbulence; during the five-year construction period (from 1850 to 1855), Panama had 20 governors.

The California gold rush of 1848, which resulted in thousands of people traveling from the east coast of the USA to the west coast via Panama (to avoid hostile Indians living in the central states), helped to make the railway a profitable venture, and it also spurred efforts to construct an interoceanic canal across Central America.

PANAMA CANAL & THE FRENCH

The idea of a canal across the isthmus was first broached in 1524, when King Charles V of Spain ordered that a survey be undertaken to determine the feasibility of constructing such a waterway. In 1878 the Colombian government awarded a contract to build a canal to the French, and the effort was led by Ferdinand de Lesseps, who was then basking in his success as the contractor-builder of the Suez Canal.

The Panama Railroad website www.trainweb.org/panama contains photographs, historical information and fascinating travelogues – one dated from 1868, written by Mark Twain.

Lesseps' company began work in 1881. Lesseps was determined to build a sea-level canal alongside the interoceanic railway, but the project proved more difficult than anyone had expected. Yellow fever and malaria killed some 22,000 workers, there were insurmountable construction problems and financial mismanagement drove the company bankrupt by 1889.

One of Lesseps' chief engineers, Philippe Bunau-Varilla, formed a new canal company, but at the same time the USA was planning its own canal somewhere through Central America. Nicaragua seemed the most likely site, but taking over the canal in Panama was also a possibility. The French, unable to complete the canal, finally agreed to sell the concession to the USA. In 1903 Bunau-Varilla asked the Colombian government for permission to conclude the sale. Colombia refused.

PANAMA BECOMES A NATION

Revolutionary sentiments had been brewing in Panama for many years, but repeated attempts to break away from Colombia had met with no success. In 1903 a civil war in Colombia created fresh discontent as Panamanians were drafted to fight and their property was confiscated by the Colombian government for the war effort.

The Path Between the Seas: The Creation of the Panama Canal, by historian David McCullough, is an excellent book that gives a vivid portrayal of the triumphs and horrors surrounding the canal's creation. The 700-page tome reads like a suspense novel.

When the Colombian government refused to allow the transfer of the canal treaty to the USA, it not only thwarted US and French interests but those of Panama too. Bunau-Varilla, who had a lot to gain financially if the sale went through, approached the US government to back Panama if it declared its independence from Colombia.

A revolutionary junta declared Panama independent on November 3, 1903, with the support of the USA, which immediately recognized the new government. Colombia sent troops by sea to try to regain control of the province, but US battleships prevented them from reaching land.

1821	1855
Simón Bolívar leads the northern swath of South America to independence from Spain; Panama becomes part of Gran Colombia	Thousands of laborers die during the US construction of a railway across the isthmus

THE FIRST CANAL TREATY

Bunau-Varilla, who became Panamanian ambassador to the USA, moved quickly to preempt the arrival in Washington, DC, of an official delegation from Panama that was slated to negotiate the terms of the canal treaty. On November 18, before the delegation arrived, he signed the Hay-Bunau-Varilla Treaty with US Secretary of State John Hay. It gave the USA far more than had been offered in the original treaty that was rejected by the Colombian government. The treaty's 26 articles awarded the USA 'sovereign rights in perpetuity over the Canal Zone,' an area extending 8km on either side of the canal, and a broad right of intervention in Panamanian affairs. The treaty was ratified over the Panamanian delegation's protests.

The treaty led to friction between the USA and Panama for decades, partly because it was overly favorable to the USA at the expense of Panama and partly due to lingering questions about its legality. Colombia did not recognize Panama as a legitimately separate nation until 1921, when the USA paid Colombia US$25 million in 'compensation.'

For all things canal-related visit www.pancanal.com, with historical information, photographs and even webcams of the canal in action.

THE USA BUILDS THE CANAL

Construction began again on the canal in 1904. The project, one of the greatest engineering feats in the world, was completed despite disease, landslides and many other difficulties. More than 75,000 workers took part in its construction, which took 10 years. Canal heroes included Colonel William Crawford Gorgas, who managed a massive campaign to eliminate yellow fever and malaria, and two chief engineers, John F Stevens and Colonel George Washington Goethals. The first ship sailed through the canal on August 15, 1914. See Panama Province (p117) for more details on the canal.

RISE OF THE MILITARY

The US military intervened repeatedly in Panama's political affairs until 1936, when the Hay-Bunau-Varilla Treaty was replaced by the Hull-Alfaro Treaty. The USA relinquished its rights to use its troops outside the Canal Zone and to seize land for canal purposes, and the annual sum paid to Panama for use of the Canal Zone was increased.

During the next three decades, there was a growing disenchantment with American involvement in Panamanian affairs and a desire for sovereignty over the canal. The conflict reached boiling point in 1964 during a student protest that left 27 Panamanians dead and 500 injured. (Now commemorated as Día de Los Mártires, National Martyrs Day.)

As US influence waned, the Panamanian army grew more powerful. In 1968 the Guardia Nacional deposed the elected president and took control of the government; the constitution was suspended, the national assembly was dissolved and the press censored. The Guardia's General Omar Torrijos Herrera emerged as the new leader.

Torrijos conducted public-works programs on a grand scale, including a massive modernization of Panama City, which won him the support of much of the populace but also plunged Panama into huge debt.

You'll find the best collection of historical Panama canal photographs at www.canalmuseum.com The website also has background information about the country and links to many related sites.

How Wall Street Created a Nation: JP Morgan, Teddy Roosevelt and the Panama Canal, by Ovidio Diaz Espino, probes deeply into the dark alliances and backroom deals that culminated in the canal's construction.

1977 Canal Treaty

US dominion over the Canal Zone, and the canal itself, were continuing sources of conflict between Panama and the USA. After years of negotiation

1878	1903
The French are granted the rights to build a canal; malaria and yellow fever claim 22,000 lives before the French declare bankruptcy	With US backing, Panama declares independence; the US is granted sovereign rights over the proposed canal zone

The recently published *Emperors in the Jungle*, by John Lindsay-Poland, is a revealing look at US military involvement in Panama over the past century, with topics ranging from chemical weapons testing to the 1989 invasion.

that foundered in a series of stalemates, a new treaty was finally accepted by both sides in 1977. It was signed by Torrijos and US President Jimmy Carter.

The treaty provided that US control of the canal would be phased out, with Panama assuming ownership and control of the canal on December 31, 1999. It also provided for the phasing out of US military bases in Panama. In 1978 the US Senate attached extenuating conditions that grant the USA the right of limited intervention and rights to defend the canal beyond the 1999 date. The treaty finally went into effect on October 1, 1979. A separate treaty ensures that the canal shall remain open and neutral for all nations, during both peace and war.

MANUEL NORIEGA

Torrijos was killed in a plane crash in 1981. In September 1983, after a brief period of leadership by Colonel Rubén Darío Paredes, Colonel Manuel Antonio Noriega took control of the Guardia Nacional and then of the country itself.

Noriega, a former head of Panama's secret police and a former CIA operative, quickly began to consolidate his power. He enlarged the Guardia Nacional, significantly expanded its authority and renamed it the Panama Defense Forces. He also closed down all media that criticized him, and he created a paramilitary 'Dignity Battalion' in every city, town and village, its members armed and ready to inform on any of their neighbors showing less than complete loyalty to the Noriega regime.

DID YOU KNOW?

General Omar Torrijos was hugely popular after negotiating the treaty that would turn the canal over to Panamanian control. He did have enemies, however, and rumors abound that his death in a plane crash was no accident.

In early 1987 Noriega became the center of an international scandal. He was publicly accused of involvement in drug trafficking with Colombian drug cartels, murdering his opponents and rigging elections. Many Panamanians demanded Noriega's dismissal, protesting with general strikes and street demonstrations that resulted in violent clashes with the Panama Defense Forces.

Relations with the USA went from bad to worse. By February 1988 the USA had indicted Noriega for drug trafficking and involvement in organized crime. In the same month president Eric Arturo Delvalle attempted to dismiss Noriega, but Noriega still held the reins of power, and Delvalle ended up fleeing Panama after being deposed himself. Noriega appointed a substitute president.

Noriega's regime became an international embarrassment. In March 1988 the USA imposed economic sanctions against Panama, ending a preferential trade agreement, freezing Panamanian assets in US banks and refusing to pay canal fees. A few days after the sanctions were imposed, there was an unsuccessful military coup. Noriega responded by stepping up violent repression of his critics, including the increasing numbers of antigovernment demonstrators.

The US Army's School of the Americas, previously based in Panama, trained some of the worst human rights abusers in Latin America – including Manuel Noriega. For information on the school's history visit www.soaw.org.

Presidential elections were held once again in May 1989. When Noriega's candidate failed to win, Noriega declared the election null and void. Meanwhile, Guillermo Endara, the winning candidate, and his two vice-presidential running mates were badly beaten by some of Noriega's thugs; the bloody scene was captured by a TV crew and its broadcast infuriated the nation. An attempted coup in October 1989 was followed by even more repressive measures.

1914	1968
The canal is completed, owing to the efforts of 75,000 laborers – many thousands of whom died during the construction	The Panamanian army overthrows president-elect Arnulfo Arias after 11 days in office; General Omar Torrijos becomes Panama's leader

On December 15, 1989, Noriega's legislature declared him president. At the same time Noriega announced that Panama was at war with the USA. The following day, an unarmed US marine dressed in civilian clothes was killed by Panamanian soldiers.

OPERATION JUST CAUSE

US reaction was swift and unrelenting. In the first hour of December 20, 1989, Panama City was attacked by aircraft, tanks and 26,000 US troops in a mission they called 'Operation Just Cause.' US President George Bush Sr said the invasion had four objectives: to protect US lives, to maintain the security of the Panama Canal, to restore democracy to Panama and to capture Noriega and bring him to justice.

Shortly before the invasion, there had been an attempt to kidnap Noriega, but he had gone into hiding. On Christmas Day, the fifth day of the invasion, he went to the Vatican nuncio to request asylum. He remained in the Vatican embassy for 10 days. Outside, US soldiers reinforced diplomatic pressure on the Vatican to expel him by setting up loudspeakers in front of the embassy and blaring rock music (Van Halen and Metallica among the selections) to unnerve those inside. Meanwhile, angry crowds near the blocked-off embassy urged Noriega's ousting.

The chief of the Vatican embassy finally persuaded Noriega to give himself up by threatening to cancel his asylum. Noriega surrendered to US forces on January 3, 1990. He was flown immediately to Miami, where he was tried on numerous criminal charges and convicted in April 1992 on eight charges of conspiracy to manufacture and distribute cocaine. In July 1992 he was sentenced to 40 years in prison.

Today Noriega is serving his sentence in a Florida prison, and will likely be released on good behavior in 2007.

T-INVASION PANAMA

After Noriega's ousting, Guillermo Endara, the legitimate winner of the 1989 election, was sworn in as president, and Panama attempted to put itself back together. The country's image and economy were in shambles, and its capital had suffered damage not only from the invasion itself but from widespread looting.

However, the Endara government did not turn out to be a panacea, and the economy foundered under him. In the following election in 1994, president Ernesto Pérez Balladares won by a narrow margin over Mireya Moscoso, the wife of former president Arnulfo Arias (he was in his late 60s and she was 23 when they were married). Arnulfo Arias, a legendary autocrat, was elected president three times in the 1940s and 1960s and was overthrown by the army each time (indeed, he was cheated out of a fourth victory in 1984). Off-and-on Panamanian resident Rubén Blades, an internationally renowned salsa star and Harvard-educated lawyer, came in third.

Pérez Balladares allocated unprecedented levels of funding for education, health care, housing projects and infrastructure improvements, but was viewed as corrupt, and in the spring of 1999 voters rejected his attempt to change constitutional limits barring a president from serving two consecutive terms.

God's Favorite: A Novel, by Lawrence Wright, blends fact and fiction in a humorous tale chronicling Noriega's final days as Panamanian strongman. Minor characters include Colombian drug boss Pablo Escobar and US general Oliver North.

Panama: The Whole Story, by Kevin Buckley, is an excellent book about Noriega and the events leading up to the 1989 invasion.

America's Prisoner: The Memoirs of Manuel Noriega, cowritten with Peter Eisner, seems particularly relevant in today's political climate – Noriega discusses the US role in regime change throughout Latin America.

1983

Following Torrijos' death in a plane crash in 1981, former CIA operative Manuel Noriega rises to power and an era of repression begins

1989

The US invades Panama; Noriega flown to Miami where he was later convicted on charges of conspiracy and drug trafficking

THE CANAL CHANGES HANDS

On December 31, 1999 the USA relinquished control of the Panama Canal. The US also closed its military bases, taking with them an economic impact of up to US$350 million; 4000 Panamanians employed by the US military lost their jobs. Polls taken before the withdrawal showed that a majority of Panamanians did not want the US to pull out completely because of the economic consequences. This sentiment conflicted with the desire to cast off this last vestige of colonialism.

Many were skeptical about Panama's ability to run the canal, yet Panama defied expectations, wracking up impressive safety records and decreasing transit time for ships passing through the canal by more than 10%.

However, the canal has not been without its problems. Forest surrounding the canal, which was vital to prevent silt buildup, was cleared, in part to build the megalithic Gamboa Rainforest Resort. Even worse, there were rumors of logging virgin forest within the Panama Canal's 'protected' watershed, and there was also the lethal garbage left by the US to be dealt with. Target practice by US planes has left an estimated 105,000 unexploded bombs scattered throughout 7800 acres of rain forest; the US claims that it cannot remove them without destroying the forest.

DID YOU KNOW?

Rumor has it that Rubén Blades will play a prominent role in the new Torrijos administration. He's currently slated to become either the minister of culture or the minister of tourism.

PANAMA IN THE 21ST CENTURY

In 1999 Mireya Moscoso, the wife of three-term president Arnulfo Arias, was elected as the country's first female president on a populist platform. Moscoso had ambitious plans for the country and promised to improve education, health care and housing for the 36% of Panama's 2.8 million who live in poverty. She also promised to generate jobs and reduce the unemployment rate.

As Panama celebrated its centenary in 2003, Moscoso had an approval rating under 30% – an all-time low. Many viewed her as an incompetent president who couldn't fulfill a single campaign promise.

The figures were damning. At the end of 2003 unemployment was at 18%, with underemployment at 30%. The budget deficit had ballooned under her, and social security, that lifeline for the poor, was predicted to go bankrupt in 2014. She angered many over her wasteful spending: as parts of the country went without food she paid US$10 million to bring the Miss Universe pageant to Panama.

During her term, thousands marched in the streets to protest the privatization of social security. In spite of her insistence that she would bail out the ailing agency – created by her husband in 1941 – no one believed her. She was also accused of looking the other way during Colombian military incursions into Darién – implying indifference to the terrorism occurring inside the country's borders.

At the time of writing, the Revolutionary Democratic Party (PRD) candidate Martín Torrijos (son of former leader Omar Torrijos), who had previously lost to Moscoso, had just won the election of 2004 and Panamanians were looking forward to a new regime.

1999	2004
The US turns the canal over to Panama and closes all of its military bases in the country	Martín Torrijos, son of Panama's former ruler, is elected president in fair elections

The Culture

THE NATIONAL PSYCHE

At the crossroads of the Americas, the narrow isthmus of Panama bridges not only two continents but two vastly different paradigms for Panamanian culture and society: one clings to the traditions of the past, while the other looks to the modernizing influences of a growing economy. These forces often tug in opposition to the Panamanian national character, creating some serious doubts about the country's future.

In some ways this disorientation is only natural given the many years that Panama has been the object of another country's meddling. From the US-backed independence of 1903 to the strong-armed removal of Noriega in 1989, with half-a-dozen other interventions in between, the USA left a strong legacy in the country. Nearly every Panamanian has a relative or at least an acquaintance living in the USA. Parts of the country seem swept up in mall-fervor, with architectural inspiration straight out of North America. Many deck themselves out in US clothes, buy US-made cars, and take their fashion tips from Madison Avenue.

Others are not so ready to embrace the culture from the north. Indigenous groups like the Emberá and Kuna struggle to keep their traditions alive, as more and more of their youth are lured into the Western lifestyles of the city. On the Península de Azuero, with its colonial homes, Spanish festivals and traditional dress and customs, tradition still lives on, but local villagers raise the same concerns about the future of their youth and their festivals.

Given the clash between old and new, it's surprising the country isn't suffering from a serious case of cognitive dissonance. Somehow, the exceptionally tolerant Panamanian character weathers many contradictions – the old and the new, the grave disparity between rich and poor and the gorgeous natural environment and its rapid destruction. Much of this tolerance begins in the family, which is the cornerstone of Panamanian society, and plays a role in nearly every aspect of a person's life. Whether among Kuna sisters or Panama City's elite, everyone looks after each other. Favors are graciously accepted, promptly returned and never forgotten.

This mutual concern extends from the family into the community – at times the whole country seems like little more than one extended community. In the political arena, the same names appear time and again, as nepotism is the norm rather than the exception. This goes hand-in-hand with Panama's most persistent problem: corruption. Panamanians view their leaders' fiscal and moral transgressions with disgust – and are far from being in the dark about issues. Yet they accept things with patience – and an almost fatalistic attitude. Outsiders sometimes view this as a kind of passivity, but it's all just another aspect of the complicated Panamanian psyche.

A People Who Would Not Kneel: Panama, the United States and the San Blás Kuna, by James Howe, describes the struggles the Kuna underwent in order to gain the independence they enjoy today.

Inauguración de La Fe (Inauguration of La Fe), by Consuelo Tomás, is a collection of tales depicting the idiosyncrasies of the popular neighborhoods of Panama City. Tomás is a deft writer with a playful but biting sense of humor.

DID YOU KNOW?

The housing shortage in Panama is estimated at 200,000 homes.

PANAMA'S SUPER STAMPS

In the world of stamp collecting, Panama is a top producer. The teams of engravers and painters, lithographic artists and graphic designers who create the nation's postal issues are widely regarded as among the world's best. Panamanian stamps not only capture the country's history, places, people and nature but also honor world events and figures.

LIFESTYLE

In spite of the skyscrapers and gleaming restaurants lining the wealthier districts of Panama City, nearly a third of the country's population lives in poverty, with 700,000 people in extreme conditions, struggling just to satisfy their basic dietary needs. Those hardest hit by poverty tend to be in the least populated provinces: Darién, Bocas del Toro, Veraguas, Los Santos and Colón. Among them you'll find indigenous villages, Afro-Antilliano towns and mestizo settlements, in a wide variety of living situations. There are also many poor residents of Panama City's slum, where an estimated 20% of the urban population lives. Countrywide, 9% of the population live in *barriados* (squatter) settlements.

In the Emberá villages of Darién, traditional living patterns persist much as they have for hundreds of years. The communities are typically made up of 30 to 40 *bohíos* (thatched-roof, open-sided dwellings). The kitchen occupies one corner and has an oven made of mud. The community survives on subsistence agriculture, hunting, fishing and raising poultry. This is much the same for the Teribe in the Bocas del Toro province. In Wounaan and Emberá communities, the men often practice woodcarving (from the dark *cocobolo* hardwood), while the women weave baskets. Among many of these towns, the life expectancy is about 10 years below the national average and the majority of people lack access to clean water and basic sanitation.

For the *campesinos* (farmers), life is hard. A subsistence farmer in the interior might earn as little as US$900 a year, far below the national average of $6700 per capita. The dwelling might consist of a simple cinderblock building, with a roof and four walls and perhaps a porch. Families have few possessions, and every member assists with working the land or contributing to the household. The best times are those spent at family gatherings, or at regional festivals – often associated with religious holidays – where food, music and dancing will be a big part of the equation. Saturdays are usually spent with the spouse and kids, and Sundays are big drinking days among friends.

The middle and upper class largely reside in Panama City environs, enjoying a level of comfort similar to their economic brethren in Europe and the USA. They live in large homes or apartments, have a maid, a car or two, and for the lucky few a second home on the beach or in the mountains. Cell phones are de rigueur. Vacations are often enjoyed outside of the country in Europe or the USA. Most middle-class families can speak some English (and often send their children to English-speaking schools).

Celebrations, weddings and family gatherings are a social outlet for rich and poor alike, and those with relatives in positions of power – nominal or otherwise – don't hesitate to turn to them for support.

POPULATION

Of Panama's three million souls, 57% live in urban areas. The majority of the population (65%) is mestizo, which is generally a mix of indigenous and Spanish descent. In truth many non-black immigrants are also thrown into this category, including a sizable Chinese population: some estimate that as much as 10% of the population is of Chinese ancestry. There are also a number of other sizable groups. About 14% of Panamanians are of African descent, 10% of Spanish descent, 5% of mixed African and Spanish descent and 6% are indigenous.

Black Panamanians are mostly descendants of English-speaking West Indians such as Jamaicans and Trinidadians, who were brought to Panama as laborers. Of the several dozen native tribes that inhabited Panama

Loma ardiente y vestida de sol (Burning and sun-drenched hill) is an imaginative novel by Rafael Pernett y Morales, which takes a bold look at Panama City's poor, mainly the squatters.

DID YOU KNOW?

Torrijos helped end the historical monopoly of power by white Panamanians.

Magnificent Molas: The Art of the Kuna Indians, by Michel Perrin, contains photographs of 300 fabric works of art. Perrin describes the vivid relationship between Kuna art and culture.

when the Spanish arrived, seven now remain. The Kuna are found along the Caribbean coast between Colón Province and Colombia. The Emberá and Wounaan inhabit the jungle of the eastern Panamá province and the Darién, while the Ngöbe-Buglé can be found in Chiriquí, Veraguas and Bocas del Toro. The Teribe and Bokotá inhabit the Bocas province, while the Bribri are found both in Costa Rica and in Panama along the Talamanca reserve. Each of these groups maintains its own language and culture. The Ngöbe-Buglé are Panama's largest tribe and number about 125,000; the Kuna, who govern their ancestral territory as the autonomous region of the Comarca de Kuna Yala and send representatives to the legislature, are the most politically organized.

Sadly, Panama's most recent immigrants are Emberá refugees from Colombia, fleeing heavy fighting occurring in the Chaco region. More than 1200 fled in the first two months of 2004 alone.

The website www .dulenega.nativeweb.org has stories and poems of the Kuna people, as well as a complete list of publications about their culture.

SPORTS

Owing to the legacy of US marines, baseball is a favorite in Panama. Although there are no professional teams in Panama, the amateur leagues host games in stadiums throughout the country. Panamanians have their favorite teams, but are usually more interested in their favorite players in the US major leagues. Mariano Rivera, the record-setting Panamanian pitcher for the New York Yankees (who recently signed a US$21 million, two-year contract) is a household name. The batting champ, Rod Carew, is another (former) Panamanian star – inducted into the Hall of Fame in 1991. Roberto Kelly, who played for the Yankees for many years, is also fondly remembered.

Throughout the country, you'll see kids playing pickup baseball games. A shortage of green space in Panama City means you may stumble across a few street games while you're passing through. In the interior, kids play soccer as much as baseball, and plenty of youth leagues provide the setting.

Boxing is another popular spectator sport; it has been a source of pride to Panamanians (and to Latin Americans in general) ever since Roberto Durán, a Panama City native and boxing legend, won the world championship lightweight title in 1972. He went on to become the world champion in the welterweight (1980), light middleweight (1983) and super middleweight (1989) categories.

DID YOU KNOW?

Panamanian jockey Laffit Pincay holds the world record in wins with over 9500 (breaking Willie Shoemaker's previous record of 8883).

MULTICULTURALISM

Panama is a rich melting pot of cultures with immigrants from many parts of the globe and a diverse indigenous population. Shortly after the Spanish arrived, slaves were brought from Africa to work in Panama's mines and perform grunt labor in the colony. Slaves that escaped set up communities in the Darién jungle, where their descendents (*cimarrones*) still live. Subsequent waves of immigration coincide with both the construction of the Panama Railroad, built in 1850, and the work on the Panama Canal (both the French effort in the late 1800s and the American completion in the early 1900s). During that time thousands of workers were brought from the West Indies, particularly Jamaica.

Workers also came from the East Indies and from China to labor – and many to die – on these massive projects. The majority of the Chinese settled in Panama City, where you can see two Chinatowns (one near Casco Viejo, the other in modern El Dorado). There are two daily Chinese newspapers and even a private school for the Chinese. The term for Chinese

Cuentos de Bocas del Toro, by José Maria Sanchez, is a collection of stories, full of protagonists driven by the sensuous excesses of the tropical jungle and sea. The Bocas setting is where the author was born and raised.

Panamanians is 'Once' (pronounced '*awn*-say'). Mixed offspring – and mixed marriages – are much more common today. Among the East Indian community, Hindus complain that their culture is disappearing: where once it was common for young men to return to India to find a bride, this is no longer the case. This intermixing of races happens across the nation, although indigenous groups and whites – representing each end of the economic scale – are least likely to marry outside of their group.

Although Panama is a much more racially tolerant society than many other countries, there is distrust among groups – particularly between indigenous groups and mestizos. This stems largely from mestizo land grabs – by loggers, ranchers and settlers – that have pushed indigenous communities off their lands. Many also see the government as corrupt and largely indifferent to their plight.

Class distinctions also persist. While politicians from the president on down take pride in mingling with the public and maintaining some semblance of a classless society, the whites *(rabiblancos)* control the majority of the wealth and nearly all of the power. Within that group are several dozen wealthy families who are above the law – people able to escape arrest by mentioning the names of others who could complicate life for a lowly police officer.

In Panama members of a certain class marry only members of that same class. And at the almighty Union Club – *the* social club of Panama City – memberships are rarely given to people with dark skin.

Racism is abhorrent no matter where it's found, but racism in Panama is mild compared to the brand found in many other countries. Panama has no counterpart to the Ku Klux Klan; there are no skinheads committing hate crimes. For all its inequities, Panama is closer to the ideal in this respect than most developed nations.

DID YOU KNOW?

Formal marriage is rare outside of the middle and upper classes. Some estimate that 60% of children are born to short-term unions.

The Tailor of Panama, by John Le Carré, is a page-turning spy novel centering on the US handover of the Panama Canal. It was made into a film with some fine footage of Panama City.

MEDIA

Panama has a number of daily newspapers – ranging from sensationalist rags to astute independents. In Panama City, the biggest medium is television. Some 75% of all homes own one. Views tend to represent business and the oligarchy. Nationwide, radio is the most important medium. Among 90 radio stations, most Panamanians have two or three favorites, and morning talk shows are very popular, representing a wide range of viewpoints.

Panama still has some horrendous laws that make freedom of the press nothing more than a myth. Government officials who take offense from criticism directed against them can have the journalist imprisoned, for 'not showing them respect.' This is a legacy of Noriega, who used such laws to suppress the voices of critics, and many international human-rights and press-advocacy organizations have decried Panama as supporting one of the most repressive regimes in the Americas because of the various 'gag laws' that bureaucrats can use to stifle opposition.

In recent years as many as 90 journalists and writers nationwide were facing potential prison sentences for publishing material that 'offended the honor' of one or another public figure. A typical incident occurred in August 2003 when two journalists from *El Panamá América* were sentenced to prison for one year (later commuted to a US$600 fine) for 'harming the dignity and honor' of supreme court justice Winston Spadafora. They were punished for an article which described Spadafora's use of public funds to build a road to Iturralde, which led almost exclusively to Spadafora's private estate.

DID YOU KNOW?

According to the UN, in Panama 33% of local representatives and corporate managers are women.

In 2002 Victor Ramos of La Prensa was brought to justice for a political cartoon involving Perez Balladares, the former president. After Balladares boasted publicly about all of the 'little toys' at his disposal – a private ocean-front residence, a plane and a helicopter among other things – Ramos' cartoon placed the former president's list next to another that itemized the scandals that had dogged his political career. Among the well-documented scandals was a US$51,000 campaign check that Balladares received in 1994 from a Colombian drug trafficker and the mysterious disappearance of millions of dollars allocated for the construction of a bridge over the Panama Canal. Although prosecutors targeted Perez Balladares in corruption investigations, they claimed there was insufficient evidence to prosecute him.

In spite of President Moscoso's pronouncement to repeal these laws during her term, she and her cronies used these 'gag laws' to suppress dissent. It's unclear whether the current administration under Torrijos will employ the same tactics.

Getting to Know the General, by Graham Greene, is a biased but fascinating portrait of General Omar Torrijos, one of Panama's more popular leaders – and father of current president Martin Torrijos.

RELIGION

The many religions of Panama can best be observed by walking the streets of the capital. Among the scores of Catholic churches, you'll find breezy Anglican churches filled with worshippers from the West Indies, synagogues, mosques, a shiny Greek Orthodox church, an impressive Hindu temple and a surreal Baha'i house of worship (the headquarters for Latin America).

Freedom of religion is constitutionally guaranteed in Panama, although the preeminence of Roman Catholicism is also officially recognized, with 77% of the country filling its ranks. Children in school study theology – although it's not compulsory. Protestant denominations account for 12%, Muslims 4.4% and Baha'i 1.2%. Additionally, the country has 3000 Jews (many of them recent immigrants from Israel), 24,000 Buddhists and 9000 Hindus.

In addition, the various Indian tribes have their own belief systems, although these are fading quickly due to the influence of Christian missionaries. As in other parts of Latin America, the evangelical movement is spreading like wildfire.

Although Catholics are the majority, only about 20% of them attend church regularly. The religious orders aren't particularly strong in Panama either: only about 25% of Catholic clergy are Panamanian. The rest are foreign missionaries.

Ancient Arts of the Andes, by Wendell C Bennett, discusses the Indian art of Panama, which is related to the pre-Columbian art of the Andes.

WOMEN IN PANAMA

As Mireya Moscoso prepared to leave office in 2004, she was one of only 12 female heads of state in the world. This historic achievement places Panama ahead of many other countries in both the developed and the developing world. Women here enjoy more opportunities than they do in many Latin American countries. The PNF (Feminist National Party) was founded in 1923 – one of the first feminist parties in Latin America. It was strongly critical of the government in pushing for social reforms for women and children, and helped women secure the right to vote in 1941. In 1981, Panama ratified the law that eliminated all forms of discrimination against women.

In spite of these advances, women still face many obstacles in Panamanian society. Machismo and gross stereotypes are more prevalent in rural areas than in urban ones, but even in the cities women have to face lower wages (67 cents to every man's dollar), sexual harassment (70% of women reported at least one instance) and are nearly twice as likely to

The Art of Being Kuna: Layers of Meaning Among the Kuna of Panama, edited by Marilyn Salvador, is a collection of essays and photographs that provide an excellent introduction to the art and culture of the Kuna.

When New Flowers Bloomed: Short Stories by Women Writers from Costa Rica and Panama, edited by Enrique Levi, is a good selection of works by contemporary Panamanian writers.

be unemployed. Although women make up 46% of the workplace – and in spite of Mireya's accomplishment – they make up only 10% of the country's legislature.

Overall, women are having fewer children and are having them later in life. Many postpone motherhood to enter the workplace – a pattern that exists in Europe and the USA. Panama also has a growing number of single mothers, particularly at the bottom income bracket (37% of lower income households are headed by women). Women also have no right to an abortion (it's illegal in Panama), and teenage pregnancy is high (girls aged 15 to 19 account for 10% of all births).

In indigenous communities, women face many hardships, including poor access to health care and a low level of prenatal care. Prevailing stereotypes also means girls are less likely to attend school (among indigenous populations 53% of women are illiterate, compared to 36% of men). Women enter motherhood at much younger ages and bear more children than their mestizo counterparts. At the same time, they are expected to work and help support the household.

Eric Jackson's website www.thepanamanews .com is the best English-language website about current events in Panama, with travel, arts, business and sports sections.

One of the most positive signs that things are improving for indigenous women is the 2004 election of a female governor over the Comarca de Emberá–Wounaan. She was chosen by the general congress, made up of both Emberá and Wounaan in the Darién Province.

ARTS

Panama's art scene reflects its ethnic mix. A slow spin on the radio dial or a hard look at Panamanian nightclubs will reveal salsa; Latin and American jazz; traditional Panamanian music from the central provinces; reggae; and Latin, British and American rock 'n' roll.

The country has a few impressive painters and writers, some of whom are internationally recognized. There is also fair representation in dance, theater and other performance arts, which are managed by the Instituto Nacional de Cultura (INAC).

Traditional Panamanian products include woodcarvings, textiles, ceramics, masks and other handicrafts.

Literature

Several of Panama's best novelists wrote around the mid-century. *El Ahogado* (The Drowned Man), a 1937 novel by Tristán Solarte (pen name for Guillermo Sánchez Borbón, a well-known poet, novelist and journalist), ingeniously blends elements of the detective, gothic and psychological genres, along with a famous local myth. *El Desván* (In the Garret), a 1954 novel by Ramón H Jurado, explores the emotional limits of the human condition. *Gamboa Road Gang,* by Joaquín Beleño, is the best work of fiction about the political and social events surrounding the Panama Canal.

Artesania Ocueña, just outside of Ocú, is a local women's co-op that sells a range of traditional embroidered items. Learn more about them and even shop on their website, www.artesania socu.bizland.com.

Music

Salsa is the most popular music in Panama, and live salsa is easy to find, particularly in Panama City (see p108). The country's most renowned salsa singer, Rubén Blades, is something of a national hero. A kid from the barrio, Blades has had several international hits and has appeared in a few motion pictures. He ran for president in 1994, finishing third.

Jazz, which was brought to Panama from the US, and calypso music from the West Indies can also be heard in clubs in Panama. Rock 'n' roll, in both English and Spanish, is played on most Panamanian FM radio stations, and some decent bands play it in Panama City clubs.

The jazz composer and pianist Danilo Pérez is widely acclaimed by American and European jazz critics.

Los Rabanes is the most popular rock 'n' roll group in the country. Panamanian folkloric music *(típico)*, in which the accordion is dominant, is well represented by Dorindo Cárdenas, the late Victorio Vergara (whose band lives on as Nenito Vargas y los Plumas Negras) and the popular brother-sister pair of Sammy and Sandra Sandoval.

DID YOU KNOW?

Danilo Perez's highly recommended album, *Panamonk,* puts a Latin spin on many Thelonius Monk compositions.

Handicrafts

Panama's handicrafts are varied and often of excellent quality. The Wounaan and Emberá Indians in Darién Province produce some beautiful woven baskets. These tribes also sell carvings of jungle wildlife from *cocobolo*, a handsome tropical hardwood, and tiny figurines from the ivory-colored *tagua* nut.

The Kuna of the Comarca de Kuna Yala are known worldwide for their *molas* – the blouse panels used by women in their traditional dress and sold as crafts. *Molas* symbolize the identity of the Kuna people to outsiders, and their colorful and elaborate designs often depict sea turtles, birds and fish.

Ocú and Penonomé produce superior Panama hats. *Polleras* (elaborate traditional outfits of Spanish origin) are handmade in Guararé and in villages around Las Tablas. Also found on the Azuero are festival masks (in Villa de Los Santos and Parita) and pottery (in La Arena).

Many of the handicrafts mentioned here can be purchased in Panama City (p110).

Painting

Trained in France, Roberto Lewis (1874–1949) became the first prominent figure on Panama's art scene. He painted portraits of the nation's leaders and allegorical images to decorate public buildings; among his most notable works are those in the Palacio de las Garzas in Panama City. In 1913 Lewis became the director of Panama's first art academy, where he and his successor, Humberto Ivaldi (1909–47), educated a generation of artists. Among the school's students were Juan Manuel Cedeño and Isaac Benítez, as well as the painters who would come to the fore in the 1950s and 1960s. This group includes Alfredo Sinclair, Guillermo Trujillo, Eudoro Silvera and others. Most of these artists are still active today, and their works are occasionally shown in local galleries.

To learn about contemporary Panamanian artists, with photographs of their work, visit the Spanish-language www.epasa .com/arte.

BUYING A MOLA

A *mola*, a traditional Kuna handicraft, is made of brightly colored squares of cotton fabric laid atop one another. Cuts are made through the layers, forming basic designs. The layers are then sewn together with tiny, evenly spaced stitches to hold the design in place. *Mola* means 'blouse' in Kuna, and Kuna women make *molas* in thematically matching but never identical pairs. A pair will comprise the front and back of a blouse.

Regardless of the design, Kuna believe the very best *molas* should always have the following characteristics:

- Stitches closely match the color of the cloth they are set against.
- Stitches are very fine and neatly spaced.
- Stitches are pulled evenly and with enough tension to be barely visible.
- Curves are cut smoothly and the sewing follows the curves of the cut.
- Outline strips are uniform in width, with no frayed edges.

The largest Panamanian art exposition – the Bienal de Arte – is held every two years at the **Museo de Arte Contemporáneo** (Av San Blás at Av de los Mártires) in Panama City (p89).

Photography

Panama has several gifted photographers, including Iraida Icaza, Stuart Warner and Sandra Eleta. Icaza, who lived for many years in Tokyo and now resides in New York, makes abstract art using photographic equipment. Her work is bold and innovative.

Warner, who has spent much of his life in Asia, the Middle East, Europe and the USA, captures the human spirit in beautiful landscapes and portraits.

Sandra Eleta's portraits of the black inhabitants of Panama's Caribbean coast (particularly of Portobelo, where she resides part of the year) have made her one of the most important photographers in Latin America.

DID YOU KNOW?

When Paul Gauguin laid eyes on Isla Taboga in 1887, he wanted very much to live there. Unfortunately, his earnings from laboring on the canal prevented it. So he went to Tahiti instead.

Environment

Although still largely undiscovered, Panama is slowly gaining fame for its vast tropical forests, hundreds of pristine islands and the astounding biodiversity stretching its full length. More and more visitors arrive on the isthmus with one thing in mind: experiencing the wildlife, which the country has in spades. Unfortunately, Panama also has grave environmental threats, coming from the hands of loggers, developers and indifferent or corrupt government agencies, who don't understand that the country's finest gem – its natural beauty – is rapidly disappearing.

THE LAND

Panama is both the narrowest and the southernmost country in Central America. The long S-shaped isthmus borders Costa Rica in the west and Colombia in the east. Its northern Caribbean coastline measures 1160km, compared to a 1690km Pacific coastline in the south, and its total land area is 78,046 sq km. By comparison, Panama is slightly bigger than Ireland or Austria, and roughly the same size as South Carolina.

While traveling around Panama, one must remember that the isthmus of the western hemisphere runs west to east; that Colón, on the Caribbean Sea, is not only north but also west of Panama City; and that in the capital city the sun appears to rise out of the Pacific Ocean, and set in the direction of the Caribbean.

Panama is just 50km wide at its leanest point, an impressive statistic given that it separates two great oceans. The Panama Canal, which is about 80km long, effectively divides the country into eastern and western regions. The provinces of Herrera, Los Santos and Veraguas are often referred to as the 'central provinces' or as 'the interior,' as in the interior of the country.

Two mountain chains run along Panama's spine, in the east and in the west. The highest point in the country is 3478m Volcán Barú, in western Chiriquí Province. Barú, Panama's only volcano, is dormant although hot springs around its flanks testify to continuing underground activity.

Like all the Central American countries, Panama has large, flat coastal lowlands. In some places these lowlands are covered in huge banana plantations, particularly in the area from Changuinola to Almirante in Bocas del Toro Province.

Panama's 480-odd rivers drain into the Pacific Ocean or Caribbean Sea. The 1518 islands off its coasts comprise the two main island groups, the San Blás and Bocas del Toro archipelagos, both in the Caribbean, but most of Panama's islands are in fact on the Pacific side, small and often unmapped. Even the Panama Canal has islands, including Isla Barro Colorado, which is home to a world-renowned rain forest research station operated by the Smithsonian Tropical Research Institute.

WILDLIFE

Panama's astounding natural beauty is one of its star attractions. Its rain forests, cloud forests, coral reefs, pristine islands and numerous other natural habitats teem with wildlife. The reason for the country's rich biodiversity owes a great deal to its geological history.

Around 65 million years ago, North and South America were joined by a land bridge not unlike what exists today. But around 50 million years

DID YOU KNOW?

In April 2004, Panama, Costa Rica, Colombia and Ecuador signed an agreement creating a Pacific Marine corridor to preserve the area's ecosystems.

A Neotropical Companion, by John Kricher, is an excellent book – and a great read – for learning about ecology, evolutionary theory and biodiversity in the New World tropics.

DID YOU KNOW?

Capybaras maintain a strict social hierarchy with one dominant male ruling over a mixed group of 25. Subordinate males often serve as sentries to keep watch for jaguars.

ago, the continents split apart and remained separate from one another for many millions of years. This isolation created in South America a unique evolutionary landscape. New families of primates flourished – having arrived, most likely, from West Africa – and there was an astonishing diversification of many species (including saber-toothed marsupial carnivores and elephant-sized ground sloths). The lands soon gave rise to many bird families (toucans and hummingbirds included), unique neotropical rodents (agoutis and capybaras) and groups like iguanas, poison dart frogs and basilisks. In North America things happened quite differently, as North America collided repeatedly with Eurasia, exchanging animal species that had no relatives in South America (horses, deer, raccoons, squirrels and mice).

Monkey's Bridge: Mysteries of Evolution in Central America, by David Rains Wallace, tells of the colorful evolutionary unfolding of fauna and flora on the isthmus beginning three million years ago and ending in the present.

The momentous event that would change natural history for both continents occurred around three million years ago when the land bridge of Panama arose. Species from both continents mingled as northern animals went south and southern animals went north. Many found their homes in the lush forests and wetlands along the isthmus, where the great variety of plant species created ideal conditions for nourishing wildlife.

Today, the interchange of species between North and South America is limited to winged migrations, which can be breathtaking to behold (see following section).

Animals

Panama's biodiversity is staggering. It boasts the largest number of bird species in Central America (940 species). There are 218 mammal species, 226 species of reptile, 164 amphibian species, and 125 animal species found nowhere else in the world.

Lonely Planet's Watching Wildlife: Central America, by Luke Hunter and David Andrew, gives details of animal species found in Parque Nacional Darién and other areas; a gallery describes dozens of species found throughout Central America.

Bird watchers consider Panama one of the world's best birding sights. Quetzals, macaws, amazons, parrots and toucans all have sizable populations here, as do many species of tanager and raptor. The best bird-watching sites in the country are at Pirre Station (p285) and Cana valley (p286) in Parque Nacional Darién (p283), where you can see four species of macaw, golden-headed quetzals and black-tipped cotingas. Another fantastic birding spot is Parque Nacional Soberanía (p121), where hundreds of species have been spotted along the 17km Pipeline Rd.

One of the most sought-after birds is the harpy eagle, the national bird of Panama. With a two-meter wingspan and weights of up to 20 pounds, this raptor is the world's most powerful bird of prey and a truly awesome sight. The bird is recognized by its size (huge), its broad, black chest band with white underneath, its piercing yellow eyes and its prominent, regal crests.

The harpy's powerful claws can carry off howler monkeys and capuchins, and it also hunts sloths, coatis, anteaters and just about anything that moves. A harpy eagle needs 30 sq km to survive and it's best spotted in the Parque Nacional Darién around Punta Patiño (p288).

Birds of Tropical America, by ornithologist Steven Hilty, is an excellent natural history of tropical birds, with a wealth of information about tropical diversity and the structure of the rain forest bird community.

More famous than the harpy eagle is the elusive, emerald-green quetzal, which lives in habitats throughout Central America – although some of the best places to see it are in Panama. The male has an elongated wing covert (train) and a scarlet breast and belly. Females have duller plumage. Parque Nacional Volcán Barú (p216) is a top spot for sighting them, as is PILA (Parque Internacional La Amistad, p247). They are best spotted in the breeding season from March to June when males grow their spectacular trains and start calling for mates.

Panama's geographical position also makes it a crossroads for migratory birds. Out of the country's 940 bird species, 122 occur only as long-distance migrants (that is, they don't breed in Panama). From August to December, North American raptors migrate south into Central America

SEA TURTLE NESTING

Turtle	Coast	Nesting Season	Peak	Hot Spots
Leatherback	both	Mar-Jul (Caribbean) Oct-Mar (Pacific)	April-May (Caribbean) Nov-Jan (Pacific)	PN Isla Bastimentos (p242) San-San Pond Sak Wetlands (p246)
Loggerhead	Caribbean	May-Sep	no peak	PN Isla Bastimentos (p242) San-San Pond Sak Wetlands (p246)
Green	both	May-Oct (Caribbean) Jun-Dec (Pacific)	Aug-Oct (Caribbean)	PN Isla Bastimentos (p242) San-San Pond Sak Wetlands (p246)
Hawksbill	both	Apr-Oct (Caribbean) Apr-Nov (Pacific)	Jun-Jul (both coasts)	PN Isla Bastimentos (p242) San-San Pond Sak Wetlands (p246)
Olive ridley	Pacific	year-round	Jun-Nov	Isla de Cañas (p182)

by the *millions*. At times, there are so many birds that they make a black streak across the sky. The canopy tower in Panama's Parque Nacional Soberanía (p121) is a particularly good vantage point for watching the migration. If you visit Bocas del Toro keep an eye out for kettling hawks. October is the best month to see them in such numbers. The migration of turkey vultures over the islands in early March and again in October is another striking sight. These big, black-bodied, red-necked birds can streak the sky and are able to soar for long periods without a single flap as they migrate between southern Canada and Tierra del Fuego.

Primate lovers are also drawn to Panama. Among the country's many species – including white-faced capuchins, squirrel monkeys, spider monkeys and howler monkeys – are some fascinating varieties. The Geoffroy's tamarin, for instance, is found nowhere else in Central America. These tiny, gregarious monkeys can live in groups of up to 40 in lowland forest, and many weigh less than a pound. They're identified by their whistles and chirps, mottled black-and-brown fur, white chests, and of course their diminutive stature. They can be spotted in Parque Natural Metropolitano (p89), Isla Barro Colorado (p122) and Parque Nacional Darién (p283).

Big cats prowl the jungles of Panama – though you'd be extremely fortunate to catch even a glimpse of one. Jaguars, pumas, ocelots, jaguarundis and margays are all found on the isthmus. The jaguar is the biggest of the bunch and is the largest cat in the Americas. Jaguars (and pumas) both need large tracts of land in order to survive. Without them the big cats gradually exhaust their food supply (which numbers 85 hunted species) and perish. They are excellent swimmers and climbers and are more commonly spotted resting on sunny riverbanks.

Panama's offshore waters host a fascinating assortment of creatures. Reefs are found off both coasts, and aquatic species in Panamanian waters include jacks, snappers, jewfish, eels, sailfish, sea bass, puffer fish, rays, lobsters, caimans and octopuses. Visitors to the national marine parks might spot humpback whales, reef sharks, bottlenose dolphins, or killer or sperm whales. Whale sharks and white-tip sharks also visit.

One of Panama's biggest coastal draws is the sea turtle. Of the world's seven different species, five can be seen in Panama at various times throughout the year (see table). All sea turtles originally evolved from terrestrial species, and the most important stage of their survival happens on

Bird watchers should visit the Panama Audubon Society's website http://panamaaudubon .org/history.html, which features articles about the study of birds and the conservation of their habitat.

DID YOU KNOW?

A breeding male quetzal will hop backwards off his perch to avoid damaging his train, which can grow up to 75cm long.

land when they come to nest. Although you'll need a bit of luck and a lot of patience, the experience of seeing hatchlings emerge is unparalleled.

Arribadas (or 'arrivals') are rare events when thousands of female sea turtles flood the beach to lay their eggs. This happens occasionally on Isla de Cañas (p182) when 40,000 to 50,000 olive ridleys come to nest. This chance event most likely occurs in the wet season (usually September to October), during the first and last quarter of the moon. No one knows exactly why these *arribadas* occur.

Endangered Species

According to the World Conservation Monitoring Centre, there are over 100 species threatened with extinction within Panama. Among the animals appearing on its 'red list' for Panama are the jaguar, the spectacled bear, the Central American tapir, the American crocodile, all five species of sea turtle that nest on Panamanian beaches and dozens of birds, including several eagle species and the military and scarlet macaws.

The Panamanian legislature has implemented laws to curb illegal hunting and logging, but the laws are widely ignored due to an absence of enforcement. For example, keeping a parrot, toucan or macaw in a cage is a fineable offense in Panama. Yet not only can you see them in cages outside many residences, but many hotel managers apparently believe that tourists enjoy seeing large tropical birds in itty-bitty cages.

You can help reduce the threat to Panama's endangered species. If you see caged animals at a hotel, complain to the manager, take your business elsewhere and report the crime to **ANCON** (☎ 314-0060). Also, refrain from eating *tortuga* (sea turtle), *huevos de tortuga* (turtle eggs), *cazón* (shark), *conejo pintado* (paca), *ñeque* (agouti), *venado* (deer) or iguana if you see them on a menu.

Obviously, buying jaguar teeth, ocelot skins or objects made from turtle shells directly contributes to these animals' extinction.

Plants

Tropical rain forest is the dominant vegetation in the canal area, along the Caribbean coast and in most of the eastern half of the country. Parque Nacional Darién (p283) protects much of Panama's largest tropical rain forest region. Other vegetation zones include grassland on the Pacific coast, mountain forest in the highlands, alpine vegetation on the highest peaks and mangrove forest on both coasts and around many islands. Among the flora, Panama has over 10,000 species of plant, including 1200 orchid species, 678 fern species and 1500 species of tree. Orchids can be spotted all over the country, particularly in highland areas. Excellent spots to find orchids are in Guadalupe (p220) and Santa Fe (p190).

NATIONAL PARKS

Today Panama has 11 national parks and more than two dozen other officially protected areas. About 25% of its total land is set aside for conservation. In many of the national parks and protected areas, you'll find mestizo and indigenous villages scattered among them. In the most successful scenarios, the communities help protect and maintain the park and its wildlife. Panama's most accessible and rewarding parks for the visitor are listed in the boxed text on p46 & p47.

To enter a national park, travelers must pay US$3 (US$10 if it's a national marine park) at ANAM (Autoridad Nacional de Ambiente; Panama's national environmental authority) headquarters in Panama

City (p80), at a regional ANAM office or at an ANAM ranger station inside the park being visited. Permits to camp or stay at an ANAM ranger station (US$5 to US$10) can be obtained in the same places as well.

ENVIRONMENTAL ISSUES

Panama has just over 25% of its land set aside for conservation, with 44.4% of its country covered by forest (according to 2003 figures published by the EIU Country Report). It has set aside more land for habitat protection than any other Central American country, and Panama's forests contain the greatest number of species of all the New World countries north of Colombia. But it's doubtful whether Panamanians will be able to live in harmony with their wilderness areas in the years to come. A little over 50 years ago, 70% of Panama's land was covered by forest, which gives a quick indication of one of the country's gravest environmental problems: deforestation.

Trees are being felled at an alarming rate, with the Darién serving as the ecological ground zero. A 2003 study conducted by the administrator of ANAM showed that in the previous 10 years 80,000 hectares of rain forest had been hacked down in the Darién Province alone.

Much of the population in Panama seems unconcerned with the rain forest's ongoing destruction. In fact there's still a large sector of Panamanian society that believes it's manly to cut down trees. If you listen in on conversations among common folk in Los Santos Province, for example, it won't be long before you overhear talk about the good old days when you could cut down trees as wide as cars. The urge to log goes well beyond economic welfare. In this province women compete with trees for men's hearts. As a result, there's hardly a patch of forest remaining there, and the *hombres* are so anxious to fell more trees that they're moving to the Darién, where big trees still abound.

Additionally, Panama's national parks are staffed by few park rangers, and many of the rangers aren't given patrol vehicles or radios, although their areas of coverage are colossal. In Parque Nacional Darién, for instance, there are never more than 20 rangers assigned to protect 576,000 hectares – an area larger than some countries. These rangers are unarmed and poorly paid, and spend most of the day trying to figure out what they are going to eat for dinner. Meanwhile illegal hunting, settling and logging take place in their park. Unless the Panamanian government gets serious, it may not be long before the country's 'protected' areas are nothing more than paper parks.

Shortly before the turn of the millennium, the government learned that the Panama Canal was beginning to silt up from soil erosion – a result from logging and increasing urbanization in the canal watershed. Realizing the threat to the country's most important waterway (which contributes 7% to Panama's GDP), the government passed legislation – in 1999 and in 2002 – which doubled water resources for the canal, placing five new areas under protection and paving the way for a third shipping lane. This would allow the passage of post-Panamex vessels, which are currently too large for the canal. The government did nothing about Darién, however, and continues to ignore its destruction.

Panama's environment continues to bear the brunt of political game-playing. President Moscoso tried for months to ram through unpopular legislation that would build a road through a national park between Boquete and Cerro Punta. Many Panamanians were astounded at her choice to build the road straight through a Unesco World Heritage site, and the

NATIONAL PARKS

Protected Area	Features
San-San Pond Sak Wetlands	lush swamps, long stretches of beach & 4 species of sea turtle
Parque Internacional La Amistad	Unesco World Heritage site, quetzals, harpy eagles & numerous endemic species
Lagunas de Volcán	forest, wetlands in the highland, rose-throated becard, pale-billed woodpecker
Parque Nacional Volcán Barú	Panama's highest point at Barú volcano (3478m), views of both oceans & the resplendent quetzal
Parque Nacional Marino Isla Bastimentos	coral reefs, wetlands, mangrove swamps, white-sand beaches & 200 tropical fish species
Parque Nacional Marino Golfo de Chiriquí	25 islands & 19 coral reefs, howler monkeys, scarlet macaws, sea turtles & whales
Parque Nacional Coiba	coral reefs, virgin rain forest, white-sand beaches, scarlet macaws, humpback whales & howler monkeys
Parque Nacional Omar Torrijos	forest straddling the Continental Divide, waterfalls, golden frogs, rare bird species
Refugio de Vida Silvestre Cenegón del Mangle	coastal wildlife refuge, scores of migratory birds roosting in mangrove trees
Parque Nacional Sarigua	dry forest, salt marsh, mangrove swamps, archaeological zone, a sad monument to environmental devastation
Parque Nacional Cerro Hoya	forest at the headwaters of three rivers, endemic plant species & animals, carato parakeet
Refugio de Vida Silvestre Isla de Cañas	island nesting site for olive ridley sea turtles: over 30,000 annually
Refugio de Vida Silvestre Isla Iguana	small island ringed with coral reefs, nesting sea turtles & humpback whales
Parque Nacional y Reserva Biológica Altos de Campana	highlands & picturesque cliffs overlooking the Pacific, golden frogs & rare birds
Monumento Nacional Isla Barro Colorado	rain forest–covered island with astounding wildlife, 102 mammal species & 381 bird species
Parque Nacional Soberanía	world-famous rain forest inside canal watershed, 525 bird species, 105 mammals
Parque Natural Metropolitano	rain forest near Panama City, trails, scenic overlooks, 250 bird species
Reserva Natural Punta Patiño	private natural reserve with mangrove swamps, beaches & rain forests teeming with wildlife
Parque Nacional Darién	Unesco World Heritage Site: Central America's greatest tropical rain forest, world's top bird watching

Activities	Best Time to Visit	Page
boat trip, camping, turtle watching	Apr-Sep (turtle nesting)	p246
hiking, camping, bird watching, visiting indigenous villages	any, drier Nov-May	p247
bird watching	any, drier Nov-May	p218
hiking, camping, wildlife watching	any, drier Nov-May	p216
diving, snorkeling, camping less rain, calmer seas	Feb-Mar & Sep-Oct	p242
snorkeling, diving, boat tours	any, drier Nov-May	p206
snorkeling, diving, fishing, surfing	drier Nov-May	p195
hiking, horseback riding, wildlife watching & camping	any, drier Nov-May	p153
bird watching	any, drier Nov-May	p168
exploring the ecological ruin	any, drier Nov-May	p166
hiking (poorly marked trails)	Nov-May	p197
wildlife watching	Aug-Nov (nesting season)	p48
snorkeling, wildlife watching	any, drier Nov-May	p181
hiking, camping, bird watching	any, drier Nov-May	p135
guided tours through STRI (Smithsonian Tropical Research Institute)	any, reserve early	p122
hiking, bird watching, wildlife watching	any, drier Nov-May	p121
hiking, bird watching, wildlife watching	any, drier Nov-May	p89
hiking, bird watching, wildlife watching	any, drier Nov-May	p288
hiking, camping, wildlife watching, bird watching	any, drier Nov-May	p283

mayor of Panama City even alleged that she was primarily interested in boosting property values on land she owned along the route. Moscoso denied the allegations and threatened the mayor with a lawsuit for criminal defamation. A later investigation by the daily newspaper *El Panama America*, however, revealed that Moscoso served as president of a holding company that owned land near the site of the proposed road. As her term neared its conclusion, there appeared to be little chance of the legislation going through, so a group of about 50 men took it upon themselves to start chainsawing the path. Word of their actions quickly spread, and within a few hours a group of local officials and environmentalists, the Boquete mayor and five police officers confronted the invaders and stopped them after they had felled just over 100 trees. Some 12 participants in the raid were accused by prosecutors and police of violating a 1976 law that prohibits the felling of trees or exploiting the natural resources in a national park. So far no one has been charged, but attorney Fidel Murgas, who represents environmentalist clients, filed private criminal charges against the invaders (permitted under Panamanian law).

NATIONAL PARKS & OTHER PROTECTED AREAS

SIGHTS & ACTIVITIES	(pp46-7)
Bosque Protector de Palo Seco	1 B2
Corredor Biológico de la Serranía Bagre	2 G3
San-San Pond Sak Wetlands	3 B1
Humedal El Golfo de Montijo	4 C3
Humedal Lagunas de Volcán	5 A2
Monumento Natural de Los Pozos de Calobre	6 D2
Monumento Natural Isla Barro Colorado	7 E1
Parque Internacional La Amistad	8 A1
Parque Nacional Camino de Cruces	9 E2
Parque Nacional Cerro Hoya	10 D4
Parque Nacional Chagres	11 E1
Parque Nacional Coiba	12 B3
Parque Nacional Darién	13 G3
Parque Nacional Marino Golfo de Chiriquí	14 B3
Parque Nacional Marino Isla Bastimentos	15 B1
Parque Nacional Omar Torrijos	16 D2
Parque Nacional Portobelo	17 E1
Parque Nacional Sarigua	18 D3
Parque Nacional Soberanía	19 E1

Deforestation

'What's the big deal? It's just a bunch of trees – they'll grow back,' is a comment you might hear when discussing Panama's environmental plight. The reasons for preserving the forest are numerous, and impact not only plants and animals, but the health of the planet as well (see box on p50).

Panama's natural vegetation was originally almost all forest, but much of this has been cleared, mainly for pasture and agriculture. The destruction of a rain forest not only wipes out animals that inhabit it but also kills many migratory animals (such as bats, butterflies and birds) that move with their seasonal food supplies. It also threatens the traditional cultures of Emberá and Wounaan tribes, as their lands rapidly disappear around them.

The process of destruction happens in several phases. And to get an idea of Panama's ecological future, one need only glimpse what's happening in the Darién. The region north of Yaviza (the town where the Interamericana presently ends) was covered with virgin forest just over three decades ago. All that changed when the highway was extended from Chepo to Yaviza. At first only loggers used the extension, but settlers and ranchers followed.

A Guide to the Birds of Panama, by Robert Ridgley and John Gwynne, is the foremost field guide to Panama's birds. The comprehensive volume also includes a list of avifauna of Costa Rica, Honduras and Nicaragua.

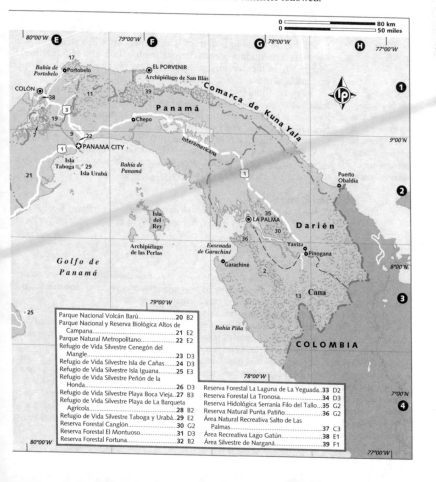

Parque Nacional Volcán Barú	20 B2
Parque Nacional y Reserva Biológica Altos de Campana	21 E2
Parque Natural Metropolitano	22 E2
Refugio de Vida Silvestre Cenegón del Mangle	23 D3
Refugio de Vida Silvestre Isla de Cañas	24 D3
Refugio de Vida Silvestre Isla Iguana	25 E3
Refugio de Vida Silvestre Peñón de la Honda	26 D3
Refugio de Vida Silvestre Playa Boca Vieja	27 B3
Refugio de Vida Silvestre Playa de La Barqueta Agrícola	28 B2
Refugio de Vida Silvestre Taboga y Urabá	29 E2
Reserva Forestal Canglón	30 G2
Reserva Forestal El Montuoso	31 D3
Reserva Forestal Fortuna	32 B2
Reserva Forestal La Laguna de La Yeguada	33 D2
Reserva Forestal La Tronosa	34 D3
Reserva Hidrológica Serranía Filo del Tallo	35 G2
Reserva Natural Punta Patiño	36 G2
Área Natural Recreativa Salto de Las Palmas	37 C3
Área Recreativa Lago Gatún	38 E1
Área Silvestre de Narganá	39 F1

The Botany and Natural History of Panama, edited by William G D'Arcy and Mireya D Correa, is a collection of research papers that covers a wide body of work, including the results of aviary experiments and instructions on how to construct aerial walkways in rain forest canopies.

The loggers initially sought big trees within easy reach, felling all the giants near the highway and trampling young trees with their machinery. Once the giant trees were gone, the loggers cut roads perpendicular to the highway, which led into tall stands of hardwoods. After those stands were chopped down and removed, more roads were cut and yet more stands were leveled.

Right behind the loggers were settlers – thousands of them – poor people looking to eke out a living by turning into cropland the trampled vegetation left by the loggers. With the mature trees gone, all that was required to create cropland was an ax and a match; after some crackling and sizzling and a lot of smoke, the would-be subsistence farmers had fields for planting. Panamanian law encourages homesteading.

As if to punish those who set fire to the forest, the topsoil that had been held in place by roots washed easily away in the rains. The earth beneath the topsoil proved nutrient deficient. After two or three years, the soil couldn't support a decent harvest and little more than grass grew on it. But grass is what cattle eat, so in came ranchers, buying fields that frustrated farmers could no longer use.

This succession of loggers, farmers and ranchers continues in northern Darién Province, although now the loggers must drive far up the side roads they've made to find trees. The farmers are still a step behind the loggers, unintentional nomads employing the slash-and-burn method so widespread in the developing world. And everywhere the settler-farmers go, ranchers move in behind them.

A good website to learn about the astounding natural riches of Isla de Coiba is www.coibapanama.com, which contains photographs as well as links to conservation organizations in Panama.

Today, nearly all that remains of the forests of northern Darién – a complex, multilayered, fragile and wondrous ecosystem that had been evolving for *millions* of years – are cow pastures. Around these pastures are struggling farmers and loggers closing in on the last trees still standing. Today, even a person using binoculars can't see much Darién forest from the highway.

As if bent on speeding the Darién's destruction, the Panamanian government is currently paving the Interamericana all the way to Yaviza (in 2004, the pavement ended at Las Aguas Frías).

Soil Erosion

Deforestation has resulted in yet another serious problem for Panama: soil erosion. Huge, exposed tree roots prevent heavy rains from washing

---

BIOPROSPECTING FOR GOLD

In October 2003, the scientific journal *Ecological Society of America* published an article on one of the most fascinating scientific research projects ever undertaken in Panama – one that could have long-lasting implications for rain forest conservation around the globe.

Several US scientists developed a program in Panama of 'bioprospecting' or scouring the rain forest for compounds that may one day become new drugs. They set up six labs and hired Panamanian scientists – cell biologists and chemists – to develop and run experiments. Although the labs have funding far below those in the USA and Europe, researchers have already begun producing remarkable results and have published their findings in a number of academic journals.

The result of all this places a great deal of importance on the rain forest's biodiversity (where research – and by necessity conservation – equals possible cures for widespread diseases). It is also slowly attracting the attention of large pharmaceutical companies – which spend US$40 billion a year on research – and could lead to a huge investment in helping to both unlock the mysteries of the rain forest and consequently preserve them. This would make conservation both the end and the means.

LOGGING THE DARIÉN

Trees are still being felled in Darién Province, and many are transported by truck along the Interamericana to two huge mills: one is in Chepo, and the other is in 24 de Diciembre, a village near Tocumen. On a single day in the dry season, you can count dozens of lumber trucks passing by.

An even greater number of Darién trees, which are clear-cut, are moved to the mills by barge. Still others are sprayed with a chemical that prevents rot and floated down rivers to the mills. The chemical has killed most of the fish in the rivers used by loggers.

The deforestation has also resulted in severe water shortages from Chepo to Yaviza during the dry season and other environmental problems. Regardless, Panamanian politicians agreed in 2000 to pave the Interamericana to Yaviza, which will permit logging trucks to work the Darién year-round and accelerate the region's destruction. In Panama, loggers have a lot of influence.

away the thin layer of nutrient-rich topsoil found in tropical forests. Take out the trees and the next big storm to hit the denuded area will carry the topsoil into rivers and out to sea, leaving only the nutrient-deficient lower soil where the vibrant jungle once stood.

When you consider that 50% of the country's soil is of poor quality to begin with and that 75% of it is on hillsides, the seriousness of the problem becomes apparent. And yet ranchers, who have deforested most of the Pacific slope from the Costa Rican border to Yaviza, are still allowed to clear-cut forest to create pasture for their cattle.

Isla de Coiba

Currently, one of the hottest environmental topics in Panama is the fate of Isla de Coiba (p195). This rain forest–covered island is set in one of the largest marine parks in the world, with a mind-boggling array of marine life, and scientists have compared it to the Galapagos Islands. Owing to the presence of a penal colony, this island and its surrounding waters remained untouched, but now that the prison is being phased out, developers and members of the government see glorious tourism possibilities for this ecological gem. What they have in mind is building a few hotels, perhaps a megaresort or two on the island and in nearby Santa Catalina, plus a cruise ship dock and so on. President Mireya Moscoso signed a law in 2002 allowing developers to exploit the island. No one knows for sure what will happen now that her term is over. If building commences, it will undoubtedly have a devastating effect on the delicate ecosystem there.

DID YOU KNOW?

Less than 5% of the world's tropical forests are protected within national parks or reserves.

Other Ecological Concerns

Water pollution from agricultural run-off threatens fishery resources. Likewise, pollution from human contaminants is widespread – particularly in the central provinces, where rivers are often used as garbage dumps. Throughout the Archipiélago de San Blás, many view the ocean as a natural toilet and build outhouses on the water. Throwing cans, bottles and plastic containers into the sea is also common, although certain groups (like Dobbo Yala) are educating people about ecological sensitivity.

Another major environmental problem in Panama today is the destruction of the mangrove swamps that play an important role in stemming beach erosion and in maintaining balance in delicate marine ecosystems. Mangroves throughout Panama are being cut down to make room for shrimp farms, resorts and urban development.

In spite of the majority of Panamanians being indifferent to the environmental devastation occurring within the country, there are a few

Plants & Animals in the Life of the Kuna, by Jorge Ventocilla, is one of the first works on ethnobiology written from an indigenous perspective. It discusses the archipelago's plant and animal life and the ecological dangers ahead.

organizations striving to protect the country and its biodiversity, which cannot always be said for ANAM, the largely useless National Environment Authority. The following resources are good places to learn about Panama's natural (and threatened) riches.

A Panama Forest and Shore: Natural History and Amerindian Culture in Bocas del Toro (Boxwood Press, 1983), by Burton L Gordon, is an academic's look at western Panama based on the author's observations of Bocas del Toro during seven field trips.

ANCON (National Association for the Conservation of Nature; Map p72; ☎ 314-0060; www .ancon.org in Spanish; Apdo 1387, Panamá 1, República de Panamá) Founded in 1985 by academic and business leaders, ANCON has played a major role in the creation of national parks and on many occasions has spurred ANAM into action. Ancon Expeditions, although no longer part of the nonprofit organization, still leases land from the conservation organization and employs some of the top naturalist guides in the country. See also p90.

Asociación Napguana (☎ 227-5886; napguana@pty.com; Av Justo Arosemena & Calle 41a, Casa 3-38, Calidonia, Panama City) An NGO founded and run by the Kuna working on preserving the ecology of the islands and other development issues.

Conservacion del Parque Nacional Volcán Barú (☎ 263-4963; www.volcanbaru.cjb.net, http://usuarios.lycos.es/quetzales, in Spanish) Works in conservation of Volcán Barú National Park.

The Smithsonian Tropical Research Institute's website, www.stri.org, contains information about current research in the rain forest labs, upcoming seminars and recent publications about tropical ecology and biodiversity topics.

Corredor Biológico Mesoamericano del Atlántico Panameño (☎ 232-6601; www .cbmap.org; 2nd fl, building 500, Av Ascanio Villalaz, Curundu) Conservation organization allied with the Central American Environment and Development Commission.

Dobbo Yala (☎ 261-7229; www.dobboyala.org.pa; El Carmen Casa No 13-B, Nvo Reparto, Urb Linares) This NGO is run by indigenous professionals, who work in conservation and development projects in indigenous communities.

Institute for Tropical Ecology and Conservation (☎ 352-367-9128 in USA; www.itec-edu .org) In addition to offering courses and research grants on tropical ecology, ITEC works with marine turtles and promotes local environmental education and antipollution in the Bocas del Toro area.

PEMASKY (Project for the Study and Management of Wild Areas of the Kuna Yala; ☎ 316-1236; geodisio@yahoo.com) This grassroots movement, led by the Kuna, has helped keep settlers and loggers out of Kuna Yala mainland rain forests.

Panama Outdoors

Although Panama City has its charms, most people come to Panama to experience the riches of its rain forests, rivers, and islands – well over 1300 in all. There are some spectacular adventure opportunities to be had in Panama, whether you want to snorkel coral reefs or surf 4m faces. Incredible hikes can be had in the mountains (where on a clear morning you might see both oceans), or in the lowland jungle. Bird watchers can pick from a variety of forests and national parks to experience the rich diversity of Panama's 900-plus bird species. You'll find world-class fishing all over the Pacific coast, and spectacular river rafting through the majestic Ríos Chiriquí and Caldera, where rapids rate from beginner to class-five. Those who'd rather just soak up the sights and sounds of the rain forest can take a boat ride along one of the country's vibrant waterways.

To read about early attempts and successes at crossing the Darién Gap, visit www.outbackofbe yond.com, which also features photographs from the expeditions.

HIKING

Hiking opportunities abound in Panama. From Boquete, you can hike to the top of Volcán Barú, Panama's highest peak, from which you can see both oceans on a clear day. There are also plenty of other walks around Boquete, where the narrow roads wind up and down slopes among coffee plantations. The Sendero Los Quetzales (p220) is a trail that leads from Boquete over Volcán Barú to Guadalupe on the other side; it's a six-hour hike through lovely forest. The more adventurous can opt for the Sendero El Pianista, a hike that crosses the Continental Divide en route to the Caribbean Sea. Cerro Punta (p219), on the other side of Barú, also has some lovely hikes with access to the fine Parque Internacional La Amistad (PILA; p247), which stretches all the way to Bocas del Toro Province. For off-the-beaten-path exploring, enter PILA via the Naso community of Wetso (p247).

The little town of El Valle, nestled into the Valle de Antón about a two-hour drive west of Panama City, is a fine place for walking. Many trails lead into the hills around the valley; they are well defined, as the local *campesinos* (peasants) frequently use them.

SAFETY GUIDELINES FOR WALKING

Before embarking on a walking trip, consider the following points to ensure a safe and enjoyable experience:

- Pay any fees and possess any permits required by local authorities (ANAM).
- Be sure you are healthy and feel comfortable walking for a sustained period.
- Obtain reliable information about physical and environmental conditions along your intended route (eg from park authorities).
- Be aware of local laws, regulations and etiquette about wildlife and the environment.
- Walk only in regions, and on tracks, within your realm of experience.
- Be aware that weather conditions and terrain vary significantly from one region, or even from one track, to another. Seasonal changes can significantly alter any track. These differences influence the way walkers dress and the equipment they carry.
- Ask before you set out about the environmental characteristics that can affect your walk and how local, experienced walkers deal with these considerations.

Near Panama City on the shores of the canal, Parque Nacional Soberanía contains a section of the old Sendero Las Cruces (Las Cruces Trail), used by the Spaniards to cross between the coasts. Here, too, is a short and easy but interesting nature trail, the Sendero El Charco, which is signed from the highway (see p121). Parque Natural Metropolitano, on the outskirts of Panama City, also has some good walks, including a nature trail and a 'monkey trail' (p89).

The lovely rivers, waterfalls and virgin cloud forests around Santa Fé (p190) make for some fine exploring, though there's not much infrastructure here (which can be good or bad depending on what you have in mind). Other excellent hikes can be found in Parque Nacional Omar Torrijos (p153), and also in Darién (p287), but these should only be undertaken in the dry season, and only with an experienced guide. Always get the latest information on the security situation, and don't even think about crossing the Darién Gap into Colombia on foot.

To read about the first historic crossing of the Darién Gap, try to find Kip Ross' article entitled 'We Drove Panama's Darien Gap,' from *National Geographic* 119, no 3 (March 1961): 368-89.

DIVING & SNORKELING

There are many decent dive spots – and several very good ones – off both coasts of Panama. The best diving and snorkeling, hands down, is near Isla de Coiba, which is the centerpiece of a national marine park. A few tour operators go there from Panama City (p90). There's also a dive operator in Santa Catalina (p193), and plenty of local fishermen in Santa Catalina who can take you out to the best spots if you have your own gear.

Parque Nacional Marino Golfo de Chiriquí (p206), near David, and the Archipiélago de las Perlas (p126) also offer excellent snorkeling and scuba diving possibilities. Sea turtles, white-tipped reef sharks and numerous other intriguing creatures ply the waters just off the beach of the Hotel Contadora Resort, a large hotel on Isla Contadora, the most popular of the Pearls. The Archipiélago de las Perlas (p126) on the Pacific side is a decent diving spot, as is the area near Portobelo on the Caribbean side. On the Pacific side you'll be looking for reef sharks, groupers and sea turtles near shore, and sailfish, amberjacks and dog-toothed snappers further out.

Bocas del Toro (p231) offers diving, but visibility is usually poor. The Comarca de Kuna Yala (p266) has many fine coral reefs, but the Kuna prohibit dive operators from working there. Visitors will have to be content with snorkeling, which is quite good.

The Darkest Jungle: The True Story of the Darién Expedition and America's Ill-Fated Race to Connect the Seas, by Todd Balf, tells the harrowing tale of the 1854 expedition that ended in tragedy in the untamed jungle.

There's also good diving near Bahía Piña, Punta Mariato and Punta Burica on the Pacific side, and Isla Escudo de Veraguas, Cayos Zapatillas and Portobelo on the Caribbean side. If you've dived some of the world's top spots, these sites won't wow you, but for most divers they're appealing and they can surprise. At Portobelo (p257), for example, it's possible to dive a 110-foot cargo ship and a C-45 twin-engine plane.

When you're making travel plans, bear in mind that the Caribbean Sea is calm during the dry season (mid-December to mid-April). During the rainy season (mid-April to mid-December), the Caribbean can be treacherous due to high winds and strong currents. On the Pacific side, strong winds are common during February and March.

DECOMPRESSION CHAMBERS

Warning: as there are only four decompression chambers in the entire country – one in Colón, one at Lago Gatún and two in Panama City – divers should avoid taking unnecessary risks. If you stay down too long or come up too fast, you'll be in serious trouble.

It's possible to dive the Pacific and Atlantic Oceans in one day. **Scuba-panama** (☎ 261-3841; www.scubapanama.com; cnr Av 6a C Norte & Calle 62 C Oeste, El Carmen, Panama City) offers bicoastal dives. There are a number of organizations that offer dives for experienced divers as well as courses for the novice. The following dive agencies offer PADI-certified courses up through Dive Master and provide equipment and transportation to dive sites: Starfleet Eco-Adventures (p231); Scuba Coiba (p193); Twin Oceans Dive Center (p259); and Jimmy's Caribbean Dive Resort near Nombre de Dios (p265).

SURFING

The best surf breaks in Panama are generally Santa Catalina, Teta and Río Mar (all on the Pacific side), though there are some excellent breaks in the Archipiélago de Bocas del Toro and elsewhere. All three Pacific-side breaks are reef breaks, and all three break both ways. The right break at Santa Catalina has no equal in Central America when the southern swells appear.

The best months for Santa Catalina (p193) are February and March, but the surf breaks here year-round. The face of a typical wave at Santa Catalina is 2m; during February and March waves with 4m faces are fairly common, and waves here are at their best during medium to high tide, when rides approaching 150m are possible. Surf booties are a must due to the volcanic rock beneath the surf. The water is never cold, but a Lycra vest is recommended during February and March, due to strong offshore winds.

Playa Teta is popular with Panamanian surfers due to its beauty and its proximity to Panama City, but its ride is nowhere near as sweet as Santa Catalina's. The face of a typical wave at Teta is 2m, and there are often long stretches between big waves. When there are big southern swells coming all the way from New Zealand, Teta is a fantastic place for getting barrel, with faces reaching 4m. The bottom is both rocky and sandy; booties aren't really needed. The best months for Teta are May, June, July and August, but even during these months the waves can be disappointing.

Playa Río Mar (p138), near Teta in Panamá Province, is only really surfable during medium to low tide, as the waves generally don't break during high tide. What is special about this place is the length as well as the ease of the ride, which can last 100m. The bottom is mostly rocky and strewn with broken oyster shells so booties are recommended. Like Teta, this beach is accessible and popular. The best months to surf here are May to August.

For consistently good breaks, try Playa Venao, also on the Pacific side. Waves there break both ways and are at their best when they are about 2m in height. Any larger and they close out without offering much of a ride. The bottom is sandy; no booties are needed.

On the Caribbean side, the islands of Bocas del Toro offer some of the best and most varied surfing in Panama, best between December and March. The top breaks in Bocas are Isla Carenero and Silverbacks. Isla Carenero is a reef break near Bocas town that often presents 200m-long peeling lefts with great tubes. It breaks over shallow reef and is comparable to the well-known Restaurants break in Tahiti. Silverbacks, off Isla Bastimentos, is home to waves up to 5m tall on good swells. Silverbacks is known for a large, powerful right with a big drop and big tube but a relatively short ride, breaking over reef and comparing to Hawaii's big-wave spots; only experienced surfers should surf it.

See the Panama Surfer's Map (pp56–7) for more information on Panamanian surf sites. For surfing tours contact **Panama Surf Tours** (☎ 507-672-0089, in USA 800-716-3452; www.panamasurftours.com). This company is run by Panama native Jon Hanna, a former national champion who knows Panama's surf scene as well as anyone.

SURFER'S MAP

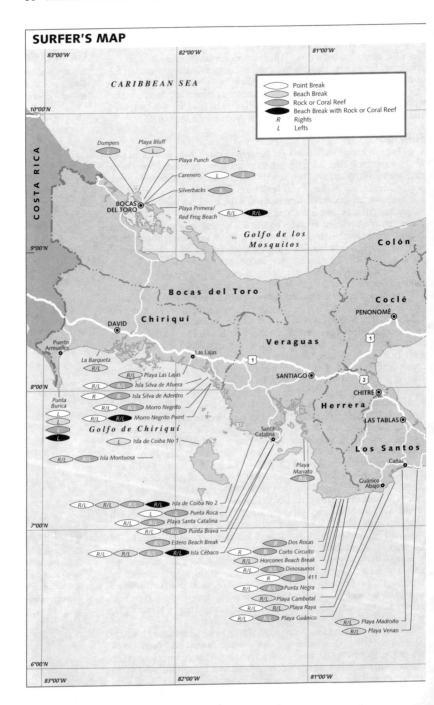

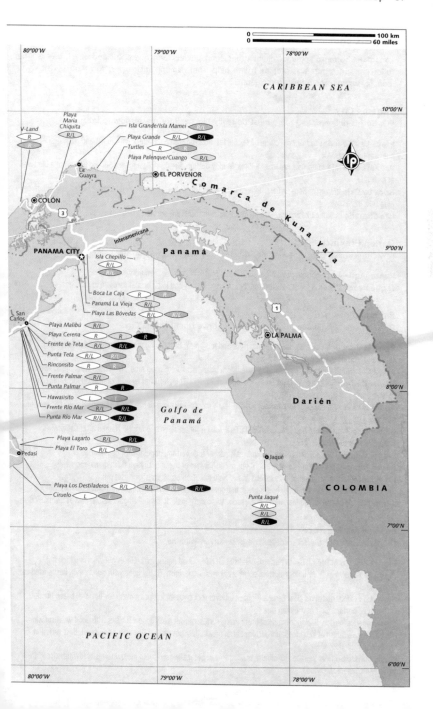

PANAMA SURF REPORT

Panama is home to some excellent tubes, long peelers, and fine-point and beach breaks. The following surf report was prepared with help from Panama surf expert Jon Hanna. Visit www .panamasurftours.com for further details.

Panama City

PC's surf is polluted, and there must be really big swell for these spots to break.

Playa Las Bóvedas In front of Palacio de las Garzas. Rock-bottom point break with rights and lefts. Best at medium to high tide.
Panamá La Vieja In front of Panamá La Vieja. Muddy bottom. Breaks right and left. Surfing limited to a big swell at high tide.
Boca La Caja In front of Boca La Caja, an area with many thugs. Rock-bottomed right break surfed at medium to high tide.
Isla Chepillo In Bahía de Panamá. Two point breaks over rocks, one surfable at all tides.

Darién Province

Few surfers have ever ventured into this territory, which is way off the beaten path.

Punta Jaqué A rock-bottom point break with rights that is best at medium tide.
Jaqué Beach Break A black-sand-bottom beach break, rights and lefts, best at medium to high tide.

Panamá Province

Fine surf sites, beginning about a 45-minute drive from Panama City.

Playa Malibu Near Gorgona. Sand-bottom right and left break; best during medium to low tide. Consistent, good tubes and long rides when good swell.
Playa Cerena In Coronado, past security gate. Right point break with good tubes, long rides when good swell.
Frente de Teta Rock/sand bottom break at mouth of Río Teta. Long lefts at low tide, rights and lefts at medium to high tide.
Punta Teta Point break over rock to south of Río Teta's mouth. Lefts and rights. Good tubes, rides. Best at medium tide going up.
Rinconsito Rock-bottom point south of Punta Teta, long right break on good swell. Named after California's famous Rincón break.
Frente Palmar South of San Carlos. Beach break, partial rock bottom, popular with beginners.
Punta Palmar Rock-bottom point break. Right peeling waves at medium to high tide when good swell.
Hawaiisito Rock-bottom point break. Lefts at full high tide. Only small swell or closes out.
Frente Río Mar Somewhat rocky beach break in front of Río Mar. Rights, lefts. Best at medium to high tide.
Punta Río Mar South of Río Mar, near jutting rocks. Walk and paddle at low tide. Rights best. Breaks at low tide only.

Los Santos Province

This province is home to some of the best surf in Panama.

Playa Lagarto At Pedasí. Beach bottom. Breaks at all tides. Good rights, lefts. Closes out when surf too big.
Playa El Toro Near Pedasí. Rock-bottom point break with lefts, rights. Really good with good swell. Best surfed at medium tide.
Playa Los Destiladeros Near Pedasí. Right point over rock bottom, left point over rock bottom, beach break with pebble bottom. Best at medium tide.
Ciruelo Before Venado. Rock-bottom point break, rarely surfed, can get really good left tubes with good swell, no wind.
Playa Venao South of Venado. Sand-bottom beach break. This spot catches just about any swell. Best surfed at medium to high tide.
Playa Madroño Near Venado. 30-minute walk. Surf can get really good, with hollow tubes at low tide. Need to arrive early, before the wind.

Playa Guánico South of Venado. 45-minute hike. Two rock-bottom point breaks with rights, lefts; one beach break with rights and lefts.

Playa Raya One hour past Venado. Waves 4m to 5m on big swells, with big tubes. Many big sharks here too.

Playa Cambutal Beyond Tonosí. Beach break with rights, lefts. Catches about any swell. Best at medium to high tide.

Punta Negra West of Playa Cambutal, around the first point. Point break over rocks, best during medium to high tide.

411 West of Punta Negra. Locally famous point break with long right over rock ledge. Best during medium to high tide.

Dinosaurios Next to 411. Rock-bottom break with rights, lefts at medium to high tide. Can get very big surf.

Horcones Beach Break West of Dinosaurios. Sand-bottom beach break with rights, lefts. Good most tides.

Dos Rocas Near Horcones. Rock-bottom point break beside two jutting boulders. Can get good rights at medium tide.

Corto Circuito At road's end toward Cerro Hoya. Rock-bottom point break with powerful peak. Breaks over a rock ledge and throws a huge tube, then peels for about 100m with a great wall.

Veraguas Province

Veraguas has some of the best surf in Central America.

Playa Santa Catalina South of Sona. Famous surf. Sharp rock bottom right and left break. Main wave is the right. Incredible tubes, long rides with lots of power. Surfed mostly medium to high tide.

Estero Beach Break Fifteen-minute walk from Santa Catalina. A long beach break, has lefts and rights over sand bottom. Beginners generally surf the beach break at low tide.

Punta Brava Just west of Estero. Point breaks at low tide over sharp rock bottom. Has lefts and rights, but the lefts are best. Very powerful. Has a great tube section. Booties needed.

Punta Roca Thirty minutes' walk from Santa Catalina. Left point break surfed at low tide over a rock-bottom ledge, with short rides but big hollow tubes.

Isla Cébaco Island near Santa Catalina. Four breaks, with rights and lefts. Area known for sharks, huge snappers, groupers.

Playa Mariato Faces Isla Cebaco. Soft rock-bottom break with lefts, rights.

Chiriquí Province

Chiriquí has several remote islands with very good surf. Need tour operator to arrange.

Isla de Coiba Many surf spots, but most are unsurfed and difficult to get to, even with a boat.

Isla Montuosa Isle opposite Hannibal Bank from Coiba. Good right rock bottom point with solid waves and very consistent. Up to 5m. Catches just about any swell.

Isla Silva de Afuera Two breaks: one left, one right. Right is big peak breaking over a shallow rock ledge at medium tide; can throw a big tube, with steep drops and no wall. Other break is a good left that breaks over a rock reef at medium tide. This spot catches almost any swell.

Isla Silva de Adentro A right-hand break over rock reef that can get really good with a good swell.

Morro Negrito Near Morro Negrito town, difficult access. About five breaks, variety of lefts and rights. Good tubes.

Playa Las Lajas East of David. Beach-bottom break with rights and lefts, but in infrequent waves.

La Barqueta Near David. Beach-bottom break with rights and lefts. Breaks at all tides, but medium to high is best.

Punta Burica On Costa Rican border. Four left points that break along the point for long, tubing rides. Catches any swell. Better wave than Pavones of Costa Rica, and uncrowded.

Archipiélago de Bocas del Toro

Excellent surfing with great variety, but limited to December through March.

Dumpers Isla Colón. Reef-bottom left break with a very steep drop, big tube and short ride. Reef is sharp and tricky. Dangerous for beginners.

Playa Punch Isla Colón. Reef-bottom left and right break with good tubes and fun sections to hit the lip and do crazy airs. Popular with beginners, but booties recommended for the reef.

Playa Bluff Isla Colón, road's end. Long beach renowned for board-breaking powerful surf. The tubes here are incredible.

Carenero Isla Carenero, 5-minute boat ride from Bocas town. Reef break with 200m peeling lefts, with great tubes. Boat drop-off, pickup at reef. Booties recommended.

Silverbacks Isla Bastimentos. Reef bottom with waves up to 5m on good swells. Large right with big drop, big tube, but relatively short ride. Not for beginners.

Red Frog Beach & Playa Primera Isla Bastimentos; walk across island. Both sand and reef bottom breaks with lefts and rights.

Colón-Portobelo Area

The best surf for this area is from December through March.

Playa Maria Chiquita In front of Maria Chiquita. Beach break with lefts and rights, but limited to big swell.

Isla Grande In front of La Guayra, best reached by water taxi. Reef bottom break with three peaks, rights and lefts.

Isla Mamei Next to Isla Grande, reached by boat or paddling from Isla Grande. Left-hand point break over shallow reef.

Playa Palenque/Cuango In front of Cuango village. Beach break with rights and lefts. Surfers seldom seen here.

Playa Grande Mainland, east of Isla Grande. Beach break with some reef. Waves break left and right.

Turtles Paddling distance from Playa Grande. Waves are great; unreal tubes, if it is glassy with a big swell.

V-Land Near Devils Beach, in Sherman. Unbelievable right-point reef break with great tubes when big swell and glassy.

WILDLIFE WATCHING

The Tapir's Morning Bath: Mysteries of the Tropical Rainforests and the Scientists Who Are Trying to Solve Them, by Elizabeth Royte, is a fascinating introduction to tropical ecology and a travelogue documenting Royte's 'education' on Isla Barro Colorado.

The bio-rich terrain of the isthmus boasts some astounding settings for spotting animal life. Parque Natural Metropolitano (p89) is a good place for seeing Geoffroy's tamarins and agoutis. Parque Nacional Soberanía (p121) also has its share of agoutis and monkeys (white-faced capuchins, mantled howlers) as well as two species of sloth. If you take a boat trip along the Panama Canal, you can sometimes spot capybaras and American crocodiles basking along the shore. Isla Barro Colorado (p122) is a fine place to see agoutis, coatis and red-tailed squirrels. You might also see howler monkeys, white-faced capuchins and spider monkeys. The island has a healthy population of ocelots, pumas and jaguars. If you're lucky you might spot the tracks of these nocturnal predators.

Bird Watching

Panama offers magnificent bird watching. The Panama Audubon Society, which does an annual bird count, consistently counts more species of bird in Panama than are recorded anywhere else in Central America. This is due to two factors: Panama's location relative to two continents and its narrow girth. Birds migrating between North and South America tend to be funneled into a small area. Many North and South American species are represented, both native and migratory. Panama also has many endemic species of avifauna.

The famous resplendent quetzal, symbol of Central America, is more abundant in western Panama than anywhere else in the region. It can be seen around Volcán Barú, notably in the hills around Boquete and Cerro Punta, where it is common much of the year.

Other birds of particular interest include the three-wattled bellbird, the harpy eagle, the great green macaw and the king vulture – the list goes on and on. All told, 940 species (native, migratory and endemic) have been identified in Panama.

To see birds in Panama, just get a good set of binoculars and get out on a trail. The Pipeline Rd (p121) trail near Panama City is a favorite with birders; more than 500 species were sighted there in a single day during a 1996 Christmas bird count. Most birds are seen around dawn and just afterward, so avid birders will want to arrive just before daylight.

Cana Valley in Darién is another of the world's top birding destinations. Prime attractions include four species of macaw, harpy eagles, black-tipped cotingas and golden-headed quetzals.

A Guide to the Birds of Panama is extremely helpful (see Books, p49). Helpful organizations include the **Panama Audubon Society** (☎ 224-9371; www .panamaaudubon.org) in Panama City, which organizes birding expeditions. Companies offering birding services include Ancon Expeditions of Panama, Pesantez Tours and Iguana Tours, which are all based in Panama City (see Tours, p90).

The Magical Web: The Tropical Forest of Barro Colorado, by Christian Ziegler (photographer) and Egbert Leigh, contains gorgeous photographs of plant and animal life on one of the world's most biologically rich islands in the rain forest.

RIVER RAFTING & KAYAKING

There are three kinds of river running in Panama, all of which are awesome. You can go white-water rafting on the Ríos Chiriquí and Chiriquí Viejo, where trips are offered by the country's top rafting outfit, **Chiriquí River Rafting** (☎ 720-1505; www.panama-rafting.com; Av Central, downtown Boquete, Chiriquí Province).

You can run the same rivers and others in kayaks. Kayaking tours during the rain season (April–November) are offered by **Kayak Panama** (☎ /fax 993-3620, www.kayakpanama.com), based at XS Memories, an American-run hotel and sports bar located in Santa Clara in Coclé Province. English, German and Spanish are spoken.

For sea kayaking, an excellent new outfit based in Boquete that makes overnight trips into the Golfo de Chiriquí, is **Exploration Panama** (☎ 720-2470; www.explorationpanama.net). Although they aren't specifically a sea-kayaking outfit, they work with the top kayakers from Chiriquí River Rafting.

Nantahala Outdoor Center (☎ 800-232-7238, in the USA; www.noc.com) offers several very popular kayaking adventures in Panama every year.

BOATING TRIPS

Nearly 500 rivers lace the rugged landscape of Panama. Visitors interested in exploring some of these lush, jungle-shrouded waterways have a variety of options.

Panama Jet Boat Explorer (☎ 720-4054; www.panamajetboatexplorer.com) operates a variety of day trips in the Bocas del Toro Province, which involve cruising up jungle rivers and stopping in Ngöbe Buglé villages. It's owned by a safety-conscious American expat, and comes well recommended.

Ancon Expeditions of Panama (☎ 269-9414; www.anconexpeditions.com), located in Panama City (p90), offers numerous tours in the Darién involving travel by riverboat and/or dugout, as well as trips up the Río Teribe in Bocas del Toro Province. It also offers an excellent day trip, the 'jungle boat adventure,' which consists of a cruise up the Panama Canal, passing close to the shoreline for maximum wildlife viewing, followed by a trip around some of the pristine islands of Lago Gatún. This is a good choice for kids.

Those who are interested in seeing Panama's famous waterway can take a full or partial canal transit.

For those looking for more off-the-beaten-path adventure, there are loads of opportunities. In the Darién, you can take a boat trip up the Río Sambú (p289), or cruise from La Palma to Río Mogué. Wetso (p247) and Las Delicias (p246) are indigenous villages where locals can take you on river trips.

In Bocas del Toro, you can hire a motorized canoe to take you out to some of the untouched islands in the archipelago. Península Valiente

The Panama Guide, by Nancy Schwalbe Zydler and Tom Zydler, is the best cruising guide to the isthmus of Panama. It offers piloting directions, charts, anchorages, history, and even instructions for transiting the Panama Canal.

and Escudo de Veraguas aren't easy to get to, but for adventurers, they're just the ticket.

FISHING

Panama has 1518 islands, 2988km of coast and 480 major rivers that empty into the oceans, so there's no problem finding a fishing spot.

For deep-sea fishing, Panama offers three world-class areas: Bahía Piña and the Las Perlas and Coiba archipelagos. All three sites are served by fishing outfits.

Piña is served by the upscale Tropic Star Lodge (p290), which boasts more than 50 current world records.

In the Archipiélago de las Perlas, the only outfit running fishing tours is based at the island resort of Isla San José (p131).

The Coiba group is served by Coiba Adventure Sportfishing and Coiba Explorer Panama; the former offers shipboard lodging, the latter shipboard and beachfront lodging (see Parque Nacional Isla de Coiba, p195).

Bocas del Toro (p223) also has fishing possibilities, with several outfits offering boat and equipment rental.

Other angling possibilities include bass fishing in Lago Gatún and trout fishing in the rivers running down Volcán Barú near the towns of Boquete, Volcán, Bambito and Cerro Punta. See Chiriquí Province (p219) for information on trout fishing.

CYCLING

Cycling is an excellent way to see most of Panama (although riding in Panama City is not recommended). The roads here are the best in Central America, which doesn't mean much once you leave the Interamericana. The highway is in good condition from the Costa Rican border to Panama City, while intersecting roads range from good (the pavement to Santa Fé, p190) to poor (the road to Santa Catalina, p193). Many of the roads are being improved (the road from the Interamericana to Pedasí, for instance, will be freshly paved by the time you read this). The major factor when considering a lengthy bike ride is the weather. No matter what bike you're on, it's not safe to ride in the rain, and it rains frequently from mid-April to mid-December. On the Caribbean side, count on rain year-round.

It is possible to bring your own bike by air and this is definitely the thing to do if you plan on seeing the country by bike. The one decent biking store is in **Panama City Bicicletas Rali** (☎ 263-4136; www.rali-carretero.com in Spanish; Via España), where you can buy bikes and accessories and have repairs done. Most airlines will fly a bike as one of your pieces of checked baggage if you box it. However, boxing a bike gives baggage handlers little clue as to the contents, and the box is liable to be roughly handled, possibly damaging the bike. An alternative is wrapping it in heavy plastic or bubble wrap – baggage handlers are likely to drop or throw the bike in this case. Airlines' bicycle-carrying policies vary a lot, so ask around.

Be advised that while Panamanians are required to license their bicycles, foreigners are not. However, foreigners are required to be able to demonstrate proof of ownership. Police in Panama have been known to confiscate bikes from foreigners who were unable to show such proof.

Food & Drink

Panama's resplendent coastline and verdant interior produce a culinary bounty, from tropical fruits to *frutas del mar* ('fruits of the sea'). In fact, in Panama (which means 'abundance of fishes'), the sea has always been the great provider for the people, though the ways in which plates of fish, crab, shrimp and lobster are prepared allow for plenty of regional variations – whether it's the West Indian flavors at play in Bocas del Toro or the traditional indigenous cooking methods of the Kuna people.

Throughout the country you'll find good food among some spectacular settings, including quaint seaside restaurants on the Caribbean, hilltop verandas in the mountains and island retreats in the Pacific. You'll find the greatest variety of cuisine in Panama City, where French, Italian, Lebanese and Japanese restaurants lie scattered among many traditional Panamanian eateries. Boquete and Bocas del Toro also have a wide selection of restaurants. The growing number of expats in each community means you'll have a surprising number of international food choices, as well as excellent regional specialties.

New World Kitchen: Latin American and Caribbean Cuisine, by Norman Aken, contains only one purely Panamanian recipe, but you'll find dozens of other 'Pan-Latin' and 'Pan-Caribbean' dishes that show culinary influences from the isthmus.

STAPLES & SPECIALTIES

The national dish of Panama is *sancocho*, a fairly spicy chicken-and-vegetable stew. *Ropa vieja* (literally 'old clothes'), a spicy shredded beef combination served over rice, is another common and tasty dish. Rice – grown on dry land – is the staple of Panama and is seemingly served with everything.

As elsewhere in the Americas, meat figures prominently in the Panamanian diet. In addition to staples like *bistec* (steak) and *carne asado* (roast meat), you'll encounter specialties like *carimañola*, which is a roll made from ground and boiled yuca that is filled with chopped meat and then deep fried. Far more commonplace – in restaurants, snack bars and just about anywhere food is sold – are empanadas, which are corn turnovers filled with ground meat and fried. If you get them fresh, they're a fine treat. Another favorite is the tamale, which is cornmeal with a few spices and chicken or pork that's wrapped in banana leaves and boiled.

Gallo pinto, which means 'spotted rooster,' is traditionally served at breakfast and consists of a soupy mixture of rice and black beans, often with a pig's tail thrown in for flavor. This dish, lightly spiced with herbs, is filling and tasty, and it sometimes comes with *natilla* (a cross between sour cream and custard) or *huevos fritos/revueltos* (fried/scrambled eggs).

Another item you might see at breakfast is a side of *tortillas de maíz*. Unlike those found in Mexico and Guatemala, Panamanian tortillas are much thicker, and are essentially deep-fried cornmeal cakes. They go quite nicely with eggs or roast meat. *Hojaldras* are also served at breakfasts and available at snack bars. Not unlike a donut, this deep-fried mass of dough is served hot, which you then cover with sugar.

For a handful of Panamanian recipes, including one for *sancocho*, Panama's national dish, visit www.boyds.org/recipes.htm

At lunch (*almuerzo*), many Panamanians opt for simple *comida corriente* (also called *casado*), the meal of the working class. This is an inexpensive set meal containing various items. Beef, chicken or fish is served alongside *arroz* (rice), *frijoles* (black beans), *plátano* (fried plantain), chopped *repollo* (cabbage) and maybe an egg or an avocado.

Vegetables don't grow well in the tropics, and yuca and plantains take the place of leafy greens at most Panamanian eateries. Among the variations are *patacones*, fried green plantains cut crossways in thin pieces,

TRAVEL YOUR TASTE BUDS

Some of Panama's best cuisine can be found on the Caribbean coast in Bocas del Toro (p223). There you can find delicious freshly caught seafood – usually served alongside coconut rice. In Boquete, don't miss the rainbow trout served at many restaurants. You'll also find excellent coffee grown at nearby plantations as well as strawberries, which make some lovely *batidos* (fruit shakes). Elsewhere in the Chiriquí region you'll encounter specialties like *almojabanos*, which are similar to *tortillas de maíz*, except hand-rolled into the form of small sausage-sized pieces. *Carne ahumada*, which is smoked, dried ('jerked') meat, is another Chiriquí favorite. A variety of smoked meats is available on the Península de Azuero, where Panama's cowboy is most evident.

covered in salt and then pressed and fried. You'll also encounter *tajadas*, ripe plantains sliced lengthwise and fried, and *plátanos maduros* (also called *plátonos en tentación*), which are ripe plantains sliced lengthwise and baked or broiled with butter, brown sugar and cinnamon.

Unlike vegetables, fruits are plentiful in Panama, and the climate is just right for nourishing a range of tasty specialties. Papayas, mangos, pineapples, melons, passion fruit, soursop (or custard apple) and regional specialties like *mamón* (a delectable cousin of the lychee) are among the many items you'll see at markets and in grocery stores.

Seafood is also abundant in Panama. On the Caribbean coast and islands, common everyday foods include shrimp, Caribbean king crab, octopus, lobster and fish such as corvina. In areas along the Caribbean coast, you'll find a West Indian influence to the dishes, and seafood is often mixed with coconut milk; coconut rice and coconut bread are other Caribbean treats. Unfortunately, lobster is heavily overfished, and you may want to skip it.

Among seafood, the fresh-tasting ceviche (marinated raw fish) is popular all over the country. Classic Panamanian ceviche includes sea bass or *conchas* (shellfish), chopped onion and *ají chombo* (one of the hottest chili peppers in the world), marinated in lemon juice. Increasingly, ceviche in Panama is offered with *langostinos* (jumbo shrimp) or *pulpo* (octopus) in lieu of corvina or shellfish.

In Panama City you'll often see men pushing carts and selling *raspados*, cones filled with shaved ice topped with fruit syrup and sweetened condensed milk. This is no gourmet dish, but it's a favorite among Panamanians, particularly the under-10 crowd.

Many bars serve *bocas*. These are little, savory side dishes such as black beans, ceviche, chicken stew, potato chips and sausages, and they make a nice appetizer before dinner.

You'll find excellent ceviche throughout the isthmus. To get a handle on preparing this delicious seafood dish, take a look at *The Great Ceviche Book* by Douglas Rodriguez.

DRINKS
Alcoholic Drinks

The national alcoholic drink is made of *seco*, milk and ice. *Seco*, like rum, is distilled from sugarcane, but it doesn't taste anything like the rum you know. This is the drink of *campesinos* (rural residents). Order a *seco con leche* in a martini lounge in Panama City and you'll likely receive some odd looks, but for a taste of real Panama, don't leave the country without trying one.

By far the most popular alcoholic beverage in Panama is *cerveza* (beer), and the most popular local brands are Soberana, Panamá, Balboa, Cristal and Atlas. None of these is very flavorful, but when served ice-cold on a hot day, they do the trick. A large Atlas at a typical cantina can cost as little as US$0.50; the same beer can cost you US$2.50 at a decent restaurant.

Ceviche is a Panamanian favorite; for half a dozen different recipes go to www.geocities.com /NapaValley/4192 /recipes.html.

A notch below *cerveza* on the popularity index are the hard liquors, often referred to by both sexes as *baja panties* (panty lowerers). Of these, rum, scotch and vodka are the big sellers. Wines are not terribly popular. Those that are offered generally come from Chile, France or the USA and the quality is poor. In all but the best restaurants, red wine is served cold. However, Panama City has a growing number of places where you can find good wines – both in restaurants and in wine shops. Vintages from California, France, Spain, Italy and Argentina are all represented, although the variety is not huge.

There's a drink that *campesinos* in the central provinces particularly like: *vino de palma,* which is sap extracted from the trunk of an odd variety of palm tree called *palma de corozo*. This collected sap can be drunk immediately (it's delicious and sweet) or fermented (which goes down like firewater).

You'll find dozens of Panamanian recipes in Spanish at www.critica.com.pa/archivo/recetas.

Most bars in Panama have a happy hour – drinks are half-price during certain late-afternoon hours, typically 4pm to 6pm or 5pm to 7pm. Some nightclubs (like Rock Café, p108) offer 'open bars,' which means you pay a cover charge and then the drinks are free. Generally only bottom-shelf local brands are served at open bars.

Nonalcoholic Drinks

Fresh fruit drinks, sweetened with heaped tablespoons of sugar and mixed with water or milk, are called *chichas* and are very common. These drinks originated in Chiriquí Province and are now popular throughout Panama. At Niko's Cafe in Panama City (p99), for example, more than a dozen different *chichas* are sold. Fruit drinks to try include *piña* (pineapple), *sandía* (watermelon), *melón* (cantaloupe), *zarzamora* (blackberry), *zanahoria* (carrot), *cebada* (barley) and *tamarindo* (a slightly tart but refreshing drink made from the fruit of the tamarind tree).

A nonalcoholic drink found in Panama and nowhere else is the *chicheme*. This delicious concoction consists of milk, sweet corn, cinnamon and vanilla. Many Panamanians believe *chicheme* has certain health-giving properties and think nothing of driving many kilometers to buy it in La Chorrera, a city in Panamá Province that produces the best *chicheme* (see p134).

Perhaps the healthiest drink available in Panama is the one served in its natural container: coconut juice. On certain stretches of the Carretera Nacional (National Hwy) on the Península de Azuero and on some islands in the Comarca de Kuna Yala, you'll see people selling coconut juice from little stands. You'll recognize the stands by the piles of coconuts beside them. For US$0.25 the vendor will hack a hole in a coconut and serve it to you. The juice is sweet and pure, and quite good for the digestion. When you're through with the juice, ask the vendor to split the coconut in half. If you're lucky, the meat that it contains will be delicious – some coconuts have tasty meat, some don't.

DID YOU KNOW?

The output of Panama's largest *seco* factory, Seco Herrerano, is 36,000 1L bottles every day.

Coffee is traditionally served very strong and offered with cream or condensed milk. Café Durán is the most popular of the local brands, and it's quite good. Cappuccinos are increasingly available in Panama City; you can also find them in David and Boquete. Tea (including herbal tea) is available in the cities but difficult to find in towns. Milk is pasteurized and safe to drink. The usual brands of soft drinks are available.

You'll find dozens of recipes for Panamanian cuisine at www.czbrats.com/Menus/recmenu.htm.

WHERE TO EAT & DRINK

Panama has eating establishments to suit every budget. At the low end are cafés (coffee shop or diner) and *cafeterías* (simple eateries), which are

---

DOS AND DON'TS

■ When you enter a restaurant, and when you sit down at a table, it's polite to say, *'buenos dias'* or *'buenas tardes'* to those sitting next to you.

■ When you leave a restaurant, it's polite to say *'buen provecho'* (bon appetit) to those near you.

■ It's customary to leave a 10% tip, which is usually included on the bill. Look to see if the *propina* (tip) has been added.

■ Don't eat animals that are endangered or at risk of being endangered. These include *tortuga* (sea turtle), *huevos de tortuga* (turtle eggs), *cazón* (shark), *conejo pintado* (paca), *ñeque* (agouti), *venado* (deer) or iguana.

■ *Langosta* (lobster) is heavily overfished, particularly in the Comarca de Kuna Yala. By eating lobster, you may be contributing to its extinction in these waters. In particular, try to avoid eating lobster during the mating season from March to July.

---

generally places to find inexpensive plates, sometimes served buffet-style (as is the case with the popular Panama City chain Niko's Café), and sometimes served as *comida corriente* (set meals) at informal sit-down establishments. In either case, meals rarely cost over US$3, and service is usually friendly, but to-the-point. In Panama City and in other areas of notable foreign influence, cafés might also connote coffee shops. Cappuccinos, snacks and even light meals can be found in these places.

Panaderías are bakeries, and are a good choice for a quick bite. Most have a few tables and a countertop where you can peer at the goods. Coffee and other drinks are available at most bakeries.

Restaurante is a term that, like its English counterpart, covers a wide spectrum of dining options. Most restaurants open for lunch from noon to 3pm and dinner from 6pm to 10pm. On weekends, restaurants in Panama City stay open until midnight or even 2am, depending on their location. Not all places open for breakfast. Those that do open at 7am or 8am. Even at the best places in Panama City, you rarely need reservations. If there's a wait, by the time you finish a cocktail at the restaurant bar (or one nearby), your table will be ready.

Eating & Drinking in Latin America: A Menu Reader and Restaurant Guide, by Andy Herbach and Michael Dillon, is a sensible choice if you plan to travel in other parts of Latin America. The guide features local specialties and unusual dishes.

Speaking of bars, finding a place to drink isn't difficult in Panama, though in rural areas this may be a bare-bones cantina without a lot of ambience. In the city, mid-level bars (ones that you could take your mother to) tend to open around 4pm. Some open at noon.

Travelers can also put together some fine meals at the supermarkets. Panama has many giant American-style supermarkets. These are short on charm, but quite nice when you want to put a meal together. Many also have *cafeterías* attached where you can get hot, cheap meals on a dime.

VEGETARIANS & VEGANS

The best places for vegetarians to eat are in Panama City, which has a handful of places where you can put together a meatless meal. Ethnic places – notably Lebanese, Thai and Chinese – are good places to look. Travelers who eat fish can do quite well in Panama, as most menus serve as much fish as meat. Panamanian dishes often contain 'hidden' meat products: vegetable soups usually are made from meat stock, and *patacones* are often fried in lard. Some creativity will be a prerequisite for vegans to eat well here. In addition to international cuisine, keep an eye out for supermarkets and vegetable stands, where you can get the ingredients to put your own meal together.

WHINING & DINING

Only a handful of Panamanian restaurants has high chairs or special kids' menus. All the same, most Panamanians are quite accommodating to diners with children. Reservations are rarely needed for most establishments. The only particularly busy times you should be mindful of are Friday and Saturday nights from 7pm to 9pm.

Cities with the widest varieties of restaurants are Panama City, Bocas del Toro, Boquete, and to a lesser extent David. In any of these towns, it's easy to find something for even the most finicky child.

Nearly every town has at least one pizzeria, which is where you're most likely to see parents with children or teenagers. And in Panama City and David, American fast-food franchises as well as the food courts inside the malls are popular eating spots for families.

Supermarkets in Panama boast a wide range of products, and are great spots for loading up on snack items before a bus trip.

Very few visitors to Panama – and that includes kids as well as adults – have a problem with sickness from food preparation. Cleanliness and hygiene are particularly high in Panama, and the tap water is safe to drink in most provinces (Bocas del Toro being a notable exception).

For more information on traveling with kids, see the Directory chapter (p294).

The Book of Latin American Cooking, by Elisabeth Lambert Ortiz, contains over 500 recipes from all over Latin America.

HABITS & CUSTOMS

Panamanians tend to have a small repast at breakfast time – usually just coffee and a roll. Those in the countryside sometimes have bigger meals with eggs, *carne asado* and tortillas. Generally, lunch is the big meal of the day, often followed by a short siesta to beat the heat of the day. Dinner usually consists of soup or salad and bread.

Panamanians are open and informal, and treat their guests quite well. If you have the good fortune to be invited into a Panamanian's home, you can expect to be served first, receive the biggest portion and perhaps even receive a parting gift. On your part, flowers or wine are a fine gift

---

PANAMA'S TOP FIVE

■ **Miraflores Restaurant** (p119; Miraflores Locks, Panama Province) This breezy restaurant just outside of Panama City is one of the few places in the world where you can dine on fresh seafood as 4-million-ton vessels pass slowly through the Miraflores Locks.

■ **Roots** (p241; Bastimentos, Bocas del Toro Province) Overlooking the Bahía de Almirante, with a fresh sea breeze, this longtime Bocas favorite serves tasty plates of grilled fish with coconut milk, rice and beans, and other Creole dishes to the backdrop of reggae. Roots is the perfect place to while away the afternoon after a trip to some of Bastimentos' lovely beaches.

■ **Dulceria Yely** (p180; Pedasí, Los Santos Province) In the sleepy hamlet of Pedasí, this charming bakery is a favorite of both surfers and former president Mireya Moscoso. Delicious pastries, fresh cakes and *uvita* (a local fruit of the Península de Azuero with a taste like cherry; literally 'little grape') juice are among the offerings.

■ **ASAELA Women's Co-Op Restaurant** (p221; Las Nubes, Chiriquí Province) Just inside the lush Parque Internacional La Amistad, this tiny restaurant serves hearty home-cooked Panamanian dishes. Hummingbirds and the wildlife of the rain forest provide the ambience. This is a fine prelude to a hike through virgin forest.

■ **Millennium** (p276; Isla Tigre, Comarca de Kuna Yala) Dine on seafood caught the same morning at this simple thatched-hut restaurant on Isla Tigre, one of the most traditional of Kuna islands.

to bring, though the best gift you can offer is extending a future dinner invitation to your hosts.

EAT YOUR WORDS

Don't know your *pipas* from your *patacones*? A *batido* from a *bolita*? Get beneath the surface of Panama's plentiful cuisine by learning the lingo. For pronunciation guidelines, see p325.

Useful Phrases

Another (beer) please.	*Mas una (cerveza), por favor.*	mas *oo*-na ser-*ve*-sa, por fa-*vor*
Do you have a menu (in English)?	*Hay una carta (en inglés)?*	ai *oo*-na *kar*-ta (en een-*gles*)
I'd like ...	*Quisiera ...*	kee-*sye*-ra ...
I'm a vegetarian.	*Soy vegetariano.*	soy ve-khe-te-*rya*-no
The bill, please.	*La cuenta, por favor.*	la *kwen*-ta, por fa-*vor*

Menu Decoder

almojabanos – similar to *tortilla de maíz*, except hand-rolled into the form of small sausage-sized pieces

batido – milkshake made with fresh fruit, sugar and milk

bocas – savory side dishes or appetizers

bolitas de carne – snack of mildly spicy meatballs

carimañola – a deep-fried roll made from chopped meat and boiled yuca

carne ahumada – smoked, dried ('jerked') meat

ceviche – marinated raw fish or shellfish

chichas – heavily sweetened fresh fruit drinks

chicheme – nonalcoholic drink consisting of milk, sweet corn, cinnamon and vanilla

comida corriente – also called casado; set meal of rice, beans, plantains and a piece of meat or fish

corvina – a flavorful white fish; Panama's most popular fish dish

empanada – corn turnover filled with ground meat, chicken, cheese or sweet fruit

gallo pinto – literally 'spotted rooster'; a soupy mixture of rice and black beans

hojaldres – fried dough, similar to a donut; popular with breakfast

huevos fritos/revueltos – fried/scrambled eggs

licuado – shake made with fresh fruit, sugar and water

mondongo – tripe

patacones – fried green plantains cut crossways in thin pieces, covered in salt and then pressed and fried; served frequently

pipa – coconut water, served straight from the husk

plátano maduro – also called *plátanos en tentación*; ripe plantains sliced lengthwise and baked or broiled with butter, brown sugar and cinnamon; served hot

raspados – shaved ice flavored with fruit juice

ropa vieja – literally means 'old clothes'; a spicy shredded beef combination served over rice

seco – alcoholic drink made from sugar cane

sancocho – a somewhat spicy chicken-and-vegetable stew; Panama's national dish

tajadas – ripe plantains sliced lengthwise and fried

tamales – ground corn with spices and chicken or pork, wrapped in banana leaves and boiled

tasajo – dried meat cooked with vegetables

tortilla de maíz – a thick, fried cornmeal tortilla

Despite the self-aggrandizing title, *Latin Ladles: Fabulous Soups and Stews from the King of Nuevo Latino Cuisine*, by Douglas Rodriguez, is an excellent recipe book of both traditional and reinvented soups. In here, you'll find recipes for *sancocho* and *seco de chivo*.

Food Glossary

BASICS

azúcar – **sugar**	*hielo* – **ice**
cuchara – **spoon**	*mantequilla* – **butter**
cuchillo – **knife**	*pane* – **bread**

plato – **plate**
sal – **salt**
servilleta – **napkin**
sopa – **soup**

taza – **cup**
tenedor – **fork**
vaso – **glass**

MEALTIMES
desayuno – **breakfast**
almuerzo – **lunch**

cena – **dinner**

> *The Latin American Kitchen*, by Elisabeth Luard, contains a wealth of information about the essential ingredients of the region and a rich variety of dishes from all across Latin America. Contains over 200 recipes.

FRUITS & VEGETABLES
aguacate – **avocado**
ensalada – **salad**
fresa – **strawberry**
guanábana – **soursop (custard apple)**
manzana – **apple**

maracuyá – **passion fruit**
naranja – **orange**
piña – **pineapple**
zanahoria – **carrot**
zarzamora – **blackberry**

SEAFOOD
camarón – **shrimp**
filete de pescado – **fish filet**
langosta – **lobster**

langostino – **jumbo shrimp**
pescado – **fish**
pulpo – **octopus**

MEATS
bistec – **steak**
carne – **beef**
chuleta – **pork chop**

hamburguesa – **hamburger**
salchicha – **sausage**

DRINKS
agua – **water**
bebida – **drink**
café – **coffee**
cerveza – **beer**

leche – **milk**
ron – **rum**
vino – **wine**

COOKING TERMS
a la parilla – **grilled**

frito – **fried**

Panama City

CONTENTS

History	72
Orientation	74
Information	75
Dangers & Annoyances	81
Sights	81
Courses	90
Panama City for Children	90
Tours	90
Festivals & Events	91
Sleeping	92
Eating	98
Drinking	106
Entertainment	108
Shopping	110
Getting There & Away	112
Getting Around	113

A teeming capital in the heart of Latin America, Panama City is both a gateway to the country's natural riches and a vibrant destination in its own right. Scattered throughout the city lie colonial neighborhoods, monolithic skyscrapers and windswept ruins of old Spanish settlements.

The city's geographic diversity is rivaled only by its cultural diversity. Urbanites here hail from Colombia, Spain, Cuba, Jamaica, the Middle East, Europe, Asia and the USA, with a broad selection of the country's indigenous groups added to the mix.

Given the ethnic diversity, it's no surprise that the capital boasts a wide array of restaurants, from traditional seafood served Bocas del Toro style, to sushi, Thai, French and Italian. You can rub elbows with the working class in old-school diners or linger with the nouveau riche in elegant bistros near the sea. One setting that boasts a mix of both is Casco Viejo, Panama City's colorful colonial district. Here, an air of Old Havana lurks about the aging but beautiful churches, the scenic plazas and cobbled streets. Casco Viejo also has its share of nightlife – as do Bella Vista and the Causeway – and music and dancing are a big part of life in Panama City. The pulse of the city can be measured by the rhythms of salsa and merengue, and there are ample opportunities to sample the wide variety of ways to spend a sleepless night.

Not far from the city you'll find some impressive adventure opportunities – from hiking through tropical rain forest to exploring charming island villages. You can sail along the Panama Canal or skirt along its jungle-clad perimeter on a train ride to Colón. And wherever you head to from here, Panama City's charming cafés and restaurants, air-conditioned cinemas and stylish nightclubs are a splendid ending to a few days (or weeks) in the forest.

HIGHLIGHTS

- Exploring historic **Casco Viejo** (p81), an edgy neighborhood with colonial buildings, beautiful churches and vibrant nightlife

- Dining in the city's excellent restaurants (such as **Eurasia**, p99), which serve everything from French eclectic to rustic Colombian and Panamanian, of course

- Soaking up the sights and sounds of the rain forest at **Parque Natural Metropolitano** (p89), 265 hectares of jungle just 10 minutes from downtown

- Party like a (Panamanian) rock star at **S6is** (p108), one of the dozens of bars and nightclubs featuring salsa, merengue, indie rock and electronica

- Reconnecting with the past at the ruins of **Panamá Viejo** (p83), the original Panama City (circa 1519) before it was sacked by pirates in the 1600s

- POPULATION: 446,000
- ELEVATION: SEA LEVEL
- AREA: 2561 SQ KM

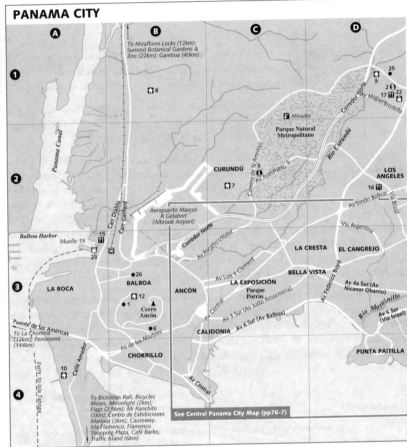

PANAMA CITY

HISTORY

The city was founded on the site of an Indian fishing village by the Spanish governor Pedro Arias de Ávila in 1519, not long after explorer Vasco Núñez de Balboa first looked upon the Pacific and claimed it and everything it touched as the property of Spain.

The Spanish settlement, known as Panamá, quickly became an important center of government and church authority. It was from Panamá, too, that gold and other plunder from the Pacific Spanish colonies were taken along the Camino Real (King's Highway) and the Sendero Las Cruces (Las Cruces Trail) across the isthmus to the Caribbean.

This treasure made Panamá the target of many attacks over the years. In 1671 Welsh buccaneer Sir Henry Morgan and 1200 of his men ransacked the city. A terrible fire ensued – no one knows for certain whether it was set by the pirates or by fleeing landowners – leaving only stone ruins. Now known as Panamá Viejo (Old Panama), these ruins can still be seen today.

Three years after Morgan's assault, the city was reestablished 8km to the southwest, down the coast at what is now the San Felipe district (or Casco Viejo, as it is popularly known). The Spaniards believed that the new site, on a small peninsula, would be easier to defend; a shallow sea flanked the city on three sides and a moat was constructed on

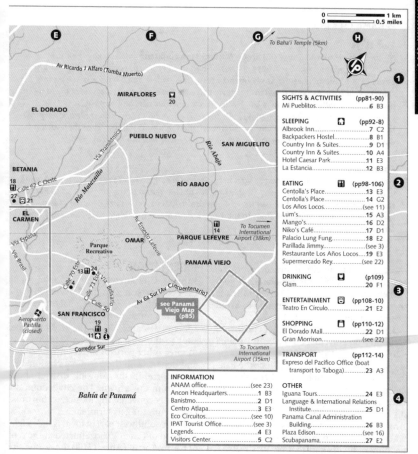

SIGHTS & ACTIVITIES   (pp81-90)
Mi Pueblitos.............................6 B3

SLEEPING   (pp92-8)
Albrook Inn...............................7 C2
Backpackers Hostel....................8 B1
Country Inn & Suites..................9 D1
Country Inn & Suites................10 A4
Hotel Caesar Park....................11 E3
La Estancia..............................12 B3

EATING   (pp98-106)
Centolla's Place........................13 E3
Centolla's Place........................14 G2
Los Años Locos....................(see 11)
Lum's.....................................15 A3
Mango's..................................16 D2
Niko's Café.............................17 D1
Palacio Lung Fung....................18 E2
Parillada Jimmy....................(see 3)
Restaurante Los Años Locos....19 E3
Supermercado Rey................(see 22)

DRINKING   (p109)
Glam.......................................20 F1

ENTERTAINMENT   (pp108-10)
Teatro En Circulo......................21 E2

SHOPPING   (pp110-12)
El Dorado Mall........................22 D1
Gran Morrison......................(see 22)

TRANSPORT   (pp112-14)
Expreso del Pacifico Office (boat
    transport to Taboga)...........23 A3

OTHER
Iguana Tours............................24 E3
Language & International Relations
    Institute...............................25 D1
Panama Canal Administration
    Building................................26 B3
Plaza Edison.......................(see 16)
Scubapanama...........................27 E2

INFORMATION
ANAM office.........................(see 23)
Ancon Headquarters...................1 B3
Banistmo.................................2 D1
Centro Atlapa...........................3 E3
Eco Circuitos......................(see 10)
IPAT Tourist Office...............(see 3)
Legends...................................4 E3
Visitors Center.........................5 C2

the fourth side, separating the city from the mainland. The new city was named Nueva Panamá (New Panama).

Unlike Panamá Viejo, Nueva Panamá was protected by a massive stone-and-brick wall 7m to 14m high and more than 3m wide, with watchtowers every 75m. Access was gained through three massive gateways. So expensive were the fortifications of Nueva Panamá that the council of Spain, auditing the accounts, wrote to inquire whether the wall was constructed of silver or gold. Perhaps the defenses were excessive, but Nueva Panamá was never sacked.

The streets of the new city were laid out at right angles around a central plaza. A cathedral, governor's house and bishop's palace would eventually face the plaza, and many churches and convents were gradually constructed throughout the town. The famous church of Santo Domingo, now in ruins, was built in the 1670s and the cathedral, with its two imposing towers, was completed in 1760. The presidential palace, leading businesses, and municipal offices and those of foreign legations were constructed within a short distance of Parque Catedral.

Unlike Nueva Panamá, the Camino Real overland trade route was attacked repeatedly, and the principal Caribbean port at Portobelo was destroyed. In 1746 the Spaniards stopped using the route altogether, and Panama City gradually declined in importance. It was not until the Panama Railroad was completed in

PANAMA CITY IN...

Two days
Go for an early morning hike in **Parque Natural Metropolitano** (p89), keeping an eye out for sloths, monkeys and more than 250 species of bird life. For lunch, head out to the **Miraflores Locks** (p119), and dine at the lovely open-air restaurant, where you'll have a prime view of big ships traveling the **Panama Canal** (p119) down below. In the evening, feast at one of the excellent restaurants in **Bella Vista** (p98), a short walk from numerous bars and nightclubs.

On the second day, visit **Casco Viejo** (p81) for a walk through the city's most historic neighborhood. Take a Panamanian siesta in late afternoon, then return to the district in the evening for dining at the charming **Café de Asís** (p99) or the decadent **Manolo Caracol** (p99).

Four days
Follow the two-day itinerary, then on your third day add in a trip to **Isla Taboga** (p123), a charming island village just a boat ride away. By day four, it's time to return to the jungle. Head to **Parque Nacional Soberanía** (p121) or **Isla Barro Colorado** (p122) to get a taste of some of Panama's spectacular wildlife. At night, return to the city for dining and dancing at **the Causeway** (p86), for a taste of urban wildlife.

the 1850s that the city returned to prominence. The railroad was popular with gold rushers from the US East Coast who made their way to California via Panama to avoid hostile Indians in the central USA.

Panama was declared independent of Colombia on November 3, 1903, in Panama City's Parque Catedral; the city then became the capital of the new nation. Since the Panama Canal was completed in 1914, the city has grown in importance as a center for international business and trade. Indeed, today it's by far the wealthiest capital in Central America, and many visitors express shock when they see its many skyscrapers and the plethora of luxury cars that ply its streets.

The city's only major setback in recent times occurred in 1989, when it was invaded by the USA to oust dictator Manuel Noriega from power. The capital suffered damage both from the invasion itself and from looting. Many residential blocks of the Chorillo district were also lost to combat-ignited fire.

But by the start of this century, Panama City had never looked better, thanks in large part to a sweeping beautification program undertaken by its mayor. Visitors will be pleased to learn that the city entered the millennium with a new domestic airport, a new central bus terminal, an expanded international airport and a new seaport – all of which are easy to maneuver and make it that much simpler to visit the impressive capital city and points beyond.

ORIENTATION
Panama City stretches about 20km along the Pacific coast, with the Bahía de Panamá to the south, the Panama Canal to the west, protected forest to the north and the stone ruins of Panamá Viejo (the city's original site) to the east. Buses from Panama City to most other parts of the country arrive at and depart from the Terminal Nacional de Transporte, in the Albrook district about 3km from downtown. The city's domestic airport is conveniently located a short distance from the bus terminal.

In the southwest part of town is the neighborhood of Casco Viejo. Situated at the foot of Cerro Ancón (Ancón Hill), it was the site of Nueva Panamá, built after Henry Morgan sacked the original settlement of Panamá.

From Casco Viejo, two major roads head east through the city. The main road, Av Central, runs past the cathedral in Casco Viejo to Parque Santa Ana and Plaza Cinco de Mayo; between these two plazas, traffic is diverted and the avenue is a pedestrian-only shopping street. At a fork further east, the avenue becomes Av Central España; the section that traverses El Cangrejo, the financial district, and heads eastward toward Tocumen International Airport is called Vía España. The other part of the fork becomes Av 1 Norte (also called Av José D Espinar), Av Simón Bolívar and finally Vía Transístmica (Transisthmian Hwy) as it heads out of town and across the isthmus toward Colón.

Av 6 Sur branches off Av Central not far out of Casco Viejo and undergoes several name changes. It is called Av Balboa as it curves around the edge of the bay to Punta Paitilla, the bay's eastern point, opposite Casco Viejo; it then continues under various names past the Centro Atlapa (Atlapa Convention Center) to the ruins of Panamá Viejo.

In 2000, two expressways opened in Panama City, facilitating travel to the domestic airport, the central bus terminal and the country's main international airport. Corredor Norte links the Curundu district of town to the Autopista Panama–Colón, a partially completed toll road to Colón, and to Av Martin Sosa, which extends southeast toward downtown. (Efforts to link Panama City and Colón entirely by high-speed highway were cut short in 2000, when the government stopped funding the project after only a third of it was completed.)

Corredor Sur, the other major expressway, links the Punta Paitilla district southeast of downtown to the town of Tocumen, which is home to Tocumen International Airport.

To the north of the city is forest that has been designated for conservation because it is part of the watershed for the Panama Canal.

Maps

For highly detailed maps, go to the **Instituto Geográfico Nacional 'Tommy Guardia'** (Map pp76-7; ☎ 236-2444, 236-1844; Av Simón Bolívar; ☷ 8am-4pm Mon-Fri), opposite the Universidad de Panamá. It has an excellent map collection, including topographical maps, city maps, tourist maps and more. Most cost less than US$7.

INFORMATION
Bookstores

Allegro (☎ 226-6967; Calle 73 Este near Calle 50) Stocks English books and CDs.

Claro COM (Map pp78-9; ☎ 200-0055; Av Eusebio Morales; ☷ 8am-11pm Mon-Sat, 9am-9pm Sun) An Internet café and coffee shop stocking a number of Spanish and English magazines and books.

El Hombre de la Mancha (Map pp78-9; ☎ 263-6218; Av 3a Sur; ☷ 10am-9pm Mon-Sat) A Spanish-language bookstore favored by Panamanians. There's an Internet and coffee shop on the 2nd floor.

Exedra Books (Map pp78-9; ☎ 264-4252; www.exedra books.com in Spanish; Vía España at Vía Brasil;

☷ 9:30am-9:30pm Mon-Sat, 11am-8:30pm Sun) One of Panama's best bookstores featuring a large selection of English titles, works by Panamanian authors, an art gallery and a pleasant café. The bookstore holds readings and discussions throughout the month.

Farmacia Arrocha (Map pp78-9) The large pharmacy chain has numerous branches around the city, including several on Vía España, and stocks books and magazines, in both English and Spanish.

Gran Morrison (Map pp78-9) With seven locations around the city (including one on Vía España near Calle 51 Este) this department store carries a selection of books, magazines and postcards in Spanish and English, including Lonely Planet titles.

Legends (Map pp72-3; ☎ 270-0096; cnr Calle 50 & Calle 71 Este; ☷ 9:30am-6:30pm) Legends has magazines in English and Spanish, books by Panamanian authors, art books, CDs and a few English titles.

Librería Argosy (Map pp78-9; ☎ 223-5344; Vía Argentina near Vía España) A bookstore and cultural institution. The interesting and ebullient Greek-born owner offers a fine selection of books in English, Spanish and French. Be advised, however, that many of the prices are steeply marked up.

Librería Cultural Panameña (☎ 223-6267; near western end of Vía España) Has a good literature selection.

Librería El Campus (☎ 223-6598; Av José de Fábrega) In front of the Universidad de Panamá.

Tupper Center (Map pp76-7; ☎ 212-8000; near Av de los Mártires, Ancón district; ☷ 10am-4:30pm Mon-Fri) The Smithsonian Tropical Research Institute (STRI) bookstore, opposite the Legislative Palace, has a nice selection of books on wildlife and the environment.

Emergency

Ambulance	☎ 228-2187, 229-1133
Fire	☎ 103
Police	☎ 104

Internet Access

Internet cafés are plentiful in Panama City, especially in **El Cangrejo** banking district.

@ljan (Map pp78-9; Calle Maria Icaza off Vía España, El Cangrejo; per hr US$0.75; ☷ 8am-11pm Mon-Sat, 9am-9pm Sun)

Claro COM (Map pp78-9; Av Eusebio Morales, El Cangrejo; per hr US$1.50; ☷ 8am-11pm Mon-Sat, 9am-9pm Sun)

Cyber Café Cibeles (Map pp78-9; Vía Argentina, El Cangrejo; per hr US$0.75; ☷ 9am-1am)

Digital Net (Map pp78-9; Vía Veneto, El Cangrejo; per hr US$0.75; ☷ 9am-1am)

Evolution Planet (Map pp78-9; Calle D, El Cangrejo; per hr US$0.75; ☷ 9am-4am)

La Red (Map pp76-7; Av Central, Casco Antiguo; per hr US$1; ☷ 10am-midnight) Facing Plaza Santa Ana.

PANAMA CITY

CENTRAL PANAMA CITY

INFORMATION

Autoridad Nacional del Ambiente (ANAM)	**1** C1
Banistmo ATM	**2** C3
Centro Médico Paitilla	**3** F4
Earl S Tupper Tropical Sciences Library	(see 13)
HSBC ATM	**4** A4
Immigration Office	**5** B3
Instituto Geográfico Nacional (Tommy Guardia)	**6** E1
La Red	**7** A5
Lavandería América	**8** B4
Main Post Office	**9** A4
Ministerio de Hacienda y Tesoro	**10** C3
Pesantez Tours	**11** G4
Post Office	**12** C3
Smithsonian Tropical Research Institute	**13** A3
Tupper Center	(see 13)
US Embassy	**14** D4

SIGHTS & ACTIVITIES (pp81–90)

Museo Afro-Antilleano	**15** B4
Museo Antropológico Reina Torres de Araúz	**16** A4
Museo de Arte Contemporáneo	**17** A4
Museo de Ciencias Naturales	**18** B3

SLEEPING 🏠 (pp92–8)

Casa de Carmen	**19** G2
Gran Hotel Soloy	**20** B3
Hotel 2 Mares	**21** C3
Hotel Acapulco	**22** C3
Hotel Andino	**23** C3
Hotel Bella Vista	**24** D3
Hotel California	**25** D3
Hotel Caribe	**26** C3
Hotel Centroamericano	**27** C3
Hotel Costa Inn	**28** D3
Hotel Doral	**29** A4
Hotel Internacional	**30** A4
Hotel Latino	**31** C3
Hotel Lisboa	**32** C3
Hotel Marparaíso	**33** C3
Hotel Montreal	**34** E2
Hotel Plaza Paitilla Inn	**35** F4
Hotel Ribadavia Star	**36** C3
Hotel Roma	**37** C3
Hotel Venecia	**38** C3
Hotel Veracruz	**39** B3
Miramar Inter-Continental	**40** E3
Pensión Las Palmeras	**41** D3
Residencial Turístico Volcán	**42** B3

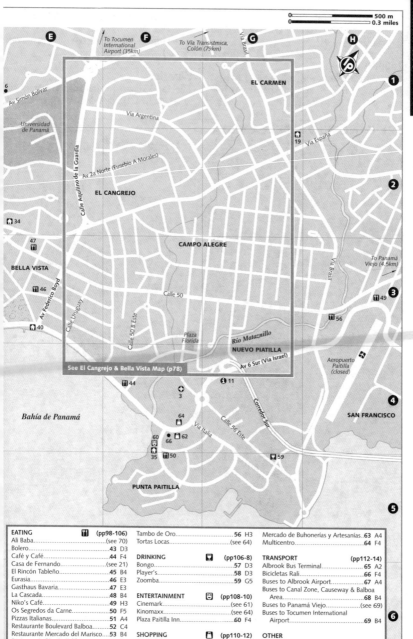

EATING 🍴 (pp98–106)
Ali Baba...(see 70)
Bolero...**43** D3
Café y Café.....................................**44** F4
Casa de Fernando.........................(see 21)
El Rincón Tableño..........................**45** B4
Eurasia..**46** E3
Gasthaus Bavaria............................**47** E3
La Cascada.....................................**48** B4
Niko's Café....................................**49** H3
Os Segredos da Carne..................**50** F5
Pizzas Italianas..............................**51** A4
Restaurante Boulevard Balboa......**52** C4
Restaurante Mercado del Marisco..**53** B4
Restaurante Rincón Tableño..........**54** C3
Restaurante y Pizzeria Napoli No 1..**55** A4

Tambo de Oro................................**56** H3
Tortas Locas..................................(see 64)

DRINKING 🍷 (pp106–8)
Bongo..**57** D3
Player's..**58** D3
Zoomba...**59** G5

ENTERTAINMENT 🎬 (pp108–10)
Cinemark......................................(see 61)
Kinomaxx......................................(see 64)
Plaza Paitilla Inn...........................**60** F4

SHOPPING 🛍 (pp110–12)
Albrook Mall.................................**61** A2
Gran Morrison...............................**62** F4

Mercado de Buhonerías y Artesanías..**63** A4
Multicentro....................................**64** F4

TRANSPORT (pp112–14)
Albrook Bus Terminal.....................**65** A2
Bicicletas Rali................................**66** F4
Buses to Albrook Airport...............**67** A4
Buses to Canal Zone, Causeway & Balboa
   Area..**68** B4
Buses to Panamá Viejo.................(see 69)
Buses to Tocumen International
   Airport.......................................**69** B4

OTHER
Panama Yacht Club........................**70** D4
Plaza Paitilla Shopping Center.......(see 62)

Tourism & Internet Cafe (Map p80; Av Central, Casco Antiguo) Internet, information about Casco Viejo and cheap long-distance phone calls.

Laundry

Lavamáticos (laundromats) are easy to find in the city; they're also inexpensive. Most charge US$2.25 to wash and dry a load.

Lavandería América (Map pp76-7; Av 4a Sur, La Exposición; 6:30am-9pm)

Lavamático Tanita (Map p80; Calle 9 Oeste, Casco Viejo; 7am-9pm) Beside Parque Herrera.

Libraries

The **Earl S Tupper Tropical Sciences Library** (Map pp76-7; ☎ 212-8113; near Av de los Mártires, Ancón district;

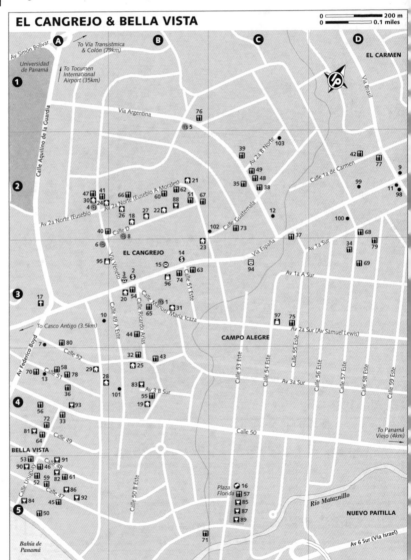

EL CANGREJO & BELLA VISTA

10am-4:30pm Mon-Fri), opposite the Legislative Palace at the Smithsonian Tropical Research Institute (STRI) center, is a world-class resource for information on tropical biology and conservation. Technical seminars are held in English at noon every Tuesday.

Medical Services

Medicine in Panama, especially in Panama City, is of a high standard. **Centro Médico Paitilla** (Map pp76-7; Calle 53 near Av Balboa) has excellent physicians who speak English and Spanish.

Money

The easiest way to get cash is through the 24-hour ATMs that are abundant throughout the city. Just look for the red *sistema clave* signs. For banking services, try:
Banco Nacional de Panamá (☎ 238-4161; Tocumen International Airport) The only bank in Panama City that exchanges foreign currency.
Banistmo (Map pp78-9; 269-5555; Calle 50; 8am-3:30pm Mon-Fri, 9am-noon Sat) Changes Amex traveler's checks with no fee, charges US$5 per transaction for other traveler's checks.

Panacambios (Map pp78-9; ☎ 223-1800; ground fl, Plaza Regency Bldg, Vía España; 8am-5pm Mon-Fri). Near the Hotel Riande Granada; buys and sells international currencies.

Post

Post offices are scarce in Panama. Alternatively, many hotels sell stamps and some will mail guests' letters.
Main post office (Map pp76-7; Av Balboa at Av B; 7am-5:45pm Mon-Fri, 7am-4:45pm Sat) Opposite the Mercado de Mariscos. Post restante items are held for 30 days.

Branches include:
Vía España (Map pp78-9; Plaza Concordia mall) Across from Gran Morrison; enter at the base of the overpass.
Av Central España (Map pp76-7; btwn Calles 33 & 34) Opposite the church in La Exposición.

Telephone

Phonecards for local and international calls can be purchased at pharmacies. Look for the 'Telechip Total' cards, which can be used with any phone. Cards come in denominations of US$3, US$5, US$10 and US$20. Internet cafés are the cheapest way to make long

INFORMATION
@ljan.	1	B3
Banistmo.	2	B3
Cable & Wireless.	3	B3
Claro COM.	4	A2
Cyber Café Cibeles.	5	B1
Digital Net.	6	A3
Edificio Banco Nacional de Panamá.	(see 2)	
El Hombre de la Mancha.	7	A3
Evolution Planet.	8	B2
Exedra Books.	9	D2
Farmacia Arrocha.	10	A3
Farmacia Arrocha.	11	D2
Librería Argosy.	12	C2
Margo Tours.	13	A4
Panacambios.	14	B3
Post Office.	15	B3
UK Embassy.	16	C5

SIGHTS & ACTIVITIES (pp81-90)
| Iglesia del Carmen. | 17 | A3 |

SLEEPING (pp92-8)
Coral Suites Aparthotel.	18	B3
DeVille Hotel.	19	B4
Hotel Continental.	20	B3
Hotel El Parador.	21	B2
Hotel Marbella.	22	B2
Hotel Riande Granada.	23	B3
Las Vegas Suites.	24	A2
Panama Marriott.	25	B4
Sevilla Suites.	26	B2
Suites Ambassador.	27	B2
The Bristol.	28	A4
The Executive Hotel.	29	A4
Torres de Alba.	30	A2
Voyager International Hostel.	31	B3

EATING (pp98-106)
Aladino's.	32	B4
Athen's.	33	A4
Athen's.	34	D3
Boquitos del Mar.	35	C2
Café Santé.	36	A4
Café Sitton.	37	C2
Cafetería del Prado.	38	C2
Cafetería Manolo.	39	C2
Cafetería Manolo.	40	A2
Caffé Pomodoro.	41	A2
Carlitos.	42	D2
Casa Vegetariano.	43	B4
Costa Azul.	44	B3
Crêpes & Waffles.	45	A5
Darna Coffee Bar.	46	A5
Delicias del Pueblo.	47	A2
El Mundo del Pan.	48	C2
El Trapiche.	49	C2
Fisch.	50	A5
Ginza Teppanyaki.	51	B2
Greenhouse.	52	A5
Groovey Café.	(see 30)
Habibi's.	53	A5
Joyería La Huaca.	54	B3
La Cocotte.	55	B4
La Mexicanita.	56	A4
Le Bistrot.	57	C5
Le Sandwich de Paris.	58	A4
Limoncillo.	59	A5
Machu Picchu.	60	B2
Madame Chang.	61	A5
Martin Fierro.	62	B2
Niko's Café.	63	B3
Nobu.	64	A4
Parillada Jimmy.	65	B3
Restaurant 1985.	66	B2
Restaurant Matsuei.	67	B2
Restaurante de las Americas.	68	D2
Restaurante y Pizzeria Napoli.	69	D3
Restaurante-Bar Tinajas.	70	A4
Rincón Suizo.	(see 66)
Romanaccio.	71	B5
Royal Thai.	72	A4
Siete Mares.	73	A2
Supermercado Rey.	74	B3
Sushi Itto.	75	C3
Te Conté.	76	B1
Tip Top.	77	D2
Tomato.	78	A4
Trattoria d'America.	79	D3
Tre Scalini.	80	A3

DRINKING (pp106-8)
BLG.	81	A4
Deep Room.	82	A5
El Pavo Real.	83	B4
La Kava.	84	A5
Liquid.	85	C5
Opah.	86	A5
Oz.	87	C5
Punto G.	88	B2
Rock Café.	89	C5
S6is.	90	A5
Skap.	91	A5
The Spot.	92	A5
The Wine Bar.	(see 24)
Traffic Island.	93	A4

ENTERTAINMENT (pp108-10)
| Alhambra Cinema. | 94 | C3 |

SHOPPING (pp110-12)
Flory Saltzman Molas.	95	A3
Gran Morrison.	96	B3
Reprosa.	97	C3

TRANSPORT (pp112-14)
| Aeroperlas. | 98 | D2 |
| Bicicletas Rali. | 99 | D2 |

OTHER
Aeroperlas Office.	100	D2
Ancon Expeditions.	101	B4
Latin Dance.	102	C2
Spanish Learning Center.	103	C2

PANAMA CITY

CASCO VIEJO

0 — 100 m
0 — 0.1 miles

INFORMATION
French Embassy	1 C4
IPAT counter	(see 4)
Lavamático Tanita	2 B2
Tourism & Internet Café	3 B2
Tourist Police	4 C3

SIGHTS & ACTIVITIES (pp81–90)
Casa de la Municipalidad	5 B1
Hotel Central	6 C2
Iglesia Catedral	7 B2
Iglesia de La Merced	8 B2
Iglesia de San Francisco	9 C2
Iglesia de San José	10 B2
Iglesia y Convento de la Compañía de Jesús	11 B2
Iglesia y Convento de Santo Domingo	(see 15)
Instituto Nacional de Cultura	12 C4
Mercado	13 B1
Ministerio de Gobierno y Justicia	14 C3
Museo de Arte Religioso Colonial	15 C3
Museo de Historia De Panamá	(see 18)
Museo del Canal Interoceánico	16 B2
Palacio de las Garzas	17 C3
Palacio Municipal	18 B2

SLEEPING (pp92–8)
Casa Grande	19 B2
Casa Mar Alta	20 C3
Casco Viejo Properties	21 C3
Hotel Herrera	22 B2
Pensión Colón	23 A1
The Lion House	24 B2

EATING (pp98–106)
Café Coca Cola	25 A1
Café de Asís	26 C2
El Arca	27 C3
Manolo Caracol	28 C3
Mostaza	29 C3
Restaurante Las Bóvedas	30 C4

DRINKING (pp106–8)
844	31 C3
Blu	32 C3
Salon Madrid	33 A1
Take Five	34 C3

ENTERTAINMENT (pp108–10)
Teatro Anita Villalaz	35 C4
Teatro Nacional	36 C2

TRANSPORT (pp112–14)
Cargo Boats to Colombia	37 C1

distance calls. Many charge around US$0.15 per minute for calls to the US; US$0.25 to US$0.50 for calls to other countries.

Cable & Wireless (Map pp78–9; ground fl, Banco Nacional Bldg, Vía España; ☉ 7:30am-9:30pm) Telephones are available to make international calls; fax service also available.

Tourist Information

IPAT (Map pp72–3; ☎ 226-7000; www.panamainfo.com; Vía Israel, San Francisco; ☉ 8:30am-4:30pm Mon-Fri) Panama's tourism bureau is headquartered at the Centro Atlapa in the San Francisco neighborhood. Enter at the rear of the large building. All the IPAT offices give out free maps and, occasionally, information on things to see and do. The usefulness of a given office depends on the individual employees. Generally, more specific questions yield more useful information. Few IPAT employees speak English.

There are also IPAT counters at:
Albrook Airport (☎ 315-0831)
Casco Antiguo (☎ 211-1959; Av Central & Calle 3)
Panamá Viejo (☎ 226-4419; Vía Cincuentenario)

Autoridad Nacional del Ambiente (ANAM; Map pp76–7; ☎ 315-0855; Bldg 804, Albrook district, Ancón; ☉ 8am-4pm) ANAM can occasionally provide maps and information on national parks, but are not organized to provide much assistance to tourists. It's best reached by taxi. The office on muelle (pier) 19 is often unstaffed.

Travel Agencies

Agencia de Viajes Continental (☎ 263-5531; viajeswong@cwpanama.net; Calle 55, El Caribe Bldg, El Cangrejo) Enjoys a sterling reputation. English and Spanish are spoken.

Ancon Expeditions of Panama (Map pp78-9; ☎ 269-0415; www.anconexpeditions.com; Calle 49 A Este near Av B Sur) Great place for purchasing domestic airline tickets.

Eco Circuitos (Map pp72-3; ☎ 264-4821; www.eco circuitos.com) Inside the Country Inn & Suites, Causeway.

Margo Tours (Map pp78-9; ☎ 264-8888; www. margotours.com; Av 3a Sur, El Cangrejo) Next to Restaurante-Bar Tinajas.

DANGERS & ANNOYANCES

Use common sense when you're in a poor neighborhood such as Casco Viejo, Calidonia or La Exposición: avoid empty or dimly lit streets; don't use big bills in places where a thug is likely to be watching you; and if you drive, always lock your car and don't leave valuables in plain sight – and that includes car radios.

Casco Viejo, one of the city's most fascinating areas, has bicycle police patrolling the streets by day, so it's safer than it's been in the past. These cops are on the lookout for tourists so don't be afraid to ask them for directions or about the safety of a particular street. Many will even escort you (whether you want it or not) to your next destination. At night, always take taxis around Casco Viejo (any restaurant or bar can call one for you).

There are occasional reports of robbery near the ruins of Panamá Viejo. Don't go after sunset, and always keep an eye out. High-crime areas best avoided altogether include Curundu, El Chorillo, Santa Ana, San Miguelito and Río Abajo.

When walking the streets of Panama City, be aware that drivers do not yield to pedestrians. Sometimes it's best to approach intersections like Panamanians – look both ways then run like hell.

SIGHTS

Panama's major sights are found in **Casco Viejo**, where visitors can discover some of the city's old churches, plazas and colonial buildings by strolling the old streets. Other areas of note are sprinkled throughout the city. In the south, the **Causeway** has numerous restaurants, bars and fine vantage points on the edge of the ocean. Further east on the way to the airport is **Panamá Viejo**, where the ruins of Spain's first settlement lie.

Casco Viejo Walking Tour

One of the more interesting parts of the city is **Casco Viejo** (also called Casco Antiguo and San Felipe; Map p80), with its mix of colonial architecture, cobblestone streets and ethnic diversity. Some, though only a few, of the buildings have been restored, and in those buildings you can sense how magnificent the area must have looked in past years. This area is gradually being gentrified, and a handful of artists have settled in the colonial area. Sadly, the area is still run-down and, as mentioned earlier, it's dangerous to walk here at night. Even in daylight, take care when walking down side streets.

The capture and plunder of Panamá (the original Panama City) by the pirate Sir Henry Morgan in 1671 convinced the king of Spain that the city was unsafe from buccaneers, and he ordered that it be rebuilt on another site. Three years later, efforts to create a new city began on a rocky peninsula at the foot of Cerro Ancón, 8km southwest of the original city. The new location was easier to defend, and reefs prevented ships from coming up to the city except at high tide. Casco Viejo was surrounded by a massive wall, which is how it got its name (Casco Viejo means 'Old Compound'). Some of the old stone-and-brick wall and original Spanish cannons can still be seen today.

In 1904, at the time construction began on the Panama Canal, all of Panama City existed where Casco Viejo stands today. The city's population was around 30,000 (about the same population as the original city of Panamá when Morgan sacked it). Since that time, the population of Panama City has increased exponentially, and the city has spread so far to the east that Casco Viejo is now merely a district in the southwestern corner of the modern capital city.

You could start a walking tour in Casco Viejo at the **Paseo las Bóvedas** (1; Promenade of Vaults), on the southern tip of the peninsula. A walkway runs along the top of the seawall built by the Spaniards to protect the city. From here you can see ships lining up to enter the canal and the Puente de las Américas (Bridge of the Americas), which arches over the southern entrance of the so-called path between the seas.

Below the wall, on the tip of the peninsula, is **Plaza de Francia (2)**, where large stone tablets tell the story (in Spanish) of the canal's construction and the role of the French in building it. The plaza is dedicated to the memory of the 22,000 workers, most of them from France, Guadeloupe and Martinique, who died trying to create a canal. Most were killed by yellow fever and malaria, and among the busts of the Frenchmen involved is a monument to Carlos J Finlay, who discovered how mosquitoes transmit yellow fever. His work led to the eradication of the disease in Panama.

On one side of the plaza are nine restored **dungeons (3)** that were used by the Spaniards and, later, by the Colombians. Although they now contain an art gallery and **Restaurante Las Bóvedas** (3; p105), a French restaurant/jazz spot, you can still see the dungeons' original stonework. Also on the plaza are the **Teatro Anita Villalaz** (p110) and the **Instituto Nacional de Cultura** (3; INAC; ☎ 211-4034; Plaza de Francia; ❂ 8:30am-4pm Mon-Fri), Panama's National Institute of Culture, which is responsible for maintaining the country's museums and other cultural institutions. INAC has a small gallery on the 1st floor that displays works by Panamanian artists.

Leaving the plaza to walk up Calle 1 Oeste, you'll soon come to the **Museo de Arte Religioso Colonial** (4; ☎ 228-2897; Av A at Calle 3; admission US$1; ❂ 8am-4pm Tue-Sat) in a chapel of **Iglesia y Convento de Santo Domingo** (4; cnr Calle 3 & Av A), which was built in 1756. With the exception of the museum, the church and convent now stand in ruins. This museum contains sacred artifacts from the colonial era, including sacred paintings and sculptures from various parts of the country, dating from the 16th, 17th and 18th centuries. Among the exhibits is a golden altar from the former chapel of the monastery that dates from the 18th century.

Just inside the doorway of the ruins is the Arco Chato, a long, flat arch that stood for centuries with no internal supports. Sadly, the Arco collapsed in 2003. It reportedly played a part in the selection of Panama over Nicaragua as the site for the canal; its survival was taken as proof that the area was not subject to earthquakes.

Turning north along Calle 3a Este, you'll pass the **Ministerio de Gobierno y Justicia (5)**, and behind it the **Teatro Nacional (6**; ☎ 262-3525; admission US$0.50; ❂ 8am-4pm Mon-Fri), built in 1907. The ornate interior has been restored, and it boasts red and gold decorations; a once-magnificent ceiling mural by Roberto Lewis (one of Panama's finest painters), that's been allowed to collapse in recent years; an impressive crystal chandelier; and several tiers

of seats. Performances are still held here. To find out about them or just to have a look at the theater, go around to the office door at the side of the building.

Opposite the theater is the **Iglesia de San Francisco (7**; ☎ 262-1410; ❂ 8am-4pm), facing onto **Parque Bolívar (8)**. In 1826 in a schoolroom opposite this park, Simón Bolívar held a meeting urging the union of the Latin American countries. After many struggles against Spanish domination, Bolívar succeeded in liberating Bolivia, Colombia, Ecuador, Peru and Venezuela, and he created Gran Colombia, which encompassed all these states. Although Bolívar was unable to keep Gran Colombia together, he is nonetheless venerated as a hero throughout Latin America.

On Av Alfaro one block north and two blocks west from Parque Bolívar is the presidential palace, called the **Palacio de las Garzas** (**9**; Palace of the Herons) for the great white herons that strut about here. The president of Panama lives on the upper floor. A few blocks further west are the **Muelle Fiscal** (**10**; the port) and the bustling **mercado** (**11**; market) – where you can buy everything from livestock to fruits and vegetables.

Two blocks south of the palace, at the center of Casco Viejo, is Parque Catedral, later renamed **Plaza de la Independencia (12)**, the central plaza where Panamanian independence was declared on November 3, 1903. In addition to the cathedral, the plaza is fringed by several other historic buildings. Many years ago canal officials and other dignitaries stayed at the nearby **Hotel Central (13)**, which was a very luxurious place back in those days. The Hotel closed in 2000 and is unlikely to reopen any time soon.

On the southern side of the plaza is the building that was once the headquarters of the French company that first worked on the canal; in 1997 it became the site of the excellent **Museo del Canal Interoceánico** (**14**; Interoceanic Canal Museum; ☎ 211-1995; Plaza de la Independencia, Casco Viejo; admission US$2; ⓨ 9:30am-5:30pm Tue-Sun). Widely known only as the Panama Canal Museum, this museum is a must-see and is housed in an elegant building built by the French in French colonial style in the mid-1870s. It opened as a hotel and later became the headquarters of the French and, later still, US canal commissions. The museum, which opened in 1997, contains such varied displays as Spanish armor and weapons, rifles from California's gold-rush days (many US prospectors passed through the city on their way to California), the desk at which Panama's declaration of independence was signed in 1903 and many Panama Railroad and Canal exhibits. The museum presents a detailed history of the railroad and canal through the use of panels covered with well-presented text (in Spanish only), paintings and photos. There are many artifacts as well. English-speaking guides are available when given six hours' notice; the museum also has audio tours available.

Next door, on the top floor of the **Palacio Municipal** (**15**; City Hall), is the **Museo de Historia de Panamá** (**15**; ☎ 228-6231; admission US$1; ⓨ 8:30am-

3:30pm Mon-Fri). This not terribly impressive museum contains exhibits on the history of Panama from Spanish colonial times until 1977, the year the USA agreed to turn over control of the canal to Panama.

A half-block south of the plaza on Calle 7 are the ruins of another church, the **Iglesia y Convento de la Compañía de Jesús (16)**. Walk to the end of the block to rejoin Av A, and then walk a block west to arrive at the **Iglesia de San José (17)**. Its famous Altar de Oro (Golden Altar) is the only thing of value salvaged after Henry Morgan sacked Panamá in 1671. When word came of the pirate's impending attack, according to local tales, a priest painted the altar black to disguise it. The priest told Morgan that the famous altar had been stolen by another pirate and even convinced Morgan to donate handsomely for its replacement. Morgan is said to have told the priest, 'I don't know why, but I think you are more of a pirate than I am.' Regardless of the accuracy of this story, the baroque-style altar, made of carved mahogany painted and veneered with gold, escaped the pirates' attention and was eventually moved to its present site.

A block further west is **Parque Herrera (18)**, which is vivacious and picturesque with plenty of shoeshines, shade trees, benches and bustling people. A block north, on Av Central two blocks west of the cathedral, is the **Iglesia de La Merced (19)**.

Walk out of Casco Viejo along Av Central, past the **Casa de la Municipalidad (20)**, a neoclassical building that was restored in 1981. After a couple of blocks you'll come to **Parque Santa Ana (21)**, with its Iglesia de Santa Ana. Parque Santa Ana marks the beginning of the Av Central shopping district; it is surrounded by simple restaurants and there are buses to the financial district.

A few blocks north of Parque Santa Ana, you'll enter the bustling pedestrian shopping area, chock-full of hawkers shouting their wares in front of air-conditioned stores and no-nonsense eateries. You'll reach the end of your walk at the small **Plaza Cinco de Mayo (22)**, a busy turnabout with buses leading to the canal, El Cangrejo and other points around the city.

Panamá Viejo

At the eastern edge of the city are the ruins of **Panamá Viejo** (Map p85). Founded on August

15, 1519, by Spanish conquistador Pedro Arias de Ávila, the city of Panamá was the first European settlement along the Pacific. For the next 150 years it profited mainly from Spain's famed bullion pipeline, which ran from Peru's gold and silver mines to Europe via Panamá. Because of the amount of wealth that passed through the city, the Spaniards kept many soldiers here, and their presence kept the buccaneers away.

For many years Panamá was the metropolis of the Pacific. In addition to being a gateway for the bullion of Peru, it was the entrepôt for the silks and spices of the Orient. From Panamá, these riches were carried across the isthmus to be loaded onto the Spanish galleons at Nombre de Dios or Portobelo. The towns of Venta de Cruces and then Chagres, where the road crossed the Río Chagres, were halfway stations on the road to the northern coast. The Spaniards used to pack bars of silver and gold over this road, which came to be called Sendero Las Cruces. Also used to transport goods was the Camino Real, a land route running from Panamá to Portobelo. It was near Venta de Cruces that the English pirate Sir Francis Drake held up a train of 190 pack mules on the night of February 14, 1573, and made off with tons of gold and silver.

Nearly a century later, in 1671, 1200 pirates led by Henry Morgan ascended the Río Chagres as far as Venta de Cruces and then proceeded overland to Panamá. The city was not fortified, but it was protected on three sides by the sea and marshes. On the land side was a causeway, and a bridge in its middle permitted tidal water to pass underneath. But to the bewilderment of historians, when Morgan and his men neared the city, the Spanish soldiers left this natural stronghold and confronted the buccaneers in a hilly area outside town.

It was the first of their many mistakes. When the two forces met in battle, the Spanish infantry left their ranks after mistaking a repositioning of some of Morgan's men for a retreat. The Spanish soldiers ran after the pirates, leaving a high position for a gully. French sharpshooters within Morgan's band were delighted by the development and opened fire on the Spaniards from nearby knolls. The first volley of musket fire dropped about 100 soldiers, and the Spanish force fell to pieces.

'Hardly did our men see some fall dead and others wounded but they turned their backs and fled and it was not possible to stop them,' reported the Spanish president at the time, Don Juan Perez. Morgan had control of the town within hours.

At the time Panamá fell, the city contained a magnificent cathedral, several beautiful churches and eight convents. There were more than 200 warehouses stocked with foreign goods, 200 residences of European elegance and 5000 houses of the common sort. The city also possessed a mint, a large hospital, the king's stables and a slave market. When Morgan left, little more than building material remained. Nearly everything of value was plundered by the pirates and divvied up later or was destroyed by a fire set by either the pirates or defiant townspeople.

For the next three centuries, what remained of the abandoned city – mostly beams and stone blocks – served as a convenient source of building materials. Yet most of the remnants of the one-time metropolis were still intact as recently as 1950, when the limits of modern Panama City reached the ruins in the form of a squatter settlement. But by the time the government declared the ruins a protected historic site, 26 years later, most of the old city had been dismantled and overrun.

Today much of Panamá Viejo lies buried under a poor residential neighborhood. So little of the original city remains that its size, layout and appearance are the subjects of much conjecture. What follows are details agreed upon by experts.

The city was founded on a coastal bar alongside a shallow cove. The primary government buildings were at the mouth of the cove, which was rather spacious at the time and could be used as a port; today it is largely mangroves. The cathedral was erected nearby. The major Catholic religious orders – the Franciscans, Dominicans, Jesuits and Augustines – had churches and convents in town. The best houses and most of the convents were built on the narrow strip of land along the beachfront.

The colonial city seems to have followed a grid plan, with blocks of various sizes and a main square; the visible remains of Panamá Viejo are certainly laid out that way. The lots tended to be narrow, and the houses often

PANAMÁ VIEJO

0 ———— 400 m
0 ———— 0.2 miles

To Vía España (2.5km)

Río Abajo

Av 6 Sur (Av Cincuentenario)

Calle de Santo Domingo

Approximate Scale
& Orientation

Calle del Obispo

Calle de La Empedrada

Av 6 Sur (Av Cincuentenario)

To Panama
City (6.5km)

Bahía de Panamá

INFORMATION
IPAT tourism office......................1 A3

SIGHTS & ACTIVITIES   (pp81–90)
Aguadero Salubre (Public Water
  Receptacle)..............................2 B3
Antigua Casa del Obispo (Old Bishop's
  House)......................................3 B2
Cabildo de la Ciudad (City Hall)...4 C3
Casa Alarcón..............................5 C2
Casa de los Genoveses (Slave
  Market).....................................6 D2
Casas de Terrín...........................7 C2

Casas Reales (Royal Houses)...................8 D3
Catedral de Nuestra Señora de la Asunción
  (Our Lady of the Assumption
  Cathedral)..9 C2
El Camino Real (King's Highway)...........10 A3
Ermita de San Cristóbal (Hermitage of St
  Christopher)..11 A2
Fortín de la Natividad (Nativity Fort)......12 A3
Hospital de San Juan de Dios (Hospital of St
  John of God)..13 B3
Iglesia de San José (Church of St Joseph)..14 C1
Iglesia y Convento de la Compañía de
  Jesús..15 C3
Iglesia y Convento de la Concepción......16 C3
Iglesia y Convento de La Merced............17 A3
Iglesia y Convento de San Francisco........18 B3
Iglesia y Convento de Santo Domingo (Church
  and Convent of St Dominic) 19 C2

Mal Llameda Piedra del Sacrificio...........20 B3
Museo de Sitio Panamá Viejo..................21 C3
Plaza Mayor (Grand Plaza)......................22 C3
Possible Bread Oven...............................23 B1
Puente del Matadero (Bridge of the
  Slaughterhouse).................................24 A3
Puente del Rey (Bridge of the King)........25 C1
Wall Protecting the Casas Reales............26 D3

SLEEPING   (pp92–8)
Hostal (Inn)...27 C3

EATING   (pp98–106)
Café de la Torre......................................28 C3

SHOPPING   (pp110–12)
Mercado (Market)...................................29 C3
Mercado Nacional de Artesanías..........(see 28)

consisted of two or three stories. The suburbs that developed to the north and northwest lacked planning; common houses and hovels were scattered along crooked lanes.

It requires a fertile imagination to visualize the city before the arrival of Captain Morgan and his men. The churches, some of which faced the sea, were the most outstanding buildings. All were rectangular, with stone outer walls, timber roofs and internal wooden supports. Few had towers. The adjoining convents had inner courts surrounded by wooden galleries. It appears that the larger ones had enclosed gardens and orchards.

Most of the better houses were built of timber and placed wall to wall, with small inner courts, open-air kitchens and separate wings for the servants. Some had ground-floor galleries and balconies, and most had plain exterior walls. A few of the fancier homes were built of stone, and their ruins remain. The poor had far simpler dwellings, usually thatched huts built with inexpensive materials like reeds.

The center of power resided at the **Casas Reales** (Royal Houses; Map p85), a complex ringed by timber ramparts and separated from the city proper by a moat. Within the complex were the customs house, the royal treasury, a prison and the governor's house. Despite the obvious historical importance of the site, past governments have allowed sections of the property to be used as a landfill and for horse stables. Only scattered walls remain of the once-impressive structures.

The **Catedral de Nuestra Señora de la Asunción** (Map p85), built between 1619 and 1626, is the best-preserved building of them all. In traditional fashion, it was designed so that its two side chapels gave the cathedral a crosslike shape as viewed from the heavens. The bell tower was at the back of the church and may have served double duty as a watchtower for the Casas Reales. The main facade, which faced the Plaza Mayor (Grand Plaza), is gone. Only the walls remain.

Also facing the Plaza Mayor were the **Cabildo de la Ciudad** (City Hall; Map p85) and the **Casas de Terrín** (Map p85), houses built by one of the city's wealthiest citizens, Francisco Terrín.

Immediately north of the cathedral are the massive ruins of **Casa Alarcón** (Map p85), the town's best-preserved and largest known private residence, dating from the 1640s. Just north of the former residence is the **Iglesia y Convento de Santo Domingo** (Church and Convent of St Dominic; Map p85), the best-preserved church. The convent dates from the 1570s and the church was built 20 or more years later.

Arriving a decade or so after the Dominican friars were the Jesuits, and they built a stone church, the **Iglesia y Convento de la Compañía de Jesús** (Map p85), whose ruins are likewise visible today. Just west of the Jesuits' facilities are the spacious ruins of a church and convent, the **Iglesia y Convento de la Concepción** (Map p85), which were erected by the nuns of Nuestra Señora de la Concepción (Our Lady of the Conception). Most of the ruins, which cover the better part of two blocks, were part of the church; little remains of the convent.

Between the nuns' church and the sea was the city's sole hospital, the **Hospital de San Juan de Dios** (Map p85). Unfortunately, much of the hospital's remains were scattered when Av Cincuentenario and a side road were put in not long ago. Also bordering the avenue, two blocks west of the hospital's ruins, are the remains of the **Iglesia y Convento de San Francisco** (Map p85), the facilities erected by the Franciscans. The church faced the sea and stood on a massive base.

Continuing two blocks west along Av Cincuentenario, you'll arrive at the ruins of the **Iglesia y Convento de La Merced** (Map p85). Erected by the Mercedarian friars in the early 17th century, the buildings actually survived the fire that swept the city following Morgan's assault. The church's facade is missing because the friars dismantled it and moved it to Casco Viejo, where it can be seen today.

Further west (beyond the Bohío Turístico Restaurant) and paralleling the modern bridge is the **Puente del Matadero** (Bridge of the Slaughterhouse; Map p85), a horribly over-restored stone bridge that took its name from a nearby slaughterhouse. It marked the beginning of the Camino Real to Portobelo. A much more significant bridge is visible from Av Cincuentenario near the northern edge of town. It is called **Puente del Rey** (Bridge of the King; Map p85); built in 1617, it may be the oldest bridge in the Americas.

About halfway between that bridge and the Iglesia y Convento de Santo Domingo lies the **Iglesia de San José** (Map p85), which belonged to the Augustine order. Marking this building as special were its vaulted side chapels – an architectural feature seldom seen in Panama. The ruins of the separate adjacent chapel are gone today.

The city's ruins are not fenced and you can visit them any time. There's the fine **Mercado Nacional de Artesanías** (National Artisans Market; Map p85; 9am-6pm) beside the ruins. Sharing a building with the market is the Café de la Torre, which serves local food.

Adjacent to the artisans market is the **Museo de Sitio Panamá Viejo** (Map p85; www.panamaviejo.org in Spanish; ruins US$0.50, museum US$2; 9am-5pm), which contains a rather impressive scale model of Panamá Viejo prior to 1671. As you gaze upon it, a tape recording in Spanish or English recounts the history of the site. The museum also contains many colonial artifacts, most of which were brought from Spain. Unfortunately, all the signs are in Spanish and all the guides (every tour is guided for security reasons) speak only Spanish. It is customary to tip the guides US$1 or US$2.

At the time of research the museum was closed for renovation, though the ruins were open. Spanish speakers should check out the excellent website for more information.

Panamá Viejo buses coming from Plaza Cinco de Mayo will bring you here.

Causeway

At the Pacific entrance to the Panama Canal, a 2km *calzada* (causeway) connects the four small islands of Naos, Culebra, Perico and Flamenco to the southern tip of La Boca district.

The Causeway, which was constructed from rock that was removed to make the Panama Canal, is a pleasant respite from the noise and smog of downtown. Many people arrive in the early morning and the late afternoon to walk, jog, skate or bicycle along it. Others just soak up the fine views of downtown and the pleasant breeze at one of the Causeway's many restaurants and bars (see Eating, p98, and Drinking, p106, for more details).

There are several places to rent a bike or in-line skates (see p114 for details).

If you don't have a vehicle, it's most convenient to take a taxi to the Causeway (US$4 to US$6) and to hail another when you're ready to return to town (any of the restaurants or bars can call one for you).

FLAMENCO SHOPPING CENTER & FUERTE AMADOR RESORT & MARINA

At the end of Isla Flamenco, you'll find one of the city's newest attractions, the **Fuerte Amador Resort & Marina** (☎ 314-0932; www.fuerteamador.com). This complex contains a two-story shopping center, a marina, a cruise ship terminal and a number of restaurants and bars. At night, these open-air spots are a big draw, providing a fine setting for cocktails or a decent meal (see Eating, p98 and Drinking, p106).

CENTRO DE EXHIBICIONES MARINAS

The **Marine Exhibitions Center** (☎ 212-8000, ext 2366; admission US$1; 🕑 1-5pm Tue-Fri, 10am-5pm Sat & Sun), operated by the Smithsonian Tropical Research Institute (STRI), includes an informative marine museum with signs in English and Spanish, two small aquariums and a nature trail through a patch of dry forest containing sloths and iguanas.

There are many exhibits at the center, including a small six-sided building with sweeping views of the Bahía de Panamá that was built by Noriega for intimate gatherings. Today it houses a museum containing exhibits that mention how Panama's first peoples gradually developed a variety of strategies to harvest fish from the sea.

At the museum you can also learn about the role that Panama's marine resources play in the country's economy, and the destructive and wasteful effects of harvesting fish and shrimp by net. All of the text is illustrated with high-quality photos.

Outside the museum is something to thrill ship enthusiasts: large, intelligent illustrations of vessels that allow visitors to glance out at the ocean and identify the types of ships waiting to transit the canal. There's a telescope that you can use free of charge to peer onto the boats and get an idea of what it's like to be a crew member on these tankers.

Two large aquariums, also part of the marine center, are 50m from the museum. One contains fish from the Pacific, the other fish from the Caribbean, allowing you to compare the two sets. You'll be struck by how much more colorful, and how much smaller, are the fish from the Caribbean. Staff on hand can tell you why that is so.

Dry forests once lined Central America's Pacific coast. Relatively easy to clear and burn for agriculture, these forests have now all but disappeared. The forest that you can see from the center, which lines the shore just south of the Puente de las Américas, is one of the largest remaining dry forests in Central America. There's even some dry forest near the aquariums, with three-toed sloths among other wildlife present.

Panama Canal Murals

The story of the monumental effort to build the Panama Canal is powerfully depicted

---

MUSEO DE LA BIODIVERSIDAD

Although the **Biodiversity Museum** (www.biomuseopanama.org) was only in the initial stages of construction when this book was researched, it promises to be one of Latin America's most important museums. Designed by world-renowned architect Frank Gehry, the museum will contain eight halls, each full of multimedia exhibitions that showcase a different aspect of Panama's rich biological and ecological diversity, from its early tectonic formation to the intermingling of North and South American species, all the while placing the country in the context of the world's biodiversity. The museum is scheduled to open in 2006.

THE SECRET LIFE OF THE CAUSEWAY

All four of the Causeway islands once comprised Fort Grant, which was established in 1913 to guard the southern entrance to the canal. Between 1913 and WWII, the USA made Fort Grant into the most powerful defense complex in the world.

In 1928 two 14-inch guns with ranges up to 44km were brought to Panama. Mounted on railway carriages, they could be moved across the isthmus via the Panama Railroad to defend either entrance to the canal. The Pacific-side emplacement for the railroad guns was on Culebra. You can still see the tracks today on the driveway leading up to the Centro de Exhibiciones Marinas. The concrete rooms nearby, now used by marine-center staff, once housed the guns' ammunition. In 1941 the Japanese assault on Pearl Harbor showed that carrier-based aircraft could attack successfully far beyond the range of artillery. Suddenly obsolete, many of the big guns were retired from service even before the end of WWII.

The most distant of the four islands linked by the Causeway is Isla Flamenco, which was once a US military command post completed in January 1942 at the then-enormous cost of US$400,000.

Today, part of the Fuerte Amador shopping center is built on a massively protected bomb proof structure that was needed 'for use in case of emergency and vital to the security of important data,' according to the US general who ordered its construction. Even today, the US military will not disclose what data was so important that it needed to be stored at the center of a rock island.

The Causeway, its four islands and a chunk of the peninsula leading to the Causeway – all part of Fort Amador – was turned over to Panama in October 1979 in compliance with the Panama Canal Treaty of 1977.

in murals mounted in the rotunda of the **Panama Canal Administration Building** (Balboa Heights; ☺ 7:30am-4:15pm Mon-Fri).

The murals tell the story of the canal's construction through four main scenes: the digging of Gaillard Cut at Gold Hill, where the canal passes through the Continental Divide; the building of the spillway of the Gatún Dam, which dammed the Río Chagres and created Lago Gatún; the construction of one of the giant lock gates (the canal uses some 80 of these gates); and the construction of the Miraflores Locks near the Pacific entrance to the canal. A frieze located immediately below the murals presents a panorama of the excavation of Gaillard Cut.

The murals were created by William B Van Ingen of New York, an outstanding artist who had achieved considerable fame for his murals in the Library of Congress in Washington, DC, and those in the US Mint in Philadelphia. Van Ingen agreed to produce the murals for US$25 per sq ft; the finished murals cover about 1000 sq ft.

According to a leaflet at the administration building, Van Ingen and two assistants first made charcoal sketches of canal construction activities during two visits to Panama in 1914. Van Ingen then painted the murals

on separate panels in his New York studio. The panels were shipped to Panama and installed during a three-day period in January 1915 under the artist's personal supervision. The paintings have the distinction of being the largest group of murals by an American artist on display outside the USA.

The building is closed on weekends, but guards will usually let you in between 10am and 2:30pm if you ask them politely.

Mi Pueblitos

At the foot of Cerro Ancón, on the western side of town, **Mi Pueblitos** (My Little Villages; Map pp72-3; Av de los Mártires; admission US$1; ☺ 9am-9pm Tue-Sun) features life-size replicas of rural villages found on the Península de Azuero, in Bocas del Toro and in Darién. It also features several OK restaurants and extensive artisan shops, where you'll find handicrafts from throughout the country. The quality is usually very good to excellent, but the prices are much higher than you'd find in the crafts' cities of origin.

Folk dances accompanied by live music are staged on Fridays and Saturdays around 6pm; it's touristy but still worth a look. Note that there are two separate entrances to different exhibits.

Museums

Sadly, the establishment and preservation of museums is not a governmental priority in Panama City. Those that do exist are mostly the products of extraordinary efforts by individuals who took it upon themselves to move a bureaucratic mountain and create institutions in which Panama's human and natural histories could be preserved.

Foremost among this select group of individuals was the late Reina Torres de Araúz, the country's most distinguished anthropologist. Before she passed away in 1982 at age 49, she successfully battled for the creation of seven museums – including the anthropology museum that bears her name.

The strength of Panama City's museums lies not in a single institution or two but in their variety. In the capital city there are museums devoted to religious colonial art, natural science, Panamanian history, contemporary art, the Panama Railroad and the canal. Unfortunately, signs at all the museums are in Spanish only, and literature in other languages generally is not available.

In addition to those listed in the walking tour (p81), Panama City hosts several other interesting museums.

The **Museo Antropológico Reina Torres de Araúz** (☎ 262-8338; Av Central near Plaza Cinco de Mayo; admission US$2; 9am-4pm Mon-Fri) conveys the rich cultural heritage of Panama with a collection of pre-Colombian artifacts and exhibits.

The small **Museo Afro-Antilleano** (Map pp76-7; ☎ 262-5348; cnr Av Justo Arosemena & Calle 24 Este; admission US$1; 8:30am-3:30pm Tue-Sat) has exhibits on the history of Panama's West Indian community, particularly their work building the railroad and later the canal.

Museo de Arte Contemporáneo (Map pp76-7; ☎ 262-8012; near Av de los Mártires, Ancón district; admission free; 9am-4pm Mon-Fri, 9am-noon Sat, 9am-3pm Sun) is a privately owned museum with an excellent collection of works on paper by Latin American artists. The rest is usually not so hot, except for an occasional temporary exhibition by a national or foreign artist and the month-long Bienal de Arte, the country's largest art exhibition.

Museo de Ciencias Naturales (Map pp76-7; ☎ 225-0645; Av Cuba, btwn Calles 29 Este & 30 Este; admission US$1; 9am-3:45pm Tue-Sat) has sections on geology, paleontology, entomology and marine biology. Steel yourself for a large quantity of stuffed animals – though the quality of the taxidermy is impressive. Numerous examples of Panama's wildlife can be found here, as well as stuffed lions, tigers, rhinos and buffalo.

Parque Natural Metropolitano

Upon a hill to the north of downtown, this 265-hectare park protects a wild area of tropical forest within the city limits. It has two main walking trails – the Nature Trail and the Tití Monkey Trail – that join to form one long loop, and a 150m high *mirador* (lookout point) offering a view over Panama City, the bay and the canal all the way to the Miraflores Locks. It is the only city park in Latin America that contains tropical semideciduous forest.

Mammals in the park include marmosets, anteaters, sloths and white-tailed deer; reptiles are represented by iguanas, turtles and tortoises. There are more than 250 known species of bird here, including the lance-tailed manakin. Fish, shrimp and turtles live in the Río Curundu, which runs along the eastern side of the park.

An international team of scientists from the **Smithsonian Tropical Research Institute** (Map pp76-7; ☎ 212-8000; www.stri.org; Tupper Bldg, Av Roosevelt, Ancón district, Balboa) has set up a crane in the park to study the forest canopy; there is a complete ecosystem 30m to 50m up, including many animals that could never be studied from the ground. Unfortunately, the crane is off-limits to the general public.

The park is bordered on the west and north sides by Camino de la Amistad and to the south and east by Corredor Norte; Av Juan Pablo II runs right through the park. Pick up a pamphlet for a self-guided tour in Spanish and English at the **visitors center** (☎ 232-5516; admission US$1; 8am-5pm Mon-Fri, 8am-1pm Sat), 40m north of the park entrance. Rangers offer one-hour tours to groups of five or more (US$6 per person), but you need to call in advance.

Additionally, the **Panama Audubon Society** (☎ 224-9371; www.panamaaudubon.org) holds its monthly meeting at the visitors center from 7:30pm to 9:30pm on the second Thursday of every month. The meetings are open to the public and often feature interesting speakers. Both English and Spanish are spoken here. These meetings provide an excellent opportunity to get to know some Panamanians, to meet other birders and to learn more about birds.

The park was the supposed site of an important battle during the US invasion to oust Noriega. Also of historical significance are the concrete structures just past the park entrance. They were used by the US military during WWII as a testing and assembly plant for aircraft engines. Today one of the buildings is an environmental education center. The other structure is vacant.

COURSES
Dance
Latin Dance Company (☎ 265-7964) Located one block from Vía España near the Hotel Riande Granada, Latin Dance Company offers classes in salsa, merengue and hip-hop for students aged five to 65. Three classes are held in the evenings starting at 5:30pm, and there are several Saturday classes as well. Classes cost US$5 plus the US$5 enrolment fee. Or if you plan on sticking around for a while, sign up for 10 days (US$50) or one month (US$80) of unlimited classes.

Language
There are several Spanish-language schools in Panama City that receive positive reviews from students there.

Language & International Relations Institute (ILERI; Map pp72-3; ☎ 260-4424; www.ileripanama.com; Av Amistad, El Dorado) ILERI offers four hours of one-on-one instruction per day, five days a week. Costs start at US$300 for the first week (with lodging, meals and laundry service), then goes down for each subsequent week. The weekly rate without lodging starts at US$200 and includes field trips and activities.
Spanish Learning Center (Map pp78-9; ☎ 213-3121; www.spanishpanama.com; Calle G near Vía Argentina) This school is among the most popular choices for those wanting to learn Spanish. It has a similar structure to ILERI's: four hours of one-on-one classes daily and homestays with meals for US$375 per week. They also offer a 'backpackers special,' which includes classes with dorm stay for US$275 per week. You can also arrange for cheaper group classes if you're learning with a friend. If you plan on sticking around a while, rates go down significantly.

See the Bocas del Toro Province chapter (p232) for information on a third Spanish-language school.

PANAMA CITY FOR CHILDREN
Panama City has a variety of attractions that are suitable for kids. With excellent rain forest nearby, consider a day tour with one of the city's fine agencies (see left). Some of the best options for kids include visiting an **Emberá village**, touring the old cannon-lined forts in **Portobelo**, cruising along Lake Gatun on Ancon's **Jungle Boat Adventure**, taking a moderate hike through **Soberanía National Park** (p121) or doing a partial **canal transit** (p119). The **Panama Canal Railway** (p113) that links the two oceans provides a lovely journey along the canal and through rain forest (many agencies offer package tours, which take you on sightseeing tours once you reach rugged Colón). Kids might also enjoy a visit to the **Miraflores Locks** (p119). The new museum there has lots of eye-catching multimedia exhibitions and there's also a good restaurant overlooking the locks (with a loudspeaker giving details on each ship as it enters the lock chambers). If you need a respite from the heat (or the rain), head to **Multicentro** (p111). The mall has dozens of shops and restaurants, a movie theater and an Internet café.

TOURS
There are numerous tours available in and around the city, offered by companies of widely varying standards. Those mentioned here enjoy solid reputations in Panama. All of the following tours commence in Panama City. See Tours in the Transportation chapter (p313) for additional information.

Ancon Expeditions (Map pp78-9; ☎ 269-9415; www .anconexpeditions.com; Calle 49 near Av 3 Sur, Marbella) Ancon was created by Panama's top conservation organization and employs some of the country's finest nature guides. Unique trips include forays into the Darién jungle and overnights at Ancon lodges, as well as excellent day trips. Contact Ancon Expeditions or visit its website for a complete rundown of the company's offerings. Prices for the following tours are per person.
Barro Colorado Nature Monument This tour (US$99 including lunch) includes car transport to Gamboa, then boat transport up the Panama Canal to Barro Colorado Island, at the heart of the oldest nature reserve in the western hemisphere. The Smithsonian Tropical Research Institute guides take visitors on a tour of the jungle island and discuss the research being done there.
Panama Canal Jungle Boat Adventure Cruise in a low-profile expedition boat among the jungle-shrouded

islands of Gatun Lake near the belly of the Panama Canal. You may see white-fronted capuchins; howler, spider and night monkeys; and scores of exotic birds. Tours (US$89) include lunch on a private island as transoceanic ships pass by.

Panama City Tour & Miraflores Locks Includes a visit to Panamá La Vieja, Casco Viejo, the excellent Panama Canal Museum and, after lunch, a visit to the Miraflores Locks. The tour (US$50) is a very fine way to take in a lot of Panama City conveniently and efficiently.

Pipeline Road in Soberanía National Park Birders the world over have at least heard of the legendary Pipeline Road, a 17km jungle-flanked road/trail that repeatedly leads Central American sites for the greatest number of bird species recorded annually. The tour (US$65) includes a visit to the harpy eagle exhibit at Summit Botanical Gardens & Zoo.

Eco Circuitos (☎ 314-1586; www.ecocircuitos.com; Country Inn & Suites, Pelican Av, Causeway) Eco Circuitos maintains an excellent reputation for the quality and variety of its tours. Among many offerings it hosts day tours to El Valle (one to the Indian market on Sunday; another to the suspended Canopy tour) and a Historic Portobelo tour. Check the website for details on these tours and overnight trips to Wekso Indigenous Lodge in rain forest near Bocas del Toro and to an Emberá village near Darién. Some of the more popular offerings include:

Camino de Cruces Trail This trail was originally used by conquistadors to haul gold seized in Peru across the isthmus and was later used by Americans heading to California during the gold rush of 1849. The tour (US$65) takes visitors 13km through 4000 hectares of primarily dry tropical forest within the Metropolitan and Soberanía nature preserves.

Historic Portobelo Tour This trip includes a visit to the Spanish forts at Portobelo and its new museum, and a boat trip to Drake's Island, where some say the remains of the famous pirate Sir Francis Drake are buried. It costs US$80 including lunch, with a minimum of four people.

Kayaking the lower Chagres River (rates per person US$125/85/65 for groups of two/four/six) A leisurely kayak along the Chagres starting below the Gatun Spillway. The rain forest here is impressive, allowing ample birding opportunities and the possibility of seeing sloths and monkeys as well as marine life. Upon reaching the Caribbean, the tour continues on foot to Fort San Lorenzo. Price includes transport, box lunch and all equipment.

Iguana Tours (Map pp72-3; ☎ 226-4516; iguana@sinfo .net; Av Belisario Porras) Opposite Parque Omar, Iguana offers a number of competitive tours. These include trips to Isla Iguana off the coast of the Península de Azuero, as well as rafting, fishing and scuba expeditions.

Margo Tours (Map pp78-9; ☎ 264-8888; www.margot ours.com; Av 3 Sur) This outfit, next to the large Restaurante-Bar Tinajas, offers a wide variety of day tours: from exploring Casco Viejo on foot, to hikes through forest near Bayano Lake. It also offers overnight trips, including a scuba diving trip to Isla Coiba. Check the website for tour details.

Pesantez Tours (Map pp76-7; ☎ 263-7577; fax 263-7860; www.pesantez-tours.com; Av 6 Sur) Near the Centro Médico Paitilla, Pesantez offers the greatest number and variety of one-day tours in the Panama City area. It also offers an evening on the Chiva Parrandera, a bus with lively music and drinking, for US$20 per person.

Extreme Panama (☎ 269-7326; www.extremepan ama.com; Blvd El Dorado, Centro Comercial Camino de Cruces No 10) This youthful outfit offers a number of unusual full-day adventures, from mountain biking through the jungle (US$80), to cave exploring off Lago Bayano (US$70). It also offers overnight trips to Santa Fé, Kuna Yala and Bocas del Toro.

FESTIVALS & EVENTS

Although not as famous as the celebrations in Rio de Janeiro or New Orleans, Carnaval in Panama City is celebrated with the same level of unrestrained merriment and wild abandon during the four days preceding Ash Wednesday. From Saturday until the following Tuesday, work is put away and masks, costumes and confetti are brought to the fore. For 96 hours, almost anything goes.

The festivities formally begin with a coronation ceremony on Friday, during which a Carnaval queen and her attendants are chosen from candidates representing a variety of social clubs, volunteer organizations, neighborhoods and private groups. Throughout her reign, the queen presides at all official receptions and is the center of attention in the daily parades scheduled each afternoon.

Officially, the craziness starts slowly, with a small parade on Saturday that consists of little more than the queen and her court. Unofficially, the cork is way out of the bottle by then. Vía España fills with people, and everyone is in high spirits and partying in an atmosphere that is sexually charged and free of class distinctions. Music pours from all directions and spontaneous dancing breaks out everywhere. Masquerade characters cavort among the crowd. Colorful street vendors wander through the throngs of people, and improvised entertainment abounds. The party moves indoors at night – into cantinas, private clubs and hotels – where combos play Afro-Cuban and typical Panamanian music and the dancing and drinking continue till dawn.

The celebration, the origins of which have been obscured with the passage of time, kicks into a higher gear on Sunday, when folk dance groups decked out in Panama's national costumes join the queen and her attendants in the afternoon parade down Vía España, traveling from near Vía Brasil to near Av Federico Boyd (the exact beginning and ending points vary from year to year). To cool the sunbaked masses, fire and garden hoses are turned on the crowd at every opportunity. The amount of water sprayed on party-goers during Carnaval in Panama City during these four festive days equals the amount the city uses during the previous four *months*.

The madness peaks on Shrove Tuesday with the biggest parade of all. Floats of all sizes rule the avenue, separated by bands of gaily dressed people walking slowly in themed formations – not the least conspicuous of which is the traditional formation of transvestites. Most of them carry a razor in each hand as a warning to macho types that a punch thrown at them will not go unanswered.

Carnaval officially closes with the first rays of sunlight on Wednesday morning, when the hardiest celebrants appear on the beach of the Bahía de Panamá to bury a sardine in the sand – a symbolic gesture intended to convey the end of worldly pleasures for the Lenten season.

SLEEPING

There are dozens of hotels in Panama City with guestrooms ranging from cell-like (small, dirty and hot with shared cold-water bathrooms) to opulent (tastefully appointed chambers with fine views, acres of space, executive desk, minibar, satellite TV, Jacuzzi with separate shower etc).

In general, budget accommodations – along with many push-buttons (seedy hotels that rent by the hour) – lie scattered around La Exposición, an area that doesn't offer many other amenities. Most travelers are happier in El Cangrejo, which has a bit more traffic but a wider variety of restaurants and nightlife nearby. Mid- and upper-range lodgings comprise the offerings here. Casco Viejo, the most scenic and also the most run-down neighborhood, has a handful of accommodations ranging from scary to sumptuous.

Budget accommodations run up to US$20, mid-range lodgings from US$21 to US$65 and top-end places from US$66 to a small house payment. Prices cited in this section do not include Panama's 10% hotel tax. There are several youth hostels but no campgrounds or RV centers in the city.

Budget
CASCO VIEJO

The colonial Casco Viejo area was once home to the seediest accommodations in town. Although there are still plenty of dodgy places for hearty adventurers on a budget, the slowly gentrifying neighborhood has a growing number of options, including a lovely B&B. If you stay here, take a taxi at night as it's not safe to walk around after dark. See also Dangers & Annoyances (p81) for safety tips.

The Lion House (Map p80; ☎ /fax 228-9903; lion housepanama@hotmail.com; Av Central near Calle 8a Este; dm US$10) This brand-new hostel promises to be one of the best budget lodging options for backpackers in the city. Accommodations are in well-lit four bed dorm rooms, each with French doors opening onto a small balcony overlooking the street. Amenities here include a kitchen for guest use and a lounge area. There's an Internet café next door.

Pensión Colón (Map p80; ☎ 228-8506; cnr Calle 12 Oeste & Calle B; s/d US$9/10, with bathroom US$10/11) Colón is the only hotel on the block that doesn't rent by the hour. Originally built to house Panama Canal workers, it has a handsome lobby where one can see the original ornate Spanish tilework. Unfortunately, the place has seen many years of neglect, and the rooms have poor beds and worn floorboards. The bathrooms aren't the best and some rooms are better than others, so check a few. The pleasant roof deck affords nice views of the canal. Be advised: on weekends the bar next door rages late into the night.

Casa Grande (Map p80; ☎ 211-3316; Av Central r without/with balcony US$6/7) This lovely, colonial building has yellow trim and wrought-iron balconies – a real charmer, until you step inside. The dingy rooms share shabby bathrooms, and thin walls stop just shy of the ceiling. Still, the balconies are nice, and it's tolerable if you don't mind roughing it.

Hotel Herrera (Map p80; ☎ 228-8994; beside Parque Herrera; d without/with bathroom US$6/8) This architecturally attractive hotel is a bit more secure and the fan-cooled rooms are a little less worn than other options. Still the whole place could use a good scrubbing. Get a front-facing room for better light. Owing to a recent change in management, this place may be gone by the time you read this.

LA EXPOSICIÓN

This bustling neighborhood contains quite a few budget hotels and many mid-range ones. It has decent, inexpensive lodging but isn't particularly safe (especially at night) and is not recommended for women traveling alone. For security – and ambience – most travelers are better off staying in the livelier El Cangrejo district.

Pensión Las Palmeras (Map pp76-7; ☎ 225-0811; Av Cuba near Calle 38 Este; d US$10) In a tranquil residential neighborhood, Las Palmeras has simple but clean rooms which feature a double bed, fan and private cold-water bathroom.

Residencial Turístico Volcán (Map pp76-7; ☎ 225-5275; Calle 29 Este btwn Avs Perú & Cuba; d US$12, with air-con US$14, two beds US$16; ❄ ▣) The Volcán has battered rooms with double beds, private bathrooms, ceiling fans and TVs. Upstairs rooms with air-con are brighter. You can use the 24-hour rooftop pool at the Hotel Covadonga next door.

Hotel Centroamericano (Map pp76-7; ☎ 227-4555; Av Ecuador btwn Av 3a Sur and Av 2a Sur; s/d US$18/20) One of the best of the bunch in this area, this hotel has spotless rooms with good mattresses, decent light, hot-water bathrooms, telephone and cable TV. There's a pleasant **restaurant/bar** (⏲ 7am-10pm Mon-Sat).

Hotel Bella Vista (Map pp76-7; ☎ 264-4029; Vía España at Calle 42 Este; d without/with air-con US$14/20; ❄) The Bella Vista could use a paint job. All the same, its airy rooms with fair beds and private cold-water bathrooms aren't bad for the money. There's also a 24-hour restaurant.

Hotel 2 Mares (Map pp76-7; ☎ 227-6150; dosmares @cwpanama.net; Calle 30 Este btwn Avs Perú & Cuba s/d/tr from US$15/20/24; ❄) The Hotel 2 Mares has so-so rooms with air-con for a reasonable price. A room with a view and a king-size bed costs US$25. Many of the rooms have small Jacuzzis.

Hotel Acapulco (Map pp76-7; ☎ 225-3832; hotel acapulco@hotmail.com; Av Cuba & Calle 30 Este; s/d/tw US$20/22/24; ❄) The six-story Acapulco has spacious rooms, some with small balconies. Each air-con room has a private hot-water bathroom, writing desk, TV and telephone.

Hotel Latino (Map pp76-7; ☎ 227-3395; fax 227-3092; Av Cuba near Calle 35 Este; s/d/tr US$18/22/23; ❄) The Latino was built in the '90s but hasn't aged gracefully. Its gloomy rooms come with air-con and TV. The hotel has a simple eatery on the ground floor.

CALIDONIA

With the exception of the following, most hotels in this area rent by the hour.

Hotel Doral (Map pp76-7; ☎ 262-5144; Calle I near 17 Oeste; d US$18) A block from the Av Central pedestrian street, the Doral is a large hotel popular with Panamanian families for its price and cleanliness. Mattresses are a bit soft and the showers are cold, but the rooms have good light. Ask for one on the top floor for bayside views.

EL CANGREJO

Although most of the accommodations here are mid-range and up, there is a popular hostel in the neighborhood. Casa de Carmen (p97) also has several rooms for budget travelers.

Voyager International Hostel (Map pp78-9; ☎ 260-5913, 223-3687; www.geocities.com/voyagerih; 8th fl Di-Lido Bldg, Calle Maria Icaza near Vía España; dm US$8, d US$17; ❄ ▣) The Voyager, Panama City's first hostel, comprises two floors in a high-rise in the banking district and is a long-time favorite with young travelers. The vibe here is festive, and the setting offers wraparound views of the city, and a small outdoor lounge. The 3rd floor has small but clean private rooms, geared for couples and those wanting more privacy. The 8th floor digs are adequately maintained eight-bed dorm rooms, featuring bunk beds with very thin mattresses. Continental breakfast (coffee, bread and fruit) is included, guests have use of the kitchen and common living area, and there's Internet access. A message board lists notes from other travelers, including details on sailboats heading for Colombia.

OTHER AREAS

Backpackers Hostel (Map pp72-3; ☎ 317-1264; www .backpackerspanama.com; former military base of Clayton; dm US$10; 🔀) Near the Panama Canal, this new hostel offers a tranquil respite from the noise of downtown. Surrounded by greenery with a garden out back, the hostel has a relaxed, friendly atmosphere. Spotless rooms are equipped with fan or air-con, and the extensive list of amenities is sure to make this a travelers' favorite: there's hot water, bike rental, telephone (cards available), cable TV, stereo, video equipment, book exchange and access to laundry, tour, fax/copies and taxi services.

Mid-Range

Mid-range hotels are scattered throughout La Exposición and El Cangrejo. As mentioned earlier, most travelers are happier in El Cangrejo.

CALIDONIA

Hotel Internacional (Map pp76-7; ☎ 262 4933; hint@sinfo .net; Av Central; s/d US$20/25; 🔀) Overlooking Plaza Cinco de Mayo, the Internacional opened during the '90s and still appears to be well maintained. The rooms are bright – although the showers are gloomy – with the top floor (six) commanding the best view. Each of the 80 rooms has air-con, hot water and cable TV. There's a bar, restaurant and casino on the premises.

LA EXPOSICIÓN

Hotel Venecia (Map pp76-7; ☎ 227-7881; hotel venecia@hotmail.com; Av Perú near Calle 35 Este; s/d US$22/24, family/executive rooms US$33/39; 🔀) The Venecia is a fairly new place with a cheerily painted exterior and a prominent Venetian theme inside through its wall hangings, vases and photos. In spite of the trappings, rooms are fair here, with OK beds, cable TV, air-con and private bathrooms. Overall, it's good value for the money. There's a restaurant/bar on the premises.

Hotel California (Map pp76-7; ☎ 263-7736; www .hotel-california.ws; Av Central España near Calle 43 Este; d/tw/tr US$25/30/35) The Hotel California has 60 good, clean rooms with private hot-water bathrooms, phones and color TV. There's a smoky restaurant/bar downstairs

and free coffee in the lobby. Ask for a quiet, spacious room with a view of the bay. Members of the Peace Corps stay here for its value and safety. If you stay three nights or more, you'll save 20%.

Hotel Marparaíso (Map pp76-7; ☎ /fax 227-6767; Calle 34 Este btwn Avs 2 & 3 Sur; s/d US$20/25; 🅿 🔀) This is one of the better choices of the hotels in this price range. Built in 1999, the Spanish-run Marparaíso offers 72 spacious, clean, tastefully appointed, air-con rooms with cable TV and telephones. There are six floors in all, and rooms on the top floor seem larger than the rest. With secure parking as well, this place offers good value.

Hotel Ribadavia Star (Map pp76-7; ☎ 225-7422; www.ribadaviapanama.com; Av Perú btwn Calle 36 & 37; d/tw US$28/33, d with balcony US$35; 🖥) The Ribadavia Star has clean, well-maintained rooms with private hot-water bathrooms and cable TV. The rooms with the balcony would be a lovely extra except for the roar of traffic on the street below. Internet and laundry services are available.

Hotel Andino (Map pp76-7; ☎ 225-1162; andino@sinfo.net; Calle 35 near Av Perú; s/d US$22/25; 🔀) On a quiet street near a park, Hotel Andino has one of the more peaceful locations in La Exposición. Rooms here are clean but a little gloomy, with tiny fridges and OK mattresses, air-con, telephone and cable TV.

Hotel Caribe (Map pp76-7; ☎ 225-0404; caribe hotel@hotmail.com; Calle 28 Este at Av Perú; s/d US$28/34; 🔀 🖳) The 11-story Hotel Caribe is a friendly spot that's worth the extra cash, offering spacious air-con rooms with telephone and cable TV (and a refrigerator, if you request one). There's a pool on the roof, an ice machine on every floor and even laundry service.

Hotel Lisboa (Map pp76-7; ☎ 227-5916; fax 227-5919; cnr Av Cuba & Calle 31; s/d US$17/22; 🔀) Hotel Lisboa isn't the loveliest spot in town, but it does offer reasonable spacious rooms with air-con, a writing table, TV and phone.

Hotel Veracruz (Map pp767; ☎ 227-3022; Av Perú near Calle 30 Este; s/d/tr US$25/30/35; 🔀) Guests receive a welcome cocktail upon arrival at the Veracruz, which offers clean rooms with cable TV and air-con. All of the rooms ending with the numbers '08' have balconies. There's a restaurant on the premises and laundry service.

Hotel Costa Inn (Map pp76-7; ☎ 227-1522; www .hotelcostainn.com; Av Perú near Calle 39 Este; s/d US$40/45;

(P) (⊠) (□) (⌨) A big step up in quality and service, the Hotel Costa Inn offers comfortable rooms with air-con and satellite TV. Facilities include a gym, pool, good restaurant, secure parking and Internet access. Airport shuttle and city tours are available, and there's a travel agency on the premises: **Viajes Florencia** (☎ 225-6083). The hotel's sales manager, Carlos Ledo Vázquez, enjoys an excellent reputation for the personal attention he provides his guests. Discounts are available through website bookings.

Hotel Roma (Map pp76-7; ☎ 227-3844; www.hotel romaplaza.com; Av Justo Arosemena at Calle 33; d from US$50, ste US$100; (⊠) (□) (⌨)) The Hotel Roma has a pool on its roof and cheerful rooms with good beds, air-con, TV, phones, free Internet access for guests (from Monday to Saturday), and a pleasant restaurant on the 1st floor.

EL CANGREJO

Hotel El Parador (Map pp78-9; ☎ 214-4586; helparador@cableonda.net; Calle Eusebio Morales; s/d US$39/44, tw/tr US$55/66; (⊠) (⌨)) A few blocks from Vía España, Hotel El Parador is one of the latest additions to the city's hotel scene. The uninspiring building features a large haunting lobby, a rooftop swimming pool and a wide variety of accommodations. Of the 80 rooms, most have decent lighting and views, with good beds, cable TV and hot-water bathrooms. The 1st floor features a restaurant and bar.

Hotel Montreal (Map pp76-7; ☎ 263-4422; hmont real@cableonda.net; Vía España at Av Justo Arosemena; s/d/tr US$22/28/33; (P) (⊠) (⌨)) The large and featureless 86-room Hotel Montreal offers the usual amenities plus a rooftop swimming pool and secure parking. Rates aren't bad for the better rooms, but ask to see several as they vary in quality.

Hotel Marbella (Map pp78-9; ☎ 263-2220; hmar bella@cableonda.net; Calle D btwn Calle 55 & Eusebio A Morales; s/d US$39/44; (⊠)) The popular, well-located Hotel Marbella has small but pleasantly decorated rooms with writing/dining tables, air-con, cable TV and good beds. Laundry service is available. It offers fine value – make sure you get the corporate rate or you'll pay more.

Gran Hotel Soloy (Map pp76-7; ☎ 227-1133; hgso loy@pan.gbm.net; Av Perú at Calle 30 Este; s/d US$39/44; (⊠)) The Gran Hotel has fairly cheerful rooms with air-con and cable TV. It's not

bad value except for the location: for the same price you could stay in El Cangrejo. There's a casino on the ground floor and a **bar and dance club** (12th floor; (☾) after 5pm Thu-Sat).

Coral Suites Aparthotel (Map pp78-9; ☎ 269-3898; www.coralsuites.net; Calle D near Calle 49B Oeste; ste from US$55; (P) (⊠) (□) (⌨)) This handsome all-suites hotel features a gym, rooftop pool, laundry room, secure parking and a business center with Internet access (5¢ a minute). Suites are simple but comfortable, with fully equipped kitchen, air-con, cable TV, good beds and fine hot-water bathrooms.

Suites Ambassador (Map pp78-9; ☎ 263-7274; Calle D btwn Calle Eusebio A Morales & Calle 49 B Oeste; ste from US$60; (⊠) (⌨)) Centrally located and offering large, handsome rooms, the Suites Ambassador has the best service in town. The smallest room at this very smart hotel would be a junior suite anywhere else. Each room comes with a true sitting area and an attractive kitchenette. Use of a conference room is offered at no extra charge. A state-of-the-art security system monitors every floor, and the rooftop pool is quite inviting. Make sure you get the corporate rate when you book here, otherwise you'll pay twice as much. Weekly and monthly discounts are available.

Las Vegas Suites Hotel (Map pp78-9; ☎ 269-0722; www.lasvegaspanama.com; Av Eusebio Morales; studio/ste US$45/58; (⊠)) Located in an area full of restaurants and Internet cafés, the rooms at Las Vegas Suites offer excellent value. The hotel was totally renovated in 2000, and all rooms have kitchenettes with refrigerators, plus cable TV, new air-con units and phones. (Suites have one extra living/dining room.) The hotel's courtyard restaurant, Caffé Pomodoro, is a highlight and the Wine Bar is also quite popular (see p106). Be sure to ask for the corporate rate.

Hotel Riande Granada (Map pp78-9; ☎ 269-1068; www.hotelesriande.com; Av Eusebio A Morales near Vía España; d from US$65; (⊠) (⌨)) The Riande Granada has elegant, comfortable and recently remodeled rooms, a basic pool and a casino, bar and restaurant.

Hotel Las Huacas (☎ 213-2222; www.lashuacas .com; Calle 53 near Vía Argentina; ste from US$65/75; (⊠)) This all-suites hotel offers excellent comfortably furnished rooms with lots of amenities (air-con, cable TV, kitchenette, phone). Many of the rooms have balconies; the five deluxe suites have names like Azuero, Bocas Town, Selva del Darién. This is also a good choice for families (the two-bedroom deluxe suite costs US$86). Several rooms are disabled accessible.

Sevilla Suites (Map pp78-9; ☎ 213-0016; www.sevillasuites.com; Av Eusebio A Morales; ste with breakfast from US$65/80; P 🅟 ✖ 🖳) This six-floor, all-suites hotel immediately put other hotels in its price range on notice when it opened in 2000. All rooms feature a large cable TV, VCR, fully equipped kitchenettes and an optional sofa bed. Facilities include a gym, 24-hour rooftop pool, coin-operated laundry and covered parking. Junior suites feature one queen-size bed and some have a balcony.

OTHER AREAS

Hotel Plaza Paitilla Inn (Map pp76-7; ☎ 269-1122; www.plazapaitillainn.com; Vía Italia at Av Churchill, Punta Paitilla; s & d US$45; ✖ 🖳) This former Holiday Inn on the water is very well maintained, with tasteful if cheap furniture in its guestrooms, many of which have superb views. Rooms have bathtubs and balconies and hotel features include a handsome pool, gym, discotheque (Genesis) and popular bar. The rates here used to be much higher (around US$100), making it quite a deal.

Albrook Inn (Map pp72-3; ☎ 315-1789; www.albrookinnpanama.com.pa; Calle Hazelhurst 14, Albrook; d/ste US$40/60) Set amid lush greenery in a tranquil area removed from the chaos of downtown, the new Albrook Inn near Albrook airport is a fine choice if you're making an early morning domestic flight. Rooms are modern and spotless, with good beds, cable TV and hot-water bathrooms. The 2nd-floor suites also offer good value and come with three beds, a kitchen/lounge area with a sofa and breakfast table, and windows looking out onto the greenery. If you'll be arriving in your own vehicle, check the website for driving directions as it can be difficult navigating out here.

Top End

There's no shortage of top-end accommodations in Panama City. You can often get a better nightly rate if you use a local tour operator to reserve a room, or if you request the hotel's corporate rate.

The Executive Hotel (Map pp78-9; ☎ 264-3333; www.executivehotel-panama.com; cnr Av 3 Sur & Calle Aquilino de la Guardia; s/d US$65/72; 🖳 ✖ 🖳) The Executive has good value comfortable rooms with good light, decent beds and all the extras including free Internet hookup, buffet break-

fast and a nightly free open bar (from 6pm to 7pm). The service here generally receives high marks and the pool and restaurant add to the hotel's popularity. Try to book online otherwise you might pay more.

Torres de Alba (Map pp78-9; ☎ 269-7770; www.torresdealba.com.pa; Av Eusebio A Morales; ste US$75; ✖ 🖳) One of the newest all-suites hotels in El Cangrejo, the Torres de Alba has comfortable, decent-sized rooms with cable TV, full kitchens, washer/drier and modern baths. All the amenities are on hand, including a rooftop pool and workout center. Guests who stay five or more nights pay US$68 per night.

Hotel Continental (Map pp78-9; ☎ 265-5114; www.hotelesriande.com; Calle Ricardo Arias & Vía España; d from US$75; ✖ 🖳) The well-located Hotel Continental has handsome guestrooms with four-poster beds and a bathtub with handrails – rare features in Panama. Amenities include a lovely pool and casino. Many of the rooms have fine views. Book online (or you'll pay more), and be sure to ask for a room in the newer wing.

Hotel Caesar Park (Map pp72-3; ☎ 270-0477; www.caesarpark.com; Calle 77 Este near Vía Israel; d from US$90; ✖ 🖳) This elegant, 361-room hotel is opposite the Centro Atlapa in the San Francisco neighborhood. Part of the Westin Hotels and Resorts chain, this is where heads of state usually stay when they visit Panama. Accommodations range from fully equipped 'standard' suites to a gorgeous suite with spectacular views. Facilities include an athletic club and spa, three floodlit tennis courts, a swimming pool, three executive floors, a business center, dance club, upscale stores, casino and sports bar, and six restaurants including a pizzeria, a very popular all-you-can-eat buffet and an elegant 15th-floor dining room with spectacular city views and prime ribs to die for. Book online to get the best rates; members of Westin's Starwood Preferred Guest program (www.starwood.com) save more – it takes little time to join and membership is free.

Country Inn & Suites, El Dorado (Map pp72-3; ☎ 236-6444, in the USA 800-456-4000; www.countryinns.com; Av Miguel Brostella west of Av Ricardo J Alfaro; d/ste US$89/109; ✖ 🖳 🖳) The lodge has a country-inn feel. It has meeting rooms, a business center, free self-serve laundry, and offers free local calls and breakfast. There are excellent discounts if you book online (rooms $49), and corporate rates are available.

AUTHOR'S CHOICE

Casa de Carmen (Map p76-7; ☎ 263-4366; www.lacasadecarmen.com; Calle 1a de Carmen 32, El Carmen; dm/tr per person US$10/13.50, d US$20-30, apt US$45; 🖳) In a beautiful converted home near Vía Brasil, Casa de Carmen offers a variety of cozy rooms, each painted a different shade with matching furniture. Most rooms have private hot-water bathrooms and all have good beds and air-con (remote-controlled no less). Guests can use the kitchen, lounge area (with books, magazines, TV) or the Internet, and there's a lush patio. Adding to the familial atmosphere are the friendly owners who have a wealth of knowledge of the city and countryside. Reservations recommended.

La Estancia (Map p72-3; ☎ 314-1417; www.bedandbreakfastpanama.com; Casa 35, Quarry Heights, Ancón Hill; d/ste US$45/75; 🖳) Set in the lush forest atop Cerro Ancón (Ancón Hill), La Estancia is one of Panama City's most charming B&Bs. Simple air-con rooms are elegantly furnished, some with views of the Bridge of the Americas, others with views of the quiet lane in front, and all have hot-water bathrooms. The two spacious suites are top-notch and worth the extra money. Each has a complete kitchen, private patio, flat-screen TV and lots of space. Breakfasts are excellent here, best enjoyed on the patio. La Estancia is no longer a secret so book as far in advance as possible.

Casa Mar Alta (Map p80; ☎ 211-3427; www.casamaralta.com; Calle 2a, Casco Viejo; d low/high season US$95/155) Located in Panama City's most historic neighborhood, Casa Mar Alta is a beautifully restored 19th-century mansion with two lavish guestrooms. Each comes with TV and private bathroom, and one of the rooms has a balcony overlooking the old quarter. Guests also have access to the dining room (where breakfast is served each morning), Internet service and telephone. Several of the finest features of this penthouse – and the reasons it's often favored for magazine photo shoots – are the exquisite tile work throughout and the rooftop terrace, with its lovely views over the sea. If you're traveling with two or three people, you can book the whole place (two bedrooms) for US$155/195 in low/high season. Book well in advance.

DeVille Hotel (Map p78-9; ☎ 206-3100; www.devillehotel.com.pa; Av Beatriz Cabal near Calle 50, El Cangrejo; ste from US$155; 🖳) One of the newest boutique hotels in town, the DeVille is an elegant addition to Panama City. All 33 rooms are suites and offer luxury par excellence. Among the features in your beautifully appointed room, expect to find an antique dresser from Thailand, glistening with inlaid mother of pearl; a marble-topped antique table set with Louis XV chairs; finest-quality US-made mattresses with custom bed linen made of Egyptian cotton and goose-feather pillows; a business desk with fax machine and Internet port and a spacious bathroom lined floor to ceiling with white marble imported from Italy. The facilities include a business center, meeting rooms and a terrific French restaurant. Ask for the corporate rate for discounts of up to 50%.

The Bristol (Map p78-9; ☎ 265-7844; www.thebristol.com; Calle Aquilino de la Guardia, El Cangrejo; ste from US$195; 🖳) An elegant hotel with marble and mahogany at every turn, the Bristol prides itself on personal service and is simply overflowing with it: each guest is attended by a 24-hour butler. The lovely rooms are equipped with fax machines and separate Internet and telephone lines in addition to CD players (guests have access to the Bristol's digital library) and all the usual amenities. Guests can have a suit or dress pressed upon arrival; laundry and shoeshine services and newspaper delivery are among its list of features. Corporate rates can save you 20%.

Country Inn & Suites, Causeway (Map pp72-3; ☎ 211-4500, in the USA 800-456-4000; www.countryinns.com/panamacanalpan; Amador Av & Pelicano Av; d/ste US$110/125; 🖳 🏊) In a peaceful setting on the water overlooking the canal, this Country Inn offers lovely, modern rooms all with balconies that provide views of the Bridge of the Americas. It offers the same amenities (including a swimming pool and hot tub) as its sister hotel in El Dorado, and has a lovely tennis court. Book online to save substantially (around 40%).

Casco Viejo Properties (☎ 262-6813; Calle 2a Oeste btwn Av Central & Av B; ste with breakfast from US$85; 🖳) Although Casco Viejo Properties was still in the works at the time this was written, the apartmental rental service in Casco Viejo promises to offer a unique lodging experience in Panama City.

Beginning in February 2005, Casco Viejo Properties will begin renting newly renovated apartments in historic buildings by the night, week or longer. Run by friendly English-speaking staff, the apartments are fully serviced with maid service, kitchens, laundry, high speed Internet, cable TV and air-conditioning. One, two and three bedrooms are available, each with its own unique charm, ranging from roof-top ocean-view terraces to balconies overlooking the picturesque Parque Bolívar. The staff at this agency can also arrange transportation, tours and accommodation in the interior. Special rates are available for longer stays.

Miramar Inter-Continental (Map pp76-7; ☎ 214-1000; www.miramarpanama.com; Av Balboa near Av Federico Boyd; d from US$165; 🔀 🖭) The Miramar is competing successfully with the Caesar Park for top honors as Panama's finest convention-capable hotel. Gorgeous guestrooms contain all the creature comforts and face either the Bahía de Panamá or the gleaming financial district. The 25-story seaside hotel features an informal marina-side restaurant, a fine dining restaurant on the 5th floor, a piano lounge, bar and dance club, a private dining salon, and a business center. The inviting pool has an island in the middle, and there's a fully-equipped spa with aerobics, a beauty salon, ballrooms and even tennis courts. Inquire about promotional rates before you book. Past guests have included Hillary Clinton, Mick Jagger, Jimmy Carter, Alberto Fujimori, Sting, Ernesto Zedillo, Andres Pastrana and Def Leppard – who weren't all traveling together, by the way.

EATING

Reflecting its large immigrant population, Panama City has a wide array of restaurants. A stroll through El Cangrejo and Bella Vista (comprising Panama City's unofficial restaurant district) will reveal cuisine from Italy, Spain, Thailand, Argentina, China, France, Lebanon, Britain, Japan and Greece. Throughout the city, Panamanian specialties and seafood abound – no small indication of the city's location.

Budget

In addition to the restaurants listed here, you can eat inexpensively at one of the city's fine bakeries (see p106). For groceries and self-catering, stop in one of the locations of the giant Supermercado Rey, most of which open 24 hours, including the branch on Vía España (Map pp72–3).

PANAMANIAN

Café Coca Cola (Map p80; Av Central, Casco Viejo; meals under $6; 🕙 7:30-11pm) A neighborhood institution near Plaza Santa Ana, Café Coca Cola is an old-school diner, complete with chess-playing señores and no-nonsense waitresses. This popular air-conditioned spot serves excellent set lunches (US$3), good breakfasts (under US$2) and dinner plates. Tasty, hearty platefuls of beef, chicken and seafood are the norm.

Restaurante Boulevard Balboa (Map pp76-7; Av Balboa at Calle 31 Este, La Exposición; meals US$1.50-4.50) If you're traveling on a tight budget and looking for a cheap but filling meal, this old-time favorite is a good choice. It doesn't have much ambience but its fans don't seem to mind. It specializes in grilled sandwiches, few of which are over US$3, and burgers, which are US$1.50. Very popular is the *milanesa a caballo* (US$4.50), which consists of a breaded steak topped with two eggs served sunny-side up.

El Rincón Tableño (Map pp76-7; cnr Calle 27 Este & Av Balboa, La Exposición; meals US$2.50-4) The menu changes daily at this open-air eatery, but the type of food never does: it's always 100% working-class Panamanian. Typical items include *sopa de carne* (meat soup, 90¢), *camarones guisados* (shrimp in tomato sauce, US$2.50), and *ropa vieja* (literally, 'old clothes'; marinated shredded beef served as a stew, US$2.10). There's a choice of a half-dozen or so natural fruit juices, each priced under US$1.

Restaurante Rincón Tableño (Map pp76-7; cnr Av Cuba & Calle 31, La Exposición; meals US$2.50-4) Next to the Hotel Lisboa, this spot serves high-quality typical Panamanian food in a fan-cooled and clean environment. The waitresses here wear the traditional attire of the women of the Península de Azuero. In addition to lots of inexpensive food like *sancocho* (chicken and vegetable stew), there's a nice selection of refreshing juices (try the papaya, a local favorite).

Café Sitton (Map pp78-9; Vía España near Vía Argentina, El Cangrejo; mains US$2-5) If you ever get nostalgic for grammar school cafeteria ladies, head to Café Sitton for a convenient meal. Once inside, grab a tray and file past the piping-hot selections at this popular working-class lunch joint. The food here is hearty Panamanian fare and although it's simple, it's probably better than what

AUTHOR'S CHOICE

Eurasia (Map p76-7; ☎ 264-7859; Calle 48, Bella Vista; mains US$14-18; ⏱ noon-3pm Mon-Fri, 7-10:30pm Mon-Sat) Dining at Eurasia is a rich, sensory experience. The lavishly adorned restaurant has marble floors and nicely displayed artwork. Impeccable service and daring, fusion cuisine meld seamlessly; the inventive French chef (whose menu changes regularly) puts together appetizers like Vietnamese shrimp rolls with orange sauce, and onion soup with tofu and duck breast. Entrées similarly range across the continents with dishes such as jumbo shrimp in tamarind sauce and coconut milk with rice pilaf to tuna breaded with ajonjolí seeds and caramelized in honey. The wine and dessert selection is equally impressive.

Café de Asís (Map p80; ☎ 262-9304; Calle 3a Este, Casco Viejo; mains US$7-11; ⏱ from 6pm) Café de Asís is perhaps the most charming spot in Panama City to go for a bite or a drink in the evening. Located on the ground floor of a four-floor beautifully restored, 19th-century building, the café has outdoor tables along Parque Bolívar with the beautiful church of San Francisco de Asís part of the scenery. The house sangria is excellent and pairs nicely with anything on the menu. Some of the tasty selections include ceviche (US$5.50), nachos (US$6), and *pulpo endiablo* (deviled octopus, US$8.50).

Manolo Caracol (Map p80; ☎ 228-4640; Av Central & Calle 3 Oeste, Casco Viejo; mains US$12-16; ⏱ noon-3pm & 7-10:30pm Mon-Fri, 7-11pm Sat) On a colonial street in Casco Viejo, Manolo Caracol has just the right ambience – original tilework, with tapestries on the walls and rustic furniture – to accompany the excellent fixed-price meals. With five courses at lunch (US$10) and seven at dinner (US$17), you won't leave hungry after sampling from the many offerings. The menu changes regularly but might include fresh squash soup, marinated vegetables, grilled fish, game hen and chocolate torte.

Limoncillo (Map p78-9; ☎ 263-5350; Calle 47 near Calle Uruguay; mains US$14-16; ⏱ noon-3pm & 7-10:30pm Mon-Fri, 7-11pm Sat) A stylish place that serves magnificent dishes, Limoncillo has been one of the city's best restaurants since opening in 1999. The menu changes every few months, but you can always count on a fresh and creative assortment of plates with delicate spices: pan-roasted grouper with grilled asparagus and tamarind vinaigrette, for instance, or pork chops with olive gnocchi and sage. Panamanian chef Clara Icaza Angelini cooked at some of the best restaurants in New York before returning to her roots, and artistry clearly runs in her family. Much of the artwork in the restaurant (paintings, photographs and an occasional sculpture) was made by her relatives. Some of it is for sale; ask one of the waiters if you find something particularly striking – besides the sautéed sea scallops with Thai red curry sauce, that is.

Habibi's (Map p78-9; ☎ 213-9919; Calle Ricardo Arias, Bella Vista; mains US$5-8) The patio in front of this Lebanese favorite makes for some of the city's best al fresco dining. Habibi's serves nicely prepared plates of shaslik, shish kabob, hummus and thin-crust pizzas, and big variety platters perfect for sharing with a group. Upstairs, the cozy lounge that vaguely resembles a sheik's tent is a fine spot to enjoy a hookah, strong coffee or cocktails after the meal. A belly dancer often appears on Friday and Saturday nights to add a splash of color to the scenery.

you ate in the fourth grade. Roast chicken with rice is popular as is the jumbo shrimp with garlic. You can also pop in at breakfast time for pancakes, eggs, ham and the like. Don't neglect the donuts, pastries and sweet breads on your way out.

Casa de Fernando (Map pp76-7; Calle 30 Este, La Exposición; mains US$4-6; ⏱ 24hr) This one-room bar and restaurant has a big menu stocked with pub food: chicken sandwiches, burgers, fried fish. It's nothing spectacular but is one of the only spots in this neighborhood to get a bite at 4am.

Niko's Cafe (Map pp76-7; Calle 51 Este near Vía España; mains US$3-4; ⏱ 24hr) Spawned from the dreams of a Greek immigrant who once sold food from a cart, Niko's today is one of Panama City's most successful restaurant chains, with five locations. The secret at each is simple: serve fresh, hearty portions of inexpensive food. The cafeteria-style ambience isn't much, but you can't beat the prices. Burgers, gyros, pasta and even filet mignon are readily available, and breakfasts are hearty. Other locations are the Albrook bus terminal and Vía Israel.

Tip Top (Map pp78-9; cnr Vía Brasil & Calle 1a de Carmen; 6am-11pm) Follow the scent of delicious roasting meats to this neighborhood favorite in El Carmen. In truth, many people come from all over the area to grab a takeout portion of grilled chicken (¼ chicken US$1.50) and sides at this no-nonsense establishment.

Tortas Locas (Map pp76-7; Multicentro shopping center, Av Balboa near Punta Paitilla; noon-9pm) One of several dozen restaurant counters on the top floor food court of the Multicentro shopping center, Tortas Locas serves delicious sandwiches in a hurry. Other fast-food options here include: Chinese, Japanese, Cuban, Mexican and spots to get dessert. The ground floor of Multicentro has more upscale options.

PIZZAS

Carlitos (Map pp78-9; ☎ 200-8243; Calle 1a de Carmen, El Carmen; pizzas US$3-5) This pleasant open-air spot tucked just off the beaten path serves delicious thin-crust pizzas, which you can top with artichoke hearts, heart of palm, Roquefort cheese or with more traditional toppings. Most cost around US$3.50. The delicious and flaky empanadas (US$0.75) make nice appetizers.

Pizzas Italianas (Map pp76-7; Av Central, Calidonia; pizzas US$2-4) Along the busy pedestrian shopping street near Casco Viejo, this very basic eatery serves tasty, piping hot mini pizzas and a range of juices. The hard, plastic benches aren't the most comfortable, but you can't beat the prices.

SANDWICHES

Le Sandwich de Paris (Map pp78-9; ☎ 265-5691; Calle 51, Bella Vista; sandwiches US$4-6; noon-10pm Mon-Sat) This charming and casual spot serves tasty light fare including sandwiches, salads, quiches and crepes. The patio seating outside is pleasant, or step inside to study the photos of Paris on the wall while you have a bite.

Groovey Café (Map pp78-9; ☎ 262-1297; Vía Venetto; sandwiches US$4-6; 11am-11pm) This recently opened sandwich shop offers a wide variety of sandwiches, soups, salads and quiches in a relaxed indoor-outdoor café setting. It has deli-standards like turkey breast, heartier fare such as pulled pork, and a range of breakfast items (scrambled eggs, fruit pancakes) – none over US$3.

GREEK

Athen's (Map pp78-9; cnr Calle Uruguay & Calle 50; 11am-10pm Wed-Mon) A young crowd gathers on the covered outdoor veranda at Athen's to feast on delicious gyros, Greek salads and thin-crust pizzas – the biggest draw. Try the Kritiko's: artichokes, olives and feta cheese. The prices and freshness of the food are excellent. There's a second Athen's on Calle 56 Este.

MEXICAN

La Mexicanita (Map pp78-9; Calle 50 near Calle Uruguay; mains US$3-6) This very casual and low-priced Mexican eatery offers a wide range of traditional specialties. Tacos, burritos and enchiladas all hit their mark.

VEGETARIAN

Casa Vegetariano (Map pp78-9; ☎ 269-1876; cnr Calle Ricardo Arias & Av 3 Sur; mains US$3-5; 7am-8 pm Mon-Sat) This excellent low-key restaurant recently received a makeover, which has brightened up the place without affecting the quality of the cooking. Tasty vegetarian cuisine with an Asian flare is the norm here. Eggplant, roast tofu with vegetables, soy burgers and homemade soups are among the offerings. There's a second location in El Dorado.

Mid-Range
PANAMANIAN

El Trapiche (Map pp78-9; ☎ 269-4353; Vía Argentina, El Cangrejo; mains US$4-9; 8am-11pm) A simple but pleasant spot in restaurant-lined Vía Argentina, El Trapiche holds its own with its famous *tamal de olla* (tamale casserole), *corvina Capitán Morgan* (sea bass with white sauce containing chunks of jumbo shrimp and lobster); and *cazuela de mariscos Panamá Viejo*, which contains lots of seafood. The Panamanian fiesta platter features seven different traditional specialties.

Cafetería Del Prado (Map pp78-9; ☎ 264-2645; Vía Argentina; 24hr) This festive spot features patio-dining and filling plates of Panamanian cooking. The real draw, however, is the fact that Del Prado never closes, making it the best place in town to go for pancakes or ceviche at 4am.

Restaurante-Bar Tinajas (Map pp78-9; ☎ 269-3840; Calle 51 near Av Federico Boyd; mains US$8-12; 11:30am-11pm Mon-Sat) This large, multilevel restaurant is decorated to resemble a traditional Península de Azuero village. Popular for the Panamanian folkloric dance shows,

Tinajas attracts mostly tourists – but the dancing is excellent, just the same. Shows are staged at 9pm on Tuesday, Thursday, Friday and Saturday nights; on these nights there's a US$5 entertainment fee, as well as a US$5.50 minimum per person – easily satisfied on tasty regional fare like *pastel de yuca* (country pie made with yucca, chicken, corn, capers and raisins), *chuletas ahumadas* (smoked pork chops with honey-pineapple sauce) and *gaucho de mariscos* (fresh seafood stew, served with coconut rice).

Parillada Jimmy (Map pp72-3; ☎ 226-1096; Av Cincuentenario across from Centro Atlapa; mains US$6-11; 🕙 11:30am-11:30pm) The long open porch with high ceilings and wrought-iron chandeliers lend a farmhouse feel to this Panama City institution. The grill flares in the corner giving an indication of the specialties served here. The grilled steaks, sausages and corvina filets are good, while those who crave lighter fare can opt for sandwiches, soups (white-bean among others) or a dozen other selections from the menu. There's a second **Jimmy's** (Map pp78-9; Calle Manuel María Icaza, El Cangrejo; 🕙 24hr), but the one near Atlapa is the favorite.

SEAFOOD

Mi Ranchito (Map pp72-3; ☎ 228-0116; Isla Naos, Causeway; mains US$5-8; 🕙 11am-midnight) This charming, breezy restaurant has nice views over the water. Beneath the thatched roof you'll find an array of seafood and grilled items, with a rotating menu of daily specials. Shrimp, corvina and ceviche are quite good. There's live music from around 6:30pm Wednesday to Saturday.

Fisch (Map pp78-9; Av Balboa, Bella Vista; mains US$6-10) The ocean theme prevails in this blue-hued restaurant on the edge of the sea. The service is excellent here and the menu allows for some creative combinations of well-prepared dishes. You choose your fish (one of 10 different types, including shark), the sauce and method of preparation (grilled, with lemon and garlic is quite good) and wait for the meal to arrive. A range of cocktails and an occasional live band spice up the proceedings.

Restaurant Mercado del Marisco (Map pp76-7; Av Balboa at Calle 15 Este, Calidonia; mains US$5-8; 🕙 lunch Mon-Sat) This open-sided restaurant on the 2nd floor of Panama's two-story seafood market is a casual place boasting 'the best and freshest fish and seafood in Panama' –

and it's not far from the mark, judging by its popularity. You can feast on jumbo shrimp, squid, mussels, octopus, sea bass, lobster and tropical king crab here.

Boquitos del Mar (Map pp78-9; Vía Argentina; mains US$6-8; 🕙 11:30am-10pm Mon-Sat, 5-9:30pm Sun) This quaint indoor-outdoor restaurant serves a decent selection of seafood plates. The food isn't earth shattering, but it's tasty and fresh and has earned a few fans for its stylish simplicity. *Corvina rellena de camarones* (corvina stuffed with shrimp) is popular as is the *orgía de mariscos* (seafood orgy), a mixed seafood platter sure to satisfy at least some of your appetites.

Costa Azul (Map pp78-9; Calle Ricardo Arias near Av 3a Sur; meals US$4-10) This laid-back spot with outdoor seating serves sea bass a dozen different ways (US$6 to US$10) and the white fish guabina. It also serves more than three dozen sandwiches (US$1.50 to US$4) and a wide variety of pasta, chicken and beef dishes.

Café Barko (Map pp72-3; ☎ 314-0000; Isla Flamenco Shopping Plaza, Causeway; mains US$7-11; 🕙 11:30am-midnight) A fresh ocean breeze graces diners at this festive outdoor spot on the Causeway. The dishes here aren't always spot on, but when things are going well in the kitchen, you can be assured of top-notch seafood. The *camarones tropicales* (shrimp with coconut milk) and ceviche has earned many fans.

Centolla's Place (Map pp72-3; Av Belisario Porras; mains US$7-10) Across from Parque Recreativo Omar, you'll find seafood served up Bocas del Toro style at this very laid-back place. Specialties include *pescado relleno* (mackerel stuffed with onions, cilantro and garlic) and *cambombia* (conch with wine or garlic sauce). There's a second location on Vía España near Calle 94 Este (Map pp72-3).

INTERNATIONAL

Cafetería Manolo (Map pp78-9; cnr Vía Veneto and Calle D; mains US$5-10; 🕙 6am-2am) This laid-back restaurant is one of the more popular ones in the area for its open-air patio (perfect for people-watching), late hours and simple, reliably good food. There are plenty of big dinner plates as well as sandwiches, and the breakfast choices are extensive. A second location is nearby on Vía Argentina (Map pp78-9).

Greenhouse (Map pp78-9; ☎ 269-6846; Calle Uruguay; mains US$6-10) This stylish restaurant and lounge, opened in 2004, is a welcome addition to Panama's culinary scene. The enclosed patio puts you in touch with the tropical greenery, while inside stained-glass windows, an artfully displayed fish tank and an uber-relaxed vibe creates the setting. Pleasant but sedate waiters bring warm towels to refresh yourself with before dining on salads (Greek, heart of palm, caprese) and tasty bites from the grill (corvina, steak burgers). The wraps and quesadillas (a cheese- or meat-filled tortilla) are also popular, and there's a decent selection of vegetarian items – including the Greenhouse special, a juicy grilled portobelo sandwich. At night, the restaurant puts the electronic music up a notch, as a young good-looking crowd holds court. The martinis (often on special) are quite good here.

Tomato (Map pp78-9; ☎ 300-2003; Calle 51, Bella Vista; sandwiches US$3-4; 🕙 10am-8pm Mon-Sat) This excellent new indoor-outdoor sandwich shop serves healthy and fresh bites to a largely lunch-time crowd, who are drawn by the create-your-own salads, deli-style sandwiches (veggie and three-cheese, smoked salmon, turkey and Swiss), and freshly squeezed juices and smoothies. The simple but stylish eatery also offers homemade desserts (brownies, flan, tiramisu), a nice finishing touch.

Lum's (Map pp72-3; ☎ 317-6303; Corozal Oeste off Carretera Diablo, Bldg 340, Ancón; mains US$6-10; 🕙 from 11am Mon-Sat) In an old hangar that once housed machinery for the Panama Canal, Lum's is the expats' restaurant of choice for dining on big plates of ribs, steaks and anything else off the grill. The pool table, foosball and beers on tap attract a small crowd during the week. Lum's is near the Panama-Colon train station.

Mango's (Map pp72-3; ☎ 321-0098; Plaza Edison off Vía Brazil; mains US$6-9; 🕙 from noon) This trendy restaurant and bar remains popular with a young, slender Panamanian crowd. A wide range of selections grace the menu – sandwiches, salads, pastas – all nicely done. By night, the bar becomes a popular meeting spot.

Le Bistrot (Map pp78-9; Calle 53 Este near Calle Anastacio Ruíz Noriega; mains US$12-16; 🕙 11:30am-11:30pm) This semiformal bistro is well known for its appetizer *calamar relleno de cangrejo* (squid stuffed with crabmeat and cooked in its own ink). Other house specialties include *callos con garbanzos* (tripe with chickpeas) and

langostinos Le Bistrot (jumbo shrimp and crabmeat covered in mushroom sauce).

La Cascada (Map pp76-7; ☎ 262-1297; Av Balboa near Calle 25 Este; mains US$6-10; 🕙 11am-11pm) One of the city's quirkier restaurants, the large garden dining patio complete with koi (colorful carp or giant goldfish) is a big draw, and the bilingual menu is larger than Noriega's dossier. Plates are nearly as large and showcase the roast meats and fresh seafood.

Flags (☎ 314-1550; Calzado de Amador; mains US$6-10) Not one but four restaurants are housed under this lively open-air spot along the Causeway. You can choose from traditional Panamanian, Italian, Texas barbecue and sushi. Popular with a mix of families and couples, the restaurants generally serve very decent cuisine. The view over the bay is lovely, and you'll catch a fine breeze here most nights.

CUBAN
Bolero (Map pp76-7; ☎ 225-8731; Calle 42, Bella Vista; mains US$5-9; 🕙 noon-11pm Mon-Sat, from 7pm Sun) This elegant but understated Cuban restaurant has many fans. Chicken in mango sauce (with the requisite rice and beans) is quite nice, and strong Cuban coffee finishes off the meal well. At night the adjacent bar is a popular spot with a salsa and meringue crowd. An occasional live band puts in an appearance on Friday or Saturday night; on other nights, a DJ spins.

SPANISH
El Arca (Map p80; ☎ 228-3159; Calle 2a, Casco Viejo; sandwiches US$4-7, pizzas US$6, mains US$7-10; 🕙 noon-11pm Mon-Sat, from 7pm Sun) A lovely outdoor spot behind the French embassy, El Arca serves good thin-crust pizzas, sandwiches, tasty tapas portions and ceviches – all of which pair nicely with the delicious (and potent) glasses of sangria. There's often live acoustic music on weekend nights, with films projected as a backdrop behind the musicians. At various times throughout the year fashion shows and art openings are staged here.

PERUVIAN
Bar-Restaurante Chimborazo (Vía Jose Agustin Arango near the Hotel Caesar Park; mains US$6-9; 🕙 10am-midnight) East of downtown, this traditional Peruvian restaurant has dozens of tables, each with its own thatched roof. There are 110 items on the menu of this family business.

Among the more popular items are the *sopa de levantamuertos* (literally, 'soup to wake you from the dead,' figuratively a solution to male sexual dysfunction; a green soup of seafood, rice and cilantro), *sopa parihuela* (a spicy soup with chunks of seafood, crayfish and root), *filete de corvina a lo macho* (sea bass served with shrimp, octopus and garlic) and *langostinos* (jumbo shrimp, prepared in 10 different ways).

Machu Picchu (Map pp78-9; ☎ 264-9308; Calle Eusebio A Morales 16, El Cangrejo; mains US$7-10; 🕑 11am-3pm & 6-11pm) A favorite among Peruvian expats in the city, Machu Picchu is a simple but cozy restaurant where blue-vested waiters make the rounds among a mix of Panamanians and foreigners. The traditional menu has lots of Peruvian specialties, and the ceviche and *corvina* dishes are tops here. You can order your fish covered with pisco and cream sauce, stuffed with shrimp or half a dozen other ways.

Tambo de Oro (Map pp76-7; ☎ 263-8147; Calle 50; mains US$9-13; 🕑 11am-3pm & 6-11pm) Although it's a bit out of the way, this Peruvian restaurant is quite popular for its excellent service and fine plates. The wood-beamed ceiling and the gold, Inca-inspired artwork add some color to the whitewashed walls. The cooking is quite traditional here, and dishes like *ajo de gallina* (chicken with garlic and herbs) rate well. Upstairs is a sometimes raucous bar, where you can groove to (or hurry past) the throbbing karaoke machine.

LEBANESE

Aladino's (Map pp78-9; ☎ 263-2870; Av 3a Sur; mains US$5-8; 🕑 noon-2pm & 6-11pm Mon-Sat, noon-9:30pm Sun) Aladino's pleasant outdoor patio overlooking the street is an excellent place to feast on tasty Lebanese cuisine. Kafta, shawerma, hummus and salads are all nicely prepared from fresh ingredients. There's also a small selection of refreshing juices – try the Limonada Lebanesa. Even if you're not in the mood for a meal, the strong coffees make for a good pitstop when you're in the neighborhood.

COLOMBIAN

Delicias Del Pueblo (Map pp78-9; ☎ 214-4678; Calle 55, El Cangrejo; mains US$4-7) The smell of fresh-roasted meats fills the air at this lively Colombian restaurant in El Cangrejo. Attractive wait staff wearing straw hats move among the tables delivering regional specialties like tamales (Colombian style) and *ajiaco* (soup with chicken, capers and potatoes).

ITALIAN

Caffé Pomodoro (Map pp78-9; ☎ 269-5836; Calle 55, El Cangrejo; mains US$7-10; 🕑 7am-midnight) This popular Italian restaurant is a favorite for its excellent food and the lovely outdoor seating in the back garden. Start with antipasto like the grilled Italian bread topped with fresh tomato and basil or the smoked salmon. The main courses feature traditional pasta dishes with a handful of chicken, steak or seafood plates. It's open for breakfast and there's a takeout service next door.

THAI

Royal Thai (Map pp78-9; ☎ 263-2323; Calle Uruguay, Bella Vista; mains US$4-6) One of the only Thai restaurants in the country, Royal Thai serves traditional and decently prepared favorites like basil chicken and pad thai on their long open-air patio.

GERMAN

Gasthaus Bavaria (Map pp76-7; ☎ 265-6772; Calle 50, Bella Vista; mains US$7-11; 🕑 noon-11pm Mon-Sat) Hands down the best German restaurant in town, Gasthaus Bavaria serves tasty portions of schnitzel along with an eclectic mix of other cuisine. The best thing on the menu is the Jaeger Schnitzel, a breaded sausage with a mushroom cream sauce (not for the feint of heart). The small, cozy bar is also popular, with complimentary cheesy puffs served alongside pints of rich Warstheiner.

STEAK HOUSES

Martín Fierro (Map pp78-9; ☎ 264-1927; Calle Eusebio A Morales; steaks US$12-22; 🕑 noon-3pm & 6-11pm Mon-Sat, noon-9:30pm Sun) For beef, the name is Martín Fierro. The quality of meat served here is unparalleled; some top selections include US-imported 16oz New York rib steak, US-imported rib eye and *bife chorizo*, which is the same cut as the New York steak, but local and grass fed. A decent selection of Argentine wines accompanies the proceedings nicely.

PIZZAS

Restaurante y Pizzeria Napoli (Map pp78-9; ☎ 262-2446; Calle Estudiante at Calle I; pizzas US$4-8; 🕑 11am-11pm Wed-Mon) Just south of Av de los Mártires, Panama's oldest pizzeria serves tasty pizzas in a hurry. This classic spot has open-air tables with red-checked tablecloths and old-time waiters shuffling between the tables. The ravioli and fettuccine dishes and sandwiches are also quite good. A second location (Map pp78–9) on Calle 57 Este, near Vía España, also serves excellent pizza and pasta.

Romanaccio (Map pp78-9; ☎ 264-9482; Calle Anastasio Ruíz, Bella Vista; medium pizzas US$4-6; ☻ 11am-11pm Wed-Mon) This tiny pizzeria attracts a young crowd most nights, who come to dine on the likes of Mediterranean and four-cheese pizzas, lasagna and tortellini. The food isn't winning any awards, but is usually decent. There's a small patio for dining in front.

BRITISH
El Pavo Real (Map pp78-9; Av 3 B Sur near Calle Ricardo Arias; ☻ noon-midnight Mon-Sat) A mix of Panamanians and expats gather over games of darts or pool at this British pub/restaurant made famous by John le Carré's thriller *The Tailor of Panama*. (The British Foreign Service employee turned best-selling novelist spent a lot of time here while conducting research for his book. The pub/restaurant's owner, Sarah Simpson, is also an ex-BFS employee. Coincidence?) The food here is tasty and filling, and offerings include burgers, chicken breast sandwiches and fish 'n' chips. Bands play here periodically and there's never a cover charge.

Top End
ECLECTIC
Ali Baba (Map pp76-7; ☎ 225-0159; Panama Yacht Club, Av Balboa near Calle 40 Este; mains US$10-15; ☻ lunch & dinner) This cozy 2nd-floor landmark is popular with the business crowd during lunch hours and with couples at night. The wide variety of dishes includes Spanish paellas, thin-crust pizzas and, befitting the name, an ample selection of Middle-Eastern dishes. The restaurant has lovely views, and live music on weekends.

BRAZILIAN
Os Segredos da Carne (Map pp76-7; ☎ 263-0666; Vía Italia near Hotel Plaza Paitilla Inn; ☻ noon-10pm) The 'secrets of meat' (as the name translates) are well known at this authentic Brazilian *churrasquería* (steak house). Just like in Brazil, sharply dressed waiters bring around long skewers of some 21 cuts of meat, which

have been cooked to perfection, and slice them onto your plate. There's also a salad bar (and some seafood to accommodate sensible people). A carnivore's dream.

ARGENTINEAN
Restaurante Los Años Locos (Map pp72-3; ☎ 226-6966; Calle 76 Este, behind Hotel Caesar Park; mains US$10-16; ☻ noon-3pm & 6-11pm Mon-Fri, noon-9:30pm Sat & Sun) Grilled Argentinean cuisine is the specialty at this intimate date spot. The most popular dish is the *parrillada Los Años Locos* (mixed grilled meats; US$24 for two people). Sea bass dishes are a favorite as are the *milanesa Napolitana* (breaded tenderloin with red sauce and mozzarella au gratin). Whatever you order the portions are hearty, so come with an appetite.

SEAFOOD
Siete Mares (Map pp78-9; ☎ 264-0144; Calle Guatemala, El Cangrejo; mains US$12-18;) Artful lighting and a few impressionistic paintings scattered along the exposed brick walls sets the mood for some serious seafood dining. The speciality is lobster, though the menu features a wide variety of options (corvina, steak, shrimp), and this is one of the more popular dining rooms on this restaurant-lined street.

SWISS
Rincón Suizo (Map pp78-9; ☎ 263-8310; Calle Eusebio A Morales; mains US$12-18; ☻ 11:30am-midnight Mon-Fri, 5:30pm-midnight Sat & Sun) Sharing space beside the French Restaurante 1985, Rincón Suizo is a slice of Switzerland in the tropics. The dining room is pleasantly decorated with elements from the old country, and the friendly wait staff looks like they've just come down from the Swiss Alps. Fondues are popular selections as is the bratwurst, rack of lamb and duckbreast in tamarind sauce. Seafood dishes are also well represented.

INTERNATIONAL
Mostaza (Map p80; ☎ 228-3341; Calle 3, Casco Viejo; mains US$8-13; ☻ Tue-Sun) This lovely restaurant in historic Casco Viejo has an eclectic menu, with a prominent selection of grilled meats and fish. Filet with guava, raviolinis and grilled octopus ceviche are all excellent. On Friday and Saturday nights the restaurant has live music (usually jazz) adding to the allure of this couples' favorite.

FRENCH

Restaurante 1985 (Map pp78-9; ☎ 263-8541; Chalet Suizo, Calle Eusebio A Morales; fixed price dinner US$58; ⏰ 11:30am-midnight Mon-Fri, 5:30pm-midnight Sat & Sun) Visitors with very large expense accounts should consider a meal of unparalleled decadence at Restaurante 1985. Located inside the Chalet Suizo (Swiss Chalet), this French restaurant provides impeccable service, elegant decor and a great many traditional French selections. *Steak morilles* (steak with morel mushrooms), lobster Provençal, shrimp cognac and the many changing daily specials highlight the talents of Chef Willy Diggelmann. The wine list is equally extensive.

La Cocotte (Map pp78-9; ☎ 213-8250; Calle Uruguay near Av Balboa; mains US$16-22; ⏰ lunch Mon-Fri, dinner Mon-Sat) Fine Parisian cuisine reins supreme at this well-outfitted dining room. Chef Fabien Migny studied at the Ecole Hotelliére Belliard while simultaneously training at the renowned Restaurant Jamin de Joel Robouchon of Paris. Appetizers like *pâté de canard* meld nicely with entrées of *confit de canard* (roasted duck) or fresh salmon in a red wine sauce. Desserts include chocolate truffles, apple tarts and *crêpes soufflées au chocolat*. The fixed-price lunch (US$13) is a good way to sample Migny's cuisine without breaking the bank.

Restaurante Las Bóvedas (Map p80; ☎ 228-8058; Plaza de Francia, Casco Viejo; mains US$16-22; ⏰ closed Sun) This lovely French restaurant is set in the vaults of a 300-year-old fort which housed political prisoners for most of the 19th century. Fortunately for the crowds who converge here on the weekends, the ghosts of the past haven't had a deleterious effect on the cooking. The menu varies daily, subject to the catch of the day, but always includes a fish filet, mixed meats and a New York steak. This place is particularly well known for its *mero* (grouper). A guitarist performs in the last vault nightly except Friday and Saturday, when there's jazz (the music usually starts around 9pm).

Crêpes & Waffles (Map pp78-9; ☎ 269-1574; Calle 47 Este, Bella Vista; mains US$4-7; ⏰ noon-11pm) Crêpe and waffle lovers rejoice at this popular spot in nightlife-rich Bella Vista. Spinach, ricotta and tomato are good standbys; the more daring can opt for *lomito á la pimienta* (strips of roast beef with pepper sauce, US$6). Or skip the fried batter alto-

gether and go for decent sandwiches and desserts. There's a second location on the Causeway, in the Isla Flamenco Shopping Plaza.

JAPANESE

Sushi Itto (Map pp78-9; ☎ 265-1222; Av Samuel Lewis, just east of Calle 54 Este; 8-/13-piece plates US$9/13.50; ⏰ noon-10pm) Modern and stylish without pretensions, Sushi Itto offers traditional sushi and some combinations you'd never find in Japan (such as a maki roll with chicken inside). The combination plates are the best deals here. Some of the fish is purchased locally, but most comes from the USA and Chile.

Ginza Teppanyaki (Map pp78-9; ☎ 264-9562; Calle Eusebio A Morales; mains US$12-18; ⏰ noon-3pm & 6-11pm) At all Teppan-style Japanese restaurants, including this one, a chef prepares your food on a scalding skillet directly in front of you, making a nice mixture of freshness and entertainment. Prices aren't cheap, but the platters are quite good. The special dinner combination, which includes fish, prawns, chicken, steak, vegetables and rice, costs US$22 and serves two.

Restaurante Matsuei (Map pp78-9; ☎ 264-9562; Calle Eusebio A Morales; mains US$11-15; ⏰ noon-11:30pm Mon-Sat, 6-11:30pm Sun) Across the street from Ginza Teppanyaki, Matsuei is another long-standing traditional Japanese spot, which has been open for over 24 years. It's known for its sukiyaki, tempura and long sushi bar, one of Panama's finest. Much of the fish is imported from Miami. If you eat early, you can enjoy an all-you-can-eat sushi feast for US$20.

CHINESE

Madame Chang (Map pp78-9; ☎ 269-1313; Calle 48, Bella Vista; mains US$12-18; ⏰ noon-3pm & 6-11pm Mon-Sat, noon-11pm Sun) One of the top Chinese restaurants in town, this elegant, upscale restaurant is known for its *pato al estilo Pekin* (Peking duck), *filete 'tit pang'* (sizzling sliced beef with oyster sauce) and *pichón en pétalos de lechuga* (a combination of duck, chicken and pigeon, served on a bed of crispy rice noodles).

Palacio Lung Fung (Map pp72-3; ☎ 260-4011; Calle 62 C Oeste, Los Angeles; mains US$7-11; ⏰ 6:30am-11pm) At the entrance to the Los Angeles neighborhood, this huge restaurant serves tasty Chinese dishes at prices cheaper than you'll find elsewhere. The popular platters bring together rich combinations. One of the most popular consists of soup, pork with almonds and vegetables, beef chop suey, shrimp rolls, chicken fried rice, and jasmine tea or coffee. Dim sum is served until 11am every day.

Nobu (Map pp78-9; ☎ 265-1312; cnr Calles Uruguay & 49; mains US$7-12; ✆ noon-3pm & 6-11pm Tue-Sun) Owned by a Chinese man and his Japanese wife, Nobu offers both Chinese cuisine and sushi. This fairly elegant and popular restaurant with a lovely full bar is known for its *arroz frito Nobu* (fried rice, vegetables, pork and shrimp) and *filete Nobu* (chopped filet of beef served with oyster sauce).

ITALIAN
Restaurante de las Americas (Map pp78-9; Calle 57 Este, Bella Vista; mains US$5-9; ✆ noon-10pm Tue-Sun) This take-out only restaurant offers delicious, good value Italian cuisine. Specialties include raviolis stuffed with smoked salmon, cappellini with prosciutto and assorted other pastas.

Trattoria D'America (Map pp78-9; ☎ 223-7734; Calle 58 Este, Bella Vista; mains US$12-16; ✆ Tue-Sun) One of the top Italian restaurants in the city, Trattoria D'America combines traditional and flavorful cuisine with excellent service. The wine cellar is extensive (with Italian vintages well represented).

Tre Scalini (Map pp78-9; ☎ 269-9951; Calle 52, Bella Vista; mains US$10-15) This casual-to-dressy Italian eatery is noted for its *pasta primavera especial* (eggplant in white wine sauce, served with spaghetti or fettuccine) and *filete Tre Scalini* (filet of beef in red wine, onions, peppers and mushrooms).

Cafés & Bakeries
El Mundo del Pan (Map pp78-9; Vía Argentina) Once you step inside this small, handsome bakery, it's unlikely you'll leave empty-handed. The display windows reveal the likes of creamy key lime pie, chocolate mousse and fluffy batches of sweet breads and pastries. A fine spot to go after a meal – or skip the meal and eat cake instead!

Te Conté (Map pp78-9; Vía Argentina; ✆ 7am-9pm) This charming café has outdoor tables, perfect for watching the street scene unfold over cappuccino and a fresh pastry. Display cases hold lovely baked goods, most costing around US$0.50. Try the *goiaba* (guava) Danish.

Café Santé (Map pp78-9; Calle 51, Bella Vista; ✆ Mon-Sat) Another good spot for recharging when the energy is low, Café Santé has outdoor tables for catching the pedestrian parade on this strip. Enjoy coffee, cappuccino, pastries or light meals. For heartier fare, half a dozen restaurants lie a stone's throw away.

Café y Café (Map pp76-7; Av Balboa, Bella Vista; ✆ 7am-midnight) This pleasant new café features a variety of pastries and decadent desserts along with well-done cappuccinos and espressos.

Darna Coffee Bar (Map pp78-9; Calle Uruguay) A pleasant spot for coffee, Darna has a lovely outdoor patio. Inside the chapel-like interior offers a full bar and sit-down tables (for corvina and other seafood). You can also amuse yourself with one of the hookahs.

DRINKING
Panama City has a vibrant nightlife scene, with a range of charming open-air spots, British-style pubs and traditional salsa-infused drinking spots. Big nightlife areas are found in Bella Vista (on and around Calle Uruguay) and the Causeway, with a handful of spots in Casco Viejo.

Casco Viejo
Blu (Map p80; ☎ 228-3503; Calle 1a Oeste; ✆ from 11pm Tue-Sat) This tiny lounge in Casco Viejo was Panama City's first martini lounge. It's also one of the only spots you'll see DJs spinning records (drum 'n' bass, house) rather than fiddling with CDs. As the night wears on a more mixed crowd is attracted to this intimate spot, making for some excellent people-watching over tasty vodka infusions.

Café de Asís (Map p80; ☎ 262-9304; Calle 3a Este, Casco Viejo; ✆ from 6pm) Although a restaurant, this charming outdoor café makes a fine spot to stop in for a sangria – or coffee – in the evening, perhaps before heading to one of the neighborhood's restaurants or nightspots.

El Arca (Map p80; ☎ 228-3159; Calle 2a, Casco Viejo; ✆ noon-11pm Mon-Sat, from 7pm Sun) In addition to tapas and pizza, this lovely outdoor spot (see p102) serves delicious sangrias and a variety of other cocktails. There's occasionally live music (a couple of guitarists) on weekend nights, with films projected as a backdrop behind the musicians.

Buena Vista Social Club (Map p80; ☎ 262-9398; Av Alfaro at Calle B; ✆ 6pm Tue-Sat) This two-floor bar, lounge and sometimes live-music spot is a fine place to have a few drinks in the evening. Set on the water in lovely Casco Viejo, the upstairs lounge provides sweeping views of the bay and downtown, and occasionally a House DJ spins here. Downstairs near the bar, a salsa trio occasionally gets things going (Friday and Saturday nights, but inconsistently). It's changed names (and ownership) a number of times, so have a backup plan (Blu, 844) before making the trip over.

El Cangrejo

The Wine Bar (Map pp78-9; ☎ 265-4701; ground fl, Las Vegas Suites Hotel, El Cangrejo; mains US$7-12; ☼ 5pm-11am Mon-Sat) This stylish Italian bistro showcases the fruit of the vine, with over 200 selections. Accompanying the wine list are a wide range of bites from appetizers like smoked salmon with toasted almonds and carpaccio with capers to a broad range of cheese plates, salads and individual pizzas. It hosts live jazz from 9pm most nights.

Bella Vista

Bolero (Map pp76-7; ☎ 225-8731; Calle 42; ☼ noon-11pm Mon-Sat, from 7pm Sun) This popular Cuban bar plays salsa and merengue. Although there's no dance floor here, the young crowd occasionally dances amongst the tables when the DJ finds his groove. The attached restaurant is also recommended (p102).

La Kava (Map pp78-9; ☎ 265-4199; Calle Uruguay; ☼ Tue-Sat) The small but handsome La Kava attracts a young indie-rocker crowd, a few travelers, and a mix of other laid-back types. Local bands perform on Thursday nights, and if old Nirvana covers don't cut it, you can always retreat to the mellow lounge space in the next room.

Greenhouse (Map pp78-9; Calle Uruguay) This stylish new restaurant (see p101) and lounge attracts a young good-looking crowd, who come to this lovely spot for the tropical cocktails and martinis, which are made with precision.

Habibi's (Map pp78-9; ☎ 213-9919; Calle Ricardo Arias) The open patio is a scenic spot for Lebanese cuisine (see p99), while upstairs is a colorful lounge for imbibing *cuba libres* or taking a few hits off the hookah.

Player's (Map pp76-7; ☎ 225-4781; Calle 42; cover fee US$5; ☼ from 5pm) This fairly new British-style pub is a favorite. Unlike other pubs

in the area, this one hasn't been thrashed yet, and the dark-wood bar and gleaming fixtures lend a cozy feel to the open space. The pool table is a popular meeting spot on weeknights; at 9pm on Friday nights (and sometimes Wednesdays), rock bands draw a mix of foreigners and Panamanians.

Gasthaus Bavaria (Map pp76-7; ☎ 265-6772; Calle 50; ☼ noon-11pm Mon-Sat) This bar/restaurant serves authentic German bites (see p103) and offers a range of beers, including Warstheiner, on tap.

El Pavo Real (Map pp78-9; Av 3 B Sur near Calle Ricardo Arias; ☼ noon-midnight Mon-Sat) This popular British pub is a relaxed spot with two pool tables and decent pub food (see p104). The Peacock (as it translates) hosts live music several nights a week and never charges a cover.

The Spot (Map pp78-9; Calle 48) One of Panama City's best karaoke bars, this place attracts would-be divas and maestros who belt out Latin favorites to the often packed bar room. The Spot has a festive vibe, and it's a good place to meet Panamanians (especially if you don't mind embarrassing the hell out of yourself).

Other Areas

Lum's (Map pp72-3; ☎ 317-6303; Corozal Oeste, Bldg 340, Ancón; ☼ from 11am Mon-Sat) This giant restaurant and bar provides an ample selection of distractions – pool tables, foosball, darts, barbecued ribs (see p102) – which is perhaps one reason why it's one of the city's most popular expat hangouts. On weekends, the place is often packed as a mixed crowd comes for the live rock bands on Friday and Saturday nights. It's near the Panama-Colon train station.

Mango's (Map pp72-3; Plaza Edison, Vía Brasil) The bar at this restaurant (see Eating, p102) becomes a fairly popular gathering spot on weekend nights. DJs play a wide mix of sounds, sometimes packing the dance floor (and sometimes clearing it).

Traffic Island (Map pp72-3; ☎ 314-1040; Isla Flamenco Shopping Plaza, Amador) One of over a dozen bars out on Isla Amador, Traffic Island is perhaps the most charming of the bunch, owing to its open-air location and views across the water. Salsa and merengue set the tone for a variety of specialty drinks and if the music puts you in the mood there's plenty of nearby places to dance in the Isla Flamenco complex (p109). There's another

Traffic Island (Map pp78-9; Bella Vista on Calle 50 near Calle Uruguay), which is much sleeker and rather futuristic (if short on ocean views).

Moonlight Bistro & Lounge (Map pp72-3; ☎ 314-1226; the Causeway, Amador) This beautiful multi-level restaurant and lounge commands an impressive view out over the water. Unfortunately, it hasn't caught on among Panamanians, so it remains empty most nights. To get there, head along the Causeway in the direction of Isla Flamenco and look for it on your right.

ENTERTAINMENT

There are numerous ways to spend a moonlit (or rainy) evening in tropical Panama City. Many restaurants in town serve up live music in addition to drinks and entrées, while a handful of spots host live jazz, rock or salsa bands. The younger set opts for one of the city's many nightclubs, which open and close with alarming frequency.

For the latest on what's happening in the city, be sure to pick up a copy of *La Prensa* (www.prensa.com in Spanish). Weekend listings are available in the Thursday and Friday editions or on its website; look for the 'De Noche' section. The Sunday supplement lists information about cultural events in the capital city for the upcoming week.

As with the bars listed in Drinking (p106), most nightlife can be found in Bella Vista and the Causeway, with a few spots in Casco Viejo. Another good website for nightlife is www.delante.com (in Spanish).

The city's many cinemas make for a more sedate evening – or a daytime escape into air-conditioned splendor. Most movie houses show the latest Hollywood releases, usually in English with Spanish subtitles. For those with excellent Spanish, there are a handful of theaters around town that show plays and musicals (*Evita* was a big hit here in 2004).

Nightclubs

Panama City has a wide selection of nightclubs – gay, straight, cruisy and sedate. DJs usually pull from a broad repertoire, from salsa and meringue to UK and US '80s classics, with electronic music (house, drum 'n' bass) liberally added to the mix. Most clubs don't open their doors before 11pm, so plan your evening accordingly. As in most cities, people dress up when they go out, the

women more so than the men. Women typically don a skirt, blouse and heels for a night out dancing, while men tend to stick to slacks or jeans and a collared shirt. At some clubs, you'll be denied entrance if you're wearing sneakers or shorts.

Due to a severe parking shortage, even if you're renting a vehicle in Panama, take a taxi if you go out in the Calle Uruguay area. Also, remember to bring identification with you, as you might be asked for it.

844 (Map p80; ☎ 211-1477; Calle 1a Oeste, Casco Viejo; ☽ from 9pm Wed-Sat) In a former mansion in Casco Viejo, the many rooms of 844 provide ample lounge space. Among the hidden corners and gauzy interiors, you'll find quirky artwork and lots of cushioned bordello-esque furnishings. In spite of all the room upstairs, most people crowd around the main bar and dance to Salsa and Meringue.

S6is (Map pp78-9; ☎ 264-5237; Calle Uruguay; cover US$5-10) This small, intimate club pronounced 'seis' plays a fine selection of electronic music to a festive, mixed crowd. Unlike some of the bigger clubs, this loungey space has a laid-back vibe, making it a good choice if you want to bypass the pickup scene.

Bongo (Map pp76-7; ☎ 227-5725; Calle 42, Bella Vista; ☽ from 6pm Wed-Sat) This popular newcomer to the bar and music scene features live salsa bands on Friday nights, with DJs filling the space the rest of the time.

Rock Café (Map pp78-9; ☎ 264-5364; Plaza Florida, Calle 53 Este; cover US$5-10) One of three large clubs in the Plaza Florida, the Rock Café attracts a seriously young crowd, lured to the open-bar nights that feature all the whisky, vodka or rum you can drink with the cover charge. The throbbing dance floor – which features more salsa than rock – is often packed at this place. To satisfy that rum-induced hunger, don't miss the taco kiosk in front of the plaza.

Oz (Map pp78-9; ☎ 265-2805; Plaza Florida, Calle 53 Este; cover US$5-10; ☽ Tue-Sat) Next to Rock Café, the bar Oz has a more laid-back scene. The small warmly lit club attracts a mix of 20- and 30-somethings, and decent live bands play here throughout the week.

Liquid (Map pp78-9; ☎ 265-3210; www.liquidpanama .com in Spanish; Plaza Florida, Calle 53 Este; cover US$8-10) This sleek and popular club has lots of polished metal and tubular lighting. DJs spin heavy beats to a fairly well-dressed crowd.

Zoomba (Map pp76-7; ☎ 215-1581; Plaza Pacífica, Punta Pacífica; cover US$5-10) This club has a warmer feel than some of the other dance clubs. A good mixed crowd comes here to get down (salsa, electronic, world beats).

Deep Room (Map pp78-9; Calle 48, Bella Vista; cover US$5-10) Panama City's favored after-hours spot, Deep Room doesn't get going until sometime after 2am. The multilevel space attracts some top DJs, making it a fun dance spot if you're in the neighborhood.

Opah (Map pp78-9; Calle 47, Bella Vista) The latest incarnation of this ever-changing club attracts a mix of beautiful people and their hangers-on. The polished club is a good spot for dancing. Electronic music, '80s and salsa are the DJs' repertoire of choice.

Skap (Map pp78-9; Calle 48, Bella Vista; cover US$7-10) What it lacks in smart decor (the walls are painted orange and are otherwise bare), it makes up for in noise. This is a popular dance club with a young well-moneyed crowd, but really not one of the better ones. There's live music weekend nights.

Isla Flamenco Shopping Plaza (Isla Flamenco, Amador) At the end of the Causeway, on the last island (Isla Flamenco), you'll reach this large complex full of shops, restaurants, bars and nightclubs. It's one of the most popular new spots in the city and has a range of bars and clubs from small, packed dance spaces to more low-key watering holes. You can walk among the options and find the mood that suits you. At last count, **Bar La Baviera**, **Karnak** and **Bucaneros** were among the most popular dance spots, but that will likely have changed by the time you read this.

Live Music

Take Five (Map p80; Calle 1a near Av A, Casco Viejo; ☼ from 6:30pm Mon-Sat) With exposed brick walls and a small, intimate stage, the interior of Take Five is reminiscent of Greenwich Village jazz clubs in the early '70s. Popular with an older crowd, it's a bit upscale, so make sure you dress the part. It features live music at 10pm Friday and Saturday nights.

Restaurante Las Bóvedas (Map p80; ☎ 228-8058; Plaza de Francia, Casco Viejo) This former dungeon makes for an intimate (if somewhat haunting) setting for live jazz on Friday and Saturday nights (9pm to midnight). The acoustics are perfect, the ambience is quite fine, and there usually isn't a cover charge. Las Bóvedas is known for its *caipirinha*

(Brazilian cocktails made from cachaça, lemon juice, ice and sugar).

Restaurante-Bar Tinajas (Map pp78-9; ☎ 263-7890; Calle 51 near Av Federico Boyd; cover US$5) Catch elaborately staged Panamanian folkloric dancing at 9pm on Tuesday, Thursday, Friday and Saturday nights. Most guests have dinner during the show (see p101). These shows are popular – reservations are recommended.

See also Drinking (p106) for other establishments that have live music.

Gay & Lesbian Venues

Although Panama City is far from being a liberal or even tolerant society when it comes to the topic of gay rights, the city does have several excellent gay clubs. Be sure to check out the nightlife-rich websites www.farraurbana.com, www.rumbanight .com and www.chemibel.com, which list new gay clubs in town as well as upcoming parties (in Spanish).

BLG (Map pp78-9; ☎ 265-1624; Calle 49, Bella Vista; cover US$5-10) Top-notch DJs spin at this large, popular dance club next to the restaurant Nobu. A good, festive crowd usually packs this space, enjoying specials like free open bar with the cover charge.

Punto G (Map pp78-9; ☎ 265-1624; Calle D, El Cangrejo; cover US$5-10) This stylish, fairly new spot has a decent-sized dance floor and a glass-top veranda. Sexed-up bare-chested bartenders (in spandex and cowboy hats) serve the crowd, and the occasional tranny show makes for a fine interlude between the serious dancing. This unmarked club is next to the restaurant Ginza Teppanyaki.

Glam (Map pp72-3; ☎ 265-1624; Av Ricardo J Alfaro, Tumba Muerto; cover US$5-10) In an industrial area north of downtown, Glam is the biggest gay dance club in the country. Saturday is generally the best night to go, when a wild and celebratory crowd fills the dance floor until late in the morning. Good DJs spin house, drum 'n' bass, soul and Latin classics; and burlesque shows add to the fun. This place is best reached by taxi; it's in front of the Club de Montana.

Cinemas

Panama City's modern movie houses show mostly Hollywood films (with Spanish subtitles) for US$2 to US$4. For listings and show times, pick up a copy of *La Prensa* or go to www.prensa.com and click on 'cine.'

Alhambra (Map pp78-9; ☎ 264-3217; Vía España, El Cangrejo)

Cinemark (Map pp76-7; ☎ 314-6001; Albrook mall) Next to the Albrook bus terminal.

Cine Universitario (☎ 223-9324; Universidad de Panamá, La Cresta) One of the only places in town to see experimental and art-house films.

Kinomaxx (Map pp76-7; Multicentro shopping center) Near Punta Paitilla.

Casinos

None of the casinos are on the verge of stealing business away from the megacasinos of Las Vegas, but there are three attractive and popular houses of chance in the capital city and three others that simply serve their purpose. All are located inside top hotels. Two of the more attractive casinos can be found in **Hotel Caesar Park** and **Miramar Inter-Continental**. Three others are in **Hotel Plaza Paitilla Inn**, **Gran Hotel Soloy** and **Hotel Riande Granada**. For address details, see Sleeping (p92).

Theater

Teatro Nacional (Map p80; ☎ 262-3525; Av B at Calle 2, Casco Viejo) Casco Viejo's lovely 19th-century playhouse stages ballets and concerts in addition to plays.

Teatro Anita Villalaz (Map p80; ☎ 211-4017; Plaza de Francia, Casco Viejo) Another historic spot in Casco Viejo to see performances.

Teatro En Círculo (Map pp72-3; ☎ 261-5375; Av 6 C Norte near Vía Transístmica) One of the city's most active theaters schedules plays and musicals regularly.

SHOPPING

The city has a number of markets where you can purchase handicrafts native to regions throughout the country. Here you'll find a range of goods – described in the pages that follow – from baskets made in Emberá villages to *molas* from Kuna Yala, with woven hats, embroidery and dozens of other handmade items.

Mi Pueblitos (Map pp72-3; Cerro Ancón; admission US$0.75; ☺ 10am-10pm Tues-Sun) Scattered throughout this life-size replica of rural villages you'll encounter a huge selection of high-quality crafts – perfect for one-stop shopping. See p88 for more details. It's near the intersection of Av de los Mártires and Calle Jeronimo de la Ossa.

Mercado Nacional de Artesanías (Map p85; beside the ruins of Panamá Vieja; ☺ 9am-4pm Mon-Sat, 9am-

1pm Sun) The city's second-largest market also has an impressive selection (p86).

Mercado de Buhonerías y Artesanías (Map pp76-7; behind the Reina Torres de Araúz anthropological museum, Calidonia; ☺ 9am-5pm Mon-Sat) You'll find a small selection of goods at this bustling outdoor spot.

Gran Morrison (Map pp78-9; Vía España, El Cangrejo) The ubiquitous department store sells a small selection of handicrafts.

Artwork

The works of some of Panama's best contemporary painters and sculptors can be viewed and purchased at a number of galleries around the city. Try **Galería y Enmarcado Habitante** (☎ 264-6470; Calle Uruguay near Calle 47); **Mvsevm** (Vía Italia), near the Hotel Plaza Paitilla Inn; **Galería Bernheim** (see p112); **Legacy Fine Art** (☎ 265-8141; Centro Comercial Balboa, Av Balboa near Calle 50); and **Galería Arteconsult** (☎ 269-1523; Av 2 Sur btwn Calles 55 Este & 56 Este).

Baskets

The Wounaan and Emberá in Darién Province produce some beautiful woven baskets, most of which are exported to the USA and Europe, although many can be found in Panama. The Guaymís in Chiriquí and Veraguas Provinces also produce baskets, but they are of an inferior quality and in little demand.

The baskets of the Wounaan and Emberá are of two types: the utilitarian and the decorative. The utilitarian baskets are made primarily from the chunga palm but can contain bits of other plants, vines, bark and leaves. They are usually woven, using various plaiting techniques, from single plant strips of coarse texture and great strength. They are rarely dyed. These baskets are often used for carrying seeds or harvesting crops.

The decorative baskets are much more refined, usually feature many different colors and are created from palm materials of the nahuala bush and the chunga tree. The dyes are 100% natural and are extracted from fruits, leaves, roots and bark. Typical motifs are of butterflies, frogs, toucans, trees and parrots. The baskets are similar in quality to the renowned early 20th-century Chemehuevi Indian baskets of California.

You can often buy baskets at any of the markets (see opposite) and at Gran Morrison stores (Map pp76–7).

Discounted Goods

For a sensory-rich shopping experience, take a stroll along the pedestrian-only Av Central in Calidonia (Map pp76–7). This narrow street is packed with discount stores selling clothing, shoes, electronics, toys, fabrics (this is where the Kuna and Emberá women shop for the fabrics for their sarongs) and dozens of other items. It's a lively street scene complete with food vendors, screeching children and baritone hawkers calling out their goods.

Most anything that you can buy in other modern capital cities you can find in Panama City. Many of the stores in Colón's Zona Libre have outlets in the capital. Often these outlets can arrange to have an item from a Colón store – a particular Rolex watch or Nikon camera, for example – sent from Colón to Tocumen airport, where you can pick it up just prior to leaving the country; you can avoid the sales tax by doing business this way.

Huacas

It's possible to purchase high-quality replicas of huacas – golden objects made on the isthmus centuries before the Spanish conquest and placed with Indians at the time of burial. The Indians believed in an afterlife, and the huacas were intended to accompany and protect their souls on the voyage to the other world.

The huacas were mainly items of adornment, the most fascinating being three-dimensional figure pendants. Most took the form of a warrior, crocodile, jaguar, frog or condor. Little else is known about the exact purpose of these golden figures, but each probably held mystical, spiritual or religious meaning.

You can purchase exact (solid gold) and near-exact (gold-plated) reproductions of these palm-size objects. They are available at reasonable cost at **Reprosa** (☎ 269-0457; fax 269-3902; sales1@reprosa.com; cnr Av 2 Sur & Calle 54 Este; 🕑 9am-7pm Mon-Sat). Also available here are well-priced necklaces made of black onyx and other gemstones. If you're looking for something special to bring back for a loved one, this is the place to come.

Jewelry

Because of their proximity to mineral-rich Colombia and Brazil, the jewelry stores here often have high-quality gems at excellent prices. Beware: there are many fake gems on the world market, as well as many flawed gems that have been altered to appear more valuable than they really are. One of the city's most reputable jewelry stores is **Joyería La Huaca** (cnr Calle Ricardo Arias & Vía España) in front of the Hotel Continental. A high-quality sapphire ring there costs about one-third less than you would pay in Europe or the USA.

Malls

Panama City has a growing number of shopping malls. These air-conditioned spots can be a good place to escape the heat on a sultry afternoon. **Albrook mall** (🕑 10am-9pm Mon-Sat, 11am-8pm Sun), next to the bus terminal, has a cinema, supermarket and dozens of stores. Near Paitilla, **Multi-centro** (🕑 10am-9pm) also has a cinema and shops, along with many lovely outdoor restaurants on the 1st floor and cheaper spots on the top floor. The **El Dorado mall** (Vía Ricardo J Alfaro; 🕑 10am-9pm Mon-Sat, 11am-8pm Sun) is near one of Panama City's newer China-towns and also has restaurants, shops and a cinema. **Isla Flamenco Shopping Plaza** (🕑 10am-10pm) is small, but nearby you'll find the best selection of open-air restaurants in the city.

Molas

A popular handicraft souvenir from Panama is the *mola* – a colorful, intricate, multilayered appliqué textile sewn by Kuna women. Small, simple souvenir *molas* are widely available in Panama City and can be bought for as little as US$5, but the best ones are sold on the San Blás islands and can fetch several hundred dollars.

Flory Saltzman Molas (Map pp78-9; ☎ 223-6963; Calle 49 B Oeste) has a large selection. *Molas* are also on sale in stores inside **Hotel Caesar Park** and other upscale hotels. **Gran Morrison** stores also stock *molas*.

Wood & Tagua Carvings

In addition to producing fine baskets, the Wounaan and Emberá also carve animal figures from the wood of the *cocobolo* tree and the ivory-colored *tagua* nut (variously known as the palm seed, ivory nut and vegetable ivory). The figures made from the tropical hardwood are often near-life-size;

popular subjects are boas, toucans and parrots. From the egg-size *tagua* nut come miniature iguanas, crocodiles and birds.

The quality of both the *cocobolo* and *tagua* carvings can be very fine. A superior *cocobolo* boa, for example, is a meter or more in length, with its back polished shiny-smooth and its underside a field of perfectly carved scales. Its eyes and mouth are delicately formed and its head perfectly proportioned. The highly honed skills of a true craftsperson are readily apparent in the finest of these carvings.

A high-quality *tagua* carving is also finely carved, well proportioned and realistic, if miniature. While the natural color of *cocobolo* figures is left unchanged, the *tagua* nut – after it is carved with hand tools and polished with fine abrasives – is beautifully painted with vibrant colors, using India inks and natural plant extracts.

The best place to shop for *tagua* carvings is **Galería Bernheim** (☎ 223-0012; Madison Bldg, Calle 50 near Calle Aquilino de la Guardia). *Cocobolo* carvings can be found at **Gran Morrison** department stores.

GETTING THERE & AWAY
Air
International flights arrive at and depart from **Tocumen International Airport** (☎ 238-4160), 35km northeast of the city center. See p306 for more information about the airport and services to Panama.

International airlines serving Panama City include:

American Airlines	☎ 269-6022
Continental Airlines	☎ 263-9177
COPA	☎ 227-2672
Delta	☎ 214-8118
Grupo TACA	☎ 360-2093
LAB	☎ 264-1330
Lufthansa	☎ 223-9208
Mexicana	☎ 264-9855
United Airlines	☎ 225-6519

Flights within Panama are inexpensive and will save you lots of time getting around. Domestic flights depart from Albrook airport (☎ 315-0403); airlines providing domestic service are:

Aero (☎ 315-0888; www.aero.com.pa; Albrook terminal)
Aeroperlas (☎ 315-7500; www.aeroperlas.com; Calle 57, El Cangrejo) Panama's principal carrier.
Parsa (☎ 315-0439; Albrook terminal)

There is no bus service to Albrook airport; taxis cost around US$1.50 to US$3. All flights within Panama last under one hour. Flights listed below are one-way fares:

Bocas del Toro (US$58; 2 per day with Aeroperlas; 2 per day Mon-Fri with Aero)
Changuinola (US$59; 2 per day with Aeroperlas; 2 per day Sat, 1 per day Sun with Aero)
Chitré (US$37; 2 per day Mon-Sat, 1 per day Sun with Parsa)
Colón (US$30; 6 per day Mon-Fri with Aeroperlas)
David (US$59; 3 per day Mon-Sat, 2 per day Sun with Aeroperlas; 3 per day Mon-Sat, 2 per day Sun with Aero)
El Porvenir Kuna Yala (US$32; 1 per day with Aeroperlas; 1 per day with Aerotaxi)
El Real (US$48; 1 per day Mon, Wed, Fri & Sat with Aeroperlas)
Garachiné (US$45; 1 per day Mon, Wed & Fri with Aeroperlas)
Isla Contadora (US$30; 4 per day Sat & Sun, 2 per day Mon-Fri with Aeroperlas)
Jaqué (US$48; 1 per day Tue, Thu, Sat with Aeroperlas)
La Palma (US$40; 1 per day Mon-Sat with Aeroperlas)
Playón Chico Kuna Yala (US$38; 1 per day with Aeroperlas 1 per day Mon-Sat with Aerotaxi)
Puerto Obaldía Kuna Yala (US$53; 1 per day Thu & Sun with Aeroperlas)
Río Sidra Kuna Yala (US$32; 1 per day with Aeroperlas)
Usutupo (US$40; 1 per day with Aeroperlas)

Boat
Expreso del Pacífico (Map pp72-3; ☎ 261-0350; willifu@ cableonda.net) travels between Panama City and **Isla Taboga**. Boats (roundtrip US$8, 35 minutes) depart from Muelle (Pier) 19 in the Balboa district, west of downtown or the canal at 8:30am and 2:30pm Monday to Friday, and 8am, 10am and 4pm Saturday and Sunday.

The slower **El Calypso** (roundtrip US$8, 75 minutes) also provides service from Pier 19 although by the time you read this it will most likely be departing from the Causeway at 8:30am Monday to Saturday, and 7:45am and 10:30am Sunday.

Bus
The new Albrook Terminal, near the Albrook airport, is a convenient one-stop location for most buses leaving Panama City. The terminal includes a food court, banks, shops, a sports bar, storage room, bathrooms and showers. A mall lies next door, complete with a supermarket and cinema.

Local buses from the city's major routes stop at the terminal, and behind the station there are direct buses to and from Tocumen International Airport. To get to the station from the city, take any of the frequent buses that pass in front of the Legislative Palace or along Vía España (look for the 'via Albrook' sign in the front window).

Major bus routes are:

Aguadulce (US$5; 3hr; 33 buses daily, 6am-8pm)
Antón (US$3.35; 2hr; every 20min, 6am-6pm)
Cañita (US$3.50; 2½hr; 11 buses daily, 6:40am-5pm)
Chame (US$2.25; 75min; 37 buses daily, 5:10am-10pm)
Changuinola & Almirante (US$24; 10hr; 1 daily at 8pm)
Chitré (US$6; 4 hr; hourly, 6am-11pm)
Colón (US$2; 2hr; every 20min, 5am-11pm)
David (US$11; 7-8hr; 13 buses daily) expresos (US$15; 5-6hr; 2 buses daily, 10:45pm & midnight)
El Copé (US$5.25; 4hr; 9 buses daily, 6am-6pm)
El Valle (US$3.75; 2½hr; many buses, 7am-7pm)
Las Tablas (US$6.50; 4½hr; hourly, 6am-7pm)
Macaracas (US$7; 5hr; 5 buses daily, 7am-3:30pm)
Ocú (US$6; 4hr; 8 buses daily, 7am-5pm)
Penonomé (US$3.70; 2½hr; 48 buses daily, 4:45am-11pm)
Pesé (US$6; 4½hr; 6 buses daily, 8:15am-3:45pm)
San Carlos (US$3.75; 1½hr; 25 buses daily, 5:10am-10pm)
San José, Costa Rica Panaline (US$25; noon); Tica Bus (US$25; 11am)
Santiago (US$6; 4hr; 20 buses daily)
Soná (US$7; 6hr; 6 buses daily, 8:30am-6pm)
Villa de Los Santos (US$6; 4 hours; 18 buses daily; 6am-11pm)
Yaviza (US$14; 7-10hr; 8 buses daily, 5am-3:45pm)

Buses to Balboa, Ancón and the Canal Zone (Miraflores and Pedro Miguel Locks, Paraíso and Gamboa) depart from the bus stop on Av Roosevelt across from the Legislative Palace. All fares are less than US$1.

Car

Many car rental agencies lie clustered around Calle 49 B Oeste in El Cangrejo. Daily rates run from US$30 to US$45 per day for the most economical cars, including insurance and unlimited kilometers.

Rental car companies in Panama City include:

Avis Albrook airport (☎ 264-0722, 315-0434); Tocumen airport (☎ 238-4056)
Barriga Tocumen airport (☎ 269-0221, 238-4495)
Budget Albrook airport (☎ 263-8777, 315-0201); Tocumen airport (☎ 238-4069)
Dollar Tocumen airport (☎ 270-0355, 238-4032)
Hertz Albrook airport (☎ 264-1111, 315-0418); Tocumen airport (☎ 238-4081)
National Albrook airport (☎ 265-2222, 315-0416); Tocumen airport (☎ 238-4144)

Thrifty Albrook airport (☎ 264-1402, 315-0144); Tocumen airport (☎ 238-4955)

Train

On Carretera Gaillard, the **Panama Railway Company** (☎ 317-6070; info@panarail.com) operates a luxury passenger train from Panama City to Colón (one-way/roundtrip US$20/35, one hour), which departs at 7:15am and returns at 5:15pm Monday through Friday. It's a lovely ride, following the canal; at times the train is surrounded by nothing but thick jungle.

GETTING AROUND
To/From the Airport

Tocumen International Airport is 35km northeast of the city center. Buses to Tocumen depart every 30 minutes from Terminal Nacional de Transporte; the ones that reach the airport via Calle 50 and Vía España cost 25¢ and take about two hours, while the ones that reach the airport via Corredor Sur cost 75¢ and take about one hour. A taxi ride from downtown to the airport costs between US$12 and US$15.

When you arrive at Tocumen from abroad, look for the 'Transportes Turísticos' desk at the airport exit. Beside it is a taxi stand, with posted prices. Taxi drivers will assail you, offering rides into town for US$25, but the staff at the desk will inform you that you can take a *colectivo* (shuttle van) for US$10 per person for three or more passengers, or US$12 per person for two passengers.

Aeropuerto Albrook handles domestic flights. A taxi ride to the Albrook airport costs US$2 to US$3.

Bus

Panama City has a good network of local buses (nicknamed *diablos rojos*, or red devils), which run every day from around 5am to 11pm. A ride costs US$0.25. Buses run along the three major west-to-east routes: Av Central–Vía España, Av Balboa–Vía Israel, and Av José D Espinar–Vía Transístmica. The Av Central–Vía España streets are one-way going west for much of the route; eastbound buses use Av Perú and Av 4 Sur; these buses will take you into the banking district of El Cangrejo. Buses also run along Av Ricardo J Alfaro (known as Tumba Muerto). There are plenty of bus stops along the street, but you can usually hail one from anywhere.

Many of these buses stop at the Terminal Nacional de Transporte, the bus station near Albrook airport.

The Plaza Cinco de Mayo area has three major bus stops. On the corner of Av Central and Av Justo Arosemena, buses depart for Panamá Viejo and Tocumen International Airport. Buses for the Albrook domestic airport depart in front of the Legislative Palace. Buses depart from the station on Av Roosevelt opposite the Legislative Palace for the Ancón area (including the Causeway) and other destinations.

Taxi

Taxis are plentiful. They are not metered, but there is a list of standard fares that drivers are supposed to charge, measured by zones. The fare for one zone is a minimum of US$1; the maximum fare within the city is US$4. An average ride, crossing a couple of zones, would cost US$1.25 to US$2. Taxis can also be rented for US$8 an hour.

Watch out for unmarked large-model US cars serving hotels as cabs. Their prices are up to four times that of regular street taxis.

You can phone for a taxi:

America	☎ 223-7694
America Libre	☎ 223-7342
Latino	☎ 224-0677
Metro	☎ 264-6788
Taxi Unico, Cooperativa	☎ 221-3191

Bicycle

There are several places to rent bicycles on the Causeway, including **Bicycles Moses** (Map p72-3; ☎ 211-3671; ☼ 8am-6pm) and **Bicicletas Rali** (Map pp76-7; ☎ 220-3844; ☼ 8am-6pm), which operates at the Causeway entrance. You can rent a bicycle for US$2.50 per hour or in-line skates for US$1 per hour.

Panamá Province

CONTENTS

Around Panama City	**119**
Panama Canal	119
Canal Area	120
Cerros Azul & Jefe	122
Baha'i & Hindu Temples	123
Isla Taboga	**123**
Archipiélago de Las Perlas	**126**
Isla Contadora	128
Isla San José	131
Eastern Panamá Province	**131**
Chepo	132
Nusagandi	132
Cañita	132
Lago Bayano	133
Ipetí	133
Tortí	133
Higueronal	134
To the Darién Gap	134
Western Panamá Province	**134**
La Chorrera	134
Capira	135
Parque Nacional y Reserva Biológica Altos De Campana	135
Punta Chame	136
Beaches	136

Lush, jungle-covered islands, white-sand beaches and tiny indigenous villages are a few of the features of Panama's second largest province (after Darién), where astounding natural beauty lies at Panama City's doorstep.

The canal is one of the most famous features cutting through the province, and visitors can take a boat ride on it, hike near its jungle-clad shore or simply admire it from the viewing platform beside the Miraflores Locks. A short boat ride up the canal leads to Isla Barro Colorado, the island home to a rich variety of flora and fauna that makes it inch for inch the most studied piece of land on the planet. On the mainland east of there lies Parque Nacional Soberanía, one of the country's most accessible tropical rain forests, with enough wildlife to please any nature-seeker. Impressive forest can also be found at higher altitudes as evidenced by 950m Cerro Azul, a prime bird watching spot in mountainous terrain east of Panama City.

Along the coastline a different geography prevails, attracting both weekending beachcombers and wave-seeking surf junkies to a string of fine beaches near San Carlos, less than 90 minutes from the capital. Those seeking even more remote locales should explore the islands off the coast. The Archipiélago de las Perlas was once a hideout for 17th-century buccaneers. Today the islands attract a more sedate crowd (and the occasional Survivor series), who come to soak up the beauty of its white-sand beaches, clear blue waters and big open skies. Closer in lies the charming island village of Taboga, which has fine walks, excellent views and an allure not so far removed from the days when visitors like Gauguin sojourned here.

HIGHLIGHTS

- Laying eyes on the awe-inspiring **Panama Canal** (p119)
- Spotting feathered friends in **Parque Nacional Soberanía** (p121) along Pipeline Rd, one of the world's premier bird watching sites
- Exploring the wildlife in verdant **Isla Barro Colorado** (p122), a world-famous jungle research center in Lago Gatún
- Breathing the fresh sea air in the lovely village of **Isla Taboga** (p123)
- Surfing decent breaks and making the most of romantic hideaways on the Pacific coast like **Playa Río Mar** (p138)

Isla Barro Colorado ★
Parque Nacional Soberanía ★
★ Panama Canal
★ Isla Taboga
★ Playa Río Mar

| ■ POPULATION: 1,459,000 | ■ AREA: 11,887 SQ KM | ■ ELEVATION: SEA LEVEL TO 1000M |

History

Panama's most populous province has a rich history associated with pirates, plunder, pearls and the world's most daring engineering marvel. Throughout the 16th and 17th centuries, the Spanish used the isthmus as the transit point for shipping gold plundered from Peru back to Spain. Several routes were used and one of these was the cobblestone Camino Real (King's Hwy) that linked the city to Portobelo. For hundreds of years the trail (today a national park) was the only semblance of a road across the isthmus. The road was abandoned by the Spanish in the 1700s (in favor of shipping gold around Cape Horn), owing to repeated pirate attacks – the most famous of which was Sir Henry Morgan's sacking of Panamá Viejo in 1671.

Even before Morgan's successful raid, there were many pirates in the region. Some, including Sir Francis Drake, used Isla Taboga as a hideout and springboard for attacks. Further off the coast an even better hideout for the seadogs was the chain of islands known as the Islas de las Perlas. This archipelago with its many hidden coves and inlets attracted the attention of Balboa, who named the chain upon learning of the abundant pearls found there, though Balboa was beheaded before he set foot on the islands (see p126). By the late 1600s, the Spanish no longer had any presence there.

Today, the province of Panamá is more famed for the canal than anything else. Although the canal is considered a 20th-century construction, the idea of a trans-isthmian water route was first discussed in 1524 when King Charles V of Spain ordered a survey to be undertaken. It wasn't until the late 1800s, however, that any country dared to undertake the momentous project of carving a trench through dense jungles and mountains. Before the canal, the US built a railway across the country in response to the frenzy brought on by the gold rush as thousands of East Coasters headed to California. Construction was not easy and many thousands of workers died (estimated between 6000 and 12,000) before its completion.

The first canal attempt came from a French team. Ferdinand de Lesseps, riding on his success building the Suez Canal, put a company together and made an attempt in the 1880s. Sadly, he and his colleagues grossly underestimated the difficulties and some 22,000 workers died during the attempt. Many workers who had contracted yellow fever and malaria were housed in an enormous sanatorium on Isla Taboga. Several decades later the Americans made their attempt and after learning from the mistakes of the French, succeeded, completing the canal in 1914.

Climate

The Pacific slope of Panamá Province gets most of its precipitation in the rainy season (mid-April to mid-December). In the northern extents of the province, however, rainfall occurs throughout the year.

National Parks

Panamá Province has several national parks, which provide ample hiking and wildlife viewing opportunities. A short distance from Panama City, **Parque Nacional Soberanía** (p121) is a birder's paradise, where in a day you can see dozens of different avian species and many mammal and butterfly species. The hiking trails here are superb. Connecting the park with Panama City's Parque Natural Metropolitano is the **Parque Nacional Camino de Cruces**, the old Camino Real, a cobblestone road used to transport gold across the isthmus. Lush rain forest abounds – as it does on the biological reserve of **Monumento Nacional Isla Barro Colorado** (p122), where scientists study the area's incredibly rich biodiversity. North of Panama City lies the Parque Nacional Chagres, an important part of the canal's watershed and home of many Emberá villages. **Parque Nacional y Reserva Biológica Altos de Campana** (p135), at 1000m in elevation, lies west of Panama City. The park has forested trails with fine lookouts over both the Atlantic and the Pacific slopes.

Getting There & Away

Access to Isla Taboga is via ferry that leaves from Muelle (Pier) 19 in Panama City (p112). To reach the Archipiélago de las Perlas, you must fly (although there is talk of reviving boat services). To reach Isla Barro Colorado all arrangements must be made through the Smithsonian Tropical Research Institute (STRI) in Panama City (p89). Parque Nacional Soberanía is easily

PANAMÁ PROVINCE

PANAMÁ PROVINCE

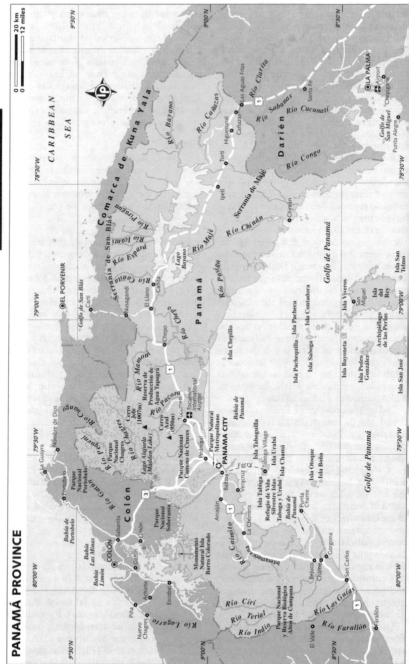

accessible by bus as are the beaches in the western part of the province.

AROUND PANAMA CITY

PANAMA CANAL

The USA's construction of the Panama Canal during the early 20th century is a true story of adventure, ordeal and accomplishment. It followed the catastrophic French attempt to cut a path between the seas, which claimed 22,000 lives. Despite all the technological advances that have taken place since the completion of the canal over 90 years ago, the lock-and-lake waterway remains one of the great engineering marvels of all time.

The canal extends 80km from Colón on the Caribbean side to Panama City on the Pacific, passing through three sets of locks, including the Gaillard Cut, a colossal excavation that cuts through the Continental Divide; and Lago Gatún, an artificial lake whose creation submerged 29 villages and huge swaths of forest and displaced 50,000 people. Each year more than 12,000 ocean-going vessels transit the canal – well over 30 a day. So significant is the canal to international shipping that ships the world over are built to fit within the dimensions of its locks: 305m long and 33.5m wide. At times a huge ship will squeeze through the locks with less than a meter to spare on each side.

Ships pay according to their weights; the average fee for commercial ships is around US$30,000. The largest passenger ships passing through the canal are assessed in excess of US$150,000 per transit. The lowest fee ever assessed was US$0.36, paid by Richard Halliburton, who swam through the canal in 1928.

Miraflores Locks

The easiest and best way to see the canal is to go to the **Miraflores Visitors Center** (☎ 276-8325; www.pancanal.com; museum admission US$10; 9am-5pm) near Panama City. The recently inaugurated visitors center features a large, four-floor multimedia museum, several good viewing platforms, a snack shop and an excellent open-air **restaurant** (11am-11pm) overlooking the locks. On the outdoor platforms, you'll be able to watch the ships pass through as a loudspeaker gives information (in English and Span-

ish) about the ships maneuvering through the locks.

To get to the locks, you can take any Paraíso or Gamboa bus from the Plaza Cinco de Mayo bus stop in Panama City. These buses, which pass along the canal-side highway that runs from the capital to Gamboa, will let you off at the 'Miraflores Locks' sign on the highway, about 8km from the city center. It's a 15-minute walk to the locks from the sign. If you have a car, there's parking at the center. Or, you can take a taxi. Even with a 30-minute visit, expect to pay no more than US$15 for the round-trip (agree on a price beforehand).

Other Locks

Further north, past the Miraflores Locks, are the **Pedro Miguel Locks**, which can be seen from the highway to Gamboa. One hundred meters beyond the locks there's a parking strip where onlookers can watch ships transit the canal. Unfortunately, you can't get a very good look at the locks from here and only authorized personnel are allowed any closer.

On the Caribbean side, the **Gatún Locks** have a viewing stand for visitors and a small replica of the entire canal that lets you place the locks in context. You can also get a good look at the locks if you cross the canal to visit Fuerte San Lorenzo. See the Colón Province chapter (p254) for more details on these locks and the nearby Gatún Dam.

Canal Tours

Canal Bay & Tours (☎ 314-1349; www.canaland baytours.com in Spanish) operates partial canal transits every Saturday morning. These boat tours depart from Muelle (Pier) 19 in Balboa, a western suburb of Panama City, travel through the Miraflores Locks to Lago Miraflores and back, and then cruise out into the bay for scenic views of the city and the Pacific approach to the canal. These fine tours last about 4½ hours and cost US$99/45 for adults/children under 12. It's a good idea to make a reservation at least a day ahead.

One Saturday a month, Canal Bay & Tours offers a full transit of the canal, from Balboa to Cristóbal, passing through all three sets of locks. The transit takes all day, from about 7:30am to 5:30pm, and costs US$149/55 for adults/children. Check the company's website for dates of upcoming transits. Be advised that many people find the full transit a bit much due to the heat and the lengthy wait times at the locks.

The one-way taxi fare to Muelle (Pier) 19 is usually US$3 to US$6.

If you take a trip to the Isla Barro Colorado area you will travel by boat along part of the canal, from Gamboa to Isla Barro Colorado, but you won't go through any locks. (See p122 for details on these trips.)

CANAL AREA

On a day trip from Panama City you could first visit the Miraflores Locks, then the Summit Botanical Gardens & Zoo, and finish by crossing into Colón Province to visit the Sendero El Charco nature trail in Parque Nacional Soberanía. The last stop is 25km from the center of Panama City but seems like a different world.

All these places are along the highway that runs from Panama City to Gamboa, the small tropical town where the Río Chagres meets the canal. Buses (one way US$0.60) passing by the Miraflores and Pedro Miguel Locks, Paraíso and Gamboa depart every 30 minutes from Plaza Cinco de Mayo in Panama City. The first bus leaves at 4:45am, the last at 10pm.

Summit Botanical Gardens & Zoo

On the highway to Gamboa, 10km past the Miraflores Locks, are the **Summit Bo-**

tanical Gardens & Zoo (☎ 232-4854; admission US$1; ⏱ 8:30am-4pm). The botanical gardens were founded in 1923 to introduce, propagate and disseminate tropical plants from around the world into Panama. They contain more than 15,000 plant species, and many of these are marked along a trail.

Also at the park is an expanding zoo that contains animals native to Central America. Its greatest attraction is its harpy eagle compound, which opened in 1998 in hopes that conditions would prove conducive to breeding; at the time of writing, there were no baby harpies to report. The harpy eagle is the national bird, and many ornithologists consider it the most powerful bird of prey. Also at the zoo is a roomy jaguar compound and a remarkably spacious cage containing lots of seemingly content macaws and other loud and large colorful birds.

Admission to the park includes a trail map. The same buses that pass by Gamboa will stop here if you ask the driver.

Parque Nacional Soberanía

A few kilometers past Summit, across the border into Colón Province, the 22,104-hectare Parque Nacional Soberanía is one of the most accessible tropical rain forest areas in Panama. It extends much of the way across the isthmus, from Limón on Lago Gatún to just north of Paraíso. It features hiking trails, the Río Chagres, part of Lago Gatún and a remarkable variety of wildlife – its known residents include 105 species of mammal, 525 species of bird, 55 species of amphibian, 79 species of reptile and 36 species of freshwater fish.

Hiking trails in the park include a section of the old **Sendero Las Cruces** (Las Cruces Trail), used by the Spaniards to transport gold and minerals by mule train between Panama City and Nombre de Dios, and the 17km **Pipeline Rd**, providing access to Río Agua Salud, where you can walk upriver for a swim under a waterfall.

Pipeline Rd is a favorite with bird watchers. A healthy cluster of golden-collared manakins is usually readily found at the end of the first 100m of the road, on the left side. Other typical sounds on the first 2km of the road come from white-bellied antbirds, black-bellied wrens, collared aracaris, keel-billed toucans and buff-throated woodcreepers. You'll likely hear a few howler

monkeys as well. In addition, you may be treated to such rarities as the tiny hawk, the hook-billed kite, the great jacamar and the black-tailed trogon. The jungle and wildlife on both sides of the road get increasingly thick as you proceed.

In order to fully appreciate the wildlife here, it's wise to hire a guide. This is one of the world's premier birding sites, and it would be a shame to give it short shrift. See p313 for a list of the country's top naturalist guides. Most charge about US$35 to guide a group of four for an entire morning on Pipeline Rd if you provide the transportation; they charge more if you don't.

A shorter, very easy nature trail is the **Sendero El Charco**. The trail is signposted from the highway, about 3km past the Summit Botanical Gardens & Zoo.

Fishing is permitted on the Río Chagres and Lago Gatún. Leaflets and information about the park, including a brochure for self-guided walks along the nature trail, are available from **Parque Nacional Soberanía** headquarters (☎ 276-6370) in Gamboa.

Canopy Tower

A former US Air Force radar station atop a hill in what is now Parque Nacional Soberanía, **Canopy Tower** (☎ 264-5720; www.canopy tower.com; d per person US$100-200) is an ecologically minded hotel surrounded by pristine rain forest. The three-story, cylindrical, enclosed tower features a viewing platform on top, a small ground-floor museum, and guest quarters with private hot-water bathrooms on the 2nd floor. Most of the rooms are attractive and comfortable, with desks, tables and chairs, firm beds and even hammocks. Two 'guide rooms' contain only a bed; guests share a bathroom with the staff. The rates vary with season and room, and rise annually. Rates include breakfast, lunch and dinner and two guided walks daily. A communal room with library, cozy sitting areas and dining tables is on the 3rd floor. A built-in steel ladder leads to the rooftop viewing deck.

The Canopy Tower offers a chance to immerse yourself in the sights and sounds of the magnificent surrounding forest. From the third and rooftop levels, you have a 360° view over some magnificent rain forest – and you can even see ships passing through the canal, a mere 2km away. The bird watching in the area is excellent, and there's lots of other wildlife in the area as well.

The Canopy Tower is also open to visitors who wish to go on a day trip. These cost US$75 per person and consist of a four-hour excursion into the forest with a bilingual guide followed by a meal. Check the website for details.

Gamboa Rainforest Resort

Near the junction of the Panama Canal and the Río Chagres, 9km past the turnoff for Canopy Tower on the road to Colón, is the US$30-million **Gamboa Rainforest Resort** (☎ 314-9000; gamboaresort.com; d from US$120). The main building's attraction is its sweeping vistas of the jungle-flanked Río Chagres – an awesome panorama of river and rain forest seen through windows three stories high. All 110 luxurious guestrooms offer slices of the same view. Flanking the driveway to the main building and lacking the gorgeous view are 65 'villas' (spiffed-up concrete duplexes really) that once housed the administrators who managed canal dredging operations a century ago.

The guestrooms are spacious with full amenities, an oversized bathroom and a hammock-strung balcony, and the resort offers a range of activities. Among the many offerings are Spa packages (per person for two nights US$460, per person for five nights US$1100), the three-night Adventure Experience (per person US$505) and the 'nature/wildlife tour' (per person for double-occupancy US$675), which is a four-night package that includes a morning boat tour of Lago Gatún, a sunrise birding tour on Pipeline Rd, and a slow ride through rain forest canopy aboard the resort's aerial tram. All packages include round-trip airport shuttle, unlimited use of kayaks, pedal boats, bicycles, the gym and tennis courts, and access to resort exhibits. The 10% hotel tax and buffet breakfast are included. At times, you may have this place to yourself.

Monumento Nacional Isla Barro Colorado

This lush island in the middle of Lago Gatún was formed by the damming of the Río Chagres and the creation of the lake. It is managed by the Smithsonian Tropical Research Institute (STRI), which administers a world-renowned research facility here. Although the 1500-hectare island was once restricted only to scientists, a limited number of guided tourists are now allowed, and a visit to the island makes a fascinating day trip from Panama City. The trip includes an STRI boat ride down an attractive part of the canal, from Gamboa across the lake to the island.

In 1923, Isla Barro Colorado (BCI) became one of the first biological reserves in the New World. Since that time, the island has become one of the most intensively studied areas in the Tropics. Home to 1316 recorded plant species, 381 bird species and 102 mammal species, the island also contains a 59km network of marked and protected trails. Visitors are only allowed on one designated nature trail to prevent them from inadvertently damaging anyone's valuable research. This 2.5km trail winds through some spectacular rain forest and ends at STRI's visitors center. The laboratories on BCI are off-limits to the public.

Tour reservations are essential; book as far in advance as possible. Reservations can be made through the Panama City visitor services office of **STRI** (Map p76; ☎ 212-8026; www.stri.org; Tupper Bldg, Av Roosevelt, Ancón district; adult/student foreigner US$70/40, adult/student Panamanian US$25/12; ☽ 8:30am-4:30pm Mon-Fri). Children under 10 are not allowed on BCI.

The boat to BCI leaves the Gamboa pier at 7:15am on Tuesday, Wednesday and Friday, and at 8am on Saturday and Sunday. There are no public visits on Monday, Thursday and on certain holidays. The entire trip lasts four to six hours, depending on the size of the group and on the weather. A buffet lunch (with vegetarian options) is included.

CERROS AZUL & JEFE

About an hour's drive northeast of Panama City is Cerro Azul, a 950m peak just south of Parque Nacional Chagres, a mountainous area of natural forest and streams. Several kilometers northeast of Cerro Azul is Cerro Jefe, a windy, cool ridge with rare elfin forest. Both peaks are popular with birders, who come looking for foothill species, including some from the Darién. Because of the difficulty of the terrain, particularly in the vicinity of Cerro Jefe, a 4WD vehicle is highly recommended. Buses do not go to this rugged area.

To reach the hills from Panama City, take Corredor Sur towards Tocumen. Corredor Sur becomes the Interamericana where it crosses the Tocumen Hwy. From this point, proceed 6.8km and look for an Xtra supermarket on the left side of the road. Just beyond the market is a police station and a turnoff, which you should take. After 1.9km you'll see a large Chinese pavilion on the left side of the road. Turn left onto another paved road. This road ascends Cerro Azul. After 9km, you will see the Las Vistas residential development; continue along the same road for 3km and you'll come to the La Posada de Ferhisse, an inn with a red-roofed, opened-sided restaurant that's very visible from the road. In this area there's some good bird watching, but it is superior on Cerro Jefe. To get there, continue on the same road another 6km until you're into the unusual elfin forest. You'll know you're in this rare forest when you find yourself surrounded by twisted, dwarfed and windswept trees. Also, Cerro Jefe is easily identified by the huge microwave tower at its summit.

Sleeping & Eating

La Posada de Ferhisse (☎ /fax 297-0197; d US$40) This place has six comfortable rooms with firm double beds, hot-water private bathrooms, a private phone and local-channel TV. There's a pool and a **restaurant** (☺ 9am-10pm) on the premises serving *tipico* (typical) food at reasonable prices.

Cabañas 4X4 (☎ 680-3076; www.cabanas4x4.com in Spanish; cabin per person US$45) If you take the road toward Cerro Jefe for 5.6km from La Posada de Ferhisse you'll see a ranger station on the left side of the road. At this point it's 7.4km to Cabañas 4X4, which you'll find by following a series of road signs with the cabins' name. Be advised Cabañas 4X4 can only be reached by a high-clearance 4WD truck and only if the road is dry. You'll come to a small wooded valley dotted with comfortable cabins that sleep from two to eight people. There are picnic areas, a pool and lots of trails that lend themselves well to bird watching.

BAHA'I & HINDU TEMPLES

On the crest of a hill on the outskirts of Panama City, 11km from the city center on the Vía Transístmica, is the white-domed **Baha'i Temple** (☎ 231-1137, 231-1191; admission free; ☺ 10am-6pm). It looks egglike from the outside, but inside it is surprisingly beautiful, with a constant breeze blowing through. This is the Baha'i House of Worship for all of Latin America. Baha'i members, who number about five million worldwide, believe in one God, and that history's great spiritual leaders – Moses, Krishna, Buddha, Zoroaster, Jesus and Muhammad – are all part of one tradition of God's progressive revelation of himself to humankind. Not surprisingly, the Baha'i is considered one of the most open-minded of faiths. Information about the faith is available in English and Spanish at the temple; readings from the Baha'i writings (in English and Spanish) are held at 10am Sunday.

An attractive **Hindu Temple** (admission free; ☺ 7:30-11am & 4:30-7:30pm), which is also atop a hill, is on the way to the Baha'i Temple.

Any bus from Panama City to Colón can let you off on the highway, but it's a long walk up the hill. A taxi ride from Panama City costs around US$10.

ISLA TABOGA

pop 970

A charming village with a whitewashed church, narrow streets and fine views out over the sea, Isla Taboga is a pleasant place to escape from the bustle of Panama City, a short boat ride away.

Taboga is part of a chain of islands that were inhabited by indigenous people who resided in thatch huts and made their living from the sea. In 1515 Spanish soldiers reached the island, killed or enslaved the Indians and took their substantial pieces of gold. This occurred just two years after Balboa first sighted the Pacific and before the city of Panama was constructed. A small Spanish colony developed on the island, and the Spaniards had the place to themselves until 1549, when Panama freed its Indian slaves and a good number chose to make Taboga their home.

Peace did not reign. Pirates, including the infamous Henry Morgan and Francis Drake, frequented the island, using it as a base from which to attack Spanish ships and towns. On August 22, 1686, the ship of Captain Townley, who was in command of English and French buccaneers, was lying in front of Taboga when it was attacked by three Spanish ships armed with cannons. During the ensuing battle, one of the Spanish ships blew up, and Townley's men were able to take the other two vessels as well as a fourth ship that had arrived as reinforcement.

The pirates' lost only one man and had 22 wounded, including Townley himself. The buccaneer commander sent a messenger to the president of Panama demanding supplies, the release of five pirates being held prisoner and ransom for Townley's many captives. When the president instead sent only some medicine, Townley said that heads would roll if his demands weren't met. When the president ignored that threat, Townley sent him a canoe that contained the heads of 20 Spaniards.

The severed heads got the president's attention, and he released the five prisoners and paid a ransom. Townley had won another battle, but he died of his wounds on September 9. For years afterward peace continued to elude the little island. As late as 1819, the pirate Captain Illingsworth and his party of Chileans landed on Taboga and sacked and burnt the village.

During the 1880s, when the French took a stab at digging a canal across the isthmus, Taboga became the site of an enormous sanitarium for workers who had contracted malaria or yellow fever. The 'Island of Flowers,' as it is sometimes called, might well have earned its name from all the flowers placed on graves here. Sadly, Taboga's centuries-old cemetery has been looted so many times that it looks like it was hit by artillery fire.

Real artillery fire also took a toll on Taboga. The US Navy used the broad hill facing the town for artillery practice during WWII. At that time the US military also installed searchlights, anti-aircraft guns and bunkers atop the island. The bunkers, abandoned in 1960, can be visited.

Today, peace has finally come to Taboga. Now the island is assailed only by weekend vacationers from Panama City and the occasional foreign tourist. There are several hotels and a few restaurants and bars on Taboga, but people primarily come just to stroll through the town's quaint streets and to hike on the island and soak up the tranquility of this overlooked gem.

Orientation & Information

A ferry serves Isla Taboga from Muelle (Pier) 19 in the Balboa district of Panama City twice daily, tying up at a pier near the north end of the island. As you exit the pier, you'll see the entrance of the Hotel Taboga to your right. To your left, you'll see a narrow street that is the island's main road. From this point, the street meanders 5.2km before ending at the old US military installation atop the island's highest hill, Cerro El Vigia.

For more information on the island, check the excellent English-language site, www.taboga.panamanow.com.

Walking Tour

One of the most pleasant ways to pass time on Taboga is to walk to the top of the island. Walk left from the pier and you will first pass a beach (unless the tide's in) on a road that's barely wide enough for a car and is mainly used by pedestrians. The road forks after 75m or so; you will want to take the high way. After a few more paces you will come to a modest **church**, in front of which is a simple square. This unassuming church was founded in 1550 and is the second-oldest church in the western hemisphere. Inside is a handsome altar and lovely artwork.

Further along you'll come to a beautiful public garden filled with flowers. At its center is a statue of the island's patroness, **Nuestra Señora del Carmen** (Our Lady of Carmen) who is honored with a procession on July 16. The statue is carried upon the shoulders of followers to the oceanside, placed on a boat and ferried around the island. Upon her return she is carried around the island, while crowds follow and everyone else watches at their windows. The Virgin is returned to her garden shrine and the rest of the day is one of rejoicing. Seemingly everyone partakes in games, fire-breathing or dancing.

Continuing along the same road another 400m you'll pass a **cemetery** that dates from the 16th century but is overgrown with weeds.

Further on, you'll notice a cross upon Cerro de la Cruz, the large hill just ahead of you. It was placed here by the Spaniards in the 16th century. The US Navy used the hillside just below it for target practice during WWII. As the road leaves the residential area, you'll see hibiscus, bougainvillea, oleander and jasmine, which earned Taboga the nickname of 'Island of Flowers.' The colors are most vibrant in April and May.

After 2km of this now-strenuous and woodsy walk, the road forks one last time. To the left are abandoned **bunkers** that were used by US troops during WWII. If you look below and to the right of the old cross you'll see a white-and-brown pile of rubble amid thickening vegetation. This is the ruins of a Spanish cannon emplacement put here 300 years ago to protect the island from pirates. The green-blue water below the ruins offers decent diving. Not visible from land but tucked into the cliff below the bunkers are two caves where Indian artifacts have been found. Up the road from the bunkers, on the road's less-traveled branch, are a radar installation and the island's secondary electrical plant, both off-limits to the public.

Beaches

There are fine beaches, all free, in Taboga in either direction from the ferry dock. Many visitors head straight for the lackluster Hotel Taboga, to your right as you walk off the ferry dock; the hotel faces onto the island's most popular beach, arcing between Taboga and tiny Isla El Morro. A day entrance fee (US$7) gives you access to the facilities; the hotel also rents kayaks, beach umbrellas and snorkeling gear. There's no need to pay the hotel simply to use the beach.

Snorkeling

On the weekends, when most people visit Taboga, you can find fishermen at the island's pier who will take you around the island in their small boats, so that you can see it from all sides and reach some of its good snorkeling spots. There are some caves on the island's western side that are rumored to hold golden treasure left there by pirates. During the week, when the small boats are nowhere to be found, you can still snorkel around Isla El Morro, which hasn't any coral but attracts some large fish.

Diving

Taboga offers typical Pacific-style diving, with rocky formations and a wide variety of marine life. The beauty of the Pacific lies in the schools of fish that roam about: on a good dive you can expect to see jack, snapper, jewfish, eels, corvina, rays, lobsters and octopuses. With a little luck, you may also come across old bottles, spent WWII-era shells and artifacts from pirate days.

Scubapanama (☎ 261-3841; www.scubapanama.com; cnr Av 6a C Norte & Calle 62 C Oeste, El Carmen, Panama City) offers periodic dive trips to the island.

Bird Watching

The islands of Taboga and nearby Urabá are home to one of the largest breeding colonies of brown pelicans in the world. The colony has contained up to 100,000 individual birds, or about half of the world population of this species. A wildlife refuge, the **Refugio de Vida Silvestre Islas Taboga y Urabá**, was established to protect their habitat. The refuge covers about a third of Taboga as well as the entire island of Urabá, just off Taboga's southeast coast. May is the height of nesting season, but pelicans can be seen from January to June.

Whale Watching

On your way to and from the island, keep an eye on the ocean. On rare occasions during August, September and October, migrating humpback and sei whales can be seen leaping from the water near Taboga in spectacular displays.

Sleeping & Eating

You'll find a number of listings on Taboga's website, www.taboga.panamanow.com, for both long- and short-term private house rental.

Vereda Tropical Hotel (☎ 250-2154; veredatropical hotel@hotmail.com; d weekdays US$45-55, weekends US$55-65) Atop a hill with commanding views, this beautiful hotel opened in 2004, and is among the most charming places to stay in Panama. Colorful rooms, some with balconies, are stylishly decorated, and have high ceilings, comfortable beds and shutters that open onto the village or the sea. The open-air restaurant, with sunny adjoining patio, serves tasty meals prepared by the talented Portuguese chef. The cocktails alone are worth a visit – try the La Vereda (tasty passion fruit juice with seco).

Hotel Taboga (☎ 264-6096; htaboga@sinfo.net; d US$44;) This 54-room hotel doesn't provide much value for the money. Rooms are simple with air-con, cable TV and hot water, and often smell mildewy. There's a pool and restaurant on the premises.

Kool Hostel (☎ 690-2545; luisveron@hotmail.com; dm US$10, house US$27) This small, friendly hostel is a good spot for backpackers. It features three clean rooms with bunk beds and shared hot-water bathrooms. Guests can use the kitchen, rent bikes or snorkel gear (per day US$5), or hire fishing tackle. Turn left as you exit the dock and continue less than 10 minutes on foot. There's a view of Cerro de la Cruz from the front door.

Restaurante Chu (mains US$3-6) This popular Chinese spot serves bowls of Chow mein, fried rice and snack foods. The open-air bar upstairs blasts salsa most weekends.

Aquario (mains US$4-7; ☒ 7am-10pm) This simple eatery with tables inside and out has an extensive menu that features good, home-cooked meals. It also has a book exchange. It's just past the basketball court; take the top path through town.

Donde Pope Si Hay (mains US$4-8) Another fine spot to go for traditional Panamanian cooking.

Getting There & Away

The boat trip to Taboga is part of the island's attraction. Visitors can take the slow **Calypso Queen** (☎ 232-5736), which departs from Muelle 19 in the Balboa district of Panama City and passes along the Balboa port, under the Puente de las Américas, and along the last part of the Panama Canal channel on its journey out to sea. Boats (round-trip US$8, 1¼ hours) depart at 8:30am Monday to Friday and return at 4:30pm. On weekends and holidays they depart at 7:45am and 10:30am, returning at 3pm and 5:45pm. Note that at the time of research, plans were in the works for this boat to leave from the Causeway, behind the Centro de Exhibiciones Marinas.

A faster boat makes the excursion in half the time. **The Expreso Del Pacífico** (☎ 261-0350) departs from Muelle 19 at 8am, 10am and 4pm from Monday to Friday, returning at 9:15am, 3pm and 5pm. On weekends and holidays it departs at 8:30am and 2:30pm, returning at 9:45am and 3:45pm. Round-trip tickets cost US$8.

ARCHIPIÉLAGO DE LAS PERLAS

In January 1979, after the followers of the Ayatollah Ruholla Khomeini had forced Shah Mohammed Reza Pahlavi to pack up

his hundreds of millions of dollars and flee Iran, the shah looked the world over and moved to Isla Contadora. It's one of 90 named islands in the Archipiélago de las Perlas, or Pearl Islands, any one of which is fit for a king – or a shah.

These islands, plus 130 unnamed islets in the Pearl chain, lie between 64km and 113km southeast of Panama City and are the stuff of travel magazines: tan-sand beaches, turquoise waters, swaying palms, colorful fish and sea turtles. And out of the oysters that abound here have come some of the world's finest pearls, including the 31-carat 'Peregrina' pearl, which has been worn by a Spanish king, an English queen and a French emperor and today belongs to actress Elizabeth Taylor. (When the pearl was found, more than 400 years ago, it was considered so magnificent that the slave who discovered it was given his freedom.)

In fact, it was pearls that initially brought the islands to the Old World's attention. Vasco Núñez de Balboa, within days of his discovery of the Pacific Ocean, learned of nearby islands rich with pearls from an Indian guide. Balboa was anxious to visit the islands, but he was told that a hostile chief ruled them, and the explorer decided to postpone the visit. He nonetheless named the archipelago 'Islas de las Perlas' and declared it Spanish property. The year was 1513, and Balboa vowed to return one day to kill the chief and claim his pearls for the king of Spain.

But before he could fulfill his vow, Spanish governor Pedro Arias de Ávila, who loathed the great explorer for his popularity with the king, dispatched his cousin Gaspar de Morales to the islands to secure the pearls spoken of by Balboa. Once on the islands, Morales captured 20 chieftains and gave them to his dogs to tear to pieces. The purportedly hostile chief, a man named Dites, initially resisted Morales and his men, but after a battle in which many Indians died, the chief saw the futility of warring with the Spaniards, and he presented Morales with a basket of large and lustrous pearls. Despite the gift, all the Pearl Indians were dead within two years.

History books do not record the circumstances of Dites' death, but they do record Balboa's. In 1517, the same year that Morales raided Las Perlas, Pedrarias (as the governor

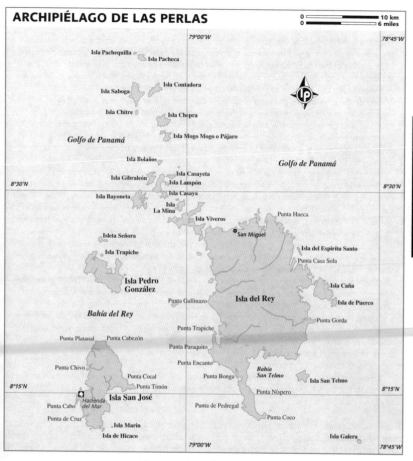

ARCHIPIÉLAGO DE LAS PERLAS

was often called) falsely charged Balboa with treason and had the loyal public servant and four of his closest friends beheaded in the Caribbean coastal town of Aclá.

In the years that followed Morales' arrival in the archipelago, the Spaniards harvested the islands' oyster beds. Because they had slain all the Indians, they found it necessary to import slaves from Africa to collect oysters. The island that was used for counting the pearls before they were shipped to Panama City – and thence to Spain – was named Contadora, which is Spanish for 'counting house.' The island has retained its name, and descendants of the first slaves who came to the Archipiélago de las Perlas presently live on the island.

Orientation & Information

Today, people inhabit no more than a dozen of the 220 islands and islets that comprise the Archipiélago de las Perlas. The largest of the group is Isla del Rey (240 sq km), followed by Isla San José (45.3 sq km), Isla Pedro González (14.9 sq km), Isla Viveros (6.6 sq km) and Isla de Cañas (3.2 sq km).

With few exceptions, tourists visit only five of Las Perlas: Isla Contadora (at 1.2 sq km), which is the most accessible, developed and visited; Isla San José, the site of a new resort; Isla Casaya (2.75 sq km) and neighboring Isla Casayeta (0.46 sq km), which are frequented by pearl shoppers; and Isla Saboga (2.96 sq km), which attracts the

PIRATES IN THE BAY

From the late 17th century, the Bahía de Panamá, home to the Pearl and Taboga island groups, was the scene of pirate exploits unsurpassed anywhere in the New World. Henry Morgan's successful 1671 sacking of the city of Panama enticed other buccaneers to enter the area and try their hands at plundering and pillaging Spanish territory and ships along the Pacific coast. Many are the stories of pirates using the Archipiélago de las Perlas as a hideout and springboard for attacks.

One of the era's most significant escapades occurred in May 1685 near Las Perlas, when the largest number of trained seamen and fighters ever assembled under a buccaneer flag in the Pacific played cat-and-mouse with a Spanish armada of 18 ships. The pirate fleet consisted of 10 French and English vessels united under the English captain Edward Blake. Because his fleet was deficient in cannons but sufficient in muskets, it was Blake's policy to avoid long-range fighting. Despite his fleet's inferior numbers, he itched for a close encounter with the Spaniards.

When the two great forces came within sight of each other on May 28, Blake ordered two of his principal ships (one led by a Frenchman, the second by an Englishman) to initiate an attack on the Spanish fleet. Fearing the Spaniards' cannons, both men refused to obey. Blake's crew exchanged shots with the Spanish vice admiral, but Blake – seeing the imprudence of continuing battle with the odds stacked against him and with some of his officers bowing out – ordered his slower ships to flee while his and another fast vessel delayed the conquistadors.

The Spaniards opened fire with their big guns, but the pirates managed some risky evasive maneuvers between rocky islets at the northern end of the archipelago, and their pursuers gave up the chase. Blake's ships anchored off the archipelago's Isla Pacheca that night, fully expecting the Spanish armada to engage them the next day. Instead, for reasons that mystify historians, the Spanish admiral ordered his fleet to return to Panamá. In the days that followed, dissent arose among the buccaneers, and the short-lived French-English pirate confederacy dissolved.

Today, little evidence of the pirates and Spaniards remains in the Archipiélago de las Perlas besides the distant descendants of the Spaniards and their slaves. Forests once felled to make ships have grown back. Storms, termites and wood worms have destroyed the old Spanish structures. Only a church and a stone dam on Isla Saboga and wells on Islas Pacheca and Chapera testify to the Spaniards' presence.

Exploiting this buccaneer reputation, the popular US show *Survivor* brought attention to the islands in Fall 2003 by setting their sensationalist series here.

occasional explorer who must check out the colonial church, despite it having been pillaged, unattractive and poorly maintained.

There is no tourist office, bank or post office on any of the islands in the Archipiélago de las Perlas, and accommodations are limited to the islands of Contadora and San José.

ISLA CONTADORA
pop 350

This small island is one of the closest in the archipelago to Panama City and is by far the most visited. There are convenient daily flights to and from the capital, a few options for lodging and eating, good snorkeling and gorgeous beaches.

Nearly all the tourist facilities are on the northern side of the island, within walking distance of the airstrip. The other side consists primarily of forest, beautiful homes and secluded beaches. Contadora is also home to the country's only official nude beach, Playa de las Suecas (Swedish Women Beach).

There's a **ULAPS Health Clinic** (☎ 250-4209; ✆ 24hr) a short walk from the airstrip. If no one answers the door, walk around to the back of the facility to the house there. It's the doctor's home and he doesn't mind being disturbed if someone's in need.

Beaches

This 1.2-sq-km island has 12 beaches, all covered with tan sand and most unoccupied except during major holidays. Five beaches are particularly lovely: Playa Larga, Playa de las Suecas, Playa Cacique, Playa Ejecutiva and Playa Galeón. Although spread around three sides of the island, all can be visited in as little as 20 minutes in a rented four-wheeler (ATV; all-terrain vehicle).

Playa Larga is always the most crowded of the beaches, as it is in front of the over-priced Hotel Contadora Resort, but it's also perhaps the best for spotting marine life. Around the corner to the south is Playa de las Suecas, where you can sunbathe in the buff legally. Continuing west 400m, you'll find Playa Cacique, a fairly large and un-visited beach. On the northern side of the island, Playa Ejecutiva is intimate except during holidays; the large house on the bluff to the east is where the shah of Iran once lived. Playa Galeón, to the northeast, is good for snorkeling.

Snorkeling

The snorkeling around Contadora can be fantastic. There are five coral fields near the island, and within them you can expect to see schools of angelfish, damselfish, moray eels, parrotfish, puffer fish, butterflyfish, white-tip reef sharks and a whole lot more. Even in the waters off Playa Larga, the most popular of Isla Contadora's beaches, you can often spot sea turtles and manta rays.

The coral fields are found offshore from the following places: the eastern end of Playa de las Suecas; Punta Verde, near the southern end of Playa Larga; both ends of Playa Galeón; and the western end of Playa Ejecutiva. Also, although there is little coral at the southwestern end of the island, there is a lot of marine life among the rocks in front and east of Playa Roca.

Snorkeling trips can be arranged at Hotel Punta Galeón Resort (see Sleeping, p129).

Four-Wheeling

Contadora lends itself to getting around in a four-wheeler. You can rent them at Hotel Punta Galeón Resort (see Sleeping, p129) for US$20 per hour.

Glass-Bottom Boat

Owned and operated by the amiable Jayson Young, Glass Bottom is a 28-foot boat with eight glass panels you know where. The Jamaican boatman takes tourists all the way around Isla Contadora, giving a detailed history of the island and a rundown of the area's marine life during the 90-minute tour (US$15).

Expect to see parrot fish, sergeant majors, puffer fish; occasionally you'll pass over sea turtles, dolphins, manta rays, sharks, even humpback whales. The boat is partially shaded, so there's relief if you start catching too many rays. This is the best-value tour on the island and highly recommended.

The boat departs from Playa Larga, but the departure time changes with varying tides. To find out when Jayson will be making his next departure, inquire at the reception desk of Hotel Punta Galeón Resort (see Sleeping, p129). Or try calling him directly (☎ 624-5126).

Sleeping

At research time, several of the hotels in Isla Contadora had become sadly run down and didn't offer much value for the money. With the exception of Cabañas de Contadora, any of the places you book below will meet you at the airport and provide transportation (via golf cart) to the resort or hotel.

Hotel Punta Galeón Resort (Map p130; ☎ 214-3719; www.puntagaleon.com; d US$165; ⚇) The best of the bunch is this centrally located hotel, which offers 48 lovely air-con rooms with cable TV, hot-water bathrooms, private phones, minibars, good beds and a sea-facing terrace. Facilities at this Colombian-owned hotel include a sauna, swimming pool, kid's pool, an open-sided restaurant and an air-con restaurant, and several viewing platforms with tables and chairs. When you leave the airport runway, walk 50m down the hill, and it's the first place you reach.

Hotel Contadora Resort (Map p130; ☎ 264-1498; www.hotelcontadora.com; s/d US$118/176) This 354-room monstrosity of French Colonial design has deteriorated. Facilities include a swimming pool, tennis courts and a nine-hole golf course, all of which are free for guests. Buffet-style meals are included, but the food is pretty bland. The hotel's greatest asset is the lovely beach in front.

Villa Romantica (Map p130; ☎ 250-4067; www.contadora-villa-romantica.com; d US$80) Overlooking the lovely beach of Playa Cacique, this small hotel has a range of clean, modern rooms with tile floors. Some rooms have waterbeds, and most have murals (castle scenes) painted on the walls. The restaurant serves a variety of seafood and meat dishes.

Casa del Sol (Map p130; ☎ 250-4212; www.panama-isla-contadora.com; s/d with breakfast US$40/50) Located in a pleasant residential neighborhood full of hummingbirds, the Casa del Sol has just one guestroom, but it's quite nice. The room is comfortably furnished with private hot-water bathroom, and a delicious breakfast is included. Guests can rent bikes (US$5 a day) or a four-wheeler (US$25 a day). The owners offer trips to unoccupied islands and snorkeling sites aboard their boat. German, Spanish and English are spoken. It's a 20-minute walk from here to the airstrip.

Cabañas de Contadora (Map p130; ☎ 265-5691; d US$33) To get to the Cabañas, take the road up the hill as you leave the airport runway. When the road forks, take the left fork and follow it for the next 200m. When the road ends, take the road to the left, and you'll soon reach the cabins on your left hand side. About a 10-minute walk from the airstrip through a lush, upscale residential neighborhood, these *cabañas* are actually four simple, side-by-side fan-cooled apartments with cool-water showers. Each apartment has a two-burner hot plate, refrigerator and microwave. If you plan on cooking, bring provisions from Panama City as the stores in Contadora don't have much.

Eating

The dining scene in Contadora is pretty weak.

Restaurante Gerald's (mains US$9-12; ☷ noon-3pm & 6-10pm Mon-Sat) Overlooking a golf course, Gerald's is a good choice for fish, seafood and grilled dishes. The small menu features items like rock lobster, grilled pork chops and fish of the day.

Punta Galeón (mains US$9-14; ☷ noon-3pm & 6-10pm Mon-Sat) Even if you're not staying at the resort, the lovely restaurant overlooking the ocean is a fine spot for a meal or a drink in the evening (there's also a bar and restaurant downstairs that's right on the beach). Among the seafood selections, the grilled *corvina* is a decent option; they also offer lighter fare, like sandwiches, and serve breakfast.

Restaurante Sagitario (meals US$2-3) For typical Panamanian food at a low, low price, head to this place where you can eat plates of simple, home cooking on the back patio.

Supermercado Contadora (☷ 8am-8pm) This tiny market sells basic provisions like eggs, macaroni and cheese, water and soft drinks.

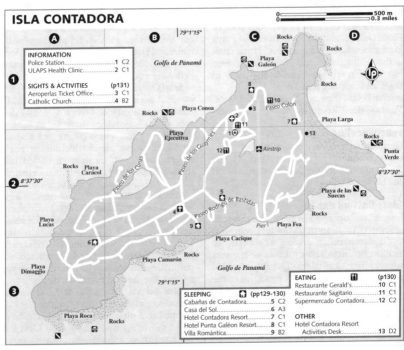

ISLA CONTADORA

0 —— 500 m
0 —— 0.3 miles

INFORMATION	
Police Station	1 C2
ULAPS Health Clinic	2 C1

SIGHTS & ACTIVITIES	(p131)
Aeroperlas Ticket Office	3 C1
Catholic Church	4 B2

SLEEPING	(pp129-130)
Cabañas de Contadora	5 C2
Casa del Sol	6 A3
Hotel Contadora Resort	7 C1
Hotel Punta Galeón Resort	8 C1
Villa Romántica	9 B2

EATING	(p130)
Restaurante Gerald's	10 C1
Restaurante Sagitario	11 C1
Supermercado Contadora	12 C2

OTHER	
Hotel Contadora Resort	
Activities Desk	13 D2

Golfo de Panamá

Playa Galeón
Playa Conoa
Paseo Colón
Playa Larga
Playa Ejecutiva
Airstrip
Punta Verde
Playa de las Suecas
Paseo de los Guaymíes
Paseo de las Colas
Playa Caracol
de Bastidas
Paseo Rodrigo
Playa Lucas
Pier
Playa Fea
Playa Cacique
Playa Dimaggio
Playa Camarón
Golfo de Panamá
Playa Roca
Rocks

79°1'15"
8°37'30"

Shopping

Oysters are still caught and pearls are still found around the Archipiélago de las Perlas. Although pearls are sometimes offered for sale on other islands, the best places to shop for them are Isla Casaya and neighboring Isla Casayeta, about 12km to the south of Contadora. Prices are generally very reasonable, and there's always room for bargaining.

When you're looking at pearls, you should know that pearl sellers tend to keep their goods in oil, so that they'll have a lovely shine when presented. Always dry the pearl that intrigues you before you buy.

Getting There & Away

Aeroperlas (☎ 250-4026 on Contadora, ☎ 315-7500 in Panama City) flies direct from Panama City to Isla Contadora (round-trip US$59, 15 minutes) at 8am and 5pm Monday to Friday; 8am, 8:50am, 9:45am and 5pm Saturday; and 8:50am, 3:30pm, 4:30pm and 5:30pm on Sunday. Flights from Isla Contadora to Panama City depart at 8:25am and 5:25pm Monday to Saturday, 9:15am on Saturday and Sunday, and 4pm, 5pm and 5:55pm Sunday.

Getting Around

Because the island is so small, there are no taxis. Many hotels shuttle guests to and from the airport via golf cart. There are also four-wheelers for rent (see p129).

ISLA SAN JOSÉ

pop 350

Most of this 45.3 sq km island is covered in a bank of rain forest that's networked by 100km of all-weather roads installed by the US military decades ago. With the exception of roads, the only development on the island is **Hacienda del Mar** (☎ 269-6634, in Panama City 269-6613; www.haciendadelmar.net; d from US$330), a gorgeous resort at cliff's edge that presently has the island and its 37 tan-sand beaches, its nine year-round rivers and its seven accessible waterfalls all to itself.

The Hacienda del Mar is the creation of Aeroperlas President George Novey, who spared no expense in the construction of his resort. Facilities include 12 luxurious cabins, each fully equipped and overlooking either the open sea or a picture-perfect sweep of beach. The main building is home to a sports bar with pool table and big-screen DirecTV. The second-story dining room has a menu that includes a range of seafood and grilled meat dishes. Dinner here with appetizer and dessert costs about US$20, and the food is delicious. Between the main building and the cabins is a lovely swimming pool.

Given the steep price tag it's comforting to know that service here is top-notch, and the charming manager speaks English, Spanish, Italian, German and French. She leads new arrivals on a tour of the resort, which includes showing guests a sea turtle hatchery that's helping to stave off the animals' extinction. She also introduces guests to the resort's many tours (which cost between US$60 and US$200 depending on the number of people).

Air transportation between Panama City and Isla San José is arranged by the Hacienda del Mar.

EASTERN PANAMÁ PROVINCE

Beyond the capital city, the Interamericana heads eastward through several small towns before arriving at the Darién Gap, that last defiant stretch of wilderness separating the continents of North and South America. The Darién Gap is the sole barrier in the way of an otherwise unbroken 30,600km highway winding from Circle, Alaska, to Puerto Montt, Chile.

Since the first Pan-American Hwy Congress met in Buenos Aires in 1925, the nations of the Americas have devoted considerable money and engineering skills to the completion of a great hemispheric road system. Today, only 150km of unfinished business prevents that system from being realized. Until recently, the governments of Panama and Colombia stood poised to construct this missing bit of pavement.

But with civil war raging in Colombia, it appears that the hemispheric highway won't be completed any time soon. Until it is, the highway on the Panamanian side of the divide will continue to end at the sweaty, ramshackle town of Yaviza, in Darién Province. Separating Yaviza and Panama City are 266km of mostly bad road and cattle country. Efforts to pave the road all the way to Yaviza, were begun in 2001 and are still several years from completion.

The drive from the capital to Yaviza takes about six hours during the dry season, longer during the rainy season, and less once the road is completely paved. For information on towns along the way beyond the Panamá–Darién border, see Darién Province (p279).

CHEPO
pop 13,600

Beyond the urban sprawl east of Panama City, the landscape becomes increasingly barren on both sides of the Interamericana. Gas stations and accommodations become somewhat scarce and the views monotonous.

Not 40 years ago the highway ended at Chepo and a sign announced the start of the Darién Gap. (Today, most Panamanians still consider all the country east of Chepo as the Darién, although much of it is actually within Panamá Province.) From Chepo to beyond the Colombian border there was only roadless jungle. To go any further by vehicle, one resorted to *piraguas* – needlelike canoes hollowed from logs. These were placed in the Río Mamoní and pushed deep into the Darién rain forest by outboard motors. The 'roads' from there on out were creeks, streams and rivers.

Today, a main road swings out from the Interamericana and into Chepo. The town, 32km past the turnoff for Cerro Azul, continues to exist mainly as a launching point into the Darién: there are two gas stations, a place to buy ice, and general stores with lots of canned goods.

Buses leave the Terminal Nacional de Transporte, in the Albrook district of Panama City, for Chepo (US$1.20, 1¼ hours) almost hourly from 6:40am to 5:10pm. The bus continues on to Cañita.

NUSAGANDI
pop 30

Just before you reach the town of El Llano and 16.2km from Chepo, you'll see the turnoff for Nusagandi, an area inside the Área Silvestre de Narganá wildlife reserve. The reserve was created by the Kuna, primarily to try to keep squatters from settling on their land. But it consists mostly of species-rich primary forest and was a perfect choice for conservation.

The road is pretty rough, and you'll need a 4WD vehicle with a strong engine and plenty of clearance. The wildlife here is impressive. This is the best spot in Panama to look for the speckled antshrike, the black-headed antthrush and the black-crowned antpitta. Various tanagers, including the rufous-winged, are numerous. There are some gorgeous waterfalls in this jungle as well.

At about the 17km mark, there's the very basic but charming **Burbayar Lodge** (☎ 264-1679; www.burbayar.com in Spanish; first/additional night per person US$114/70). This rustic place is a truly ecologically minded, low-impact lodge accommodating up to 14 guests in six simple cabins. A tiny generator provides some electricity but at night most of the light comes from gas lanterns or candles, lending an old-time feel to the setting. Hammocks are strung around the lodge to better enjoy the sounds of the rain forest. The all-inclusive lodge offers excellent meals prepared by the Spanish owner (good fresh Panamanian cuisine along with lots of fruit and salad). In addition to three meals a day, the price includes round-trip transportation from Panama City and two guided hikes a day. There's primary forest all around, with nearby waterfalls, and even a trail all the way to the coast in Kuna Yala (27km, six to eight hours). Burbayar also leads a spelunking trip to the nearby caves at Lago Bayano. This place is quite a find. Be sure to book in advance, as you can't simply show up here. The lodge is not recommended for children aged under 12. Transportation can be arranged from Panama City.

CAÑITA
pop 2200

This small town, also bisected by the Interamericana, is 8.7km beyond El Llano. It has a gas station and a public phone in town, as well as three restaurants. At one of them, thatched-roofed, open-sided **El Descanso**, the nailed-up skins of jaguars, ocelots and other animals attest to the health of the rain forest that once blanketed the area. It was felled within the last 20 years, mainly to make room for cattle ranches.

El Descanso is decent and cheap, with few meals over US$3. It's typical of the restaurants between Chepo and Yaviza: it doesn't have menus, but a server will tell you what's available. Meals typically consist of chicken or beef or pork with rice and beans. The selection is usually dependent upon which trucks have stopped by recently.

Buses leave Panama City's Terminal Nacional de Transporte for Cañita (US$2.75, 2½ hours) almost every hour from 6:40am to 5:10pm.

LAGO BAYANO

Fourteen kilometers from Cañita you'll come to Puente Bayano (Bayano Bridge), which crosses Lago Bayano. There's a checkpoint here where people heading to and from the Darién are stopped, asked to show their IDs and are sometimes searched.

Around the lake and near the highway here you'll see some healthy secondary forest. It exists to protect Lago Bayano's watershed. Lago Bayano, which supports a hydroelectric project, was created by the damming of the Río Bayano. Because the forest is owned by a utility company, it will likely remain intact.

IPETÍ

pop 550

This town, 45km east of Lago Bayano, actually consists of three towns – Ipetí-Emberá, Ipetí Kuna and Ipetí Colono – with three different cultures (Kuna, Emberá and rural Panamanian) living practically side by side. As you approach this area, be on the lookout for a faded green sign that says 'bienvenidos.' To reach the friendly Emberá village turn right at the sign and follow the dirt road for about 2km. This traditional village was just starting an ecotourism project (with the help of a Peace Corps worker). Overlooking the Río Ipetí, this small Emberá village consists of several dozen wood-sided, thatched-roof houses. They have a Casa Cultural (an open-sided building used as a meeting space), a Casa Medicinal (where healing herbs are grown) and rain forest nearby. A 45-minute walk upstream along the Río Ipetí leads to some lovely natural swimming pools with small waterfalls. You can also hire one of the villagers to take you by dugout canoe. This village hosts occasional tour groups, but you can just as easily show up on your own. If you want to stay the night, you can pitch a hammock in the Casa Cultural for around US$1. You can also ask around, as there's often a private room (with hammock) available for US$9 per night. You can buy a simple meal in town for US$2 (usually fried fish and patacones). There's also a small handicrafts store, and if you ask around you'll find someone who can give you a traditional *jagua* body painting.

Directly across the highway from the turnoff to Ipetí Emberá is Ipetí Kuna. This is a very traditional Kuna village, and many of the residents don't speak Spanish – much less English. There's a handicrafts and fruit and vegetable market along the highway, but not much infrastructure. **Igua** (☎ 595-9500), one of the Kuna chiefs here, has been recommended for leading boat tours to Lago Bayano and hikes into the rain forest.

If you continue up the road 1km you'll reach Ipetí Colono, just a few buildings scattered off the highway. Some fine horsemen hail from this village. Travelers looking for some impromptu adventure should stop in and inquire about hiring horses. You can reach virgin forest on horseback in two hours.

TORTÍ

pop 8400

In Tortí, 12km from Ipetí, you'll come across the first pensión east of Panama City – the **Hospedaje Tortí** (s/d with fan US$6/8, with air-con US$10/12; ✷). It has 25 rooms, each with a firm mattress, a portable fan, towels and soap. The four shared showers and two shared toilets are clean, and there's electricity 24 hours. The walls are cinderblock, but it's not bad value. There's usually space at the hospedaje unless you happen to arrive during Tortí's big March feria, which runs from the 25th to the 28th. It's a colorful event if you happen to be around, with a running of the bulls, horsemanship shows and lots of stands selling local treats.

Also in town are three public phones, a health clinic, police and gas stations and several restaurants. The best restaurant is **Avicar** (dishes US$1.25-4; ✷ 7am-10pm), which serves good Panamanian dishes. Andres, the friendly owner, speaks English and can tell you all about the area. A grocery store of the same name adjoins the restaurant.

Up the road, you'll reach a leather-goods store named **Echao Palante** (Going Forward; ✷ 10am-8pm daily). Inside, hard at work, you'll find Pedro Guerra. Pedro has handmade more than 5000 saddles (it takes him a day to make one) and countless belts and sandals. And his prices are low.

HIGUERONAL
pop 200

Higueronal is 10.2km from Tortí. There's a gas station, two restaurants and a public phone here. Down the road a little, the town of Cañazas offers tourists a pay phone only. There's also a military checkpoint at Cañazas. Foreigners will be asked to come inside the building, where a soldier will ask for your passport, note in his ledger your name and nationality, and then return your passport. This is done so that if something happens to you and someone is looking for you, the checkpoint will be able to inform the search party that you passed by here.

TO THE DARIÉN GAP

Crossing the border from Panamá Province into Darién Province, you'll pass the towns of Las Aguas Frías, Santa Fé and Metetí before you arrive in Yaviza. See the Darién Province chapter (p283) for details on these towns.

WESTERN PANAMÁ PROVINCE

There are many communities in the western section of Panamá Province, but the area is known primarily for its many lovely beaches. Every weekend thousands of stressed-out Panama City residents hop into their cars or board buses and head west on the Interamericana, bound for fine beaches along the Pacific.

LA CHORRERA
pop 59,900

Despite its large population, La Chorrera has relatively little to offer visitors. Still, it's a place with a past, a culture, a waterfall and a unique local drink: the *chicheme*, a nonalcoholic beverage made from milk, mashed sweet corn, cinnamon and vanilla.

Orientation

The Interamericana runs from east to west through La Chorrera, slowing to one sluggish lane in each direction as vehicles enter and exit the highway from side streets. However, most people pass the city by on the 28km-long tollway (US$0.50) that bypasses around the city.

Information

There is no tourist office in La Chorrera, but you can obtain reliable information from the **Instituto Nacional de Cultura** (INAC; ☎ /fax 253-2306; Calle Maria Leticia; ☼ 8am-5pm Mon-Fri, 10am-2pm Sat), 75m north of the Interamericana, at the east end of town (the turnoff is 100m before the Super 99 supermarket). The office, located in an art school, can tell you (in Spanish) about the town's culture and festivals (see also Festivals & Events, p135).

There's an **Internet café** just beyond the Super 99. Most **banks** in La Chorrera are conveniently located on the Interamericana halfway through town. The **post office** (Calle San Francisco) is two blocks south of the Interamericana.

Waterfalls

La Chorrera has only one true tourist attraction and, sadly, it isn't what it once was. **El Chorro** is a series of cascades on the Río Caimito, the last of which takes a 30m plunge into a broad swimming hole. Years ago the Caimito was a raging river, and its banks were swathed in pristine jungle. Today, much of the river has been siphoned off upstream and the area is poorly maintained.

To get here from the Interamericana, turn north onto Calle Larga at the Banistmo and drive 1km until you reach an intersection with a Super La Fortuna market on one side and a Mini Super Pacifico market on the other. Turn right just before the minimarket and then stay to the left on the road. The falls are at the end of this road, 1km from the intersection. You can also hire a taxi (US$1.50 each way) or hail a bus (US$0.35) with 'Calle Larga' scrawled on its windshield; they run all day.

Lago Gatún

Adventurous souls might want to venture to Lago Gatún (Gatún Lake), which is easily reached from La Chorrera. To get to the lake by car, turn off the Interamericana onto the unmarked road beside the Caja de Ahorros, which is 100m west of the Banco del Istmo and turn off for El Chorro. Proceed north 800m to the Plaza de 28 de Noviembre, on the right side of the road. Just beyond the plaza, on a corner on the left side of the street, you'll see a butcher shop called Carniceria Victor Loo. Turn left onto the street in front of Victor Loo. (The street's unmarked and no one seems to know the name, hence all these landmarks instead of street names. However, most people know this as the road to Mendoza, or *'calle a Mendoza.'*)

To reach Lago Gatún from here, stay on the road to Mendoza for the 16.9km and continue on another 5km; this will put you at lake's edge. There's a pier there and at it you can always find a boatman who will take you fishing for US$25 for two hours. When you've returned with your catch, walk from the pier up the road a little way to the Club Campetre Arco Iris, where there are some *bohíos* (thatched-roof huts). There, for a few dollars, someone will gladly cook your fish for you. Be prepared: bring at least a plate and a fork with you.

If you're relying on public transportation, back at the Caja de Ahorros store, catch a bus with 'Mendoza' or 'Mendoza/Represa' on the windshield and tell the driver that you want to go to Lago Gatún (US$1.50).

Festivals & Events

The region is known for its beautiful folkloric dances, which can best be seen during its popular fair. La Feria de La Chorrera lasts 10 days and is held in late January or early February; dates vary from year to year. The festivities also include parades, a rodeo and cockfights. La Chorrera is also known for drum dances that have their origin in African music brought by slaves.

Sleeping & Eating

Hospedaje Lamas (☎ 253-7887; Av de las Américas; d with fan/air-con US$14/18; 🆒) Near the west end of town, this place features 10 modest rooms, all with somewhat firm beds, private, cold-water bathrooms, TVs and tiled floors.

La Carreta Carbon (Interamericana; US$5-10) On the highway right before the Super 99, this pleasant thatched-roof restaurant serves good grilled meats and seafood.

Shangri La (Interamericana; mains US$5-9) For Chinese food, locals recommend this place near the eastern end of town.

Leonardo Pizzeria (Interamericana; pizzas US$4-11) A few blocks west of Shangri La, you'll find decent pizzas and pastas best enjoyed on the open-air patio out front.

El Chichemito (cnr Calles L Oeste & 26 Norte; 🕒 7:30am-10:30pm) An excellent place to try *chicheme*, the favored drink in La Chorrera, is this takeout restaurant. As you're driving west on the Interamericana, turn right onto Calle 26 Norte (just beyond the 'bbb' shoe store sign) and look for the restaurant, 30m further on the left.

At El Chichemito you can also try the *boyo chorrenano*, a sweet-corn tamale filled with marinated chicken and spices. The women who make it and other *boyos* (fillings vary; five kinds are made) insist that they're the best in town, and the number of people who flock to this corner stand evidently agree.

Getting There & Away

East- and west-bound buses stop at the Delta station, opposite the Pribanco bank and Matrox pharmacy on the Interamericana. Buses for Panama City (US$1.25, one hour) leave every eight minutes. Ask for the express bus or you'll be making frequent stops. There are plenty of taxis in town.

CAPIRA

Along the Interamericana, around the town of Capira (57km from Panama City), you'll reach an excellent cheese shop on the left hand side of the road. **Quesos Chela** (Interamericana; 🕒 10am-5pm Mon-Sat) is an institution, and few Panamanian drivers heading along this road can pass by without stopping. It's a nondescript shop that usually has piping hot fresh cheese and meat empanadas. A long counter, full of sweets and delicious cheeses (string, mozzarella, farmers, ricotta), lines the store. The cheese shop is right next door to a Texaco and a Mr Precio supermarket.

PARQUE NACIONAL Y RESERVA BIOLÓGICA ALTOS DE CAMPANA

The easy-to-miss turnoff for this national park is 25km southwest of La Chorrera, on the western side of the Interamericana. More specifically, it's at the top of a steep and windy section of the Interamericana known locally as the Loma Capana. From the turnoff, a rocky road winds 4.6km to an **ANAM ranger station** (park fee US$1; camping per night US$5) at the entrance to the park, which is located on Cerro Campana; pay fees here. Camping is allowed but there are no facilities.

About 200m beyond the station there's a lookout point from which you have a fantastic view of mostly deforested but completely un-inhabited mountains and the Pacific Ocean. Here you're at 1007m and the breeze is very refreshing.

This park requires at least several hours to be appreciated because it's best viewed on foot. Starting at the road's end, beyond the microwave tower, trails will take you into some lovely forest, which is on the much greener Atlantic slope. The difference between the deforested Pacific and the lush Atlantic slopes is nowhere more evident.

Bird watchers are almost certain to see scale-crested pygmy-tyrant, orange-bellied trogon and chestnut-capped brush-finch. The list of rare possibilities includes the slaty antwren, the white-tipped sicklebill and the purplish-backed quail-dove.

No buses go up the road leading to the park. You pretty much need to have your own vehicle, rely on the services of a guide company or do some rather serious hiking to get in. However, getting to the turnoff for the park is easy. Virtually any bus using that section of the Interamericana will drop you there; indeed, there's a bus stop beside the turnoff. Getting picked up isn't a problem during the day, either, as there are many buses that pass by the turnoff during daylight hours.

PUNTA CHAME
pop 390

The turnoff from the Interamericana for Punta Chame is immediately east of the tiny hamlet of Bejuco, 13.6km west of the turnoff for Parque Nacional Altos de Campana. The paved road that links the Interamericana to the point first winds past rolling hills, then passes flat land that consists mainly of shrimp farms and red and white mangroves, and then passes dry forest. Few people live along this 25km road because very little rain falls in the area and brackish water makes farming difficult.

Punta Chame is a one-road town on a long, 300m wide peninsula, with residences and vacant lots lining both sides. To the north is a muddy bay; to the east is the Pacific. The bay is popular with windsurfers, but there's no windsurfing equipment available for rent here. The beach on the Pacific side (Playa Chame) has lovely sand, but almost no one comes here due to its inconvenient location and its lack of facilities. Also, due to the number of stingrays

that nestle in the sand 50m to 100m from shore, locals don't swim on the bay side during low tide.

Sleeping & Eating

Decent food is available at **Hotel Punta Chame** (☎ 240-5498; fax 263-6590; cabin US$55), the only accommodation on the point, but the accommodations are pretty shabby. The beds form a U-shape when you sit on them and the rates are excessive. It has two concrete-walled cabins, three rooms in a four-unit trailer home (US$44 per unit), and two stand-alone trailer homes for rent (US$120).

As you enter Punta Chame, on the right side of the street you'll see a sign for **Fundación Amigos de las Tortugas Marinas** (☎ 227-5091 in Panama City, cellular ☎ 630-1347, 630-3612; cabin per person US$30). The Friends of Sea Turtles Foundation was founded by brother and sister Ramon and Vilma Morales in 1998 to reverse the declining numbers of sea turtles returning to nest on Punta Chame-area beaches every year. Here, there are several hatcheries, where a turtle hunter-turned savior hatches sea turtles and releases them when they are of a good size. To help finance their project, the Moraleses had several cabins built next to the hatcheries. These looked to be comfortable, but you'd be wise to bring mosquito netting.

Getting There & Away

To get to Punta Chame from the Interamericana, catch a bus at the stop at the Punta Chame turnoff (at Bejuco). A bus to the point (US$1) leaves hourly from 6:30am to 5:30pm daily.

BEACHES

Starting just south of the town of Chame and continuing along the Pacific coast for the next 40km are dozens of beautiful beaches that are popular weekend retreats for Panama City residents. About half of these beaches are in Panamá Province, while the remainder are in Coclé Province (see p139).

The beaches are quite similar to one another: all are wide, covered with salt-and-pepper sand and fairly free of litter. The waves in the vicinity of five of the beaches (Playa Malibú, Playa Serena, Playa Teta, Playa El Palmar and Playa Río Mar) attract surfers. See Surfing in the Directory (p293) for details.

BEACHES

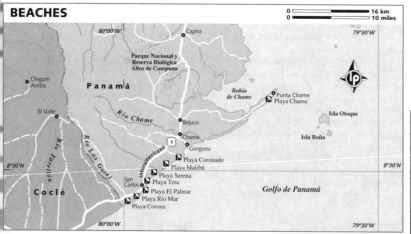

The most popular of these beaches can be reached by local bus or taxi from the Interamericana. Taxis can be hailed at the turnoffs for the beaches and are inexpensive.

Gorgona

Six kilometers southwest of the turnoff for Punta Chame is the turnoff for Gorgona, a small oceanside community with a few accommodations. The long, curving beach is mostly black sand – lots of iron and very hot. However, the surf is free of riptides and relatively safe for swimming.

There are two places to stay in Gorgona, which, except for the beach, has little to offer the tourist. **Cabañas de Playa Gorgona** (☎ 269-2433; www.propanama.com/gorgona; cabin weekdays/weekends from US$25/35;) is popular with Panamanian families. It offers 40 concrete cabins, some able to accommodate big families. All have kitchenettes and air-con, and there's a pool. The hotel also has beach property, which is open to all its guests and contains two pools, and lots of simple thatched-roofed *palapas*.

El Canadian (☎ 240-6066; cabin weekdays/weekends from US$50/60;) offers seven concrete cabins, all with air-con, firm beds, kitchenette and private cold-water bathroom. Some cabins might be better than others; ask to see at least two. The Canadian owner speaks English and Spanish. There's an adults' pool, a kids' pool and a full bar. It's a minute's walk from the beach.

A few kilometers west along the highway is **Restaurante Bar Mi Posada** (Interamericana; mains US$3-6) in Las Lajas, 200m east of the turnoff for Playa Coronado. This place is very popular and has air-con and lots of cheap, tasty food.

Playa Coronado

The turnoff from the Interamericana for Playa Coronado, an affluent beachside community, is 4km southwest of the turnoff for Gorgona. The sand is salt-and-pepper with black patches, and is very hot to the touch on a sunny day. There are far better beaches to the west.

SLEEPING & EATING

Corowalk Inn (☎ 240-1516; d weekdays/weekends US$44/66) Right at the turnoff to Coronado you'll spot this inn and shopping center. Although the location leaves a little to be desired as it's too far to walk to the beach, the place has a country inn feel to it and the rooms are quite nice – with tall ceilings, modern, comfortable furnishings and good beds.

Coronado Hotel & Resort (☎ 240-4444; www.coronadoresort.com; d from US$165) Coronado is a true resort. Its 75 standard rooms are all gorgeous and spacious with every amenity, and there are 12 grand suites, six with kitchenettes. The resort also has a top-notch beachside golf course, a good restaurant and another more elegant one, tennis courts, a weekend casino, and other luxuries such as Jacuzzis, saunas, pools, an exercise room, bars and so on. Guests are shuttled to and from its beachside property, which features a lovely pool and bar, and guests can rent kayaks, jet skis and other water toys.

There are two good restaurants in the area.

Restaurante Los Che's (Interamericana; mains US$6-12) Beside the turnoff for Playa Coronado is this attractive place with excellent but pricey food, such as sandwiches (US$4), pasta (US$5), grilled sea bass (US$8) and lobster thermidor (US$18). Los Che's is well known for its rotisserie-cooked meats and fish, and lobster and clams.

Club Turístico Malibu (mains US$7-13) This open-air spot, a few doors down from the Corowalk Inn, serves fairly decent plates of grilled corvina (US$7) and langostinos (US$12).

GETTING THERE & AWAY

To get to the Coronado Hotel & Resort from the highway, take one of the van buses that park under the mango tree beside the Texaco station at the Playa Coronado turnoff from 6am to 7:30pm daily; one departs every 20 minutes. They charge US$0.25 to take you to the Coronado Hotel & Resort. Taxis with longer hours are available in Bejuco, 9km northeast on the Interamericana. If you have your own vehicle, just head into Playa Coronado and ask the guard at the gate to point toward the hotel you want. To get a taxi back to the highway, ask your hotel to call one for you.

Playa El Palmar

This mostly white-sand beach, 10km west of the Playa Coronado turnoff and 1.8km from the Interamericana, has several hotels along the water, including a surf camp. On the weekend it is often packed with Panamanians having a good time. The turnoff for this beach is at San Carlos (take a left at the Glidden paint sign).

Hotel Palmar Surf Beach & School (☎ 240-8004; www.palmarpoint.com; camping per person US$5, tr/q/ste US$40/50/90;) This handsome spot on the beach is an excellent choice for those wanting to surf or who are interested in learning to. Rooms are basic and minimally furnished with air-con and private bathrooms. They also offer a cozy suite (with kitchen) that sleeps up to six. Surf lessons here are

US$25 per hour, and the owner can also arrange surf trips throughout Panama. There's a thatched-roof bar where you can get tidy piña coladas and listen to the waves on the shore. You can rent boards here and the English-speaking owner will pick you up in San Carlos if he knows you're coming.

Bay View Hotel & Resort (☎ 240-9621; d weekdays/weekends US$50/60) This new hotel on the beach looks lovely from the outside, but it doesn't offer much value for the money. Rooms here are basic and rather cramped and the hotel had already shown signs of wear after only a few weeks of being open. The pool is nice, as is the restaurant overlooking the beach. A wide variety of seafood is served for around US$9 a plate.

Playa Río Mar

Two kilometers west of San Carlos along the Interamericana is the turnoff for this small community, which has several hotels near the beach.

Hotel Playa Río Mar (☎ 240-8027; fax 264-2272; d weekdays/weekends US$33/43;) This unsigned place 800m from the highway is on a bluff overlooking the ocean. Located 95km from Panama City, this place is a popular weekend retreat for residents of the capital. The hotel has a pool, a bar and a restaurant. Below it is another good surfing beach. The 20 rooms each have a little table, dresser, air-con and small TV. Rooms numbered 15, 16 and 17 are best. As with many hotels along this coast, there's a chance that you'll have the place to yourself on weekdays.

Río Mar Surf Camp (☎ 240-9128; www.riomar surf.com; s/d/tr with fan US$15/19/24, s/d/tr with air-con US$24/30/35;) Surfers should consider staying at this place just a two-minute walk from the beach. Eight *cabañas* set on a pleasant lawn offer small but clean accommodations. There's a rancho in the middle of the property where you can unwind in one of the hammocks. You can use the kitchen for US$5 a day (you'll want to bring your own food or else you'll be eating in the Hotel Playa Río Mar restaurant). There are surfboards available for hire (US$10/20 for short/long boards), and the owner gives classes for US$20 per hour. He also leads surf tours around the country. See the website for details.

Coclé Province

CONTENTS

El Valle	141
Santa Clara	147
Río Hato & Farallón	148
Antón	149
Penonomé	149
La Pintada	151
Albergue Ecológico La Iguana	152
Trinidad Spa & Lodge	152
Parque Nacional Omar Torrijos & La Rica	153
Parque Arqueológico del Caño	154
Natá	154
Aguadulce	155

COCLÉ PROVINCE

Coclé – land of sugar, salt and presidents. More sugar has been refined in this province, more salt has been produced here, and more Panamanian presidents have been born in Coclé than in any other province. These are facts in which the people of Coclé take great pride, but the province isn't without a lion's share of tourist attractions as well.

Coclé is home to mountains and coast – lovely settings for exploring, relaxing or simply soaking up the scenery. The mountain town of El Valle has an Indian arts and crafts market, lovely nature scenes and intriguing petroglyphs. Further west along the Cordillera Central, the landscape is defined by peaks that resemble the famous karst formations of southern China.

The overlooked Parque Nacional Omar Torrijos has some of the most amazing forests in Panama. Orchid-covered waterfalls, lush mountain peaks and virgin cloud forest make for some beautiful hikes from the village of La Rica, located inside the park.

Away from the coast but not quite into the foothills is Penonomé, Coclé's bustling provincial capital, famous for its hats, its Carnaval and its patron saint festival. Nearby Natá is one of the oldest cities in the country, and is also home to one of the oldest churches in the Americas.

Among the province's more obscure attractions is La Pintada, where a cigar factory produces the country's best *habanos* (Havana cigars). There's also the coastal town of Aguadulce (Sweet Water), with swimming pools built in tideland.

Putting an accent on Coclé are its many festivals, ranging from an aquatic parade in Penonomé to a tomato festival in Natá. And not to disappoint those of you whose breath quickened at the earlier mention of salt and sugar, it *is* possible to tour a huge sugar refinery here, and you *can* look out upon salt flats all day.

COCLÉ PROVINCE

HIGHLIGHTS

- Horseback riding in the tranquility of mountainous **El Valle** (p144)
- Taking long walks along empty stretches of beach around **Santa Clara** (p147)
- Hiking through dense forest in **Parque Nacional Omar Torrijos** (p153) as tanagers flit about
- Browsing for souvenirs and smokes in **La Pintada** (p151), home to both an artisan market and a world-class cigar factory
- Resting in the cool interior of the splendid colonial **Iglesia de Natá** (p154), completed in 1522

★ Parque Nacional Omar Torrijos

★ La Pintada

El Valle ★

Santa Clara ★

★ Natá

| ▪ AREA: 6075 SQ KM | ▪ ELEVATION: 1626M | ▪ POPULATION: 212,100 |

COCLÉ PROVINCE

National Parks

Parque Nacional Omar Torrijos (p153) is a lovely national park that remains largely overlooked owing to its difficult access. You'll need a good 4WD, or plan on walking a bit (at least one hour) to reach the entrance. Once there you'll be rewarded with some prime bird watching through lovely forest, and the possibility of viewing both the Atlantic and Pacific Oceans. The trails here are in excellent condition.

Getting There & Around

Several of the towns listed here (Penonomé, Natá, Aguadulce) straddle the Interamericana, with many buses passing in both directions (west toward David and east

toward Panama City). Penonomé is the transit point for La Pintada, Parque Nacional Omar Torrijos and Chiguiri Arriba (Trinidad Spa & Lodge).

EL VALLE

pop 6900

This picturesque town (officially El Valle de Antón), 123km west of Panama City, is nestled in the crater of a giant extinct volcano. The volcano erupted three million years ago with such force that it blew off its top, creating a crater 5km across – one of the largest in the Americas. The crater gradually filled with rainwater, and a large lake resulted.

The lake level fell markedly between 25,000 and 10,000 BC. Eventually, through erosion or collapse, a breach opened at the present site of Chorro de Las Mozas (Young Women's Falls) and the entire lake drained. Later, Indians moved into the valley to farm its fertile soil, but to date no one has attempted to determine when they arrived.

A road suitable for 4WD vehicles was carved from the Interamericana to the valley. That horribly rutted 28km road was greatly improved in 1997. Today an elevated, paved road allows motorists to reach El Valle from Panama City in little more than two hours.

Today El Valle is a tranquil town ringed by verdant forest and jagged peaks. Sparkling creeks add to the beauty of the valley and, at 1000m, El Valle is much cooler than Panama's coastal towns.

El Valle is known for its small handicrafts market; it's also a superb place for walking, hiking or horseback riding. Many trails lead into the hills around the valley and, because they are often used by Indians, they are well defined.

Nature lovers, and birders in particular, won't be disappointed. The valley's forests offer very good bird watching (various hummingbirds abound, such as the green hermit, the violet-headed hummingbird and the white-tailed emerald), and El Valle is home to an impressive set of waterfalls and some rare golden frogs.

People who stand to gain from increased tourism to the area like to mention El Valle's *arboles cuadrados* (square-trunked trees) and La India Dormida, a set of nearby peaks that vaguely resemble the silhouette of a sleeping Indian princess – both of which require a bit of imagination.

Orientation

The road that heads north to El Valle from the Interamericana becomes Av Central once it hits the eastern edge of the valley. Av Central is El Valle's main street, along which are numerous hotels and restaurants and most of the town's businesses. Many of the roads branching off Av Central lead to yet more hotels and restaurants.

Av Central ends just west of the center of town. Here you can turn right and proceed 100m or so until the road forks. The branch to the left – Calle La Reforma – reaches the Cabañas Potosí after about 800m. The branch to the right – Calle del Macho – leads to a rain forest canopy ride and lovely waterfall (p143) and to some petroglyphs (p143).

Information

MEDICAL SERVICES

For your health needs, turn to the **Centro de Salud de El Valle** (☎ 983-6112; 24hr) near the eastern end of Av Central.

MONEY

Just east of Restaurante Santa Librada is a Banco Nacional de Panama **ATM** (Av Central).

INTERNET ACCESS

An **Internet café** (Av Central; per hr US$1; 8am-6:30pm Mon-Sat, 10:30am-2pm Sun) is on the main road near Motel-Restaurante Niña Delia.

POST

There's a **post office** (Calle del Mercado; 8am-4pm) behind the handicrafts market.

TOURIST INFORMATION

Instituto Panameño de Turismo (IPAT) operates a small **information booth** (☎ 983-6474) at the center of town next to the handicrafts market, though it is rarely staffed. Both the Residencial El Valle (p145) and Don Pepe (p145) sell good maps of the area (US$2).

Sights & Activities

HANDICRAFTS MARKET

More than anything else, El Valle is known for its **handicrafts market** (Av Central; 8am-6pm) to which Indians – mostly Ngöbe Buglé, but also some Emberá and Wounaan – bring vegetables, fruit and flowers to sell and trade and a variety of handicrafts to sell to tourists (most of whom are Panamanians from Panama City). There's a larger selection on weekends than there is on weekdays.

You can find traditional items like *bateas*, large trays carved from a local hardwood and used by the Ngöbe Buglé for tossing rice and corn. You can also find figurines, colorful baskets made from palms, gourds painted in brilliant colors, clay flowerpots, Panama hats, and birdcages made of sticks.

After browsing, be sure to visit the nearby shops beneath Residencial El Valle and Don Pepe, where you can find lots of high-quality handicrafts, some of which are made in a shop on the premises.

EL VALLE

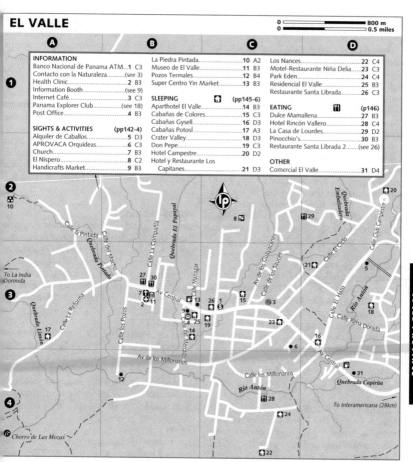

INFORMATION		
Banco Nacional de Panama ATM...**1**	C3
Contacto con la Naturaleza..........(see **3**)	
Health Clinic........................**2**	B3
Information Booth..................(see **9**)	
Internet Café......................**3**	C3
Panama Explorer Club.............(see **18**)	
Post Office.........................**4**	B3

SIGHTS & ACTIVITIES	(pp142-4)
Alquiler de Caballos.................**5**	D3
APROVACA Orquídeas..............**6**	C3
Church...............................**7**	B3
El Nispero...........................**8**	C2
Handicrafts Market.................**9**	B3

La Piedra Pintada...................**10**	A2
Museo de El Valle...................**11**	B3
Pozos Termales.....................**12**	B4
Super Centro Yin Market..........**13**	B3

SLEEPING		(pp145-6)
Aparthotel El Valle..................**14**	B3
Cabañas de Colores.................**15**	C3
Cabañas Gysell.......................**16**	D3
Cabañas Potosí......................**17**	A3
Crater Valley........................**18**	D3
Don Pepe............................**19**	C3
Hotel Campestre....................**20**	D2
Hotel y Restaurante Los Capitanes......................**21**	D3

Los Nances...........................**22**	C4
Motel-Restaurante Niña Delia.....**23**	C3
Park Eden............................**24**	C4
Residencial El Valle.................**25**	B3
Restaurante Santa Librada.........**26**	C3

EATING		(p146)
Dulce Mamallena....................**27**	B3
Hotel Rincón Vallero................**28**	C4
La Casa de Lourdes..................**29**	D2
Pinocchio's..........................**30**	B3
Restaurante Santa Librada 2.......(see **26**)	

OTHER		
Comercial El Valle...................**31**	D4

CANOPY ADVENTURE & CHORRO EL MACHO

The **Canopy Adventure** (El Valle ☎ 983-6547, Panama City ☎ 612-9176; canopy ride US$40, swim US$2, admission to falls US$2; ☑ 8am-4pm) is a suspended ride that uses cables, pulleys and a harness to allow you to view a rain forest from dozens of meters above the jungle floor. You'll be in a harness dangling among jungle trees as you ride from one platform to another (there are six in all), at times gliding over the 85m-high Chorro El Macho (The Manly Waterfall).

If you're afraid of heights or have a weak grip, pass on this adventure. Riders need to have at least a normal grip to brake themselves. Also, you must be at least 10 years old and weigh less than 200lbs. Unless you like

to expose your private parts to strangers, don't do this in a dress or short shorts.

You don't have to do the ride to admire Chorro El Macho or to take a dip in the bathing hole at its base. A large swimming pool made of rocks, surrounded by rain forest and fed by river water sits below the falls.

LA PIEDRA PINTADA

In the northwestern corner of the valley, in a neighborhood known as La Pintada (Colored Stone), is La Piedra Pintada – a huge boulder adorned with pre-Columbian carvings. Locals often fill in the grooves of the petroglyphs with chalk to facilitate their viewing, but their meaning isn't clearer. That doesn't prevent Guaymí children from

COCLÉ PROVINCE

giving their interpretation of the petroglyphs for US$2 (in Spanish only).

One of these interpreters, Seneida Milena Rivera, says she learned the 'story of the rock' at school. Amid a 10-minute explanation of the graffiti-like carvings, she took her bamboo pointing stick and identified an x carved into the rock. It represents the burial site of a powerful chief who died many centuries ago, she said. 'The site moos like a cow every time it rains,' she added.

Due to one report of theft from a vehicle near the entrance of the trail leading to the petroglyphs, it's best to come by bus even if you've got your own wheels. The site can be reached by a yellow school bus with 'Pintada' above the windshield. It passes along Av Central every 30 minutes, from 6am to 7pm (20¢ one way).

MUSEO DE EL VALLE
On the eastern side of El Valle's conspicuous church is the very modest **Museum of El Valle** (Av Central; admission US$0.25; ☉ 10am-2pm Sun), which contains exhibits of petroglyphs and ceramics left by Indians who lived in the area hundreds of years ago. There is also some religious art (the museum is owned by the church next door), mostly statues of Christ and the Virgin, and some information on El Valle's volcano.

SQUARE TREES & THE PRINCESS
Directly behind the Hotel Campestre is an intriguing thicket that supposedly contains **square-trunked trees** (arboles cuadrados). Well, they aren't round, but they're not exactly square, either. You might want to see them for yourself and then ponder, 'What's the big deal even if they are square?'

Ask any resident of El Valle to point out **La India Dormida** (The Sleeping Indian, also known as The Sleeping Indian Princess). The local will point to a mountain ridge that may resemble any number of things if you use your imagination. Ask a local to tell you the colorful myths behind the princess.

ZOO & GARDENS
About 1km north of Av Central is a zoo and gardens named **El Níspero** (☎ 983-6142; adult/child US$2/1; ☉ 7am-5pm). Most Latin American zoos are sad, cruel places. This is such a zoo. Here, for example, there are numerous eagles and hawks in a cage smaller than a walk-in closet. However, El Níspero is also one of the best places for seeing Panama's golden frogs (ranas doradas), as well as a decent collection of orchids. A taxi ride to the zoo costs about US$1.50 each way.

For the best selection of orchids (orquídeas) in the area, visit the pleasant **Aprovaca Orquídeas** (free admission; ☉ 9am-4pm daily). Some 32 volunteers work to maintain the lovely flowers inside the greenhouse (one of three in the area) and the grounds, and they welcome visitors to show off the 96 varieties of orchids cultivated. It's well worth a visit. Look for the 'Orquídeas' sign on the way into town.

POZOS TERMALES
On the west side of town (follow the signs) **Pozos Termales** (Thermal Baths; Calle los Pozos; admission US$1; ☉ 8am-5pm) is a place to soak away the afternoon. The forested complex is rustic, with two concrete swimming pools and an area (a bucket, to be more precise) for applying healing mud to one's skin.

HORSEBACK RIDING
Near the Hotel Campestre you'll see a sign for **Alquiler de Caballos** (☎ 646-5813; horse rental per hr US$3.50, with a guide per hr US$7), with a horse mural painted on the side of a building. The stable here has 30 horses, which make for some fine transportation to explore the nearby mountains. Guides speak Spanish only.

Tours
Next door to the Internet café, **Contacto con la Naturaleza** (☎ 623-4122, 629-3722; elvalle deanton@hotmail.com; Av Central) provides English- and Spanish-speaking guides for US$5 per hour. They can arrange trips to La India Dormida and overnight camping trips to other areas. Just avoid their city tour (which simply takes you to places in El Valle – Pozos Termales, the museum, the market – which you can easily visit on your own).

Based at Crater Valley Hotel (p144), the **Panama Explorer Club** (☎ 983-6939; www.pexclub .com) is an adventure tourism outfit that offers a wide range of activities. Available tours include hiking La India Dormida (US$20 per person, three to four hours), climbing and rappelling (US$20 per person, three to four hours), river kayaking (US$45 per person) and mountain biking tours (US$10 to US$15 per person). It also has an office in Panama City and offers trips from there.

Those planning a hiking or bird watching trip should stop at Cabañas Potosí (p145), where you can arrange a trip to La India Dormida for US$20. Or call top Panama guide **Mario Bernal Greco** (☎ 693-8213) directly; his mother runs the Cabañas Potosí.

Sleeping

Hotel y Restaurante Los Capitanes (☎ 983-6080; www.panamainfo.com/loscapitanes; Calle El Ciclo; d/ste from US$33/72) Features a number of handsome rooms with fine details, firm beds, spacious hot-water bathroom, TV and VCR. There are four wheelchair-accessible rooms and three lovely suites, with more on the way. There's a bar with DirecTV, an excellent restaurant (p146), a café and a children's pool. The owner-manager is a former captain in the German merchant marine, and he can arrange bike or horse rental. English, Spanish, German, Italian and French are spoken.

Hotel Rincón Vallero (☎ 983-6175; www.rinconvallero.com; Calle Espave; d/ste from US$83/105) In a lovely residential neighborhood, the Rincón Vallero has 14 comfortable rooms with air-con and private hot-water bathroom. There are also several attractive suites. Among the standard rooms, Nos 2 and 7 are tops. There's a restaurant with delicious food, and several lovely sitting areas.

Crater Valley (☎ 215-2330; www.crater-valley.com; d US$85-105; 🏊) This hotel and spa sits on beautifully tended grounds that include a pleasant swimming pool and a climbing wall. The rooms are nicely decorated with tall ceilings, colorfully painted walls and excellent beds. Some of the rooms have patios with hammocks and nice views. They also have a spa, and an adventure tourism outfit allows guests to take part in guided hikes, mountain biking and river rafting (p144).

Cabañas Potosí (☎ 983-6181; Calle La Reforma; campsites US$10, d cabin Mon-Fri US$30, Sat & Sun US$40) Cabañas Potosí lies about 1.5km west of the town center on peaceful, park-like grounds with lovely views of the craggy ridges ringing the valley. The four cabins have two beds apiece with private hot-water bathroom. You can camp here too (two-person tent provided). Excellent guides are available; English and Spanish are spoken.

Park Eden (☎ 938-6167; www.parkeden.com; Calle El Nance; d US$60-120, house from US$195) Park Eden, overflowing with country charm, is a beautiful retreat. This gorgeous home offers three very tastefully appointed rooms, plus a separate two-story house, a cottage and a little room behind the cottage. The owner is an American-trained designer, and it shows (his wife is from Ecuador). Mountain bike rental, guided hikes, and beach excursions are available.

La Casa de Lourdes (☎ 983-6450; glosinas@cableonda.net; d US$95-150; 🕒 Fri-Sun) Three lovely rooms are available for rent at this beautiful villa. Rooms are comfortable with good beds and private bathrooms and feature fine views out over the hills. The villa is foremost a restaurant (see p146).

Residencial El Valle (☎ 983-6536; residencialelvalle@hotmail.com; Av Central; s/d US$25/30) Friendly service and excellent rooms with private hot-water bath, TV and good beds come standard at this hotel. A handicrafts shop and popular restaurant are downstairs. Bikes can be rented (US$2 per hour, US$8 per day) and guides are available (US$10 per half day per person).

Don Pepe (☎ 983-6425; hoteldonpepe@hotmail.com; Av Central; s/d US$25/30) Next door to Residencial Al Valle, Don Pepe also offers big, comfortable rooms, and has a good downstairs restaurant. Bikes are also available, as is a washer and drier (US$1 per load). On a clear night, be sure to check out the view from the roof.

Los Nances (☎ 983-6126; Calle El Nance; d with breakfast US$50) This appealing private residence sits high above the valley floor and offers lovely views. The friendly English-speaking couple rents four of their bedrooms. An inviting indoor spa is available to guests.

Hotel Campestre (☎ 983-6146; www.hotelcampestre.com; Calle Club Campestre; d Mon-Fri US$44, Sat & Sun US$66, cabin US$60) The oldest hotel in town has 12 rooms in its original 1920s-era two-story lodge, plus 20 rooms in a 1990s addition. There are also three family-size cabins available. There's a restaurant, a bar, and a large fireplace in the main room.

Cabañas Gysell (☎ 983-6507; Av Central; d US$35-45) On the east side of town, Cabañas Gysell offers five comfortable rooms with private hot-water bathrooms.

Cabañas de Colores (☎ 983-6613; d from US$45) Three attractive cabins, each with the feel of a small house, lie in the owner's backyard. Each stucco-walled cabin has a lovely hot-water bathroom, double bed with a firm mattress, and local TV.

Motel-Restaurante Niña Delia (☎ 983-6110; Av Central; s/d/tr/q US$12/15/20/25) The recently renovated Motel-Restaurante Niña Delia offers excellent value for its six rooms. Each comes with good beds, TV and private bathroom (they will likely have hot water by the time you read this). They also have a good, inexpensive restaurant (below).

Aparthotel El Valle (☎ 692-2849; Calle del Mercado; ste from US$38) This complex features large, cheaply furnished suites with full kitchen, tiled floors, separate living quarters and private bathroom. An uninviting pool and gardens are out back. Discounts given for longer stays.

Restaurante Santa Librada (☎ 986-6376; Av Central; s/d US$10/15) Santa Librada has four clean rooms with soft mattresses and private cold-water bathroom.

Eating

Hotel y Restaurante Los Capitanes (☎ 983-6080; mains US$8-11; Calle El Ciclo; ⏰ 8:30am-8pm Sun-Thu, 7:30am-10pm Fri & Sat) The menu at this fine restaurant features German, French and Italian cuisine, with lots of fresh seafood. Specials change daily but always include tasty dishes like *jager* schnitzel, corvina *normandie* and a mixed plate of grilled meats (chicken, pork and meat). Don't miss the freshly baked cakes and pies or the *batidos* (fruit shakes). Warsteiner and other imported beers are available.

La Casa de Lourdes (☎ 983-6450; mains US$11-14; ⏰ 7-10pm Fri, noon-3pm & 7-10pm Sat, noon-3pm Sun) El Valle's most beautiful restaurant has the look and feel of a Tuscan villa. Situated on the back terrace with stunning views, Lourdes offers an eclectic menu of dishes like lobster and sweet corn risotto, pork chop with a port wine and guava sauce, and blackened corvina with tamarind. For dessert, decadent slices of chocolate pecan pie and bread pudding round out the menu. It's a lovely spot if you're around on the weekend. La Casa de Lourdes also rents rooms (weekends only; p145).

Hotel Rincón Vallero (☎ 983-6175; mains US$6-10; ⏰ breakfast, lunch & dinner) The cozy restaurant here is one of the El Valle's most charming. Beside a koi pond, diners enjoy plates

of fresh shrimp, sea bass, grilled corvina, chicken ravioli and grilled meats. They also have wine and cocktails.

Pinocchio's (☎ 983-6975; Av Central; pizzas US$3-8; ⏰ 11am-9pm Thu-Sun) This pizzeria makes tasty and cheap pizzas with a range of toppings. Also available here is rotisserie-cooked chicken, meaty burgers and tacos.

Dulce Mamallena (Av Central; pastries US$0.30-0.50) Next door to Pinocchio's, this place serves up fresh pastries and coffee daily.

Restaurante Santa Librada 2 (Av Central; mains US$3-4.50; ⏰ 8am-9pm) This popular restaurant serves good Panamanian food at attractive prices, such as *lomo de arroz* (roast beef with rice) and *bistec picado* (spicy shredded beef). Most sandwiches and breakfasts are under US$2. The restaurants' *sancocho de gallina* (a stew-like chicken soup) is excellent.

Don Pepe (☎ 983-6425; mains US$5-8; ⏰ 7:30am-9pm) and **Residencial El Valle** (mains US$5-8; ⏰ 7:30am-9pm), next door, both offer clean and inviting restaurants below the hotels. Dishes include ample seafood, chicken and meat entrées. They're both popular places.

Motel-Restaurante Niña Delia (☎ 983-6110; mains US$2.50-6; ⏰ 8am-8pm) You'll find a range of tasty Panamanian dishes here, from *típico* (typical) breakfasts and lunches (both US$2) to dinner plates of fresh jumbo shrimp (US$6). They also have fresh fruit juices. It's a lovely spot, with live music throughout the week.

Restaurante Dominguez (mains US$1.50-2; ⏰ 8am-3pm) This local lunch favorite just up the road from Niña Delia serves filling plates of fried chicken or fish at rock-bottom prices.

Comercial El Valle, on the eastern side of town, is the best grocery store in El Valle.

Getting There & Away

To leave El Valle you can hop aboard a bus traveling along Av Central; on average, they depart every 30 minutes. The buses' final destinations are painted on their windshields. If your next destination isn't posted, catch a bus going in the same direction and transfer when appropriate. To reach El Valle from the Interamericana, disembark at Las Uvas (marked by both a sign for El Valle and a pedestrian overpass), about 5km west of San Carlos. Minibuses pick up passengers at this turnoff and travel to El Valle (US$1 one hour, every 30 minutes).

Getting Around

Despite El Valle's small size, taxis ply Av Central all day long. You can go anywhere in town for US$2.

SANTA CLARA

The small community of Santa Clara, on the coast 11km southwest of the Interamericana turnoff for El Valle, offers visitors the loveliest beach along this stretch of coast and several cozy places to stay. The area around Santa Clara is arid and sparsely populated, with patches of thin, dry forest. If you are looking for a place with pleasing scenery where you can relax and/or explore, you'll find it here.

There are two Santa Clara turnoffs from the Interamericana; one is posted for the town and the other is posted for the beach (Playa Santa Clara). The first turnoff you'll see as you come from the east is the turnoff for town.

Activities

A few years ago, the owners of XS Memories (p147) launched **Kayak Panama** (☎ 993-3096; www.kayakpanama.com; tours per person from US$60) with canoeing guide **Sven Schiffer** (☎ /fax 993-3620; vsschiffer@cwp.net.pa). Now the foremost kayaking agency in the country, Kayak Panama offers a wide range of excursions, including trips on the Río Chame and the Río Santa Maria, salt marsh paddling tours and kayak trips from the top of the Continental Divide to the Caribbean. Tours have a three-person minimum. Kayak Panama operates only during the rainy season (April to November). English, German and Spanish are spoken.

Sleeping & Eating

If you go down the first turnoff for Santa Clara from the Interamericana for about 1km, you'll see signs for Las Veraneras and Las Sirenas.

Las Sirenas (Santa Clara ☎ 993-3235, Panama City 263-7577; traducsa@cwpanama.net; d US$80) One of the gems along this coastline, Las Sirenas is a peaceful spot consisting of 11 modern rooms with all the amenities, set on a lush hillside 150m from the crashing surf. Five rooms are particularly attractive, with very tall ceilings. All have kitchenette and dining area; there is no restaurant on the premises, making it wise to bring your own food.

Las Veraneras (☎ /fax 993-3313; lasveraneras@cwp .net.pa; cabin US$55) A little less charming than Las Sirenas, Las Varaneras consists of seven rustic two-story cabins set upon a knoll 150m from the ocean. Each of the cabins has ocean views from its front porch, a loft with a thatch roof, and four have kitchenette with fridge. There's a double bed on the ground floor and a double bed with a bunk single and a stand-alone single on the 2nd floor of each cabin. There's a beachside **restaurant** (☺ 8am-9pm) that serves cheap Panamanian plates.

XS Memories (☎ 993-3096; www.xsmemories. com; campsite per person US$3, motor home hookup with/without air-con per day US$12/8, d from US$55) Just north of the turnoff for Playa Santa Clara, 100m from the Interamericana, is this American owned and run outfit. The property contains three spacious guestrooms with air-con and private hot-water bathroom. One guestroom has a double bed and kitchenette, one has two double beds, and one has three double beds. There's also an excellent **restaurant** (☺ 8am-8pm Mon-Thu, 8am-10pm Fri-Sun) where they serve a famous burger (US$2.75) as well as sandwiches and filling plates of fish, steak or roast pork. Breakfasts are equally good. XS has 21 water, sewer and electrical hookups for motor homes, an area to pitch tents, an inviting swimming pool and a sports bar that has DirecTV.

Getting There & Away

To get to Santa Clara, just take any bus that would pass through Santa Clara and tell the bus driver to drop you in town. When it's time to leave Santa Clara, just stand at any of the bus stops in town and hail a bus going in the direction you want to go. From Santa Clara, you can catch onward buses west to Antón (US$1, 30 minutes, every 30 minutes) or Penonomé (US$1.75, one hour, every 30 minutes). It's also easy to catch a ride on buses heading as far as David (US$10, 5½ hours, every hour) and points along the way. Heading east, you can find buses to San Carlos (US$1, 30 minutes, every 20 minutes), Chame (US$1.25, 45 minutes, every 20 minutes) and Panama City (US$2.25, 1¾ hours, every 20 minutes).

Getting Around

Except late at night, there are always taxis parked beside the turnoff on the Interamericana for Santa Clara (the town, not the beach). You can take one for US$2 to get to any of the places mentioned previously. The beach is 1.8km from the Interamericana.

RÍO HATO & FARALLÓN

A few kilometers past the Santa Clara turnoff, you'll see signs for several large resorts in this area.

GHOSTS OF AN INVASION

About 1km past the Playa Santa Clara turnoff, you'll notice an open area where a wide, paved path stretches straight out from both sides of the Interamericana. This was once a key runway used by Noriega's forces, and it has some interesting history.

During the days of the Panama Defense Forces (PDF), there was a major army base here, known as Río Hato, to which the runway belonged. There were many barracks, an armory, a clinic and near the end of a 3km road that runs from the Interamericana to the coast, paralleling the runway, was Noriega's vacation home, near the hamlet of Farallón.

At 1am on December 20, 1989, the 'H-hour' of the US invasion of Panama, two F-117A stealth fighters swooped undetected out of the night sky and dropped two 2000lb bombs near the Río Hato PDF barracks. The bombing marked the first time that the USA's most sophisticated fighter plane was used in combat.

The US secretary of defense said at the time that the planes performed their missions flawlessly, precisely hitting their intended targets after flying all night from their base in Nevada. Later, the Pentagon admitted that the pilots had confused their targets, hitting one out of sequence and badly missing the second. The planes, incidentally, cost US$106 million each.

Río Hato was also where the US Army suffered its highest concentration of casualties during the invasion, but most were not the result of combat. Moments after the bombs exploded, an 850-man contingent of army rangers parachuted onto the runway. However, because they jumped from an altitude of only 150m and landed on pavement, many of them sustained serious injuries. More than two dozen members of the elite force were incapacitated by broken legs, torn knee ligaments and other injuries.

One of the most interesting things about all this is not the army's errors in planning the jump, but that the US military acted with great humanity in its bombing. Strange as that may sound, the targets the stealths were ordered to hit were empty fields near barracks filled with young Panamanian soldiers, not the barracks themselves. By dropping bombs near the barracks, the US military hoped to scare the soldiers into surrendering and thus avoid unnecessary bloodshed. In fact, hundreds of Panamanian soldiers at Río Hato did surrender immediately. For all the criticism leveled at the USA during and after the invasion, there were many such instances of restraint that went unmentioned.

Post-invasion, the site of the former PDF base is profoundly creepy. During a past visit, the camouflaged buildings, 11 in all, stood vacant among tall weeds. Their windows were blown out, their walls pockmarked by bullets. Along one long wall was a wobbly line of holes made by heavy machine-gun fire, most likely .50-caliber rounds unleashed by a helicopter gunship. Small trees grew in rooms where PDF soldiers once carried out their orders. Scattered about were the burned hulks of cars and trucks.

A kilometer or so south of the scene of the fighting is the hamlet of Farallón, which is home to a small general store and simple homes housing a few hundred people. A little further down the road, the houses become increasingly fancy and the walls around them increasingly impenetrable. Many were owned by Noriega's top officers during the 1980s. One – the abandoned two-story house on the right side of the road, pocked from top to bottom with bullet holes – was owned by the general himself.

There's an interesting little war story attached to this residence. One of the reasons US President George Bush ordered the invasion was to arrest Noriega and bring him to trial on drug-trafficking charges. A big story on the third day of the invasion was US General Maxwell Thurman's announcement that US soldiers had found more than 50kg of cocaine in Noriega's Farallón house. It wasn't until a month later, after persistent questioning from reporters, that the Pentagon admitted that the suspicious substance was actually a flour-like powder used to make tamales.

Royal Decameron Costa Blanca Beach Resort
(☎ 214-3535; r with meals per person from US$75; ☜)
is an enormous complex on the beach at
Farallón, featuring 600 rooms, plus tennis
courts, restaurants, swimming pools, dis-
cotheque and so on.

Another giant, all-inclusive resort overlooking the beach, **Barceló Playa Blanca** (www
.barcelo.com; r per person from US$100; ☜) has 219
rooms, 19 junior suites and all the amenities (swimming pools, tennis, golf, restaurants etc). As far as resorts go, many rate the
Decameron slightly higher than this one.

Back out on the Interamericana and 1km
west of the turnoff for Farallón is Río Hato,
which is home to **Hospedaje Las Delicias** (☎ 993-
3718; d with fan/air-con US$12/21), a very good-value
hotel located on the north side of the highway.
There are 10 comfortable, sponge-painted
rooms here, five with fans only and five with
air-con. All have private bathroom.

ANTÓN
pop 9000

Antón, 15km west of Farallón, is in the
center of a lush valley that's sprinkled with
rice fields and cattle ranches. It has little
to offer the tourist, except for its natural
beauty, its annual **patron saint festival** (January 13 to 16) and its folkloric festival, **Toro
Guapo** (October 13 to 15). The people of
Antón seemingly live for these events.
There's a bank, several restaurants and a
couple of gas stations in town.

Sleeping & Eating

As you drive into Anton along the Interamericana, you'll notice several hotels on
your approach to town.

Hotel Rivera (☎ 987-2245; d with fan US$20, s/d
with TV & air-con US$25/27.50; ☜) The best option
in town, with 30 rooms with good beds and
private bathroom.

Pensión Panama (☎ 239-3163; d US$10, with TV
US$12) Directly across the street from the
Hotel Rivera, this raggedy place has cinderblock walls, soft beds and private cold-
water bathroom. It was in the midst of a
renovation when we stopped in.

PENONOMÉ
pop 17,000

This provincial capital 144km west of Panama City and 16km northwest of Antón is
a bustling city with a history. The town was

founded in 1581; by 1671 it had become so
prominent that it served as the isthmus' capital after the destruction of the first Panama
City (now known as Panamá Viejo), until
Nueva Panamá (New Panama) was founded
a few years later.

Today, the city offers the tourist two
principal attractions: its annual festivals
and its traditional Panama hats.

Orientation

Penonomé straddles the Interamericana.
On the eastern side of town, the highway
forks around an Esso gas station. One
branch, Av Juan Demostenes Arosemena,
goes to the right, and the other, the Interamericana, goes to the left.

Av Juan Demostenes Arosemena is the
city's main street. Along it are two banks,
a post office and the town church. The
avenue actually ends at the church, which
faces the central plaza. During Carnaval,
the plaza and every street for three blocks
around it are packed with people.

Information

For laundry, **Lavandería El Sol** (Av Juan Demostenes
Arosemena; ☉ 8am-6pm Mon-Sat) is across the street
from the Esso gas station.

The city's principal **hospital** (Interamericana)
is at the eastern end of town.

For banking, try **BBVA** (Interamericana) or
Banco Nacional de Panamá and Banistmo,
both along Av Juan Demostenes. All have
ATMs.

The **post office** (Av Juan Demostenes Arosemen-
ais) is in the Palacio Municipal, behind the
church. There's a **mercado público** (public market;
☉ 4:30am-3:30pm) that's fun to browse near
the central plaza. There is no tourist office
in town.

Festivals & Events

Carnaval, held during the four days preceding Ash Wednesday, is a huge happening
in Penonomé. In addition to the traditional
festivities (the dancing, the masks, the costumes, the queen's coronation), floats here
are literally *floated* down a tributary of the
Río Zaratí.

Less popular but still a big crowd pleaser
is Penonomé's **patron saint festival**. This festival is generally held on December 8 and
9 (or the following Saturday if both these
dates fall on weekdays). Following a special

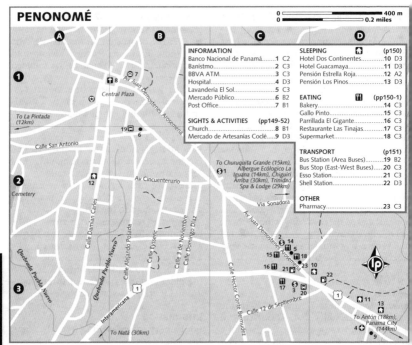

mass, Penonomé's Catholics carry a statue of the saint through the city's streets. The mass and procession seem incidental to the celebration that takes place outside the church for two days.

Sleeping

Hotel Guacamaya (☎ 991-0117; hguacamaya@cwpanama.com.pa; Interamericana; d/ste US$22/33) Near the point where the Interamericana forks, Hotel Guacamaya has the best digs in town. Among the 40 rooms and suites you'll find clean and comfortable accommodations with good beds, private hot-water bathroom and cable TV. The 'suites' are merely larger rooms (with a hair dryer) that face the highway. The quieter rooms have better views onto the mountains. Excellent value.

Hotel Dos Continentes (☎ 997-9326; fax 997-9390; Interamericana; d US$20-22) A few doors down from the Hotel Guacamaya, Hotel Dos Continentes has 61 guestrooms and a popular cafeteria. The hotel has a newly renovated section featuring tile floors, comfortable beds, good lighting and modern hot-water bathrooms.

The old part has gloomy, battered rooms short on style and comfort.

Pensión Los Pinos (Interamericana; d with fan/air-con US$12/14) At the entrance to town, this pensión has clean rooms with decent-to-soft beds and private cold-water bathroom.

Pensión Estrella Roja (Calle Damían Carles; r US$6) If you're traveling on a dime, this crummy pensión several blocks from the central plaza may be in the cards. It has OK beds, fan and thin plywood walls, with one exposed lightbulb per room. There are four showers and four toilets for 20 rooms.

Eating

Parrillada El Gigante (Interamericana; mains US$3-5) A short walk to the west of the Esso station, this pleasant, open-sided restaurant serves traditional Panamanian food, good pizzas and delicious Lebanese dishes (falafel, hot pita bread), thanks to the Lebanese owner-chef. The *sancocho de gallina* (chicken soup) is also quite good.

Restaurante Las Tinajas (Interamericana; mains US$2-3) Opposite El Gigante, this small restaurant serves typical Panamanian food (like *bistec picado* – spicy shredded beef) in a buffet style. There aren't always many options, but it's a popular place nonetheless.

Gallo Pinto (Av Juan Demostenes Arosemena; mains US$2-4) This is an inexpensive and low-key eatery. Hot sandwiches are a good choice; they also serve fried corvina and beefsteak.

The **Chinese restaurant** (Interamericana; mains US$4-6.50) at Hotel Guacamaya has a range of hearty meals (lo mein, roast tofu, shrimp with almonds), served in a nicely air-conditioned setting.

The **restaurant** (Av Juan Demostenes Arosemena; breakfast, lunch & dinner) at Hotel Dos Continentes is usually crowded. Sandwiches, steaks and seafood are among the selections.

The town's top bakery (with nice-looking cinnamon rolls) and a supermarket lie nearby the Esso station.

Getting There & Away

Buses traveling to and from Penonomé via the Interamericana use a small parking lot opposite the Hotel Dos Continentes as a passenger pick-up and drop-off point. Buses pass through in either direction every 10 to 15 minutes. Area buses, such as those to Churuquita Grande (US$1, 45 minutes, every 30 minutes), Aguadulce (US$1, 30 minutes, every 20 minutes), La Pintada (US$1, every 30 minutes), San Pedro, Chiguirí Arriba (US$1.50, 80 minutes, seven per day) and El Copé (US$1.50, one hour), use a station two blocks southeast of the central plaza. From Penonomé there are frequent buses to Panama City (US$4.25, 2½ hours, every 20 minutes) and David (US$7, 4½ hours, every 35 minutes).

Getting Around

Due to its size and importance, Penonomé has no shortage of taxis. The best place to hail one is by the Esso gas station, near the entrance to town. You can also find one near the central plaza. The fare for any destination in town is not usually more than US$3, and often it's half that.

LA PINTADA

pop 4000

This small foothill town, which boasts an artisans' market and a cigar factory, is 12km northwest of downtown Penonomé. Anyone with a real hankering for handicrafts or a love of cigars would enjoy a visit to La Pintada.

Mercado de Artesanías La Pintada

The **Pintado Artisan's Market** (983-0313; 9am-4pm) specializes in Penonomé-style Panama hats. The material used in Panamas occasionally varies from one town to the next. Here the headgear is made of *bellota* and also of *pita*, which is related to cactus. There are several *bellota* and *pita* plants growing in front of the market, so you can see what they look like.

Other items of particular interest are dolls wearing handmade folkloric costumes, *seco* bottle covers made from hat palm, and handmade brooms.

The market is easy to find. As you drive through La Pintada on the main road from Penonomé, you'll come to a very large soccer field on the left side of the road. The market is on the far side of this field.

Cigars Joyas de Panama

To get to the **Cigars Joyas de Panama** (/fax 983-0304; joyapan@yahoo.com) from the artisans' market, just drive southeast from the market, straight toward Penonomé (ignore the Pana American Cigar Co, which is en route to Joyas de Panama). You'll come to Cafe Coclé, on your right; take the well-maintained dirt road just beyond it (the road that initially parallels the paved road, not the next right). Follow this road about 1km until you see a simple thatched-roof restaurant on the right side of the road immediately followed by the open-sided cigar factory with a corrugated metal roof. You've arrived!

The factory's owner, Miriam Padilla, began growing tobacco in La Pintada with three Cubans in 1982. They went their separate ways in 1987, when the Cubans emigrated to Honduras to open a cigar factory. Left to her own devices, Miriam sent choice samples of her tobacco to tourists and other people she'd met in Panama over the years, seeking investors for a factory.

Today Miriam and her son, Braulio Zurita, are La Pintada's largest employers, employing 80 workers who make a total of 22,000 cigars a day. The employees work at rows of desks in a long, concrete-sided, aluminum-roofed, one-story building the size of a large home, which is the pride of the neighborhood.

The cigars are made in an assembly process that begins at one end of the building with leaf separation from stem, and ends at the other end of the building with the

---

PANAMA HATS

Penonomé is known throughout Panama as the place to buy the hats that bear the country's name. Unlike the better-known panamas from Ecuador, which are woven from crown to brim in one piece, this kind is made by a braiding process, using a half-inch braid of palm fiber, usually of alternating or mixed white and black.

The finished braid is wound around a wooden form and sewn together at the edges, producing a round-crowned, black-striped hat. It's a common sight in the central provinces of Panama. In the last presidential elections several of the contenders donned hats periodically to appear as 'one of the people.' The highest-quality Penonomé hats are so tightly put together that they can hold water. Prices range from US$10 up to US$150.

There's no one place to buy these hats in Penonomé. They are made in outlying towns, such as Ocú, and brought to the city for sale. Many are sold by hat vendors standing outside stores and restaurants near the Esso gas station by the entrance to town. For starters, try the Shell gas station in front of Restaurante Las Tinajas, and the **Mercado de Artesanías Coclé** (☽ 8am-4pm) at the eastern end of town.

---

packaging of the final product. From here, the cigars are shipped primarily to the USA, France and Spain.

A box of 25 of their highest-quality cigars costs US$50 in Panama and twice that outside the country. Joyas de Panama cigars also come flavored – with a hint of vanilla, rum or amaretto.

Miriam and Braulio speak English, and cigars are clearly much more than a business to them.

ALBERGUE ECOLÓGICO LA IGUANA

This **albergue ecológico** (ecological shelter; ☽ /fax 983-8056; campsites US$10, r US$30), 14km northeast of Penonomé, consists of a pleasant, open-sided **restaurant** (mains US$5-10) and guests' quarters. The shelter is set on 75 hectares that contain a modest waterfall and various tree-production projects. There's also a substantial patch of forest on the property that contains iguanas, red-nape tamarins and even a few caimans. Among the 75 species of bird that have been identified here are the white-winged dove and the rare black-and-white hawk.

The emphasis here is on outdoor recreation. Visitors are encouraged to wander the trails through the woods and get in touch with nature. The restaurant serves seafood and meat dishes. The eight guestrooms each feature one good double bed and three firm single beds, a private cold-water bathroom and ceiling fan. At last count, the *albergue* was becoming run-down and had few guests. If you come, you may have the place to yourself.

Getting There & Away

To reach the Albergue Ecológico La Iguana from the center of Penonomé, take the well-marked turnoff for Churuquita Grande, several hundred meters northwest of the Hotel Dos Continentes. Proceed 13km and begin looking for a sign announcing the retreat on the right side of the road. If you take a taxi from Penonomé, the ride will cost US$7 each way (less if you haggle).

You can also go to Penonomé's area bus station, two blocks southeast of the central plaza, and take a 'Churuquita Grande' or 'Chiguiri Arriba' bus (US$1, every 30 minutes). Both pass by the ecological shelter. Be sure to tell the driver to stop at the shelter's entrance, or they won't. To return to Penonomé, flag down any southbound bus.

TRINIDAD SPA & LODGE

Reachable by paved road and located in Chiguiri Arriba, 29km to the northeast of Penonomé, is the **Trinidad Spa & Lodge** (☎ 983-8900; www.posadaecologica.com; r US$50-75). The lodge sits atop a summit with sweeping views of green valleys and imposing peaks intermittently shrouded by clouds, looking not so much like a slice of Central America but rather the famous karst formations outside Guilin, China.

The main structure, set amid gardens that attract many species of bird, consists of a one-story lodge with four guestrooms. There is also an outstanding restaurant and bar, with breathtaking views. Vegetarian items are available, and nearly all of the food is grown organically. A selection of Chilean wines accompanies the meals. A short walk from the main building are 10 lovely rooms with sweeping views, four of which are among the very best in Panama owing to their views. Each of these rooms has terraces, private hot-water bathrooms and firm beds. All of the rooms except for one (the premier) rent for US$65 per person. The premier costs a little more (US$75), because word has slipped that it is one of former President Moscoso's favorite rooms and many Panamanian guests now request it.

The spa offers mud baths and herbal oil massages. Guests can also take guided hiking tours, ranging from easy nature walks to arduous treks and taking in river, waterfall and forest scenes. Area wildlife includes three-toed sloths, night monkeys, deer and armadillos. Four species of toucan and many species of hummingbird also live here; these can occasionally be seen from the comfort of the inn's creek-fed swimming pool.

Trinidad Spa & Lodge is a great find, well worth the time it takes to get there.

Getting There & Away

To get to the inn from central Penonomé, take the well-marked turnoff for Churuquita Grande, several hundred meters northwest of the Hotel Dos Continentes. Proceed past Churuquita Grande and follow the signs to Chiguiri Arriba and the inn.

Alternately, go to Penonomé's area bus station and take a 'Chiguiri Arriba' bus (US$1.50, 80 minutes) on its windshield. Buses depart at 6am, 10am and 11am and 12:30pm, 2pm, 4:30pm and 6pm.

PARQUE NACIONAL OMAR TORRIJOS & LA RICA

The turnoff for this **national park** (admission per day US$3, campsite US$5, r per person US$5) is on the Interamericana, 18km west of Penonomé. From the turnoff, it's another 32.8km to the park's entrance. The road, paved for the first 26km, winds through rolling countryside dotted with farms and small cattle ranches. The paved road ends at the small town of El Copé. The remaining 6.8km of the drive to the park is on a dirt road that's so bad that a 4WD vehicle with a very strong motor and excellent tires is needed. There is no public transportation to the park. If you don't have a car, catch a bus from Penonomé to El Copé (US$1.50, one hour) and transfer there in a minibus to Barrigón (US$0.50), the closest village to the park. From there it's a one-hour hike into the park.

If you're driving, take the turnoff as marked from the Interamericana and proceed 26km. You will then see a sign directing you to the park (to the right) and another to the park's Sede Administrativa (administrative office). There's no reason to go to the administrative office, so stay to the right and continue until you reach the park's entrance.

Partly because of the bad roads, the forests here are among the most beautiful in Panama and offer superb bird watching. The park starts in montane forest on the Pacific side of the Continental Divide and continues onto the Caribbean side, where the forest is noticeably more humid. Among the rare birds that have been recorded here are the golden-olive woodpecker, red-fronted parrotlet, immaculate antbird and white-throated shrike-tanager.

One of the wonderful surprises that greets visitors here is the condition of the park's trail system, which was recently given a major makeover by US Peace Corps volunteers, Autoridad Nacional del Ambiente (ANAM) rangers and members of Panama Verde (a Panamanian student ecological group). Another surprise: this park offers the easiest and surest point from which to see both the Pacific and Atlantic Oceans (from the lookout above the cabin).

There is a **ranger station** (6am-8pm) just inside the entrance of the park where visitors can pay admission and accommodations fees. There's a cabin 200m further up the road with four beds and a kitchen with basic cooking supplies. It also has a loft and living room, allowing a total of 10 to sleep comfortably if you have your own gear. Either way, you'll need a sleeping bag; it cools off at night in the mountains so bring some warm clothing as well. The cabin would be much nicer if it were further from the road.

Another excellent way of visiting the park is taking advantage of the services of the friendly Navas family. They rent rooms in their **house** (983-9130; r with meals per person US$15-20) in Barrigon, and they also have a *cabaña*, **Albergue Navas** (983-9130; r with meals per person US$15-20), in La Rica, a beautiful community inside the park. Accommodations at both places are rustic, but very well maintained and inexpensive, with all meals included. The family – Santo and Anna Navas and their sons – work as guides, as they have done in the past for scientists and birders. They help to maintain the park and its trails and their knowledge and love of the area is quite apparent.

Barrigon can be reached by car or public transportation from El Copé. From Barrington it's a two- to three-hour hike or a horseback ride to La Rica, where you'll find a cool and pleasant community with a beautiful river and swimming holes, with access to secluded, orchid-covered waterfalls, virgin rain and cloud forest, and excellent birding.

From La Rica, you can take day hikes to the summits of cerros Marta and Peña Blanca, visit the impressive waterfalls of Chorros de Tife, and even hike to the ruins of Torrijos' plane.

La Rica is remote (no phone, electricity or road), and the hiking is strenuous, but it is a nature lover's dream and comes highly recommended. All the arrangements can be made through Santo and Anna Navas (Spanish only). Call ahead, or ask around for the Navas family when you reach Barrigon.

PARQUE ARQUEOLÓGICO DEL CAÑO

This **park** (adult/child US$1/0.25; 9am-noon & 12:30-4pm Tue-Sat, 9am-1pm Sun) is one of only two archaeological sites in the country that are open to the public (the other is Barriles, in Chiriquí Province, p217). It has a museum that contains a few objects that were found nearby. There's an excavation pit in the park as well, which contains a burial site in which were found five skeletons in the exact same position as visitors see them today.

Nearby there's a field containing dozens of stone columns that were lined up and stood on end in recent years; they aren't much to look at and their significance to the lost culture is unknown.

The site was excavated during the 1920s by an American who allegedly left with most of the objects he came across. The museum contains dozens of pieces of pottery, arrowheads and carved stones. The objects are believed to date from a culture that lived in El Caño about 1500 years ago. The few signs at the museum are in Spanish only, and the site's caretaker/guide can offer no reliable information about El Caño's history.

The turnoff for the town of El Caño is on the Interamericana, about 8km north of Natá. The park is another 3km from the turnoff, down an occasionally mud-slicked road. El Caño is not served by bus, but you can take a taxi here from Natá.

NATÁ
pop 6300

In 1515 an Indian chief named Tatacherubi, whose territory covered much of what would later become northern Coclé Province, informed the Spanish conquistadors Alonso Perez de la Rua and Gonzalo de Badajoz of the wealth of his neighbor to the southwest, a chief named Natá. 'Natá has much gold, but he has few fighting men,' was the gist of that conversation.

Naturally, the conquistadors went after Natá's gold. Perez and his 30 men arrived first; Badajoz and his 130 men were not far behind. Perhaps a bit overanxious, Perez and his party soon found themselves amid a large Indian settlement. Retreat was impossible, but Perez grabbed the Indian chief and threatened to kill him, and thus forced Natá to tell his warriors to back off.

Then Badajoz and his well-armed soldiers showed up, and Natá was forced to surrender a large quantity of gold. The Christians remained for two months in the village named after the chief before they headed south and plundered more villages. Two years later, the Spaniards, led by Gaspar de Espinosa, returned to Natá and established one of the earliest European settlements on the isthmus.

The Indians, meanwhile, were enslaved. As an incentive to settle in Natá, the ruthless Spanish governor Pedro Arias de Ávila divided the village and its Indians among 60 soldiers who agreed to start a pueblo there.

Today, Natá is a quiet town, and most of its inhabitants work at the area's sugar refineries or in the fields around town. Natá's main attraction is its church, completed in 1522, making it one of the oldest in the country. There are also a number of well-preserved colonial houses here.

Iglesia de Natá

The church, which has remained close to its original state all these years, is well worth a visit. The church was extensively renovated in the late '90s. It has a fine colonial facade and a remarkable interior.

If you look closely at the altar of the Virgin, you'll notice sculpted fruit, leaves and feathered serpents on its two columns – clearly the influence of its Indian artisans. The position of the carved angels at its base signifies the power the artisans felt the angels possessed.

Notice also the Holy Trinity painting to the right of the altar. The painting was created in 1758 by the Ecuadorian artist José Samaniego. For many years it was kept from public view because it represents the Trinity as three people who all look like Christ, which is not in conformity with Church canon.

Under the floor beneath the painting are the remains of three people placed there many years ago. No one knows who they are or how many other skeletons there are beneath the church's floor. Restorers stumbled upon the remains in 1995 while working on the floor.

Father Victor Raul Martinez leads Natá's congregation and he can usually be found inside the church. He speaks English and he'll unlock a door and lead you up a narrow flight of stairs to the belfry if you politely ask him to. Once in the belfry, you'll discover four bells, all dating from the 20th century. The original bells were made of solid gold and were stolen years ago.

The choir platform above the entryway was built in 1996 to the specifications of the original. The original columns (the rough ones) that support the church's roof are made of níspero, a hardwood found in Bocas del Toro Province. The smooth columns are new and also made of níspero. The entire ceiling was replaced in 1995 and is made of pine and cedar.

The church does not have regular hours.

Festivals & Events

Natá holds its **Fiesta de Tomate** (Tomato Festival) in mid-April. Dates of the three-day agricultural fair vary each year; check with **IPAT** (☎ 226-7000; www.panamainfo.com; ⏰ 8:30am-4:30pm Mon-Fri) in Panama City.

Sleeping & Eating

Hotel Rey David (☎ 993-5149; s/d US$18/24) The only place to stay in Natá, on the main road that leads into town from the Interamericana is the Rey David. An excellent value hotel, it offers 20 comfortable rooms with air-con.

Restaurante Vega (mains US$3) Two doors up from Hotel Rey David, Restaurante Vega serves good chow mein and decent rice with shrimp.

Getting There & Away

Natá can be reached by all the buses that use this stretch of the Interamericana, except for the few nonstop buses that cruise between Panama City and Paso Canoas. Buses pass by in either direction every 15 minutes or so. Tell the driver to drop you at Natá, and they'll let you off beside the Restaurante Vega. Often there's a taxi parked in front of the café. You can catch buses eastward to Penonomé (US$1, 30 minutes, every 20 minutes), Panama City (US$4, 2½ hours, every 30 minutes) and points in between. Westward, there are regular connections to Aguadulce (US$0.50, 15 minutes, every 20 minutes), Divisa (US$1, 30 minutes, every 20 minutes), David (US$7.50, 4½ hours, every hour) and points all along the Interamericana.

AGUADULCE

pop 8300

Aguadulce's name is a contraction of *agua* and *dulce* (meaning 'sweet water'), and it is said that this bustling city was named by Spaniards who were pleased to come across a freshwater well amid the arid landscape.

Today, Aguadulce is known for its sugar, its jumbo shrimp and its salt. There are salt flats south of downtown, and until recently there was a sizeable saltworks. Unable to compete with the lower prices of Colombian salt, the saltworks here closed its doors in 1999. The flats provide excellent bird watching opportunities; you can see marsh and shore birds, particularly the roseate spoonbill and wood stork.

Just outside town are fields and fields of sugar cane. From mid-January to mid-March of each year, the cane is cut and then refined at several large refineries in the area. One of these mills, the Ingenio de Azúcar Santa Rosa (Santa Rosa Sugar Refinery, p157) offers tours – a must-do if you're in the area during the grinding season.

Generally, a place in Latin America that acquires a reputation for its crustaceans quickly overharvests them and then has none to offer. But in Aguadulce, which for years has been nationally famous for its jumbo shrimp, restaurants continue to serve them in generous portions.

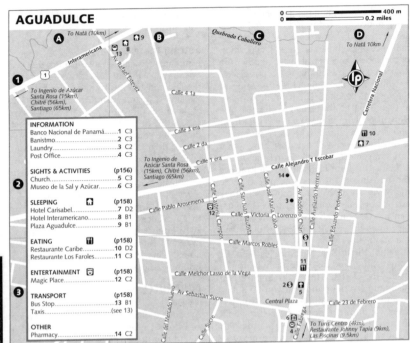

AGUADULCE

INFORMATION	
Banco Nacional de Panamá	1 C3
Banistmo	2 C3
Laundry	3 C2
Post Office	4 C3

SIGHTS & ACTIVITIES	(p156)
Church	5 C3
Museo de la Sal y Azúcar	6 C3

SLEEPING	(p158)
Hotel Carisabel	7 D2
Hotel Interamericano	8 B1
Plaza Aguadulce	9 B1

EATING	(p158)
Restaurante Caribe	10 D2
Restaurante Los Faroles	11 C3

ENTERTAINMENT	(p158)
Magic Place	12 C2

TRANSPORT	(p158)
Bus Stop	13 B1
Taxis	(see 13)

OTHER	
Pharmacy	14 C2

Orientation

Aguadulce is in hot, dry country, 10km south of Natá, 185km west of Panama City and 251km east of David. Like so many cities and towns in Panama, Aguadulce is beside the Interamericana. Its downtown, however, is a kilometer or two from the highway.

The main road into town from the highway is Av Rafael Estevez. The Hotel Interamericano marks the turnoff. There are always taxis here, and the parking lot next to the hotel is also the town's main bus stop.

To get to Aguadulce's central plaza, drive south on Av Rafael Estevez several blocks until it ends at its intersection with Calle Alejandro T Escobar. Turn left here, onto Calle Alejandro T Escobar, drive three and a half blocks to Av Rodolfo Chiari and then turn right. The central plaza and church will appear on your left, four blocks later.

Information

Banco Nacional de Panamá (Av Rodolfo Chiari) ATM
Banistmo (Av Rodolfo Chiari) ATM
Laundry (Av Rodolfo Chiari) Three blocks north of the central plaza.

Post office (Av Rodolfo Chiari) Near the central plaza, just around the corner from the Museo de la Sal y Azúcar.

Sights & Activities
MUSEO DE LA SAL Y AZÚCAR

This rather unusual **museum** (☎ 997-4280; Plaza 19 de Octubre; adult/child US$0.75/0.25; ☺ 9am-5pm Tue-Sat, 2-5pm Sun) faces the central plaza. As its name suggests, the exhibits here document the history of Aguadulce's salt and sugar industries. The museum also contains artifacts from the Colombian civil war (1899–1903), in which many Panamanians fought. These include guns, uniforms and swords.

A number of pre-Columbian artifacts are also on display, mostly ceramics and tools found in the cane fields nearby. But the majority of exhibits tell how the salt flats were developed, detail the role Aguadulce's salt and sugar have played in Panamanian life, and so on. Signage is in Spanish only.

TURIS CENTRO

This modest **recreation area** (☎ 997-3720; free admission, bike/skate rental per hr US$1/1.50, boat rental per 15min US$1.50; ☺ 11am-8pm) is 4km from downtown Aguadulce, on the road to Restaurante Johnny Tapia. Here, in the middle of salt flats and scrub brush, you can rent bikes, skates, or hire paddleboats for the small pond. There's also a children's playground and an inexpensive open-sided restaurant. A taxi here costs about US$2.

LAS PISCINAS

Las Piscinas (The Pools) are 9.5km from downtown Aguadulce, just beyond the salt flats and 250m past Restaurante Johnny Tapia. They consist of four 1.5m-high swimming pools constructed in tideland about 150m from the high-water mark. If the tide is out, you can walk over the muddy sand that separates the pools from the shore and take a dip. The water's murky (it's saltwater, after all), but it's not polluted, as the pools are nearly 10km from town. The view from the pools is mostly one of a big, beautiful sky, with distant foothills on one side and the ocean spreading out before you on the other.

The tideland is quite expansive. When the tide is out, you can walk 2km before reaching the ocean. But be careful; once the tide turns, it rises rather quickly. If you've walked a kilometer or so beyond the pools and notice the tide rising, head inland immediately. Sea lions have even been spotted swimming near the pools when the tide's in.

The best way to get to the pools is by taxi. Tell the driver to take you to Restaurante Johnny Tapia. From Johnny Tapia, walk south (away from town). On the left side of the road are mangroves, beginning a little way from the restaurant. After you've walked about 100m, you'll see a clearing in the mangroves, and through the clearing you'll be able to spot the pools (if the tide is out). Don't let the view from the road fool you; the pools are lovely in a funky way.

INGENIO DE AZÚCAR SANTA ROSA

The **Santa Rosa Sugar Refinery** (☎ 987-8101/8102; ⏱ 7am-4pm Mon-Fri, 7-11:30am Sat) 15km west of Aguadulce, is a must-see if you're in the area when the factory is in operation. The grinding season is from mid-January to mid-March. During these two months, the refinery grinds 6500 tons of sugar cane per day.

Because the land here is hilly and rocky, the cane must be harvested by hand. Four thousand people are hired to help with harvesting and production, and they bring the cane in as fast as they can, 24 hours a day, six days a week (the mill is quiet on Sunday). Most of the cane is harvested on company land, but the mill still buys about 3% of its cane from campesinos who bring it in on carts pulled by tractors and oxen. Around 135kg of cane enters the mill each second via a huge conveyer belt that's continually fed from trucks coming in from the fields. By day's end, the yield of refined sugar is around 675,000kg (1.5 million pounds). All this cane is sent through grinders that resemble a stack of studded roller pins – except that each one weighs 20 tons and is about the size of a Buick. They spin quickly, and the cane that passes through them is crushed flat.

Occasionally the machine chokes. A 10-second choke results in a pileup of 1350kg of cane, and jackhammers are required to remove the clog. To give you an idea of the grinders' power: when a choke starts to occur, railroad ties are pushed into the grinders. In the fraction of a second it takes for the ties to pass through, they are chewed up as if they were breadsticks, but even as they're pulverized, they act as battering rams, punching bunched-up cane through the machines.

Also on the property is a replica of the original house of the mill's first owner, built in 1911. This museum is nicely done and contains many exhibits; all its furniture and other articles are originals.

To book tours, ask for Gonzalo Peréz (he speaks English and Spanish). The refinery would like at least 24 hours' notice to receive visitors.

If you're driving from Aguadulce, the turnoff for the mill will be on the right-hand side of the Interamericana and marked by a sign (there's an Esso station opposite). Take the road half a kilometer, and you'll come to a white guard station with a tiny chapel in front of it. Give your name to the guard and follow instructions.

You can also take a taxi from Aguadulce (which could cost US$25 if the driver waits for you and takes you back to town), or you can catch any bus headed in the direction of the refinery and tell the driver to drop you at the Ingenio de Azúcar Santa Rosa (US$0.50, 20 minutes, every 15 minutes). Be forewarned that the walk from the guard station to the mill is more than 1km down a paved road lined with mature teak trees.

Festivals & Events

Aguadulce's big celebrations are **Carnaval**, held the four days before Ash Wednesday; its **patron saint festival**, on July 25 (or, if that's a weekday, the following Saturday); and the city's **founding day**, on October 18, 19 and 20. The Carnaval festivities are lively as are the founding day festivities. Parades, floats, Miss Aguadulce ceremonies, and lots of music, dancing and drinking characterize the events.

Sleeping

Hotel Carisabel (☎ 997-3800; fax 997-3805; cnr Calle Alejandro T Escobar & Carretera Nacional; s/d US$22/27; 🖾) Near the downtown area, the Carisabel offers Aguadulce's best accommodations. This friendly place offers 21 rooms, all with air-con, TV and private hot-water bathroom. There's a pool, a bar and a restaurant as well.

Hotel Interamericano (☎ 997-4363; fax 997-4975; Interamericana; s or d US$17; 🖾) Near Av Rafael Estevez, this popular place is good value. All 30 rooms have TV, air-con and hot-water private bathroom. There's also a swimming pool, a restaurant and a popular bar here.

Plaza Aguadulce (☎ 986-0788; Interamericana; s/d US$17/19) Next door to Hotel Interamericano, this fairly new hotel offers large, unattractive rooms that are short on natural light. The rooms are clean if uninspiring.

Eating

Restaurante Caribe (Carretera Nacional; mains US$5-8) Beside the Hotel Carisabel, this pleasant restaurant offers a range of chicken and seafood plates.

Restaurante Los Faroles (☎ 997-4176; Calle Melchor Lasso de la Vega; mains US$4-7; 😋 breakfast, lunch & dinner) Opposite the church in downtown Aguadulce, this indoor-outdoor restaurant has a large menu, but specializes in pizza. Its Hawaiian pizza has raisins and maraschino cherries in addition to the regular pineapple and ham toppings.

Restaurante Johnny Tapia (seafood US$2.50-3.50; 😋 from 8am) One of the best places to enjoy shrimp is this very casual beachside diner just past the salt flats, 9km from downtown Aguadulce. This is a basic place named for its ebullient owner-waiter. Typical offerings here include ceviche (US$2.50), shrimp salad (US$3), fresh fish (US$3.50) and fish soup (US$3.50). If the tide's out, consider taking a dip in one of the nearby pools. There's nothing fancy about either Johnny Tapia or the pools, but it's a curious place.

The **restaurant** (executive lunch US$2.50) at the Hotel Interamericano offers jumbo shrimp prepared four ways, each for US$8. The restaurant is known for its lunches, especially the *ejecutivo* (executive lunch), which includes soup, salad, rice, beans, beef and fried plantains.

Entertainment

Magic Place (Cnr Calles Lastenia Campos & Pablo Arosemena) is one of Aguadulce's more popular dance clubs, with occasional live music on weekends.

There are also several dance clubs on the Interamericana.

Getting There & Away

Buses arrive and depart from the small parking lot beside Hotel Interamericana on the highway. Destinations west include Divisa (US$1, 30 minutes, every 30 minutes), where you can change for buses to Chitré, Santiago (US$1.75, one hour, every 30 minutes) and David (US$7, four hours, every 45 minutes). Destinations east include Natá (US$0.50, 15 minutes, every 20 minutes), Penonomé (US$1, 30 minutes, every 20 minutes) and Panama City (US$5, three hours, every 20 minutes). A taxi from the parking lot into town costs US$1.

Getting Around

Taxis are the best way to get from one part of Aguadulce to another if you don't feel like walking. Fares rarely exceed US$2, although you can expect to pay a little more at night. Always agree on a price before entering a taxi.

Herrera Province

CONTENTS

Chitré	161
Playa El Aguillito	166
Parque Nacional Sarigua	166
Parita	167
Refugio de Vida Silvestre Cenegón del Mangle	168
Pesé	168
Ocú	168
San José	169
Cruce de Ocú	169

HERRERA PROVINCE

The Península de Azuero is looked upon by Panamanians as their country's heart and soul. It is here, on plains that more closely resemble rural USA than the American tropics, that the Spanish legacy is strongest. On the Azuero, fair complexions, hazel eyes and aquiline features prevail. The people have little Indian ancestry; their descent is nearly pure Spanish.

But culture on this semiarid peninsula didn't arrive with the Spaniards; it was here centuries before a teenage Italian named Cristóbal Colón got his first sailing lesson. What we know of this culture has been gleaned mainly from archaeology, and perhaps no excavation sites have told us more about the people the conquistadors encountered in Panama than the digs near Parita and those at nearby Sitio Conte, in Coclé Province (see Reconstructing the Past, p167).

Herrera Province, which is in the center of the Península de Azuero, was lush and only sparsely inhabited during the 16th century; today the country's smallest province not only contains little forest but also has the third-highest population density of Panama's nine provinces, with 44 residents per square kilometer.

Herrera has maintained its Spanish legacy mainly through Spanish festivals. The town of Ocú holds a popular patron saint festival, which begins with religious services and includes the joyous parading of a just-married couple through the streets. Las Minas and Parita are known for their feasts of Corpus Christi (Body of Christ), festivals celebrated 40 days after Easter in honor of the Eucharist. Pesé hosts dramatic public reenactments of the Last Supper, Judas' betrayal and Jesus' imprisonment during the week preceding Easter.

HERRERA PROVINCE

HIGHLIGHTS

- Sighting migratory seabirds at **Playa El Aguillito** (p166)
- Visiting pottery factories in **La Arena** (p163), where artisans produce ceramics that mimic pre-Columbian designs
- Walking historic **Parita** (p167), where you'll find pridefully maintained buildings dating back to the 16th and 17th centuries
- Visiting **Ocú** (p169) and neighboring **San José** (p169) where women make Panama hats as well as *polleras* and *montunos* (traditional embroidered dresses and shirts)
- Beholding the apocalyptic **Parque Nacional Sarigua** (p166), a sad monument to environmental devastation

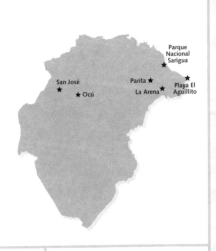

- POPULATION: 107,830
- AREA: 2341 SQ KM
- ELEVATION: SEA LEVEL TO 3478M

NATIONAL PARKS

In contrast to many of Panama's other national parks, the small **Parque Nacional Sarigua** (p166), just outside of Chitré, is not the place to encounter lush forests or abundant wildlife – which is precisely the point. The desertlike wasteland exists as a sad and potent reminder of the future of Panama if greed wins out over environmental responsibility.

The **Refugio de Vida Silvestre Cenegón del Mangle** (p168) is a mangrove forest and wildlife refuge that's a prime nesting ground for herons and other birdlife. It also contains a series of pools said to have therapeutic properties.

CHITRÉ
pop 45,400

Chitré, the capital of Herrera Province, is the largest city on the Península de Azuero and a convenient base for exploration. It is the site of some of the area's best-known festivals. If you plan to attend any festivals here, you'll have difficulty finding a place to stay if you arrive without a reservation. This is particularly true during Carnaval, when most of the city's rooms are booked months in advance.

In the vicinity of Chitré are the Parque Nacional Sarigua; the Humboldt Ecological Station at Playa El Aguillito; and, a fair walk or short bus ride away, the village of La Arena, 3km west of Chitré, where you

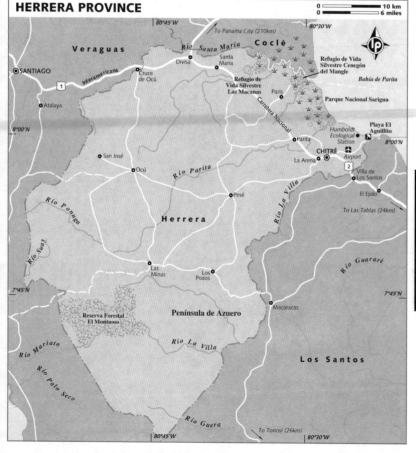

HERRERA PROVINCE

0 — 10 km
0 — 6 miles

Veraguas

80°45'W   80°30'W

To Panama City (210km)

Río Santa María   Coclé

SANTIAGO
Interamericana
Cruce de Ocú
Divisa
Santa María

Refugio de Vida Silvestre Cenegón del Mangle

Bahía de Parita

Atalaya

Refugio de Vida Silvestre Las Macanas
París

Carretera Nacional

Parque Nacional Sarigua

8°00'N

San José

Río Parita
Parita

Humboldt Ecological Station

Playa El Aguillito

8°00'N

Ocú

CHITRÉ
La Arena   Airport
Villa de Los Santos

Pesé

Río La Villa

El Ejido

To Las Tablas (24km)

Herrera

Río Ponuga

Río Suay

Río Guararé

7°45'N

Las Minas   Los Pozos

7°45'N

Reserva Forestal El Montuoso

Península de Azuero

Macaracas

Los Santos

Río Mariato

Río La Villa

Río Palo Seco

Río Guera

To Tonosí (26km)

80°45'W   80°30'W

HERRERA PROVINCE

HERRERA PROVINCE

CHITRÉ

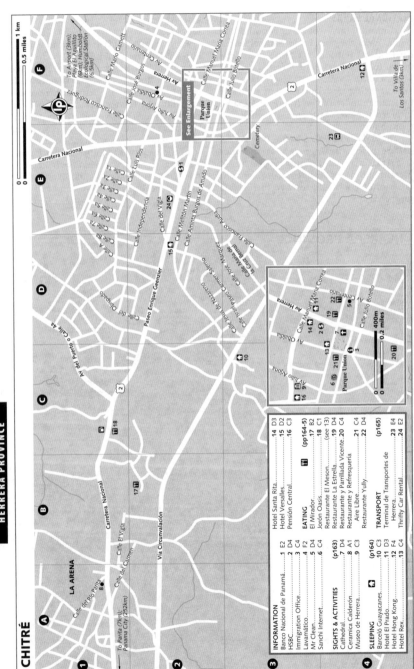

INFORMATION
Banco Nacional de Panamá...........1	E2
HSBC...2	D4
Immigration Office.........................3	C4
Lavamático....................................4	F2
Mr Clean.......................................5	D4
Sanchi Internet..............................6	C4

SIGHTS & ACTIVITIES (p163)
Cathedral......................................7	D4
Ceramica Calderón........................8	A1
Museo de Herrera..........................9	C3

SLEEPING (p164)
Barceló Guayacanes.....................10	C3
Hotel El Prado.............................11	D3
Hotel Hong Kong.........................12	F4
Hotel Rex....................................13	C4
Hotel Santa Rita..........................14	D3
Hotel Versalles.............................15	D2
Pensión Central...........................16	C3

EATING (pp164-5)
El Mirador...................................17	B2
Joron Oasis.................................18	C1
Restaurante El Meson.........(see 13)	
Restaurante La Estrella.................19	D4
Restaurante y Parrillada Vicente...20	C4
Restaurante y Refresquería	
Aire Libre.................................21	C4
Restaurante Yully........................22	D4

TRANSPORT (p165)
Terminal de Transportes de	
Herrera....................................23	E4
Thrifty Car Rental........................24	E2

can see ceramics being made. All of these sites are covered in this chapter.

Villa de Los Santos (p173), where some of the peninsula's most important festivals take place, is 4km southeast of Chitré, just inside Los Santos Province.

Orientation

The Interamericana connects with the Carretera Nacional (the National Hwy) at the town of Divisa, atop the Península de Azuero, and from there the Carretera Nacional runs southeast 37km to Chitré. From Chitré it runs 31km further to Las Tablas, in Los Santos Province, then further south toward the southern edge of the peninsula.

Chitré is the first major town the Carretera Nacional encounters as it winds southeast from Divisa, When the highway reaches Chitré, it becomes Paseo Enrique Geenzier, changing name again a dozen blocks further east, to Calle Manuel Maria Correa. The Carretera Nacional reemerges at the southern end of town.

The town's cathedral and the adjacent central square, Parque Union, are one block south of Calle Manuel Maria Correa between Av Obaldía and Av Herrera. There are numerous hotels and restaurants within a short walk of the square.

Information

For money matters, try **Banco Nacional de Panamá** (Paseo Enrique Geenzier; 9am-1pm Mon-Thu & Sat, to 3pm Fri) or **HSBC** (Av Herrera; 9am-1pm Mon-Fri), which lies just north of the cathedral. Both have ATMs. A number of Internet cafés are clustered near the Parque Union. **Sanchi Internet** (Calle Aminta Burgos de Amado; per hr US$0.75; 8:30am-11:30pm), one block west of the park, has reliable connections and keeps decent hours. There are two laundries: **Lavámatico** (Calle Luis Ríos at Calle Fabio Díaz; 9am-noon & 1:30-4pm Mon-Sat) and **Mr Clean** (Calle Melitón Martin near Av Centenario; 9am-4pm Mon-Sat), both of which will wash and dry a load for around US$3.50.

Sights

MUSEO DE HERRERA

This anthropology and natural history **museum** (996-0077; Paseo Enrique Geenzier; adult/child US$1/25¢; 8am-noon & 1-4pm Tue-Sat, 8-11am Sun) contains many well-preserved pieces of pottery dating from 5000 BC until the time of the Spanish conquest. Some of the pieces

that were found at the excavation sites outside Parita are here, although most of those artifacts are on display at the anthropology museum in Panama City.

Also on display are replicas of *huacas* (golden objects placed with Indians at the time of burial) found on the peninsula, as well as numerous photos of archeologists at work and maps showing where the pottery and *huacas* were found. Be sure to visit the museum's 2nd floor, where you'll find photos of Azuero residents, authentic folkloric costumes and religious artifacts (including the original bell of Chitré's cathedral, which was cast in 1767). Signs are in Spanish only.

CATHEDRAL

The cathedral dates from the 18th century but was substantially remodeled in 1988. The entire ceiling is made of polished mahogany and the walls are adorned with near-life-size figures of saints. Large, vivid stained-glass windows depict momentous events in the life of Jesus. The stations of the cross are marked by 4m teak crosses and intricately carved figurines. Unlike many cathedrals that impress through ostentation, this one is striking for its elegant simplicity and fine balance of gold and wood.

LA ARENA

Several kilometers west of downtown Chitré and bisected by the Carretera Nacional is the village of La Arena, which is known for its ceramics factories. The pottery made here mimics the pre-Columbian designs of the culture that once lived nearby. This is a good place to watch pottery being made.

The best of the several pottery factories is **Ceramica Calderón** (near Calle del Río Parita & Carretera Nacional), where you can buy traditional painted ceramics at low cost. These pieces are made on the premises in a workshop directly behind the roadside showroom. All the pottery is made by hand with the help of a foot-powered potter's wheel.

The artisan who makes most of the ceramics sold here is Angel Calderón, who's been making ceramics professionally for almost 50 years. If you visit Angel's shop, be sure to take a look at the ovens out back. They're quite impressive.

A taxi ride to La Arena from Parque Union costs US$2. There's also a bus service from Chitré (see p112).

Festivals & Events

Chitré's **Carnaval** festivities, held each year on the four days before Ash Wednesday (in February or March), feature parades, folkloric dancing, water fights and lots of drinking. On June 24, Chitré's patron saint festival, the **Fiesta de San Juan Bautista**, starts with a religious service followed by bullfights (the animals are merely teased), cockfights and other popular activities. And on October 19, festivities that celebrate the **Founding of the District of Chitré** (1848) include parades, historical costumes and much merriment.

Sleeping

The selection of lodging options in Chitré ranges from hot and rundown cubicles to spacious, tastefully appointed guestrooms. Room reservations for the Carnaval period must be made six months or more in advance. At the popular Hotel Hong Kong and the Hotel Versalles, reservations at Carnaval time must be made several years in advance.

Hotel Versalles (☎ 996-4422; versalles@cwp.net .pa; Paseo Enrique Geenzier near Paseo Carmen Salerno; d/ste US$25/42;) This lovely hotel is one of Chitré's best. Spacious guestrooms feature comfortable beds, air-con, cable TV, private hot-water bathrooms, phone and desks. There are also suites available, and the hotel has a swimming pool and a restaurant-bar.

Barceló Guayacanes (☎ 996-8969; isabel_s22@hot mail.com; Vía Circunvalación; s/d/ste US$39/50/77;) The newest hotel in Chitré lies just outside of town, and features a four-building complex surrounding a small artificial lake, as well as a swimming pool, disco and restaurant (opposite). The rooms are comfortable and well appointed with good beds and all the creature comforts, though the place doesn't have much charm.

Hotel Rex (☎ 996-6660; fax 996-4310; Calle Melitón Martín; s/d US$18/27;) Beside the town square, Hotel Rex has 32 air-con rooms with cable TV, phone and private hot-water bathrooms. For space, ask for room numbers 104 or 106. There's a bar and restaurant.

Hotel Hong Kong (☎ 996-4483; fax 996-5229; Carretera Nacional; s & d/ste US$30/80;) Hotel Hong Kong has well-maintained guestrooms with all the amenities, and suites with Jacuzzis and kitchenettes. Unfortunately, some of the rooms lack windows and have saggy beds. Several rooms are wheelchair acces-

sible. There are two swimming pools (one for kids) and a fine restaurant and bar.

Pensión Central (☎ 996-1856; Calle Manuel Maria Correa; s/d US$8/10) Near Av Perez, the Central offers six worn, dusty rooms with ceiling fans and private cold-water bathrooms. Some beds are better than others; ask to see several rooms.

Hotel Santa Rita (☎ 996-4610; fax 996-2404; cnr Calle Manuel Maria Correa & Av Herrera; s/d with fan US$11/16, with US$14/19) Santa Rita was one of the city's first hotels, and it's still a good value. Rooms are well maintained, with private balconies and clean hot-water bathrooms.

Hotel El Prado (☎ 996-4620; Av Herrera; s/d US$9/15, with US$15/19) Just south of Calle Manuel Maria Correa, El Prado is a clean, well-kept hotel with a 2nd-floor restaurant, sitting area and open balcony overlooking the street. The fairly worn rooms are set back from the street, so they're not too noisy; each has a private bathroom, TV and phone.

Eating

Chitré's fishermen cast from 2am to 6am and sell their haul soon after their return from the sea, so most of the seafood served in Chitré has been caught the same day. For this reason, Chitré is known throughout the peninsula as having fresh seafood – and it's surprisingly cheap.

IN TOWN

Restaurante El Meson (☎ 996-6660; fax 996-4310; Calle Melitón Martín; mains US$4-9) This restaurant at the Hotel Rex has good, reasonably priced food, with many meat and fish specialties. The *lomo al horno* (pork roast) is excellent, as is the paella, which is served only on Sunday.

Hotel Hong Kong (☎ 996-4483; fax 996-5229; Carretera Nacional; mains US$5-7; 7am-10pm) One of several Chinese restaurants in town, this one features tasty bites like shrimp chow mein, Creole-style shrimp, smoked pork chops and chicken with cashew nuts.

Restaurante y Parrillada Vicente (Av Herrera; mains US$4-7) Another excellent Chinese restaurant lies two blocks south of the cathedral. Brightly-painted walls hung with Van Gogh prints form the backdrop to excellent chow mein, chicken with sweet-and-sour sauce and roast pork. The grilled octopus is also recommended. They have many daily lunch specials.

Restaurante y Refresquería Aire Libre (Av Obaldia; mains US$3-5; 6:30am-10pm) This pleasant open-air café facing the western end of the plaza serves good inexpensive Panamanian dishes, such as *camarones al ajillo* (shrimp with garlic), as well as coffee and ice cream.

Barceló Guayacanes (996-8969; isabel_s22@hotmail.com; Vía Circunvalación; mains US$5-10) Situated on a small bluff overlooking downtown Chitré, this restaurant serves excellent seafood dishes, grilled meats and many specials, such as octopus salad. The amount of hardwood used in this spacious indoor-outdoor restaurant is astounding, including a ceiling made of spiny cedar supported by pillars of 1m-thick *guayacan* trunks. The owner of this impressive facility, which also has a hotel, bar and a large swimming pool, is one of Panama's major loggers.

Restaurante La Estrella (Av Herrera; plates US$3-4.50) is a low-key eatery that serves hearty Panamanian fare at low prices. A block east of there, **Restaurante Yully** (Calle Melitón Martín; plates US$3-4.50) is another good budget option with a range of chicken, meat and noodle dishes served buffet-style.

LA ARENA

El Mirador (The Lookout; mains US$3-7; 4pm-midnight) The highest point within 5km of downtown Chitré, this open-sided restaurant, atop a hill in La Arena, is more popular for its panoramic views and atmosphere than its food. To find the Mirador from downtown Chitré, head west on the Paseo Enrique Geenzier about 2.5km and turn left onto the road that begins just past the large 'Chino Bar' sign. At the fork, turn right and continue for another 400m until you reach the top of the hill. A taxi will cost US$2 each way.

Jorón Oasis Quite popular with locals, this typical roadside open-air restaurant is on the southern side of the Carretera Nacional, opposite the Accel gas station. The *sopa de carne* (meat soup) is very good and should be ordered with rice. The local way to eat this combination is to fill your spoon with rice and dip it into the soup.

Getting There & Away

AIR

Chitré's airport is northeast of town; follow Av Herrera north from the town square to reach it. A taxi ride there costs US$2.50.

Aeroperlas (996-4021; at airport) flies from Chitré to Panama City at 8:25am Monday to Saturday, and at 4:15pm Sunday (US$37).

BUS

Chitré is a center for regional bus transportation. Buses arrive and depart from the **Terminal de Transporte de Herrera** (996-6426), 1km south of downtown, near Vía Circunvalación. To get to the station, take a taxi (US$1 to US$2) or catch a 'Terminal' bus (US$0.25) at the intersection of Calle Aminta Burgos de Amado and Av Herrera. The terminal has a restaurant that's open 24 hours a day.

Tuasa (996-2661) and **Transportes Inazun** (996-4177) buses depart Chitré for Panama City (one way US$6, four hours, every 45 to 60 minutes from 1:30am to 6pm).

Other buses from Chitré operate from sunrise to sunset, and include the following destinations:

Divisa (US$1; 30min; many buses)
La Arena (US$0.35; 5min; many buses)
Las Minas (US$2; 1hr; every 30min)
Las Tablas (US$1; 40min; every 20min)
Ocú (US$2; 1hr; hourly)
Parita (US$0.50; 15min; every 45min)
Pedasí (US$2; 1hr; hourly)
Pesé (US$1; 20min; every 30min)
Playa El Aguillito (US$0.50; 12min; every 20min)
Playas Monagre & El Rompío (US$1; 30min; every 20min)
Santiago (US$2; 1½hr; every 30min)
Villa de Los Santos (US$0.25; 10min; every 10min)

To get to David or Panama City from Chitré, take a bus to Divisa and then catch a *directo* (direct bus) to either city. Buses leave from the Delta station that is at the intersection of the Interamericana and the Carretera Nacional. You likely won't have to wait more than 30 minutes. The bus fare will set you back US$7 or US$8. If you're trying to get to Chitré from the Interamericana, ask the bus driver to stop in Divisa. He'll know to stop near the Delta station. At the station, catch any bus heading toward Chitré.

Getting Around

If you need to travel by vehicle, a taxi is the best way to go. They're cheap – US$2 is the most you would pay in town, and most fares are US$1.

PLAYA EL AGUILLITO

Seven kilometers from Chitré's Parque Union is Playa El Aguillito, which is not so much a sandy beach as it is a mudflat created by silt deposited by two nearby rivers, the Río Parita and the Río La Villa. At low tide the mudflat stretches more than 2km from the high-water mark to the surf, and thousands of birds descend on the mud in search of plankton and small shrimp.

Most of the birds are migratory, flying between Alaska and various South American countries. For reasons that escape scientists – including Francisco Delgado, who heads the **Humboldt Ecological Station** near the northwest end of the beach (look for an 'Estacion Ecologica Alejandro Humboldt' sign) – these birds return year after year to exactly the same beach and to no others in the area.

This is rather amazing when you consider how many thousands of kilometers the birds fly during a single season and how many feeding grounds they must fly over. Playa El Aguillito regulars include roseate spoonbills, black-necked stilts, white-winged doves, yellow-crowned amazons (which are frequently seen here) and also common ground-doves (which, in Panama, are found only on this beach).

When the tide is high, these birds congregate around salt ponds to the immediate east of Playa El Aguillito.

Another reason to visit the beach and ponds is the ecological station, which was established by a group of local environmentalists in 1983. Since then, Francisco and others have banded more than 15,000 birds and monitored them with the help of scientists in other countries. Among the items on display at the station is a map showing the migratory routes of all the bird species that pass through the area.

Francisco, who speaks English and Spanish, knows as much about the birds on the Península de Azuero as anyone. If you have questions about the birds or his work, Francisco usually can be reached at his home (☎ 996-1725) and through the restaurant-bar (☎ 996-1820) beside the beach.

Getting There & Away

Playa El Aguillito is reached from Chitré via Av Herrera; it's just past the airport. A bus leaves the Chitré station for the beach every 30 minutes or so from sunrise to sunset.

The one-way fare is US$0.50. A taxi ride from town costs US$3 one way.

PARQUE NACIONAL SARIGUA

Ten kilometers north of downtown Chitré, this **national park** (entrance US$3; ☒ 8am-4pm), which was created in 1984, consists of 8000 hectares of wasteland that ANAM (Autoridad Nacional de Ambiente; Panama's national environmental authority) would have you believe is tropical desert. The park is not without attractions – the area may be the most important pre-Columbian site in Panama. The Sarigua site has been dated back 11,000 years based on shell mounds and pottery fragments and it offers some rich archaeological opportunities, although much of it has yet to be excavated.

Part of the park actually serves as the waste-disposal site for Chitré, Parita and other cities. In fact, directly behind the ANAM station (where you pay the entrance fee), you can see garbage poking up out of the ground.

The wasteland goes far beyond the pockets of urban waste buried in this national park. Sarigua is the end product of slash-and-burn agriculture. People moved into the area, cut down all the trees, set fire to the debris, planted crops for a few harvests and then left. Because the forest that had held the thin topsoil in place was removed, the heavy rain that falls here every year carried the topsoil into creeks and thence into rivers and out into the sea. What you see in Sarigua today is the nutrient-deficient rock that had been underneath the topsoil.

Shamefully, despite the example of Sarigua, the Panamanian government wants to open Darién Province and northern Veraguas Province to the same variety of wasteful and unsustainable agriculture.

Getting There & Away

To get here from the Carretera Nacional, take the Puerto Limón turnoff, a couple of kilometers northwest of Parita. After 1km you'll notice the foul smell of a nearby pig farm. After another 1km you'll come to the park turnoff. Follow the signs for 2km, until you come to a structure on the left. This is the ANAM station.

Buses do not go to the park. A round-trip taxi ride to the ANAM station from Chitré costs about US$20.

RECONSTRUCTING THE PAST

An excavation during the 1940s of tombs within 10km of Parita uncovered some of the most artistic pottery that was ever produced by pre-Columbian Indians. Brightly colored, fanciful bird and reptile designs adorn the ancient pottery. The bowls were often shaped to resemble king vultures, with finger-long wings flaring from their sides and bulbous heads and stubby tails at their ends.

The remains of a young child with a necklace of hollow gold beads were found in one large painted bowl. In another tomb scientists found long-necked bottles and 40 painted pots in the form of bird effigies. Also found in this tomb were exquisitely carved batons shaped like stylized alligators, made from manatee ribs.

Perhaps the most amazing find was an urn that contained the remains of a single man and a necklace made of 800 human teeth. Nearly all the teeth were front incisors, which means that the teeth of at least 200 people were required to make the jewelry. The circumstances under which the necklace was made remain a mystery.

Other sites near Parita have yielded large quantities of ceremonial pottery. These are mostly vessels mounted on tall pedestal bases of two types: painted globular bowls and other bowls in the form of king vulture effigies, brightly painted with outstretched wings. More than 100 nearly identical red-painted, globular jars with short necks were found in one mound.

Tantalizing but far from adequate descriptions of the people who created these objects have been left to us by Gaspar de Espinosa and Gonzalo de Badajoz, who led looting expeditions on the peninsula between 1515 and 1525. According to their writings, at that time the area was controlled by a powerful chief named Parita, of the Ngöbe-Buglé tribe.

Parita's warriors were able to prevent the Spaniards from settling on the Península de Azuero for several years, but when Espinosa led a later raid on the peninsula, he found to his pleasant surprise that Parita had recently died. Instead of confronting the chief in combat, the raiders found him lying in state in a room containing 355lbs (161kg) of gold ornaments. Also found near the dead leader were 20 Indian captives who were lashed to house posts by cords around their necks; these poor souls had been destined to be buried alive with the great chieftain. Also expected to be buried with Parita were his wives and household attendants.

Today, very few Indians live near the Parita site. Those Ngöbe Buglé who could flee went to the jungled mountains in what is now Chiriquí Province. They lived primarily by hunting and by cultivating corn, beans, manioc and bananas. So fearful were they of white people that until only a few decades ago they placed deadly traps along trails to kill or maim outsiders.

PARITA

pop 3900

This beautiful and historic town is 10km northwest of downtown Chitré, just off the Carretera Nacional. It's known to few people outside the Península de Azuero, and there are no hotels here, but the town does offer several pleasant surprises.

Sights

Parita follows a grid pattern. As you come to intersections near the town's center – which is about 500m from the Carretera Nacional – and glance both ways, you'll see buildings that look much the way they have for centuries. This town was founded in 1558, and most of the structures near its center date from at least the 18th century. The walls are thick and the beams are as solid as railroad ties. The roofs are made of red convex tiles and the fancier structures have arcades on the side facing the street.

The **church** in Parita is the only one in Panama that has its steeple located directly over its entrance rather than over a corner of the structure. This is very unusual, because bell towers are always extremely heavy and therefore are generally built on pillars that rest upon a massive foundation. It is a major curiosity to the residents of Parita that the steeple hasn't collapsed upon the entryway. Although the church was completed in 1723, you'll never see a Parita resident loitering near the entrance.

Beside the church is a grassy square in which cattle-roping demonstrations are held from August 3–7, during the town's patron-saint festivities.

Two doors down from the southeastern corner of Parita's church is a **workshop**

(☎ 974-2242/2036) that specializes in the restoration of altars. It is the only such workshop in the country. The artisans working here – Macario José Rodriguez and the twin brothers José Sergio Lopez and Sergio José Lopez – have been restoring the altars of Panama's colonial churches since the 1970s.

All three men speak some English and they are very friendly. Chances are they'll let you take a look around.

To find the home of one of the country's top **mask makers**, Darido Lopez, return to the Carretera Nacional and find the Shell station near the turnoff. Darido's house is about 100m northwest of the gas station, on the opposite side. Visitors can identify his home by the masks hanging beside his front door.

Darido has been making colorful masks for folkloric dancers since the 1960s. While he continues to make masks and satin costumes worn by dirty-devil dancers, these days most of his masks are exported to the USA and to Europe. Most cost between US$20 and US$80. (For more information on another of Panama's top mask makers, see p175.)

Getting There & Away

Parita makes an excellent day trip from Chitré. Buses for Parita leave the Chitré bus terminal station every 45 minutes from sunrise to sunset and cost US$0.50 each way (see p165). A taxi here costs about US$4.

REFUGIO DE VIDA SILVESTRE CENEGÓN DEL MANGLE

This wildlife refuge near Parita protects a mangrove forest at the mouth of the Río Santa María, an important wildlife area and nesting ground for herons. Its primary attraction is the birds, though people also claim the small pools here have health-giving properties.

The refuge is not reachable by bus; it's a 45-minute drive north of Chitré via the Carretera Nacional. Take the turnoff to **Los Pozos** (the Wells), which is signposted. After 1km the road forks at a church in the village of Paris; take the right branch and it becomes a dirt road. Proceed 3.8km on this road, after which you'll come to a sign with an arrow showing you where to go and indicating you're 1.88km from the wells. There's a viewing tower there as well as a restroom and a couple of picnic tables.

PESÉ

pop 2700

The town of Pesé, 19km southwest of Chitré, is ringed by sugarcane plantations and becomes extremely popular on Good Friday during its annual live representation of the Golgotha drama, a reenactment of Christ's crucifixion.

Pesé is home to the country's largest *seco* (a distilled liquor akin to rum) factory, **Seco Herrerano** (☎ 974-9621; fax 974-9593; free admission; 🕙 9am-5pm Mon-Sat), established in 1936. It's a rather small factory, with only 45 workers, but its output is impressive: 36,000 1L bottles every business day (Monday to Saturday). The distillery and mill are open for tours.

The mill operates only during the harvest season, which lasts from mid-January to mid-March. During this time, you can see tons of sugarcane being fed into huge presses to extract the sweet juice. The juice is then pumped into huge containers, where it ferments. What's impressive about this operation is the speed of the pressing and the power of the machinery.

If you wish to take a tour, fax your request at least a week in advance. Send it to Carlos Cedeño. Carlos speaks so-so English, so keep your request simple. Don't expect a reply and it's fine to just show up.

Getting There & Away

Pesé is 19km southwest of Chitré and the Carretera Nacional. It can be reached by bus from the Terminal de Transportes de Herrera in Chitré (US$1, 20 minutes, every 30 minutes).

OCÚ

pop 8700

This sleepy town, 49km by road southeast of bustling Santiago, is distinguished by its hat-makers and an artisans co-op in nearby San José. Not long ago, Ocú – which straddles a loop road that links it and the major Herrera Province towns of Chitré, Pesé, Los Pozos and Las Minas – used to be where Panamanians went to buy the finest Panama-style hats made in their country; now people often go to Penonomé, in Coclé Province (see p152).

There is a Banco Nacional de Panamá, a post office and a couple of decent restaurants, all located on the main street.

Hatmakers

Until the 1990s, Ocú's many hatmakers could take their intricately braided merchandise to the town square every morning and expect to have it all sold by noon. Truckers, who were major hat buyers, used to make special trips to Ocú for their headgear. But once good-quality hats became available in Penonomé, which is conveniently located on the Interamericana, the truckers stopped making the special trip, and the hatmakers began selling to vendors who resell the hats in Penonomé.

Today, there are still hatmakers in Ocú, and if you wish, you can visit some of them and see how a genuine Panama hat is made. The finest are so tightly braided that you can turn them over and fill them with water and they won't leak. The time needed to make a hat varies from one week to one month. Costs range from US$25 to US$150.

If you decide to visit a hatmaker, go see Elena Montilla and/or Ezequela Maure. They live only two houses apart at the northern end of town on the main street, Av Central. To find their houses, drive or walk about 1km on Av Central from the town plaza until you reach a fork in the road (a dirt road splits to the left, while the main paved road sweeps right; if you pass the Jorón El Tijera restaurant, in the fork of the road, you've gone too far). Ezequela's house is on the left side of the street, about four houses south of the fork. Elena's house is two doors down. None of Ocú's hatmakers speak English.

Festivals & Events

The **Festival del Manito Ocueño**, one of the country's best folklore events, is held in Ocú, usually during the third week in August (check with IPAT, p174, for dates). The three-day festival was established to maintain the region's traditional culture, and folklore groups from throughout Herrera Province present their dances in traditional dress. The fiesta's climax is a Sunday morning church wedding, after which the couple is paraded through the streets on horseback by friends and family.

Ocú is also famous for its **patron saint festival**, usually held January 20–23 (check with IPAT, as the dates are flexible). During this festival, an effigy of St Sebastian is paraded through the streets at night, and devotees walk behind the statue carrying lighted candles. This festival includes folklore programs and an agricultural fair.

Sleeping & Eating

There are several places to stay in Ocú. The best option is **Habitaciones de Juan Pablo** (☎ 974-1312; d or tw US$10) Just on the edge of town off the road connecting Ocú with the Interamericana (on the left if arriving from the Interamericana), you'll see a sign that reads 'se alquilan habitaciones' (rooms for rent), marked with a flag. Here you'll find eight basic rooms each with two double beds, a fan and clean private bathrooms. It's a friendly, family-run affair.

From here you can walk into the main square, where you'll find basic **restaurants** serving simple rural cuisine.

SAN JOSÉ

Just outside of Ocú, in the small village of San José, lies one of Panama's most organized artisan groups. **Artesanía Ocueña** (www .artesaniasocu.bizland.com) was founded in 1994 by a group of 20 members – all women – who carry on the intricate work of making *montunos* (traditional folklore outfits), *polleras* (traditional dresses from the Península de Azuero) and a range of other handmade items (tablecloths, place mats). Today the group numbers about 50, and they are receiving international attention (not least from the German government, who helped fund the construction of their workshop/studio in San José). The embroideries here are simply exquisite.

To visit the workshop, take the turnoff (the sign says 'Los Llanos') on the left side of the road as you head north of Ocú in the direction of the Interamericana. The turnoff is about 1km from the central plaza. From there it's a 15-minute drive along a crummy dirt road until you reach the community. You can also catch an 'Ocú–Los Llanos' *chiva* (rural bus; US$0.50) in front of the main plaza in Ocú. If no one's around when you stop in, ask around for **Ana Marin** (☎ 601-7430) or **Guillermina Montilla** (☎ 694-2251). The co-op also sells over the Internet.

CRUCE DE OCÚ

At the intersection of the Ocú highway and the Interamericana, there's an Accel gas station and a Texaco gas station. Between the two is a small field that borders the

Interamericana. Most buses traveling this section of the Interamericana, including the David–Panama City buses, stop beside the field to pick up and drop off passengers.

Café Daytona (7am-11pm) beside the Accel station has terrific food, including a 'Texas hamburger with cheese' for US$1.50. They also have fresh fruit shakes, Greek salad, chili con carne and a range of other filling meals. The restaurant's Greek owner and chef, Antonio Joannou, takes great pride in his inexpensive and tasty food – and it shows.

Los Santos Province

CONTENTS

Villa de Los Santos	173
Playas Monagre & El Rompío	175
Road to Las Tablas	176
Guararé	176
Las Tablas	177
Santo Domingo	179
Pedasí	179
Refugio de Vida Silvestre Isla Iguana	181
South of Pedasí	181
Isla de Cañas	182
Tonosí	183
El Charcón	183
Playas Cambutal & Guánico	183
Macaracas	183

Covering the southeastern third of the Península de Azuero, Los Santos Province is home to cowboys, statuesque people and gorgeous beaches. It was here that Panama's cry for independence from Spain was first uttered. And yet the residents of the Saints Province take great pride in their Spanish history, and showcase it in folkloric festivals that date back to the first settlers.

The Fiesta de Corpus Christi in Villa de Los Santos, and the Fiesta de Santa Librada in the provincial capital of Las Tablas, are marked by exuberant displays of traditional clothing and dances born in Spain during the Middle Ages. The most intricate *polleras* – the national costume that is an elaboration on the dresses worn by Spanish peasants during the 17th and 18th centuries – are made in the village of La Enea and in villages around Las Tablas.

As in Herrera Province, many locals in Los Santos Province look distinctly European. The people are taller, their skin fairer, and their features more chiseled than those of Panamanians elsewhere on the isthmus. Their eyes are often hazel or blue and some even have red or blond hair. In Los Santos more than in any other province of Panama, the European bloodline is apparent and the whites want to keep it that way.

Yet for at least the past 100 years, the residents of Los Santos Province have known only racial harmony, and their sense of community pride is so strong that one wonders if it's hereditary. If you meet a black, Indian or white Los Santos native in another part of the country you'll surely know it, as he or she will tell you in short order.

HIGHLIGHTS

- Traveling among the people of **Los Santos Province** – some of the friendliest and most animated in Panama

- Catching the wild celebrations at **Las Tablas'** Carnaval (p178) and **Villa de Los Santos'** Corpus Christi bash (p178), or **Guararé**'s Feria de la Mejorana (p177)

- Spotting sea turtles at **Isla de Cañas** (p182), whose beaches are visited by thousands of the amphibians each year

- Roaming **La Enea** and **Santo Domingo** (p179), where local dressmakers create *polleras,* the beautiful national costume

- Surfing great waves and soaking up the pristine beauty of **Playa Venao** (p182), one of Panama's loveliest beaches

| ▪ AREA: 3806 SQ KM | ▪ ELEVATION: SEA LEVEL TO 950 METERS | ▪ POPULATION: 86,700 |

LOS SANTOS PROVINCE

LOS SANTOS PROVINCE

Climate
The Península de Azuero follows a straight-forward rainy-dry season. During the rainy winter months (April to November) the hillsides are lush and green, while in summer (December to March) little rain falls, leaving the countryside dry and barren-looking.

National Parks
Although the province has no national parks, there is a wildlife refuge and a protected area frequented by nesting sea turtles. The **Refugio de Vida Silvestre Isla Iguana** (p181) near Pedasí has some lovely snorkeling and diving. You might also see some humpback whales in the area. **Isla de Cañas**

(p182) is a major nesting site for olive ridley sea turtles.

VILLA DE LOS SANTOS
pop 7700

The Río La Villa, 4km south of downtown Chitré, marks the boundary between the provinces of Herrera and Los Santos. Just south of the river you'll come to Villa de Los Santos (often called simply 'Los Santos'), on the Carretera Nacional.

This picturesque town, replete with many colonial structures, is where Panama's first move toward independence from Spain began on November 10, 1821. The event is honored with a museum and an annual celebration. Also worth a look is the

VILLA DE LOS SANTOS

INFORMATION		
Banco Nacional de Panamá.......**1** C1	SLEEPING	(p175)
IPAT Tourist Office.................**2** C1	Hotel La Villa.............................**9** A3
Lavamatica Chele....................**3** C1	Kevin's Hotel & Restaurant......**10** B2
Pharmacy...............................**4** C1	
Police Station.........................**5** C1	TRANSPORT	(p175)
	Buses to Chitré..........................**11** B2
SIGHTS & ACTIVITIES (pp174-5)	Buses to Las Tablas & Chitré..(see 15)
Home of Maskmaker Carlos Ivan de	Buses to Panama City................**12** C1
Leon..................................**6** B2	Buses to Panama City................**13** C1
Iglesia de San Atanacio **7** C1	Taxis..**14** C1
Museo de la Nacionalidad.........**8** C1	Taxis..**15** B2

old church. There's a good hotel and a wild bar/dance club in town too.

Information

Banco Nacional de Panamá (cnr Av 10 de Noviembre & Calle Tomas Herrera)

IPAT (☎ 966-8013; fax 996-8040; Calle José Vallarino; ⏰ 9am-4pm Mon-Fri) Provides information on any upcoming celebrations in the area.

Laundry (Calle José Vallarino; ⏰ 8am-6pm Mon-Sat, 9am-noon Sun)

Pharmacy (Calle Segundo Villarreal)

Police station (Av 10 de Noviembre)

Sights

MUSEO DE LA NACIONALIDAD

This unimpressive **museum** (Calle José Vallarino; adult/child US$1/0.25; ⏰ 9am-4:30pm Tue-Sat, 9am-1pm Sun), opposite Plaza Simón Bolívar, occupies the former house where Panama's Declaration of Independence was signed in 1821. In the years that followed, the handsome brick-and-tile residence served as a jail, a school and a legislature. It predates the town's church, but no one knows exactly when it was built.

Inaugurated as a museum in 1974, it contains artifacts related to Panama's independence, which was declared in Los Santos 18 days before it was declared by the government. It also contains objects from the era of the Spanish conquest. Pre-Columbian ceramics and colonial-era religious art comprise most of the exhibits. There's also a lovely garden courtyard.

IGLESIA DE SAN ATANACIO

Villa de Los Santos' church, alongside Plaza Simón Bolívar, opened its doors to the public in 1782, after nine years of construction. It's a fine example of the Baroque style, with lots of intricately carved wood depicting cherubs, saints, Jesus and the Virgin. Almost everything in the church is original, and some of the objects even predate the structure itself. The 12m arch in front of the altar, for example, bears its date of manufacture (1733) and the names of its two creators.

The altar is made of mahogany and rosewood and covered nearly from base to top in gold leaf. In a glass sepulcher in front of the altar is a near-life-size wooden statue of

Christ that is carried through the streets of Villa de Los Santos on Good Friday, behind a candlelit procession.

This church was granted national monument status by the government in 1938 and is truly a national treasure.

MASKS

Carlos Ivan de Leon (☎ 966-9149; Calle Tomas Herrera; ⌚ noon-1pm & 6-10pm) makes the most elaborate and frightening masks in Panama at his house near Calle Segundo Villareal. He specializes in one kind of mask, that of the devil for the famous *baile de los diablos sucios* (dance of the dirty devils). Most of Carlos' masks are sold to professional dancers, but increasingly they are being bought by European and American collectors. Several are on display at the IPAT office in Los Santos, while others appear in the lobby of the Hotel Versalles in Chitré.

Look for the house with a black front door and a sign with his family name (De Leon) nearby. Carlos speaks Spanish only.

For information on Panama's top mask makers, see Parita (p167).

Festivals & Events

The anniversary of the historic *grito* (cry), also known as the **First Call for Independence**, is celebrated in Los Santos on November 10, or the nearest Saturday to it.

The **Feria de Azuero** (Azuero Fair, late April/ early May) features folkloric dancing, agricultural attractions and competition among local singers performing regional songs.

The **Fiesta de Corpus Christi** is held from Thursday to Sunday, 40 days after Easter (May/June) and is one of the most animated in the country. It features masked and costumed dancers representing angels, devils and imps while enacting dramas.

Other notable festivals include **Carnaval**, celebrated four days before Ash Wednesday (February/March) and **Semana Santa** (Holy Week) celebrated in April.

Sleeping & Eating

In the southwestern section of town, 500m from the Carretera Nacional, **Hotel La Villa** (☎ 966-9321; fax 966-8201; s/d US$24/33; ❄ ▣) has small rooms with air-con and private bathrooms and slightly bigger standard rooms with better beds. There's also a swimming pool, a bar and a good restaurant.

Kevin's Hotel (☎ 966-8276; fax 966-9000; r US$15-21; ❄), set back from the Carretera Nacional, features a range of guestrooms with air-con, DirecTV, two double beds and private hot-water bathroom. Rooms range from mediocre to decent and are better value than the Hotel La Villa. The hotel's **restaurant** (mains US$4-7; ⌚ 8am-9pm) is very good and reasonably priced. Specials include *chuleta a la barbecue* (barbecue pork chops) and *cacerola de mariscos* (seafood casserole).

Getting There & Around

Chitré–Las Tablas buses stop on the Carretera Nacional, and Chitré–Villa de Los Santos buses stop on Calle José Vallarino half a block from the Carretera Nacional. Fares to these destinations or anywhere in the province are usually between US$0.50 and US$2.

Buses to Panama City depart from Calle José Vallarino at Av 10 de Noviembre, and also from Calle Segundo Villarreal a block and a half northeast of Plaza Simón Bolívar.

Taxis are a quick way to get around Villa de Los Santos and between Villa de Los Santos and Chitré. The fare won't exceed US$3 if you stay within these cities. Taxis can usually be found near the bus stop on the Carretera Nacional and northwest of Plaza Simón Bolívar.

PLAYAS MONAGRE & EL ROMPÍO

Ten kilometers northeast of Villa de Los Santos are the Playas Monagre and El Rompío. Both beaches are popular with fishermen, families and body surfers, but beware of possible rip currents (see Swimming Safety, p296). El Rompío is less frequented than Monagre and has less litter, but both have a lot of driftwood on them and the sand is dark and hot on sunny days. Both places have a couple of inexpensive inns, and simple, open-sided restaurants serving seafood nearby. open-air **Brisas del Mar** (meals US$7; ⌚ 7am-11pm), 50 meters from Playa Monagre, is the best restaurant in the area. Owned by an eccentric German woman, there's no menu here, but Brigitte can prepare just about anything you want (curry shrimp, tuna steaks, grilled fish with ginger, cajun-style lobster, grilled conch). Any budget can be accommodated for and meals include a salad and vegetables. Hearty breakfasts (pancakes, eggs, ham or shrimp omelets) are also served.

A bus leaves the Chitré station for Playas Monagre and El Rompío (US$1, around 20km, hourly) from sunrise to sunset. This bus passes through Villa de Los Santos on the way to the beaches and can be hailed from the Carretera Nacional in town. Look for a bus with 'Monagre' on its windshield. The fare from Villa de Los Santos to either beach is US$0.50. A taxi ride from Chitré to either beach costs about US$5; a taxi from Villa de Los Santos costs half that.

ROAD TO LAS TABLAS

The Carretera Nacional from Villa de Los Santos to Las Tablas runs mostly past small farms and cattle ranches, with almost no remaining forest in sight. Indeed, the province is the most heavily deforested in the country.

About 3km southeast of Los Santos along the Carretera Nacional is **Kiosco El Ciruelo** (🕐 6am-10pm Fri-Sun), a rustic trucker stop where everything is cooked on a wood-fire grill. Among the offerings is a traditional specialty of Los Santos Province: tamales wrapped in plantain leaves and made with corn, pork and other spices.

From Kiosco El Ciruelo, travel 5.6km southeast, and on the eastern side of the road you'll see a bright blue public phone and just beyond it a small hut, **La Casa de la Pipa** (The House of Coconut Juice), beside a large pile of coconut husks. Here you can get fresh, ice-cold coconut water for US$0.25.

As you travel the two-lane Carretera Nacional toward Las Tablas, you'll occasionally see stands with sausages dangling in front of them. The **pork sausages** made on the Península de Azuero are nationally famous for their delicious taste, but you might want to get some at one of the grocery stores on the peninsula.

If you're traveling the highway around Carnaval time, you'll also see dozens of smashed-up cars on the roadside. These once belonged to the motorists killed by drunk drivers during Carnaval. The police realize that most of the people on the road during Carnaval are intoxicated. Instead of trying to arrest all the drunk motorists, the police display the old wrecks, hoping the sight will encourage drunks to drive slowly. Try to avoid highway travel during Carnaval.

GUARARÉ

pop 4200

The tiny town of Guararé, on the Carretera Nacional between Villa de Los Santos and Las Tablas, offers little of interest to tourists, but it does have some attractions, including a museum, nearby *pollera* makers and a large annual festival.

Museo Manuel F Zárate

Zárate was a folklorist who was devoted to conserving the traditions and folklore of the Azuero region. The **museum** (adult/child US$0.75/0.25; 🕐 8am-noon & 1-4pm Tue-Sat, 8am-noon Sun), in Zárate's former home, contains *polleras*, masks, *diablito* (little devil) costumes and other exhibits. It's two blocks behind the church, about six short blocks from the main road (turn off at the gas station).

La Enea

Some of the finest *polleras* are made in this small village northeast of Guararé. The *pollera* (once the daily attire of Spain's lower classes in the 17th and 18th centuries) has today become a national costume of stirring beauty and elegance. Almost every part of the costume is made by hand, from the attractive embroidery on the blouse and skirt to the delicate filigree ornaments tucked around the gold combs in the hair.

The traditional assortment of jewelry worn with a *pollera* can cost upwards of US$20,000.

By convention, the *pollera* consists of two basic pieces: a blouse that rests upon the tops of the shoulders and a long skirt divided into two fully gathered tiers. Each dress requires no less than 10m of fine white linen or cotton cloth. Elaborate needlework in a single color enriches the white background.

One of the best-known makers of the national costume, **Ildaura Saavedra de Espina** (☎ 994-5527), lives beside Parque de La Enea, in the green-tiled house next door to the small market with 'Roxana' painted over its door. She made her first *pollera* in 1946 at the age of 16 and has been making them ever since, averaging one *pollera* every six months. Ildama sold her first dress for US$300. Today, she charges US$1800 per dress.

Anyone with a keen interest in needlecraft is welcome to visit Ildama, who speaks Spanish only. She is accustomed to strangers stopping by her home to marvel at her handiwork. If you're lucky, Ildama will show you her scrapbook, containing photos of many of the dresses she's made. Be advised that every dress is made to order. She does not have a rack of *polleras* on hand, just sections of the one she's working on.

Festivals & Events

Like most towns in Los Santos Province, Guararé is not without at least one festival, in this case the **Feria de la Mejorana**, a combined patron saint and folkloric festival held from September 23 to 27. As in all patron saint festivals, a statue of a saint is paraded through the streets.

The folkloric festival is the country's largest. Begun by Manuel Zárate in 1950 to stimulate interest and participation in traditional practices, the Feria de la Mejorana has become the best place to see Panama's folklore in all its manifestations. Dance groups from all over the country – and even some from other Latin American countries – attend this annual event, which includes a colorful parade in which participants are hauled through the streets in oxcarts.

Folkloric dances that were once part of other celebrations in other places are today sometimes seen only at this event. For example, this is the only festival in which a dance known as La Pajarita (Paper Bird) is performed. In contrast to the various exuberant devil dances, a calm, religious quality pervades La Pajarita.

Sleeping & Eating

Just off the Chitré–Las Tablas highway, the **Residencial La Mejorana** (☎ 994-5794; fax 994-5796; r US$13-48; ⊠) is a large, clean, modern hotel. The rooms are in good condition, with air-con, TV, telephone and private hot-water bathroom. Prices vary depending on the number of beds and the size of the room, but the cheaper rooms are just fine. There's a good restaurant-bar here.

Getting There & Away

Guararé is beside the Carretera Nacional, 20km south of Villa de Los Santos. La Enea is to its northeast. You can hop on any bus that travels the highway in the direction of Guararé; you'll be dropped off at the town.

To get to La Enea, take a taxi (US$2).

LAS TABLAS

pop 8600

Las Tablas is the capital city of Los Santos Province and has a fine church and a small museum devoted to former Las Tablas statesman and three-time president Belisario Porras. The city is famous for its Carnaval, widely regarded as Panama's most authentic, and also famous for its combined patron saint/*pollera* festival – a colorful mix of religious ceremony and beauty contest.

Orientation

Las Tablas is 31km southeast of Chitré via the Carretera Nacional, which becomes Av Laureano Lopez at the northern edge of town and reemerges as the road to Santo Domingo on the southeastern side of town. Av Laureano Lopez runs for nine blocks before ending at the Museo Belisario Porras, beside the central plaza.

Almost everything of interest to travelers is within five blocks of the plaza. This includes remnants of one of the finest colonial churches on the peninsula, banks, a post office, hotels and restaurants. Further out is a bus station and taxi stands.

Information

Banco Nacional de Panamá (Av Laureano Lopez, near Calle 2)

BBVA (Av Belisario Porras) ATM available

Banistmo (Calle Belisario Porras)

Laundry (Calle Doctor Emilio Castro; ⊠ 8am-noon & 1-5pm Mon-Sat)

PC Center (Calle 8 de Noviembre; per hr US$1) Near the plaza

Post office (Calle 2)

Zona Internet (Calle 8 de Noviembre; per hr US$1; ⊠ 8am-10pm Mon-Sat) Near the plaza

There is no tourist office in town.

Museo Belisario Porras

This **museum** (Av Belisario Porras; adult/child US$0.50/0.25; ⊠ 9am-12:30pm & 1:30-4pm Tue-Sat, 9am-noon Sun) opposite Central Plaza is in the mud-walled former home of three-time president Belisario Porras, during whose administration the Panama Canal opened. Porras, who is regarded as a national hero, was president for all but two years from 1912 to 1924. He is credited with establishing Panama's network of public hospitals, creating a national registry for land titles, and constructing scores of

LAS TABLAS

0 ———— 400 m
0 ———— 0.2 miles

INFORMATION
Banco Nacional de Panamá.......**1** B2
Banistmo..................................**2** A3
BBVA ATM..............................**3** B3
Lavandería Popular.................**4** C2
PC Center................................**5** A3
Post Office..............................**6** A2
Zona Internet.........................**7** A3

SIGHTS & ACTIVITIES (pp177-8)
Iglesia Santa Librada................**8** A3
Museo Belisario Porras.............**9** A3

SLEEPING (p179)
Hospedaje Mariela..................**10** B3
Hotel Manolo..........................**11** B3

EATING (p179)
Jorón Moraveal.......................**12** A2
Los Portales............................**13** B3
Panadería Tio Lucho...............**14** A3
Pizzeria Portofino....................**15** A3
Restaurante El Caserón............**16** B3

TRANSPORT (p179)
Bus Station.............................**17** B2
Taxis......................................**18** B3
Taxis......................................**19** B2

bridges and aqueducts. The museum contains many artifacts from Porras' life.

Incidentally, the huge tomb inside the museum, which bears Porras' name, is empty. Plans to move his remains here from a cemetery in Panama City were never carried out. Interestingly, all of Porras' male descendants wear their whiskers in his unusual style – a thick, prideful mustache resembling the horns of a Texas longhorn steer.

Iglesia Santa Librada

This Baroque-style **church** (Av Belisario Porras) near the central plaza opened its doors on March 9, 1789, but sustained major damage in 1950 during a fire. The walls are original as is the base of the pulpit. The painted faces on the ornate 23-karat gold-leaf altar are original, but the figurines of Christ, the Virgin and the saints were added after the blaze. Cedar wood was used in the construction of the altar, which was renovated in 2001.

Festivals & Events

Las Tablas is perhaps the best place in Panama to spend **Carnaval**, which is held during the

four days that precede Ash Wednesday. By tradition, the town is divided into two groups, *calle arriba* (high street) and *calle abajo* (low street), which compete intensely with each other in every aspect of the fiesta. Each calle has its own queen, floats and songs. Each day begins with members parading in street clothes, singing songs that poke fun at the rival group. During the parade, jokesters from both sides toss tinted water, blue dye and shaving cream at the other side. No one, onlookers included, is spared; dress expecting to get creamed.

Both sides take a rest during the heat of the day and don costumes or put finishing touches on their floats in the late afternoon. Then at dusk, the groups' parades begin on parallel streets, led by floats that are followed by musicians seated in the back of flatbed trucks, who are followed in turn by *calle* members. Every night, each *calle* has a different float and different costumes. Crowds pack the sidewalks and fireworks light up the night. The queens make their appearances on Saturday night, dressed at first in gaudily decorated costumes and later in exquisite evening gowns. Their coronation is held on Sunday. Monday is masquerade day, and Tuesday all the women in town who have *polleras* don them and fill the streets.

Another excellent time to be in Las Tablas is July 21, when the provincial capital hosts two big events: the patron saint festival and the *pollera* festival.

The highlight of the **Fiesta de Santa Librada** is the procession through the streets. The sacred event and services inside the church are accompanied by street celebrations that recall a medieval fair – gambling, dancing, singing, bullfights, and excessive eating and drinking. It's a strange juxtaposition of the sacred and the profane.

The **Fiesta de La Pollera** is a photographer's delight. Beautiful young women model the national costume as they pass through the streets, all the while being judged on their grace as well as on the artisanship, design and authenticity of their costumes.

Sleeping

Hotel Manolo (☎ 994-6372; Calle Belisario Porras; s/d without window US$17/25, with window US$20/30; ✹) This pleasant hotel was rebuilt in 2001 and offers good value in its 15 guestrooms (all on the 2nd floor, above a restaurant-bar). All rooms have air con, private hot-water bathroom, telephone and TV.

Hospedaje Mariela (☎ 994-6366; ☎ /fax 994-7422; Av Belisario Porras; d with shared bath US$9, d with fan/air-con US$12/16; ✹) Above an old-school barbershop, the Hospedaje Mariela is the best budget option, featuring a wide range of rooms. Most have decent light and all have tile floors. A few have private bathroom (some have hot water; some don't) and the beds range from shabby to fair; check a few.

Eating

Restaurante El Caserón (cnr Calles Augustin Batista & Moises Espino; mains US$4-6) This local favorite serves a range of tasty plates. Breakfast items include the popular *especial ranchero* (steak and eggs), while lunch and dinner items include chow mein, beef steaks and fish.

Panadería Tío Lucho (facing Central Plaza) This bakery has a small selection of breads, pastries, desserts and ice cream.

Los Portales (Av Belisario Porras; mains US$3-5) In a handsome colonial building, this low-key spot serves steaks, roast chicken and corvina. A tasty farm-style breakfast (US$2.60)

includes coffee, steak with sauce and corn patties.

Pizzeria Portofino (Av Belisario Porras; medium pizzas US$3.50) Popular with families and students, the simple Pizzeria Portofino serves thin-crust pizzas, *batidos* (fruit shakes), burgers and sandwiches for low prices.

Jorón Moravel (Calle 1; ☯ 7am-midnight) This pleasant and attractive thatched-roof restaurant specializes in pizzas. Sandwiches, fresh fish and many grilled items are also available.

Getting There & Away

From Las Tablas' **bus station** (cnr Av Laureano Lopez & Av Doctor Emilio Castro) buses run hourly to Santo Domingo (US$0.30, 10 minutes, 5km), Chitré (US$1, 30 minutes, 31km), Tonosí (US$3, 1½ hours, 79km) and Pedasí (US$2, one hour, 41km).

There are 10 daily departures to Panama City (US$6.50, 4½ hours, 282km) – more during holidays and festivals.

Getting Around

Las Tablas is a small town and is very walkable. Taxis are available on Calle 1, two blocks north of the central plaza and on Calle Belisario Porras at Calle Estudiante. Fares within town never exceed US$2.

SANTO DOMINGO

If you're in the market for Panama's **polleras**, the beautiful national costume, there are several places besides Guararé where the colorfully embroidered dresses are made. Keep in mind that the *polleras* may cost US$2000 apiece.

The small town of Santo Domingo, about 10 minutes from Las Tablas by car, is known for its fine *polleras*, as are the nearby hamlets of **La Tiza**, **El Cocal**, **El Carate** and **San José**. If you haven't got wheels, your best bet is to hire a taxi. The roundtrip fare to San José, the most remote of the bunch, will set you back US$40.

PEDASÍ

pop 2100

This pleasant coastal town of friendly souls, 41km southeast of Las Tablas, makes a good base to explore the local beaches. Many people make forays from here to the Refugio de Vida Silvestre Isla Iguana, a wildlife refuge that offers some fine snorkeling and diving.

Orientation & Information

The Carretera Nacional passes down the western part of Pedasí. There are some fine beaches a few kilometers to the east. A **Banco Nacional de Panama**, with ATM, is at the northern entrance to town. A new **IPAT** office (🕑 8am-8pm) lies behind the Residencial Pedasí hotel in the north of town. Eduardo Moscoso, one of the staff members there, leads tours to both Isla Iguana and Isla de Cañas. Next door is an **Internet café** (per hr US$1; 🕑 9:30am-5:30pm Mon-Fri, 9:30am-4pm Sat). The **ANAM** office in the south of town can provide information about Isla Iguana and Isla de Cañas (p182).

Sights & Activities

SCUBA DIVING

You can arrange dives through the **Pedasí Scuba Center** (☎ 995-2405; www.divenfishpanama.com), next door to IPAT. It offers diving and boating excursions to Isla Iguana or Isla Frailes (boat hire US$80, two-tank dive US$35) and other areas. The Scuba Center also rents snorkeling gear for US$10 per day.

PLAYAS EL TORO & LA GARITA

The surf at these beaches is usually safe for swimming; this is particularly true at La Garita, but El Toro is the more accessible of the two. At El Toro you can actually drive onto the beach if you have a vehicle, but La Garita is flanked by a rocky slope, and a hike of about 100m through light scrub and dirt (mud if there's been any recent rain) is required to reach the beach. Despite their proximity to Pedasí, both beaches are quite isolated and private. Neither offers much snorkeling – the water is simply too murky.

You can hire a taxi in Pedasí to reach these beaches; if you're driving from central Pedasí, turn east off the Carretera Nacional onto the paved street beside the Pensión Moscoso, and drive about 250m to the Cantina Hermanos Cedeño bar. Then take the dirt road just past the bar for 1km until the road forks. Follow the signs for 2km to the beaches.

Festivals & Events

Pedasí holds patron saint festivals on June 29 and November 25, or the nearest Saturday to them. These are fun affairs, with long parades and lots of merriment. On July 16, a celebration for fishermen is held at Playa Arenal, a beach 3km northwest of town.

Sleeping

There are three places to stay in Pedasí all of which are located on the Carretera Nacional and are good value.

Residencial Moscoso (☎ 995-2203; s/d US$6/8, with air-con & private bathroom US$14/17; 🅿) Near the center of town, Moscoso has simple, clean rooms with cable TV and shared bathroom, as well as brighter rooms with private cold water bathroom. The owner is related to Panama's former president, Mireya Moscoso, who is from Pedasí.

Residencial Pedasí (☎ 995-2322; s/d/tr US$15, 20/25) At the northern end of town, Residencial Pedasí has decent rooms fronting a tranquil courtyard, and a restaurant on the premises.

Dim's Hostal (☎ /fax 995-2303; s/d US$17/23) On the main road near the center of town, Dim's has a family atmosphere with a fine backyard, complete with hammocks and a shady mango tree. Each of the five rooms features one double bed, two single beds and a private cold-water bathroom (the only drawback).

Eating

Don't miss lovely **Dulceria Yely,** a cake shop on a side street near the Pensión Moscoso (opposite side of the street). Slices of Mrs Dalila Vera de Quintero's cakes sell for US$0.25 to US$0.50, and they are divine. Her rum cake is glorious, as is her *manjar* cake (manjar resembles caramel in taste and appearance and is a specialty of the region). Also sold here is *chicheme*, a wonderful drink made from milk, mashed sweet corn, cinnamon and vanilla (US$.30), and *uvita chichi,* a drink made from berries that grow in the region. The desserts served to Panama's president are purchased here. You can also find very tasty sandwiches (chicken or roast beef).

Restaurante JR (mains US$8-12; 🕑 noon-1pm & 6-8pm), on the opposite side of the street and 100m south of the Hotel Residencial Pedasí, this restaurant features an owner-cook-server who was a chef in France and Canada before he retired to Pedasí. The menu varies daily but often includes flaming pepper steak, chicken curry with seafood, and garlic lobster.

Refresqueria Juicy (🕑 5pm-midnight) Several blocks south but on the same side of the street as Restaurant JR, this low-key restaurant serves tasty hamburgers and empanadas.

Restaurante Angela (mains US$2.50-4), near Dim's Hostel, serves good, cheap plates of simple Panamanian cuisine.

Getting There & Away

Buses to Las Tablas leave every 45 minutes between 6am and 4:30pm (US$3, two hours). Buses to Venao and south are sporadic. Generally there's one a day at around 8pm that passes the beach en route to Cañas, returning the next morning at around 8am. A taxi costs US$12 to US$14 to Venao.

REFUGIO DE VIDA SILVESTRE ISLA IGUANA

The Iguana Island Wildlife Refuge is a 55-hectare protected island ringed by coral fields, much of which died in the 1982–83 El Niño (a change in weather patterns that shifts ocean currents and starves marine life along the eastern Pacific coast). However, the surviving coral is pretty spectacular and is shallow enough to be snorkeled.

Humpback whales inhabit the waters around Isla Iguana from June to November. These large sea mammals, 15m to 20m long, mate and bear their young here and then teach them to dive. The humpbacks are the famous 'singing whales'; occasionally you can hear their underwater sounds when diving here.

The island is supposed to be maintained by Panama's environmental agency, but the main beach is often strewn with litter. Also, the US Navy used the island for target practice during WWII, and unexploded ordnance is occasionally discovered here; it's unwise to stray off the island's beaten paths.

Isla Iguana is reachable by boat from Playa El Arenal, a beach 3km northwest of the Accel station in Pedasí. At the beach, boatman Lionel Ureña takes parties of up to eight people to the island for US$20 each way. Be sure to tell him when to return for you. Lionel speaks Spanish only.

Stop by the ANAM office in Pedasí (p180) for more information.

SOUTH OF PEDASÍ
Playa Los Destiladeros

On a bluff overlooking a lovely beach are several tall, thatched-roof **cabins** (☎ 675-9715, 211-2277; d cabin US$130) that are some of

Panama's most charming accommodations. The painstaking work that went into these cabins is apparent, from the lovely hand-carved washbasins to the front decks with sea views. Each cabin is fan cooled and allows plenty of privacy, and the price includes three meals a day. The owner and designer, Philippe Atanasiades, is one of the best chefs in Panama (and founder of several successful restaurants, including Las Bovedas in Panama City), meaning guests eat quite well here. To get here, drive through Pedasí and take the turnoff to the left in El Limon.

Resort La Playita

This **'resort'** (☎ 996-2225, 996-6551; d cabin US$60) 31km southwest of Pedasí consists of three lovely cabins, each beautifully designed with good beds and private hot-water bathroom. Guests have access to La Playita's beautiful beach with (generally) no one on it. Ask for the cabin with ocean views. One thing you should know about La Playita is that the owner has a soft spot for the avian species. There are lots of birds here – particularly ostriches, spotted pigeons and several turkeys – but watch out; the birds have the run of the grounds.

There's also a pleasant restaurant overlooking the water, and you can rent snorkeling gear (US$6) or arrange boat trips with the owner (US$30). Be advised that if you stay here on weekend days, you'll be sharing the facilities with dozens (sometimes hundreds) of revelers who come from Los Santos to party beside the beach.

Villa Marina

The next driveway past La Playita leads to **Villa Marina** (☎ 211-2277; www.playavenado.com; d/master bedroom US$85/110; 🔀), a beautiful bed-and-breakfast set right on the beach. The three cozily furnished guestrooms feature good beds with air-con and good light. Two of the guestrooms are rather small and share a hot-water bathroom, while the master bedroom is larger with a private bathroom and French doors that open toward the ocean. It's a charming spot, and the price includes three meals a day. There are hammocks, horses available for hire, and guests can use the snorkeling gear and boogie boards. The owner can also arrange boating and fishing excursions.

RESCUING THE TUNA

Thirty kilometers southwest of Pedasí, on the southern side of the road, is the entrance to the **Laboratorio Achotines** (www.iattc.org), where a group of US marine biologists studies the early life of yellowfin tuna. Their research has played a key role in the implementation of fishing quotas to protect the tuna stock in Pacific Ocean waters from California to Ecuador. Their recommendations to an international regulatory commission on the use of certain types of fishing nets have also played a direct role in reducing the number of dolphins that are killed by tuna fishing in the eastern Pacific, from 500,000 annually to 3000. The research center is not open to the general public.

Playa Venao

Playa Venao is a long, curving protected beach (no riptides) that's very popular with surfers because it almost always has waves to surf, and because the waves break both ways.

The Playa Venao turnoff is 33km by road southwest of Pedasí, or 2km past the Resort La Playita turnoff. Facilities here are limited to an open-sided restaurant-bar and very rustic *cabañas* for US$16 a night. Bring a mosquito net. An option is to bring a tent and camp beside the beach for free. Hardcore surfers sleep in their cars. There's a **public phone** (☎ 995-8107) beside the restaurant.

Getting here by bus is challenging. One bus from Cañas passes in the morning (between 8am and 9am) en route to Pedasí (US$2). The bus makes the return journey in the evening (Pedasí to Cañas) though it's much easier to take a taxi from Pedasí (US$12 to US$14).

ISLA DE CAÑAS

From the end of August through November, thousands of olive ridley sea turtles come ashore at night to lay eggs in the sand on the broad beach of Cane Island. This is one of five places that these endangered turtles nest in such numbers. The others are two beaches on the Pacific side of Costa Rica, and two beaches in Orissa, India, on the Bay of Bengal.

The turnoff for Isla de Cañas is easy to miss. It's beside a bus stop on the south side of the Carretera Nacional, 6.5km west of the turnoff for the town of Cañas; next to the bus stop, there's a brown-and-yellow sign that reads 'Bienvenidos Isla de Cañas via Puerto 2.5km.' The bus stop is served by Toyota Coaster buses that travel between Las Tablas and Tonosí hourly from 7am to 4pm.

From the turnoff, a 5km drive or hike on a dirt road takes you to the edge of a mangrove forest. There's usually a boatman

there who will shuttle you to and from the island for US$5 per party. If there's no boatman to greet you, find the truck wheel hanging from a tree at the mangrove's edge and hit it hard five times with the rusty wrench atop it. If the sun's out and the tide's up – if there's water in the mangrove – a boatman will fetch you.

Either arrive during daylight hours, or call ahead for boatman **Pedro Perez** (☎ 995-8002) and let him know (in Spanish) when you'll be arriving.

Once you reach the island, you will be approached by a guide. As a rule every foreign visitor must be accompanied by an island guide who will likely charge US$10 an hour per group when working. If they couldn't make money from the turtles in this way, these people would sell all the turtle eggs they could find on the black market. As it is, about half of the eggs that are laid on the beach are dug up and sold illegally in Panama City. The other half are placed in hatcheries.

The turtles arrive late at night, so there's no point in hiring the guide during daylight hours. Instead, agree on a meeting place and an hour when the guide can take you. When that time arrives, the guide will walk you across the island to the beach, and if you're lucky you'll arrive when many expectant mothers are arriving. Sea turtles are easily frightened, particularly by bright lights such as flashlights. Don't bring one. Instead, just let your eyes adjust to the moonlight.

There's a restaurant and some rustic **cabañas** (per person US$10) if you wish to stay on the island. Bring a mosquito net and lots of insect repellent, long pants, a windbreaker or bug jacket and mosquito coils if you have them.

You can arrange tours to the island through IPAT in Pedasí; you can get information on these tours at the ANAM office in Pedasí (p180). Expect to pay about US$30 for a small group.

TONOSÍ

pop 2400

The chief attractions in this cowboy town, 57km southwest of Pedasí, are its scenery – the town is in a green valley ringed by tan hills – and its proximity to many isolated surfing beaches.

Tonosí's streets roughly follow a grid pattern. If you arrive from the north via El Cacao, you'll be on the Carretera El Cacao until you reach the center of Tonosí. Here the highway intersects with Av Central, Tonosí's main street, which is flanked on both sides by homes.

The **Residencial Mar y Selva** (☎ 995-8153; fax 995-8185; s/d/t US$16/18/20; ✹), on the main road into town, has the town's best-value accommodation with clean, modern air-con rooms and private hot-water bathroom. On the ground floor, **Restaurante Lindy** (meals around US$3) specializes in rural Panamanian food, which is good and cheap.

The friendly **Hospedaje Irtha** (☎ 995-8316; Calle Antonio Degracia; d/tr US$5/7, tr with air-con US$15; ✹) has seven basic rooms with cement floor and shared bathroom, and a triple room with air-con. To get there take the first left past Residencial Mar y Selva, follow the street to the end, take a right and you'll see it.

EL CHARCÓN

This open-sided thatched-roofed restaurant-bar **El Charcón** (✹ 7am-11pm daily) is 1km from the Restaurante Lindy on the road to Playa Guánico. It specializes in smoked and grilled meat, mostly beef and pork. Popular dishes include *carne de res humada* (smoked beef, US$2.75), *pollo humado* (smoked chicken, US$2.50), and saltwater and freshwater shrimp. The food is very authentic for the region and good. It's a pleasant place, made all the more so because of all the lovely hardwood used in its construction.

Just below the road, 100m south of the restaurant, you'll see a slow-moving river that's home to cattle egrets, American caiman and yellow-eared turtles. Check it out, but before you do ask the owner of El Charcón for a bag of fat (US$0.25) to take with you to toss to the caiman. He'll gladly oblige.

PLAYAS CAMBUTAL & GUÁNICO

Playas Cambutal and Guánico are two excellent surfing beaches along the southern coast of the Península de Azuero. Guánico and Cambutal are about 16km and 22km away from Tonosí, respectively and both are reachable by dirt road from Tonosí, but neither is served by bus. If you don't have your own wheels, go to Restaurante Lindy and ask its owner to give you a ride and to pick you up at a certain time.

Taxi driver Ricuarte Dominguez (☎ 995-8491, 696-6414), in Tonosí, can take you anywhere you want to go and be relied upon to pick you up. He can sometimes be found at the Restaurante Lindy.

Give some thought to camping on the beaches if you're planning to be in the area during September or thereabouts. There aren't any stores near the beaches, but you can take some food with you from Restaurante Lindy or elsewhere. You'll likely see some nesting sea turtles if you're on the beaches in late August, September or early October.

MACARACAS

pop 2900

Little Macaracas, 57km northwest of Tonosí and 40km southwest of Chitré, is another small town bisected by a highway. It has nothing to offer the tourist in year-round attractions, but its annual **folkloric festival** (from January 5 to 10), featuring the drama *The Three Wise Men*, is very popular.

There are two banks in town, a couple of mediocre restaurants and one hotel, **Pensión Lorena** (☎ 995-4181; main road; s/d with fan US$8/12, with air-con US$12/14; ✹), which consists of 11 rooms above a pharmacy.

One of the main attractions here is swimming in the **Río La Villa**, just outside of town. It's pretty empty during the week, while weekends it can get crowded. To get there, take a right off the main road at the San Juan gas station. Continue for 750m until you pass over a metal bridge, then turn right into the gravel lot. The main area is a bit littered, but if you pick your way along the riverbank, you'll find your own peaceful setting.

Buses run between Macaracas and Chitré, and Macaracas and Tonosí (US$2, one hour, hourly) from 7am to 4pm.

Veraguas Province

CONTENTS

Santiago	188
Iglesia San Francisco de Veraguas	189
Santa Fé	190
Ceramica La Peña	193
Las Palmas	193
Soná	193
Santa Catalina	193
Parque Nacional Coiba	195
Parque Nacional Cerro Hoya	197

Panama's third-largest province, near the center of the country, is the only province that has both Caribbean and Pacific coastlines. Veraguas was also the site of the Spaniards' first attempt to obtain a footing in the continental New World; it was here that Christopher Columbus tried to establish a colony. Veraguas remains today a land of tremendous natural beauty, with robust rivers and stunning peaks. Nearly 500 years after Columbus' arrival, the area is still one of the least-developed regions on the isthmus.

Most of Veraguas Province's people make their living through farming or ranching. From an airplane, the Caribbean and Pacific slopes of Veraguas look as different from each other as Canada's Rocky Mountains do from Australia's Great Sandy Desert. Heavy rainfall, virgin forest, and little evidence of people characterize the Caribbean slope. Most of the Mosquito Coast of Veraguas can be reached only by boat, completely isolated from towns on the other side of the Cordillera Central. The Pacific slope of Veraguas – from the summit of the Cordillera to the Pacific Ocean – is an environmentalist's nightmare. Perhaps 5% of the original forest remains; most of it was hacked down to create cattle farms.

Off the Pacific coast but still within the province is Panama's largest island, Isla de Coiba, which is both part of a national park and home to residents of a federal penal colony who live on beaches in huts. The diving around Coiba and neighboring islands is excellent, and the fishing is world-class. Also world-class are some of the waves that curl up to nearby Playa Santa Catalina, which is more of a lava field than a beach, at the end of a bad road near the western edge of the mouth of the Golfo de Montijo. Waves with 5m faces that offer 150m rides are not uncommon here in April, July and August.

HIGHLIGHTS

- Snorkeling, scuba diving and exploring the astounding natural beauty of **Parque Nacional Coiba** (p195)

- Swimming in mountain streams, hiking to virgin forest and seeing the magnificent orchids of **Santa Fé** (p190)

- Surfing great waves and soaking up the laid back vibe of **Santa Catalina** (p193)

- Visiting the fine **Iglesia San Francisco de Veraguas** (p189), one of the Americas' best examples of baroque art and architecture

- Hiking or horseback riding through **Alto de Piedra** (p192), a vast forested wilderness near Santa Fé

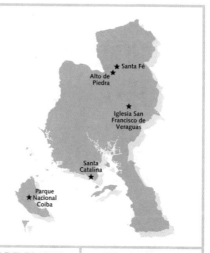

- AREA: 10,050 SQ KM
- ELEVATION: SEA LEVEL TO 3478M
- POPULATION: 209,100

VERAGUAS PROVINCE

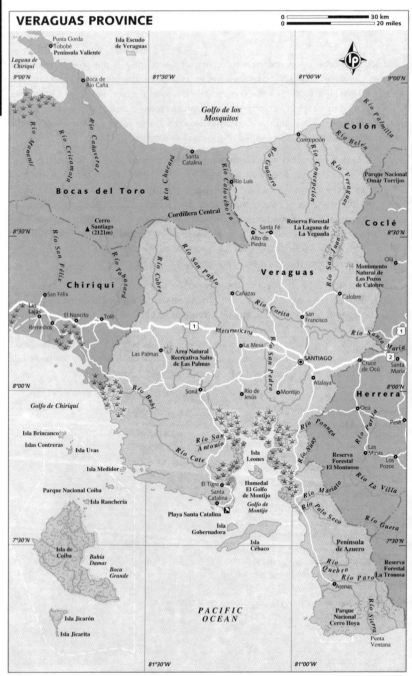

History

Columbus' first three voyages westward toward Asia were in search of land; his fourth and final voyage was undertaken to find a water passage that would, by Columbus' calculation, pass south of Asia into the Indian Ocean. To the north the admiral had found Cuba, which he believed was part of eastern Asia. To the south he had found South America, which he described in his log book as a 'New World' as yet unknown to Europeans. Columbus believed that the Atlantic Ocean flowed through a strait between them, and he was determined to find it.

For this venture, in which he proposed to sail around the world, Columbus chartered four small vessels. The year was 1502, and the great explorer spent most of it commanding his little worm-eaten fleet up and down the Caribbean coast from Venezuela to Nicaragua. Unable to find a strait, but seeing gold on Indians in the region and hearing of rich mines, the admiral cast anchor at the mouth of the Río Belén – the river that today constitutes the boundary between Veraguas and Colón Provinces. He was determined not to return to Spain empty-handed.

In February 1503 Columbus gave orders to establish a colony on a hill beside the river's silt-filled mouth. The Quibian, the area's native inhabitants, disapproved. Armed with spears, the Indians massacred an exploratory party that had gone up the Río Belén. When Spanish corpses came floating down the river, Columbus, fearing an attack, loaded the ships and set sail for Hispaniola (island of modern-day Dominican Republic and Haiti).

In his journal, Columbus wrote: 'I departed, in the name of the Holy Trinity, on Easter night, with the ships rotten, worn out, and eaten with holes.' Three years later the admiral died in an inn in Valladolid, Spain, of diseases he had acquired during his voyages. He died believing he'd seen Asia, unaware that he'd found instead the second-largest landmass on Earth, composed of the two continents of the western hemisphere.

Several other expeditions were attempted over the next 30 years and ended in similar disaster. The conquistadors, not ones to forget reports of gold in Veraguas, returned to the area two decades later and eventually overcame the Indians and the torrential rains of northern Veraguas. They found gold, established mines and, in 1560, at the town of Concepción, 10km west of the Río Belén, they set up a headquarters and a smelter for the mines. African slaves were brought in to extract the gold (most of the Blacks who live in Veraguas Province today are their descendants).

By 1590 the mines were spent. Many miners left for newfound gold deposits in Colombia. Others escaped or were set free and took to farming throughout Pacific Veraguas and the Península de Azuero. Today, the people on the peninsula fall into three main groups: black-skinned descendants of the slaves, fair-skinned descendants of the conquistadors, and people of mixed ancestry. Many of the Indians who had lived on the peninsula died by Spanish swords and from Old World diseases. The rest retreated to the slopes of the Cordillera Central, where their descendants live today.

Climate

South of the Cordillera Central, rains fall heavily during the months between April and November. Everything is particularly lush then, and dirt roads in the mountains are impassable. In the Caribbean coastal regions, rain falls heavily throughout the year making them inaccessible.

National Parks

Parque Nacional Coiba (p195) is one of the largest marine parks in the world. It contains Panama's largest island, the 493-sq-km Isla de Coiba and astounding biodiversity, in spite of the fact that much of the island has yet to be formally studied. For informal trips into the park and onto the island, most visitors base themselves at Santa Catalina (p193).

The 32,577-hectare **Parque Nacional Cerro Hoya** (p197) is on the southwestern side of the Península de Azuero, and has some of the last remaining forest on this peninsula. Unfortunately, the park has little infrastructure and getting there is a challenge.

Getting There & Around

Santiago, which is on the Interamericana, is the main transit point through the province. Both Panama City–bound and David-bound buses stop regularly in Santiago. To reach Santa Catalina, you'll have to pass through Soná as there are no direct buses from Santiago.

VERAGUAS PROVINCE

SANTIAGO

pop 34,800

Santiago, 250km from Panama City, is bisected by the Interamericana, and its central location – just north of the Península de Azuero and about halfway between Panama City and Costa Rica – has made it a hub of rural commercial activity.

This town is a good place to break up a long drive from the Costa Rican border to the capital or to get your vehicle serviced if you encounter mechanical problems. Other than that, Santiago offers little to the tourist. Most of the town's commerce and services – including stores, banks, gas stations, restaurants and hotels – are along the Interamericana and Av Central, which splits off from the highway.

Information

Most of the banks lie a few blocks east of Av Central.

Autoridad Nacional de Ambiente (ANAM; ☎ 998-0615; Interamericana; 🕙 9am-5pm Mon-Fri)

Hal's Internet (Calle 10; per hr US$1; 🕙 8:30am-11pm Mon-Sat) Near Av Central.

Instituto Panameño de Turismo (IPAT; ☎ 998-3929; 🕙 9am-5pm Mon-Fri) On the northern side of Av Central, 500m west of its junction with the Interamericana; maps and brochures available.

Sleeping

Hotel Plaza Gran David (☎ 998-3433; fax 998-2553; s/d US$19/25; 🅿 🌊) This hotel offers good-value, spacious rooms with air-con, tile floors, good beds and private hot-water bathroom. It's one of the more peaceful settings for Santiago. All rooms face onto the swimming pool.

Hotel Galería (☎ 958-7950; fax 958-7954; r US$39; 🅿) Some of the best rooms in town are at this hotel on the Interamericana north of the Av Central intersection. Each room has air-con, a large TV, firm mattresses, and a private bathroom with hot water. There's a restaurant and gym, but no swimming pool.

Hotel Piramidal (☎ 998-3123; fax 998-5411; s/d/tr US$22/28/31; 🅿) At the junction of the Interamericana and Av Central, this popular hotel has 62 boxy rooms lined up row after row. The rooms have air-con and 39-channel cable TV, and there's a restaurant and a bar here.

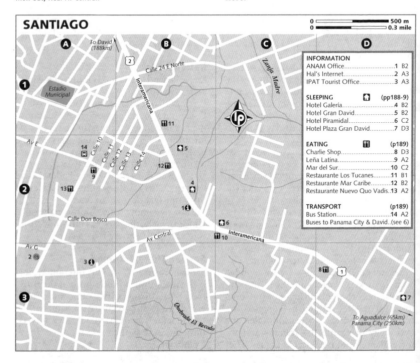

SANTIAGO

INFORMATION	
ANAM Office	1 B2
Hal's Internet	2 A3
IPAT Tourist Office	3 A3

SLEEPING 🏠	(pp188-9)
Hotel Galería	4 B2
Hotel Gran David	5 B2
Hotel Piramidal	6 C2
Hotel Plaza Gran David	7 D3

EATING 🍴	(p189)
Charlie Shop	8 D3
Leña Latina	9 A2
Mar del Sur	10 C2
Restaurante Los Tucanes	11 B1
Restaurante Mar Caribe	12 B2
Restaurante Nuevo Quo Vadis	13 A2

TRANSPORT	(p189)
Bus Station	14 A2
Buses to Panama City & David	(see 6)

Hotel Gran David (☎ 998-4510; fax 998-1866; s/d with fan US$10/14, with air-con US$16/22; ✷) Of the cheapies in town, this is the most palatable option, with fairly clean rooms, tile floors, adequate beds and private hot-water bathroom. It's on the Interamericana about 500m north of the Av Central intersection.

Eating

Mar del Sur (cnr Av Central & Interamericana; mains US$7-14; ✷ lunch & dinner) For superb Peruvian-style seafood, head to Mar del Sur. The ceviche is particularly good and served the Peruvian way – very spicy.

Charlie Shop (mains US$4-7; ✷ breakfast, lunch & dinner) This pleasant outdoor spot has a large menu that features sandwiches (salami and mozzarella) and fruit shakes, as well as seafood and grilled meats. It also has an inexpensive takeaway stand in front.

Restaurante Los Tucanes (mains US$4-7; ✷ breakfast, lunch & dinner) This popular self-serve restaurant is a favorite for David–Panama buses passing on the Interamericana. In addition to daily specials such as roast chicken, chicken parmesan and shrimp *criolla* (tomato and onion sauce), it serves salads and hot sandwiches.

Restaurante Nuevo Quo Vadis (Calle 10; mains US$6-8) Among the options at this long-time seafood favorite are tasty shrimp with curry sauce and the *fantasía marinera*, a mixed seafood platter. Nuevo Quo Vadis' paella, served only on Sunday, is very popular.

Restaurante Mar Caribe (mains US$4-7; ✷ lunch & dinner) Across the street from Hotel Gran David, this restaurant is popular with locals for reliably decent seafood.

Leña Latina (chicken kabob US$2; ✷ 4-11pm) On a quiet neighborhood street, this long narrow porch makes a charming open-air setting for fresh-roasted chicken or steak kabobs in the evening. Look for the glowing embers of the oven and the torches burning out front.

Getting There & Away

From the **bus terminal** (☎ 998-4006) in front of the Hotel Piramidal, buses depart for David (US$6, three hours) hourly from 9am to 2am, and for Panama City (US$6, four hours) hourly from 3:15am to 9:15pm.

Buses to destinations in Veraguas depart from Santiago's bus station on Calle 10, near Av E. For Santa Fé, buses depart half-hourly from 5am to 6pm (US$2, 1½ hours).

You can also hail these on the turnoff from the Interamericana, north of Calle 24. Buses to Soná (from where you can get a bus to Santa Catalina) depart half-hourly from 7am to 6pm (US$1.50, one hour).

Getting Around

Taxis are the way to travel within Santiago. They are easy to hail and they go anywhere in town for US$2 or less.

IGLESIA SAN FRANCISCO DE VERAGUAS

In the small town of **San Francisco**, 16km north of the Interamericana on the road from Santiago to Santa Fé, is one of the best and oldest examples of Baroque art and architecture in the Americas that was created by Indians using native materials. Unlike most Baroque churches, the altar and interior of this church are colorfully painted.

The highly ornate altar is made of ash and bitter cedar. Carved into the altar and elsewhere around the church are the usual images – the crucifixion, the Virgin, the saints – but also throughout the church are finely carved and well-preserved images of the artisans and prominent Indians. Their faces are cleverly inserted into the religious scenes; some appear atop the bodies of cherubs.

One large carving includes items that had special meaning for the Indians or otherwise impressed them – an eagle piercing its own heart with its beak, three large dice, a Spanish sword, a lantern and a human skull.

The captivating altar (most colonial altars in the Americas were brought over from Europe) and the church were constructed within a few years of each other; the date of completion is estimated to be 1727, but no one is certain.

The steeple, incidentally, is not original. The original bell tower survived until 1942, when it suddenly collapsed without warning. Unfortunately, the new one doesn't resemble the old one. The original served two purposes, one good, one evil – it was, of course, used for religious purposes, but the Spaniards also used it as a lookout tower to monitor the movements of the Indians and slaves in the community.

Near the church in San Francisco is **El Chorro del Espíritu Santo** (Holy Spirit Waterfall), which has a fine swimming hole. To get to it, follow the road as it winds around the church, and then take the road just behind the church. After a few hundred meters, take the first right; after another several hundred meters the road will bring you to the small cascades.

Getting There & Away

To reach the church, head 16km north on the San Francisco turnoff from the Interamericana, until you reach the police sub-station (you'll see a stop sign there, and the station is conspicuously located on the main road). Veer right, proceed 400m, and then turn right again at the Supermercado Juan XXIII de San Francisco. Another 100m on, you'll see the church on the left.

A bus leaves the Santiago station for San Francisco (US$1, 25 minutes, every 30 minutes from 7am to 6pm).

If you're short on time, an alternative is to hire a taxi in Santiago to take you to the church and, if you wish, on to Santa Fé. Expect to pay US$12 roundtrip to and from San Francisco, and another US$18 if you hire the taxi to take you all the way to Santa Fé.

SANTA FÉ
pop 3000

This tiny mountain town remains one of the untouched gems of Panama. It lies in the shadow of the Continental Divide, 52km north of Santiago and 36km from San Francisco. At an altitude of 1000m, it's much cooler than the lowlands, and is still green. Much of the forest remains as it did when the Spaniards founded the town in 1557. Sweeping panoramas of lush mountainsides, waterfalls and mountain streams make Santa Fé an ideal destination for hikers, bird watchers and those simply wanting to soak up the beauty of the mountains.

Orientation & Information

Town planning is not evident in Santa Fé. The road that heads north to town from Santiago and the Interamericana, winding through lovely valleys along the way, branches out in three directions at the southern edge of town. The middle 'branch' forks yet again after a few more blocks.

None of the streets in town have names, and that's just fine with Santa Fé residents;

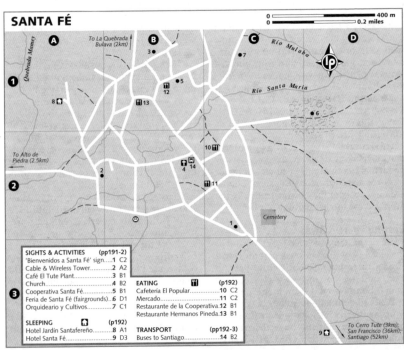

SANTA FÉ

To La Quebrada Bulava (2km)

Quebrada Mamey

Río Mulaba

Río Santa Maria

To Alto de Piedra (2.5km)

Cemetery

To Cerro Tute (3km); San Francisco (36km); Santiago (52km)

SIGHTS & ACTIVITIES	(pp191-2)
'Bienvenidos a Santa Fé' sign.....1	C2
Cable & Wireless Tower............2	A2
Café El Tute Plant.....................3	B1
Church....................................4	B2
Cooperativa Santa Fé................5	B1
Feria de Santa Fé (fairgrounds)..6	D1
Orquideario y Cultivos..............7	C1

SLEEPING	(p192)
Hotel Jardin Santafereño...........8	A1
Hotel Santa Fé........................9	D3

EATING	(p192)
Cafetería El Popular.................10	C2
Mercado................................11	C2
Restaurante de la Cooperativa.12	B1
Restaurante Hermanos Pineda.13	B1

TRANSPORT	(pp192-3)
Buses to Santiago...................14	B2

everybody here seems to know where everybody else lives. And the structures in town that aren't homes – the mayor's office, the cooperative, the church and so on – can be counted on two hands.

Although there's no tourist office (not to mention a bank, laundry or gas station), there are several individuals who can provide information: the first is Bertha de Castrellón from Orquideario y Cultivos (p191); the other is Eudosia Rodriguez, the friendly owner and manager of the Hotel Santa Fé (p192).

Sights & Activities
ORQUIDEARIO Y CULTIVOS
Santa Fé is known throughout Panama for its orchids, and in Santa Fé the person to see about these flowers is **Bertha de Castrellón** (☎ 954-0910), who has an impressive collection of them (no fewer than 265 species) in her backyard and enjoys showing them to enthusiasts. Among her orchids are some of the largest and some of the smallest varieties in the world.

Most of the orchids are handsomely displayed in hanging coconut shells. They include a lovely lavender orchid found only in the hills around Santa Fé. Bertha, who speaks a little English, can tell you a great many things about her plants if you can communicate with her in Spanish. She also has a wealth of information about the area and was running for mayor in 2004.

To get to Bertha's house, take the right 'branch' at the point where the Santiago–Santa Fé road forks at the southern edge of town. Then take the second right and proceed 100m or so further, until you see a driveway flanked by a sign that reads: 'Orquideario y Cultivos Las Fragacias de Santa Fé.'

There are two other things you should know about Bertha: she and her brother are the area's top birding guides, offering tours of nearby Cerro Tute (p192), where there's a lovely set of waterfalls, a cliff with wind currents that seemingly prevent anyone from falling off, and fine bird watching; and, when Bertha claps, her green parrot bobs up and down and whistles US and Panamanian popular songs.

Although Bertha does not charge a fee for showing her orchids, feel free to leave a donation. Please remember you are visiting a home, so be considerate: don't show up

before 9am or after 5pm, and if you call out to her from her gate and there's no answer, assume she's not home. Don't open the gate unless she instructs you to do so.

COOPERATIVA SANTA FÉ
The **Santa Fé Cooperative** (🕙 6am-8:30pm) and the cooperative's store above the Restaurante de la Cooperativa (p192) sell hats made of mountain palm (called *palmilla*) that are much more durable than hats found elsewhere in Panama – and they cost much less (from US$5 to US$15). They are not as refined as the hats available in Ocú and Penonomé, but if you're looking for a rugged hat in classic Panama style, you can't do better.

While in the cooperative, you might want to pick up some Café El Tute, the locally grown coffee.

MERCADO
Much larger than the Cooperativa is the open-air market just past the entrance to town. In addition to fruits and vegetables, you'll find woven handmade bags, a wide range of hats, leather goods and many other items. It's a fun place to browse.

RIVERS & WATERFALLS
Not far from Santa Fé there are a number of lovely waterfalls (including one that's pictured on IPAT's Veraguas glossy publication) and empty mountain streams that make this area so charming. The most accessible swimming spots are within walking distance from town. Head along the same road as Bertha's, and you'll soon reach several spots that make for a nice dip. Continuing on, you'll reach a bridge – cross it, take the second turnoff on the right and you'll find a place to rent inner tubes (US$1), allowing you to float idly down the river.

Behind the Café El Tute coffee factory (p192), there's a lovely swimming hole, **La Quebrada Bulava**, about 30 minutes' walk away. Ask one of the local kids to show you the way.

El Salto is among the most impressive falls in this area. It lies about 30 minutes south of Santa Fé along a bad road fit only for 4WD (and only during the dry season). There are also three waterfalls that you'll reach by entering Alto de Piedra. Ask for a guide at the **Hotel Santa Fé** (☎ 954-0881; santafeexplorer@hotmail.com); Edgar Toribio and

Fidel are both recommended. Extreme Panama (p91) based in Panama City, also leads tours to this area.

CERRO TUTE & ALTO DE PIEDRA

There are two heavily forested mountainous areas near town that offer some fine birding. Many specialties of eastern Chiriquí and Veraguas Provinces can be found here, including the rufous-winged woodpecker and the crimson-collared tanager. Both areas require a 4WD vehicle, a horse or strong legs.

The turnoff for **Cerro Tute** is a few kilometers south of town, on the western side of the Santiago–Santa Fé road. There are trails here, but you'd be wise to go with someone who knows the area well, such as Bertha de Castrellón (p191); or Edgar Toribio from Hotel Santa Fé (p192).

Alto de Piedra, reachable by a road that leaves the western side of town, is an excellent place to explore on horseback. The best place to ask for a steed and a guide is at the hotel Santa Fé. Horse hire is around US$5 per hour. This vast, mountainous and forest-covered area contains many thousands of hectares of pristine wilderness and ranges from the northern edge of Santa Fé to the Caribbean Sea. The entire northern portion of the province – the area where Columbus, Nicuesa and the other Spanish explorers had so much trouble – contains not a single road and is sparsely inhabited. The edge of the awesome forest is only a couple of kilometers from town, and the forest becomes a jungle once you clear the ridge and proceed down the Caribbean slope.

Café El Tute Plant

If you've never been to a coffee processing plant, this is your chance. At the northern end of town, this small factory produces coffee from beans grown around the region. You can stop in for a free tour (in Spanish) to get an idea of how it all comes together. Among other things you'll learn that the plant produces two distinct types of coffee. Café El Tute is the better of the two, made from 100% Arabica beans. Café Santa Fé is an inferior grade produced here, with coffee beans as well as other additives – such as corn.

Festivals & Events

Agricultural Fair This lively event is hosted by the producers of northern Veraguas from 28 January to 2 February. If you're in the area don't miss it. It features traditional dancing, horse races, lots of food stands and an occasional boxing match or rodeo competition. Held in the Féria de Santa Fé in the east of town.

Orchid Exposition Collectors from all over Panama display their finest orchids in the Féria de Santa Fé at this popular event each August; the IPAT office in Santiago (☎ 998-3929) can provide you with the precise date, as can Bertha, the orchid lady.

Sleeping & Eating

Hotel Santa Fé (☎ 954-0941; d/tw US$13/15, r with air-con US$25; 🅿) This delightful hotel is on the Santiago–Santa Fé road, just south of Santa Fé. The clean and cozy 21-room hotel (on the left side as you drive into town) sits on a bluff and overlooks a gorgeous valley.

All rooms have cold-water private bathrooms, and some have air-con, which isn't needed much in this climate. There is a good restaurant-bar on the premises. This is also the best place in town to arrange a tour or horseback riding. Eudosia, the friendly owner, has a great appreciation for Santa Fé, and can give recommendations and directions for reaching some of the town's nearby attractions. Fidel and Edgar are recommended local guides in the area. There is a map of Santa Fé in the hotel's main office.

Hotel Jardín Santafereño (d US$10) On the western edge of town, a good walk from the center, is this bare-bones, budget hotel. It offers four *cabañas* with worn, soft beds and private cold-water bathroom, and a cheap restaurant. However, it's on the highest point in town, nestled in a forest and very tranquil. Not bad if you're used to roughing it.

In addition to the restaurants at the two hotels, there are three places to eat near the center of town. The best of the three is **Restaurante de la Cooperativa** (mains US$3; 🕑 6am-7pm), which serves fish, pork, beef and chicken with a side of rice and vegetables.

Neither **Restaurante Hermanos Pineda** (🕑 breakfast, lunch & dinner) nor **Cafetería El Popular** (🕑 breakfast, lunch & dinner) will be winning culinary awards anytime soon, but their prices are painless; at either place, expect to pay US$2.50 for a plate of chicken, rice and beans, and a soft drink.

Getting There & Away

Buses from Santa Fé to Santiago (US$2, 1½ hours) depart every 30 minutes from 5am to 6pm.

Buses leave the Santiago station for Santa Fé (US$1.50, 1½ hours, hourly from 7am to 4pm). A taxi ride from Santiago costs US$40.

CERAMICA LA PEÑA

This **artisans' market** (⏱ 9am-4:30pm Mon-Fri) is on the Interamericana, 8km west of Santiago. Here you can find wood carvings and baskets made by the Emberá and Wounaan peoples of the Darién, and woven purses and soapstone figurines made by Ngöbe Buglé people living in the area, as well as ceramics from the town of La Arena in Herrera Province and masks from the town of Parita, also in Herrera Province. There's also a workshop on the premises where you can occasionally see ceramics being made.

LAS PALMAS

There's nothing of special interest in sleepy Las Palmas, a town 10km south of the Interamericana and 32km northwest of the town of Soná. But if you love waterfalls and have your own wheels, you'll want to know about the nearby cataract and its enticing swimming hole. The scene is set amid light forest, and you'll likely have the place to yourself.

To get to the **falls** from the Interamericana, take the Las Palmas turnoff and drive 10km. Bypass the first road into town, but turn left at the second road just before the town's cemetery. Follow this dirt road for 1km and then take the fork to the right. This last kilometer to the falls, along a much rougher road, requires a 4WD vehicle. If you aren't driving one, it's best to play it safe and walk the last kilometer to the falls. Be sure to lock up and take your valuables with you.

If you are coming from Soná, drive 32km along the road that leads toward the Interamericana and turn right just beyond the cemetery. Then follow the directions in the preceding paragraph.

Keep in mind that there is no place to stay in Las Palmas, and the few restaurants in town are mediocre at best.

SONÁ

pop 10,100

Soná, 45km west of Santiago, is set in a farming region bisected by the road that links the Interamericana to El Tigre and other small communities on the peninsula that comprises

the western shore of the Golfo de Montijo. Soná's chief feature is its bars – about one in every five businesses here is a cantina.

If that sounds good to you, you might like to know that there are two places to stay in Soná. **Pensión Min** (☎ 998-8331; tw US$7), on the main road, has 10 basic fan-on-a-stand twin rooms with shared cold-water bathroom. **Hotel Águila** (d with fan/air-con US$11/14; ✷), near the center of town on a side street a stone's throw from the main road, has slightly better rooms.

Buses from Soná to Panama City (US$7, five hours) depart the bus terminal on the main road in the middle of town at 8:30am, 10:30am, 1:30pm and 4pm daily. Buses to Santiago leave the terminal every 20 minutes from 4:30am to 6:30pm (US$1.50).

SANTA CATALINA

Sixty-six km south of Soná is Santa Catalina, where several hundred people lead simple lives in simple homes near a beach that attracts surfers from around the globe. **Playa Santa Catalina** is a major break, where you can nearly always find a decent wave to ride. At its best it's comparable to Oahu's Sunset Beach. The best waves are generally from December to April (see p55 for more information). The town has a laid-back feel to it with one good outdoor pizzeria that forms the nexus of the dining and nightlife scene.

Santa Catalina is also the best place to hire a boat out to Isla de Coiba. There's now a dive operator in Santa Catalina, and a host of local boatmen who will take you out snorkeling among the rich aquatic life around Parque Nacional Coiba (p195). Another lovely day trip is to Isla Cébaco, featuring white-sand beaches, crystal-clear waters and good surf.

Orientation & Information

To get to the oceanside surf hotels from the bus station, take the dirt road on the left side of the road into Santa Catalina just before the road ends. Each hotel has its own sign marking the turnoff. There is only one public phone, and there are no banks in Santa Catalina. Make sure you arrive with cash – no one takes credit cards.

Activities

SCUBA DIVING

Scuba Coiba (☎ 263-4366; www.scubacoiba.com) Run by an experienced Austrian dive master,

Scuba Coiba offers divers a chance to experience some of the spectacular marine life around Isla Coiba. Two-tank dives cost US$70 per person. Diving in the park costs more as the distance is much greater. He offers day trips (US$130) as well as two-day trips (US$320), which include entry into the national park, lodging at the ANAM station on Coiba and meals. There's a two-person minimum for these trips. You can also get PADI-certified here for US$225. Snorkeling gear is available for hire (US$6 per day). It's located on the main road into town, between the restaurant La Fonda and Cabañas Rolo.

SURF LESSONS

Amigos del Pacífico (1½hr lesson US15) This surf school is run by three friends (Valentin, Gabrielle and Felix), and offers classes for those who'd like to learn the sport. Classes are typically held in the mornings from 9am to noon and the afternoons from 2:30pm to 6pm. Ask for them at Cabañas Rolo (p194) or the Surfers' Paradise Camp (p194).

Tours

Many of the local fishermen make excellent guides and can take visitors to some superb snorkeling and spearfishing spots and some great surf breaks. Their lifelong knowledge and love of the area is apparent. You'll need some basic Spanish, but contracting with locals is the best way to support the community. Look for them on the beach and ask around. You can also find locals who will lead horseback riding tours.

For sailing trips, **Surfkats** (☎ 632-3797; www .surfkats.com) offers excellent value. This Canadian-run outfit leads overnight and up to six-day excursions to great surf breaks. Prices start at US$230 per person for a two-day trip and includes all meals. Sailing on their fleet of 35-foot vessels is a striking way to experience this gorgeous coastline.

Many accommodations also offer tours (see below).

Sleeping

IN TOWN

Cabañas Rolo (☎ 998-8600; per person US$7) One of Santa Catalina's only locally owned hotels, these eight cabins are a favorite of surfers. Each has one to three good beds, a fan, and a shared cold-water bathroom. It's easy to find, near the end of the only road into town. Ask for Rolo Ortega, the friendly owner; he speaks Spanish and English, cooks meals by request (typically US$3), rents surfboards (US$10 per day), and can arrange fishing trips and gear rental. For a day-long snorkeling or fishing excursion, expect to pay US$200 for a small group to Coiba, US$150 to Isla Cébaco.

Sol y Mar (☎ 596-1521; per person US$7) As you're coming into town, you'll pass a blue building on the right (about 150m before Rolo's). You'll find basic cabins with shared bathroom and kitchen access. Nicer cabins with terrace, private bathroom, air-con and sea views (US$35) are due for completion in mid-2005. Luis da Silva, the friendly multilingual Portuguese owner, also leads boating tours around Santa Catalina. Overnight trips to Isla Coiba cost US$250 per group (plus the park fee of US$10 per person and the ANAM cabin rental of US$10 per person). A day-long fishing and snorkeling trip to Cébaco costs US$120.

BEACH

You can reach the following places by taking the turnoff on the left after arriving in town. (It's the only other road in town.) The following are arranged in the order in which you'll reach them.

Casablanca Surf Resort (☎ /fax 226-3786; per person US$5-35; 🏕) Casablanca contains a number of housing options in a park-like setting bordering the beach. The nicest is the house with five beds, air-con and fans; there's also a duplex with three beds in each unit (fan only); and five stand-alone cabins (fan only). The house and duplex feature tiled roofs, concrete floors and walls, and cold-water bathroom, and are comfortable and clean. The cabins are similar except that they have thatched roofs. Mosquitoes are a problem here. Camping is available for US$3 per person (tents provided).

Punta Brava (☎ 614-3868; www.puntabrava.com; per person/d US$15/30; 🏕) This pleasant spot overlooking the beach has five connected *cabañas* capable of sleeping six each. Rooms are simple, with air-con and private bathroom, and there's a sea-view terrace **restaurant** (lunch/dinner US$4/5). There's also a nicer, more spacious room with fan and sea views in the main house. Surfboards are available for rent.

Surfers' Paradise Camp (☎ 595-1010; surfcatalina@ hotmail.com; per person US$10) On a breezy bluff overlooking the ocean, you'll find eight rustic and basic wooden rooms on offer here. Breakfast and dinner are available. The rooms at Rolo's are more comfortable, but the sea views at Surfers' Paradise Camp are nice. Surfboards and snorkeling equipment are available for hire (each US$10 per day).

Eating

There are several places to buy excellent fresh fish to prepare yourself. One is in town in a small building across from the building that says 'hielo.' In the morning, you can also buy fish right off the boats along the beach.

The no-name **restaurant** (dishes US$2) on the corner of the turnoff to the beach hotels has simple Panamanian dishes of rice and beans with chicken, meat or fish. Look for the toucan.

Restaurant La Fonda (☎ 316-4022; dishes US$1-2; ⊗ 6-11pm) This small restaurant in town (just before Rolo's) offers fresh and healthy cuisine at good prices. Tuna sandwiches, fresh *batidos,* and fruit with granola are among the offerings. The coffee is also quite good.

Pizzeria Jamming (pizza US$3-5; ⊗ 6:30-11pm Tue-Sun) On the road to the beach-facing hotels, this pizzeria offers delicious thin-crust pizzas made from fresh ingredients, any of which go nicely with the cold beer on hand. This stylish, open-air rancho is Santa Catalina's liveliest gathering spot; it gets crowded, so arrive early.

Getting There & Away

To reach Santa Catalina from Panama City, first take a bus to Soná (see p112). From Soná, three buses serve Santa Catalina daily, leaving at 5am, noon and 4pm (US$3). Unless the driver is pushed for time, he will take you to any one of the hotels listed for an additional US$1. If you miss the bus, you can hire a taxi from Soná to Santa Catalina for US$25.

From Santa Catalina, three buses serve Soná daily. They leave at 7am, 8am and 2pm. In Santa Catalina the bus stops near the Restaurant La Fonda – a conch-shell's throw from Cabañas Rolo. If you're staying at one of the other hotels, it's a 1km walk to them on mostly flat terrain. There are no taxis in town.

PARQUE NACIONAL COIBA

In the Golfo de Chiriquí is Panama's largest island, 493-sq-km **Isla de Coiba**. The island is part of a protected scenic area and for decades had been the site of a federal penal colony. In 1991 it became the centerpiece of a 2700-sq-km national park, over 80% of which is oceanic. Today only a handful of prisoners are left, scattered around the densely forested island. Also on Isla de Coiba are crocodiles, snakes and the country's last cluster of scarlet macaws.

On the northern end of the island is an **ANAM ranger station** (with five basic cabins, each with four beds), an attractive beach, and a lovely cove with mediocre snorkeling. Beside the cove is a tiny island that you can snorkel around during high tide; if you choose to do this, be warned that the current on the island's far side is sometimes very strong. If you're a poor swimmer, do not venture outside the cove.

A few prisoners work at the ANAM station – preparing meals, washing clothes, and even leading tourists on snorkeling jaunts in the cove. They are allowed to roam freely in the vicinity of the station and to chat with guests. They're a pretty nice bunch. There are two other areas on or very near the island that are worth a visit: a healthy **mangrove forest** close to Punta Hermosa in the west, and the tiny island of **Granito de Oro**, where the snorkeling is excellent. Both the mangroves and Granito de Oro can be reached only by boat.

The marine life in the park is simply astounding. Over 23 species of dolphin and whale have been identified. Humpback whales are often seen in the park, as are spotted and bottle-nosed dolphins. Killer whales, sperm whales and Cuvier's beaked whales are also present in park waters, but in fewer numbers.

Seventeen species of crocodile, turtle and lizard, as well as 15 species of snake (including the very dangerous fer-de-lance and the coral snake), are found in the park. Although the list is far from complete, to date 147 species of bird (including the Coiba spinetail, a little brown-and-white bird found only on Coiba) have been identified on the island. Scarlet macaws are among the species that nest on Coiba.

Coiba is home to the second-largest eastern Pacific coral reef and the finest diving

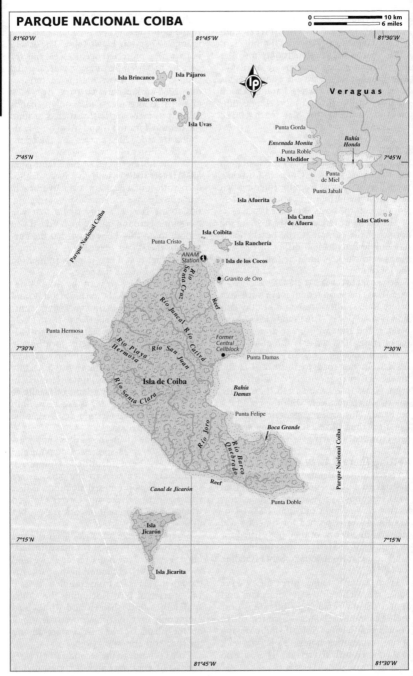

PARQUE NACIONAL COIBA

| 0 _____ 10 km |
| 0 _____ 6 miles |

81°60'W   81°45'W   81°30'W

Isla Brincanco   Isla Pájaros

Islas Contreras

Veraguas

Isla Uvas

Punta Gorda

Ensenada Monita   *Bahía Honda*

Punta Roble
Isla Medidor

7°45'N   7°45'N

Punta de Miel

Punta Jabalí

Isla Afuerita

Isla Canal de Afuera   **Islas Cativos**

Parque Nacional Coiba

Isla Coibita

Punta Cristo   Isla Ranchería

ANAM Station   Isla de los Cocos

Río Santa Cruz   ● Granito de Oro

Río Juncal   *Reef*

Punta Hermosa   *Río Cativa*

Former Central Cellblock

7°30'N   *Río Playa Hermosa*   *Río San Juan*   Punta Damas   7°30'N

Isla de Coiba

Río Santa Clara   *Bahía Damas*

Punta Felipe

Río Joro   *Boca Grande*

Río Barco Quebrado   *Parque Nacional Coiba*

Reef

Canal de Jicarón   Punta Doble

Isla Jicarón

7°15'N   7°15'N

Isla Jicarita

81°45'W   81°30'W

and snorkeling to be found along the Pacific coast from Colombia to Mexico. The entire island is covered with a heavy virgin forest, except for the former prison camps and along the lower courses of the larger streams where there are swampy woodlands. Rocky headlands project along the coast, and there are sandy beaches broken by mangroves at river mouths.

In addition to Coiba (50,314 hectares), islands within the park include Isla Jicarón (2002 hectares), Isla Brincanco (330 hectares), Isla Uvas (257 hectares), Isla Coibita (242 hectares), Isla Canal de Afuera (240 hectares), Isla Jicarita (125 hectares), Isla Pájaros (45 hectares) and Isla Afuerita (27 hectares).

Diving, Snorkeling & Fishing

In addition to the local operators in Santa Catalina (p194), excursions are available with the following companies.

Ancon Expeditions (Panama City ☎ 269-9414/5; www.anconexpeditions.com; El Dorado Bldg, Calle 49A Este) Ancon provides guided tours to Coiba upon request. Prices vary depending on group size, length of stay and other factors. Contact the company for prices.

MV Coral Star (USA ☎ 800-215-5169; www.coralstar .com) This 115-foot luxury live-aboard ship cruises the islands in and around Parque Nacional Coiba, carrying its passengers to some great dive spots. In addition to diving, guests can sea kayak, fish, snorkel or explore the beaches and rain forests on uninhabited islands. Accommodations consist of two master staterooms on the main deck, two deluxe and four standard cabins on the lower deck. Weekly all-inclusive rates start at US$1750 per person.

Coiba Adventure (☎ 999-8108 in Panama City, USA ☎ 800-800-0907; www.coibadventure.com) This sportfishing operation is run by Tom Yust, and he's widely regarded as Panama's top sportfishing captain. Tom runs a personal-ized operation. Rates vary depending on the time of year, boat used and the size of the party, but in general expect to pay between US$2600 and US$5000 per week including all expenses.

PARQUE NACIONAL CERRO HOYA

On the southwestern side of the Península de Azuero, this 32,577-hectare park protects the headwaters of the Ríos Tonosí, Portobelo and Pavo, as well as 30 endemic plant species, and fauna that includes the carato parakeet. It contains some of the last remaining forest on a huge peninsula that is one of the most agriculturally devastated regions of Panama. Although the park was created in 1984, much of the forest had been chopped down prior to that time, and it will be a long time before the park really looks like a park.

There are no accommodations for visitors in or near the park, and the trails into it are ill defined.

The best way to get to the park is by boat from Playa Cambutal. There, it's always possible to find a boatman to make the two-hour trip; the cost is generally US$60 to US$80 per party (one way). If you happen to come upon a boat going from Playa Cambutal in Los Santos Province to the park or to Punta Ventana nearby, the ride could cost as little as US$5 per person.

It's also possible to reach the park by a road that winds along the western edge of the Península de Azuero. However, even with a 4WD vehicle (dry season only), visitors are only able to get as far as Restigue, a hamlet south of Arenas, at the edge of the park. Unfortunately, two of the park's main attractions are its waterfalls and rivers, which are reduced to trickles during the dry season.

In short, until the park is more accessible and facilities are developed for tourists, the attractions don't warrant the special effort needed to see them.

Chiriquí Province

CONTENTS

History	201
Climate	201
National Parks	201
Getting There & Away	201
Getting Around	201
Lowlands	**202**
David	202
Around David	205
Paso Canoas	205
Playa Barqueta	205
Golfo de Chiriquí	206
Punta Burica	206
East to Veraguas Province	207
Highlands	**208**
Boquete	208
Parque Nacional Volcán Barú	216
Around Parque Nacional Volcán Barú	216
Buena Vista	216
Volcán	217
Lagunas de Volcán	218
Santa Clara	218
Paso Ancho	219
Bambito	219
Cerro Punta	219
Guadalupe	220
Parque Internacional La Amistad	221
Río Sereno	221
Finca la Suiza	221

CHIRIQUÍ PROVINCE

Chiricanos claim to have it all, and there's an element of truth in what they say: Panama's tallest mountains are in Chiriquí Province, as are some of its longest rivers. The province is home to spectacular rain forest, and yet it is also the country's top agricultural and cattle-ranching region. Two of the country's largest islands and one of the world's biggest copper mines are in Chiriquí Province as well.

But it is the pleasant climate and beauty of several mountain towns that make the province a favorite vacation spot of Panamanians. Mention Boquete, Cerro Punta or Guadalupe to Panama City residents, and they'll tell you how cool and lovely these towns are. Nestled in a valley at the foot of Volcán Barú, the country's tallest mountain, Boquete is also famous for its delicious oranges and coffee.

All of this makes for some excellent exploring for visitors. In Boquete, there are the simple pleasures of watching the sun set over charming towns in the mountains. And there's also serious white-water rafting, with over 20 different runs within a two-hour drive. Numerous hiking opportunities lie nearby, from day hikes into Parque Internacional La Amistad (PILA) to four-day treks to the Caribbean coastline. At the other end of the province lies the lovely, untouched Golfo de Chiriquí, with beautiful white-sand beaches, and a rich variety of sea life.

With so much to offer, it's no surprise that some Chiricanos dream of creating an independent República de Chiriquí. Their fiercely independent spirit goes back several hundred years. See the history section (p201) to learn more.

HIGHLIGHTS

- Basking in the cool, mountain climate of **Boquete** (p208), a village set in one of the country's most picturesque valleys

- Whale-watching, snorkeling and island-hopping in the pristine national marine park in the **Golfo de Chiriquí** (p206)

- Hiking the verdant **Sendero Los Quetzales** (p211), one of Central America's loveliest nature trails

- White-water rafting along the **Ríos Chiriquí** and **Chiriquí Viejo** (p210), with abundant wildlife

- Spotting rare birds and soaking up the sounds of the rain forest at **Parque Internacional La Amistad** (p216) or **Parque Nacional Volcán Barú** (p216)

| ■ AREA: 8653 SQ KM | ■ ELEVATION: SEA LEVEL TO 3478M | ■ POPULATION: 395,200 |

CHIRIQUÍ PROVINCE

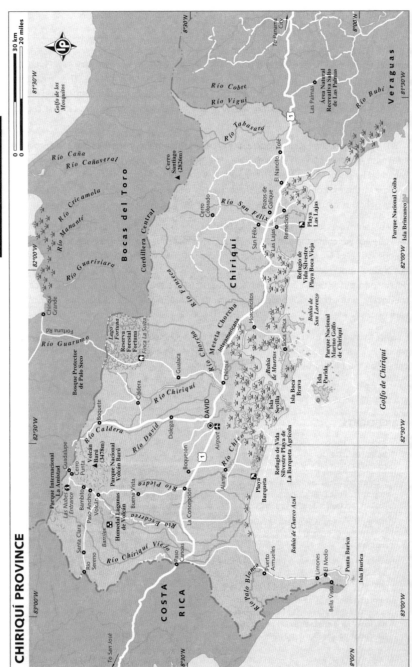

HISTORY

When the Spaniards first visited the area in the 1520s, they were astonished by what they found. Instead of one or two Indian tribes, they found many small groups living in relative isolation. Often separated by only a few kilometers, these groups still had distinct languages and religions. They fought among themselves and later against the Spanish.

In the early 17th century, Spanish missionaries led by Padre Cristóbal Cacho Santillana decided to convert the Indians and had 626 natives rounded up and placed in two towns he had founded. Santillana identified six distinct languages among this group, and he had started to record a vocabulary of the most common words when measles brought by the colonists swept through the towns and killed half the Indians.

The survivors, having had enough of the Spaniards, took to the hills, but the fate was sealed for many of the tribes. Of the Cotho, Borisque, Dorasque, Utelae, Bugabae, Zune, Dolega, Zariba, Dure and others, only the Ngöbe Buglé survived. Today they are the most populous of Panama's seven indigenous groups.

During the 17th century and into the 18th century, pirates attacked Chiriquí. It was just outside Remedios in 1680 that English buccaneer Richard Sawkins, attempting to lead an assault against the well-defended city, was fatally wounded. Six years later, pirates coming down from Honduras sacked the towns of Alanje and San Lorenzo. And Miskito Indians behaving like pirates invaded the region in 1732, plundering and burning the city of David.

In the 19th century, another sort of foreigner moved in – farmers from the USA and Europe who viewed the climate and slopes of the Chiriquí highlands as prime for coffee, timber and other crops.

And the Ngöbe Buglé? Today, they live on a large reservation in the Chiriquí highlands and are seeking statehood. Their lives revolve around subsistence agriculture, just as they did when white people first arrived nearly 500 years ago. But these days the Indians have political clout, and their future is in their own hands.

CLIMATE

Given its geographic diversity, the climate varies considerably throughout the Chiriquí Province. In the lowlands, David remains hot and humid year-round, with marked rainfall from mid-April through mid-December. Just an hour north of there, in the mountain valley of Boquete you can expect much cooler temperatures year-round (getting as low as 40°F at times). The province's rain patterns follow that of David, though a foggy afternoon drizzle blankets the valley even in the dry season.

NATIONAL PARKS

Along the coastline south of David, the impressive **Parque Nacional Marino Golfo de Chiriquí** (p206) is a 14,740-hectare national marine park that protects 25 islands and numerous coral reefs. The aquatic life is astounding.

The 14,300-hectare **Parque Nacional Volcán Barú** (p216) surrounds Panama's only volcano. Its fertile soil nourishes a wide variety of plant and animal life, making it a fine destination for hikers and bird watchers. Volcán Barú's summit, at 3478m, is Panama's highest peak.

The 407,000-hectare **Parque Internacional La Amistad** (p221) is shared with Costa Rica, and happily this side of PILA remains largely undiscovered. It has several excellent day hikes, or you can hire indigenous guides to lead you on overnight excursions. The most accessible entrance to the park lies near Cerro Punta (p219), though the park can also be entered near Changuinola (p244).

GETTING THERE & AWAY

The gateway to Chiriquí is David, with daily flights to Panama City. It's also possible to fly to David from Bocas or Changuinola. The majority of travelers coming from Bocas take the scenic (though white-knuckled) bus journey from Changuinola or Almirante, which are connected by boat service to the islands. David also has regular bus service to the Costa Rica border, along the heavily trafficked Interamericana (Río Sereno, p309, is a much more pleasant border). You can also drive the Interamericana in the other direction to reach provinces east of Chiriquí.

GETTING AROUND

Although David offers few attractions, it is a major transit point for going into the mountains. A regular bus service connects the city with Boquete and with Guadalupe. Note that there is no road between Guadalupe and Boquete. Travelers will have to return to David to go from one to the other (or hike the Quetzal trail, p206). Access to the Golfo de Chiriquí is via Boca Chica, at the end of a long, rugged road accessible only by 4WD (taxis are available – see p206).

LOWLANDS

DAVID
pop 83,300

Panama's second most populous city, David is the capital of Chiriquí Province and the center of a rich farming region. It has plenty of places to stay and eat, but few tourist attractions – and David is hot and sticky all year. Travelers stop here mainly on their way to or from the Costa Rican border at Paso Canoas, 54km away. David is also used as a springboard for visits to Boquete and Volcán, Parque Nacional Volcán Barú and islands in the Golfo de Chiriquí.

Orientation

David is about halfway between Panama City and San José, Costa Rica – it's about six hours by road from either place. The Carretera Interamericana does not enter the town but instead skirts around its northern and western sides. The city's heart is its fine central plaza, the Parque de Cervantes, about 1.5km southwest of the highway.

Information
BOOKSTORES
Livraría Regional (Av Bolivar) Next to the cathedral, David's best (and rather modest) bookstore stocks a handful of titles in English, mostly coffee-table books on Panama.

CONSULATE
Costa Rican consulate (☎ /fax 774-1923; cosurica@chiriqui.com; cnr Calle B & Av 1 Este; ☺ 8am-3pm Mon-Fri) In the center of the city, opposite the Restaurante El Fogon.

INTERNET ACCESS
Internet Fast Track (Av 2 Este; per hr US$1; ☺ 24hr)
Planet Internet (Calle Central; per hr US$1; ☺ 9am-midnight)

LAUNDRY
Lavamática El Cisne (Av 5 Este; wash & dry US$1.50) Next to Pensión Costa Rica.

MONEY
ATMs (Visa/MC/Plus/Cirrus) are available at the following:
Banistmo With branches on Calle C Norte near the park and on Av Obaldía north of the bus station.
HSBC (Av Central) Near Calle C Norte.

POST
Post office (Calle C Norte; ☺ 7am-6pm Mon-Fri, to 4:30pm Sat) A block behind the central plaza.

TOURIST OFFICES
Autoridad Nacional de Ambiente (ANAM; ☎ 775-7840; fax 774-6671; ☺ 8am-4pm Mon-Fri) The office is near the airport, where you can get information and permits to camp in the national parks.
IPAT (☎ 775-2839; Av Central; ☺ 8:30am-4:30pm Mon-Fri) Information on Chiriquí Province, including maps of Boquete.

Sights & Activities

David is within an hour's drive of many good places to visit, including Boquete (p208), Volcán (p217), Cerro Punta (p219) and Playa Las Lajas (p207).

There is a **market** in David that's worth a look if you've never seen a traditional Latin American market. It faces the junction of Avs Bolívar and Obaldía; produce is far cheaper here than what you'd pay in a supermarket.

Festivals & Events
Feria de San José de David This big international fair is held for 10 days each March; contact the IPAT tourist office for exact dates, as they vary from year to year.
Concepción A half-hour drive west of David, Concepción celebrates its patron saint's day on 2 February (or the following Saturday if the 2nd lands on a weekday).

Sleeping
BUDGET
Pensión Clark (☎ 774-3452; Av Francisco Clark; s/d US$8/12) Northeast of the bus station, this pleasant family-run guesthouse offers six clean, well-kept rooms, with a lush garden and hammocks out back. At times, nobody is around to check you in. English is spoken.

Purple House (☎ 774-4059; www.purplehousehostel.com; cnr Calle C Sur & Av 6 Oeste; dm/r US$7/17-21; 💻) This brightly-painted hostel offers clean quarters in bunk beds, use of kitchen and living space (with DVDs and Internet). The tables on the patio are a good place to meet

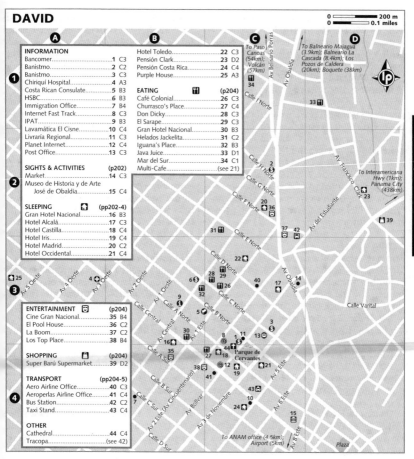

DAVID

0 — 200 m
0 — 0.1 miles

INFORMATION	
Bancomer	1 C3
Banistmo	2 C2
Banistmo	3 C3
Chiriquí Hospital	4 A3
Costa Rican Consulate	5 B3
HSBC	6 B3
Immigration Office	7 B4
Internet Fast Track	8 B3
IPAT	9 B3
Lavamática El Cisne	10 C4
Livraría Regional	11 C3
Planet Internet	12 C4
Post Office	13 C3

SIGHTS & ACTIVITIES	(p202)
Market	14 C3
Museo de Historia y de Arte José de Obaldia	15 C4

SLEEPING	(pp202-4)
Gran Hotel Nacional	16 B3
Hotel Alcalá	17 C3
Hotel Castilla	18 C4
Hotel Iris	19 C4
Hotel Madrid	20 C2
Hotel Occidental	21 C4

Hotel Toledo	22 C3
Pensión Clark	23 D2
Pensión Costa Rica	24 C4
Purple House	25 A3

EATING	(p204)
Café Colonial	26 C3
Churrasco's Place	27 C4
Don Dicky	28 C3
El Sarape	29 C3
Gran Hotel Nacional	30 B3
Helados Jackelita	31 C2
Iguana's Place	32 B3
Java Juice	33 D1
Mar del Sur	34 C1
Multi-Cafe	(see 21)

ENTERTAINMENT	(p204)
Cine Gran Nacional	35 B4
El Pool House	36 C2
La Boom	37 C2
Los Top Place	38 B4

SHOPPING	(p204)
Super Barú Supermarket	39 D2

TRANSPORT	(pp204-5)
Aero Airline Office	40 C3
Aeroperlas Airline Office	41 C4
Bus Station	42 C2
Taxi Stand	43 C4

OTHER	
Cathedral	44 C4
Tracopa	(see 42)

CHIRIQUÍ PROVINCE

To Paso Canoas (54km); Volcán (57km)

To Balneario Majagua (3.9km); Balneario La Cascada (8.4km); Los Pozos de Caldera (20km); Boquete (38km)

To Interamericana Hwy (1km); Panama City (438km)

Calle Varital

Parque de Cervantes

To ANAM office (4.5km); Airport (5km)

Plaza

---

other travelers, and the English-speaking owners have much information about the city and region.

Pensión Costa Rica (☎ 775-1241; Av 5 Este; s/d US$6/9, with bathroom US$9/11) Costa Rica offers fan-cooled rooms with a subterranean feel, but rooms can be suffocating on hot days.

Hotel Iris (☎ 775-2251; fax 775-7233; Calle A Norte; d US$12, with ⊠ US$15, tw US$20) The faded three-story Iris has 70 worn rooms with good beds and private bathrooms. It's well located, across from the park.

MID-RANGE

Hotel Castilla (☎ 774-5260; fax 774-5246; Calle A Norte; d Sun-Thu/Fri & Sat US$30/40, ste US$66; ⊠ 🖵) Near the Parque de Cervantes, this excel-

lent, centrally-located hotel offers one of the best values in David. Every room in this three-story, 70-room hotel is cheerful and equipped with air-con, phone, private hot-water bathroom and 50-channel TV.

Gran Hotel Nacional (☎ 775-2222; Calle Central; s/d US$50/58; P ⊠ ⊇) This large hotel has many amenities including a restaurant, pizzeria, casino, safe parking and a large swimming pool. The 75 rooms feature phones, good beds, 50-channel TV and private hot-water bathrooms.

Hotel Toledo (☎ 774-6732; fax 774-6733; Av 1 Este; s/d US$18/25; ⊠) The friendly Toledo has 28 clean rooms with private hot-water bath-rooms, color TVs and firm beds. Ask for a room with windows.

Hotel Madrid (☎ 775-2051; fax 774-1849; Calle F Norte; s/d US$18/24; 🕸) Madrid has decent but dark downstairs rooms and breezier rooms with a view upstairs. All have hot-water bathrooms.

Hotel Occidental (☎ 775-4068; fax 775-7424; Av 3 de Noviembre; s/d US$20/26; 🕸) On the east side of Parque de Cervantes, the Occidental has 40 rooms with private bathrooms. The rooms are a bit worn, but it still offers excellent value. There's a bar and a popular restaurant on the ground floor.

Hotel Alcalá (☎ 774-9018; fax 774-9021; Av Bolívar; s/d US$20/25) Three blocks northeast of Parque Cervantes, Alcalá is rundown on the outside, but the rooms are clean and comfortable, if nondescript. There's a restaurant downstairs.

Eating

Java Juice (Av Francisco Clark; mains US$2.50-4; 🕙 11am-11pm Mon-Sat, 4-10pm Sun) Ice coffee, fresh-fruit smoothies, healthy salads and juicy grilled burgers are the fare at this charming outdoor café northeast of the bus terminal.

Mar del Sur (Calle J Norte; mains US$7-11; 🕙 dinner only Tue-Sat) This elegant Peruvian restaurant serves excellent ceviche and seafood dishes. Try the tasty blackened corvina with capers.

Multi-Cafe (Av 3 de Noviembre; meals US$3; 🕙 closed Sun) This restaurant at the Hotel Occidental serves the most extensive buffet in town at decent prices.

Churrasco's Place (Av 2a Este; comida corriente US$1.75; 🕙 lunch & dinner) Churrasco's is popular with locals for its grilled meats and good, inexpensive lunch specials. Open late.

Gran Hotel Nacional (Calle Central; buffet US$4.50; 🕙 11:30am-9pm Mon-Sat) Facing the hotel of the same name, the Nacional serves the best pizza in town, along with the usual selection of traditional Panamanian dishes. The good all-you-can-eat lunchtime buffet is a big draw.

Café Colonial (Calle C Norte; rolls US$0.50) For inexpensive cappuccino, cinnamon rolls and croissants, head to this simple bakery.

El Sarape (Calle D Norte; mains US$4-6) Beneath a thatched roof, open-air El Sarape serves tasty Mexican dishes like jumbo burritos. It's a pleasant spot in the evening.

Helados Jackelita (Calle E Norte; US$0.35-0.85) This open-air snack stand is a local favorite for its cheap ice-cream cones and fresh juices (such as carrot juice).

Don Dicky (Calle C Norte; mains US$2-3) Divey but decent, Don Dicky sells traditional plates for next to nothing. Outdoor dining.

Iguana's Place (Calle C Norte; mains US$4-8) This popular spot has a fine open-air patio where Davidians come to enjoy fresh-roasted meats off the grill.

Super Barú (cnr Avs Francisco Clark & 3 de Noviembre) This has large deli and produce sections, and a well-stocked pharmacy. There's a small area where you can enjoy a dessert or cold beverage.

Entertainment

Normally pool tables and alcohol make a sordid combination, but **El Pool House** (Av del Estudiante), near the bus terminal, and **Los Top Place** (Av 2 Este), 150m west of the park, are both fine places to enjoy a few games. Popular with the younger set.

La Boom (Av Obaldía) is David's largest disco, featuring a sleek dance floor that packs young crowds on Friday and Saturday night.

The **Cine Gran Nacional** (Av 1 Este) shows the latest Hollywood films with Spanish subtitles.

Getting There & Away

AIR

David's airport, the Aeropuerto Enrique Malek, is about 5km from town. There are no buses to the airport; take a taxi (US$2).

Aeroperlas (airport ☎ 721-1195; Panama City ☎ 315-7500; David ☎ 775-7779; www.aeroperlas.com; Calle Central near Av Bolívar; 🕙 8am-5pm Mon-Fri, to 3:30pm Sat) flies from David to Panama City (US$57) at 7am, 11:30am and 5pm Monday through Friday, 8:30am and 5pm Saturday, and 9:30am and 5:15pm Sunday. The airline also flies from David to Bocas del Toro town (US$26) on Isla Colón at 8am Monday to Friday.

Aero (airport ☎ 721-0841; Panama City ☎ 315-0888; David ☎ 775-0812; www.aero.com.pa; Calle D Norte) flies from David to Panama City (US$57) at 7:35am, noon and 5:10pm Monday through Friday; 8:15am, 11:45am, 5:10pm on Saturday, and 9:15am and 5:10pm Sunday.

BUS

From Panama City, buses depart for David regularly (US$11, 7 to 8 hours, 13 per day). There are also two daily expresses (US$15, 5 to 6 hours, 10:45pm and midnight).

The David **bus station** (Av del Estudiante) is about 600m northeast of the central plaza. It has a small office where you can leave luggage for US$0.50 a day, and a **restaurant** (⊙ 5am–midnight).

David is a transportation hub for western Panama and has buses to many places:

Almirante (US$9; 4hr; hourly, 5am-6:30pm)
Boquete (US$1.40; 1hr; every 30min, 6am-9:30pm)
Caldera (US$1.50; 45min; hourly, 8:15am-7:30pm)
Cerro Punta (US$2.65; 2¼hr; every 20min, 5am-8pm)
Changuinola (US$10; 4½hr; hourly, 5am-6:30pm)
Chiriquí Grande (US$6; 3hr; hourly, 5am-6:30pm)
Guadalupe (US$2.65; 2½hr; take the Cerro Punta bus, which continues on to Guadalupe)
Horconcitos (US$1.50; 45min; 11am & 5pm)
Las Lajas (US$2, 1½hr; 4 per day 11:45am-5:20pm; from Las Lajas take a taxi, US$5, to the beach)
Panama City (US$11; 7-8hr; every 45min, 6:45am-8pm) express (US$15; 6hrs; 10:45pm & midnight)
Paso Canoas (US$1.50; 1½ hr; every 10min, 4:30am-9:30pm)
Puerto Armuelles (US$2.75; 2½hr; every 15min, 5am-9pm)
Río Sereno (US$4; 2½hr; every 30min, 5am-5pm)
Santiago (US$6, 3hr; hourly, 7am-9pm)
Volcán (US$2.30; 1¾hr; take the Cerro Punta bus)

Tracopa (☎ 775-0585) operates direct buses between David and San José, Costa Rica. Buses depart every day at 8:30am from the David bus station and arrive in San José about eight hours later. From San José, buses depart for the return trip to David at 7:30am. The fare is US$12.50 one way. Bus tickets can be purchased up to two days in advance.

Getting Around

David has local buses and plenty of taxis. Taxi fares within the city are around US$1; the fare to the airport is US$2.

There are numerous car-rental agencies at David's airport. If you want a 4WD vehicle, request a *cuatro por cuatro*. See p205 for details on car rental. Companies include the following:

Avis	☎ 774-7075
Budget	☎ 775-5597
Chiriquí	☎ 774-3464
Hertz	☎ 775-6828
Hilary	☎ 775-5459
Mike's	☎ 775-3524
Thrifty	☎ 721-2477

AROUND DAVID
The Road to Boquete

If you're heading up to Boquete (p208), there are a few attractions along the way.

The **Balneario Majagua**, 3.9km north of the Interamericana on the road to Boquete, is a cool place to swim in a river with a waterfall. There's also a bar here with a dance floor. Another place to cool off is the **Balneario La Cascada**, 8.4km from the Interamericana, also with a bar. Both of these places can get uncomfortably crowded on the weekends.

The small town of **Dolega,** about half-way between David and Boquete boasts a fine second-hand bookshop. The **Book Mark** (⊙ 9am-5pm Tue-Sun) stocks mostly English-language titles (with a handful in Spanish), including some old and rather obscure works. It's worth stopping in for a browse.

Los Pozos de Caldera (admission US$1) are natural hot springs famous for their health-giving properties, especially for rheumatism sufferers. The springs are on private land near the town of **Caldera**, which is 14km east of the David–Boquete road (closer to Boquete); a sign marks the turnoff. To get to the springs, take a bus or drive to the town of Caldera (the turnoff to Caldera is 13km south of Boquete). From where the bus drops you off continue to the end of town, where you'll see a sign indicating the turnoff to the springs. You'll turn right along this rugged dirt road, accessible by 4WD only. If you're walking it's about 45 minutes from here. Continue along the road until you reach a suspension bridge. Cross it, and take the first left leading up the hill. After 100m, you'll see a gate which marks the entrance to the property. If you're driving, don't leave anything in the car. There have been reports of break-ins here. The springs themselves aren't anything fantastic, but the pleasant Rio Caldera is a stone's throw away, making a pleasant spot to cool off. Hourly buses run from both David and Boquete (both US$0.75, 45 minutes) to the town of Caldera.

PASO CANOAS

See Border Crossings (p306) for information on this major border town.

PLAYA BARQUETA

This long and lovely dark-sand beach southwest of David has a handful of development along its shoreline. Capping the eastern end is the **Las Olas Resort** (☎ 772-3000; www.lasolasresort.com; s/d US$120/144, ste s/d US$130/170; ⊠ ⊛). It features 31 standard guestrooms, six standard suites and two double suites, all with terraces that have ocean views. Rooms are comfortable and well maintained with good beds and TV. Facilities are extensive, and include a gourmet restaurant, a bar, a poolside restaurant-bar, a workout center, a spa and a gift shop. Las Olas offers a range of activities, from yoga classes on the beach to horseback riding. Be advised that the surf in front of the resort is dangerous due to riptides. The hotel is next to an ecological reserve in the mangroves designed to protect migratory birds. Room rates are cheaper in the low season (April to November).

GOLFO DE CHIRIQUÍ

South of David, the Golfo de Chiriquí is home to the **Parque Nacional Marino Golfo de Chiriquí**, a national marine park with an area of 14,740 hectares protecting 25 islands, 19 coral reefs and abundant wildlife. Attractions include beaches, snorkeling, swimming, diving, surfing, bird watching and big-game fishing.

The 3000-hectare **Isla Boca Brava** lies just off the coast. It's a lovely island with 12km of trails. Three species of monkey, four species of sea turtle and 280 recorded bird species inhabit the island. Offshore coral reefs provide excellent opportunities for snorkeling, and there are picturesque beaches.

Situated on an idyllic spot overlooking the sea, **Restaurante y Cabañas Boca Brava** (☎ 676-3244; r US$10, cabin US$18-35, hammock per person US$3) is the only place to stay on the island. There are four spacious cabins with private bathrooms and four rustic rooms with shared bathrooms. Owners Frank and Yadira Köhler speak English, German and Spanish. Reservations are not accepted, but they'll always find you a place to stay if you're willing to sleep in a hammock.

The breezy **restaurant-bar** (meals US$4) features a large selection of seafood (such as red snapper), and Frank can arrange any number of excursions around the islands, involving snorkeling, whale-watching or just lounging on a gorgeous uninhabited island (prices range from US$12 to US$70 depending on the tour and the number of participants). From the restaurant, you're a stone's throw from the boundary of the national marine park.

Getting There & Away

To reach the island, drive or take a bus to the Horconcitos turnoff, which is 39km east

of David (US$1.50; 45 minutes; 11am and 5pm daily). You can take any bus going by the turnoff (any bus heading from David to Las Laja, San Felix, Santiago or Panama City), as long as you tell the driver to drop you at the Horconcitos turnoff.

From the turnoff, take a pickup-truck taxi 13km to the fishing village of Boca Chica (US$15; one hour). If you see no taxis at the turnoff, walk into Horconcitos and call either **Jovené** (☎ 653-1549) or **Roberto** (☎ 628-0651); both are taxi drivers in the area. The Purple House in David (p202) can also arrange transport from the hostel to Boca Chica (US$8 one way). At the Boca Chica dock, hire a water taxi (per person US$1) to take you 200m to the island.

If you drive your own vehicle, you can safely leave it near the village dock, but the road between Horconcitos and Boca Chica is impassable save for 4WD vehicles.

PUNTA BURICA

This lush peninsula jutting into the Pacific is a lovely spot for absorbing the beauty of both the rain forest and the coastline. Four years in the making, **Mono Feliz** (☎ 595-0388; mono_feliz@hotmail.com; cabin 1st night/every night thereafter per person US$20/15; campsite per person per day US$5; ☻) offers visitors a chance to enjoy this untouched natural beauty. Wildlife is a key feature here, and the Mono Feliz (happy monkey) certainly has its share of its namesake. Among the species that regularly wander through the seven-hectare property are Central American squirrel monkeys, white-faced capuchins and howler monkeys. Other wildlife includes a variety of birdlife, iguanas, armadillos, anteaters, sloths and butterflies.

Facilities include three stand-alone cabins, two in the garden and one on the beach. They also have a large pool (fed by cool spring water, and you may be surrounded by monkeys at times), fresh water showers and an outdoor kitchen for guest use. Those who'd rather not cook can pay US$20 per day extra for three home-cooked meals, ranging from fresh seasonal fish to conch or lobster when available (individual meals available for US$6/8/10 breakfast/lunch/dinner). Beds have mosquito nets. Camping on the beach is also available (bring your own gear), and you have access to pool and bathrooms.

The friendly American and Canadian owners (Allegra and John or 'Juancho' as he's known to locals) offer a range of activities including nature walks (an excursion to Isla Burica at low tide is a highlight), bird watching, fishing, surfing (several boards available) and horseback riding. Remedial massage and yoga is available for guests in need of deeper relaxation. All activities except horseback riding (US$5) are free. English, French and Spanish spoken. Please note that email and phone messages are only checked every two weeks, but the owners won't turn away anyone who simply shows up.

Getting There & Away

Owing to its isolation, Mono Feliz requires a bit of work getting there. You'll first need to go to the small coastal town of Puerto Armuelles. Departures from David to Puerto Armuelles leave every 15 minutes (US$2.75, 2½ hours). Be sure to arrive in Puerto Armuelles no later than noon. The bus drops you off in the *mercado municipal*, and from there you'll take a truck to Bella Vista. Trucks generally operate around low tide (local papers often list tide charts or you can check www.pancanal.com/esp/eie/radar/balboa-tides-2004.pdf). From Bella Vista it is approximately a one-hour walk down the hill to Mono Feliz. You can also exit at El Medio, the last stop before the trucks go inland to Bella Vista. From El Medio it's an hour's walk along the beach. Mono Feliz is directly in front of the island Isla Burica. There are also 'Mono Feliz' signs from El Medio onward.

If you have a 4WD, you can drive directly to Mono Feliz in the dry season (mid-December to mid-April). From Puerto Armuelles keep heading south along the coast towards Costa Rica. Go through the Petroterminal and then veer directly onto the beach (attempt this only at low tide). About 15km along you will pass though Limones, Puerto Balsa and then, around 20 minutes later, El Medio. Keep going on the beach for another 10 minutes and you will see where the dirt road starts, marked with a 'Mono Feliz' sign. Keep to this road and 30 minutes later, when you cannot go any further, you will reach Mono Feliz.

EAST TO VERAGUAS PROVINCE
Meseta Chorcha

On the northern side of the Interamericana, 24km east of David, is the enormous Meseta Chorcha (Chorcha Plateau), which photog-

raphers won't want to miss. As you approach the plateau from the west, you'll see a white streak running down its glistening granite face. As you come closer, you'll see that the streak is an extremely tall waterfall.

Unfortunately, the highway's as close to the falls as you can get without trespassing. The land between the highway and the foot of the falls belongs to a rancher who doesn't like strangers on his property.

Playa Las Lajas

Playa Las Lajas, 62km east of David and 13km south of the Interamericana via a paved road, is one of several lengthy, palm-lined beaches along this stretch of the Pacific coast. This tan-sand beach is quite popular on the weekends but often empty during the week. The waves are perfect for body surfing without much undertow, and the sand is cool.

There's one place to stay at this beach, and it's **Las Lajas Beach Cabins** (☎ 720-2430 & 618-7723; dm/d US$6.50/35, cabin US$25). The cabins consist of nine small rustic *cabañas* right on the beach, a clam's toss from the surf. The cabins have concrete floors with walls of bamboo and a thatched roof. There are windows on all sides, and each *cabaña* contains a double bamboo bed (a two-inch foam mat and sheets are provided). The bathrooms are communal in a nearby concrete structure. There is also an additional concrete structure 50m back from the beach with six private rooms and two dormitories (one for women, one for men). If you've got a tent and want to camp, you can do so here and use the facilities for US$5 per tent.

Back where the road dead-ends at the beach (about 800m from the cabins) sits old **La Estrella del Pacifico** (dishes US$2.50), the only restaurant in the area. Simple fish dishes are decent, and with the great ocean view, the slow service doesn't seem so intolerable.

To get here, take any bus from David (US$2, 90 minutes) that travels by the Las Lajas turnoff on the Interamericana, except an express, and ask the driver to drop you at the Las Lajas turnoff. At the turnoff, take a taxi (US$5) the 13km to where the road reaches the sea. Turn right and proceed 1.5km until you arrive at the cabins.

At the turnoff to Las Lajas, there's **Restaurante El Cruce** that's open 'early til late' every night. Buses stop here every 30 minutes from 5am to 4:30pm.

Ngöbe Buglé sell **handicrafts** in a wooden-walled structure 500m west of the restaurant and about 50m south of the Interamericana. (Most of the residents of San Félix, 3km north of the Restaurante Le Cruce, are Ngöbe Buglé.)

Cerro Colorado

One of the world's largest copper mines is an hour's drive north of the Interamericana via a private road that begins nearly opposite the Playa Las Lajas turnoff. Mineralogists estimate that there's approximately 1.4 million tons of copper in Cerro Colorado. The open-face mine is not open to tours.

Pozos de Galique

The Pozos de Galique (Springs of Galique) are three no-frills hot springs, each of which can accommodate several people, at the end of a 3.8km badly rutted dirt road that winds north from the Interamericana. If you usually enjoy hot springs, you'll likely enjoy these – especially if you reach them in the early morning (before the day heats up) and bring lots of cold drinks.

The easy-to-miss turnoff for the road to the springs, which requires a 4WD vehicle, is 27km east of the Interamericana turnoff for Horconcitos and 4km east of the turnoff for Playa Las Lajas. The turnoff is 30m west of a small bridge with 'Galique' written on it.

Rock Carvings

About 5km west of the town of Tolé is a turnoff for El Nancito, a small community known for its carved boulders. Local people say the carvings were made more than 1000 years ago, but no one really knows; the rocks have yet to be studied. Few people even know about them.

From the Interamericana, turn north onto the road to El Nancito, and when you reach the 'Cantina Oriente' sign, turn west and drive 75m. You'll come across some rather large boulders with figures carved into them. The largest of the boulders is on the far side of a barbed-wire fence, behind a cattle chute. There are many other carved boulders in the area.

No buses stop in El Nancito. If you are relying on public transportation take any bus that passes by El Nancito, ask the driver to drop you at the turnoff on the Interamericana, and then hike the 1.5km to the boulders. Be careful doing this in the late afternoon; you'll have difficulty catching a return bus after sunset.

HIGHLANDS

BOQUETE
pop 4100

Nestled in a craggy mountain valley at 1060m, with the sparkling Río Caldera running through it, Boquete is known throughout Panama for its cool, fresh climate and pristine natural setting. It's a fine place for walking, bird watching, and enjoying a respite from the heat of lowland David, 38km south. *Bajareque*, which roughly translates as 'slow drizzle,' is the name locals give to the light rainfall that visits this pleasant town almost every afternoon.

Flowers, coffee, vegetables and citrus fruits flourish in Boquete's rich soil. The coffee is considered the country's finest, and Boquete oranges (grown from November to February), originally brought from Riverside, California, are known for their sweetness.

Nights are chilly here, and temperatures can drop to near freezing. Visitors should pack some warm clothes if they plan to do any camping.

Orientation

Boquete's central area consists of only a few square blocks. The main road, Av Central, comes north from David, passes along the western side of the central plaza and continues up the hill past the church.

Information
INTERNET
Chevita.com (Av Central; per hr US$1; ◷ 8:30am-10pm Mon-Sat, 9am-9pm Sun) Across from the church.
Internet Kelnix (Av Central; per hr US$1) Near the central plaza.
McNet (per hr US$1) Attached to the Kalima All Suites (p213).

LAUNDRY
Lavamático Las Burbujas (Av Central; wash small/large US$2/4) Just opposite and a little downhill from the church.

MEDICAL SERVICES
Centro Medico San Juan Bautista (☎ 720-1881) On the main road just south of Café Ruiz, English-speaking Dr Leonido Pretelt is highly recommended.

BOQUETE

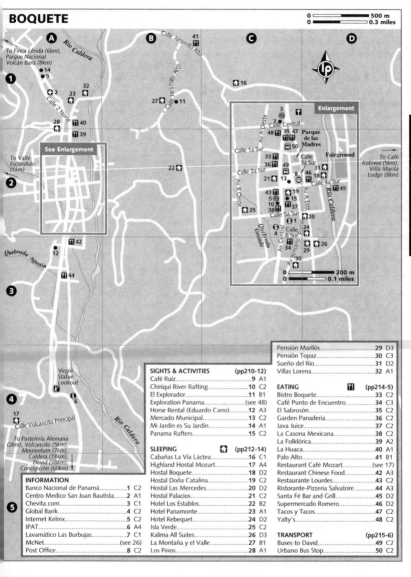

INFORMATION
Banco Nacional de Panamá.............................1 C2
Centro Medico San Juan Bautista..................2 A1
Chevita.com...3 C1
Global Bank...4 C2
Internet Kelnix...5 C2
IPAT..6 A4
Lavamático Las Burbujas................................7 C1
McNet...(see 26)
Post Office..8 C2

SIGHTS & ACTIVITIES   (pp210-12)
Café Ruíz...9 A1
Chiriquí River Rafting..................................10 C2
El Explorador...11 B1
Exploration Panama..............................(see 48)
Horse Rental (Eduardo Cano)......................12 A3
Mercado Municipal.......................................13 C2
Mi Jardín es Su Jardín..................................14 A1
Panama Rafters..15 C2

SLEEPING   (pp212-14)
Cabañas La Vía Láctea..................................16 C1
Highland Hostal Mozart................................17 A4
Hostal Boquete..18 D2
Hostal Doña Catalina....................................19 C2
Hostal Las Mercedes.....................................20 D2
Hostal Palacios...21 C2
Hotel Los Establos..22 B2
Hotel Panamonte..23 A1
Hotel Rebequet...24 D2
Isla Verde...25 C2
Kalima All Suites...26 D3
La Montaña y el Valle...................................27 B1
Los Pinos..28 A1

Pensión Marilós..29 D3
Pensión Topaz..30 C3
Sueño del Río...31 D2
Villas Lorena...32 A1

EATING   (pp214-5)
Bistro Boquete...33 C3
Café Punto de Encuentro..............................34 C3
El Sabrosón..35 C2
Garden Panadería...36 C2
Java Juice...37 C2
La Casona Mexicana......................................38 C2
La Folklórica...39 A2
La Huaca..40 A1
Palo Alto..41 B1
Restaurant Café Mozart..........................(see 17)
Restaurant Chinese Food..............................42 A3
Restaurante Lourdes.....................................43 C2
Ristorante-Pizzeria Salvatore........................44 A3
Santa Fé Bar and Grill..................................45 D2
Supermercado Romero..................................46 D2
Tacos y Tacos...47 C2
Yalty's..48 C2

TRANSPORT   (pp215-6)
Buses to David..49 C2
Urbano Bus Stop...50 C2

CHIRIQUÍ PROVINCE

MONEY
Banco Nacional de Panama (Av Central) and **Global** (Av Central) Opposite each other, they keep similar hours (8am-3pm Mon-Fri, 9am-noon Sat); both have ATMs.

POST
Post office (7am-6pm Mon-Fri, to 5pm Sat) On the eastern side of the plaza.

TELEPHONE
McNet (to USA per min US$0.25) Make long-distance phone calls here; attached to Kalima All Suites (p213).

TOURIST OFFICE
IPAT (9:30am-6pm) Before arriving in Boquete (about 1.5km south of town), this office sits atop a bluff overlooking town. You can pick up maps here (though they often

run out) and obtain information on sites. A balcony affords a wonderful view of the river valley, and the pleasant café serves Boquete's mountain-grown coffee. On the 2nd floor is an exhibit detailing the history of the region (Spanish only).

Sights & Activities

Boquete, with its flower-lined streets and nearby forest, is ideal for walking, hiking and birding. The town lends itself well to picturesque strolls. The more ambitious might fancy climbing 3478m **Volcán Barú** in the nearby national park; there are several entrances to the park, but the easiest access is from Boquete (see Parque Nacional Volcán Barú, p216).

A stroll around town will allow you to see the **Parque de las Madres** – with its flowers, fountain and children's playground – and the **fairgrounds** and **river**. You'll also come across an old railway and an exhibition wagon – leftovers from the days when a train linked Boquete with the coastal town of Puerto Armuelles.

Kotowa Coffee Estate (☎ 720-1430; www.my roaster.com; tour US$14, 2½hr) offers the best coffee-estate tour in the area. It features a description of the estate's history (beginning with a Canadian's arrival in 1918). There's a full tour of the production facilities, with emphasis on the estate's environmentally friendly methods of production, as well as a tour of the estate's original processing mill. At the cupping session, guests learn what to look for in high-quality coffee. The estate requests 24 hours' notice prior to your visit.

Café Ruíz (☎ 720-1392; www.caferuiz.com; tour US$14, 3hr), on the main road about 600m north of the town center, offers a tour that includes transportation to a nearby coffee plantation, a presentation on the history of coffee in Boquete, and a description at the processing plant of how fresh-picked coffee beans are prepared for roasting. Next, you're led to the roasting facility where you'll learn the methods involved in the final processing of the beans for consumer use. The tour rounds out with a cupping session. Tours depart at 9am daily except Sundays and holidays, but you have to make advance reservations – most easily done over the Internet or by phone if you speak Spanish.

Mi Jardín es Su Jardín (admission free; ☼ daylight hr), just uphill from Café Ruíz, is a magnificent garden surrounding a luxurious private estate. The residence is off-limits to the public, but you are free to stroll about the garden.

El Explorador (☎ 775-2643; Calle Jarmillo Alto; US$2; ☼ 10am-6pm daily mid-Dec to mid-Apr, Sat & Sun only mid-Apr to mid-Dec) is a cafeteria and gardens in a hilly area 45 minutes' walk from the town center. The cafeteria serves breads, hot chocolate, coffee drinks, chicken and fried bananas. Reached by a path behind the cafeteria, the gardens are designed to look like something out of *Alice in Wonderland* as they wander through a forested area and over an itty-bitty bridge. Unfortunately, the place has been poorly maintained and doesn't hold much appeal.

Finca Lérida, located northwest of town, is a coffee farm owned by the Collins family. Bordering the farm is prime habitat for the quetzal, the national bird of Guatemala that's nearly extinct there but has found refuge in Chiriquí Province. In all, nearly 900 bird species have been identified in these woods. The Hotel Panamonte (p213), also owned by the Collins, offers tours of Finca Lérida. The per-person cost of US$150 (party of one), US$75 (party of two) or U$65 (party of four to six people) includes lunch and transportation. The quetzals are most likely to be seen January through August.

Every Saturday, hundreds of Ngöbe Buglé Indians from outlying areas descend upon the central plaza to buy bolts of material, rubber boots etc at the **Mercado Municipal**.

WHITE-WATER RAFTING

Those who seek a bit of adventure shouldn't miss the excellent white-water rafting within a two-hour drive of Boquete. There are two rivers that are used by a reputable white-water rafting outfit in the area. The Río Chiriquí and the Río Chiriquí Viejo both flow from the fertile hills of Volcán Barú and are flanked by forest for much of their lengths. At some places waterfalls can be seen at the edges of the rivers, and both pass through narrow canyons with awesome, sheer rock walls.

The Río Chiriquí is most often run from May to December, and the Chiriquí Viejo is run the rest of the year; the rides tend to last four and five hours, respectively. Bring along plenty of sunscreen. (See the boxed text p214 for more information.)

The country's best white-water rafting outfit, **Chiriquí River Rafting** (☎ 720-1505; www.panama

-rafting.com), in downtown Boquete, switches between the rivers, depending on rainfall, the age and experience levels of its clients and other factors. The company's owner, Hector Sanchez, speaks English and Spanish, and is very safety-conscious (see Panama's Top Guides p313). Some stretches of the river are ideal for beginners and families with children age eight and over; others are only for the most experienced. All-day trips are offered for US$75 to US$100, depending on the river, with a minimum of four people. If you don't have four people, you can call the company, and it will try to team you with others to meet the minimum. Stop by the office in Boquete to see the options.

Panama Rafters (☎ 720-2712; rafting4kev@cwpanama.com) across the street offers excursions at similar prices.

HIKING TOURS
The lovely scenery, cool climate and abundance of natural attractions make Boquete an ideal spot for hiking. **Feliciano Gonzalez** (☎ 624-9940, 632-8695; felicianogonzalez255@hotmail.com) offers numerous hiking tours, and he comes highly recommended. Although his English is still a work in progress, Feliciano is a very personable fellow and has a great deal of knowledge about the area. In addition to a **city tour of Boquete** (2 people US$30; 3-4hr), he offers some other popular tours:

Boquete to Bocas (2/3 people US$250/350) This difficult hike lasts three to four days and requires camping along the way. The trail begins outside of Boquete and ends at the Caribbean, crossing over the Continental Divide. A shorter three-hour hike along this *sendero* is also available, which passes through pristine cloud forest and prime quetzal habitat in Parque Internacional La Amistad to the top of the Continental Divide and (clouds permitting) a view of the Pacific and Atlantic oceans.

Hot Springs of Caldera (1 or 2 people US$20, each additional person US$10) This five-hour tour involves a visit to some petroglyphs near Caldera, followed by a therapeutic dip in the hot springs near the town of Caldera, and a refreshing plunge in the gorgeous Río Chiriquí.

Sendero Los Quetzales (1/2/3 people US$20/30/40) This difficult hiking tour lasts six hours, which are spent walking one of the country's premier hiking trails and a trail renowned for quetzals.

Volcán Barú (1/2 people US$50/60) This challenging hike leads to the summit of Panama's only volcano. You'll travel by car to the eastern entrance and from there hike 11km to the peak. Allow at least 10 hours for this trip.

Another recommended guide for hikes around the Boquete area is **Ludwig Shiwanov** (☎ 720-2078, 683-8954; ludwigshiwanov@yahoo.com). For bird watching contact **Hans & Terry** (☎ 720-3852; habbusdekwie@cwpanama.net), a friendly Dutch couple who lead tours around Boquete.

TRUCK TOURS
Boquete Mountain Cruisers (☎ 720-4697; boquetecruisers@hotmail.com) This expat-owned outfit offers two daily tours in its open-air trucks. The first leaves at 8:30am (per person US$20) and makes a number of stops in and around Boquete. Highlights include coffee, basalt formations, waterfalls, country drives and views. The second tour departs at 2pm (per person US$15) for the Caldera hot springs. Both tours last four hours. Call for reservations. Trips include pickup at your hotel.

HORSEBACK TOURS
Eduardo Cano (☎ 720-1750; Av Central; per hr US$8) offers guided horseback tours for US$8 an hour (US$5 for the horse and US$3 for himself, as he likes to say). Friendly Eduardo speaks Spanish only, but that doesn't matter. If you're a party of one and don't speak Spanish, as many of his parties are, you'll just have to make do with the tranquility and beauty of the mountains.

BOAT TOURS
Exploration Panama (☎ 720-2470; www.explorationpanama.net; Av Central) This new outfit offers a wide variety of excursions in and around the Golfo de Chiriquí. Aboard a 50ft vessel, which is a former US Coast Guard Search & Rescue ship, you can take a 'jungle cruise' (per person US$75, four-person minimum), exploring the mangroves, small rivers and coastal forests south of David. Ron Mager, the owner-captain of *Exploration Panama*, also offers sea-kayaking trips (led by personnel from Chiriquí River Rafting), fishing trips, and scuba-diving trips – and he's a very safe and reliable captain (he has his US Coast Guard license and is a former Green Beret). His ship can accommodate up to six passengers on overnight trips, which allow for excursions into some gorgeous unexplored waters.

GOLF
El Valle Escondido (☎ 720-2897; www.valleescondido.biz; 9 holes US$20, 18 holes US$30) Offers carts, a

CHIRIQUÍ PROVINCE

full-service shop and beautiful greens. To get to Valle Escondido, take a left at Calle 5a Sur, proceed two blocks and take a right on Av B Oeste. Follow the signs, and you'll reach the complex 1km later.

Festivals & Events

The town's annual festival, the **Feria de las Flores y del Café** (Fair of Flowers and Coffee), held for 10 days each January, draws people from near and far. In April, the town hosts a smaller **orchid fair**. Contact IPAT (p209) for exact dates of both events, as they vary.

Sleeping

Because of the cool climate, all the accommodations in Boquete have hot showers.

BUDGET

Pensión Marilós (☎ 720-1380; marilos66@hotmail .com; cnr Av A Este & Calle 6 Sur; s/d US$7/10, with bathroom US$10/16) Marilós is a favorite with budget travelers from around the world. It's a good place to stay – family run, clean and comfortable, with kitchen access for guests. Owner Frank Glavas has a wealth of knowledge of Boquete and can arrange excursions throughout the area.

Hostal Boquete (☎ 720-2573; s/d US$11/15) Off Calle 4a Sur, this pleasant hotel has clean rooms with private bathrooms and a lovely terrace overlooking the Río Caldera. Excellent value.

Sueño del Río (☎ 720-2736; s/d US$6/12) Also off Calle 4a Sur, this family house rents a couple of rooms and offers home-cooked meals for US$2. Rooms are basic but well maintained.

Hostal Palacios (☎ 720-1653; per person US$6.50) Facing the plaza, this friendly, centrally located guesthouse features rooms varying in quality, some with private bathrooms. Some rooms are better than others, but the place offers a good value. Guests have kitchen access.

Pensión Topaz (☎ /fax 720-1005; schoeb@chiriqui .com; Av Belisario Porras; s/d US$10/15, with bathroom US$20/25; ▣) Topaz offers eight lovely rooms, a swimming pool and an organic garden. Six of the rooms have private bathrooms, and two rooms share an outdoor solar-heated bathroom. A wonderful breakfast is available for US$4. The gracious hosts speak English, Spanish, German and French. You can pitch a tent here too (US$5).

Hotel Rebequet (☎ 720-1365; Calle 6 Sur; s/d US$22/33, annex r US$15) Opposite Pensión Marilós, the friendly Rebequet has attractive rooms with private bathrooms, TV and fridge. The annex next door has smaller rooms, clean but featureless. Rebequet also rents four rooms in a secluded spot a few blocks away with fine views (per person US$7); good for those seeking a bit of solitude. Ask at the Rebequet to have a look.

Hostal Las Mercedes (☎ 660-3138; rdarios44@ hotmail.com; cnr Av A Este & 5a Sur; d US$10-15) Las Mercedes has nice clean rooms in a family house. Guests can use the kitchen and living room, and the owner can arrange tours around the region.

Hostal Doña Catalina (☎ 720-1260; s/d US$5.50/11, with bathroom US$10/22) On the central plaza, the old blue Hostal Doña Catalina has bare, shabby rooms downstairs with shared facilities. Upstairs rooms with bathrooms are a bit better, and the balcony overlooking the park is nice. The local owners are friendly.

MID-RANGE

Highland Hostal Mozart (☎ /fax 720-3764, coyaldps@ hotmail.com; Calle Volcancito Principal; cabin from US$26, r US$45) Near IPAT, this beautiful spot offers lovely views from its cabins out over the hills (to the Pacific on a clear day). The cabins are simple but nicely designed, each with a private bathroom, wardrobe and a terrace in front for enjoying the view. Inside the house, there are several cozily furnished rooms with lots of windows. You can also camp (US$5), and rent a tent (one/two people US$7/10). There's a delightful veranda restaurant (p214) where Peruvian food is often served, and bicycles are available for rent. German, English and Spanish are spoken. A taxi ride to here from downtown Boquete costs US$1.

Isla Verde (☎ 720-2533; islaverde@cwpanama.net; Av B Oeste; small/large cabin US$50/65) These centrally located cabins offer some of the loveliest accommodations in Boquete. Set in a beautiful, lushly landscaped area are six modern, comfortable two-story *cabañas*, with tall ceilings, a kitchen and roomy bathroom (three of the *cabañas* are wheelchair-accessible). The three largest *cabañas* can accommodate up to six people; the others can accommodate four people. Hosts can also arrange horseback riding tours.

Hotel Los Establos (☎ 720-2685; www.valleescon lido.biz/losestablos/index.htm; d/ste US$110/230) This elegant B&B has the air of a Tuscan villa. Although it was originally built for stables, the lavish quarters here bear no trace of horses. Each of the four guest bedrooms and two suites is well furnished with a terrace outside of each room. Guests can use the video library, outdoor glass-enclosed Jacuzzi (for six), golfing green, patio, and grand salon (pool table), and have access to Valle Escondido's facilities (p211).

Villa Marita Lodge (☎ 720-2165, www.panamainfo .com/marita; d US$55) These seven stand-alone cabins on the edge of a plateau overlook three coffee farms and have striking views of Volcán Barú. Proudly maintained, each gorgeous cabin contains a cozy sitting area. There's a restaurant that's open to guests and a large common room. It's very reasonably priced, and accepts children of all ages. English and Spanish are spoken.

Hotel Panamonte (☎ 720-1327; www.hotelpana monte.com; d from US$65) At the northern end of town, this beautiful old hotel with dollhouse-like charm lies in perfect harmony with its surroundings. The hotel has handsomely furnished guestrooms, and the fine restaurant-bar with stone fireplace makes a nice stop for a meal or a cocktail in the evening. The hotel has a day spa, and offers guided tours for quetzal viewing (see Finca Lérida, p210). A variety of other nature tours and a coffee farm tour are also offered here.

Cabañas La Vía Láctea (☎ 720-2376; www.lavia lactea.biz; Calle Jaramillo Alto; d/tr from US$45/55) Just outside of town, these cabins sit at the edge of the pretty Río Palo Alto. Built in 2003, the six-sided guestrooms feature tile floors, good lighting, decent beds, private bathrooms and small, fully equipped kitchens. A plan to add a gazebo/lounge area near the river was due to finish in mid-2005.

Kalima All Suites (☎ 720-2884; www.kalimasuites .net; d US$40) This new all-suites hotel offers good value for money. The six suites (which can accommodate from two to six) are well maintained with tile floors, a living and kitchen area and a terrace in the back. A popular Internet café is next door (p208).

La Montaña y el Valle (☎ 720-2211; www.coffee estateinn.com; Calle Jaramillo Alto; d US$90) Also called the Coffee Estate Inn, these three luxury bungalows each come with a well-equipped kitchen, spacious living room/dining area,

separate bedroom, bathroom and private terrace with valley views. Below the bungalows is a working coffee estate with trails into a lovely patch of forest; the price includes estate coffee roasted daily, and coffee and nature tours. No children younger than nine years are allowed.

Momentum (☎ 720-4385; www.momentum-panama .com; s/d US$35/45, d cabin US$60; 🖳 🕿) Situated 8km south of Boquete (30km from David), Momentum offers four large, stand-alone cabins that all face Volcán Barú. Cabins feature two large rooms with full kitchens and bathrooms, and each is wheelchair-accessible. There are also two rooms available inside the main house for rent. Guests have full use of the facilities (solar-heated pool, small workout area, laundry, Internet access), and there's a 1km running track circling the property. It's a very peaceful place, situated on the edge of a canyon (which you can hike down into) with the Rio Cochéa running below. On clear nights you'll have spectacular views of the stars. From here, it's a US$3 cab ride to Boquete. Momentum is also one of Panama's only openly gay- and lesbian-friendly resorts (though it's open to anyone).

El Valle Escondido (☎ 720-2897; www.valle escondido.biz; d US$90) In a large, gated expat community on the edge of town, El Valle Escondido has several pleasant cabins for rent, and guests can take advantage of the many amenities here: 18-hole golf course, athletic center, equestrian center, holistic medicine services, spa, restaurant, coffee shop and so on. Cabins have tall ceilings, kitchenettes with a little breakfast table, DirecTV (satellite TV), and huge bathrooms.

Villas Lorena (🖂 720-1848; jrshydro@sinfo.net; d low-/high-season US$40/50) This large, two-story apartment building beside the Río Caldera offers spacious and fully equipped two-level guest quarters with living rooms and two bathrooms apiece. The place is simply furnished and has tile floors, but it's good value for money.

Los Pinos (☎ 775-1521; www.lospinosboquete.com; d/tr US$50/70) This interconnected complex features five two-story apartments that can accommodate up to eight people each. Downstairs is the kitchen, two bedrooms, bathroom and a small outdoor terrace. Upstairs is another bedroom and a bathroom. The rooms are cheaply furnished and

CHIRIQUÍ IS FOR KAYAKERS

John Miller has made more first descents of Panama's white-water rivers than anyone else. The teacher of instructors for US-based Nantahala Outdoor Center, the world's largest kayaking school, John's an expert kayaker – especially when it comes to Panama's rivers. He prepared the following report for Lonely Planet's readers:

'There are other rivers in Panama, but nothing compares to Chiriquí. And if someone wants to paddle in Panama, this is where they should go.

The Chiriquí Province of Panama has three elements that make it a paddler's paradise: terrain, rainfall and accessibility. During the rainy season (mid-April through mid-December), the area around Boquete has over 20 different runs within a two-hour intro drive of this small mountain town, varying from easy Class 1 or 2 to scary Class 5. The Cordillera Central ranges from over 10,000ft near the Costa Rican border in the west to around 6000ft at the border with the Veraguas Province in the east. The river gradient is steep and consistent almost to the Pacific Ocean, resulting in long continuous stretches of white water. In addition, Volcán Barú towers over Boquete at 11,500ft on the Pacific side of the Cordillera Central. This dormant volcano tends to attract rainfall and has six runnable rivers draining its flanks.

Most of the watersheds in this area are small, but thanks to the bountiful precipitation in the rainy season, they are usually runnable every day during the rainy season. During the dry season, only the two biggest watersheds, the Río Chiriquí and the Río Chiriquí Viejo, have enough water to be runnable, and most of the paddling in Panama is found in these two watersheds. By far, the best time of year to paddle is from September through November.

Almost all of the rivers in this area follow a very predictable pattern. They are very steep and continuous at the higher elevations, tending to be small, steep streams. As the rivers flow down the mountains, the gradient gradually levels off, and the rivers pick up tributaries and grow in volume and width. As you approach sea level, the rivers are high-volume but also drop or pool. You can generally gauge how difficult the run will be by the elevation. The hardest runs start as high as 5000ft while anything below 1000ft tends to be no harder than Class 3.'

lacking in style, but the place gets decent light and is well maintained. There's a small playground in front.

Eating

Boquete has many inexpensive restaurants to choose from, and coffee here is among the best in Panama.

Bistro Boquete (Av Central; mains US$3-7; ☻ 11am-10pm) This handsome, low-key bistro in the center of town serves a range of eclectic cuisine: from light, flavorful meals – curry chicken salad – to big plates such as chili-rubbed filet mignon with potatoes and vegetables. The menu is well rounded and features a number of sandwiches and salads, as well as plates of trout and salmon. Don't miss the rich dessert selection (brownies, cheesecake, lemon pie). There's also a full bar.

Palo Alto (Calle Jaramillo Alto; mains US$6-12; ☻ noon-9pm Tue-Sun) A newcomer to Boquete's culinary scene, this charming open-air spot has an idyllic setting along the rushing Río Palo Alto. The menu features a large mixed selection and receives high marks. Trout with ginger sauce, grilled pork chops and jumbo shrimp, as well as lighter fare (soups, salads and sandwiches) are among the offerings. There's also a small but decent selection of wines.

Café Punto de Encuentro (Calle 6 Sur; meals US$3-4.50; ☻ 7am-noon) Just east of the main road two blocks south of the plaza, Encuentro serves tasty breakfast (omelets and pancakes) in a pleasant garden setting with hummingbirds passing nearby. There's also an English-language book exchange.

Restaurant Café Mozart (mains US$7-10; ☻ 8am-2pm & 6-10pm) This charming restaurant and hotel (p212) offers lovely views out over the valley from the open-air restaurant. Dishes here are made with a great deal of care and feature an ever-changing menu, pulling from Peruvian and German specialties. The owner always has a dish for vegetarians. On the last Saturday of the month, she sponsors a culinary fest highlighting a different part of the world.

La Folklórica (Av Central; mains US$5.50) On the main road just north of the church, this pleasant restaurant and antique store serves excellent, home-cooked dishes such as trout with garlic and herbs. The lush scenery through the picture window is quite nice, as is the coffee.

Café Ruiz (7am-6pm) The outdoor patio at Ruiz makes a good spot to sip locally-produced coffee and watch the mist move across the mountains (see also p210).

Pastelería Alemana (8am-noon) On the main road 2km south of town, this gorgeous spot serves decadent fresh-baked pies (apple, lemon, pineapple), sweetbreads and good coffees (including an iced mocha).

La Casona Mexicana (Av Central; mains US$4-6) A block south of the plaza, La Casona serves decent Mexican food in a colorful interior. There are ample vegetarian options. Save room for the outstanding strawberry *batido* (milkshake).

La Huaca (720-1343; Av Central; pizzas US$6-7; Wed-Mon) North of the plaza, La Huaca is set in a beautifully restored colonial-style building with river and mountain views. It's a favorite for the tasty stone-baked pizzas. The pool tables by the bar make a nice spot for a game. They also deliver.

Java Juice (Av Central; sandwiches US$3; 9am-10pm) This pleasant café has a small patio in front that makes a fine spot for a light repast – veggie burgers, fresh salads, juices and tasty *batidos* (blackberry, banana, melon and strawberry among others). As indicated by the name, this is also a good place to get your caffeine fix (iced cappuccinos and moccaccinos).

Yalty's (Av Central; mains US$3-5; 7:30am-6pm) A favorite among expats, this low-key restaurant is a regular slice of Americana. Big breakfasts (French toast, crepes and pancakes), deli-style sandwiches (smoked turkey and pastrami) and homemade soup are among the popular selections.

Ristorante-Pizzeria Salvatore (Av Central; pizzas US$5-11; lunch & dinner) Six blocks south of the central plaza, Salvatore offers good pizza in a pleasant environment, with tables inside and out. The menu also features pastas and seafood.

Pizzería La Volcánica (Av Central; pizzas US$3.50-10; lunch & dinner) Near the plaza, the low-key Volcánica serves OK pizzas and Italian dishes at low prices.

Santa Fe Bar & Grill (Calle 4a Sur; mains US$4-6; 7am-6pm Tue-Sun) Beside the Río Caldera, this Southwestern USA–themed restaurant serves hearty burgers, barbecue sandwiches, potato skins and other things you wouldn't expect to find in a Panamanian mountain town. Outdoor seating and ample windows make full use of the impressive natural setting.

Trattoria Villa Florencia (Calle Volcancito Principal; mains US$5.50-10; noon-midnight Sat, Sun & holidays) The view out over the hillsides with Italian ballads playing in the background may make you think you're in Umbria at this charming open-air spot (4km from the center of Boquete). Italian cuisine is the fare here, though it pales in comparison to the view (stick to the fresh *pomodoro* pasta and you should be fine).

Restaurant Chinese Food (Av Belisario Porras; dishes US$2-5) This popular spot near the Pensión Topaz may not look like much from the outside, but inside Restaurant Chinese Food is a clean and pleasant place serving hearty portions of you-know-what. It offers lunch specials (roast pork, fish, beef), and other dishes such as chow mein and sweet-and-sour pork.

El Sabrosón (Av Central; mains US$2-3) Two blocks north of the plaza, this simple eatery offers regional food, served buffet style.

Tacos y Tacos (Av A Este dishes US$2-5; 11:30am-9pm Mon-Thu, to 10pm Fri-Sun) Located behind the larger El Sabrosón restaurant, this informal eatery offers good Mexican food at rock-bottom prices.

Restaurante Lourdes (Av Central; mains US$3-6) Serving hearty plates of chicken and trout in a no-frills dining hall, Lourdes is a safe bet for cheap, reliable cooking.

The area's fresh produce is sold at the **mercado municipal**, on the northeastern corner of the plaza. **Supermercado Romero** (Av A Este), a block east of the plaza, has all your basic groceries. Among the several bakeries in town, **Garden Panadería** (Av Central) is one of the best.

Getting There & Around

Buses to Boquete depart David's main bus terminal regularly (US$1.40, one hour, every 30 minutes, 6am to 9:30pm). Buses to David (US$1.40) depart from the northern side of Boquete's plaza every 30 minutes from 5am to 6:30pm. A taxi between David and Boquete costs around US$12.

Boquete's small size lends itself to easy exploration, and walking is a great way to see the area. The local *(urbano)* buses winding through the hills cost US$0.50. They depart on the main road one block north of the plaza. Taxis charge US$1 to US$2 to get to most places around town.

PARQUE NACIONAL VOLCÁN BARÚ

Volcán Barú is Panama's dominant geographical feature of western Panama. Its fertile volcanic soil and the temperate climate of its mid-altitude slopes support some of Panama's most productive agriculture, especially in the areas around Cerro Punta and Boquete. Large trees dominate the volcano's lower slopes, giving way on the upper slopes to smaller plants, bushes, scrub and alpine wildflowers.

Volcán Barú is no longer active; its last eruption was about 500 years ago. It has not one but seven craters. Its summit, at 3478m, is the highest point in Panama, and on a clear day it affords views of both the Pacific and Caribbean coasts.

The 14,300-hectare Parque Nacional Volcán Barú contains walking trails and provides ample possibilities for hiking, mountain climbing and camping. The park is home to abundant wildlife, including pumas and the *conejo pintado,* a raccoon-like animal. The resplendent quetzal is often seen here, especially from January to May.

There are entrances to the park on the eastern and western sides of the volcano. The eastern access to the summit, from Boquete, is easiest. The road from town to this entrance is paved, but if you plan on driving the unpaved road from the entrance to the summit, you'll need a 4WD vehicle and a winch. To reach this entrance from central Boquete, turn west on Calle 2 Norte and continue along this paved road for 7.5km, until it forks. Take the left fork, which forks again in 600m; here you'll want to take the gravel road to the right. A taxi from Boquete to the entrance costs US$5.

It takes most hikers six hours to summit Barú and five hours to make it back down. It is a strenuous hike best accomplished early in the morning, initially by the light of the moon. Within an hour after sunrise, the summit's usually shrouded in clouds, and hopes of seeing both oceans are dashed. There is no water en route, so bring plenty, and pack warm clothes and a windbreaker, as it is cold as well as lonely at the top.

AROUND PARQUE NACIONAL VOLCÁN BARÚ

A road branches off the Interamericana at Concepción (1200m) and climbs steadily through the towns of Volcán (1500m), Bambito (1600m) and Cerro Punta (1800m) until it stops at Guadalupe (2130m), on the western side of Volcán Barú. It's a good, paved road the entire way, frequently traversed by buses from David.

As in Boquete, the climate here is cool and the air is brisk. The farmland around Cerro Punta has rich, black volcanic soil and is a great area for walking. As you near Cerro Punta, everything starts to look European, with meticulously tended agricultural plots and European-style houses with steep-pitched tin roofs. A Swiss colony was founded here many decades ago. Later immigrants included Croatians, and you can still hear their language spoken in the area.

This area produces not only abundant cool-climate crops, including vegetables, fruits, strawberries and flowers, but also livestock and thoroughbred racehorses. You'll pass several *haras* (stables) where racehorses are bred along the Cerro Punta road.

As on the Boquete side of Volcán Barú, there are accommodations that range from budget to expensive. And you can camp in the national park, or in the more remote Parque Internacional La Amistad. Another option is to visit this area on a day trip from David; buses run frequently between David and Cerro Punta via Volcán and Bambito (see p204).

BUENA VISTA

In this small community, 16km north of Concepción near the road to Volcán, is one of the nicest couples you'd ever meet. Canadians Dorothy and Claus Claassen built and later sold Cocomo on the Sea, a gorgeous B&B in Bocas del Toro town, and now run the **Buena Vista B&B** (☎ 770-5605, 697-5024; claassendc@email .com; d/ste US$40/45; ☒). They relocated to Buena Vista to a house with engrossing views of the Pacific Ocean and Volcán Barú, and now rent two charming rooms adjacent to their home. Each contains a hot-water bathroom, a sofa and other furnishings, and a queen-size bed with orthopedic mattress; the suite has a kitchenette. There's also an aboveground swimming pool. It is available for rent 15 November through 15 May, three-night minimum stay; and the whole house can be rented the rest of the time. Buena Vista makes a good base for forays into other Chiriquí highlands communities.

VOLCÁN

pop 7400

As you head north from Concepción, this is the first town you'll encounter, 32km uphill from the Interamericana turnoff. Clinging to the flanks of the giant Volcán Barú, the town is dwarfed by its namesake. There isn't a lot to do in Volcán itself, but the town has a pleasant feel and makes a good base for excursions.

Orientation & Information

The road that links Concepción and Volcán forks in the center of town: one arrow points left toward Río Sereno, on the Costa Rican border (47km); the other points right toward Cerro Punta (16km).

There's no IPAT in Volcán, but there is a **Highland Adventures** office (☎ /fax 771-4413; ecoaizpurua@hotmail.com; Av Central, Volcán; ☼ 7am-8pm) – look for a 'Turismo Ecologico' sign. This tour company offers guided tours and activities, including rappeling beside a river, bicycle rides, a photo safari, kayaking, water tubing and climbing Volcán Barú. Most of the tours run about US$30 per person and are good value. The guides speak English and Spanish.

On Av Central, there is a **pharmacy**, a **laundry** and a **health clinic**. **Internet** access is available at the Hotel y Restaurante Don Tavo (per hour US$1) and Volcan.net (per hour US$1, 100m up the road from Don Tavo) – a more reliable Internet café. **Banistmo** is located just before Highland Adventures; it cashes traveler's checks and gives cash advances on Visa cards.

Sights & Activities

On the western side of the Concepción–Volcán road, 3km south of Volcán, you'll see **Arte Cruz Volcán – Artesania en Madera** (☎ 623-0313; ☼ 8am-noon & 1-5:30pm), where artist José de la Cruz González makes fine-quality signs, sculptures and furniture out of wood, and etchings on crystal and glass. José was trained in fine arts in Italy and Honduras, and his work has been commissioned by buyers worldwide. Visitors are welcome, and José is happy to demonstrate and explain his art.

Small items are for sale, and he can make you a personal souvenir in just a few minutes.

The ruins of the pre-Columbian culture at **Barriles** are about a five-minute drive from the center of town. The ruins are on private land, but the family who lives on the land allows visitors to see the ruins. Major artifacts from the archaeological site, including statues, *metates* (flat stone platforms used for grinding corn), pottery and jewelry are displayed in the Museo Antropológico Reina Torres de Araúz in Panama City (p76).

Just past Volcán, on the way to Bambito, is one of the entrances to Parque Nacional Volcán Barú (opposite).

Other attractions around Volcán include springs, rivers, trout fishing, a botanical garden, coffee plantations (Cafetales Durán, with a million coffee bushes!), racehorse ranches and habitats of the quetzal and other exotic birds. Hiking trails in the area include one to the top of Cerro Punta; the Sendero Los Quetzales (the Quetzals' Trail), which crosses the national park to Boquete (see p220); the Sendero del Tapir (Tapir Trail), which leads to a place where many tapirs live; and a number of others. Also nearby are the Lagunas de Volcán (p218).

On weekends, a **market** is held at the San Benito school in Volcán; handicrafts are sold, as well as ordinary items at good prices. All proceeds benefit the school.

Sleeping

The following hotels are listed in the order that you pass them driving west to Río Sereno.

Motel California (☎ 771-4272; d US$20-30) Just past the turnoff to Cerro Punta, the California has 15 clean, basic doubles with hot-water private bathrooms.

Oasis Place (☎ /fax 771-4644; s/d US$10/15) A little beyond Motel California, Oasis has basic rooms with inconsistently good beds; ask to see several. The bar at Oasis gets noisy some nights. The owner also rents more-pleasant rooms out of her home.

Hotel y Restaurante Don Tavo (☎ /fax 771-5144; volcan@chiriqui.com; s/d/tr US$28/37/50; 🖳) Further along, Don Tavo offers nicer digs in 17 rooms set around a garden with private hot-water bathrooms. Internet is available for US$1 per hour.

Valle la Luna (☎ /fax 771-4225; s/d/tr US$24/31/36) About 1.6km from the center of Volcán, you'll reach a family-friendly place with five cabins, each with private bathrooms and kitchens. The accommodations are a bit worn here. In front there's a small café.

Cabañas Las Huacas (☎ 771-4363; cabin US$27-90) About 2.3km from the turnoff Las Huacas features the most impressive accommodations in town. Five charming two-story cottages, each with a kitchen and hot-water bathroom, lie scattered around the woodland setting. There's a goose pond and beautiful mountain vistas. Cabins can accommodate from two to eight people.

Hotel Dos Ríos (☎ 771-4271; fax 771-5794; d from US$50) Furthest from central Volcán, the Dos Ríos has the look and feel of a hunting lodge. The entire hotel is made of teak, and all 24 guestrooms face a creek and the mountains.

Eating

Restaurante Cerro Brujo Gourmet (☎ 629-5604; mains US$10-13) On the way into town, 1km off the main road (look for the signed turnoff before reaching the fork in the road), Cerro Brujo is set on attractive grounds and offers excellent fresh-cooked dishes. You can also **camp** (per person US$5) on the grounds; call to let the owners know you're coming.

Restaurante Castrejón (comida corriente US$1.75) Next to the gas station, this popular local eatery brings good meals to your table in a hurry.

Acropolis (mains US$4-5) Across from the Shell station near the Hotel Las Huacas, Acropolis serves superb plates of Greek food (souvlaki, moussaka and pastitsio), with some fantastic baklava for dessert. It's a charming little spot and the friendly owners, Elisabet and George Babos, have a wealth of information about Volcán and the rest of Panama. George is a native of Greece and speaks Spanish, English and Greek. One traveler described his meal here as the best Greek food he'd had outside of Greece.

Nearby Acropolis there are several other local favorites. The most popular is the pleasant **Mary's Café** (mains US$3-5), just up the road, where you can find good, inexpensive Panamanian dishes. Nearby, **Lorena** (mains US$3-5) has outdoor tables and similar offerings.

The restaurant at the **Hotel Dos Ríos** (mains US$5-8) serves good food that's reasonably priced. It's open for breakfast, lunch and dinner, and items include sandwiches, chicken and fish or meat dishes.

The food at the **Hotel y Restaurante Don Tavo** (Av Central; mains US$4-7) is reasonably priced and includes pizza, spaghetti, soups, sandwiches, chicken and beef dishes.

Getting There & Away

Buses from Volcán to David depart from the Shell station on Av Central every 15 minutes from 5am to 7:30pm (US$2.30, 1¾ hours). There are also pickup truck taxis available by the Río Sereno–Guadalupe fork in the road. A trip to one of the hotels in the area costs US$1 to US$2.

LAGUNAS DE VOLCÁN

At 1240m, the Area Silvestre Protegida Lagunas de Volcán, 4.5km from Volcán, is the highest lake system in Panama. The two lakes here swell after a big rain and are quite picturesque, with lush, virgin forest at their edges and Volcán Barú rising majestically in the background.

The lakes and the woodland around them are excellent sites for bird watching. On the lakes, the birds of special interest are the masked duck and the northern jacana. At water's edge, keep an eye out for the rose-throated becard (rare), pale-billed woodpecker, and mixed flocks of tanagers, flycatchers and antbirds.

To get to the lakes from the Concepción–Volcán road, turn west onto Calle El Valle (near central Volcán) and follow the signs. No buses go to the lakes, but you can hire a taxi in Volcán to bring you here. If you take your own vehicle, be advised that there have been reports of thefts of belongings from vehicles here.

SANTA CLARA

About 30km from Volcán, on the highway to Río Sereno, you'll reach the tiny town of Santa Clara, which is little more than a grocery store and a gas station. A few hundred meters past the gas station, on the left-hand side, you'll see a sign for **Finca Hartmann** (☎ 775-5223; www.fincahartmann.com; cabin US$70). A working farm that produces shade-grown coffee, Finca Hartmann is set on highland forest with a rich variety of wildlife on the grounds. The owner Ratibor Hartmann and his sons and daughter are ardent supporters of conservation, and Smithsonian-affiliated scientists have done research on the land. Currently the family rents rustic but hand-

ORCHIDS A-BLOOM

About 600m beyond the Hotel Los Quetzales at the turnoff to the Cabañas Los Quetzales cabins (p220) lies the **Finca Dracula Orchid Sanctuary** (☎ 771-2070; tour US$7), one of Latin America's finest and most varied orchid collections, with more than 2000 species.

some cabins for those wishing to enjoy the fantastic surroundings. Although there's no electricity here, the cabins have clean potable spring water, flush toilets and hot showers. The hiking and bird watching is superb here – over 280 species spotted on the land. At elevations between 1300 and 2000 meters, there are a number of accessible dirt roads that pass through many habitat types on the property, and that are excellent for hiking and birding. Sr Hartmann is a good host with a wealth of information. Ask to see his 'museum' (a lifetime's collection of Panamanian insects and pre-Columbian artifacts).

PASO ANCHO

On the road to Cerro Punta, the first settlement you'll come to is Paso Ancho, where you'll find a great house to rent. **Las Plumas** (☎ 771-5541; www.las-plumas.com; house US$66) is set on 2.3 hectares of land, and provides a tranquil setting for those wishing to explore the area. A friendly Dutch couple rents out a small guesthouse, which makes a nice mountain retreat. The house can accommodate four persons and has two bedrooms, a living room with fully functional kitchen, hot water bathroom, patio and DirecTV. It's excellent value for money. Dutch, German, Spanish and English spoken.

BAMBITO

Seven kilometers past Volcán on the road to Cerro Punta, Bambito is barely a town at all. Its only noticeable feature is the large Hotel Bambito. Opposite it is the **Truchas de Bambito** (admission US$0.50) rainbow trout farm, where thousands of trout are raised in outdoor ponds with frigid water from the nearby river. You can buy fresh trout here (per lb US$2.60).

The **Hotel Bambito** (☎ 771-4265; bambito@chiriqui.com; s/d US$138/154; 🖳 🕿) has spacious rooms and numerous suites. It features

a swimming pool, sauna, hot tub, tennis courts, business center, massage service, horseback riding, mountain bikes, a restaurant, Internet access, a lounge and more.

Past the trout farm, **Cabañas Kucikas** (☎ 771-4245; www.cabanaskucikas.com; cabin from US$66) has 18 spacious A-frame cottages that are set around 36 hectares of park-like grounds with children's play areas, barbecue sites and a river that provides decent trout fishing. Cottages of various sizes, sleeping two to 10 people, have kitchens and hot-water bathrooms. This is a charming place, and decent value if you're traveling in a group.

Located in the hamlet of Nueva Suiza, 3.3km past the Hotel Bambito on the road to Cerro Punta, is the **Hostal Cielito Sur B&B** (☎ 771-2038; www.cielitosur.com; US$65-75; 😊 Nov-Sep). This lovely B&B is a terrific find. Four spacious guestrooms featuring private hot-water bathrooms with bathtubs, living rooms with fireplaces, and riverside patios are excellent value. There's also a *bohío* (rustic hut) with hammocks and a bathhouse with a Jacuzzi. The prices include a country-style breakfast. This B & B is owned by a friendly Panamanian-American couple.

In Bambito, about 1.5km north of the Hotel Bambito, you'll find a small store named Alina that sells all sorts of fruit jam, candy, and strawberry *batidos*. It's a charming spot.

CERRO PUNTA

At an altitude of 1800m, this small town is surrounded by beautiful, rich agricultural lands. About 7km north of Bambito, it offers spectacular views across a fertile valley to the peaks of Parque Internacional La Amistad, a few kilometers away. This is a great place for taking in natural scenery.

Visitors come here primarily during the dry season (January to April) to visit the two nearby parks (Volcán Barú and La Amistad) and to enjoy the beauty of the surroundings. During this time, quetzals are often seen right on the road; though they can be seen here year-round, they tend to live further down in the mountains during the rainy season.

Other attractions in Cerro Punta include **Fresa de Cerro Punta** and **Fresas Manolo**, where strawberries are grown, and **Panaflores** and **Plantas y Flores**, where flowers are raised for commercial sale; you can visit all of these places.

CHIRIQUÍ PROVINCE

The main road continues through Cerro Punta and ends at Guadalupe, 3km further. Another road takes off to the west, heading for the Las Nubes entrance to Parque Internacional La Amistad (see opposite), 6.8km away; the turnoff is marked by a large wooden sign.

Sleeping & Eating

Hotel Cerro Punta (☎ /fax 771-2020; hotelcer@hotmail .com; s/d US$22/28) On the main road, this charming hotel has 10 decent rooms with big windows, nice views and good light. All rooms have private hot-water bathrooms, and the hotel has an excellent restaurant. Whether you stay here or not, drop by for a blended fruit drink. The local strawberries are the best you'll ever taste, and the strawberry drink is divine, as are the carrot, orange and rhubarb drinks. The pies and jams are homemade and quite good. For breakfast, try the pancakes with strawberry compote (US$2.50).

La Primavera (David ☎ 774-1060; d US$15) Half a kilometer down the road to Las Nubes (look for the *'bienvenidos a tierras altas'* sign), this family-run pension is basic, offering shabby rooms with hot-water bathrooms.

The **supermarket** (d US$15) across from the police station has upstairs rooms for rent. They're clean and well maintained with decent beds and private bathrooms. The billiards hall right next door stays noisy on weekends.

Several decent restaurants in town serve *comida corriente* for under US$2: **3R**, just up the road from the Hotel Cerro Punta and **Elsa's**, which has outdoor seating and a more pleasant ambience. Look for her sign on the road to Las Nubes.

Getting There & Away

A bus runs from David to Cerro Punta en route to Guadalupe (US$2.75; 2¼ hours; every 15 minutes, from 5:30am to 6pm), stopping at Volcán and Bambito along the way. If you're coming from Costa Rica, you could catch this bus at the turnoff from the Interamericana at Concepción. If you're in Volcán, catch one of these buses at the parking lot opposite the Shell station.

GUADALUPE

Guadalupe is at the end of the road, 3km past Cerro Punta. It's a glorious area where you can walk among meticulously tended farms and gardens and enjoy the climate. The little community is full of flowers, and the agricultural plots curling up the steep hillsides are dreamy. Please do respect the signs that read: 'Esteemed Visitor: we are making all Guadalupe a garden – please don't pick the flowers.'

Sendero Los Quetzales

Two kilometers past Cerro Punta on the road to Guadalupe, a sign points the way to the Sendero Los Quetzales. Keep following the 'Los Quetzales' signs all the way through Guadalupe to reach the trail. One of the most beautiful in Panama, this trail goes at least 10km to Boquete, crossing back and forth over the Río Caldera. A guide is not necessary, as long as you stay on the well-trodden path. Bear right at most forks.

For details on how to get there, see Cerro Punta, p219.

Sleeping & Eating

In the center of town, the **Hotel Los Quetzales** (☎ 771-2182; fax 771-2226; www.losquetzales.com; dm/d US$12/55) is the ideal place to enjoy this tranquil community. The hotel consists of 10 rooms, two dormitories (separated by gender), a restaurant, bar, lounge and spa. Every room features a tall ceiling, cheerful decor and private hot-water bathrooms. Additionally, there are five cedar-walled suites, containing a romantic fireplace, a kitchenette, a bathtub, sofas, and a rain forest–facing balcony. All guests have access to the full-service spa and can use the trails around the Cabañas Los Quetzales (see details following) inside the Parque Nacional Volcán Barú, less than an hour's walk from the hotel; the hotel can also provide transportation. Also on the premises are three riverside whirlpool spas. Horses and bikes are available for rent; you can also camp here for US$10. The owner speaks fluent English and Spanish.

In addition to food at the hotel, Guadalupe has a couple of tiny restaurants, which serve simple plates for around US$2.

The Hotel Los Quetzales also rents four lovely cabins inside the Parque Internacional La Amistad called the **Cabañas Los Quetzales** (☎ 771-2182; fax 771-2226; www.losquetzales .com; cabin US$75-135). Each cabin has a fully equipped kitchen and separate bedrooms, a hot-water bathroom, a fireplace, kerosene lanterns and large canopy-level terraces. Best of all, they're tucked away in the forest. Here you can hike through lush foliage – or just enjoy the tranquility (and hummingbirds) right outside your door. The cabins hold up to six or eight people, and costs include transportation from the Hotel Los Quetzales, trail guides for exploring the forest, and use of horses, ponchos and boots. A cheaper option is the **geodesic dome** (US$44). Set at canopy level in primary cloud forest, this large space sleeps four (in two double beds). For a bit extra the hotel can provide you with food (raw or cooked). Make reservations, especially during the dry season (November to April).

PARQUE INTERNACIONAL LA AMISTAD

This 407,000-hectare park, half of which is in Panama and half in Costa Rica, has three Panamanian entrances: one at Las Nubes (near Cerro Punta on the Chiriquí side), one near Wetso (near Changuinola; see p246), and a third at the upper Guadalupe area (a 10-minute walk from Cabañas Los Quetzales (see earlier).

There's a ranger station at Las Nubes where tourists can stay (see following). Permits are required to camp in the park; they're available for US$5 at the ranger station. Entrance to the park costs US$3, and parking an additional US$1.

There are three main trails that originate at the Las Nubes ranger station. One is a 1.4km trail that winds up to the **Mirador la Nevera**, a lookout point at 2500m. A second trail winds 1.7km to **La Cascada**, a 45m-high waterfall with a lovely bathing pool. A third trail, named **Sendero El Retoño** (Rebirth Trail), loops 2.1km through secondary forest.

If you plan to spend much time at Las Nubes, be sure to bring a jacket. This side of the park, at 2280m, has a cool climate. Temperatures are usually around 75°F in the daytime and drop to about 38°F at night.

Sleeping & Eating

A **ranger station** at Las Nubes has a dormitory room with bunk beds where tourists can stay for US$5 per night. Due to the popularity of these beds among school groups from Canada and the USA, reservations are well advised. To reserve a spot, call the **ANAM**

(☎ 775-3163, 775-7840) in David or the co-op **restaurant** (☎ 771-2566) at the park entrance. Guests have access to the kitchen; stock up on provisions in Cerro Punta. You'll also need to bring your own bedding.

The delightful **restaurant** (dishes US$2; ✓ 9am-4pm Mon-Sat), run by a local women's co-op, sits near the entrance of the park. It has outdoor seating on a wooden patio where you can watch hummingbirds buzzing nearby. You can get plates of fresh-cooked foods like soup, rice and beans, and grilled cheese. In addition to bottled water, it has hot tea, which is quite refreshing on a chilly day, and its homemade jams are also recommended. The co-op restaurant is also a good place to inquire about local guides who can lead inexpensive excursions into primary rain forest.

RÍO SERENO

pop 19,600

At Volcán, a paved road heads west to Río Sereno (47km), on the Costa Rican border. The road winds through lush valleys sprinkled with coffee fields, teak plantations and stands of virgin forest. A sparkling river occasionally appears at the roadside, and just as quickly disappears back into the foliage. Travelers coming from the border crossing at Río Sereno usually have a very favorable first impression of Panama.

See Border Crossings (p306) for further information.

FINCA LA SUIZA

Located high in the Talamanca range to the east of Boquete, amid cool, fresh air, is one of those easily overlooked places that guidebook writers, hikers and birders just love to find. **Finca La Suiza** (☎ 615-3774, afinis@chiriqui .com; s/d US$28/36) consists of 200 hectares of mostly mountain rain forest, accessed by hiking trails that originate at a lodge. Inside the lodge are three lovely rooms with two single beds each, rocking chairs, reading lamps, private hot-water bathrooms, and (on cloudless days) views to the Pacific Ocean, Costa Rica and Volcán Barú.

There are four trails through this pristine property, presenting hikers and birders with easy access to spectacular rain forest. Highlights include waterfalls, dipping ponds and superb vantage points across the forest canopy. Be advised that the owners keep dogs that roam freely at night, and for

CHIRIQUÍ PROVINCE

early-morning bird watching, you'll need to ask for them to be tied up.

Use of the trail system is US$8 for guests' entire stay, and nonguests pay US$8 per day. Payment is in cash only. English, German, French and Spanish are spoken. A bird list is available to guests, as are breakfasts and dinners. There are assigned eating times for all meals, which is not a problem for easy-going folks but come prepared if you want any snacks during your stay; there are no food stores nearby.

For phone calls, the best time to call is between 7pm and 9pm. The lodge and trails are closed June, September and October – the area's wettest months.

Getting There & Away

The lodge is located 1km from the Chiriquí–Chiriquí Grande road, atop a steep driveway. If you're driving, call ahead and you'll be met at the end of the driveway, where you can park within the property and be taken by 4WD to the lodge.

If you're traveling by bus between David and Almirante or Changuinola, just tell the bus driver to drop you at Finca La Suiza. If you arrive unannounced, leave your luggage with the workers beside the finca's entrance and walk up. Your luggage will be brought to you.

The lodge is 40km from Chiriquí and 60km from Chiriquí Grande.

Bocas del Toro Province

CONTENTS

Archipiélago de Bocas del Toro **227**
Isla Colón & Bocas del Toro 227
Isla Carenero 238
Isla Bastimentos 239
Other Islands 241
Parque Nacional Marino
   Isla Bastimentos 242
Changuinola Canal 242
Mainland **242**
Bosque Protector Palo Seco 242
Almirante 243
Changuinola 244
Around Changuinola 246
Guabito 247

Famed for the large Archipiélago that lies inside its borders, the Bocas del Toro Province is rapidly becoming Panama's top tourist destination. Visitors come to the islands to soak up the laid-back Caribbean vibe that Islas Colón and Bastimentos offer. In addition to the simple charm of Bocas del Toro town, the islands offer snorkeling among coral reefs, surfing on great breaks, and sailing. The abundance of rain forest covering the islands makes for some great exploring. You can hike through huge swaths of rain forest among wide jungle-flanked rivers and arrive at an empty stretch of gorgeous white-sand beach with waves crashing on the shore.

The province is more than just the archipelago – though inhabitants of the island might disagree. In the interior of the province, there's gorgeous virgin rain forest where a handful of Ngöbe-Buglé settlements lay scattered. The abundance of wildlife, jungle rivers and waterfalls make it a choice destination for those who want to get off the beaten bath.

Bocas del Toro Province is bordered by the Caribbean Sea to the north, Veraguas Province to the east, Chiriquí Province to the south and Costa Rica to the west. Most of the province is on the slopes of the Talamanca and Central Mountain Ranges, but the majority of its inhabitants live in low-lying areas along the coast and on islands. The Archipiélago de Bocas del Toro lies at the mouth of the Laguna de Chiriquí, beginning 35km from the Costa Rican border. The chain consists of 68 islands and numerous mangrove keys. Around them are fields of coral, a titanic variety of marine life and emerald green waters.

HIGHLIGHTS

- Soaking up the village charm of slow-paced **Bocas del Toro** town (p227)
- Exploring the untouched beaches and lush forests around **Isla Bastimentos** (p239)
- Gliding by boat through the wildlife rich **San-San Pond Sak Wetlands** (p246)
- Hiking through tropical forest and visiting indigenous villages near **Las Delicias** (p246)
- Exploring the **Parque Internacional La Amistad** (p247), home to jaguars, Ngöbe-Buglé villages and spectacular jungle rivers

| POPULATION: 94,000 | ELEVATION: SEA LEVEL TO 3300M | AREA: 8745 SQ KM |

History

When Christopher Columbus visited the territory in 1502, on his fourth and final New World voyage, it was inhabited by many nomadic tribes. He was so taken by the beauty of the area that he affixed his name to many sites: Isla Colón (Columbus Island), Isla Cristóbal (Christopher Island), Bahía de Almirante (Admiral's Bay; the major port of Almirante) and other locations. Because little gold was found in Bocas del Toro, the Spaniards did not colonize the region, and the Indians were spared their wrath for a while.

During the 17th century the archipelago became a haven for pirates, mainly because the Spaniards didn't have a presence here. The buccaneers repaired their ships on the islands, built others with wood from their forests and fed upon the many sea turtles that nested on the beaches. Even today most of the archipelago is flush with virgin rain forest, and four species of sea turtle continue to lay their eggs on its beaches, just as they have for thousands of years. The pirates are said to have buried treasure on a number of the islands, but to date none of this loot has been found (or at least reported).

During the 17th and 18th centuries, most of the Indians were killed in battles among themselves, by Old World diseases brought by the Spaniards and by Spanish swords. Some Indians intermarried with French Huguenot settlers who arrived on the coast of Bocas del Toro around the end of the 17th century. By 1725 many of the Indians and Huguenots had been killed in fights with Spanish militiamen sent to dislodge the French settlers.

In the early 19th century, blacks from the USA and Colombia's San Andrés and Providencia Islands arrived as slaves of wealthy landowners looking to reestablish themselves in the province. When slavery was abolished, in 1850, the former slaves stayed and eked out a living as fishermen and subsistence farmers. Jamaican blacks joined them toward the end of the 19th century, as the province's banana industry began to develop.

Bocas del Toro's banana industry dates from 1890, when three American brothers arrived here and founded the Snyder Brothers Banana Company. They planted banana trees all along the shores of the Laguna de Chiriquí, at the mouth of which is Isla Colón. Because of its central location, Isla Colón quickly became the heart of this new activity. In 1899 the United Fruit Company planted itself in the town of Bocas del Toro on Isla Colón and bought the Snyder Brothers Banana Company.

In the years that followed, United Fruit and smaller growers established banana plantations, most of which still exist, over a vast area stretching from the archipelago to the Costa Rican border. The company constructed bridges and roads and even dug a 15km canal to ease the transportation of bananas to the sea, where they were loaded onto ships for export (mainly to the USA). The company also built houses, restaurants, clinics and schools for its workers.

Today, United Fruit, which was purchased and renamed several times, is part of the multinational Chiquita Brands International. Chiquita's workers in Bocas del Toro Province grow and export three-quarters of a million tons of bananas annually; they comprise the largest workforce in the province and the most diverse workforce in the country. On the payroll are: descendants of American, Colombian and Jamaican blacks; the descendants of blacks from the French Antilles who arrived in Panama to work on the railroad and, later, the canal; members of at least four of Panama's seven Indian groups; and many people of mixed indigenous and Spanish ancestry.

Climate

Bocas gets an incredible amount of rain. Like other regions along the Caribbean coast, rainy and dry seasons don't mean much, as it can downpour for days on end in the 'dry' season. The least rainy time of year is mid-August to mid-October, when the seas are calm, and February and March.

National Parks

In the Archipiélago de Bocas del Toro, **Parque Nacional Marino Isla Bastimentos** (p242) protects various areas of the Bocas archipelago, and is an important nature reserve for many species of Caribbean wildlife. Turtles nest on its beaches and its abundant marine life makes for great snorkeling and diving.

On the mainland the enormous **Parque Internacional La Amistad** (p247) lies near the

BOCAS DEL TORO PROVINCE

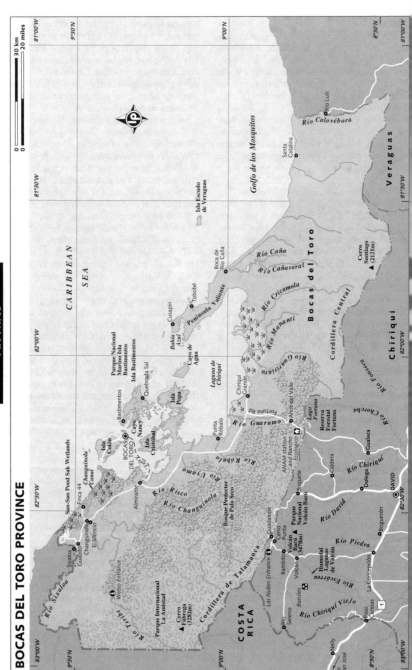

border of Costa Rica (both country's share this park). PILA, as the park is called, is home to several different indigenous groups, pristine rain forest and abundant wildlife. The infrastructure at this end of the park isn't as developed as it is at the Chiriquí entrance (p198).

Near the border with Chiriquí Province, the **Bosque Protector Palo Seco** (p242) contains lush cloud forest set high in the Talamanca range. Several hiking trails and nearby lodging allow visitors to immerse themselves in the area's rich biodiversity.

Language

In Bocas Province, the Ngöbe-Buglé language is still commonly spoken, although many from this group also converse in Spanish. On the islands, you'll also hear Gali-Gali, the distinct Creole language of Bocas del Toro Province that combines English, Spanish and Ngöbe-Buglé. This rich dialect originated with the Jamaicans who were brought over to harvest bananas. Additionally, some blacks speak Patois, a mixture of Afro-Antillean English, Spanish and Gali-Gali, which is most spoken on Isla Bastimentos. In the interior you'll hear Naso, which is the language of the Teribe tribe.

Dangers & Annoyances

Unlike in most other places in Panama, tap water is not safe to drink in the province. Riptides can be dangerous out on the islands. See p229 for more information.

Getting There & Away

The only way onto Isla Colón – the gateway to the archipelago – is by boat or by plane. There is a regular *lancha* (motorboat) service from Almirante (p243) and Changuinola (see p245). The majority of visitors arrive on the island on a 50-minute flight from Panama City. You can also fly in from David.

Getting Around

Boat services between the islands in Bocas del Toro is frequent, but rather informal. There are many boat operators, and most charge a fixed rate to get between Bocas del Toro, Isla Carenero and Isla Bastimentos.

In the interior, *chivas* (buses) are the means of getting to and from rural areas.

ARCHIPIÉLAGO DE BOCAS DEL TORO

The archipelago consists of six large, mostly forested islands and scores of smaller ones. The large islands are Isla Colón (61 sq km), Isla Popa (53 sq km), Isla Bastimentos (51 sq km), Isla Cristóbal (37 sq km), Cayo de Agua (16 sq km) and Isla Solarte (Cayo Nancy; 8 sq km). Of these islands, four are among the country's 10 largest. Only Isla Colón has roads, but accommodations and food are available on Islas Colón, Bastimentos, Solarte and Carenero. Cayo Zapatilla Sur also has accommodations.

The archipelago is a biologist's fantasy. It and the adjacent shore represent an isolated pocket of lowlands, semicircled by the foothills of the Talamanca range and by marshes at the mouths of the Ríos Changuinola and Cricamola. Because of its isolation, the wildlife in the lowlands of western Bocas del Toro Province includes many species not found outside the region. For example, there is a red frog on Isla Bastimentos that lives nowhere else.

A beautiful, conifer-like tree dominates the forest canopy of the larger islands, giving a unique look to their jungle. The jungle's interior has abundant lianas, vine tangles and forest palms, all of which are maintained by the region's rainy climate.

Culturally, the islands and the lowlands around them support a distinct group of Indians, the Ngöbe-Buglé. They still live by fishing and subsistence farming, travel mostly by canoes and reside in wooden, thatched-roof huts without electricity or running water. While many of their *cayucos* (canoes) are powered by outboard engines, most locals paddle or use sails made from rice sacks. Since this tribe usually does not live in groups but in widely scattered huts at the water's edge, *cayucos* remain the Ngöbe-Buglé's chief mode of transportation.

ISLA COLÓN & BOCAS DEL TORO

Isla Colón is by far the most visited and developed of the Bocas del Toro islands. On its southeastern tip is its major town and the provincial capital, **Bocas del Toro** (population 4300), which offers tourists a pleasant and convenient base from which to explore the

BOCAS DEL TORO PROVINCE

ARCHIPIÉLAGO DE BOCAS DEL TORO

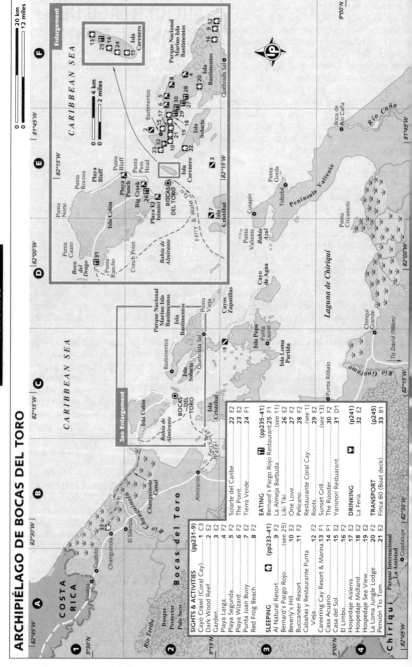

SIGHTS & ACTIVITIES	(pp231–9)
Cayo Crawl (Coral Cay)	1 C3
Dark Wood Reef	2 E2
Garden	3 E2
Playa Larga	4 F2
Playa Segunda	5 F2
Playa Wizard	6 F2
Punta Juan Buoy	7 F2
Red Frog Beach	8 F2

SLEEPING	(pp233–41)
Al Natural Resort	9 F2
Bernard's Pargo Rojo	(see 25)
Beverly's Hill	10 E2
Buccaneer Resort	11 F2
Cabañas y Restaurante Punta Vieja	12 F2
Careening Cay Resort & Marina	13 F1
Casa Acuario	14 F1
Casa del Sol	15 E2
El Limbo	16 E2
Hospedaje Aislenis	17 E2
Hospedaje Midland	18 E2
Hospedaje Sea View	19 E2
La Loma Jungle Lodge	20 F2
Pensión Tío Tom	21 E2
Solarte del Caribe	22 E2
The Point	23 E2
Tierra Verde	24 F1

EATING	(pp235–41)
Bernard's Pargo Rojo Restaurant	25 F1
La Almeja Barbuda	(see 11)
Liki Tiki	26 E2
One Love	27 F2
Pelicano	28 F2
Restaurante Coral Cay	(see 1)
Roots	29 E2
Sunset Grill	(see 13)
The Rooster	30 F2
Yarisnori Restuarant	31 D1

DRINKING	
La Feria	(p241)
	32 E2

TRANSPORT	
Finca 60 (Boat deck)	(p245)
	33 B1

Parque Nacional Marino Isla Bastimentos (p242) and other nearby sites. The town, the archipelago and the province as a whole all share the same name – Bocas del Toro.

Bocas del Toro town (or simply Bocas town) is where most of the archipelago's accommodations and restaurants are found, as well as the dive operators. The town is a slow-paced community made up mostly of English-speaking black people of West Indian ancestry and Spanish-speaking Latinos.

Bocas town is a great place to hang out for a few days. On the nearby islands and reefs are wonderful opportunities for swimming, snorkeling and diving, or lounging on white sandy beaches fringed by reeds and coconut palms. Water taxis (or *taxis marinos),* readily available in this small town of wooden houses built by the United Fruit Company, will take you to remote beaches and snorkeling sites. The town's relaxed, friendly atmosphere seems to rub off on everyone who visits, making it easy to meet locals and travelers.

Relaxed as it is, Bocas is in the middle of a major development boom, with new hotels and restaurants opening every other week, making the information here particularly susceptible to change.

Orientation

Bocas town is laid out in a grid pattern. Most of the hotels, restaurants and bars are on the main street, Calle 3. Perpendicular to the numbered streets are lettered avenues, from 'A' to 'H.' The only airport in the archipelago is on Av E, four blocks from the main street.

Information

EMERGENCY

Police ☎ 104, 757-9217
Fire ☎ 103

INTERNET ACCESS

Bocas Internet café (Calle 3; per hr US$2; ☉ 8am-10pm) 15 computers.
Bravo Center (Calle 3; per hr US$2; ☉ 10am-7pm) Five fast computers in air-con splendor.
Don Chicho's (Calle 3; per hr US$2; ☉ 8am-9pm Mon-Fri, 9am-8pm Sat & Sun) Next to the restaurant of the same name.
IPAT tourist office (Calle 1; per hr US$0.50; ☉ 10am-5pm Tue-Sat) In back of the IPAT office you'll find eight computers.

INTERNET RESOURCES

The Bocas del Toro website at www.bocas.com has useful information in English.

LAUNDRY

Lavandería Emilio de Gracia (☉ 8am-6pm Mon-Sat, 8am-noon Sun) In back of the Hotel Scarlett, Emilio washes and dries for US$3.
Lavandería (next door to Om Café) Another laundry that charges similar prices.

MAPS

An excellent map of Bocas (US$2) is available at the Bocas Internet café and many of the hotels.

MEDICAL SERVICES

Farmacia Rosa Blanca (Calle 3) A tiny pharmacy/general store near the boat dock.
Hospital (☎ 757-9201; Av G near Calle 10; ☉ 24hr) The island's only hospital has a 24-hour emergency room.

MONEY

It's wise to bring some cash with you to the island as many places don't accept credit cards, and the ATM at Bocas del Toro's only bank is sometimes down. Try:
Banco Nacional de Panamá (☉ 8am-2pm Mon-Fri, 8am-noon Sat) Next to the park, the BNP exchanges traveler's checks, and it has a 24-hour ATM.

POST

Post office (Calle 3) Located inside the large governmental building beside the park.

TELEPHONE

Cable & Wireless (Calle 1) In addition to the pay phones around town, international calls can be made from this phone office.

TOURIST INFORMATION

IPAT tourist office (☎ 757-9642; ipatbocas@cwp.net.pa; ☉ 10am-6pm Tues-Sat) In the new building on the eastern waterfront, IPAT provides limited information. On the 2nd floor there's a fine exhibit that describes the natural and anthropological history of Bocas.
ANAM office (☎ 757-9442; Calle 1) It's not really set up as a tourist information office, though they can answer questions about the national park or other protected areas. If you want to camp out in any of the protected areas, you must first get a permit from this or any other ANAM office.

Dangers & Annoyances

On many of the beaches the surf can be quite dangerous, with strong riptides; use

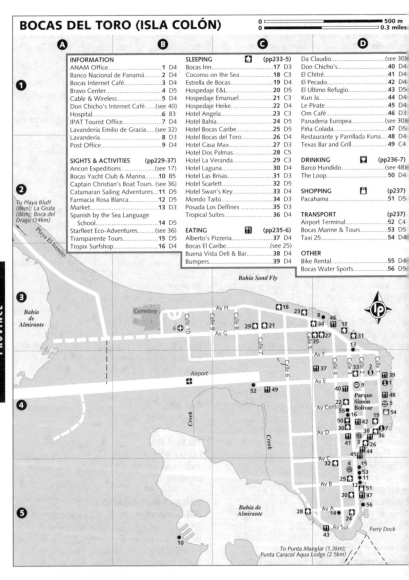

BOCAS DEL TORO (ISLA COLÓN)

0 — 500 m
0 — 0.3 miles

INFORMATION
ANAM Office....................................1 D4
Banco Nacional de Panamá.........2 D4
Bocas Internet Café.......................3 D4
Bravo Center...................................4 D5
Cable & Wireless............................5 D4
Don Chico's Internet Café......(see 40)
Hospital...6 B3
IPAT Tourist Office.........................7 D4
Lavandería Emilio de Gracia...(see 32)
Lavandería.......................................8 D3
Post Office.......................................9 D4

SIGHTS & ACTIVITIES   (pp229-37)
Ancon Expeditions...................(see 17)
Bocas Yacht Club & Marina.......10 B5
Captain Christian's Boat Tours..(see 36)
Catamaran Sailing Adventures...11 D5
Farmacia Rosa Blanca..................12 D5
Market..13 D3
Spanish by the Sea Language
  School..14 D5
Starfleet Eco-Adventures........(see 36)
Transparente Tours......................15 D4
Tropix Surfshop............................16 D4

SLEEPING   ⌂   (pp233-5)
Bocas Inn.......................................17 D3
Cocomo on the Sea......................18 C3
Estrella de Bocas..........................19 D4
Hospedaje E&L..............................20 D5
Hospedaje Emanuel......................21 C3
Hospedaje Heike...........................22 D4
Hotel Angela.................................23 D4
Hotel Bahía....................................24 D5
Hotel Bocas Caribe.......................25 D5
Hotel Bocas del Toro....................26 D4
Hotel Casa Max.............................27 D3
Hotel Dos Palmas.........................28 C5
Hotel La Veranda..........................29 C3
Hotel Laguna.................................30 D4
Hotel Las Brisas............................31 D3
Hotel Scarlett................................32 D5
Hotel Swan's Key..........................33 D4
Mondo Taitú..................................34 D4
Posada Los Delfines......................35 D3
Tropical Suites..............................36 D4

EATING   🍴   (pp235-6)
Alberto's Pizzeria.........................37 D4
Bocas El Caribe........................(see 25)
Buena Vista Deli & Bar.................38 D4
Bumpers...39 D4

Da Claudio...............................(see 30)
Don Chico's....................................40 D4
El Chitré...41 D4
El Pecado.......................................42 D4
El Ultimo Refugio.........................43 D5
Kun Ja..44 D4
Le Pirate..45 D4
Om Café...46 D4
Panadería Europea...................(see 30)
Piña Colada....................................47 D5
Restaurante y Parrillada Kuna....48 D4
Texas Bar and Grill.......................49 C4

DRINKING   🍸   (pp236-7)
Barco Hundido..........................(see 48)
The Loop..50 D4

SHOPPING   🛍   (p237)
Pacahama.......................................51 D5

TRANSPORT   (p237)
Airport Terminal...........................52 C4
Bocas Marine & Tours..................53 D5
Taxi 25..54 D4

OTHER
Bike Rental.....................................55 D4
Bocas Water Sports......................56 D5

---

caution when going out into the waves. If you get caught in a riptide, swim parallel to the shore and don't panic; you'll be out of the pull quickly.

Bocas town has a water treatment plant, but locals say the tap water isn't to be trusted. The water is certainly fine for brushing your teeth, but you're probably

best off siding with caution and purchasing bottled water for drinking.

If you plan to go scuba diving in the area, take a good look at the equipment. There have been some unfortunate accidents in Bocas in the last few years.

The Bar El Encanto occasionally turns up its music and keeps it there until very late. It ou're planning on staying at nearby Hospedaje E & L or the Hotel Bahía, you might consider bringing ear plugs just in case.

Sights & Activities

BOCA DEL DRAGO

Located on the western side of Isla Colón, Boca del Drago is one of the best beaches on the island, though the surf can be rough at times. Just offshore from the beach is a patchy coral-and-sand sea bottom that offers good snorkeling when the sea is calm and the water clear.

Boca del Drago isn't nearly as nice as Red Frog Beach or Playa Larga on Isla Bastimentos, where there's a good chance of encountering sea turtles if you camp out or make a night hike from one of the island's hotels. However, the surf at those beaches makes swimming unsafe.

The most leisurely way of getting here is by bicycle (see p238 for rental information) or you can also take a water taxi with **Bocas Marine & Tours** (Calle 3), taxi (round-trip US$15) or bus service (US$2, 25 minutes). See p237 for details.

OTHER BEACHES

There are plenty of other beaches around Isla Colón, reached by a road that skirts up the eastern coast from town. There's no public transportation to them, but a taxi will take you there, and you can arrange for the driver to come back for you at an appointed time.

Playa El Istmito, also called Playa La Cabaña, is the closest to town. It's on Bahía Sand Fly, and the *chitras* (sand flies) that live here have an itchy bite. Repellent is available in town. This is not the most attractive beach; better ones are further north.

Further up the coast are **Big Creek**, **Punta Puss Head** and **Playa Punch**, which is dangerous for swimming but good for surfing. After Punta Bluff, the road takes you along **Playa Bluff**, which stretches all the way to Punta Rocosa. Endangered sea turtles nest on Playa Bluff from around May to September.

DIVING & SNORKELING

Be aware that although the Cayos Zapatillas are within the boundaries of a national marine park, they don't make for particularly good dive/snorkel trips due to strong currents. Better sites include Cayo Crawl (also called Coral Cay and Coral Key, a lovely reef in shallow water with lots of fish, coral and lobster), which is south of Isla Bastimentos; Dark Wood Reef (with many nurse sharks and occasional hammerheads), north of Bastimentos; Hospital Point, a 50-foot wall off Isla Solarte (also called Cayo Nancy); and the base of the buoy near Punta Juan (with some beautiful coral), north of Isla Cristóbal. Of these, only the Punta Juan buoy and Hospital Point are also good for snorkeling. Another superior spot for snorkeling is The Garden, near Isla Solarte; there's lots of coral there.

Be forewarned that the archipelago's waters are notorious for poor visibility. Sometimes the visibility is good (15m or more); more commonly it's limited to 3m. More than 40 rivers expire around the islands, and they unload a lot of silt into the sea after heavy rains in the mountains. If it's rained a lot in recent days, don't expect good visibility.

Two agencies offering diving in Bocas are **Starfleet Eco-Adventures** (☎ 757-9630; www.explore panama.com/starfleet.htm; Calle 1) and **Bocas Water Sports** (☎ /fax 757-9541; www.bocaswatersports.com; Calle 3). Both offer two-tank dives for about US$50 per person (two person minimum; includes all equipment), and both offer PADI open-water-diver certification for around US$195. Starfleet offers instruction in English, German and Spanish, and enjoys a sterling reputation.

There are a number of agencies that offer snorkeling trips to several destinations around the islands. See Tours, p232.

KAYAKING & SURFING

For tooling around in the bay, sea kayaks can be rented from Bocas Water Sports (per hour/day US$3/10). You can rent fairly thrashed surfboards from a shack on the main street facing the park (per day US$8). There are a number of decent breaks on the islands (mainly from December through March). Popular spots include Playa Punch and Playa Bluff on Isla Colón, the back side of Isla Carenero and Red Frog Beach and Playa Primera on Isla Bastimentos.

BIRD WATCHING

While the bird watching on the islands isn't as good as that on the mainland, it can still be rewarding. Particularly rare birds, or at least those poorly known to Panama, have

BOCAS DEL TORO PROVINCE

been recorded on the islands in recent years, including the semiplumbeous hawk, white-tailed kite, zone-tailed hawk, uniform crake, olive-throated parakeet, red-fronted parrot-let, lesser nighthawk, green-breasted mango, chestnut-colored woodpecker, snowy cotinga, brown-capped tyrannulet, yellow-bellied elaenia, stub-tailed spadebill, purple martin, tree swallow and black-cowled oriole.

In early March and October thousands of turkey vultures can often be seen gliding just above the forest canopy on the large islands. These are big black birds with featherless heads and reddish necks. They are masterful fliers, often soaring for long periods without a flap, tilting from side to side to take ad-vantage of every favorable air current. These birds range from Canada to Chile. Many of the northern birds winter in Central Amer-ica and northwestern South America.

SAILING
Catamaran Sailing Adventures (☎ 757-9710; movida@cwp.net.pa; Calle 3) In addition to cata-maran excursions (below), Marcel Schmitt offers classes for those wanting to learn how to sail (per hour US$25).

Courses
Spanish by the Sea Language School (☎ 757-9518; www.spanishbythesea.com; Calle 4) This language school offers affordable Spanish classes in a casual setting. Rates for group/private les-sons are US$70/100 for two hours a day five days a week, US$100/145 for three hours a day and US$130/190 for four hours a day.

Other rates include US$9 per hour for one-on-one lessons, US$7 per hour for two stu-dents, and US$6 per hour for three or more students. This language school also offers a 'traveler's survival Spanish course' (US$40) that includes six hours of instruction over two or three days, phrasebook included.

Owner-instructor Ingrid 'Ins' Lommers speaks English, Spanish, Dutch, French and German. The school offers students two rooms for rent (opposite).

Tours
The most popular tours in the area are all-day snorkeling trips, which give visitors a taste of the rich marine life in the area. The most popular goes to Dolphin Bay, Cayo Crawl, Red Frog Beach and Hospital Point. Most trips depart at 9:30am and return around

4:30pm. Snorkeling trips typically cost US$15 per person per day including gear. The further from Bocas del Toro a trip goes the more it costs. A trip to the distant Cayos Zapatillas costs US$40, including lunch, a laze on the beach and a jungle walkabout on Cayo Zapatilla Sur. Note that if you go into the marine park, there's a US$10 charge in addition to the tour fee.

If you're concerned about being exposed to too much direct sunlight, when select-ing an operator for a tour, be sure to ask whether the boat you'll be on has a cover. Operators include:

Ancon Expeditions (Av H, Bocas Inn near the end of Calle 3) Offers an all-day snorkeling tour that includes Cayo Zapatilla, Punta Vieja, Cayo Crawl, Red Frog Beach and Punta Hospital for US$15 to US$25, depending on the number of people. If you'll be in Panama City and you're tinkering with the idea of spending a few days in Bocas, consider Ancon Expeditions' three-day, two-night 'Bocas del Toro Adventure' (US$365). It includes air transportation to and from Bocas, two nights at the Bocas Inn, all meals, and tours to Isla de los Pájaros (Island of the Birds), Cayos Zapatillas (within a marine national park), and a protected frog sanctuary on Isla Bastimentos.

Bocas Water Sports (☎ /fax 757-9541; www.bocas watersports.com; Calle 3)

Captain Christian's Boat Tours (☎ 591-2881; www .ccboattours.com; Calle 1)

Catamaran Sailing Adventures (☎ 757-9710; movida@cwp.net.pa; Calle 3) This 42-foot catamaran offers a nice alternative to motorboat tours. The Boca del Drago tour stops en route at Punta Caracol, for snorkeling and starfish gazing, followed by lunch at Yarisnori, and return-ing in the afternoon. There's another tour to Dolphin Bay followed by snorkeling at Cayo Crawl and one other sight. A good-sized sack lunch is included. Both cost US$25. You can also arrange overnight sailing trips.

Panama Jet Boat Explorer (☎ 604-7736; www.pan amajetboatexplorer.com; per person US$140-200, 4-person minimum) This Boquete-based outfit (see also p211) offers a number of day-long adventures exploring some of the rivers and indigenous villages around the Bocas area. One of the more popular offerings is the eight-hour 'Jungle River Experience' (per person US$200, 4-person minimum), which departs Bocas del Toro town, across Admiral's Bay (Bahía de Almirante), to Chiriquí Lagoon (Laguna de Chiriquí). Along the route you'll pass manglar-covered cayos before traveling by river up to indigenous Ngöbe communities. There you'll disembark from the jet boat and take a three-hour cayuco (native kayak) trip down the river, allowing visitors the chance to see a wider variety of animal life including monkeys and possibly manatees and crocodiles. Trip includes sack lunch. Other trips include pportunities for snorkeling (equipment included) and ore extensive visits to indigenous communities.

tarfleet Eco-Adventures (☎ 757-9630; www xplorepanama.com/starfleet.htm; Calle 1)

ransparente Tours (☎ 757-9600, cellular ☎ 687- 913; Calle 3) In addition to snorkeling, Transparente also ents a 40-foot sportfishing boat (per day US$400) with eshwater shower for family tours of the islands and for ortfishing.

Many 'tours' are really little more than boat ransportation to a pretty spot. If you have our own snorkel gear (or if you rent it), ou can also get the local boatmen to take ou to many good snorkeling spots around he area in their small, motorized canoes. They know many good spots, and this op- ion can be cheaper than the dive compa- ies' trips. Agree on a price before you go.

estivals & Events

Bocas town observes all of Panama's holi- lays and a few enjoyable local ones besides. Annual events are celebrated in Bocas town nd on Isla Bastimentos.

While the rest of Panama is celebrating he **Día del Trabajador** (Worker's Day) on May Day (May 1), the **Palo de Mayo** (a Maypole lance) is done by young girls in Bocas town nd on Isla Bastimentos.

Everyone in Bocas town makes a pilgrim- age to La Gruta, the cave in the middle of he island, for a mass in honor of the Virgen lel Carmen on **Día de la Virgen del Carmen**, on he third Sunday in July.

Feria del Mar (the 'fair of the sea') is a four- lay festival held on Playa El Istmito, north of Bocas town, from September 28 through October 2.

Fundación de la Provincia de Bocas del Toro, held on November 16, celebrates the found- ng of the province in 1904 with parades and other events. It's a big affair, attracting people from all over the province, and the Panamanian president also attends.

Día de Bastimentos (Bastimentos Day) is celebrated on November 23 with a parade and drumming on Isla Bastimentos.

Sleeping

The town of Bocas has become a major tourist draw. Both expats and locals run ho- tels, and a few Bocas residents rent rooms out of their houses. You'd be wise to make a reservation before arriving, especially from

December to April, and during national holidays and local festivals.

IN TOWN – BUDGET

Hospedaje Heike (☎ 757-9708; Calle 3; s/d/tw US$9/15/16) Near the center of town, Heike offers good value in seven charming 2nd- floor rooms with fans, mosquito nets, furni- ture and two shared hot-water bathrooms.

Mondo Taitú (☎ /fax 757-9425; www.mondotaitu .com; Av H; dm/s US$8/12) This old wooden build- ing has a charming feel to it and is a popu- lar spot with 11 basic, clean and well-swept guestrooms. Each has two to four good beds and a fan. Shared hot-water bathrooms are downstairs, and there's a communal kitchen and an outdoor patio. The bar here has a wide selection of tropical concoctions.

Hospedaje Emanuel (☎ 757-9958; Av G; r per per- son US$7; ❄) Basic, fairly clean rooms with fan and private cold-water bathroom are available at this family style house. Most rooms contain a double bed and a single above it, bunk-bed style. There's also a room with air-con (US$15).

Spanish by the Sea Language School (☎ 757- 9518; spanishbythesea@hotmail.com; Calle 4; dm US$6) This language school offers rooms to non- students on a space-available basis. The rooms are basic but comfortable with ceil- ing fans, good beds, shared bathrooms and a communal kitchen.

Hotel Scarlett (☎ /fax 757-9290; Calle 4; s/d US$10/15, with air-con US$15/20; ❄) The Scarlett offers modern digs without much character. Rooms are bright, clean and spacious with private cold-water bathrooms.

Hotel Las Brisas (☎ /fax 757-9248; Av H; d with fan/ air-con/seaview US$21/26/47; ❄) On the northern end of Calle 3, this rambling old place offers a variety of rooms, most with tall ceilings, worn fixtures and saggy mattresses (test a few). The haunting place has wood floors and a small balcony in back over the water. Ask to see the more modern and pricier rooms.

Hospedaje E & L (☎ 757-9206; Calle 3; dm/d US$6/12) Near the southern end of town, this family run place offers seven basic rooms in a poorly constructed, concrete-walled, metal-roofed building. Most guestrooms have good beds, fans, and private cold-water bathrooms. Guests can use the kitchen.

Hotel Bocas Caribe (Calle 3; bed with/without bath US$6/5) Small, gloomy rooms with little venti- lation is what's in store for guests at the Bocas

Caribe. Accommodations are dormitory-style, so you may have a room to yourself or may end up sharing it with whoever shows up. The downstairs restaurant serves decent plates of Italian food (see Eating, p236).

IN TOWN – MID-RANGE & TOP END

Hotel Casa Max (☎ 757-9120; casamax1@hotmail.com; Av G; d from US$35) This Dutch-owned hotel is in a beautiful, wooden two-story building containing 10 cheerful and spotless guestrooms, each tastefully done. All rooms have private hot-water bathrooms, and several have balconies. Morning coffee and fresh fruit are available free of charge to guests.

Posada Los Delfines (☎ 757-9963; www.posadalosdelfines.com; Av G; d/tr/ste US$35/50/60; ❄) This pleasant hotel features a range of rooms, some with charming balconies overlooking the street. All the rooms are colorfully designed and have air-con, TV and private baths. The smallest rooms, however, feel a little cramped. A pleasant restaurant sits in front of the hotel, and there's a spa next door.

Hotel Bocas del Toro (☎ 757-9018; www.bocas.com; Calle 1; d/tr/q US$52/76/99; ❄) On the water, the Hotel Bocas del Toro shows beautiful craftsmanship. Ten spacious guestrooms all come with air-con and private hot-water bathrooms. Several have fine seaviews.

Hotel La Veranda (☎ 757-9211; www.bocas.com; Calle G; d US$29-50) This lovely residence-turned-inn was built in 1910 and has been maintained with pride, down to its gleaming hardwood floors and pretty antique windows and doors. None of the six guestrooms are alike, except that all contain early-20th century regional furniture and firm new mattresses. Several rooms have shared baths, while others have private bathrooms.

Tropical Suites (☎ 757-9081; www.tropical-suites.com; Calle 1; ste with/without seaview US$125/100) This new, all-suites hotel over the water features spacious, well-designed rooms with tile floors, kitchens (with rangetop and refrigerators), flat-screen TVs and air-con. Large modern bathrooms come equipped with Jacuzzis. Service here is excellent, and among the amenities is a coin-operated laundry and the island's only elevator. Discounted rates for longer stays.

Hotel Angela (☎ /fax 757-9813; www.hotelangela.com; Av H; d US$35-65; ❄) This handsome seaside hotel offers 12 elegant rooms with good beds, air-con and private hot-water bathrooms. The hotel features pleasant sitting areas and a very amiable owner. The deluxe rooms with balcony and oceanview are worth the extra money. A pleasant restaurant and bar over the water makes a fine place for a bite in the evening.

Hotel Dos Palmas (☎ 757-9906; Av Sur; s/d US$22/28) Proudly touting the hotel as '100% Bocatoreño,' the friendly owners of Dos Palmas offer eight rooms with private hot-water bathrooms, good beds and ceiling fans. The hotel sits entirely over the water, and there's a seaside porch with hammocks, tables and chairs.

Hotel Bahía (☎ 757-9626; www.panamainfo.com/hotelbahia; Calle 3; d US$44; ❄) This building was originally built in 1905 by the United Fruit Company to serve as its local headquarters. Today, the hotel has been restored and you can see the original splendor of this fine building. The American pine lining the halls is original, as are the oak floors. During renovation the 18 guestrooms were modernized, though the new fixtures conform to the originals in design. Every room has air-con and a private hot-water bathroom and some have balconies with oceanviews.

Bocas Inn (☎ /fax 757-9226 in Bocas, ☎ 269-9414; www.anconexpeditions.com; Av H near the end of Calle 3; d with/without seaview US$66/55; ❄) Managed by Ancon Expeditions, the waterside hotel features seven guestrooms with air-con, firm mattresses, dressers, nightstands and private hot-water bathrooms. The newest rooms are quite spacious, with lovely hardwood floors, and are worth the extra money. Some of the rooms have seaviews, and there are communal seaside porches as well as a restaurant and bar. Full packages including lodging, all meals and day tours start at US$90 per person.

Cocomo on the Sea (☎ 757-9259; www.panamainfo.com/cocomo; Av H; d with breakfast US$55-65) This attractive seaside inn has four fine rooms, two with oceanviews, with access to seaside terraces strung with hammocks. These rooms were built with attention to detail, from the soundproof roofs that squelch the noise of driving rains to matching decor and orthopedic mattresses. Rates include breakfast and free use of the kayaks. No children under eight or pets are allowed. English is spoken.

Hotel Laguna (☎ 757-9091; www.bocas.com; Calle 3; d from US$50; ❄) This two-story hotel has 15 ttractive rooms with lots of wood details, ood beds, air-con and hot-water private athrooms. There's also two suites with itchens.

Estrella de Bocas (☎ 757-9011; feryleriz@yahoo om; Calle 1; r/ste from US$25/60; ⚒) This two-story otel is clean but cheaply furnished with a aded look about it. It features several small asic rooms and eight furnished suites. All he rooms open onto a lovely balcony that verlooks a courtyard. The suites all have iny kitchenettes, with living room, air-con nd TV.

AROUND THE ISLAND

Punta Manglar (☎ 757-9541, www.bocas.com; dm IS$12, cabin US$30-50; ⚒) A 10-minute boat ride rom town, the Punta Manglar consists of ive wooden cabins and a restaurant/bar, all uilt on stilts over the water and connected y walkways. One room has a double bed, air-con and a hot-water private bathroom. The others have a mixture of double beds nd bunk beds and can hold four to six eople each, but they have cold-water pri- ate bathrooms and fans only. There's also n 8-bed dorm for budget travelers. All of he rooms have oceanfront porches, and he reef right out front offers quality snor- eling. This place has occasional trouble with gnats, particularly at sundown.

Punta Caracol Aqua Lodge (☎ 612-1088; www puntacaracol.com; s/d with breakfast & dinner in low sea- son US$195/215, high season US$240/260) Continuing another 10 minutes by boat past the Punta Manglar in the direction of Boca del Drago you'll reach five pleasant two-story *cabañas* – built entirely over the water of wood and *penca* (palm tree leaves) in conformity with traditional Caribbean architecture. Unlike the Punta Manglar, these *cabañas* were built far enough away from the nearby man- groves to escape visits by biting gnats. The upper room in each *cabaña* is the bedroom, with a king-size bed and mosquito netting (mostly for decor). There's a comfortable living room on the ground floor with two sofa beds and an adjacent terrace facing the open sea and distant jungled hills. A sea breeze keeps the rooms pleasant most of the time. Solar panels power this low-key resort, and a septic tank handles waste. The price includes full breakfast and an excel- lent dinner of seafood prepared Spanish or Caribbean style.

Eating
IN TOWN
Bocas town is small but has a wide variety of places to have a meal, from sweet-smelling bakeries to traditional Italian eateries and places serving fresh seafood.

Alberto's Pizzeria (☎ 757-9066; Calle 5; pizzas US$4- 10; ⏱ 5-11pm Mon-Sat) Alberto's has earned many admirers for the delicious pizzas and calzones served at this low-key spot.

Om Café (Av H; mains US$4-8; ⏱ 8am-noon & 5:30- 10pm Thu-Tue) There are only a handful of tables at this handsome outdoor Indian restaurant, but the authentic *palak paneer* (US$4), and tasty lassis (US$1.75) make it worth the wait. Breakfasts here are excel- lent, with banana pancakes and yogurt and granola among the offerings.

Panadería Europea (Av D; baked goods US$0.75-1.50; ⏱ 7am-noon Mon-Sat) Sample the island's best baked goods at this sweet-smelling bakery attached to Da Claudio. Huge, fluffy cin- namon rolls, sweet breads and donuts are all highly addictive.

El Pecado (mains US$8-13; ⏱ 5pm-10pm) This trendy upstairs restaurant near the park serves some of Bocas' best cuisine. El Pec- ado specializes in Thai-Panamanian com- binations, such as filet of fish smothered in coconut milk-based curry (US$8). The chicken satay is also quite tasty.

Piña Colada (Calle 3; mains US$6-9) Near the dock, this pleasant open-air spot on the water serves tasty eclectic cuisine (mango chicken served in a bread bowl, US$6.50), and strong tropical drinks (banana monkey, US$3.50).

Da Claudio (☎ 757-9091; mains US$6-10) Below the **Hotel Laguna**, Da Claudio serves great breakfasts, including pancakes with choco- late and banana, and yogurt and fruit. The talented chef prepares Italian and German cuisine for lunch and dinner. A wide selec- tion of imported beers is available.

El Ultimo Refugio (☎ 640-1878; Av Sur; mains US$8- 12; ⏱ 11:30am-10pm) This rustic, mellow place on the edge of the sea specializes in sea- food dishes like fresh octopus and calamari, red snapper, and spicy shrimp in coconut sauce. It also serves filet mignon and tasty vegetarian tacos. It's a popular place and is one of the few restaurants where you might need reservations.

Arco Iris (Av G; mains US$3-5) This charming out- door snack spot serves Italian ice cream, club sandwiches, roast chicken and fruit shakes.

Buena Vista Deli & Bar (Calle 1; mains US$5-7; ⓨ noon-9:30pm) Another laid-back spot over the water, Buena Vista serves delicious sandwiches (like teriyaki chicken breast or grilled vegetable on foccacia bread) and tasty seafood dishes (giant prawns with Thai coconut curry). The full bar with DirecTV gets crowded with expats during major sporting events.

Restaurant Bahiá (☎ 757-9626; Calle 3 inside Hotel Bahiá; mains US$7-11) Serves an excellent selection of Caribbean dishes in an open-air setting.

Bocas El Caribe (Calle 3; mains US$3-4) Italian-owned, El Caribe serves cheap, decent meals that don't feature rice *or* beans. Old-country favorites include lasagna (US$3.50), pasta primavera (US$1.75) and pizza by the slice (US$0.50).

Kun Ja (Calle 1; mains US$4-7) This local favorite serves good, cheap Chinese food, such as a nicely flavored chop suey with chicken.

Don Chicho's (Calle 3; plates US$2-4.50) This local favorite on the main street prepares decent inexpensive Panamanian food, served cafeteria-style. For cheap bites, try the rice and beans, with a side of yucca. Don't overlook the excellent cakes and pies (try the Key Lime, US$0.75).

Restaurante y Parrillada Kuna (Calle 1; mains US$6-8) Just past the entrance to Barco Hundido, you can find a range of fresh seafood dishes liked grilled snapper or sautéed shrimp. Breakfasts are also quite tasty.

Le Pirate (Calle 3) Seafood is served in large quantities at this seaside restaurant. Sometimes it's tops, other days the cook is a little off. It also offers a fine selection of fruit drinks, and there's a full bar.

Bumpers (Calle 1; mains US$4-6; ⓨ 7am-10pm) Over the water, this pleasant Canadian-owned spot is a good lunch or dinnertime choice for the filling fish or chicken specials served with potato salad, coleslaw and rice. It also serves tasty burgers (the Caribbean chicken burger with Monterey Jack cheese and a pineapple slice is quite good).

Texas Bar & Grill (Av E; mains US$6-8) For a slice of good, down-home cooking, head to this small eatery near the airport. A few picnic tables in front and the sound of a sizzling grill form the setting to dining on hearty portions of baby back ribs, steak and grilled tuna, with all the fixings.

Super Gourmet (Av E) A grocery store that stocks a small but decent selection of imported and locally grown items. You' find cheeses, Italian sausage, chorizo, fres ceviche, juices and flash-frozen fish filet and steaks. At the time of research, Supe Gourmet was next to the Banco Naciona de Panamá, but it is planning to move to bigger space and open a full-service deli.

AROUND THE ISLAND

Yarisnori Restaurant (mains US$6-9; ⓨ 7:30am-7pm Overlooking the beach at Boca del Drago this charming, open-air seafood restauran is a local favorite. Grab an outdoor tabl on the sand, and feast on ceviche followe by fish, jumbo shrimp, octopus or lobste Afterwards, take a dip, or soak up some su on the lovely beach nearby. See p231 fo details on getting here.

Liki Tiki (mains US$4-7; ⓨ noon-10pm) Thi beach bar sits on Playa El Istmito, an makes a charming spot to have lunch o dinner, or to while away the afternoo over a few tropical cocktails. The restauran serves decent seafood with Caribbean an Mexican accents. In addition to big plates there are snacks and sandwiches. On week ends you might catch a pickup volleybal game on the beach out front.

Drinking

Barco Hundido (Calle 1) Bocas' liveliest night spot, this open-sided, thatched-roof bar i also called The Wreck Deck after the sub merged banana boat that rests in the clea Caribbean water in front. A short boardwalk extends from the bar over the vessel to ar island seating area that's perfect for stargaz ing. The American owners usually crank the rock 'n' roll, which is just fine for the medley of expats and locals who come here.

Mondo Taitú (Av H) This small, charming bar boasts the best tropical cocktails in Bocas Mondo's talented bartender mixes some potent and tasty concoctions, with ingredients like coconut milk, fresh juices and plenty of alcohol. For a free drink, order one of the tequila suicides (a snort of salt a squeeze of lime in the eye and a shot o cheap tequila).

Liki Tiki (Playa El Istmito; ⓨ noon-10pm) This beach bar, 15 minutes north of town, provides a fine setting for drinks – day or night (see also above).

Bar El Encanto (Calle 3) This lively locals' bar is ruled by a young crowd and features oc-

:asional live music, with DJs playing reggae and other island hits.

Shopping

You'll find *molas* and a range of other hand-crafts for sale by local Kunas at stands near the park.

Pacahama (Calle 3) Features arts made by most of Panama's indigenous peoples plus handicrafts produced by the native peoples of Colombia, Guatemala and Nicaragua, including Guatemalan textiles, Nicaraguan hammocks and baskets made by the Emberá Indians of Darién.

Tropix Surfshop (Calle 3) Sells custom-made surfboards and a few used boards. You'll also find bikinis and other island apparel here.

Getting There & Away

AIR

Bocas del Toro has a fine little airport, with daily flights to and from Panama City, and weekday flights to and from David. **Aero-perlas** (☎ 757-9341 in Bocas) offers daily flights from Panama City to Bocas (one way US$58) at 8:30am and 1pm Monday to Friday, 7am and 3pm Saturday, and 8am and 3pm Sunday. See Panama City (p112) for more information. Flights from Bocas to Panama City depart at 9am and 2:30pm Monday to Friday, 8am and 5pm Saturday, and 9:25pm and 5pm Sunday.

Aero (☎ 757-9841 in Bocas) also has flights between Panama City and Bocas at 9am Monday to Friday, and 6:30am Saturday and Sunday. Return flights are at 9am Monday to Friday and 6am Saturday and Sunday.

BOAT

If you don't fly into Bocas you'll have to take a water taxi from either Almirante or Changuinola. These towns are connected by bus to David and to the Costa Rican border at Sixaola/Guabito (for schedules and fares see Almirante, p244, and Changuinola, p245). From David buses stop first in Almirante, then in Changuinola. Buses from the border go to Changuinola then Almirante.

The boat ride to Changuinola travels through the old canal formerly used by the banana plantations. It's a scenic trip that's well worth taking. **Bocas Marine & Tours** (☎ 757-083; Calle 3) operates a daily boat service (one way US$5, 45 minutes). Boats from both Bocas and Changuinola depart at 7am, 8am,

9:30am, 11am, 12:30pm, 2pm, 3:30pm and 5:30pm.

Boats coming from either direction can let you off in Boca del Drago (one way US$3), but make sure your captain knows you're going there. If you go for the day, be sure to arrange a pick-up time with the secretary and the driver (the last boat back leaves at 6:10pm).

Bocas Marine & Tours also runs an hourly boat service to Almirante. (one way US$3) from 6am to 6:30pm. **Taxi 25** (☎ 757-9028) near the IPAT office also operates water taxis between Almirante and Bocas (US$3, 20 minutes), leaving every half hour from 6am to 6:30pm.

The **Ferry Turistico Palanga** (☎ 615-6774), which carries passengers and vehicles, operates between Almirante and Bocas (passengers/vehicles US$1.50/20, 1½ hours) on Wednesday, Friday, Saturday and Sunday. It leaves Almirante at 9am and Bocas at 5pm.

A short dinghy trip from town is the fairly new **Bocas Yacht Club & Marina** (☎ 757-9800; www .bocasmarina.com), which features world-class floating concrete docks capable of holding 100 boats up to 100 feet in length (rental cost is US$8 per foot per month). Facilities include showers, a laundromat, water, electricity, security, maintenance, parts, full-service haul-out facilities, a fuel dock, a gazebo and barbecue area. Every second Friday, the expat crowd gathers for lively parties.

Getting Around

To reach nearby islands, hire the boatmen operating motorized canoes along the waterfront. Find them at the dock next door to Bocas Marine & Tours or beside Le Pirate (opposite). Round-trip rates are US$4 to the near side of Isla Bastimentos or US$7 to Red Frog Beach, on the far side. A trip to Isla Carenero costs about US$1.

Bocas Marine & Tours (Calle 3) has four daily boat departures to Boca del Drago (one way US$3) at 9:30am, 11am, 12:30pm and 5:20pm. Boats return at 10:10am, 1:10pm, 2:30pm and 4:10pm. If you go for the day, confirm your pick-up time with the driver.

Although there are official times for buses to Boca del Drago – 6:45am, 9am, 10:30am, 12:30p, 3pm and 4:15pm – it's pretty irregular. Generally the bus makes three to four trips a day between Bocas town and Boca del Drago, with the last one arriving late afternoon.

On the main street facing the park there's a place where you can rent bicycles (per day US$6) and motorbikes (per day US$25).

There are also pickup truck taxis along Calle 3, which can zip you up to Boca del Drago or along the road to Playa Bluff. Negotiate a price before you go.

ISLA CARENERO

A few hundred meters from Isla Colón is the small sparsely populated island of Isla Carenero, which in recent years has become popular with business folk hoping to lure tourists off Isla Colón and into their establishments.

The island takes its name from 'careening,' which in nautical talk means to lean a ship on one side for cleaning or repairing. It was on Careening Cay in October 1502 that ships under the command of Christopher Columbus were careened and cleaned while the admiral recovered from a bellyache.

Sleeping & Eating

Bernard's Pargo Rojo (☎ 757-9649; www.pargorojo .net; cabin US$30, mains US$6-12) This popular open-air restaurant and bar has an excellent location right on the water, straight across from Bocas town. The charming view is matched by the excellent cooking of owner Bernard Bahary, originally from Iran and a real character. Meals vary with the catch of the day, but a variety of delicious sauces is always offered (like tasty fish curry). Bernard also serves a traditional Iranian meal upon request. Beside the restaurant there are five rustic cabins, with plank floors and walls and thatch roofs. Each has a private hot-water bathroom, a downstairs bed and a loft with another bed. Guests have free use of the kayaks.

Casa Acuario (☎/fax 757-9565; joberg1301@cwp .net.pa; d US$75; 🞖) This handsome house by the water has four gorgeous guestrooms with lovely seaviews, air-con, DirecTV and snorkeling off the porch. There's a beach next door and friendly American owners. Guests are welcome to use the kitchen.

Tierra Verde (☎ 757-9042; www.hoteltierraverde .com; s/d/tr US$45/50/55) Offering excellent value for money, this lovely three-story building sits just back from the beach in a shady area full of palm trees. The seven spacious rooms feature beautiful wood details and windows that allow ample light, and have good beds and private hot-water bathrooms. On the

1st floor there's a cozy lounge with DirecTV just outside is a shade-covered porch.

Careening Cay Resort & Marina (☎/fax 757-924. www.careeningcay.com; 2-/4-person cabin US$45/65) Thi American-owned and -run place has fou large stand-alone cabins with porches, eacl with a hot-water private bathroom, a divide separating a parents' room (with queen bed from a kid's room (with two bunk beds), and a table and chairs. The marina has 26 berth to 55 feet (20-foot maximum width) witl 120/240V, 60Hz power, pressurized wate showers, dinghy dock, garbage disposa shaded work areas, and access to a laundr fax and email services. The dockage rate c US$0.25 per foot per night (US$7.50 per foo per month) includes normal power and wate usage; rates improve with longer stays.

The Sunset Grill (dishes US$5-10; 🕑 7-9am, 11an 2pm & 4-10pm) This restaurant at the resort i worth a trip over from Isla Colón, especiall for Tuesday night's Texas barbecue (US$9.50 and Wednesday night's Mexican (US$8 Regular fare includes Philly steak sandwiche and cheeseburgers (US$5), a variety of sea food plates (US$8), grilled pork tenderloi (US$9) as well as USDA Select steaks. It als serves hearty American breakfasts.

Buccaneer Resort (☎ 757-9042; www.buccane -resort.com; cabañas $65-85; 🞖) On a lovely strip c beach, this place offers four suite *cabañas* an eight smaller *cabañas*. Each is elevated an features polished hardwood floors and wall a romantic thatch roof, screened porch, ceil ing fan, sitting area, and modern tiled bath room with air-con. The four suite *cabaña* which contain living rooms, are honeymoo material – very romantic and private.

La Almeja Barbuda (just in front of Buccaneer Resor An open-sided restaurant perched over th water where you'll find excellent seafoo and grilled meats. It's one of the most pop ular expat hangouts in Bocas.

Doña Mara Restaurante y Hospedaje (☎/fa 757-9551; d US$55) This is a peaceful spot, bu it's a bit expensive for what you get. The si guestrooms, all with air-con, hot-water bath rooms and local TV, have the feel of a cit hotel, and are arranged in a U layout wit only the two end rooms having a seaview There's a **restaurant** (🕑 8am-11pm) next door.

Getting There & Away

To get to Isla Carenero you'll have to find reliable looking boatman (fare US$1). Try th docks by Bocas Marine & Tours (p237) or your favorite seaside restaurant.

ISLA BASTIMENTOS

pop 1500

Isla Bastimentos is a 10-minute boat ride from Bocas town. There are two communities on the island, the larger being the village of Bastimentos which has no roads, only a concrete footpath with rustic wooden houses on both sides. Though it's near to Isla Colón, the language here is very different.

Until the 1990s, most of Bastimentos' adults were hard-working people who traveled to Almirante daily to tend to banana fields. Owing to the collapse of the banana industry, by the turn of the millennium less than two dozen of the island's residents were still working the fields. Most of the residents had taken to fishing, farming small plots or just hanging out.

On the southeastern side of the island is the Ngöbe-Buglé village of Quebrada Sal (Salt Creek). Between Quebrada Sal and Bastimentos a wide swatch of rain forest falls within the Parque Nacional Marino Isla Bastimentos, which is the terra firma section of a mostly marine park. You can explore the park, but go only with a local guide (children who know the area often offer their services), as it's possible to get lost.

The island has several beautiful beaches. You can walk from Bastimentos to **Playa Primera** (also called Wizared Beach) in 20 minutes or so. Other fine beaches along the northern side of the island include **Playa Segunda** and the lengthy **Playa Larga**, where sea turtles nest from April to August. Playa Larga is inside the national marine park, but some locals continue to kill turtles there for meat and shells and rob their nests of eggs.

Sights & Activities

Nivida is the name of a cave recently discovered by one of Bastimentos' residents. and it is one of the island's most fascinating natural wonders. Getting to the sight is half the adventure: go to Roots restaurant (p241) to arrange a trip with Oscar, a very reliable guide; tours (minimum four people) cost US$25 per person. You'll travel by small motorboat up a channel in the Bahía Honda area, through lush vegetation full of wildlife. A short walk through the jungle leads to the cave, inside which you'll spend about 1½ hours explor-

ing this massive subterranean phenomenon, passing nectar bats, wading through water (at times chest deep) and taking a dip in the cavern lake. Oscar provides helmets with lanterns. Avoid touching *anything* inside the cave. On the way back he usually makes a stop at a jungleside bar (aka the swamp bar). He also offers a more physically challenging hike through the rain forest to Laguna de Bastimentos (known as 'the jungle lake').

On the southeastern edge of Isla Bastimentos is the Ngöbe-Buglé village of **Quebrada Sal**, at the end of a long canal cut through mangrove forest. The community consists of 60 thatch-and-bamboo houses, an elementary school, handicrafts store, general store and soccer field.

Sleeping

La Loma Jungle Lodge (☎ 592-5162; www.the junglelodge.com; d w meals US$45) Located near the Ngöbe-Buglé community of Bahía Honda, this lodge is set on 23 hectares of jungle stretching from Bahía Honda up to the highest point on Bastimentos. Scattered throughout the property are six stand-alone cabins in beautiful natural settings. They're rustic but stylish, and each has a double bed with a private bathroom. Solar power provides the energy for the lights and fans, and much of the building material was taken from sustainable sources – fallen trees and *penca* thatch. The organic garden here produces much of the food, and all meals (and afternoon tea) are included in the price. Guests also have access to a large network of trails, freshwater rock pools and wildlife observation stations. There are traditional wooden canoes available for paddling around. For an additional fee guided tours are available, including hikes to Laguna de Bastimentos, cave tours, and trips to the deserted beaches of Blue Fields.

El Limbo (☎ 620-5555; www.ellimbo.com; d with breakfast & dinner US$45) Every room is different at El Limbo, with lots of unique touches such as headboards made of driftwood and seashells arranged in room corners for artistic effect. It offers eight rustic but attractive rooms in a two-story wooden lodge with electricity, good cross-ventilation and private bathrooms. There's a fine beach and reef out front. The rate includes breakfast, dinner and the use of snorkeling equipment. Tours to Salt Creek and Cayos Zapatillas are available for US$15 per person.

Cabañas y Restaurante Punta Vieja (cabañas per person US$5) Consists of several very basic and small raised *cabañas*, with one light bulb each, and a shared rustic shower and bathroom. There's a simple and inexpensive restaurant built on stilts over the water 25m from shore. It serves dishes such as grilled fish (US$5), whole lobster (US$9) and octopus (US$7). Apart from its rates, the most appealing things about this place are: its owner, Alberto Livingston (who goes by the name Ñato, which means man with little nose); the seaview, with mesmerizing, nonstop breakers; and the waves, which surfers would appreciate most of all. Ñato, who's about the friendliest man you'll ever meet, speaks Gali-Gali and a little Spanish.

Tranquilo Bay Resort (☎ 757-9967; www.tran quilobay.com; 🐛) Still under construction at the time of writing, this resort offers a stunning location overlooking the zapatillos on Isla Bastimentos. Once complete, it will be an all-inclusive resort featuring six spacious aircon, concrete-walled, zinc-roofed *cabañas* with all the amenities, and a restaurant. Visit the website for more information.

The Point (☎ 757-9704; cabin US$40) At the northern tip of Bastimentos lie two cabins and a nicely designed house, all overlooking the sea, with the crashing waves a few meters from the doorstep. Each of the cabins has impressive views, beautiful wood details, a refrigerator and private hot-water bathrooms. One or two of the rooms in the house are available for rent for US$75. These are also handsomely designed, with ample space and a cozy feel. Guests have free use of kayaks, and you can surf right off the tip (bring your own board). This is also an ecologically sensitive place with a septic system, rather than plumbing that flushes into the sea.

Hotel Bastimentos (s/d US$5/10) On a hill off the main path, this hotel has clean, pleasant rooms with shared bathrooms. Rooms with a view cost slightly more. The balcony is a nice spot to lounge or meet other travelers.

Hospedaje Sylvia (☎ 757-9442; s/d US$5/10) Sylvia offers five small rooms with fans, clean shared bathrooms and a good common area. The rooms upstairs are less cramped. Breakfast is quite good (omelettes US$3, French toast US$2.50), and you can order sandwiches for lunch if you're making a boat tour.

Hospedaje Aislenis (☎ 757-9410; s/d US$7/12) This basic locally owned spot is built on pilings over the water and features five small but clean and well-swept, all-wood rooms, two with private bath and three with shared baths. Small windows open over the water (no view) and hammocks are strung on the end of the dock. The friendly family that runs the place also offers boat tours around Bocas.

Hospedaje Midland (s/d/tw US$8/10/12) Another locally owned spot, Midland has modest concrete cabins that are clean and well maintained with private bathrooms. Upstairs is a pleasant, open-air restaurant with a thatch roof and hammocks strung about.

Hospedaje Sea View (s/d US$7/10) This small family run hotel has three basic rooms with private bath and a small deck on the water.

Beverly's Hill (☎ 757-9923; s/d US$10/15) Rooms in clean cabins set amid a lush garden make Beverly's excellent value; it's also one of the few environmentally friendly hotels on Bastimentos. You'll find it as you're walking north, past Tío Tom's on your right side.

Casa del Sol (d without/with bathroom US$12/17) At the end of the footpath beyond Beverly's Hill, Casa del Sol has small, cozy upstairs rooms and darker, more spacious rooms downstairs with a shared kitchen.

Pension Tío Tom (☎ /fax 757-9831, tomina@cwp .net.pa; d with/without private bathroom US$20/10) This traveler's favorite has five rooms with good cross-ventilation and a relaxing deck on the water. One room has a private hot-water bathroom; the others share a bathroom. The food here is delicious, and offerings include rabbit in a red wine cream sauce served with vegetables (most dinners are US$5). The friendly owners rent snorkel gear (per day US$5) and offer tours. Spanish, English and German are spoken.

Pelicano (☎ 757-9830; s/d US$10/14) Run by an Italian-Panamanian couple, Pelicano has basic cabins with fans and private coldwater bathrooms. The seaside restaurant serves Italian dishes and seafood.

Al Natural Resort (☎ 623-2217; alnaturalbocas@ cwp.net.pa; d with meals & transport first/second night US$85/60) This all-inclusive resort set against the forest contains five elegant but rustic *cabañas* on the beach. Each has seaviews, a private bathroom and mosquito nets. There's a communal dining area and an inviting sunbathing platform at the end of a dock, with a coral reef in front. The price includes three meals daily, wine with dinner and round-trip transportation from sla Colón, as well as the use of kayaks and vindsurfing and snorkeling equipment. Although Al Natural was once one of the most charming getaways on the islands, readers have complained that the standards here have slipped in recent years, and the resort no longer offers good value for the money.

ating & Drinking

Roots (mains US$3-5; ♥ Wed-Mon) Lovely sea-iews and the backdrop of reggae are part of the charm of this pleasant, locally owned estaurant over the water. Popular dishes include rice and beans with coconut milk and chicken, and plates of grilled fish. It's also a fine place for a drink in the evening. Co-owner Oscar Powell has done much for the community of Isla Bastimentos, and he's a personable fellow with a sharp sense of humor. He currently offers one of the more unique tours on Bocas to a cave that he discovered. See p239 for details.

The Rooster (mains US$3.50-4.50; ♥ Sat-Thu) This inexpensive, low-key spot, which is also known as Pete's Place, serves excel-ent food. The friendly, garrulous owner who bills himself as the 'anti-fried guy') is a talented and creative cook and everything that comes out of his kitchen tastes fresh and healthy – whether it's his pork chops, veggie burgers, Chinese-style chicken with vegetables or eggplant schnitzel. He always has vegetarian options, and likes introduc-ing people to the island's rich fruits and vegetables, like piva or breadfruit.

One Love (mains US$3.50-6) Another of Basti-mentos' top eating spots, One Love special-izes in simple, fresh and very tasty plates of seafood. It's a simple spot in the south of town, easily identified by the painting of Bob Marley on the yellow building.

La Feria This large, blue barnlike structure is built partially over the water and is the seat of Bastimentos' nightlife. After the sun sets it's an easy spot to find; just follow the sound of reggae. *Bocatoreños* from all over come to the wild parties called Blue Mon-days (held on Monday of course).

Restaurante Coral Cay (dishes US$6-12; ♥ 8am-pm) An island unto itself, this place is a clus-ter of thatched-roof *bohios* on stilts beside a clump of mangrove and a field of coral reef. This is a terrific place to relax, lay in the sun, snorkel and eat, and the boat ride out is an adventure. Dishes include filet of fish

in either a Jamaican curry or a tomato sauce (US$6), octopus in coconut milk with side dishes (US$10), lobster with butter and garlic (US$12) and shrimp in white salsa (US$6). When you're meeting fellow travelers, talk a few into making the trip out here – that way you can split the cost of the water taxi. Beer and some booze are available.

Getting There & Away

At the time of writing there was no reliable shuttle service between Isla Bastimentos and Bocas del Toro town. Your best bet is to go to Transparente Tours (see p233) or Bocas Marine & Tours and ask to be taken to Isla Bastimentos.

For the return trip, either make arrange-ments with the boatman who brought you over (if the boatman seems reliable), or stop by Roots or one of the other businesses mentioned here.

OTHER ISLANDS

The archipelago has many other beautiful islands, all with good snorkeling spots.

Isla Solarte, also called Cayo Nancy, is dis-tinguished by Hospital Point, named for the United Fruit Company hospital that was built here in 1900 when the company had its headquarters in Bocas town. The hospital was established to isolate victims of yellow fever and malaria; at the time it was not yet known that these diseases, then rampant in the area, were transmitted by mosquitoes. The hospital complex eventu-ally included 16 buildings. It was here for only two decades, however; when a fungus killed United Fruit's banana trees, the com-pany moved its banana operations to the mainland and abandoned the hospital.

Solarte del Caribe (☎ 757-9032; www.solarteinn .com; d/ste with breakfast US$65/110) This lovely, well-crafted and recently constructed lodge enjoys the privilege of being the sole hotel on the island. It has the air of a country inn, with a spacious open-sided dining room, a relaxing furnished lounge (called the 'great room') and guestrooms that make ample use of light. Rooms are small but cozy and feature ceiling fans and screened windows, with lovely hardwood floors, good beds and private bathrooms with flushing compost toilets. There are also two-room suites with separate kitchenette/dining areas. Breakfast is included, and the restaurant also serves lunch and dinner. It's about a 15-minute boat ride to Bocas town.

Swan Cay, also called Isla de los Pájaros, is home to a great many birds and, not surprisingly, is popular with bird watchers. Most hope to see red-billed tropic birds and white-crowned pigeons. Nearby are **Wreck Rock** and **Sail Rock**, which are responsible for the premature retirement of more than a few boats whose skippers mistakenly chose to sail at night in unfamiliar waters.

The **Cayos Zapatillas** are touted by tour operators for snorkeling, despite strong currents in the area. The two keys, Cayo Zapatilla Norte and Cayo Zapatilla Sur, have beautiful white-sand beaches and pristine reefs. Nearly every meter of the south key, incidentally, was dug up in the early 20th century on the rumor that Captain Henry Morgan had buried treasure here. None was found. There is an ANAM station on the south key and it's often possible to stay at it. Check with the ANAM office in Bocas town (p229).

PARQUE NACIONAL MARINO ISLA BASTIMENTOS

Panama's first marine park, established in 1988, was **Parque Nacional Marino Isla Bastimentos** (entry US$10). Protecting various areas of the Bocas archipelago, including parts of large Isla Bastimentos (especially Playa Larga) and the Cayos Zapatillas, the park is an important nature reserve for many species of Caribbean wildlife.

Its beaches are used as a nesting ground by four species of sea turtle. The abundant coral reefs, great for snorkeling and diving, support countless species of fish, lobster and other forms of sea life. The lagoons are home to animals such as freshwater turtles and caimans, and there is still more wildlife in the forests. Unfortunately, poaching also occurs in the park.

If you want to camp out anywhere in the park, you are required to first obtain a permit from ANAM in Bocas del Toro (p229). For information on Isla Bastimentos, see p239.

CHANGUINOLA CANAL

In 1903 a 15km canal connecting the Río Changuinola and Bahía de Almirante was dug parallel to the Caribbean shoreline, running within several hundred meters of it for most of its length. The work was begun six years earlier by the Snyder Brothers Banana Company to facilitate the barging of bananas from the fields to ships. The 30m-wide channel allowed transfer of the heavy fruit without interference from the open sea.

The canal, which sliced through dense rain forest, was abandoned years ago, and until the mid-1990s it was a bird watcher's dream. Today, much of the jungle on both sides of the waterway has been cleared for cattle pasture, though there is still wildlife in the area. Bocas Marine & Tours offers boat service between Changuinola and Bocas (see p237).

MAINLAND

The mainland of Bocas del Toro Province is awesome. As in the Darién, there is forest in parts of Bocas del Toro Province that is able to support jaguars and the world's most powerful bird of prey, the harpy eagle, both of which require enormous amounts of territory to survive.

The mainland is an explorer's dream. Its jungles teem with wildlife and are pocketed with small indigenous villages. Some months of the year, in the dead of night, sea turtles lumber out of the choppy surf and onto the beaches north of Changuinola to lay eggs and then head back to the water until the same time next year.

In Parque Internacional La Amistad, half of which is in Panama and half in Costa Rica, are 407,000 hectares of rain forest that contain seven of the 12 classified life zones. It's possible to ride some of its rivers for hours and only see a handful of human beings. Bribri or Teribe Indians float downstream on rafts made of balsa wood held together by vines. These crude one-trip rafts have been used by the Indians for generations.

BOSQUE PROTECTOR PALO SECO

Located 29km south of Chiriquí Grande on the road to David (also called 'Fortuna Road' because the road passes by Lago Fortuna reservoir), the **Bosque Protector Palo Seco** (BPP; Panamanians/foreigners US$1/3) is a lush cloud forest, covering more than 160,000 hectares. It's set high in the Talamanca range, and the wildlife here includes monkeys, sloths, armadillos, butterflies, and great birdlife, including ashy-throated bush-tanagers, Panama's only known site for them.

An ANAM station lies at the entrance to the Bosque, and here you can pay the park admission fee and obtain information about current hiking conditions. ANAM maintains three trails in the park, each about 45 minutes in duration, allowing visitors the chance to get a taste of the region's natural wonders (one of the trails is named 'Los Tucanes,' in honor of the sometimes sighted bird, while another trail offers panoramic views of the valley below).

ANAM has rustic facilities for those interested in staying the night inside the center (per person US$5), but be sure to bring your own food and bedding. Guests have access to the kitchen as well as bathrooms. To ensure they have room for you, contact the Changuinola **ANAM office** (☎ 758-6603, 767-9485).

Just down from the ANAM station is the home of **Isabel & Onel Guerra-Martinez** (bed with/without meals US$30/10), who also provide food and lodging for guests. Accommodations are rustic, but clean and well maintained with flush toilets and showers. The friendly family can cook your meals; they also provide tours of the area (Spanish only).

Across the road from them is the sign for **Willie Mazu Rancho Ecologico** (☎ 442-1340 in Panama City; panabird@cwpanama.net; mattress with/without meals US$45/25), which consists of a large, thatched-roof structure under which four-person tents are pitched. The tents contain mattresses, and guests have access to cooking facilities and a clean bathroom and shower. You can bring your own food or buy your meals here. In the vicinity is a crystal-clear stream that's very refreshing after a long hike. There are several trails on the property, one of which leads to a lovely set of waterfalls and bathing pools. There's also a stand about 100m further up the road that sells cucumbers and bananas and other fresh fruits.

The last place to stay in the area is the *cabaña* owned by the doctor and his wife who run the NGO called **Mocelva** (☎ 774-4934; hapenagosg@hotmail.com; lodging & 3 meals US$27). It's up the road from the other spots at kilometer 67 and the sign at the entrance is marked 'Celestine.' This lovely cabin is set in the forest, with two trails running behind it. At the time this was written, the cabin lacked beds – you'll have to sleep on the floor of the cabin (bring sleeping bags). The price of lodging also includes three meals – prepared by a local Ngöbe-Buglé villager – and

guided walks along the trails (also led by the Ngöbe-Buglé).

All of these sights lie less than 17km from Lago Fortuna, a picturesque reservoir that serves a power plant. All around the reservoir is some of the finest forest in Panama, which is strictly protected because it serves as the watershed for the Fortuna Dam. The bird watching here is superb as it is in Bosque Protector Palo Seco. Keep an eye out for the bat falcon, wedge-billed woodcreeper and golden-winged warblers.

To get there from David take any bus in the direction of Changuinola or Almirante (US$4, hourly from 5am to 6:30pm). Tell the driver you want to stop just before Altos del Valle, the community just past the places mentioned above. Disembark at kilometer 68.5, which is right by the ANAM station. Don't try to reach these areas at night because they're set back from the road and easy to miss. Getting a ride out of the area basically requires catching one of the buses heading in the direction you're going. Buses pass every 45 minutes to an hour heading north to Changuinola (US$5, 2 hours) and south to David (US$4, 2 hours).

ALMIRANTE

pop 12,800

For travelers, this port town is the jumping-off point for a boat ride to Bocas del Toro town or a bus or taxi ride to Changuinola. For residents, Almirante means bananas – Chiquita bananas. Most Almirante residents are in the banana business, and the vast majority are poor folk who toil in the fields. These people inhabit the board-and-tin hovels you'll see throughout town.

Getting There & Away

BUS

Buses to Changuinola (US$1, 35 minutes, hourly) run from near the canal used by Almirante's water-taxis from 6am to 10:30pm. The bus terminal is on the other side of the train yard if you're coming from Bocas and heading north; when exiting the water taxi, turn left on the canalside road and follow the sidewalk around the train yard.

Buses to David (US$10, every 45 minutes) leave from a bus stop at the edge of the new highway from 5:30am to 7:30pm. To find the bus stop, find the bus terminal and walk 1km north on the paved street heading out of town. Or take a taxi to the bus stop; there's usually one at the terminal, and the cost shouldn't exceed US$1.50.

BOAT

Two companies – **Bocas Marine & Tours** (☎ 758-4085) and **Taxi 25** (☎ 757-9062) – operate water taxis between Almirante and Bocas town (US$3, 35 minutes). In Almirante, you can easily walk from one to the other. The water taxis leave when they're at least half full, so avoid the company that has an empty waiting area. Taxis more or less leave Almirante hourly, from 6:30am to 6:30pm.

The **Ferry Turistico Palanga** (☎ 758-3731) operates between Almirante and Bocas, carrying passengers as well as motor vehicles. The ferry runs between Almirante and Bocas on Wednesday, Friday, Saturday and Sunday, leaving Almirante at 9am and Bocas at 5pm (passengers/vehicles US$1.50/20, 1½ hours).

CHANGUINOLA

pop 41,700

Halfway between the Costa Rican border and the Archipiélago de Bocas del Toro, this city has been transited by many tourists, but few ever overnight here in this humid town.

From Changuinola it's easy to get to the Río Teribe, from which you can enter the Parque Internacional La Amistad. If you head in the opposite direction (north, toward the coast), you can visit some verdant wetlands that end at a Caribbean beach where sea turtles lay their eggs. Closer to the border, you can reach the indigenous community of Las Delicias, set in the heart of gorgeous rain forest.

Orientation

The city can be described as tall and slim. The main street, Av 17 de Abril (also called Av Central), runs north to south, and most of the hotels and restaurants are along this long, two-lane avenue, from which the rest of the city stems. There's an airport near the northern end of town, and the bus station is near the city center – close to restaurants, bars, markets and hotels.

Vast banana plantations flank the city. Most sites of interest to the traveler are easily reached on foot. Taxis are cheap and it's a good idea to use them after dark.

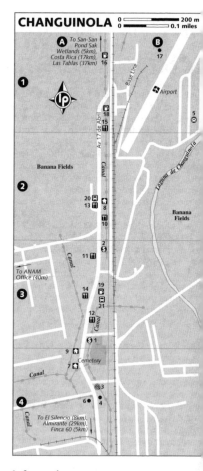

Information

There's an Internet café at **Farmacia Universal** (Av 17 de Abril), the best pharmacy in the city in the south of town, and another one right next to a **lavanderia** (Av 17 de Abril).

The town has a Banco Nacional de Panamá, a Banistmo and an immigration office, all on Av 17 de Abril. There is also a post office in town. There's no tourist office, but the police are helpful and friendly; they speak only Spanish, however.

The **ANAM office** (☎ 758-6603, 767-9485; 8am-4pm Mon-Fri), near the center of town, should be able to provide information on San-San Pond Sak, Las Delicias, Bosque Protector Palo Seco and Parque Internacional La Amistad. Some English is spoken here.

BOCAS DEL TORO PROVINCE

INFORMATION		
Banco Nacional de Panamá	1	A3
Banistmo	2	A3
Internet Café	3	A4
Laundry	4	A4
Post Office	5	B1

SIGHTS & ACTIVITIES		(p244)
Immigration Office	6	A4

SLEEPING	🅰	(p245)
Hotel Carol	7	A4
Hotel Chalet Suizo	8	A2
Hotel Semiramis	9	A4

EATING	🍴	(p245)
El Buen Sabor	10	A1
Grocery Store	(see 11)	
La Huaca	11	A3
Pharmacia Universal	12	A3
Pizzeria Aladino	13	A2
Restaurant/Bar Chiquita Banana	14	A3
Steak y Mar	15	A1

TRANSPORT		(pp245-6)
Accel Gas Station	16	A1
Airport Terminal	17	B1
Delta Gas Station	18	A1
Shell Gas Station	19	A3
Taxis	(see 21)	
Terminal Urraca	20	A2
Transporte Sincotavecop	21	A3

Sleeping

Hotel Semiramis (☎ 758-6006; Av 17 de Abril; s/d/tr US$23/28/32) This hotel features 20 clean, fully equipped rooms with decent beds and tile floors. There's a restaurant in front.

Hotel Carol (☎ /fax 758-8731; Av 17 de Abril; d with/without hot water US$18/11) This recently rebuilt hotel features a range of clean rooms. The cheapest are a little small.

Hotel Chalet Suizo (☎ 758-8242; Av 17 de Abril; raul avi@cwp.net.pa; d US$12-16) The wooden-floored rooms are worn, but they have decent light.

Eating

Pharmacia Universal (Av 17 de Abril; sandwiches US$2-3) This air-conditioned pharmacy has a small counter in front where you can order tasty hot *emparedados* (sandwiches), and *batidos* (fruit shakes) for US$1.

Restaurant/Bar Chiquita Banana (Av 17 de Abril) Opposite the bus station this local favorite serves good, cheap Panamanian food but surprisingly no bananas. (Indeed, bananas are hard to find in town.)

Pizzeria Aladino (Av 17 de Abril; medium pizza US$5.50) A simple, air-conditioned spot serving decent pizzas.

Steak y Mar (Av 17 de Abril; mains US$6-10) The mirrored windows may be off-putting, but this modest air-con place serves excellent seafood. Locals consider it the best spot in town.

El Buen Sabor (Av 17 de Abril; pastries US$0.35-0.95) An old, fan-cooled bakery that sells banana bread and other sweet breads, as well as donuts, cakes and pies.

There are supermarkets along Av 17 de Abril; **La Huaca** is among the best of the bunch. The branch near Banistmo also has a café.

Getting There & Away

AIR

Aeroperlas (☎ 758-7521 in Changuinola) flies to Panama City (US$59, 80 minutes) at 8:50am and 2:30pm Monday to Friday, 8:45am and 4:40pm Saturday, and 9:30am and 5:15pm Sunday. Flights from Panama City to Changuinola leave at 8:30am and 1pm Monday to Friday, 7am and 3pm Saturday, and 8am and 3pm Sunday (US$59, 80 minutes). On each of these flights, it stops first in Bocas town. Flights to David (US$32, 30 minutes) leave at 1:10am Monday through Friday. Flights from David to Changuinola (US$32, 30 minutes) depart at 10:10am Monday to Friday.

Aero (☎ 758-9841) flies from Panama City to Changuinola (US$59, 80 minutes) at 6:45am and 2pm Monday to Friday, 6:30am and 1pm Saturday, and 1pm Sunday. From Changuinola to the capital, flights depart at 8:15am and 3:30pm Monday to Friday, 8am and 2:30pm Saturday and 5pm Sunday.

To reach the airport, you can either walk or take a taxi (US$1).

BOAT

The water taxi service to Bocas del Toro (US$5, 45 minutes) runs along the old banana canals – it's a lovely trip. **Bocas Marine & Tours** (☎ 758-9858 in Changuinola) has boats departing from the water taxi dock (known as Finca 60) at 7am, 8am, 9:30am, 11am, 12:30pm, 2pm, 3:30pm and 5:30pm. Bocas del Toro-bound boats stop in Bocas del Drago if passengers request it. *Colectivo* buses run regularly from the bus station in town to Finca 60 for US$0.40. Or take a taxi (US$3 to US$5).

BUS

The two bus stations in Changuinola are a stone's throw apart. From Terminal Urraca, buses to David (US$8) depart hourly from 5am to 6pm via Almirante (US$1). There is one bus daily to Panama City (US$24), leaving at 7am and arriving at 6pm.

At Transporte Sincotavecop, there are buses to Guabito (US$0.70, every 20 minutes) from 6am to 7:30pm, El Silencio (US$0.50, every 20 minutes) from 5am to 8:30pm, Almirante (US$1, every 20 minutes) from 6am to 10pm, David (US$8, every 40 minutes) from 5:15am to 7pm, and San José in Costa Rica (US$8, one bus daily), departing at 10am and arriving 3:30pm.

TAXI
Taxis can be found at the city bus station. A taxi ride from Changuinola to the Costa Rican border at Guabito takes about 15 minutes and costs US$5.

AROUND CHANGUINOLA
San-San Pond Sak Wetlands
These fantastic wetlands, also called Humedal de San-San Pond Sak, are 5km north of central Changuinola and harbor a great variety of flora and fauna. The fresh water of San-San is one of the few known Central American habitats for manatee, in addition to sloths, river otters, white-faced monkey, caiman, iguanas, conejo pintado poison-dart frogs and the more than 60 bird species inhabiting the wetlands. At the beach green, leatherback, loggerhead and hawksbill turtles come in to lay their eggs.

This protected area is administered by a conservation organization called AAM-VECONA, which works with ANAM. The US$3 park entry fee helps support the conservation organization. To arrange a trip, stop by the Changuinola **ANAM office** (☎ 758-6603) or contact **AAMVECONA** (☎ 758-9461) directly. Trips cost from US$25 to US$35 depending on the size of your group, with a further nightly fee of around US$8. The wetlands make a fine day trip for those looking for a bit of off-the-beaten-path adventure; there's also rustic accommodations out on the beach. On a tour of the wetlands you'll travel by 4WD to San San Puente (US$2, 10 minutes from Changuinola), from where you'll take a slow boat tour through an area rich with vegetation and excellent birdlife.

Once you reach the beach you can rent a tent or stay in the rustic house on stilts. It has three rooms, simple showers, a flush toilet (fed by rainwater) and a cooking area. Solar panels provide the electricity. There may or may not be bedding (ask at ANAM). At night you can accompany conservationists out to observe the turtle nesting sites. If you want to volunteer, this is an excellent place to do it.

Regardless of the house, bring your own food and drink, a sleeping bag or blanket, mosquito net, and bug spray. The chitras and mosquitoes here will show no mercy. Dress warmly; it does cool off at night.

Las Delicias
Set in a hilly area of lush rain forest, the small indigenous community of Las Delicias lies along the Sixaola River, 20km from Guabito (the border of Costa Rica). Among the attractions here are waterfalls, abundant wildlife and impressive lookout points over the Sixaola River Valley and the Talamanca Mountains. It's part of the protected area managed by the Las Delicias community. These local residents have recently shifted their source

---

TURTLES' TRAGIC TROUBLES

Four of the world's eight sea turtle species nest on the beaches of the Archipiélago de Bocas del Toro, particularly the long beaches on the northern side of Isla Bastimentos. The loggerheads appear from April to September, the leatherbacks in May and June, the hawksbills in July and the greens in July and August.

Sea turtles leave the water only to lay their eggs. Two months after the eggs are laid, the hatchlings break loose from their shells, leave their sandy nests and enter the sea – if they are not first eaten by raccoons, birds or dogs. Many hatchlings, which are guided to the sea by moonlight, die because people using flashlights unintentionally steer the tiny turtles into the rain forest, where they are preyed upon or get lost and die from starvation or the heat.

The turtles also have human predators to contend with. Throughout Panama, many still eat turtles and/or their eggs, which is why they are now threatened with regional extinction. AAM-VECONA (Association of Friends and Neighbors of the Coast and its Environment, in Spanish) is one community-based organization that is working toward their preservation. They're based in the San-San Pond Sak Wetlands. To take a trip with them or to volunteer, see p246.

f income from harvesting and logging to reservation and ecotourism. Visiting them s one way you can make a very positive contribution to the environment.

There's much to see here, and the Teribe are quite proud of their wildlife. On a day trip o the area, you'll get the chance to take a boat our through the Sixaola and Yorkin Rivers, ollowed by a hike through rain forest or possibly a horseback ride (up to you). The villagers will then prepare a lunch – it's usually resh fish, and amazingly good. Prices for an outing are quite reasonable, at around US$20 per person. At the time this was written, they vere planning to offer cabins for overnight visitors (US$16 per person). Hardy travelers can also string a hammock up at one of the anchos (bring bug spray and a mosquito net). Remember, this is a rustic, untouched place. There's no electricity here, and you'll need your own water (or a purifier).

You can make arrangements through the Changuinola **ANAM office** (☎ 758-6603) or by phoning **Las Delicias** (☎ 600-4042) directly. To get there, take a bus from Changuinola to Las Tablas (US$1.60, 1½ hours) and from there a chiva to Las Delicias (US$0.90). You can also negotiate a price with one of the 4WD taxis in Changuinola.

Wetso & Parque Internacional La Amistad

The 407,000-hectare **Parque Internacional La Amistad** (park entry fee US$3) was established jointly by Panama and Costa Rica – hence its name, La Amistad (Friendship). In Panama the park covers portions of Chiriquí and Bocas del Toro Provinces and is home to members of three Indian tribes: the Teribe, the Bribri and the Ngöbe-Buglé.

The park, slightly more than half of which is in Panama, contains some gorgeous rain forest that remains home to a recorded 90 mammal species (including jaguars and pumas) and more than 300 bird species (including resplendent quetzals and harpy eagles). Most of the park's area is rather remote, high up in the Talamanca Mountains.

In addition to the Wetso entrance, it's possible to enter the park from Chiriquí Province in Las Nubes near Cerro Punta. See p221 for details.

To get near the park you first have to catch a bus from Changuinola to the hamlet of El Silencio. From there you take a 45-minute boat ride up the Río Teribe. In El Silencio there's often a *colectivo* boat, which will cost about US$5 per person; if you have to hire the boat yourself it will cost US$15 to US$25. If you go to the ANAM office in Changuinola (p244) and tell the people there you want to go to Wetso, ANAM can radio ahead and make sure there is someone at the river's edge.

Once on the river you'll pass hills blanketed with rain forest and intermittent waterfalls; the backdrop is always the glorious Talamanca range. The jungle comes all the way down to the river water. There are a few sandbars, but the current's too swift for crocodiles. You're likely to see iguanas lounging in trees (though you'll have to look hard for them) and lots of birds. After about 45 minutes on the river, you'll see a sign on the right bank that announces your arrival at Wetso, which is actually a protected area but still some ways from the park.

Before the US invasion in 1989, Wetso was named Pana-Jungla and was the jungle-survival training facility for Panamanian soldiers. Many of the old structures (barracks, mess hall, chapel, armory, serpentarium etc) are still there, though dilapidated.

There's a 3.5km loop trail at Wetso that cuts through secondary and virgin rain forest, with excellent bird watching. You can also take a dip in the river, but be careful not to wade out very far, or the current will carry you downstream. Keep in mind that the guides at Wetso, all of whom are Indians raised in the area, speak only Spanish and Naso, their first language.

There's a rustic **guest lodge** (lodgings per person US$12, meals US$3-4) in Wetso that is run by and benefits the Teribe (Naso) Indians. They can prepare meals for you and lead you on guided tours through the jungle. It's a five-hour hike from Wetso into Parque Internacional La Amistad. Contact ANAM or call the organization **ODESEN** (Organización para el Desarrollo Sostenible Ecoturístico Naso; Organization for the Sustainable Development of Naso Ecotourism; ☎ 620-0192).

GUABITO

For information on entry requirements at the border crossing between Panama and Costa Rica at Guabito (Sixaola on the Costa Rican side), see Costa Rican Border Crossings in the Transportation (p309).

BOCAS DEL TORO PROVINCE

Colón Province

CONTENTS

Colón	252
Around Colón	254
West of Colón	255
Portobelo	257
Isla Grande	261
Playa Blanca	263
Nombre de Dios	263
Jimmy's Caribbean Dive Resort	265

Panama's fourth most populous province has a very rich history. In the colonial era, gold and silver pilfered from indigenous peoples of Panama and Peru were stored at the Caribbean coastal towns of Nombre de Dios and Portobelo until ships arrived to take the bullion to Spain. For decades these were the wealthiest towns on Earth, veritable treasure troves that attracted scores of pirates.

Today you can visit the ruins of the forts that stood guard over Portobelo. These impressive Spanish ruins and the old colonial buildings of the town were declared a United Nations World Heritage site in 1980. Today they make for a fascinating visit. Many visitors also use the area as a base for scuba-diving trips. Good diving lies just outside of Portobelo; several operators (such as Jimmy's Caribbean Dive Resort and Scubaportobelo) go further out to some exceptional diving.

Northeast of Portobelo lies the picturesque island of Isla Grande. This is a popular weekend getaway for many urbanites from Panama City, and offers a selection of hotels and restaurants overlooking the crashing waves. The absence of cars ensures a level of tranquility at the sleepy village.

Several of the Panama Canal's most impressive features are found in this province. The Gatún Locks are the canal's largest set of locks, and allow visitors to see the impressive engineering at work, as ships are raised and lowered 26 meters.

The province also provides some fine exploring for those looking to get off the beaten path. Escobal, a small village west of Colón, has some fine camping, hiking and fishing opportunities. Near Portobelo, there are some great hiking opportunities through rain forest full of wildlife, crystal streams and hidden waterfalls. Local guides can lead the way.

COLÓN PROVINCE

HIGHLIGHTS

- Wandering through historic **Portobelo** (p257), home to the well-preserved ruins of several colonial forts
- Soaking up the natural beauty of **Isla Grande** (p261), a popular weekend getaway ringed by fine snorkeling and dive sites
- Admiring the engineering of **Gatún Locks** (p254), the largest of the Panama Canal's three sets of locks
- Taking in the past at **Fuerte San Lorenzo** (p255), built of cut coral and still displaying its old cannons
- Laying eyes on the impressive **Gatún Dam** (p255), once the world's largest earthen dam

| ■ AREA: 4890 SQ KM | ■ ELEVATION: SEA LEVEL TO 979M | ■ POPULATION: 204,200 |

COLÓN PROVINCE

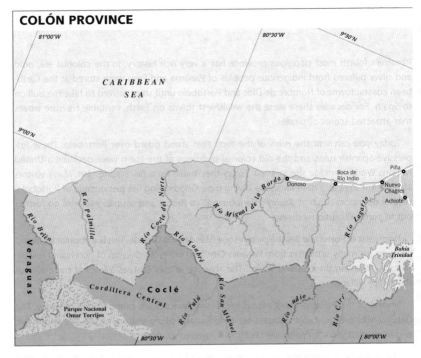

History

The town of Nombre de Dios played a major role in Spain's involvement in the New World. Goods from Spain were unloaded there and sent across the isthmus to the city of Panama. Moving in the opposite direction were gold and silver taken from Indians on the isthmus and in Peru. During the 200 years in which Nombre de Dios and, later, Portobelo acted as temporary warehouses for pilfered riches, the ports came under repeated attack from English, French, Dutch and Welsh pirates. Many attacks were successful, as were the assaults on galleons that tried to reach Spain after taking on a king's treasure.

The Spaniards built forts to protect their fortunes, but the forts weren't enough. In 1572 the English privateer Francis Drake easily entered Nombre de Dios – 'the treasure house of the world,' as he called it – and was deciding which riches to plunder when a wound forced his retreat. Drake returned to Nombre de Dios in 1596, and this time his men not only emptied the treasure house but also torched the town.

In 1671 the Welsh buccaneer Sir Henry Morgan took Fuerte San Lorenzo, at the mouth of the Río Chagres, then crossed the isthmus and sacked Panamá. In 1739 Portobelo, which was plundered twice during the 17th century, was destroyed by British admiral Edward Vernon. After this blow, Spain abandoned the Panama crossing in favor of sailing around Cape Horn to the southern coast of the isthmus.

From then until the mid-19th century, the Caribbean coast of Panama was quiet. That changed in 1848 with the California gold rush, when thousands of people traveled from the east coast of the USA to the west coast via Panama. The Panama Railroad was built between 1850 and 1855 to profit from these travelers.

In 1881 a French company began work on a sea-level canal across the isthmus, but it gave up the effort eight years later after the monetary costs had proved too great, and yellow fever and malaria had killed 22,000 workers. Twenty-five years later, the US effort to build a lock-and-lake canal was successful, and the sleepy backwater town

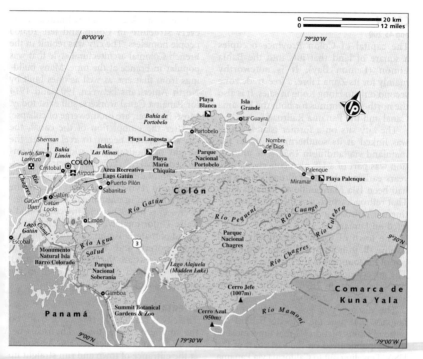

of Colón, at the Caribbean terminus of the canal, was transformed into a vibrant provincial capital.

Colón received another big boost in 1948, when a free-trade zone was created within its borders. Today, the Zona Libre is the largest free-trade zone in the Americas. It links producers in North America, the Far East and Europe with the Latin American market. More than 1600 companies and several dozen banks conduct business in the high-walled, 482-hectare compound in the southeastern corner of town, but not much wealth crosses the walls into the city itself, which remains largely rundown.

Climate
Owing to its location on Panama's northern Caribbean coast, Colón gets an awful lot of rain year-round. Terms like 'rainy' and 'dry' seasons don't apply here.

Dangers & Annoyances
Although the city of Colón isn't as dangerous as it used to be, crime is still a problem. It's unwise to walk around at night, and even during the day you should exercise caution. Some travelers prefer to bypass the city altogether; however, if you're sensible it's unlikely you'll encounter any problems.

Getting There & Away
One of the more scenic ways to arrive in Colón is via the restored Panama Railway Company train (see p113). There are also short flights from Panama City and dozens of daily buses traveling between the two cities.

Getting Around
From Colón, buses travel within the province along two routes: buses along the 'Costa Arriba' route head northeast to Portobelo and Nombre de Dios (some going all the way to Miramar); while the 'Costa Abajo' buses travel beside Lago Gatún to Escobal then north to Achiote. Travelers from Panama City heading to Portobelo or Isla Grande can bypass Colón city by taking a bus as far as Sabanitas and transferring to a Costa Arriba bus there.

COLÓN

pop 45,200

The capital of Colón Province occupies a square of land that juts into the Bahía Limón (Lemon Bay). It is noteworthy mainly for its Zona Libre, a free-trade zone second only to Hong Kong in sales. It is also the northern terminus for both the Panama Canal and the Panama Railroad.

The city sits on a former island, which was linked at its southernmost tip to the mainland via landfill in 1852. The unification was part of a US plan conceived three years earlier to build a railroad from what had been Isla Manzanillo to Panama City. That railroad, which was the first transcontinental railroad in the world, was completed on January 27, 1855.

The town of Colón was initially called Aspinwall, in honor of William Aspinwall, one of the founders of the Panama Railroad. The government of Colombia changed the name to Colón in 1890, and the adjacent area was named Cristóbal.

The discovery of gold in California in January 1848 was the impetus behind the railroad's construction. At that time, most of the US public lived on the east coast of the USA. Traveling out to California via Panama was cheaper, quicker and less dangerous than traveling through the USA's vast heartland, which was home to many hostile Indians. Gold seekers took steamships from the east coast to the mouth of the Río Chagres and walked the Sendero Las Cruces to the Pacific coast (a distance of approximately 80km); then boarded ships bound for California. The Panama Railroad eliminated the long walk.

From its 1855 completion until the arrival of a transcontinental railroad in the USA in 1869, the Panama Railroad was the only rapid transit across the continental western hemisphere. During this time, Colón became a real city, as scores of businesses opened to accommodate the travelers.

When the US transcontinental railroad was established, Colón suddenly became an economically depressed city, and it remained that way until 1881, when the French began construction of the interoceanic canal. The French enterprise brought with it a new batch of laborers and revived the sluggish economy.

The French were four years into their project when a fire, set by a Colombian hoping to spark a revolution, burned nearly every structure in Colón and left 10,000 people homeless. The city was rebuilt in the French Colonial architectural style that was popular in France at the time. Many buildings from that era, as well as ones built by North Americans between 1904 and 1914 for Panama Canal workers, still exist today. Most, however, are on the verge of collapse.

After the completion of the canal, the city's economy began to reel under the weight of thousands of suddenly unemployed canal workers and their families. The Zona Libre was created in 1948 in an attempt to revive the city, but none of the US$10 billion in annual commercial turnover seems to get beyond the compound's walls. Unfortunately, the Zona Libre is an island of materialism in a sea of unemployment, poverty and crime (Colón's rates in all three areas are the highest in Panama). Colón can be a dodgy place even in the daytime; take care if walking around.

Orientation

The city is reached via two major roads on the southern side of town. The roads become Av Amador Guerrero and Av Bolívar at the entrance of town and run straight up the grid-patterned city, ending near Colón's northern waterfront.

Perpendicular to these avenues are, primarily, numbered streets. Calle 16 is the first of these you'll cross as you enter the city from the south; Calle 1 is at the northern end of town. As you enter town, you can turn right on Calle 13 and drive approximately eight blocks to reach the main entrance of the Zona Libre. If you continue another three blocks you reach Colón 2000, the city's cruise ship port. If you turn left on Calle 13, you'll pass the passenger train terminal; another 200m is the port of Cristóbal.

Information

Given Colón's high rate of crime, the safest place to withdraw money is the **BNP** ATM in the Colón 2000 cruise ship port.

Sights

ZONA LIBRE

In Colón's sprawling, free-trade zone are the showrooms of 1650 companies and the branch offices of 21 banks. Here, you can

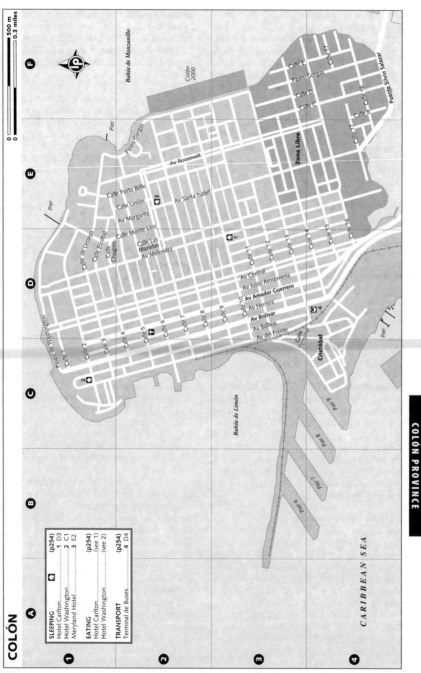

COLÓN

SLEEPING	(p254)
Hotel Carlton	1 D3
Hotel Washington	2 C1
Meryland Hotel	3 E2

EATING	(p254)
Hotel Carlton	(see 1)
Hotel Washington	(see 2)

TRANSPORT	(p254)
Terminal de Buses	4 D4

Bahía de Manzanillo

Colón 2000

Calle E
Paseo Gorgas
Calle D
Calle C

Zona Libre

Calle 17
Calle 16
Calle B
Calle 17
Puente Silvio Salazar

Pier

Paseo Gorgas

Av Roosevelt

Calle Porto Bello
Calle Limón
Av Margarita
Av Santa Isabel

Pier

Calle de Lesseps
Calle Escobal
Calle Monte Lirio
Calle Chagres
Calle Las Marietas
Av Melendez

Av Central
Av Justo Arosemena
Av Amador Guerrero
Av Herrera
Av Bolívar
Av Balboa
Av del Frente

Calle 11
Calle 12
Calle 3
Calle 10
Calle 14
Calle 15
Calle 16

Cristóbal
Calle Terminal

Paseo de Washington

Calle 1
Calle 2
Calle 3
Calle 4
Calle 5
Calle 6
Calle 7
Calle 8
Calle 9

Bahía de Limón

Pier 6
Pier 7
Pier 8
Pier 9

CARIBBEAN SEA

500 m
0.3 miles

buy items at wholesale prices and avoid paying taxes.

The Zona Libre doesn't make for compelling window-shopping. Most items for sale are utilitarian rather than luxurious, and little effort is put into presentation, because the big buyers here know what they want.

COLÓN 2000

In December 2000, the self-proclaimed 'Caribbean cruise port of shopping and entertainment' called Colón 2000 opened on the east side of Colón. It's a rather modest affair with a couple of restaurants, souvenir shops and a grocery store.

Sleeping & Eating

There are quite a few hotels in Colón, but most are located in unsafe areas. Those mentioned here have guards and secure parking.

Hotel Carlton (☎ 441-0111; fax 447-0114; Calle 10; d/tw/tr US$30/35/45; ☒ ℗) This four-story hotel is the closest to the Zona Libre and every one of its 64 comfortable rooms contains at least one firm bed, air-con, cable TV, a hot-water private bathroom and a phone.

Meryland Hotel (☎ 441-7128; cnr Calle 7 & Av Santa Isabel; s/d US$44/50; ☒ ℗) This hotel has 79 comfortable guestrooms with air-con, private hot-water bathroom, cable TV, telephone and good beds.

Hotel Washington (☎ 441-7133; fax 441-7397; Calle 2; s/d/tr US$50/59/70; ☒ ☛ ℗) This bills itself as the grand dame of Colón's hotels – and indeed it was once grand – but today it's only a monstrosity in need of millions of dollars worth of updating. In spite of its wear, its guestrooms are popular and come with air-con, cable TV, telephone and private hot-water bathroom. There is a restaurant, a swimming pool and a casino on the premises.

Getting There & Away

AIR

Aeroperlas (☎ 403-1038) flies from Colón to Panama City (US$36, 15 minutes) at 9:10am Monday to Friday, and 5:35pm Monday to Thursday. Flights from Panama City to Colón depart at 8:45am Monday to Friday and 5:10pm Monday to Thursday.

BUS

Colón's **bus terminal** (☎ 441-4044; cnr Calle Terminal & Av Bolívar) serves towns throughout Colón Province, including the following:

Escobal/Cuipo (US$1/1.50, 1hr, hourly, 10am-7pm)
La Guayra (US$2.25, 1½hr, hourly, 6:30am-6pm)
Nombre de Dios (US$3, 1½hr, 66km, hourly, 6:30am-6pm)
Palenque (US$4, 2hr, 78km, hourly, 6:30am-5:30pm)
Portobelo (US$1.30, 1hr, 43km, hourly, 6:30am-9pm, to 6pm Sun)

Additionally, there are buses departing this terminal for Panama City (US$2, two hours, every 20 minutes) and vice versa.

TRAIN

The **Panama Railway Company** (Panama City ☎ 317-6070) operates a luxury passenger train from Panama City to Colón (one-way/roundtrip US$20/35, one hour). It leaves the capital at 7:15am and returns from Colón at 5:15pm. It's a lovely ride, with the tracks following the canal, and at times traversing thick jungle.

Getting Around

If you visit Colón, don't walk any further than you must. If you arrive by bus, it's best to take a taxi from the station to your destination.

AROUND COLÓN
Gatún Locks

The **Gatún Locks** (admission free; ☒ 8am-4pm), 10km south of Colón, raise southbound ships 25.9m from Caribbean waters to the level of Lago Gatún. From there, ships travel 37km to the Pedro Miguel Locks, which lower southbound ships 9.3m to Lago Miraflores, a small body of water that separates the two sets of Pacific locks. The ships are lowered to sea level at the Miraflores Locks.

Not only are the Gatún Locks the largest of the three sets, but their size is mind-boggling. In his superlative book *The Path Between the Seas*, David McCullough notes that if stood on its end, a single lock would have been the tallest structure on Earth at the time it was built, taller by several meters than even the Eiffel Tower. And each chamber could have accommodated the *Titanic* with plenty of room to spare.

The amount of concrete poured to construct the locks at Gatún – 1,820,000 cubic meters – was record-setting. That amount of concrete is enough to build a wall 2.4m thick, 3.6m high and 213km long. The concrete was brought from a giant mixing plant to the construction site by railroad cars that ran on a circular track. Huge buckets that were maneuvered by cranes carried the wet concrete from the railroad cars and poured it into enormous steel forms. The forms themselves were moved into place by locomotives. It took four years to build the locks.

Today you can see the locks in action. From a well-placed viewing stand opposite the control tower, you can watch southbound ships enter the two lower chambers at sea level, rise to the level of Lago Gatún in three steps and then steam onto the lake en route to the Pedro Miguel and Miraflores Locks. The whole process takes from one to two hours.

Just before you reach the viewing stand, you'll see a model of the entire canal and photos of it under construction. Additionally, you will be given a brochure in English or Spanish that provides information about the canal.

Buses to the Gatún Locks leave the Colón bus terminal hourly (US$1.25, 20 minutes). If you arrive by taxi, however, you can stop here before heading on to Gatún Dam – another 2km away. A taxi ride from Colón to the locks and dam and back should cost no more than US$15 per party. Agree on a price before leaving.

Gatún Dam

The Gatún Dam, which was constructed in 1908 to shore up the Río Chagres and to create Lago Gatún, was the world's largest earthen dam until the Fort Peck Dam was built in Montana (USA) in 1940. And until Lake Mead was formed by the 1936 completion of the Hoover Dam on the Nevada–Arizona (USA) border, Lago Gatún was the world's largest artificial body of water. When the Gatún Dam's spillway is open, the sight is quite a rush. The guard at the entrance to the Gatún Locks speaks English and can tell you if the spillway is open.

Power generated by the dam drives all the electrical equipment involved in the operation of the Panama Canal, including the locomotives that tow ships through the locks. Another interesting bit of information: when Lago Gatún was created, it submerged 262 sq km of jungle. Also submerged were entire villages (the people were relocated) and the original tracks of the Panama Railroad.

For directions on reaching the dam, see Gatún Locks, above.

Fuerte San Lorenzo

Fuerte San Lorenzo (Fort San Lorenzo; www.wmfpanama.org in Spanish; ☀ 8am-4pm) is perched at the mouth of the Río Chagres, on a promontory west of the canal. It was via this river that the pirate Henry Morgan gained access to the interior in 1671, enabling him to sack the original Panama City (the ruins of that destroyed settlement, today known as Panamá Viejo, are still visible).

Like the fortresses at Portobelo, this Spanish fort is built of blocks of cut coral, and displays rows of old cannons. A British cannon among the Spanish ones bespeaks the time in the 17th century when British pirates overcame the fort. Much of San Lorenzo is well preserved, including the moat, the cannons and the arched rooms. The fort commands a wide view of the river and bay far below.

There is no fee to enter this or any of Panama's other forts. There's no bus service to the fort, but you can take a taxi there from Colón (about US$20). If you're driving, go to the Gatún Locks, continue past the stoplight near the northern entrance to the locks and then follow the signs directing you to the dam, 2km away. Drive over the dam and follow the 'Fuerte San Lorenzo' signs. These will lead you to the entrance of **Sherman** (☎ 433-1676; www.sanlorenzo.org.pa), a former US military base, where you'll be asked to show ID. Once you've done this, you will be allowed to proceed the remaining 9km to Fuerte San Lorenzo.

WEST OF COLÓN

The many small coastal communities west of Colón (Piña, Nuevo Chagres and Boca de Río Indio, to name a few) are relatively unattractive with little to offer the tourist. The beaches along this stretch of coast are strewn with litter and the surf contains lots of riptides. There are no banks, post offices, hotels or restaurants to speak of.

However, southwest of Colón, along the banks of the Lago Gatún, is the fishing village of Escobal, which with the help of the US Peace Corps has put together a homestay program for tourists, and a host of activities that will no doubt interest some adventurous readers.

Escobal

This small, laid-back town (population 2181) lies in the Panama Canal watershed rain forest bordering Lake Gatún. Inhabited mostly by the descendants of former canal builders and people who were displaced with the flooding of the Río Chagres, Escobal contains one of the most densely diverse populations in Panama. Here, residents are as likely to be the descendants of Haitians, Jamaicans or Colombians as they are Panamanians. And many of the people living in Escobal today hail from the Península de Azuero and have more in common culturally with Spaniards than they do with the Afro-Antilleans who comprise the majority of the population of nearby Colón.

ACTIVITIES

From the community campsite (see above), you can arrange **fishing trips** (per person $10) onto the lake (usually for peacock bass); boat tours of Lake Gatún (where you might spy white-faced and black monkeys, perhaps a caiman), horseback riding in the forest, or bird watching.

FESTIVALS & EVENTS

During the months of January and February, every Friday, Saturday and Sunday night, the town celebrates its Afro-Antillean heritage through Los Congos, a yearly tradition which communicates the slave folklore through song and dance.

SLEEPING & EATING

The friendly Escobolanians are one of the main reasons to visit Escobal. There are no hotels in town, so some of the people have literally opened their homes to visitors. A **homestay program** (s/d US$6/10) created in early 2001 allows for tourists to be placed in private residences, where they are assured of a bed, a fan and a simple local breakfast. You also have the option to **camp** (per person US$2) beside a family's home and use their bathroom (tent not included).

Interested readers should contact homestay program coordinators **Granville 'Bill' Eversley** (☎ 434-6020), who speaks English and Spanish, or **Saturnino Díaz** or **Aida Gonzalez** (☎ 434-6017/6106), who speak Spanish. If you show up in Escobal unannounced, go to the Restaurante Doña Nelly (there are only three restaurants in Escobal) and ask for Saturnino or Aida, the restaurant's owners.

There's also a community-based **campsite** (La Propriedad de Tuñon, also called La Propriedad de Placido; cabin US$10) on a peninsula surrounded by a beautiful, well-stocked freshwater lake. The campsite offers rustic cabins with electricity and running water. There are clean bathrooms with showers, hammocks, picnic tables and access to the lake for swimming and canoeing (on-site canoes for rent).

The town has three restaurants, which offer traditional Colón cuisine (fish with coconut rice and fried vegetables). There are also several food markets and a couple of cantinas.

Achiote & San Lorenzo Protected Area

About 13km north of Escobal is the picturesque village of Achiote, a friendly community with a mixed population of black, Spanish and Indian descent. The great attraction of Achiote is its proximity to the 10,000-hectare **San Lorenzo Protected Area** (www.sanlorenzo.org.pa). The area is renowned for its bird watching, with access to secondary forest teeming with plant and animal life. You can take some lovely walks to waterfalls and natural ponds, visit organic shade-grown coffee farms, and hike to splendid lookouts with views of the protected area and the Río Chagres.

The best way to explore the area is to hire one of the local guides, operating with the ecotourism group Los Rapaces, named for the raptors that migrate seasonally overhead every autumn and spring. At the time this was written, Los Rapaces was developing more trails in the area. **Fermina Moreno** (☎ 635-9973) is the local contact of the organization and is a great source of information about the area. Other local birding guides are **Julian de La Cruz** (☎ 601-7388) and **Michael Castro** (☎ 648-3480). Guides generally charge US$15 per group for a two-hour hike.

Visitors can also stop in the **Centro El Tucán** (☎ 628-9000, 226-6602; ☷ 8am-4pm Mon-Fri). This community learning and visitors center lies on the main road, 2km from the San Lorenzo Protected Area.

The center has an exhibition room, and an excellent documentation center on the flora and fauna, human ecology and history of the area. You can pick up a map of the

San Lorenzo National Park and surrounding attractions here.

Fuertes Davis & Espinar

Just before reaching Colón from Panama City, there's a turnoff called Quatro Altos that leads to the former US military bases of Fort Davis and Fort Gulick, which were handed over to Panama as part of the Carter-Torrijos Treaty of 1977. At both, you'll still see former military buildings that the Panamanian government is allowing to deteriorate while it decides what to do with them.

However, at Fuerte Espinar (called Gullick before the handover), a Spanish hotel chain has converted Building 400 into a giant hotel, the **Meliá Panamá Canal** (☎ 470-1100; www.solmelia.com; d from US$75; 🖳). The US$30-million hotel, which features guestrooms with all the amenities, a cluster of swimming pools with a swim-up bar, and numerous reasonably priced tours (fishing, kayaking and night safaris among them), occupies a finger of land that juts into Lago Gatún.

Building 400 used to be home to the US Army School of the Americas, which was established in 1949 and trained more than 34,000 Latin American soldiers before moving to Fort Benning, Georgia, in 1984. The school was created to keep communism out of Latin America, and quickly that translated into teaching Latin American soldiers how to thwart armed communist insurgencies.

The school graduated some of the worst human-rights violators of our time, including former Argentine President Leopoldo Galtieri, who 'disappeared' thousands during Argentina's Dirty War of the 1970s; and El Salvador's Roberto D'Aubuisson, who led death squads that killed Archbishop Oscar Romero and thousands of other Salvadorans during the 1980s. Not too surprisingly, the Meliá's staff has painted over all evidence that the hotel has ever been anything but an upscale fun center.

At former Fort Davis, travelers who have business in Colón but who don't want to stay there or at the Meliá will find a very attractive alternative in the **Davis Suites** (☎ 473-0639; www.davis.suites.8k.com; ste US$55; 🖳). There are 10 spacious suites with two or three beds, a kitchenette and a living room in each. Every suite comes with air-con, a private hot-water bathroom and cable TV. The friendly staff here can arrange kayaking and hiking tours into the lush area nearby.

To get there, follow the signs from the Quatro Altos turnoff. Be advised that there are few taxis in the area; Meliá staff can call one for you.

PORTOBELO
pop 4100

This bayside town, 99km from Panama City and 43km from Colón, was given the name 'Puerto Bello' (Beautiful Port) by Christopher Columbus in 1502 on account of the beauty of its natural harbor. As often happened with Spanish names, this one was abbreviated over time.

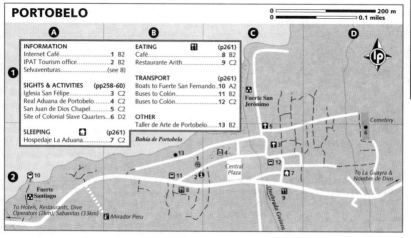

PORTOBELO

0	200 m
0	0.1 miles

INFORMATION
Internet Café.................................1 B2
IPAT Tourism office.....................2 B2
Selvaventuras...........................(see 8)

SIGHTS & ACTIVITIES   (pp258–60)
Iglesia San Félipe........................3 C2
Real Aduana de Portobelo..........4 C2
San Juan de Dios Chapel.............5 C2
Site of Colonial Slave Quarters....6 D2

SLEEPING   🛏   (p261)
Hospedaje La Aduana................7 C2

EATING   🍴   (p261)
Café...8 C2
Restaurante Arith.......................9 C2

TRANSPORT   (p261)
Boats to Fuerte San Fernando...10 A2
Buses to Colón..........................11 B2
Buses to Colón..........................12 C2

OTHER
Taller de Arte de Portobelo......13 B2

Fuerte San Jerónimo

Cemetery

Bahía de Portobelo

Central Plaza

Fuerte Santiago

To Hotels, Restaurants, Dive Operators (2km); Sabanitas (33km)

Mirador Peru

Quebrada Guinea

To La Guayra & Nombre de Dios

Portobelo consisted of not more than 10 houses when Juan Bautista Antonelli visited in 1586. Antonelli designed many fortresses in the Spanish Indies and was sent to examine the Caribbean ports. After the celebrated Italian engineer noted how well Portobelo's bay lent itself to defensive works, King Félipe II ordered that Nombre de Dios be abandoned and Portobelo colonized.

Despite the order, it wasn't until after Drake's 1596 attack on Nombre de Dios that a gradual transfer took place. In addition to Portobelo, two other forts were built beside the bay. But in spite of these defenses, Portobelo suffered numerous invasions at the hands of buccaneers and the English navy.

However, not all of the invasions were the products of superior tactics or numbers. In 1679 the crews of two English ships and one French vessel united in an attack on Portobelo. They landed 200 men at such a distance from the town that it took them three nights of marching to reach it. As they neared Portobelo, they were seen by a farmer, who ran ahead to sound the alarm. But the pirates followed so closely behind that the town had no time to prepare. Unaware of how small the buccaneer force was, all the inhabitants fled.

The pirates spent two days and nights in Portobelo, collecting plunder in constant apprehension that the Spaniards would return in great numbers and attack them. However, the buccaneers got back to their ships unmolested and then distributed 160 pieces of eight to each man. At the time, one piece of eight would pay for a night's stay at the best inn in Seville.

Today Portobelo is a sleepy town. Most of its inhabitants make their living from the sea or tending to crops. Their homes are situated among the ruins of military buildings, half of which retain some of their original form. The other half are simply small piles of cut stone or coral, and their origins have been obscured by time.

In addition to the ruins in and about the town, Portobelo is popular for its scuba diving. There are eight major dive sites in the area (including a 110-foot cargo ship and a C-45 twin-engine plane), and their quality ranges from fair to good. There is no exceptional diving in the vicinity of Portobelo, but few people leave here unhappy because the diving offers very good value.

There is only one modest pension in Portobelo and several hotels on the Sabanitas–Portobelo road into town. Likewise, there are a couple of simple restaurants in town and several good places along the Sabanitas–Portobelo road.

Orientation

Portobelo consists of about 15 square blocks of mostly rundown homes and businesses beside a paved, two-lane road. That road intersects with the Panama City–Colón road at the town of Sabanitas, 33km to the west.

East of Portobelo, the road forks after 9km. The right branch of the road extends 14km further east to Nombre de Dios; the left branch extends 11km to the hamlet of La Guayra, where visitors can hire boats to take them to Isla Grande, a few minutes' ride away.

Information

The **IPAT tourist office** (☎ 448-2200; Calle Principal; ☻ 9am-5pm), just off the main road through town, has a small display of paintings focusing on the Congo in the back room (only Spanish is spoken). Across the street from there is an **Internet café** (per hr US$1.50; ☻ 8:30am-4pm Mon-Fri).

Sights & Activities
FORTS

To defend his bullion and galleons from pirates, King Félipe II ordered forts be constructed at Portobelo. By 1601 two had been built, both near the mouth of the bay: Fuerte San Félipe was on the northern side, and on the southern side was Fuerte San Diego. In the years that followed, many more fortresses would be erected, some on the sites of earlier, less substantial forts.

Today the remnants of Fuerte San Jerónimo and Fuerte Santiago can still be seen near town, and the ruins of **Fuerte San Fernando** occupy a grassy flat across the bay from town. Sadly, most of San Fernando was taken by Americans who used its walls to create the breakwater protecting the northern end of the Panama Canal. Boats can be hired at the water's edge (see Tours, p259) near Fuerte Santiago for the trip across the bay to this fort.

Fuerte Santiago is the first fort you'll see as you near town from the west. It was built after British admiral Edward Vernon's 1739 attack and contains many musket ports. Several of its walls are 3m thick, made entirely of cut coral – or 'reef rock,' as the Spaniards called it. Coral was used because it is as tough as granite and yet as light as pumice, and can be shaped with a saw. The ruins at Fuerte Santiago include an officers' quarters, an artillery shed, a sentry box, a barracks, and batteries.

On a hill overlooking Santiago and much of the bay is a small but well-preserved watchtower called **Mirador Perú** built at the same time as Santiago. There are steps carved into the hillside to reach the lookout.

Fuerte San Jerónimo, closer to the center of town, was the largest fortress ever built to protect the bay. If you're short on time, San Jerónimo is more complete and makes for a better visit than Santiago. Beyond its impressive gateway are the remains of the officers' quarters, a barracks and a guardroom. Facing the mouth of the bay are 18 cannon embrasures. Some of the original cannons remain exactly where the Spanish troops left them when they returned home in 1821 – the year Panama declared its independence from Spain.

REAL ADUANA DE PORTOBELO

The handsome, two-story Royal Customs House of Portobelo was originally built in 1630 to serve as the *contaduría* (counting house) for all the king's gold. It was in this building that the treasure brought across the isthmus was recorded and stored until it could be placed on galleons and sailed to Spain.

According to early records, the building was originally called the King's House, and 253 soldiers were assigned to it. The structure was severely damaged twice – by cannon fire in 1744 and by a strong earthquake in 1882.

The **Real Aduana** (admission US$1; 8am-4pm) consists of two main rooms, which are now used as exhibition halls. One room displays dozens of robes donated by believers, which are placed on the statue of the Black Christ every October when thousands of followers worship the icon (see p260). Most of the robes are made of purple velvet. Among the donors are boxer Roberto Duran and salsa star Ismael Rivera.

The other room contains replicas of Spanish-colonial rifles, sketches of Portobelo's forts, many photos taken of the *contaduría* during the 20th century, and a couple of dozen rusty cannon balls. Signage is in Spanish only.

Don't forget to visit the building's 2nd floor, which features an intriguing collection of photos and drawings of the Spanish-colonial fortresses that exist throughout Latin America. Also, don't overlook the bronze cannon at the entrance; it was recovered from a sunken galleon and bears a Spanish coat of arms, and the date of manufacture (1617).

DIVING & SNORKELING

The diving around Portobelo may not be spectacular, but offers good value for money. There are two dive operators on the Sabanitas–Portobelo road, west of town. There's a third outfit, Jimmy's Caribbean (p265), closer to Nombre de Dios. With any of these operators, it's best to let them know you're coming.

Twin Oceans Dive Center (☎ 448-2067; www .twinoceans.com; 1/2 dives US$60/80, open-water course incl equipment US$210) Run by a professional outfit with 20 years of diving experience in Panamanian waters, Twin Oceans (located in the Coco Plum hotel, see p261) has a wide range of dives and courses available. In addition to half a dozen dive sites around Portobelo (between five and 25 minutes by boat from Twin Oceans), it also arranges longer trips to Isla Coiba (p195). Spanish and English are spoken.

Scubaportobelo (☎ 261-3841; www.scubapanama .com; 1/2/3 people incl equipment US$127/96/86, open-water course incl equipment beginner/advanced US$100/174) This outfit has a wide variety of rental equipment, and on-site tank refill is available. They offer diving instruction and are part of Scubapanama, which offers dives in the canal and in the Pacific.

Tours
BOAT TRIPS

Next to Fuerte Santiago (p259), there are boat operators who can take visitors across the bay to the **Fuerte San Fernando** (per person US$2). There are also three nearby beaches that make for a lovely trip: **La Huerta**

COLÓN PROVINCE

THE STORY OF THE BLACK CHRIST

Many tales have attempted to explain the origins of the Black Christ statue in Portobelo's church and the festival that honors it. One story has it that a ship bound for Cartagena, Colombia, from Portobelo tried to leave the port five times, but on each occasion a mighty storm appeared and blew the ship back to the town's edge, nearly sinking it in the process. The terrified crew are said to have lightened their vessel by tossing a heavy box overboard. On their sixth attempt to sail out of the bay, no storm appeared and they were able to go on their way unchallenged.

According to this tale, several fishermen found the discarded box floating off Portobelo and were shocked to discover a statue of a black Christ inside it. They are said to have placed it in Portobelo's church out of respect. As word got around about the dark wooden statue, which stands 1.5m high, the figure took on a mythic reputation.

A second story claims that Portobelo fishermen found a box floating at sea during a cholera epidemic. It contained a black Christ statue that, out of respect, the men placed inside the town church. Almost immediately, so goes this story, the epidemic passed, and people who had been reeling from the terrible disease quickly recovered.

These are just some of the stories. Regardless of the veracity of any of them, the Black Christ Festival on 21 October makes for an interesting time. It begins with the parading of the statue and continues all night, as many people in purple robes – some wearing crowns of thorns and carrying crosses – roam around dancing, gambling and drinking.

(US$5), **Puerto Frances** (US$6), and **Playa Blanca** (US$10). The beaches don't have a lot of sand, but the water here is generally quite clear. Prices listed here are for the roundtrip, with a three-person minimum.

HIKING

SelvAventuras (☎ 442-1042, 688-6247; www.geocities.com/selvaventuras) On the main road into town, this adventure outfit is run by two local Portobelans (Jose Antonio and Jose Alfredo), who both lead excursions into pristine rain forest. They know the area well, and lead hikes to some impressive places including **Catarata de Rio Piedras** (a 45m waterfall), **Salto de Tigre** (another gorgeous waterfall and swimming hole) and to **Rio Iguanita**, where you'll pass four waterfalls and arrive at a crystalline rain forest-enshrouded swimming hole. Trips start at US$15 per person; you'll need some Spanish.

Festivals & Events

The **Black Christ Festival** (21 October), in honor of the statue housed in the Iglesia de San Félipe, is a fascinating event to witness. Pilgrims arrive from all over Panama to dance and celebrate in honor of Jesus, many wearing purple (the color of the robe Christ wore). The exact origins of this festival and the Black Christ statue it celebrates are a matter of speculation: many fanciful stories exist (see the boxed text above), but any definitive church records were likely lost in the fire that followed Henry Morgan's sacking of Panamá in 1671. Regardless, on each anniversary of the statue's discovery, it is taken from the Portobelo church and paraded around town. The parade begins at 6pm, and street festivities follow.

Los Congos, a festivity in which Black people assume the role of escaped slaves and run around taking 'captives,' is held in Portobelo and sometimes elsewhere in the province during Carnaval, on New Year's Eve and on patron saint days (March 20 in Portobelo). 'The Congos' is both the name of the festivity and the name of the people who maintain this intriguing tradition, which is based around a satire of colonial Spaniards.

The tradition dates from the days of Panama's slave trade, when some Black slaves escaped into the jungle and formed communities there. The satire consists of taking someone prisoner and demanding a huge ransom, but the prisoner is freed when he or she pays a token ransom, perhaps only US0.50. The celebrants are generally dressed in outlandish outfits that include tattered clothes and hats that resemble crowns. Many of them also carry wooden swords, and appear frighteningly animated.

Los Congos usually perform before audiences that assemble to watch them 'captivate' people, but sometimes a really crazy-looking group of men wielding wooden swords will descend upon a person who's just walking down the street and demand thousands of dollars (but they'll settle for a few coins). Sound bizarre? It is. If you ever find yourself an innocent 'victim' of this tradition, try not to freak out.

Sleeping

As you approach Portobelo from Sabanitas, you'll pass several spots on the left side of the road.

Coco Plum (☎ 264-1338; www.cocoplumpanama .com; s/d/tr US$35/45/55; ⋈) This new lodge has 12 simple but comfortable rooms, each with air-con, private bathroom and TV. There's a good open-air restaurant, as well as the dive outfit Twin Oceans Dive Center (p259).

Scubaportobelo (☎ 261-3841; cabin Sun-Thu US$30, Fri-Sat US$50; ⋈) Features basic cabins with air-con and private cold-water bathroom.

Hospedaje La Aduana (☎ 448-2925; d with fan/ air-con US$10/15; ⋈) Located in town, this very basic but clean place has five rooms – two with private bathroom, two with shared bathroom, and one with private bathroom and air-con.

You'll find that many local families also rent out spare rooms for around US$5 to US$10. Ask at the IPAT tourist office (p258) or at SelvAventuras (see opposite).

Eating

There are several good restaurants along the Sabanitas–Portobelo road, and a couple of local favorites in town. All are open for breakfast, lunch and dinner.

As you travel toward Portobelo, the first place you'll come to is **Restaurante Los Cañones** (meals US$6), which is over the water and faces a lovely inlet. The menu includes red snapper, sea bass, squid, clams and baby shrimp. The dish that this restaurant is really known for is octopus, slowly cooked to perfection in a spicy tomato-based sauce and served on a bed of coconut rice.

The next place you'll come to is **Restaurante Grupo Marin** (mains US$6-9) located at the water's edge with lovely views. You'll find excellent seafood here, and the restaurant has earned its share of admirers from Panama City.

Continuing on toward Portobelo, you'll spot the open-air **Las Anclas** (dishes US$6-10), in front of the Coco Plum hotel. In addition

to tasty seafood dishes, it also serves fresh juices.

Closer to town, on the right side of the road, is **Restaurante La Torre** (dishes US$6-10), which advertises 'cheeseburgers in paradise' and delivers the goods. English is spoken at this breezy, Colombian-owned restaurant, and the seafood here is excellent. Try the conch in coconut sauce or jumbo shrimp.

In town, **SelvAventuras** (⋈ 9am-5pm Mon-Sat) is a pleasant coffee shop. It's also the place to arrange an excursion into some of the area's lovely rain forest (see opposite).

A few hundred meters east of SelvAventuras is the pleasant thatched-roof **Restaurante Arith** (mains US$3-5). You can find reliably good home-cooked meals here. Fish or octopus, served with coconut rice, are among the offerings.

Getting There & Away

Buses to Portobelo depart Colón's bus terminal every 30 minutes from 4:30am to 6pm (US$2.30). To go to Panama City from Portobelo, you must first get to Colón or to Sabanitas and transfer there.

Getting Around

There are occasional taxis in Portobelo, but not many. The best way to travel the Sabanitas–Portobelo road is to flag down any of the buses headed in your direction. No public transportation is available after dark.

ISLA GRANDE

pop 1000

This island, 15km east of Portobelo, is a popular weekend destination for Panama City dwellers. The inhabitants of this island are of African descent and most make a living from fishing and coconut production.

The French built a lighthouse on the island in 1893, which sent red, green and white light over 100km out to sea. The lighthouse still functions today, but its light is now white, and it is visible for only 70km.

Activities

There are some lovely **beaches** on the northern side of the island that can be reached by boat (hire a water taxi at the dock in front of Cabañas Super Jackson, p263), or on foot (there's a water's-edge trail that loops around the 5km-long, 1.5km-wide island, as well as a slippery cross-island trail).

There are also some fine snorkeling and dive sites within a 10-minute boat ride of the island. **Isla Grande Dive Center** (☎ 223-5943) offers a variety of dives around the island and in the Archipiélago de San Blás. It's 50m west of Cabañas Super Jackson.

For US$30, one of the boatmen in front of Cabañas Super Jackson will take you on a half-day adventure. The possibilities are quite appealing. There are **mangroves** east of Isla Grande that make for fun exploring, and you could also go **snorkeling** and take a picnic to a beach on the mainland or a small secluded island.

About 200m east of Cabañas Super Jackson is Club Turqueza – a restaurant-bar from which it's possible to make a sailing excursion with **San Blás Sailing** (☎ 214-3446, 687-8521) to the San Blás islands aboard a 41-foot yacht or a 42-foot catamaran. Prices range from US$85 to US$180 per person per day and include drinks, meals, lodging, use of snorkeling equipment, kayaks, surfboards and more.

Festivals & Events

Carnaval (Sat-Tue before Ash Wednesday, 40 days before Easter Sunday) Locals dance the conga with ribbons and mirrors in their hair, the women wearing traditional *pollera* dresses and the men in ragged pants tied at the waist with old sea rope. Along with the dancing, there are satirical songs about current events and a lot of joking in the Caribbean calypso tradition.

San Juan Bautista (24 June) Celebrated with swimming and canoe races.

Virgen del Carmen (16 July) Honored with a land and sea procession, baptisms and Masses.

Sleeping & Eating

There are many places to stay on Isla Grande and they run the gamut from crummy to charming to overpriced. In general, prices are much higher on weekends.

Cabañas Super Jackson (☎ 448-2311; d with fan/air-con US$20/35; ✷) The closest place to the main pier, this has five basic rooms with concrete walls and clean-swept floors. All rooms have private bathroom. The hotel is beside a small store selling ice-cold beverages.

Hotel Isla Grande (☎ 225-6722; fax 225-6721; d with fan/air-con US$40/60; ✷) About 200m west of Super Jackson, Isla Grande consists of several multilevel blocks of rooms, each with a fan, private bathroom and an ocean view. There are also 10 popular oceanside

cabins with air-con. In general, the place is fairly run-down. A sandy beach surrounded by barbed wire runs along behind the hotel (access US$3 for nonguests).

Cabañas Cholita (☎ /fax 448-2962; d/tr US$40/50; ✷) To the east of Super Jackson, Cholita offers 14 oceanside rooms, all with air-con, good mattresses and private cold-water bathroom. The **restaurant** (lunch/dinner US$6) here is one of the island's best.

Posada Villa Ensueño (☎ 448-2964; d/tw/tr US$40/45/60) With 16 attractive rooms; there's even a large lawn for campers (US$10 per tent per night, use of showers and toilets included).

Sister Moon Hotel (☎ 226-9861, 448-2182; d from US$50; ✷) Continuing on the path another 10 minutes, you'll reach these lovely cabins perched on a hillside at the end of the island. Surrounded by swaying palms with crashing waves below, these cabins are the most charming on the island. Each has fabulous views from its porch (and hammock), with simple but nicely designed interiors including private bathroom. There's a decent restaurant right over the water as well as a swimming pool. Cheaper rates available during the week.

Bananas Village Resort (☎ 263-9766; www.bananasresort.com; s/d US$110/150; ✷) On the northern side of the island, Bananas includes an open-sided restaurant, a bar, a swimming pool, and a long, clean beach. Accommodations consist of eight two-story houses with three guestrooms apiece (two downstairs and one upstairs). All of the houses are backed by jungle and fronted by the sea. Rooms are cheerful, with white wicker furniture, French doors and a safe. Rates include all meals and boat shuttle from the mainland. The resort often lowers its rates from April 15 to October 15.

The pickings are generally slim at the island's stand-alone restaurants, which seem to specialize in bland, overcooked food. The exception is **Club Turqueza** (dishes US$7), east of Posada Villa Ensueño, which offers *huevos rancheros* served with homemade marmalade and bread, salad niçoise, and many seafood and crêpe dishes.

Getting There & Away

Buses to La Guayra (the coastal hamlet where visitors can hire boats to get to Isla Grande) leave from the Colón bus terminal hourly from 6:30am to 6pm (US$2.25). These buses can be boarded at Sabanitas, the turnoff for Portobelo, La Guayra, and Nombre de Dios.

In La Guayra, there are always skippers hanging about near the water's edge, waiting to take people to the island. The 10-minute boat ride costs US$1 per person.

PLAYA BLANCA

A few kilometers west of Isla Grande is lovely **Playa Blanca** (Panama City ☎ 232-4985; cell ☎ 613-1558; per person with/without meals & boat transportation US$150/250), which consists of a seaside lodge with a breezy common area, and five guestrooms with private hot-water bathroom. This relaxing four-hectare retreat is situated on a roadless peninsula, and faces a small private cove with an inviting white-sand beach.

The retreat's main attraction is the peaceful setting and fine snorkeling that's available in the cove a shell's toss away. There's a pristine coral reef close to shore and another, significantly deeper one about 100m farther out. These may be the least-disturbed reefs between Colón and the Archipiélago de San Blás.

The comfortable guestrooms can each accommodate one couple. There are two fully equipped kitchens. Mosquito netting accompanies each bed, and electricity is supplied by solar panels. Meals are hearty and feature barbecued chicken, fish, pasta or beef and local vegetables and fruits. The food's not fancy, but it is delicious and filling. There's plenty of beer and wine to go around.

The retreat, which is owned and run by a couple of retired US military officers, is connected by 'land line,' which is slightly different from your usual telephone line. To place a call directly to the retreat, dial ☎ 441-0672, followed by 7801 after you hear a chime.

NOMBRE DE DIOS

Nombre de Dios, 23km east of Portobelo, has a colorful history but isn't much to look at today. There are no ruins from the Spanish settlement to be found, although people here still occasionally pick up the silver-cross coins used by the Spaniards 400 years ago. There's a salt-and-pepper beach, but it's nothing special.

History

From 1519 to 1598, this settlement was the northern terminus of trade across the isthmus. It was here in 1510 that Nicuesa ordered his small fleet to land after they failed to establish a colony at the mouth of the Río Belén in Veraguas. Leading a fleet of sick and starving men, Nicuesa looked upon the seemingly fruitful shore near the northernmost point of the isthmus and exclaimed, '¡Paremos aqui, en el nombre de Dios!' ('Let us stop here, in the name of God!'). His followers, sensing something auspicious in his words, decided to call the place Nombre de Dios even before they landed.

A PIRATE'S GRAVE

According to some, Francis Drake's body lies near Nombre de Dios in a leaden coffin at the bottom of the ocean. The English pirate led the sacking of Nombre de Dios in January 1596, but later that month he died of dysentery that he'd acquired in the Tropics. The captain was buried at sea within striking distance of the scenes of his earlier exploits, his descent to the ocean floor accompanied by a thunderous salute fired by his fleet.

In Drake's honor, two of his own ships and his share of the Nombre de Dios treasure were sunk near the spot. A nearby point and a small island were named after him, and a sermon was read aboard Drake's ship, the *Defiance*, with all of the captains of his fleet in attendance. It went like this:

Where Drake first found, there last he lost his name,
And for a tomb left nothing but his fame.
His body's buried beneath some great wave,
The sea that was his glory is his grave.
On whom an epitaph none can truly make,
For who can say, '*Here* lies Sir Francis Drake?'

About 280 settlers made it to Nombre de Dios (800 men had left Hispaniola in November 1509), and they used what little strength they had to build a blockhouse and huts. For many weeks the men lived on rotten provisions; on a good day they fed upon alligator.

One day a scouting party from the Spanish colony at Antigua, in the Darién, stumbled upon Nombre de Dios. By this time only 60 settlers remained; the rest had died of disease or hunger. The survivors told the scouts nasty stories about Nicuesa, who was more concerned about establishing a capital than he was about his men. The scouts returned to Antigua with horror stories about Nombre de Dios and its leader.

Nicuesa and 17 men reached Antigua a few days after the scouts, but they were told not to come ashore. The settlers at Antigua wanted nothing to do with Nicuesa. But the governor was stubborn, and the next day he and his party paddled to shore. The men were seized, placed on the worst vessel in the harbor and forced to sail. The rotting craft left Antigua on March 1, 1511, and the ship and its passengers were never seen again.

It was rumored that the worm-eaten vessel wrecked on the coast of Veraguas, where these words were found carved into a tree: *'Aqui anduvó perdido el desdichado Diego de Nicuesa'* ('Here wandered lost the wretched Diego de Nicuesa'). Another version has it that, while landing on the coast for water, Nicuesa and his men were captured by Indians, barbecued and eaten. According to a third version, a tree was found in Cuba inscribed with the words *'Aqui feneció el desdichado Nicuesa'* ('Here died the wretched Nicuesa') carved into it.

The 43 miserable survivors who were barely standing at Nombre de Dios were soon rescued and taken to Antigua by that colony's leader, Vasco Núñez de Balboa. Eight years later, in 1519, the city of Panamá was founded, and later that year Nombre de Dios was resettled. Nombre de Dios soon became the Caribbean terminus of trade across the isthmus, and so it remained until the late 1590s, when nearby Portobelo took over that role.

But even in its heyday as a trading center, Nombre de Dios was a dreadful place. It rained most days, and the heat was excessive.

According to a 16th-century historian, the town was so unhealthy that Indian women living there became barren, and even the native fruits refused to grow. Strong men are said to have died before their time, and disease always claimed the lives of Spanish children. The town was known as a graveyard for travelers. It is fitting that Drake, who spent so much of his life in the Tropics, died of dysentery within days of sacking Nombre de Dios.

Following Francis Drake's attack on Nombre de Dios and the rise of Portobelo at the end of the 16th century, the town was all but abandoned, and it remained a backwater hamlet for the next 300 years. At that point it gradually revived to a community of about 2000 people, most of whom were the descendants of slaves. People still died like flies in Nombre de Dios until the beginning of the 20th century, when Americans arrived to dredge sand from the harbor for use in concrete for the Gatún Locks. The Americans built a public hospital, screened houses, dug wells and improved sanitation.

Orientation & Information

As you enter the town, you'll pass some very rustic houses on both sides of the road. After 100m, a short road curves to the left, toward the ocean, where there are more homes.

If you stay on the main road, 50m or so past the first turnoff you'll reach a second road that turns toward the ocean. In 75m this road reaches the center of town, marked by a small plaza.

The one pay phone in town is near the plaza. There is no post office or bank.

Sleeping & Eating

Casa de Huespedes (☎ 448-2068; r with shared/private bathroom US$4/5) Facing the plaza, this place has nine rooms, each of which contains a standing fan. This no-frills place is clean and offers good value; ask for Alejandrina Vega.

There are a couple of simple restaurants nearby.

Getting There & Away

Buses to Nombre de Dios (labeled 'Costa Arriba') depart from Colón's bus terminal (US$3, 90 minutes, hourly from 6:30am to 6pm). These same buses can be boarded at Sabanitas, which is the turnoff for Portobelo, La Guayra and Nombre de Dios.

Buses from Nombre de Dios to Sabanitas (US$2.50, 80 minutes) leave hourly from 6am to 4pm.

JIMMY'S CARIBBEAN DIVE RESORT

Five kilometers east of Nombre de Dios, you'll see the turnoff for **Jimmy's Caribbean Dive Resort** (☎ 682-9322; www.caribbeanjimmysdiveresort.com; divers/nondivers 4 nights US$589/489; ☒). It's another 3km along a dirt road before you reach these five lovely cabins on the ocean's edge. Each comes with good beds, air-con, private bathrooms and a small porch that opens onto the sea. An excellent restaurant-bar is next door serving a variety of fresh seafood plates, pastas and grilled meats. Bands play here on weekends. Jimmy's offers jungle excursions, horseback riding and fishing trips, although the majority of people come here to dive. You'll find some superb diving – shore dives, reef dives, wreck dives and cavern dives among the offerings. Rates include two tanks per day, lodging, three meals a day, horseback riding and other activities, as well as transport to and from the Panama City airport. At the time of writing Jimmy's was building a 15-room motel due for completion in mid- to late 2005.

Comarca de Kuna Yala

CONTENTS

El Porvenir	272
Nalunega	272
Ogobsibu	272
Wichub-Walá	272
Ikuptupu	273
Cartí Suitupo	273
Nusatupo & Río Sidra/Mamardup	274
Kuanidup	274
Naranjo Chico	274
Cayos Los Grullos, Holandéses & Ordupuquip	275
Río Azúcar	275
Narganá & Corazón de Jesús	276
Isla Tigre	276
Isla Iskardup	277
Isla Tupile to Isla Uaguitupo	277
Ustupo Ogobsucum	277
Isla Pino	278
Mulatupo Sasardí	278

The Comarca de Kuna Yala is an autonomous region that comprises the Archipiélago de San Blás and a 226km strip of Caribbean coast from Colón Province to Colombia. The southern boundary of the *comarca* (district) consists of two strings of jungle-clad mountains, the Serranía de San Blás (highlands of the San Blás) and the Serranía del Darién (Darién regions).

Many of the nearly 400 islands of San Blás are uninhabited, covered by coconut trees and ringed by white-sand beaches with the turquoise Caribbean lapping at the shore. These contrast sharply with the inhabited islands, where acre-sized cays are packed with bamboo huts and people, allowing barely enough room to maneuver among the detritus-lined pathways.

The islands are home to the Kuna, who run San Blás as a *comarca* with minimal interference from the national government. The Kuna have governed the region since the 1920s, when the Panamanian government granted the tribe the right of self-rule following a Kuna uprising that led to the death of 22 Panamanian policemen and 20 Kuna who had befriended them. Today, the Kuna not only govern themselves but have two representatives in the Panamanian legislature, as well as the right to vote in Panamanian elections.

A visit to the islands necessarily involves mingling with the Kuna, which many visitors consider to be the best part of the experience. They have much to share with visitors from the simple beauty of their islands to their rich cultural traditions.

HIGHLIGHTS

- Attending annual *feria* on **Isla Tigre** (p276), one of the most traditional Kuna islands

- Soaking up the sun, surf and sand on **Isla Uaguitupo** (p277), which hosts one of the island's best hotels

- Meeting the Kuna, a fiercely independent people who maintain their traditions in a changing world

- Discovering the beauty of romantic **Isla Aguja** (Needle Island; p273), with its postcard-perfect sand and surf, and friendly locals

- Snorkeling around **Wreck Reef** (p275), a coral-rich site that's become a graveyard for many a boat

★ Wreck Reef
Isla Aguja ★ ★ Isla Tigre
(Needle Island) ★ Isla Uaguitupo

COMARCA DE KUNA YALA

| ▪ AREA: 2360 SQ KM | ▪ ELEVATION: SEA LEVEL TO 748M | ▪ POPULATION: 32,450 |

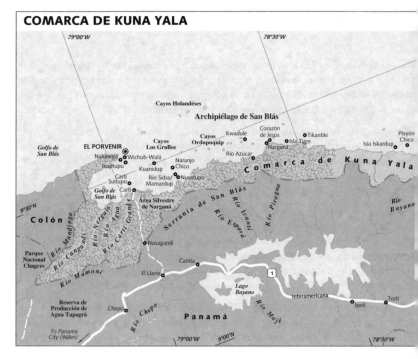

COMARCA DE KUNA YALA

Climate

The best time to visit the *comarca* is May through November, when the winds are stronger and the temperatures are generally lower. When there's no breeze and the mercury rises, the humidity sets in, and life on the San Blás islands can be miserable. During January and February, the seas can be rough.

Getting There & Away

AIR

At the time of research only **Aeroperlas** (☎ 315-7500; www.aeroperlas.com) was flying between Panama City and the islands of the *comarca*. Demand far exceeds supply, so book as far in advance as possible. Note that planes may stop at other islands in the archipelago, loading and unloading passengers or cargo before continuing on. Be sure to ask the name of the island you're on before you leave the plane. All flights depart from Albrook airport early in the morning. Prices listed are one-way.

Achutupo (US$40, 1hr, 1 daily, 6am/7:20am)
Ailigandi (US$40, 55min, 1 daily, 6am/7am)

Cartí (US$34, 45min, 1 daily, 6am/6:55am Mon-Sat, 7am/8am Sun)
Corazón de Jesús (US$34, 30min, 1 daily, 6am/6:40am Mon-Sat, 7am/7:40am Sun)
El Porvenir (US$31.50, 25min, 1 daily, 6am/6:35am)
Mulatupo (US$45, 1hr, 1 daily 6am/7:10am)
Playon Chico (US$38, 35min, 1 daily, 6am/6:45am)
Puerto Obaldía (US$52.50, 1hr, 1 daily, 6am/7:15am Thu & Sun)
Río Sidra (US$31.50, 45min, 1 daily, 6am/6:55am Mon-Sat, 7am/7:55am Sun)
Tupile (US$38, 40min, 1 daily, 6am/6:50am)
Usutupo (US$40, 85min, 1 daily, 6am/7:35am)

Boatmen await the arrival of planes to shuttle people to their island destination (US$2 to US$5). Be sure to make reservations before coming to Kuna Yala.

BOAT

Diehard adventurers may consider taking a collective boat from Miramar (p251) in Colón Province to an island near Porvenir. There's usually one boat in the morning, though it doesn't always make the journey (US$5 to US$10, two hours). Try to find

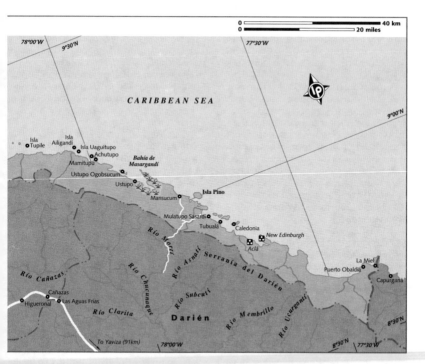

out about the condition of the seas before boarding these vessels, which are not the most seaworthy. In January and February, the seas can get especially rough. To get to Miramar, take a bus to Colón and transfer to a Miramar (or 'Costa Arriba') bus; Miramar is the last stop on the road.

CAR
Only one road leads into the district, the rugged El Llano–Cartí road that connects the town of El Llano, on the Carretera Interamericana 70km east of Panama City, to the San Blás coastal hamlet of Cartí.

The road begins near El Llano at the turnoff for Nusagandi, a forest reserve just inside the Comarca de Kuna Yala. The reserve begins at the southern boundary of the district, 20km north of the Interamericana. A few kilometers north of the district boundary is the rustic Burbayar Nature Lodge (p132).

The lodge is reachable only by a 4WD vehicle with a powerful engine, a winch and good off-road tires. Beyond the lodge, the remaining 20km to Cartí is on a road that

even a German assault tank would have difficulty traversing. For all practical purposes, the El Llano–Cartí road ends at the lodge.

Getting Around
In addition to guides available in Panama City (p90), you can hire local guides when you're out on the islands. Any hotel can make the arrangements.

Intrepid travelers can try their luck on Colombian merchant boats. These travel the Caribbean Sea between Colón and Puerto Obaldía, stopping at inhabited San Blás islands to pick up and drop off people and goods. These fleets are occasionally used for drug trafficking, and travel by these often overloaded boats is neither comfortable nor safe.

Kuna Indians
The Kuna have lived in eastern Panama for at least the last two centuries, but scholars don't agree on their origin. Language similarities with people who once lived several hundred kilometers to the west would indicate that the Kuna migrated eastward.

However, oral tradition has it that the tribe emigrated from Colombia after the 16th century, following devastating encounters with other tribes armed with poison-dart blowguns.

Some scholars contend the Kuna were well established in eastern Panama at the time the conquistadors arrived, due to Spanish chroniclers indicating that the Indians they met used the Kuna words *ulu* for 'canoe' and *oba* for 'corn.' These scholars also note that many geographic names in eastern Panama during the colonial epoch were Kuna. Nearly all the rivers in Darién Province have Kuna names, for example, although the Emberá and Wounaan Indians live there now.

No matter where the Kuna came from, scholars agree that life on the islands is relatively new for the Indians. Historians at the end of the 18th century wrote that the only people who used the San Blás islands at that time were pirates, Spaniards and the odd explorer.

Today there are an estimated 70,000 Kuna: 32,000 live on the district's islands, 8000 live on tribal land along the coast and 30,000 live outside the district. So communal are the island Kuna that they inhabit only 40 of the nearly 400 keys; the rest are mostly left to coconut trees, sea turtles and iguanas. On the inhabited islands, so many traditional bamboo-sided, thatched-roof houses are clustered together that there's scarcely room to walk between them.

The Kuna like to say that their archipelago consists of 'one island for every day of the year.' In fact, there are nearly 400 islands in the chain, all small creations of sand and palm rising barely far enough above the blue-green Caribbean to escape complete inundation by breakers during storms. Reefs to the north and east prevent destructive waves from striking the islands. From the tourist's perspective, there are two kinds of San Blás islands: the white-sand, palm-sprinkled, magazine-cover beauties, and the overcrowded keys where feces and rubbish are found just a few meters from shore.

Few of the islands are more than 10km from the district's mainland, and all the heavily inhabited islands are very close to the coast in order for the Kuna to access agricultural areas and vital natural resources, such as water, firewood and construction materials. Also on the mainland are the giant trees from which the Indians make their chief mode of transportation – the *cayuco*, a dugout canoe made from a burned and hollowed-out trunk. There are nine towns on the mainland, all within 100m of the sea; there are no restaurants or hotels in these towns.

The Kuna still adhere to traditions that astonish tourists. For example, a Kuna woman is not given a name until she has had her first menstrual period, at which time a party is held, the young woman's hair is cut short and her parents select a name for her with the help of a medicine man. Until that day the young woman answers to a nickname.

Most Kuna women continue to dress as their ancestors did. Their faces are distinguished by a black line painted from the forehead to the tip of the nose. A gold ring is worn through the nose. A length of colorful printed cloth is wrapped around the waist as a skirt, topped by a short-sleeved blouse covered in brilliantly colored *molas* (traditional Kuna textiles). A printed head scarf and many necklaces, rings and bracelets complete the daily outfit. To make themselves more attractive, the women also wrap their legs, from ankle to knee, in long strands of colorful beads.

The Kuna sometimes appear unfriendly to tourists, and understandably so, because most visitors view them as oddities that must be photographed. Cruise ships visit several islands, and when the ships arrive, the number of people on an already congested island can triple, leaving barely enough room for anyone to turn around. Nonetheless, virtually two-thirds of the populace (the tourists) are trying like crazy to photograph the other third (the Kuna). It's a pretty ugly scene that's repeated time and again.

In addition, the behavior of many tourists is appalling to the Kuna. For example, Kuna women dress conservatively, always keeping their cleavage, bellies and most of their legs covered. In their opinion, to do otherwise would be offensive. Yet many foreign women arrive in Kuna villages in bikini tops and short shorts, not only embarrassing themselves in the eyes of the Indians but also showing disrespect for Kuna sensibilities. Likewise, local men don't go shirtless and travelers who do so risk offending Kuna sensibilities. As a result of repeated violations of their privacy and sensibilities, the Kuna often ask that travelers pay a visitation fee and fees for photographs taken of them (see below).

Until the late 1990s, the district's principal currency was the coconut. (In recent years, the sale of *molas* replaced the sale of coconuts as the Kuna's number one revenue source.) The Kuna grow coconuts like crazy: in a good year they'll harvest more than 30 million of them. They barter away most of these to Colombians, who make the rounds of Kuna towns in old wooden schooners, each of which can hold 50,000 to 80,000 coconuts. In return for the fruit, the Colombians give the Kuna clothing, jars of Nescafé, vinegar, rice, sunglasses, canned milk, batteries, soups and other goods.

In Colombia the coconuts are used in the production of candy, gelatin capsules, cookies, shampoos and other products. Colombia has many processing plants for the fruit, but Panama, oddly, has none. The Colombians also sell Kuna coconuts to other South American countries.

The Kuna are shrewd businesspeople. Because, until recently, their economy was based on the sale of coconuts, they protect it by selling the fruit at a predetermined price to prevent their buyers from playing one Kuna off another to bring down the cost. Every year the tribe's chiefs agree on one price for coconuts. If a Kuna is found selling coconuts at another price, the tribe punishes that person. By price fixing and enforcement, the chiefs prevent price wars among the Kuna. Price wars would hurt the community by lowering the standard of living, and they could even force some Kuna out of business.

In another protectionist move, the chiefs passed a law a few years ago prohibiting outsiders from owning property in the district. Thus they promptly forced out the handful of foreigners living on the islands without compensation. As a result of that law, there are fewer than a dozen places to stay on the islands, because few Kuna have enough money to construct even a basic hotel. None of the hotels that do exist are fancy.

Visiting the Comarca

On most of the heavily inhabited islands, the Kuna require tourists to register and pay a visitation fee (US$3 to US$5) upon arrival. The price varies from island to island, and the visitor is expected to pay it regardless of whether he or she stays a week or only half an hour. If you arrive on a populated San Blás island, you might be expected to present your passport and pay a visitation fee as well.

With few exceptions, visitors must also pay for any photo they take of Kuna. If you want to take someone's photo, be sure to first ask his or her permission, and be prepared to pay at least US$1 per subject (some Kuna expect to be paid US$1 per photo).

Another thing visitors should know is that all the uninhabited islands are privately owned. It's usually OK to use the island, but be prepared to pay a small fee if the owner shows up. Some largely uninhabited islands have a single family living on them; if you spot such an island and like it, you can usually visit it for a few hours if you pay the family US$2. Unless you speak Kuna, your boatman might have to do the talking for you. Not all Kuna speak Spanish, and very few speak English.

If you want to camp on an uninhabited island, US$5 a night per couple will usually do the trick. But camping on such islands isn't wise because you run the risk of encountering drug traffickers in the night. The Kuna do not allow the Panamanian coast guard or US antidrug vessels to operate in the archipelago, so the uninhabited islands are occasionally used by Colombian drug traffickers running cocaine up the coast.

There are only a handful of lodgings on the islands, and none on the mainland. Most of these are basic, although a couple are quite comfortable. Most densely populated islands in the district have a store selling basic items, as well as coin telephones from which you can place domestic and international calls. Though the phones are public, there's usually a Kuna standing nearby charging a telephone tax of up to US$1 per call.

Festivals & Events

One of the big holidays in Kuna Yala is the commemoration of the anniversary of the Kuna Revolution of 1925. This is celebrated on February 25, which marks the day when the Kuna rebelled against the Panamanian police who had been occupying the islands and expelled them from the *comarca*.

Sometimes the event is remembered through a reenactment of the rebellion.

From October 10 to 12 there is the celebration of the traditional dance, Nogagope. Both of these are particularly celebrated on Rio Tigre (p276).

EL PORVENIR

pop 1900

El Porvenir, at the northwestern end of the district, is the gateway to the San Blás islands. Visitors to the keys tend to fly here, proceed directly to the island's small dock and take a boat elsewhere. That 'elsewhere' is more often than not the Hotel San Blás, on the nearby island of Nalunega; the Kuna Niskua Hotel, on the island of Wichub-Walá; or the Ukutupu Hotel, on an artificial island known simply as Ukutupu.

There's a police station, two public phones and a few homes on El Porvenir, as well as a hotel with a restaurant: **El Porvenir Hotel** (☎ 229-9000, ☎ /fax 221-1397, ask for Mrs Bibi; r per person Oct-Mar/Apr-Sep US$25/30). Most of its 13 rooms contain three twin beds, and each has a toilet, a cold-water shower, one light and one power outlet. Electricity is provided from 6pm 'until all of our guests have gone to bed.' The hotel's walls are concrete and its roof is corrugated tin – nothing fancy – but the place is cool and pleasant.

NALUNEGA

pop 350

This island, with its many traditional Kuna homes close together, is similar to the inhabited San Blás islands found further south and east in the archipelago. However, Nalunega is considerably cleaner than the others because the owner of its sole hotel pays several boys to keep the small island free of litter. There was no public phone on this island at the time of research.

Hotel San Blás (☎ 262-9812; r per person US$35) is the best value and most popular hotel in the district. It has 29 simple but OK rooms; most are bamboo-and-board adjoining rooms with sandy floors, thatched-roofs and shared bathrooms. The guestrooms above the open-sided dining area and the adjacent general store are cooler and cleaner than the others because their floors are not sandy; although the sea is a stone's throw away, the views from these rooms are mostly of thatched-roofs. Ask to see several rooms, as their appeal and the firmness of the beds varies substantially. The price includes three meals and a boat tour. You can use the beach of a nearby private island for US$1 a day.

The hotel's owner, Luis Burgos, speaks English, and the food he provides is the best on the islands – expect lobster, though king crab is occasionally served. If Luis knows you're coming, he'll arrange for a boatman to meet you on El Porvenir. Luis opened his hotel in 1972, at which time it consisted of three Spartan huts, and Luis served triple duty as cook, maid and boatman. Today he is the largest employer on Nalunega, with a staff of four.

The Hotel San Blás can set you up with a guide for touring nearby islands, taking boating/hiking trips in and out of the Mandigo River. Juan Armando Iglesius speaks Spanish, Kuna, English and Italian and comes highly recommended.

OGOBSIBU

This tiny island hosts the **Coco Blanco Cabañas** (☎ 265-6335, 613-3551; s/tr/q US$110/180/320), which consist of four lovely bamboo cabins, each with a private bathroom and shower in an ecologically sensitive lodge, complete with septic system. Two cabins have two beds, one cabin has four beds, and the other has one double bed. The beach here is quite nice, and there's a grassy area for games of football or volleyball. The price includes three meals, snorkeling gear and one or two boating trips. The informal restaurant features excellent cuisine, with grilled vegetables making a regular appearance beside dishes like shark, octopus and lobster. The friendly Sanchez family lives on the other side of the island; otherwise guests will have the place to themselves. This is best reached by flying through El Porvenir.

WICHUB-WALÁ

This small and unusually clean inhabited island with one public telephone is a five-minute boat ride from El Porvenir, and is home to the **Kuna Niskua Lodge** (☎ 225-5200, 299-9011; iguabi@hotmail.com; r without/with bathroom US$40/45). It has 12 fine rooms in a two-story thatch-and-bamboo structure with shared bathrooms. These rooms are in the middle of the island and do not have ocean views, but they are nicer than the rooms at the

Hotel San Blás and there's a very pleasing dining room. Rates include meals and two snorkeling tours. The guide Orlando Diaz is particularly recommended. There are also three rooms with private bathroom. Snorkel gear is available for rent at US$5 per day. Travelers who stay at the Voyager Hostel in Panama City (p93) can get discounts at the Kuna Niskua Lodge. Inquire at the Voyager.

Just east of Wichub-Walá, on an un-named island about the size of two basket-ball courts, is the very rustic **Cabañas Turisticas Yery** (Panama City ☎ /fax 255-0463; r per person US$27). It consists of two leaning, thatched-roof-and-bamboo lodges, each containing four tiny bathroomless rooms with swaying beds, and there's no electricity. Don't come expecting five-star accommodations. The rate includes meals and a boat tour.

IKUPTUPU

One hundred meters from Wichub-Walá is the tiny artificial island of Ikuptupu, home to the **Ikuptupu Hotel** (Panama City ☎ /fax 220-9082; r per person US$35). The hotel was a research facility used by the Smithsonian Tropical Research Institute from 1974 to 1998. Ikup-tupu consists of a basketball court-sized island, from which several boardwalks con-nect to 16 bamboo-sided, tin-roofed and linoleum-floored guestrooms, all built over the water. All bathrooms are shared (and toilets 'flush' directly into the sea, a reality that disturbs some guests). The rate includes meals and a boat tour. For isolation and sea views, this beats Nalunega, Ogobsibu and Wichub-Walá. But if you want to mingle with or at least observe the Kuna, you're better off at one of the other places.

CARTÍ SUITUPO

Cartí Suitupo is the island closest to the coastal hamlet of Cartí. The hamlet is dis-tinguished by the fact that it is the only town in the district reachable by road, although that road (the El Llano–Cartí road; see Get-ting There & Away p268) is really more of a wide, horribly rutted jungle trail. A mere 100m separates the two Cartís. There's an airstrip near the hamlet, and from it you can travel by boat to Cartí Suitupo and thence to other islands.

Cartí Suitupo is very typical of the in-habited islands from here to the Colombian border; it's the size of three football fields, crowded with bamboo houses and terribly polluted. Cartí Suitupo is also one of the San Blás islands that are visited by explora-tory boats from cruise ships. Packed with tourists, these boats visit an average of five times a month.

If you speak Spanish, it's very easy to get from Cartí Suitupo to a pristine, sparsely populated island. Just talk to Tony Adams Harrington, who has been chosen by the local population as the island's sole guide. He will find you shortly after your arrival on Cartí; *wagas* (foreigners) don't go un-noticed on the inhabited islands for more than a few nanoseconds.

For US$5 per person, Tony can arrange for a boatman to take you to nearby **Isla Aguja** (Needle Island) and pick you up later. The fee pays for the boatman, but it would

---

MOON CHILDREN

Few Kuna marry outside their villages. The result is an inbred people – usually short, large-headed and thick-necked – with the world's highest incidence of albinism. Albinos' eyes are dark pink, their hair yellow-white and their skin pale pink. When seen amid their brown-skinned, black-haired relatives, Kuna albinos are quite captivating.

In some societies, albino children are viewed as freaks of nature and are ostracized by their peers. Not so in Kuna society. Kuna children are taught that albinos are special people – children of the moon – and that they are destined to be leaders.

As a result, the moon children of the Comarca de Kuna Yala are not only the most popular kids in the tribe, but they are also the most recalcitrant due to their big egos. Kuna children have a lot of confidence as it is, but when you tell some of them that they are particularly gifted – and they surely do look different – they can become very confident indeed.

Unsurprisingly, an unusually high percentage of moon children put their abundant confidence to work for them and actually become community leaders – a fact that further supports the notion that they really are special people.

be wise to give Tony a tip as well, just to ensure he'll remind the boatman to pick you up at the specified time. There are only two families living on gorgeous Isla Aguja, and the beach and swimming there are lovely. There are lots of leaning palm trees, gentle surf lapping against the shore and golden sand. The few friendly souls who live here will make your visit all the more pleasant.

NUSATUPO & RÍO SIDRA/MAMARDUP

Nusatupo and Río Sidra/Mamardup (the communities of Río Sidra and Mamardup share an island) are densely populated islands 15km east of Cartí Suitupo. Only a few minutes' boat ride apart, they are served by an airstrip that's a few kilometers away on the mainland. Nusatupo, which has a hotel, is the closer of the islands to the airstrip. Río Sidra/Mamardup has no tourist services at all, but it does have two public phones (at the time of research there were no phones on Nusatupo).

On Nusatupo, **Hotel Kuna Yala** (Panama City ☎ 315-7520, ask for Manuel Alfaro; r per person US$40) has three rooms with concrete floors, a tin roof, no fans, and a shared bathroom with an over-the-water toilet. The kitchen service here is excellent, and the portions of fruit and seafood are generous. The rate includes three meals daily and a boat ride to and from several snorkeling sites. If requested, a guide will take you to a Kuna cemetery and on a jungle tour of the mainland free of charge (tip suggested). Because of its proximity to the keys mentioned in the following sections, people who don't mind roughing it a little will find this place to be a good deal.

KUANIDUP

This little island, 30 minutes by motorized *cayuco* from the airstrip serving Río Sidra/Mamardup, is home to a cluster of seven bamboo-and-thatch cabins, lots of palm trees, a few iguanas, soft white sand and little else. It's a beautiful island with a lovely beach for swimming. Hammocks are hung between some trees, and it's awfully easy to fall asleep in one as your mind drifts from the lapping surf to the arcing sea-sky horizon to the swaying palms above you. This island, and others around it, are the stuff of travel-magazine covers and faraway dreams.

Each of the stand-alone cabins at **Cabañas Kuanidup** (☎ 635-6737, 641-1570, 227-7661; kuanid uppanama@yahoo.com.mx; r per person US$45) has two firm beds, a lantern, a platform to place your bag on and sandy floors. A short walk away are pairs of showers, sinks and toilets, and beyond those is a small kitchen and dining area. The rate includes three meals daily (the food here is usually nothing special) and one snorkeling trip. The friendly owner, who speaks English, also owns a nearby uninhabited island where, he says, it's OK to sunbathe in the buff – and quite a few guests do.

Nearby, **Robinson's Cabins** (☎ 299-9058; cabin per person US$17.50) are set on an uninhabited island, surrounded by a fine sandy beach. The accommodations consist of rustic bamboo huts with hammocks and include three meals a day. There's fine snorkeling off the island, but the friendly Robinsons can also take you to other islands in the area. Spanish and some English spoken. To visit the island you must also pay a one-time community fee of US$6, and boat transportation (US$10 per person).

NARANJO CHICO

Three kilometers northwest of Río Sidra/Mamardup is the relatively large, lovely and sparsely populated island of Naranjo Chico (Little Orange, which is also known as Narascandub Pipi, its Kuna name). **Cabañas Narascandub Pipi** (per person incl meals US$40-50) has four sand-floored thatch-and-bamboo *cabañas* that leak during downpours, have no electricity, and share cold-water bathrooms. But the two families here (one owns one *cabaña*, another owns the other two) couldn't be nicer, which is important because the rate is steep. If the cost isn't terribly important to you and you don't mind the basic accommodations, you'll surely love the beach, the snorkeling and the sheer beauty of the island and its surroundings.

There's no phone on Naranjo Chico. The best way to make reservations for the Cabañas Narascandub Pipi is by calling ☎ 256-6239, and reserving through Yuligsa del Valle, a friend of the owner.

Nearby, on the island of Yandup, guests can stay at the lovely **Cabañas Yandup** (☎ 261-7229; cabin per person US$60) in one of four comfortably fitted thatched-roof cabins. There's good snorkeling off the island and a sandy beach, and guests receive good care at this low-key spot. The price includes three excellent meals and excursions (including walks in the jungle and trips to other beaches). It's run by an indigenous nonprofit organization Dobbo Yala (www.dobboyala.org.pa), which is involved in conservation and sustainable development in indigenous communities throughout the country.

CAYOS LOS GRULLOS, HOLANDÉSES & ORDUPUQUIP

The dozen or so sparsely inhabited islands known as Cayos Los Grullos are 10km northeast of Río Sidra/Mamardup, at the lower left (southwestern) corner of a triangle of three island groups. Topping the triangle is Cayos Holandéses (Dutchmen Keys), north of Los Grullos. Cayos Ordupuquip make up the lower right (southeastern) corner of the triangle. These groups, popular with yachties, are 12km from one another, separated by calm blue-green water. There are no tourist facilities on these islands.

All of the islands in these groups are lovely, but the Cayos Holandéses are best because they are the closest to a shallow reef that makes for some interesting snorkeling – not so much for fish and corals as for numerous pieces of wreckage. This ridge of rocks, sand and coral, 100m north of Cayos Holandéses, is called **Wreck Reef**, and it earned its name by snaring all kinds of vessels over the years. The reef's been able to do that because it's pretty far from the closest island, and though the water south of the reef is barely 1m deep, the ocean floor north of the reef plunges 100m in half that distance – or, from a sea captain's perspective, the ocean floor rises 100m to a dangerously shallow depth in half that distance. Wreck Reef's distance from the islands and the presence of deep water so close to the reef have fooled many experienced sailors.

Most crafts that smack into the reef these days belong to drug traffickers and contraband smugglers operating at night. These people are alerted to the presence of the reef by the loud, crunching sound of rock and coral taking bites out of their hulls. Over time, the surf that crashes against these wrecks breaks them up, and their cargo is tossed into the surrounding sand.

In 1995 a smugglers' boat filled with TV sets slammed into the reef at night, and the crew abandoned ship. The smugglers had hoped to bring the TVs (bought in Colón's Zona Libre) into port at Cartagena, Colombia, without paying any import taxes. The next morning, scores of Kuna in *cayucos* helped themselves to the TVs. The smugglers were never caught, and today their rusting, looted boat is perched on the reef like a trophy.

Historically, most of the boats claimed by Wreck Reef were the victims of *chocosanos* ('storms that come from the east' in Kuna). *Chocosanos* are ghastly tempests that whip up monstrous waves that can overrun entire islands. Such waves have swept many San Blás Indians and their homes out to sea. The violent storms are always preceded by a purple-black eastern sky and a lack of breeze and birdsong.

As soon as it's evident that a *chocosano* is approaching, the Kuna – particularly the older ones – combat it by blowing into conch shells. The sound alerts their benevolent god, who tries to disperse the threatening storm. If he fails, as he sometimes does, the eerie stillness is broken by ground-shaking thunderclaps, howling winds, pounding downpours and a vengeful sea. At the southern end of Wreck Reef is a freighter that lies with its hull fully exposed and its deck flat against the ocean floor – a big vessel that was flipped like a pancake by a mighty *chocosano*.

RÍO AZÚCAR

This typical, jam-packed island is close to the mainland and has no lodgings or places to eat. It is the only San Blás island that hosts **Carnaval** festivities, held during the four days preceding Ash Wednesday. This is mainly because celebrating in style – and they do celebrate in style here – takes money, and the Kuna have very little of it. But every year a wealthy and benevolent Panama City lawyer gives generously to the island's Carnaval fund, and the people respond enthusiastically with four days of dancing, singing and costume-wearing. Needless to say, the lawyer never has to pay for his fishing trips when he vacations in the area.

Like most heavily populated islands in the district, Río Azúcar has a public coin-operated telephone from which you can place domestic and international calls. There's also a clinic with a US-trained doctor, and a very modest store on Río Azúcar that sells batteries, soups and other household products. You can buy sodas at these stores, but bottled water is rarely available.

Also on Río Azúcar is a simple church showing its age, built in 1945 by Italian engineers at the direction of a Spanish priest. The priest is long gone, but the islands have no shortage of Merki (American) missionaries who want the Kuna to forget their storm-clobbered god and accept Jesus as their lord.

NARGANÁ & CORAZÓN DE JESÚS

The inhabited islands of Narganá and Corazón de Jesús are 5km northeast of Río Azúcar and reachable by a coastal airstrip. The two islands are linked by an arcing wooden footbridge perhaps 70m long. At the southwestern end of the bridge is **Narganá**, home to the district's only courthouse, its only jail and its only bank. There are also a few policemen on the island; if any ask for your passport, politely present it. Jotting down tourists' names in little books gives them something to do.

Corazón de Jesús is the most westernized of the San Blás islands – few Kuna practices are observed here, and most of the structures are made of concrete and tin instead of bamboo and thatch.

Information

It is possible to have money wired to **Banco Nacional de Panamá** (Narganá; ☼ 8am-3pm Mon-Fri, 9am-noon Sat), but be aware that the service takes 24 hours. It is also possible to cash American Express traveler's checks here.

Sleeping & Eating

Narganá has a new hotel, aptly named the **Nargana Lodge** (r with fan US$10, r with air-con & bathroom US$15; ✲). It's a basic hotel that's good value and has eight rooms, two with air-con and private bathroom, and six with fan and shared bathroom. **Millennium** and **Nali's Café** are good restaurants on the island. At either one you can have a lobster feast (US$7 to US$10) if you give them enough notice. Most plates are around US$3 and feature rice and beans served with fish or chicken. At Nali's you can rent movies to watch there. There's also a food store where you can buy vegetables – something of a rarity on the islands.

There are no places to stay on Corazón de Jesús.

ISLA TIGRE

This surprisingly clean, very traditional Kuna island is 7km east of Narganá. Here, Kuna women can be readily seen in their doorways offering *molas* to passersby; on other islands women often stay out of sight if they know tourists are moving about. On most inhabited San Blás islands, narrow dirt pathways separate the homes. Here, however, the walkways are unusually wide. This island is very vibrant culturally, perhaps owing to the island's fairgrounds, and travelers interested in seeing some of the Kuna's traditional celebrations would do well to stay at Isla Tigre.

Information

The Kunas on Isla Tigre ask that visitors come to the tourism commission when arriving on the island so that they can explain the community rules – one of which is being respectful with photography. You will be charged US$50 if you brandish a video camera, even if you say that you won't be using it. Photos of Kuna cost US$1 here, as elsewhere in the district.

Festivals & Events

February 4 is the anniversary of the **foundation of Rio Tigre** and February 25 the anniversary of the **Kuna Revolution**. On Isla Tigra this event is remembered through an emotional re-enactment of the rebellion against the Panamanian police and is staged by the local group, Morginnit.

The traditional dance, **Nogagope**, is celebrated from October 10 to 17, when groups from other communities come to Rio Tigre and dance for three days straight. The annual *feria* is from October 13 to 16 and includes more dancing, as well as art expositions and various games and sports events such as canoe races.

Sleeping & Eating

Cabañas Tigre (public phones ☎ 229-9006, 299-9092, ask for Adelberto Martinez, say you'll call back in 15 min & do so; r per person US$10) features five sand-floored bamboo-and-thatch *cabañas* on an attractive beach. Two of the *cabañas* have single beds, two have double beds, and one has no bed. Hammocks can be requested. Bathrooms are shared. Kayaks are available for US$5 a day from December to March, and there's snorkeling gear for the nearby reefs.

There is a small **restaurant** (lobster US$7, fish or octopus US$3) on the island. There is also a *refresquería* (refreshment stand) where the locals eat.

ISLA ISKARDUP

This idyllic island, the size of a soccer field and at the center of a cluster of unpopulated islands, is occupied by **Sapibenega 'The Kuna Lodge'** (Playón Chico ☎ 299-9116/7, ask for Paliwitur Sapibe, say you'll call back in 1hr & do so; r per person US$75). This 'lodge' isn't a lodge at all, but rather a large open-sided restaurant-bar with 13 stand-alone water's-edge cabins. Together, they represent the finest retreat in the archipelago. Four plank-floored, bamboo-walled, thatched-roof cabins have twin beds, seven cabins have two twin beds, and two cabins have two full-size beds. Each cabin is well constructed and raised a foot off the ground to help keep internal temperatures down. Windows, which are rarely found in the *comarca*, abound in all of the cabins, letting in breezes and gorgeous sea views. Every cabin has a private bathroom with a flush toilet, tiled shower, overhead lights and 24-hour solar-powered electricity. The rate includes all meals and a daily boat tour to a snorkeling site and a private beach.

Owner-manager Paliwitur Sapibe speaks English, Spanish and Kuna and offers numerous excursions, including: a daylong hike through mainland jungle to a waterfall and mountaintop (US$15); a boat trip (six hours each way) up a jungle-flanked river to a truly spectacular waterfall, overnighting in a hammock under a *palapa* with a meal prepared by an accompanying chef, and stopping along the river to swing on lianas, Tarzan-style (US$25); and a four-hour fishing adventure beyond the reef using the Kuna fishing tools of nylon, hook and stone (US$15). A visit to Playón Chico, a densely inhabited island great for *mola*-browsing or investigating the Kuna lifestyle, costs a mere US$5. Lobster, octopus, crab, flan and a delicious coconut dessert are typically served at the restaurant.

ISLA TUPILE TO ISLA UAGUITUPO

The ocean can be treacherous along the central part of the archipelago, particularly in the 15km stretch of roiling blue sea from densely populated Isla San Ignacio de Tupile past equally crowded Isla Ailigandí to within 1km of Isla Uaguitupo (Dolphin Island). Here, 3m swells are the norm. If you've been frightened by the sea in the northern part of the archipelago, you can expect to be terrified as you ride these waves. If you plan to travel these waters in a motorized *cayuco* and have any doubts about your boatman, consider hiring another one before attempting this trip.

Isla Ailigandí

Ailigandí is a densely populated island. Visitors can stay at the **Hotel Palmera** (public phones ☎ 299-2968/9, ask for Bolívar Arango, who speaks Spanish and Kuna; r per person US$10). The hotel is a two-story building with five rooms and shared bathrooms. There are two or three decent beds, and much-needed windows in each room. Downstairs there's a restaurant that serves simple plates of fish.

Isla Uaguitupo

Uaguitupo is a pleasant, grassy little isle, 100m from the island of Achutupu (which is served by a coastal airstrip). Taking up almost all of Uaguitupo is **Dolphin Island Lodge** (☎ 225-8435; www.dolphinlodge.com; s/d/tr per person US$110/95/86), which consists of nine new and very comfortable concrete-floor stand-alone cabins with private cold-water bathroom with environmentally friendly flush toilet. There's a pleasant open-sided restaurant that serves good food and faces long sets of breakers. Included in the rates are all meals, plus a tour of Achutupu and one or two snorkeling sites. Dolphin Island Lodge receives a substantial number of repeat foreign visitors. English is spoken here and the owner-managers are very accommodating; for example, if you want to find a boat and a guide for some serious exploring, they'll gladly hook you up with a boatman.

USTUPO OGOBSUCUM

pop 5000

This island, 15km southeast of Uaguitupo, has the largest population (5000) of all of the San Blás islands. Ustupo Ogobsucum, widely known as simply Ustupo (the same name used by a tiny community on the mainland a short distance away), is crowded and unattractive, and offers little of interest to the visitor.

Should you decide to visit Ustupo Ogobsucum, you must immediately go to the police station, which is in a two-story structure beside two very tall radio antennae. There you must present your passport and your tourist card or visa, whichever pertains to you (see p303), and pay US$5. Next, you must ask permission from the island's chiefs to wander around the island. If you don't speak Spanish or Kuna, you will have a very difficult time explaining yourself, as none of the chiefs speak any English. If they don't like the way you look, your request will be rejected.

Lodgings on Ustupo Ogobsucum consist of the **Motel Awibe Kuna** (no phone; r per person US$7). This is a concrete, two-story structure with six partitioned cubicles in one decent-size but fanless room. There's a worn mattress on a swaying steel frame in each cubicle and bars on all the windows. The shower consists of a bucket of water in a public area outside the motel, and the toilet is a hole in a board over the ocean with just a little privacy.

ISLA PINO

Isla Pino (Pine Island), named for the lovely forest that covers most of the island, is 25km southeast of Ustupo Ogobsucum (or 1½ hours by 15-horsepower boat). As you approach the 2km-long, 1.5km-wide island, you'll note that it looks astonishingly similar to a whale.

There's a sleepy little town on the western side of Isla Pino, and its 300 inhabitants spend the better part of the day trying to beat the oppressive heat by staying in their hammocks in their thatched houses. When they work, they harvest coconuts and fish.

There are no hotels on the island. In fact, there are no services in town of use to the tourist, except a small provisions stand that

also serves some snacks, beer and soda – nothing much, but the beverages go down nicely in this hot place.

If you're up for a walk, you can take a trail that winds around the island. It skirts dense jungle that's home to large boas, wild rabbits and red-naped tamarins, among other creatures you probably don't have at home.

MULATUPO SASARDÍ

This typical San Blás island, 7km south of Isla Pino, is far removed from the cruise-ship scene, and its 4000 residents actually see very few tourists. The Kuna here are extremely friendly, particularly the children, many of whom will come up to shake your hand and say, 'Hello, mister' or 'Hello, lady' in English (it's about all the English they know).

The place to pay the visitation fee is a two-story building (one of just a few here) facing the island's basketball court. The chiefs usually hang out in this building, and it's important to ask them for permission to see the island. They speak Spanish and Kuna, and will give you permission as long as you're not doing something offensive to them, such as going about in a bikini top or shirtless.

There's a place to stay on the island: the very basic **Isla Herrera Hotel** (Panama City ☎ 262-5562, ask for the hotel; r per person US$20). You bathe here by dipping a bucket into a big barrel and pouring water over yourself. The barrel is behind a family's home near the hotel, as is the toilet, an over-the-sea contraption.

Also on the island is the **Restaurante Mi Pueblo** (chicken & fries US$3) which is run by a Kuna woman who has a smile that could melt a glacier. The chicken is delicious.

Darién Province

CONTENTS

To the Darién Gap	283
El Real	285
Pirre Station	285
Cana	286
La Palma	288
Reserva Natural Punta Patiño	288
Río Sambú	289
Tropic Star Lodge	290
Jaqué	291
Playa de Muerto	291

The Darién is one of the wildest *and* most ravaged areas in the Americas. It is the biggest province in Panama and the country's most sparsely inhabited with fewer than three people per square kilometer. Home to Panama's most spectacular national park and to its worst scenes of habitat destruction, it is two worlds, divided into north and south.

The heavily logged northern Darién has suffered serious environmental damage. Southern Darién – the area south of Yaviza – is the antithesis of the north. Here wildlife abounds and the only 'roads' are jungle-flanked rivers. Most of the southern Darién is within Parque Nacional Darién – 576,000 hectares containing sandy beaches, rocky coasts, mangroves, freshwater marshes and four mountain ranges covered with double- and triple-canopy jungle.

The park is *the* attraction of the Darién. The bird watching here is among the world's finest, with places where you can see four species of macaw fly by with outstanding frequency. The harpy eagle, the world's most powerful bird of prey, resides here, as do giant anteaters, jaguars, ocelots, monkeys, Baird's tapirs, white-lipped peccaries, caimans and American crocodiles.

The southern Darién is an adventurer's dream, offering spectacular opportunities for rain forest exploration by trail or river. It's a place where the primeval meets the present – where the scenery appears much as it did a million years ago. Indians perfected the use of poison-dart guns here and still maintain many of their traditional practices. It's a place for travelers with youthful hearts, intrepid spirits and a yearning for something truly wild. If you've been growing old in a concrete jungle, spend some time in this verdant one – even if it's only for a few days. It's sure to rejuvenate your spirit.

HIGHLIGHTS

- Laying eyes on the majestic **Parque Nacional Darién** (p281), home to vast jungles, jaguars, crocodiles and remote Indian tribes
- Spotting harpy eagles in **Reserva Natural Punta Patiño** (p288), a lush jungle reserve on the edge of Golfo de San Miguel
- Watching the sun rise over verdant **Cana Valley** (p286), where macaws abound and jungle trails lead to abandoned mining trains
- Hiking through virgin rain forest in wildlife-rich **Pirre Station** (p285), which offers spectacular jungle trails
- Taking jungle hikes, dining on fresh lobster and mingling with the locals at **Playa de Muerto** (p291), a traditional Emberá village on the Pacific coast

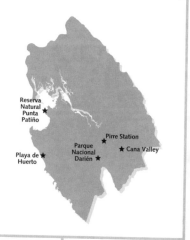

Reserva Natural Punta Patiño ★

Pirre Station ★

Parque Nacional Darién ★   ★ Cana Valley

Playa de ★ Huerto

- AREA: 16,671 SQ KM
- ELEVATION: SEA LEVEL TO 1875M
- POPULATION: 53,000

Emberá & Wounaan Tribes

Living within the boundaries of Parque Nacional Darién are the Chocóes, as they are commonly called. These Indians emigrated here from the Chocó region of Colombia, and they continue to live much the same way they have for thousands of years.

Anthropologists place the Chocóes in two linguistic groups: the Emberá and the Wounaan. But with the exception of language, the two peoples' cultural features are virtually identical – no great surprise considering their shared origins and environment. The external pressures placed on them (chiefly encroachment by white settlers and habitat destruction by loggers) are virtually identical as well. The tribes, however, prefer to be thought of as two separate peoples.

Some historians contend that the Emberá emigrated from northern Ecuador and southern Colombia beginning in 1830, and that the Wounaan emigrated from the Río San Juan area of Colombia (where the greatest concentration of them lives today) around 1910. Other historians say the tribes arrived much earlier. The Indians themselves aren't sure, as they have no written history.

In Panama, by far the greatest number of Emberá and Wounaan live in the Darién. They reside deep in the rain forest beside rivers, particularly the Ríos Sambú, Jaqué, Chico, Tuquesa, Membrillo, Tuira, Yape and Tucutí. They also live, in far smaller numbers, in Panamá and Colón Provinces. Their total population in Panama is estimated to be around 8200.

The Emberá and Wounaan practice subsistence agriculture, followed by hunting, fishing and poultry raising. They also create plantations to grow commercial crops appropriate to the areas in which they live, and they commercially cultivate rice and maize, but to a lesser extent.

Increasingly, the Emberá and Wounaan are replacing their traditional attire with Western wear. Except for a few older individuals, the men have set aside their loincloths for short pants and now prefer short-sleeved shirts to going around barechested. The women, who traditionally wore only a skirt, increasingly don bras, and some have taken to wearing shirts as well.

All of the women used to wear wide silver bracelets and elaborate necklaces made of silver coins, but that practice too is disappearing as tourists offer the Indians more money than they've ever seen to buy their family jewelry. Many Emberá and Wounaan still stain their bodies purplish black with juice from the *jagua* fruit, which is believed to have health-giving properties and to ward off insects.

Emberá and Wounaan homes are well suited to the environment. Built on stilts 3m to 4m off the ground, the floors consist primarily of thin but amazingly strong strips of palm bark. The stilts protect occupants and food from pesky ground animals and swollen rivers.

To permit breezes to enter, more than half of the typical Indian home is open-sided. The roof is made of thatch, which keeps the rain out and acts as good insulation against the tropical sun. The kitchen occupies one corner and has an oven made of mud. A log with stairs carved into it provides access to the home. Emberá and Wounaan grow medicinal plants and edible vegetables and roots around their homes. Pigs and poultry are often raised in pens beneath the elevated houses.

The government of Panama has erected concrete schoolhouses in many of the Indians' villages. Today most Emberá and Wounaan children spend their mornings in class and their afternoons working the land. For fun, they swim in the rivers.

The Emberá and Wounaan are very good woodcarvers and basket weavers. Traditionally the men carved boas, frogs and birds from the dark *cocobolo* hardwood. More recently they have taken to carving tiny figurines (typically of iguanas, turtles, crocodiles and birds) from the ivory-colored *tagua* nut. The women are among the world's finest basket makers. (See p110 for more information about Emberá and Wounaan products.)

The Emberá and Wounaan also produce incredibly fine dugout canoes, which they call *piraguas*. The boats have very shallow bottoms, so they can be used during the dry season when the rivers run low. The Panama Canal Authority employs Emberá and Wounaan craftsmen to make the *piraguas* used by officials to reach the higher parts of the canal's watershed. Most of the Indians' *piraguas* are powered by paddles, but the canal authority *piraguas* are motorized.

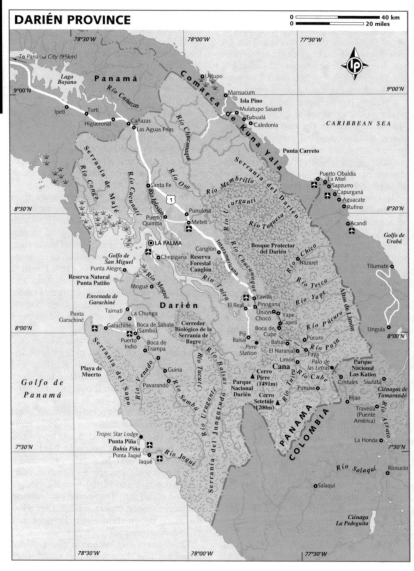

DARIÉN PROVINCE

Until it left Panama in the late 1990s, the US Air Force turned to the Emberá and Wounaan for help, but for an entirely different reason: jungle survival. Because the Indians have the ability to not only survive but to thrive in tropical wilderness, quite a few of them were added to the corps of instructors that trained US astronauts and air force pilots at Fort Sherman, near Colón.

Before the introduction of the gun, the Emberá and Wounaan were expert users of the *boroquera* (blowgun), and they envenomed their darts with lethal toxins from poisonous frogs and bullet ants. Many scholars believe that it was these people who forced the Kuna out of the Darién and into the Caribbean coastal area they now inhabit.

The Emberá and Wounaan are about the toughest people you'll ever meet, yet their smiles could melt silver. Emberá and Wounaan children are friendly and fun-loving; if you want to score points with them (and their parents), bring along a Polaroid camera and plenty of film. Lots of people take photos in Indian villages, but few ever leave the Indians with pictures of themselves.

Climate

Darién Province has two drastically different seasons: the rainy season and the dry season. During the rainy season (mid-April to mid-December) the amount of precipitation here is astounding, with most months boasting more than 500mm. In the dry season there's very little rainfall. As in most other parts of Panama, the temperature here is fairly constant year-round, averaging 25°C to 30°C.

National Parks

Parque Nacional Darién is Panama's crown jewel, boasting 576,000 hectares of wildlife-rich rain forest. The heart of this Unesco World Heritage site is Cana (p286), a former mining valley. The remote Pirre Station (p285) is also inside the park.

The **Reserva Natural Punta Patiño** (p288) is a 26,315-hectare wildlife reserve on the southern shore of the Golfo de San Miguel. It's one of the best places in the country to see the harpy eagle, Panama's national bird.

Dangers & Annoyances

Travel beyond Yaviza toward the Colombian border is possible only on foot or by boat and is extremely risky. This area is known to be frequented by Colombian paramilitaries, drug traffickers, guerrillas and bandits. In recent years tourists have been shot, missionaries have been abducted, and local residents have been robbed, raped and murdered with machetes in towns east and southeast of Yaviza. Two British nationals traveling near the border in 2000 were held hostage by Colombian rebels for nine months before being released.

The US State Department warns travelers not to cross an invisible line that extends from Punta Carreto in Kuna Yala to Yaviza and south to Punta Piña. The area from Nazaret to Punusa is like a low-intensity war zone. The paramilitaries and rebels move in big groups armed with rocket launchers, flamethrowers and machine guns. Panamanian border police buzz the sky in helicopter gunships and tote AK-47s. Travel to the towns of Pinogana, Yape, Boca de Cupe and Paya is foolhardy at best. As of May 2004, however, the tourist haunts of Cana, Bahía Piña and Punta Patiño remained unaffected by the hostilities.

Getting There & Away

The 266km drive from Panama City to Yaviza along the Interamericana passes through Chepo, El Llano, Cañita, Ipetí, Tortí, Higueronal and smaller, unmapped communities in Panamá Province before crossing into the Darién; see the Panamá Province chapter (pp115–138) for details on those towns.

All of the towns to Yaviza are served by buses originating from Panama City's bus terminal. There are five buses daily to Yaviza, with the first departure at 4:15am and the last at 2pm (US$14, six hours). Be sure to tell the bus driver your destination.

Travelers can also fly into the region. **Aeroperlas** (in Panama City ☎ 315-7500) flies to La Palma (US$40), El Real (US$48), Jaqué (US$48), Garachiné (US$50) and Bahía Piña (US$50).

Getting Around

In the jungles of the Darién, rivers are the means of getting from one point to another, with dugout canoes providing the transport. In La Palma you can hire a motorized boat for US$120 to US$200 per day, which can take you to the Río Mogué or the Río Sambú. From either of these rivers you'll have to negotiate with indigenous villages (in Mogué or La Chunga) to take you further upriver in *cayucos* (dugout canoes). Hiring boats in Río Jaqué is possible but strongly ill-advised owing to the dangers of guerilla activity. A shorter (and cheaper) boat trip goes from Puerto Quimba to La Palma (p284).

TO THE DARIÉN GAP
Las Aguas Frías

Near the border of Panamá and Darién Provinces are the towns of Las Agua Fría Uno and Agua Fría Dos (3km southeast of Uno). There's no phone in either town. Agua Fría Dos has a gas station and a place with a sign out front that reads 'Pensión Interiorana,' but its rooms are only rented to longterm tenants. Agua Fría Uno is 7km southeast of Cañazas.

Santa Fé
pop 5900

In this town, 21km southeast of Agua Fría Dos and 3km from the Interamericana, there are two hotels, both along the main road into town (leading off the Interamericana). On the left side of the road is **Motel Honee Kaiba** (☎ 299-6727; s/d/tw US$6/8/10), which has 14 grim rooms with so-so beds, ceiling fans and private cold-water bathroom. There are also four crappy rooms with shared bathroom for the same price.

About 500m further on as you continue into Santa Fé, you'll come across the **Habitaciones Rosned** (☎ 299-6434; r with fan/air-con US$7/15) on the right side of the road. Here you'll find some of the best accommodations in the area. The seven rooms are well-maintained with tile floors and modern private bathrooms. One of the rooms is large enough to accommodate three or four. Downstairs is a bakery and a general store.

Punulosa
pop 200

This community is notable for its border police checkpoint. Here, motorists traveling in either direction are stopped and asked where they are coming from and where they are going. Sometimes travelers headed southeast are asked to present their identifications; if you're a foreigner, your ID is your passport. The soldier will return your identification to you in a few minutes. Occasionally, a soldier will give a foreigner a brief lecture about the dangers near the border. That's because these soldiers are the ones sent into the dangerous area to search for tourists every time one disappears.

Metetí
pop 6400

This town is 1km southeast of Punulosa. There's a gas station here, plus a public phone, a bank and a hotel. **Hotel Felicidad** (☎ 299-6188; r with shared/private bathroom US$8/15), above the Felicidad restaurant, offers 33 rooms. Although there's one other hotel between here and Yaviza, this is the last decent place before the end of the road. There

are several restaurants in Metetí; **La Felicidad** (meals US$2.50-4.50) is the best of them.

From Metetí, you can take a turnoff for Puerto Quimba, a port on the Río Iglesias; the road between Metetí and Puerto Quimba is 19.7km long. At the time of writing, it was one of only two paved roads in Darién Province, the other being the stretch of the Interamericana up to Aguas Frias. At Puerto Quimba it's possible to board a boat to La Palma, the provincial capital. Boats to La Palma leave hourly from 7:30am to 6:30pm (US$2.50); they depart from La Palma hourly from 5:30am to 12:30pm, and from 2pm to 5pm. There is a pickup truck shuttle service between Metetí and Puerto Quimba every 30 minutes from 6am till 9pm (US$1.25).

Traveling to La Palma by boat from Puerto Quimba is an excellent alternative to flying straight in from Panama City. The scenery along this 30-minute river trip is of jungle and mangroves – very nice.

Yaviza
pop 3300

The Interamericana just kind of fizzles at the town of Yaviza. No sign announces that you've reached the famous Darién Gap. The highway ends and then there's just a narrow stretch of dirt road beside which trucks, buses and a few cars park. And the town seems filled with people who appear to have nothing but time on their hands.

There are a couple of awful-looking restaurants in this town at the meeting of the Ríos Chucunaque and Chico. There's one hotel, the **Hotel 3 Americas** (r US $8), which has 10 rooms with fans, worn beds, stained walls and a common bathroom. There's a loud bar next door, and the town is hot as Hades. Welcome to the end of the road!

If you just want to see some of the Darién and don't have a compelling reason to be in Yaviza, you're encouraged to take the turnoff at Metetí, proceed to Puerto Quimba and go by boat to La Palma (p288). The scenes from the boat to La Palma will give you a good sense of the wild frontier that still exists in much of Darién Province, whereas the views from the highway between Metití and Yaviza convey mostly destruction. From La Palma, restless spirits can travel deeper into the heart of Darién if they so desire.

EL REAL

pop 1300

El Real dates from the days of the early conquistadors. They constructed a fort here, beside the Río Tuira, to prevent pirates from sailing upriver and attacking Santa María. Gold from mines in the valley of Cana, to the south, was brought to Santa María and stored until there was a quantity sufficient to warrant assembling an armada and moving the bullion to Panama City.

Today, this hot and humid place is one of the largest towns in the Darién. It's nothing special, but it is home to the closest airstrip to the Pirre ranger station, south of town, which offers excellent bird watching (see opposite). There's an Autoridad Nacional del Ambiente (ANAM; National Environment Authority) office in town where you can get permission to visit Pirre Station. The best way to locate this office is to ask someone to point you toward it, as none of the wide paths in town have names.

El Real has no bank. The only hotel, **El Mazareno** (r per person US$8), has seven mildewy rooms with U-shaped mattresses, and shared toilets that don't flush thoroughly.

Aeroperlas (in Panama City ☎ 315-7500) flies from El Real to Panama City at 10:55am on Monday, Wednesday and Friday (US$48, 75 minutes), with a stop in La Palma along the way.

PIRRE STATION

Pirre is an ANAM ranger station just inside the Parque Nacional Darién, 13km south of El Real as the lemon-spectacled tanager flies. It is, to steal a line from naturalist guide Hernán Araúz, 'Panama's foremost theater of life.' Pirre is of particular interest to birders, although most of the bird species represented here can also be found in Cana Valley, an excellent bird watching area that lies further south (see p286). Specialties at Pirre include the crimson-bellied woodpecker, the white-fronted nunbird and the striped woodhaunter.

If you intend to visit Pirre Station, you must first get permission from the ANAM office in El Real (see opposite) and pay US$3; if no one's at the office when you arrive, ask around for Narciso 'Chicho' Bristan, who can take care of business.

The area around Pirre is the most accessible section of the park, and the station's strength is that two good hiking trails originate from it. One trail leads to Pirre Mountain ridge, which takes most hikers two days to reach. Tents are pretty much a necessity. The other trail winds through jungle to a series of cascades about an hour's hike away. Neither trail should be attempted without a guide, as they are not well marked and if you get lost out here, you're finished. You can hire a ranger as a

---

THEY DROVE THE DARIÉN GAP

In 1960 – back when the Carretera Interamericana reached only as far as Chepo, 52km east of Panama City – a group of adventurers sought to become the first people to drive between North and South America. Their destination: Bogotá, Colombia, 433km from Chepo by land – 297km of it through primeval jungle in a region called the Darién. Those 297km then formed the Darién Gap.

The adventurers consisted of a distinguished crew of six men and two women, as well as nine local woodsmen – who were hired to cut a path through the jungle for the vehicles, a US-built jeep and a British Land Rover. Also on board for most of the trip was Kip Ross, a *National Geographic* writer whose fascinating article on the expedition appeared in the society's March 1961 journal.

All told, the entire enterprise took four months and 28 days. The team crossed 180 rivers and streams and was forced to improvise bridges over 125 of them, built mainly from the trunks of palm trees. At times progress was slowed to 5km a day. Although several major vehicular mishaps occurred, no snakebites or serious injuries were sustained.

Among the group were historian Amado Araúz and his wife, Reina, the finest anthropologist Panama has produced. (Amado provided much of the information on the Emberá and Wounaan Indians that appears in this book.) Reina founded nine museums and wrote the definitive books on Panama's tribes before cancer took her life at the age of 48. Their son, Hernán Araúz, is now widely regarded as the country's top nature guide (see p290).

guide (contact the ANAM office, p285), or you can hire one of the excellent naturalist guides from Ancon Expeditions (p90) in Panama City.

Fifteen kilometers separate the station and Cana Valley, and between the two there's nothing but virgin rain forest. Unfortunately, no trails link Pirre Station and Cana, although trails lead from both sites to the Pirre Mountain ridge. Contact Ancon Expeditions of Panama (p90) if you're considering a Pirre to Cana trek.

At Pirre Station are **barracks** (cots per person US$10) with a front room with fold-out cots for visitors, a dining area that consists of two tables and four benches beside a very rustic kitchen, a *palapa* (open-sided shelter) with a few chairs, and one outhouse. Bathing is done in a nearby creek. There is no electricity at the station. Like Cana, Pirre is relatively cool and not very buggy.

If you plan on eating, you must bring your own food. The rangers will cook your food for you (US$5 a day is most appreciated), but you must provide bottled water. However, if you've got a water-purification system or tablets, the water in the creek should be OK, and there are lots of lemon trees in the vicinity of the station. Be sure to try the *zapote* growing at the station. This fruit has a fleshy orange meat with the appearance, taste and texture of mango. It's highly addictive.

Beware: most of Parque Nacional Darién is prime fer-de-lance territory, and these very deadly snakes have been found near the station. Always wear boots and long trousers when you're walking in camp at night or entering the forest at any time.

Getting There & Away

Pirre Station can only be reached by hiking or by a combination of hiking and boating. The hike from El Real takes three hours. You can also take a one-hour canoe ride from El Real to the village of Piji Baisal and then hike for one hour from Piji Baisal to Pirre Station.

First, you'll need to get to El Real (p285), which can be reached by plane or boat. Then, if you prefer to hike, take the 'road' connecting El Real and Pirre Station. This road is covered with 2m-high lemongrass. Hiking this barely discernible road takes about three hours and pretty much requires

a guide. The ANAM station in El Real can help you find a local guide (expect to pay about US$20).

The alternative is to hire a boatman to take you up the Río Pirre to Piji Baisal. Expect to pay about US$40 plus the cost of gasoline. From Piji Baisal, it's a one-hour hike to the station. Again, you'll need a guide to lead you to the station, as no signs mark the way.

CANA

Cana, a valley nestled in foothills on the eastern slope of Pirre Ridge, is the most isolated place in the Republic of Panama and home to some of the world's finest bird watching. About 60 Panamanian bird species can be found only in Parque Nacional Darién, and Cana is at the park's lush heart.

In addition to four species of macaw, Cana is known for its harpy eagles, black-tipped cotingas, dusky-backed jacamars, rufous-cheeked hummingbirds and golden-headed quetzals. Many bird species can be found much more easily here than elsewhere in Panama. Cana is also home to jaguars, pumas, ocelots and margays, but you'd be extremely fortunate to see one of these cats. They avoid people and generally prowl at night.

Although the town of Santa Cruz de Cana, which was founded by Spaniards in the 16th century, has been completely overgrown, the valley is not entirely devoid of human habitations. There's an airstrip at the eastern end of the valley, and a short walk from it there's a border-police station, as well as an ANAM/ANCON field station (see opposite).

History

A survey of Cana determined that a lake covered most of the valley's floor during prehistoric times. Experts speculate that the lake emptied when an earthquake created a divide that allowed the water to drain; such was the case at El Valle in Coclé Province. As you enter the valley by air, you can still see a marshy area and some ponds – remnants of the prehistoric lake.

During the early 16th century, Spaniards discovered gold in the valley, and in the years that followed they mined the place using regional Indians as well as slaves brought from Africa. Las Minas del Espíritu Santo (Mines of the Holy Spirit), as they were called, at one time filled the valley with 20,000 people. They lived in the town of Santa Cruz de Cana, which has long since been reclaimed by the jungle.

One of the longest rivers in the Darién, the Río Tuira, runs northward past Cana and out to the Pacific Ocean. The Spaniards used to send supplies to the Cana Valley via the Tuira, and they sent gold from the valley to Santa María, on the western bank of the river, for safekeeping until boats arrived to transport the precious metal to Panama City.

Naturally, the vast quantities of gold at Santa María attracted pirates, and the town fell numerous times. When the Spaniards left Panama in the 1820s, the mines were abandoned.

An English outfit visited Cana in the early 20th century and discovered that there was still gold to be found in the hills. They ran train tracks from the valley to Boca de Cupe, 20km away, and moved men, supplies and gold along them in small locomotives and in freight cars. When these Englishmen cleared out, 20 years later, they left their trains behind. Today you can find several rusting locomotives, numerous freight cars and many mines amid Cana's dense jungle.

Hiking

Three trails begin near the ANAM/ANCON field station (see right): the Cituro Trail, the Machinery Trail and the Stream Trail.

The **Cituro Trail** begins at the northeastern corner of the station and winds a couple of hundred meters through secondary forest, paralleling some old railroad tracks and passing a rusted-out locomotive with the brand name 'Cituro' forged into it.

The **Machinery Trail** is a loop trail that begins at the western edge of the station and winds several hundred meters through secondary forest to the remains of another abandoned Cituro locomotive, a very overgrown smelter and other pieces of mining machinery.

The **Stream Trail** is glorious but short – only 50m – running from behind the field station to a small creek where you can take a refreshing dip.

Beside the valley's grass-and-dirt airstrip, which is about 100m from the field station, the mouths of two more trails disappear into the dense rain forest: the Pirre Mountain Trail and Boca de Cupe Trail.

The **Pirre Mountain Trail**, starting near the western end of the airstrip, offers a six-hour ridgeline hike to a campsite high above the Cana Valley. The campsite is in cloud forest, and it's cool and refreshing at night. If you're traveling to Cana with a tour operator's assistance and want to camp along the ridge, let the operator know in advance so that it can arrange tents for you.

The **Boca de Cupe Trail** runs north from Cana to the town of Boca de Cupe, a two- to three-day hike. However, because of bandits, guerrillas and paramilitaries in the vicinity of Boca de Cupe, use of this trail is not recommended. Be advised too that the trail crosses the knee-deep Río Cupe six times. It initially passes through secondary and thereafter only virgin jungle.

Please resist the temptation to explore the old mines in the area. At least one tourist who wandered into an old Cana mine developed a life-threatening respiratory illness after inhaling something nasty in the tunnel.

Sleeping

The valley's **ANAM/ANCON field station** is a wooden structure that was built by gold workers during the 1970s and enlarged in mid-1998 by the wildlife conservation group ANCON. Tourists can stay at the barrackslike station, at the eastern end of Cana Valley, but only if they have arranged their trips through Ancon Expeditions (upwards of US$2400 per person for two weeks; see p90 for further details). Although Cana is managed by ANAM, the station is maintained by ANCON (parent to Ancon Expeditions), and ANCON does not allow other tour operators to use the facility.

Each room contains two or three firm beds and a shelf on which to place a candle at night, but nothing more. Food is provided for guests. There's no electricity and it's shared bathrooms only, but the place is clean and pleasant and cool at night. When you consider the awesome hiking and the bird watching possibilities in the area, the station is outstanding.

Getting There & Away

Except for a several-day hike, the only way into the valley is by chartered aircraft. Even if you arrive on foot, Ancon Expeditions (p90) has a monopoly on the valley's sole lodgings so you need to contact that company to make arrangements. At the time of writing, Ancon Expeditions offered an excellent five-day, four-night package that included an English-speaking guide, all meals, accommodations (including tent camping along the Pirre Mountain Trail, with all provisions carried by porters) and transportation to and from Panama City. Contact Ancon Expeditions (p90) for rates.

LA PALMA

pop 4200

La Palma is the provincial capital and is also the most populous town in the Darién. La Palma is at the mouth of the Río Tuira, where the wide river meets the Golfo de San Miguel. It was actually the San Miguel gulf, not the much larger Golfo de Panamá, that Balboa saw when he became the first European to set eyes on the Pacific.

Despite its lofty position as capital of the largest province in Panama, La Palma doesn't offer much to see or do. It's pretty much a one-street town, with the street following the sweeping river bank. Every facility of possible interest to the traveler is on this street, within 300m of the airstrip. La Palma is home to the only bank in the Darién, the Banco Nacional de Panamá. There's also a hospital, a port and a police station (if you intend to go anywhere near the Colombian border and you speak Spanish, you should talk to the police here first), as well as three hotels, three bars and several food stands. By far the busiest places are the airstrip and the small port.

Most travelers visit La Palma for one of two reasons: they're here to catch a plane to somewhere else or they're here to take a boat ride to somewhere else. The two most popular boating destinations are the Ancon nature reserve and lodge at Reserva Natural Punta Patiño (right) and the Emberá villages along the banks of the Río Sambú (p289).

You can visit these destinations on your own; if you speak Spanish, you can usually find someone near the dock who owns a boat and is willing to go on an adventure with you for the right price (US$120 to US$200 per day, gas included). Most people, however, prefer to make these trips with a guide, so that everything is conveniently prearranged (see Transportation, p313, for information on Panamanian tour companies).

Sleeping & Eating

Hotel Biaquira Bagara (Casa Ramady; ☎ /fax 299-6224; r with shared/private bathroom US$15/20) This is the best of the three hotels in La Palma. It's run by the friendly Ramady family, who live in a home beneath the 13 rooms they rent. Six rooms have cold-water private bathroom with bathtub. Several of the clean, fan-cooled rooms have private balcony. Some beds are firmer than others; ask to see several rooms. There's also a lovely sitting area facing the river. This place is a godsend after a week or two in the jungle.

Pensión Tuira (s/tw US$10/15) These accommodations offer 11 small rooms with decent beds and fan.

La Pensión Takela (☎ 299-6490; s/d with shared bathroom US$10/12, with private bathroom US$12/14) Like the other two, this hotel is at river's edge. It has nine fan-cooled rooms, three with private bathroom and old TV. It is the worst of the three.

Refresquería Guivi (☺ 8:30am-8pm) This is owned and run by Viola Maria Avila, who's very friendly and a good cook. Among her offerings are chicken stew with spaghetti and rice (US$2), beer and sodas.

Getting There & Away

Aeroperlas (Panama City ☎ 315-7500) flies from La Palma to Panama City at 10:30am on Monday, Wednesday and Friday (US$40). Flights from Panama City to La Palma depart from Albrook at 9:30am on Monday, Wednesday and Friday (US$40) and arrive around 10:20am.

RESERVA NATURAL PUNTA PATIÑO

Punta Patiño, on the southern shore of the Golfo de San Miguel 25km from La Palma, is known mainly for its 26,315-hectare **wildlife preserve**, which is owned by the conservation group ANCON. The only way to reach the preserve, short of hacking your way through many kilometers of jungle, is by boat.

The boat ride is definitely part of the Punta Patiño experience. The ride begins at La Palma and takes you into the gulf but not too far from shore. You'll likely pass shrimp boats and fishermen in dugouts using nets. After about 45 minutes, you'll pass the mouth of the Río Mogué, which is flanked primarily by virgin forest. There's an **Emberá village** on the bank of the Mogué, about 30 minutes upriver by boat. The village is home to about 400 people and remains fairly traditional.

About 10 minutes after you leave the mouth of the Mogué and head south along the coast, you'll pass the small community of **Punta Alegre**. *Alegre* means 'happy,' and this does seem to be a pretty content community despite the poverty in which the 500 or so African-descent inhabitants live. Most of the adults make their living fishing from dugout canoes in the gulf. Their music, which relies heavily on bongo drums, is pure West African. If you're lucky, some of the men and women here will bring out their guitars and drums.

There are no places to stay in Punta Alegre, but there are a couple of simple restaurants. Punta Alegre's food, which typically consists of fresh fish and prawns, is quite tasty.

A handful of Emberá families live at the southern end of Punta Alegre. And it's a good place to get a *jagua*-juice 'tattoo,' in the same manner that the Emberá paint themselves. The juice stains the skin for about a week. Consider getting painted if you're only days from going home and there's someone you'd like to surprise with your 'permanent tattoo.'

Continuing south another 20 minutes, you'll reach an expansive beach. A 400m-long dirt road winds from the beach to the restaurant and cabins near the center of the Punta Patiño ANCON preserve, passing a swamp with several crocodiles and a meadow frequented by capybaras, the world's largest rodents.

The preserve contains lots of species-rich primary forest, but the jungle is a fair walk from the cabins and it's pretty buggy. The panorama of the gulf from the dining and viewing area, which is perched atop a ridge near the cabins, is spellbinding, particularly at daybreak. The cabins, all of which have private bathrooms, are quite comfortable. There's no good place to go swimming nearby, however.

Visitors to the preserve are treated to guided night and morning nature hikes. During the day, they can explore by boat the mangroves lining the gulf, chat with fishermen at work (all are friendly but none speak English) or drop by Punta Alegre.

Getting There & Away
If you prefer, you can get to ANCON's preserve on your own without booking a guided tour through Ancon Expeditions, the organization's for-profit arm, but you must notify Ancon Expeditions in advance so that it can reserve a cabin for you (see p90 for contact information). If you visit without Ancon Expeditions' help, lodging and three daily meals will cost you US$90 per person per day. You can hire boats in La Palma to reach Punta Patiño; expect to pay your boatman about US$120 to US$150 per day.

Ancon Expeditions offers a package tour to Punta Patiño that includes the roundtrip airfare between Panama City and La Palma, a boat ride up the Río Mogué to the Emberá village, a visit to Punta Alegre, hikes in the preserve, guide service and all meals. The three-day, two-night adventure costs about US$600 per person (party of two) and substantially less per person for larger parties.

RÍO SAMBÚ
The mouth of the wide, brown Río Sambú is 1½ hours by fast boat south of Punta Patiño. Traveling it is a heart-of-darkness experience: you pass through spectacular jungle inhabited by jaguars and mountain lions and Indians who until recently did most of their hunting with blowguns. The river meanders for many kilometers toward the Colombian border, passing Emberá villages along the way. The further you go up the river, the more traditional are these Indian villages.

Boats and boatmen can be hired in La Palma, or you can travel with a guide (see p290). When you reach the Río Sambú, you will need to hire a dugout canoe to get further upriver. During the rainy season, the river is navigable by dugout all the way to Pavarandó, the most inland of the eight Emberá communities on the Sambú.

Prior to 1990 or 1991, the indigenous people living beside the river led traditional Emberá lives – they grew corn, rice, plantains and other crops; they fished the river and went about dressed in the manner of their ancestors (the women bare-breasted and wearing colorful knee-length skirts, the men wearing only loincloths).

Today, the Sambú continues to provide the Emberá with fish, traditional methods of agriculture are still practiced, and the

Emberá still reside mainly in open-sided thatched-roof houses atop stilts. But western attire is replacing traditional dress, outboard motors are increasingly seen on the Indians' dugouts and Christianity brought by missionaries is replacing traditional Emberá religious practices.

At night, you can make camp where you please if you have a tent. However, unless you've brought an individual tent for your boatman, he will prefer an alternative – making a deal to sleep on the floor of an Emberá family's home. If you can speak Spanish, finding a family to move in with for the night isn't difficult, and even getting a hot meal is easy. Money talks, and it talks loudly in these Emberá villages. Expect to pay US$10 per person for shelter and US$5 for food.

Before you go to sleep, apply insect repellent liberally to avoid waking up with hundreds of bites. Be forewarned: a trip far up the Río Sambú is not everyone's cup of tea. Even before you reach the river, you will be on a boat rather a long time under a broiling tropical sun. And if riding in a boat that's loaded down with leaking gasoline cans bothers you, you should probably pass on the Sambú: you'll need to bring several large containers of gasoline along from La Palma to fuel the canoe that you'll hire upriver.

There are other minor hardships, like the lack of showers and toilets. But the Sambú offers you true adventure, something that may not even be possible anywhere in the Tropics 50 years from now. Even if you travel deep into the Amazon, you'd be hard-pressed to find such wilderness and such people these days.

Getting There & Away
If you speak Spanish, you can travel up the Sambú without the assistance of a tour operator. But if you or your traveling companions don't speak the language, you'll want to hire a guide. You will need to do this because the boat you'll hire in La Palma to reach the Sambú will sit too low in the water to navigate the upper portions of the river; to get any further upriver, you must negotiate the use of a shallow dugout in one of the Emberá villages. If you don't speak fluent Spanish, these negotiations could prove futile. Be advised that when you rent a boat anywhere in Panama, you're also hiring its

owner to operate the vessel. Remember too that you must bring enough gasoline from La Palma to fuel your dugout.

As for guides, only one name jumps to mind when the destination is the Darién: **Hernán Araúz** (☎ 269-9414, cellular 625-5755; birder@sinfo.net). Hernán is widely regarded as *the* guide for Panama's wild eastern province. He has 10 trans-Darién expeditions to his credit, and he has a wealth of knowledge about the rivers, the indigenous tribes and the wildlife – especially the birds – of Darién.

TROPIC STAR LODGE
Overlooking Bahía Piña, near the southern tip of the Darién, is one of Panama's legendary institutions: **Tropic Star Lodge** (USA ☎ 800-682-3424; www.tropicstar.com; ☒). This is the only lodge that serves Bahía Piña, and more International Game Fish Association (IGFA) world records have been broken in the bay than anywhere else.

The facilities include stand-alone cabins, a pool, a restaurant, a bar and porch with lovely bay views, and even a so-called 'palace' that was built by a Texas oil tycoon as his home away from home in 1961. The facilities are on a manicured hillside overlooking the protected bay and the lodge's fleet of 31ft Bertrams, the Ferraris of sportfishing boats.

Everything here is done just right, from the superb multicourse dinners to the professional fishing guides, and there's a sense of camaraderie among the guests, many of whom are millionaires and/or celebrities.

Weekly packages include the use of a boat with a captain and mate, all meals, and fishing tackle and leaders. Rates vary with the number of people in a boat. From April to September: US$7495/4195 per person for one/two people in a boat and US$3395/2895 per person for three/four people in a boat. The rates go up from January to March.

Getting There & Away
Aeroperlas (in Panama City ☎ 315-7500) flies from the capital to the Bahía Piña airstrip at 9:15am Tuesday, Thursday and Saturday (US$44). A short dirt road links the Bahía Piña airstrip to the Tropic Star Lodge. Flights to Panama City depart Bahía Piña at 10:25am, stopping at Jaqué at 10:40am on Tuesday, Thursday and Saturday.

Hotels

Usually there is no shortage of places to stay in Panama, although getting a hotel room during Carnaval, Semana Santa (Easter week) and other holiday times can be difficult in some places. Finding a room on a popular island (Isla Grande, for example) can be tough on a lovely weekend during the dry season. Hotel accommodations can also be tight if there is a special event going on in a particular town.

Some travelers prefer to make advance reservations everywhere; this is generally possible and is recommended in the better places and in the increasingly popular Bocas del Toro town on Isla Colón. Sending emails to make reservations is the most common way of booking a room.

Before accepting a room, ask to see several. The same prices are often charged for rooms of widely differing quality. Even in the US$10-a-night cheapies it's worth looking around. If you are shown a horrible airless box with just a bed and a bare light bulb, you can ask to see a better room without giving offense. You'll often be amazed at the results. Naturally, hotels want you to rent their most expensive rooms; if you're on a tight budget, make a habit of asking if economical rooms are available. (Some Panamanian hotels have them but don't post their lowest prices.)

Lodges

A handful of lodges lies scattered about the country, most notably in Darién and Guadalupe (p220) in Chiriquí Province. Although these places aren't cheap, they provide an excellent opportunity to be surrounded by nature with access to some spectacular hiking and wildlife-watching nearby.

Rental Accommodations

You can arrange short- or long-term rental accommodations through **Haciendas Panama** (☎ 612-5577). This agency has lovely homes for rent in Coronado, Cañazas and Santa Catalina. Prices start at US$200 a night and guesthouses can sleep from five to 14.

Resorts

Panama also has a growing number of all-inclusive resorts, which often include meals, activities, private beach access and all the amenities. These can be a good option for those with children, as most resorts offer plenty of diversions for kids and adults.

ACTIVITIES

Panama has scores of ways to spend a sun-drenched afternoon, from hiking through lush rain forests to snorkeling among coral reefs. The diving, surfing, bird watching and fishing are just a few of Panama's star attractions. For a complete list of what the country offers, see p53.

BUSINESS HOURS

Opening hours for travel agents, tour operators and other businesses are normally 8am to noon and 1:30pm to 5pm weekdays,

---

PRACTICALITIES

- Panamanians use the metric system for weights and measures, except that they pump gasoline by the *galón* (gallon) and occasionally use pounds and miles.

- Electrical current is 120 volts in Panama City and 110 volts, 60Hz elsewhere. Plugs are two-pronged, the same as in the US and Canada.

- The most widely circulated daily newspaper in Panama is *La Prensa* (www.prensa.com in Spanish).

- The *Panama News* (www.thepanamanews.com) is published in English every two weeks and distributed free in Panama City.

- There are three commercial TV stations in Panama (channels two, four and 13) and two devoted to public broadcasting (five and 11). Most hotels mid-range and up have cable TV with Spanish and English channels.

- Popular radio stations in Panama (the signal's best in and near the capital) include 97.1 and 102.1 (salsa), 88.9 (Latin jazz), 88.1 (reggae), 94.5 (traditional Panamanian), 106.7 (Latin rock) and 98.9 (US rock).

and 8am to noon Saturday. Government offices, including post offices, are open 8am to 4pm weekdays and don't close for lunch. Most banks are open 8:30am to 1pm or 3pm weekdays; some have Saturday hours as well. Shops and pharmacies are generally open from around 9am or 10am until 6pm or 7pm Monday to Saturday.

Grocery stores keep longer hours, opening around 8am and closing around 8pm or 9pm. A handful of grocery stores in Panama City stay open 24 hours.

Restaurants usually open for lunch from noon to 3pm and dinner from 6pm to 10pm. Those that offer breakfast open from 7am to 10am. On Sundays, many restaurants close. In Panama City and David, restaurants open later on Friday and Saturday nights, until about 11pm or midnight. Most bars are open from around noon to 10pm, later on Friday and Saturday nights (typically 2am). Nightclubs in Panama City open around 10pm or 11pm and close at 3am or 4am.

CHILDREN

Panamanians have a family-oriented culture, and will generally be very accommodating to travelers with children. The same can't be said of many businesses owned by expats, who state very clearly the age requirements of their guests.

High chairs in restaurants are a rarity in Panama, but safety seats in hired cars can be provided upon request. For diapers, creams and other supplies, the best places to stock up are in Panama City and David. Fresh milk is rare and may not be pasteurized. Packet UHT milk and powdered milk are more common. Most of Panama is quite safe to travel with children. The places that present greater health risks include Bocas del Toro, where dengue fever is present, and the Darién region, where malaria and yellow fever, though rare, still exist.

Among its rain forests, beaches and waterways, Panama has some fantastic sights for children. The Panama Canal is a favorite, and kids are likely to enjoy the interactive new museum at the Miraflores Visitors Center (p119). A cruise up the canal is another option, though the full-transit tour is not recommended, owing to its length. Many Panamanian families enjoy outings to Isla Taboga (p123), where there is both beach and fine walking opportunities, along

with plenty of snacking spots. The boat ride out there is quite nice as well.

A number of tours, some low-intensity, can be an enjoyable way for you and your children to see Panama's lush environment. You can visit Emberá villages along the Río Chagres (see p90), hike along Pipeline Rd (p121), or take a boat tour into thick rain forest, with great wildlife-viewing opportunities. Tour outfits such as Ancon Expeditions (p90) will help make arrangements.

And if the kids (or you) simply need a day off, there's always the cinema, shopping and food courts in the nicely air-conditioned Multicentro (p111).

Older kids can take advantage of river rafting in Chiriquí (p210), horseback riding in El Valle (p144) or Boquete (p211) and snorkeling in Bocas del Toro (p231).

The supermarkets are excellent in Panama, and you can find just about any product you'd find in the US. For more ideas about making the most of your family travels, get a hold of Lonely Planet's *Travel with Children*.

CLIMATE CHARTS

Much of Panama falls into the pattern of rainy season (mid-April to mid-December) and dry season (mid-December to mid-April). This is true for the Pacific slope, but the Caribbean side can get rain throughout the year. For more information see p13.

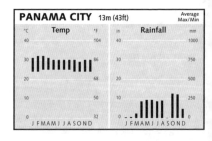

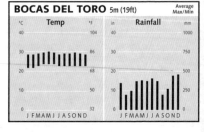

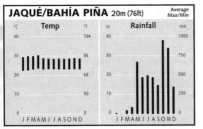

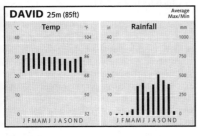

COURSES

Panama offers only several intensive Spanish-language programs: two in Panama City (p90) and the other in Bocas del Toro (p232). Those who want to go out dancing in some of the capital's nightclubs should learn the right moves: take a few salsa or merengue classes while in Panama City. See p90 for details.

CUSTOMS

You may bring up to 200 cigarettes and three bottles of liquor into Panama tax free. If you try to leave Panama with products made from endangered species – such as jaguar teeth, ocelot skins and turtle shell – you'll face a steep fine and jail time.

DANGERS & ANNOYANCES

Crime is a problem in certain parts of Panama City, namely the districts of Chorrillo and Calidonia. It can also be dangerous to stroll the Casco Viejo district at night. In general, use common sense; stay where it's well lit and there are plenty of people.

Colón has some upscale residential areas, but most of the city is a sad slum widely known for street crime. If you walk around, even in the middle of the day, well-meaning residents will inform you that you are in danger. Unless you've just got to visit Colón's Zona Libre, it's best to avoid the city altogether.

Parts of Darién Province are extremely dangerous. Many people, including tourists and missionaries, have been kidnapped and/or murdered in the vicinity of the Colombian border.

Plying the waters of the Archipiélago de San Blás are numerous Colombian boats that run back and forth between the Zona Libre in Colón and Cartagena, Colombia. It has been well documented that some of these boats carry cocaine on their northbound voyages. If you decide to ride on one of these slow cargo boats, be forewarned that your crew may be trafficking drugs.

Hiking Safety

You should be adequately prepared for hiking trips. Always carry plenty of water, even on short journeys, and always bring adequate clothing; jungles *do* cool down a lot at night, particularly at higher elevations. Hikers have been known to get lost in rain forests – even seemingly user-friendly ones such as Parque Nacional Volcán Barú. A Panamanian hiker who entered that park in 1995 was never seen again; it's assumed that he got lost, died of hypothermia and was fed upon by various creatures.

Never walk in unmarked rain forest; if there's no trail going in, you can assume that there won't be one when you decide to turn around and come back out. Always let someone know where you are going, in order to narrow the search area in the event of an emergency.

Police

Police corruption is not as big a problem in Panama as it is in some other Latin American countries. However, it's not unheard of for a Panamanian police officer to stop a motorist for no obvious reason, accuse him or her of violating a law, and levy a fine to be paid on the spot. If there are people around, making a big scene will sometimes fluster the officer into letting you go. Most of the time, however, you become an unwilling participant in a waiting game.

Your best option, unless you want to try to wait out the officer, is to negotiate the fine down. Most officers will insist the fine is US$20. However, US$5 is the going rate for 'getting out of trouble.' Failure to pay anything can result in your being led to jail with the officer insisting you really did break some law.

Swimming Safety

Sadly, in recent years there have been several deaths in Bocas del Toro Province and on other beaches around the country owing to strong currents. Tourist brochures do not mention the drownings that occur every year in Panamanian waters. Of these, about 80% are caused by rip currents. A rip current is a strong current that pulls the swimmer out to sea. It occurs when two currents that move parallel to the shore meet, causing the opposing waters to choose the path of least resistance, which is a path out to sea. It is most important to remember that rip currents will pull you *out* but not *under*.

If you find yourself caught in a rip current, stay calm and swim parallel to the shore to get out of it – rip currents dissipate quickly. When the current dissipates, swim back in at a 45° angle to the shore to avoid being caught by the current again. Do not try to swim directly back in, as you would be swimming against the rip current and would only exhaust yourself.

If you feel a rip current while you are wading, try to come back in sideways, thus offering less body surface to the current. If you cannot make headway, walk parallel to the beach so that you can get out of the rip current.

Thefts & Muggings

Tourist-oriented crime is uncommon in Panama, but it does happen, particularly in the districts of Chorrillo and Calidonia. Be smart; avoid carrying all your money in one place, avoid entering areas that appear unsafe, and adhere to the rule 'if a deal seems too good to be true, it probably is.' This last rule is a reference to Panama's confidence artists – people who defraud others after gaining their trust – of which there are many.

If you elect to go bar-hopping in Casco Viejo at night, play it smart and follow this advice: leave your watch, jewelry and expensive clothing at the hotel; take only the amount of money you think you'll need, and then a little extra tucked away in a shoe; and be sure to carry photographic ID (it's the law). If you look like you don't have anything of value on you, you're less likely to interest a mugger.

It is a good idea to carry an emergency packet somewhere separate from all your other valuables. It should contain a photocopy of the essential pages of your passport. On the back of the photocopy you should list important numbers, such as your traveler's checks' serial numbers, airline ticket numbers, and credit card and bank account numbers. Also keep one high-denomination bill with this emergency stash.

If you are robbed, you should get a police report as soon as possible. This is a require-

---

SAFETY GUIDELINES FOR DIVING

Before embarking on a scuba diving, skin diving or snorkeling trip, carefully consider the following points to ensure a safe and enjoyable experience:

- Possess a current diving certification card from a recognized scuba diving instructional agency (if scuba diving).

- Be sure you are healthy and feel comfortable diving.

- Obtain reliable information about physical and environmental conditions at the dive site (eg from a reputable local dive operation).

- Be aware of local laws, regulations and etiquette about marine life and the environment.

- Dive only at sites within your realm of experience; if available, engage the services of a competent, professionally trained dive instructor or dive master.

- Be aware that underwater conditions vary significantly from one region, or even site, to another. Seasonal changes can significantly alter any site and dive conditions. These differences influence the way divers dress for a dive and what diving techniques they use.

- Ask about the environmental characteristics that can affect your diving and how local trained divers deal with these considerations.

ment for any insurance claims, although it is unlikely that the police will be able to recover the property. If you don't speak Spanish and are having a hard time making a police report, your embassy can often advise and help.

Panama has a long history of business-related crimes, particularly with regard to real estate. If you want to sink money into any kind of Panamanian business, make sure you check it out *thoroughly*. Don't invest more in Panama than you can afford to lose.

DISABLED TRAVELERS

The **Instituto Panameño de Habilitación Especial** (IPHE; Panamanian Institute for Special Rehabilitation; ☎ 261-0500; Camino Real, Betania, Panama City; ✆ 7am-4pm) was created by the government to assist all disabled people in Panama, including foreign tourists. However, the law does not require – and Panamanian businesses do not provide – discounts to foreign tourists with disabilities.

Panama is not wheelchair friendly; with the exception of wheelchair ramps outside a few upscale hotels, parking spaces for the disabled and perhaps a few dozen oversize bathroom stalls, accommodations for people with physical disabilities do not exist in Panama. Even at the best hotels, you won't find railings in showers or beside toilets.

If you have a disability and want to communicate with another disabled person who might have been to Panama recently, consider becoming a member of **Travelin' Talk Network** (TTN; in USA ☎ 303-232-2979; www.travelintalk.net; membership per year US$20). This organization offers a worldwide directory of members with various disabilities who communicate among themselves about travel.

Another helpful website is **Gimp on the Go** (www.gimponthego.com), reported to be the most informative of the free Internet-based newsletters written for persons with disabilities who love to travel.

Other organizations include:
Access-Able Travel Source (☎ 303-232-2979; www.access-able.com; PO Box 1796, Wheat Ridge, CO 80034) An excellent website with many links.
Mobility International USA (☎ 541-343-1284; fax 541-343-6812; www.miusa.org; PO Box 10767, Eugene, OR 97440) Advises disabled travelers on mobility issues and runs an educational exchange program.

Society for Accessible Travel & Hospitality (SATH; ☎ 212-447-7284; www.sath.org; 347 Fifth Ave, Suite 610, New York, NY 10016) Lobbies for better facilities and publishes *Open World* magazine.

EMBASSIES & CONSULATES
Panamanian Embassies & Consulates

Panama has embassies and consulates in the following countries:
Canada (☎ 613-236-7177; fax 613-236-5775; 130 Albert St, Suite 300, Ottawa, Ontario K1P 5G4)
Colombia (☎ 257-5067, 257-5068; fax 257-5068; Calle 92, No 7-70, Bogotá)
France (☎ 1-47-83-23-32, 1-45-66-42-44; fax 1-45-67-99-43; 145 Av de Suffren, 75015 Paris)
Germany (☎ 228-36-1036; fax 228-36-3558; Lutzowstrasse 1, 53173 Bonn)
Mexico (☎ 5-250-4229; fax 5-250-4045; Schiller 326, 8th fl, Colonia Chapultepec-Morales, CP 11570, Mexico DF)
UK (☎ 171-493-4646; fax 171-493-4499; 48 Park St, London W1Y 3PD)
USA (☎ 202-483 1407; fax 202-483-8413; 2862 McGill Tce NW, Washington, DC 20008)

Embassies & Consulates in Panama

More than 50 countries have embassies or consulates in Panama City. Their addresses and telephone numbers can be found in the Panama white pages, listed under 'Embajada de' followed by the country name in Spanish. Many embassies appear in the yellow pages under 'Embajadas' or 'Consulados.' With the exception of the United States and France, you'll find most embassies in the Marbella district of Panama City. Costa Rica also has a consulate in David.

Ireland, Australia and New Zealand have no consulates or embassies in Panama.
Canada (☎ 264-9731; fax 263-8083; World Trade Center, Calle 53 Este, Marbella)
Colombia (☎ 264-9266; World Trade Center, Calle 53 Este, Marbella)
Costa Rica David (☎ /fax 774-1923; Calle C Sur btwn Avs 1 and 2 Este); Panama City (☎ 264-2980; fax 264-4057; Av Samuel Lewis)
France (☎ 228-7824; Plaza de Francia, Las Bóvedas, Casco Antiguo)
Germany (☎ 263-7733; World Trade Center, Calle 53 Este, Marbella)
Holland (☎ 264-7257; Calle 50, Marbella)
UK (Map pp78-9; ☎ 269-0866; Swiss Tower Calle 53 Este, Marbella)
USA (Map pp76-7; ☎ 207-7000; Avs Balboa & Calle 37, La Exposición)

FESTIVALS & EVENTS

Panama has a range of colorful festivals that encompass everything from traditional folkloric fests to indigenous celebrations. For the lion's share of the country's revelry, head to the Península de Azuero, where some of Panama's most famous events take place. For more details see Chitré (p164), Ocú (p169), Villa de Los Santos (p175), Guararé (p177), Las Tablas (p178) and Pedasí (p180).

The following events are the country's better known celebrations:

February/March
Carnaval On the four days preceding Ash Wednesday, costumes, music, dancing and general merriment prevail in Panama City and on the Península de Azuero towns of Las Tablas, Chitré, Villa de Los Santos and Parita.

March/April
Semana Santa On Holy Week (the week before Easter), the country hosts many special events, including the re-enactment of the crucifixion and resurrection of Christ; on Good Friday, religious processions are held across the country.

May/June
Corpus Christi Forty days after Easter, this religious holiday features colorful celebrations in Villa de Los Santos. Masked and costumed dancers representing angels, devils, imps and other mythological figures enact dances, acrobatics and dramas.

October
Festival of the Black Christ On October 21, thousands of visitors come to honor the black Christ in Portobelo.

FOOD

See the Food & Drink chapter (p63) to get an in-depth look at Panama's cuisine. For price listings in the Panama City Eating section, we signify budget restaurants as having main dishes costing US$5 and under, mid-range as costing US$6 to US$10 and top-end as costing more than US$10.

GAY & LESBIAN TRAVELERS

Other than the gay float during Carnaval in the capital, there are few open expressions of homosexuality in Panama. As in other Latin American countries, gay men and lesbians remain closeted or else suffer a great deal of discrimination.

Panama City has a few gay and lesbian clubs (not openly advertised, however). Outside Panama City, gay bars are hard to come by. In most instances, gays and lesbians just blend in with the straight crowd at the hipper places and avoid cantinas and other conventional lairs of homophobia. There are several Panamanian websites for gays and lesbians that focus on Panama City, upcoming events and parties, new club openings and political issues about town. You'll need at least a little Spanish to maneuver these sites:

- www.farraurbana.com
- www.chemibel.com
- www.rumbanight.com

HOLIDAYS

National holidays (*días feriados*) are taken seriously in Panama, and banks, public offices and many stores close. Public transportation tends to be tight on all holidays and the days immediately preceding or following them, so book tickets ahead.

There is no bus service at all on the Thursday afternoon and Friday before Easter, and many businesses are closed for the entire Semana Santa (Holy Week, the week before Easter). From Thursday to Easter Sunday, all bars are closed and alcohol sales are prohibited. Beach hotels are usually weeks ahead for the Semana Santa, though a limited choice of rooms is often available.

The week between Christmas and New Year's, along with the first week of the year, tend to be unofficial holidays. In addition, various towns have celebrations for their own particular days throughout the year. These other holidays and special events are not official holidays, and businesses remain open.

All the official national holidays are listed below, and most are celebrated on Monday to create long weekends. When holidays fall on a Thursday or Friday, they are celebrated on the following Monday; holidays that happen to fall on Tuesday or Wednesday are usually celebrated the prior Monday.

New Year's Day January 1
Martyrs' Day January 9
Good Friday, Easter March/April
Workers' Day May 1
Founding of Old Panama (Panama City only) August 15
Hispanic Day October 12
National Anthem Day November 1
All Souls' Day November 2
Independence Day November 3
First Call for Independence November 10
Independence from Spain November 28
Mothers' Day December 8
Christmas Day December 25

Upcoming dates for **Carnaval** (Friday to Tuesday) are as follows:

2005   February 4–8
2006   February 24–28
2007   February 16–20
2008   February 1–5

INSURANCE

Signing up for a travel insurance policy to cover theft, loss and medical problems is a good idea. Some policies specifically exclude dangerous activities, which can include scuba diving, motorcycling, even trekking.

You may prefer a policy that pays doctors or hospitals directly, rather than you having to pay on the spot and claim later. If you have to claim later, ensure you keep all documentation.

Check that the policy covers ambulances or an emergency flight home. For information on medical insurance see p316.

INTERNET ACCESS

Most travelers make constant use of Internet cafés and free Web-based email such as **Yahoo** (www.yahoo.com) or **Hotmail** (www.hotmail.com). Internet cafés are plentiful in Panama, with locations in Panama City, David, Boquete, Volcán, Bocas del Toro, Pedasí, Portobelo and Santiago, to name a few towns you might be passing through. Most charge around US$1 to US$2 per hour, though at the time this guide was researched, many places were charging as little as US$0.50 per hour.

If you're traveling with a laptop or handheld computer, be aware that your modem may not work once you leave your home country. The safest option is to buy a reputable 'global' modem before you leave home, or buy a local PC-card modem if you're spending an extended time in any one country. For more information on traveling with a portable computer, see www.teleadapt .com.

LEGAL MATTERS

The legal drinking age in Panama is 18, which is strictly enforced in Panama City and generally ignored elsewhere. In Panama you are presumed guilty until found innocent. If you are accused of a serious crime, you will be taken to jail, where you will likely spend several years before your case goes before a judge. Some valuable advice: stay away from people who commit crimes.

For example, you can expect to go to jail if the car you are in is stopped and found to contain illegal drugs, even if they aren't yours and you don't do illegal drugs.

In Panama penalties for possession of even small amounts of illegal drugs are much stricter than in the USA, Europe, Australia and most everywhere else. Defendants often spend years in prison before they are brought to trial and, if convicted (as is usually the case), can expect sentences of several more years in prison. Most lawyers won't even accept drug cases because the outcome is certain: conviction.

If you are jailed, your embassy will offer only limited assistance. This may include a visit from an embassy staff member to make sure that your human rights have not been violated, letting your family know where you are and putting you in contact with a lawyer (whom you must pay yourself). Embassy officials will not bail you out.

Remember that you are legally required to carry identification at all times. This should be a photographic ID, preferably a passport.

MAPS

International Travel Maps (☎ 604-687-3320 in Canada; www.itmb.com) publishes an excellent 1:800,000 color map showing the geographical features, cities, towns, national parks, airports and roads of Panama.

At the Instituto Geográfico Nacional 'Tommy Guardia' in Panama City (p75) you can buy topographical maps of selected cities and regions. Various free tourist publications distributed in Panama also have maps; however, as yet there are no good maps available for hiking trails.

MONEY

Panama uses the US dollar as its currency. The official name for it is the *balboa,* but it's exactly the same bill, and in practice people use the terms *'dólar'* and *'balboa'* interchangeably. Panamanian coins are of the same value, size and metal as US coins; both are used. Coins include one, five, 10, 25 and 50 *centavos* (or *centésimos*); 100 *centavos* equal one *balboa*. Most businesses won't break US$50 and US$100 bills and those that do may require you to present your passport. For exchange rates, see inside the front cover. For information on costs, see p14.

ATMs

Throughout Panama, ATMs are readily available except in the most isolated places. Look for the red 'sistema clave' signs to find an ATM. They accept cards on most networks (Plus, Cirrus, MasterCard, Visa, Amex). Most Panamanian banks charge a US$3 fee for every ATM transaction, and the amount that can be withdrawn at one time varies from bank to bank. Some have a US$200 limit, others a US$500 limit.

Credit Cards

Widely accepted at travel agencies, upscale hotels and many restaurants, credit cards can be problematic almost everywhere else. In short, carry enough cash to get you to the next bank or ATM. There are several places where it's essential to show up with cash. Among tourist destinations, the following places have no banks, and it's a long way to the nearest ATM: Santa Catalina, Santa Fé, Boca Brava, Isla Contadora, Isla Grande and Portobelo. At the time of research, very few businesses on Bocas del Toro accepted credit cards. Find out if your hotel does *before* you go to avoid any unpleasant surprises.

Moneychangers

The only bank that exchanges foreign currency is the Banco Nacional de Panamá counter at Tocumen International Airport. Once you have left the airport, the only place to change foreign currency for dollars is a *casa de cambio* (exchange house). There is one in Panama City but few elsewhere.

Taxes

A tax of 10% is added to the price of hotel rooms; when you inquire about a hotel, ask whether the quoted price includes the tax. Hotel prices given in this book include the 10% tax. A 5% sales tax is levied on non-food products.

Tipping

The standard tipping rate in Panama is around 10% of the bill; in small cafés and more casual places, tipping is not necessary. Taxi drivers do not expect tips.

Traveler's Checks

Although they can be cashed at a few banks, traveler's checks are rarely accepted by businesses, and traveler's checks in currencies other than US dollars are not accepted anywhere in Panama. Some banks will only accept American Express traveler's checks. The banks that do accept traveler's checks typically charge an exchange fee equal to 1% of the amount of the check.

PHOTOGRAPHY
Film & Equipment

The prices of high-end camera equipment in Panama are competitive, particularly in the Zona Libre in Colón, although the savings are not terribly impressive. The inventory, however, can be excellent, especially for Nikon equipment.

Filmwise, Panama City has everything, but outside the capital city you'll be hard-pressed to find Kodachrome 64 or Fuji Velvia slide films – the really good stuff. At the many Supercolor stores in Panama City (check the phone book for addresses and phone numbers), not only can you find Fuji Velvia, but it's well priced.

Film processors in Panama reportedly do good work. If you're going to be in Panama a while and are anxious to see your photos, consider having one roll developed in Panama and examining the results before submitting additional rolls.

Photographing People

Panamanians make wonderful subjects for photos. However, most people resent having cameras thrust in their faces, and some attach price tags to their mugs. In the Comarca de Kuna Yala, subjects typically expect US$1 per photo. As a rule, you should ask for permission if you have an inkling your subject would not approve.

Technical Tips

Tropical shadows are very strong and come out almost black on photographs. Often a bright but hazy day makes for better photographs than a very sunny one. Photography in open shade or using a fill-in flash will help. Polarizing filters reduce glare and accentuate colors.

You will need high-speed (400 ISO or faster) film or flash equipment and/or a tripod if you want to take photographs within a rain forest – the amount of light penetrating the layers of vegetation is remarkably low. Pros prefer high-quality but super-slow (50 ISO) Fuji Velvia slide film and a tripod to the convenience of high-speed film that produces grainy images.

As a general rule, the best time for shooting is when the sun is low – the first and last two hours of the day. Remember, too, that flash equipment is forbidden in Panama's churches and museums.

POST

Airmail to the USA takes five to 10 days and costs US$0.35 (postcards US$0.25); to Europe and Australia it takes 10 days and costs US$0.45 (postcards US$0.40). Panama has neither vending machines for stamps nor drop-off boxes for mail. You may be able to buy stamps and send mail from an upscale hotel to avoid going to the post office and standing in line.

Most post offices are open from 7am to 6pm weekdays and from 7am to 4:30pm Saturday. General delivery mail can be addressed to '(name), Entrega General, (town and province), República de Panamá.' Be sure the sender calls the country 'República de Panamá' rather than simply 'Panamá,' or the mail may be sent back.

SHOPPING

A remarkable variety of imported goods, including cameras, electronic equipment and clothing, is sold in Panama, both in Colón's tax-free Zona Libre and in Panama City. The giant stores in the Zona Libre cater mostly to mass buyers, and most of them will not sell individual items (see p252).

Panama City gives tourists and foreigners a better shopping opportunity, offering a wide selection of high-quality handicrafts and traditional artwork.

The favorite handicraft souvenir from Panama is the *mola,* a colorful, intricate, multilayered appliqué textile sewn by Kuna women of the Archipiélago de San Blás. Small, simple souvenir *molas* can be bought for as little as US$5, but the best ones are sold on the islands and can fetch several hundred dollars.

It's possible to purchase high-quality replicas of *huacas* – golden objects made on the isthmus centuries before the Spanish conquest and placed with Indians at the time of burial. These range in price from US$5 to more than US$1000.

Other handicrafts that can be purchased include wood carvings (from the *cocobolo*

tree), *tagua* carvings (from the egg-sized *tagua* nut) and baskets. These are all made by the Wounaan and Emberá tribes.

Panama City's Avenida Central is a mecca for bargain hunters. Shop around and bargain, as there's a lot of competition. Those interested in textiles should explore this street, as this where the Kuna and Emberá women shop for fabric that will be made into clothing and *molas.*

For masks, you can find Panama's best mask makers in the Azuero Peninsula towns of Parita (p167) and Villa de Los Santos (p175). The peninsula is most famous, though, for its *polleras,* the lacy, frilly, intricately sewn dresses that are considered Panama's national dress. You can buy one, but they're not cheap: some cost more than US$1000, owing to the hundreds of hours that go into them.

Other handicraft and shopping destinations that visitors should be aware of include the following:

Boquete (p208) Mountain-grown coffee, oranges and a few handicrafts.
El Valle (p142) Daily craft market of indigenous goods. Sundays are the best days to go.
Penonomé (p152) Wide selection of hats in the Panama style.
San José (p169) Women's co-op that makes *polleras, montunos,* tablecloths and other handmade items.
Santa Fé (p191) Inexpensive market featuring woven hats and bags, locally grown coffee and a few leather goods.

In Panama City all the Gran Morrison chain department stores have handicraft and traditional art sections. Other places where visitors can shop for handicrafts in the capital city are mentioned on p110.

SOLO TRAVELERS

Traveling alone isn't uncommon in Panama, and there are plenty of places to meet other travelers. Bocas del Toro (p227) is particularly suited to meeting other travelers. This is best accomplished by simply enjoying some of the island's attractions – snorkeling trips, surf beaches and seaside restaurants, among others. Language schools, both in Bocas and in Panama City, are another good spot to meet other travelers while in Panama, as are the country's few hostels.

Traveling solo is a bit more expensive than traveling with a friend. Single rooms generally cost only slightly less than doubles.

TELEPHONE

Panama's country code is ☎ 507. To call Panama from abroad, use the country code before the seven-digit Panamanian telephone number. There are no local area codes in Panama.

Telephone calls to anywhere within Panama can be made from pay phones. Local calls cost US$0.10 for the first three minutes, then US$0.05 per minute. You can buy Telechip phonecards at pharmacies, corner shops and Cable & Wireless offices (the national phone company) in denominations of US$3, US$5, US$10, and US$20. You then plug this into the phone and dial the local number. Some public phones accept both cards and coins, but many accept only cards. Note that calling cell phones (which typically begin with a '6') is much pricier (US$0.35 for the first minute, then US$0.10 per minute thereafter).

International Calls

Travelers wishing to make international calls can do so with a phonecard or via an Internet café. They can purchase a phonecard – either a *tarjeta* mentioned above – or a Telechip Total card, which has a scratch-off code and can be used from any phone – whether public or private. They come in denominations of US$1, US$3, US$5, US$10, and US$20. Buy at least US$5 for an international call.

Another way of making a long-distance call is through some of the Internet cafés found throughout the country. Many have one or two private phone booths where you can talk. Average prices for these places at time of research was US$0.20 a minute to the US, US$0.50 a minute to Europe and US$0.75 a minute to Asia and Australia.

Connecting to an international operator from a residential, business or pay phone is easy. To connect with a local international operator, simply dial ☎ 106. For an international operator in the USA, dial ☎ 108 (MCI), ☎ 109 (AT&T), ☎ 115 (Sprint) or ☎ 117 (TRT). To reach a Costa Rican operator, dial ☎ 107; for a Colombian operator, dial ☎ 116.

Most hotels, however, require that you make international calls via a switchboard so they can charge an outrageous connection fee; in the pricier hotels this fee can be US$4 or more – even if you are simply asking to be connected to an international operator.

Cable & Wireless offices throughout Panama offer international telephone, telegraph, fax, and sometimes email and modem services.

TIME

From the last Sunday in October through the first Sunday in April, Panama time is in line with New York and Miami. Because Panama does not observe daylight saving time, during the rest of the year (April through October), Panama is one hour behind New York. Panama is five hours behind Greenwich Mean Time (GMT) and one hour ahead of the rest of Central America. If you're coming from Costa Rica, be sure to reset your watch.

TOILETS

Panamanian plumbing generally is of high quality, although on some Comarca de Kuna Yala islands and elsewhere you'll find signs beside the toilets asking you to place your used paper in the trash bins provided instead of flushing it away. That's because narrow piping was used during construction and the owners fear clogging. Putting used toilet paper into a trash bin may not seem sanitary, but it is much better than clogged bowls and overflowing toilet water.

In Kuna Yala and in some parts of Bocas del Toro, whatever you flush goes straight out to sea.

Public toilets can be found mainly in bus terminals, airports and restaurants. In Spanish, restrooms are called *baños* and are often marked *caballeros* (gentlemen) and *damas* (ladies). Outside the cities, toilet paper is not always provided, so you may want to consider carrying a personal supply.

TOURIST INFORMATION

The **Instituto Panameño de Turismo** (IPAT, Panamanian Institute of Tourism; ☎ 226-7000; www.ipat.gob.pa; Centro Atlapa, Vía Israel, San Francisco, Panama City) is the national tourism agency. In addition to this head office, IPAT runs offices in Bocas del Toro, Boquete, Colón, David, Paso Canoas, Penonomé, Portobelo, Santiago, Villa de Los Santos, Las Tablas, El Valle and Pedasí. There are smaller information counters at the ruins of Panamá Viejo, in Casco Viejo, and in both the Tocumen International Airport and the Albrook domestic airport.

IPAT has a few useful maps and brochures, but often has a problem keeping enough in stock for distribution to tourists. Most offices are staffed with people who speak only Spanish, and the helpfulness of any particular office depends on the person at the counter. Some employees really try to help, but others are just passing the time. As a general rule, you will get more useful information if you have specific questions.

Panama provides tourist information in the United States (☎ 800-231-0568), and IPAT literature and other information is sometimes available at Panamanian consulates and embassies (see p297). Be forewarned: IPAT publications tend to be rich with inaccuracies. Many Panamanian businesses are developing websites, so the Internet is also a good tool for pre-trip research.

VISAS & DOCUMENTS
Onward Tickets

Travelers officially need onward tickets before they are allowed to enter Panama. This requirement is not often checked at Tocumen International Airport, but travelers arriving by land should anticipate a need to show an onward ticket.

If you're heading to Colombia, Venezuela or another South American country from Panama, you may need an onward or round-trip ticket before you will be allowed entry into that country or even allowed to board the plane if you're flying. A quick check with the appropriate embassy – easy to do by phone in Panama City – will tell you whether the country that you're heading to has an onward-ticket requirement.

Passports, Tourist Cards & Visas

Every visitor needs a valid passport and an onward ticket to enter Panama, but further requirements vary by nationality and change occasionally. Anyone planning a trip to Panama would be advised to contact the Panamanian embassy or consulate nearest them to obtain the latest information on entry requirements. Ticketing agents of airlines that fly to Panama and tour operators that send groups there often can provide this information.

At the time of writing, people holding passports from the following countries needed to show only their passports to enter Panama: Argentina, Austria, Belgium,

Chile, Costa Rica, Denmark, Egypt, El Salvador, Finland, France, Germany, Greece, Guatemala, Holland, Honduras, Hungary, Israel, Italy, Luxembourg, Paraguay, Poland, Portugal, Northern Ireland, Scotland, Singapore, Spain, Switzerland, UK, Uruguay and Wales.

People from the following countries needed a passport and a tourist card: Antigua, Australia, Bahamas, Barbados, Belize, Bermuda, Bolivia, Brazil, Canada, Colombia, Granada, Guyana, Iceland, Ireland, Jamaica, Japan, Malta, Mexico, Monaco, New Zealand, Norway, Paraguay, San Marino, South Korea, Suriname, Sweden, Taiwan, Tobago, Trinidad, the USA and Venezuela.

Citizens from countries that do not appear on this list will need to obtain a visa, available at Panamanian embassies or consulates. Contact the one nearest you or call the **immigration office** (☎ 507-227-1448, 225-8925; fax 227-1227, 225-1641) in Panama City.

A tourist card costs US$5, and it's available at the airport or at border posts upon arrival (though land border posts occasionally run out of them). Most airlines serving Panama issue the tourist cards before you arrive, as does the Tica Bus company (see p310.). You can also obtain a tourist card before you leave home at Panamanian embassies and consulates (p297).

No matter where you are coming from, you will be given a 30-day stamp in your passport when you enter Panama. This means you are allowed to remain in Panama for 30 days without having to obtain further permission from the authorities. After 30 days, visas and tourist cards can be extended at *migración* (immigration) offices.

Those entering Panama overland will probably be asked to show an onward ticket and a show of sufficient cash (US$500) or a credit card.

In the event that you lose your passport while in Panama, you'll need proof of when you entered the country to be able to leave it. That proof, oddly enough, does not come from an immigration office but from the airline you flew in on. You need to go to the airline's main office in Panama City and request a certification of your entry date *(certificación de vuelo)*. There's no charge, but you'll likely be asked to come back the next day to pick it up. When you leave the country, along with your new passport (obtained from your embassy in Panama City), you'll present your *certificación de vuelo* to an immigration agent.

Visa Extensions

Visas and tourist cards are both good for 30 days. To extend your stay, you'll have to go to an office of Migración y Naturalización in Panama City, David, or Chitré. You must bring your passport and photocopies of the page with your personal information and of the stamp of your most recent entry to Panama. You must also bring two passport-size photos, an onward air or bus ticket and a letter to the director stating your reasons for wishing to extend your visit. You will have to fill out a *prórroga de turista* (tourist extension) and pay US$10. You will then be issued a plastic photo ID card. Go early in the day as the whole process takes about two hours.

If you have extended your time, you will also need to obtain a *permiso de salida* (permit) to leave the country. For this, bring your passport and a *paz y salvo* (a certificate stating you don't owe any back taxes) to the immigration office. *Paz y salvos* are issued at Ministerios de Economia y Finanzas, found in towns with immigration offices, which simply require that you bring in your passport, fill out a form and pay US$1.

These documents can be obtained in Panama City or in David at the following locations:

Migración y Naturalización office David (☎ 775-4515; Calle C Sur nr Av Central, 🕑 8am-8pm Mon-Fri); Panama City (☎ 225-1373; Av Cuba & Calle 29 Este, La Exposición; 🕑 8am-3pm Mon-Fri)

Ministerio de Economia y Finanzas, Dirección de Ingresos (☎ 207-7748; cnr Via Españ & Calle 52 Este, Panama City) For a *paz y salvo*.

WOMEN TRAVELERS

Female travelers find Panama safe and pleasant to visit. Some Panamanian men make flirtatious comments or stare at single women, both local and foreign, but comments are rarely blatantly rude; the usual thing is a smiling *'mi amor,'* (my love) an appreciative hiss or a honk of the horn. The best way to deal with this is to do what Panamanian women do – ignore the comments and don't look at the man making them.

Panamanians are generally fairly conservative in dress. Women travelers are advised to avoid skimpy or see-through clothing. And although Emberá women in the Darién go topless, it would be insulting for travelers to follow suit.

Women traveling solo will get more attention than those traveling in pairs or groups. Although assault and rape of foreign travelers is rare, avoid placing yourself in risky scenarios. Don't walk alone in isolated places, don't hitchhike and always pay particular attention to your surroundings.

For more information on traveling solo see p301.

WORK

It's difficult for foreigners to find work in Panama. The government doesn't want them to take jobs away from Panamanians, and the labor laws reflect that sentiment. Basically, the only foreigners legally employed in Panama work for their own businesses, possess skills not found in Panama or work for companies that have special agreements with the Panamanian government.

Small boats transiting the Panama Canal sometimes take on backpackers as deckhands (line handlers) in exchange for free passage, room and food. Inquiries can be made at the Panama Canal Yacht Club in Colón; some boat owners post notices in pensions. The official rate for line handling is US$55 per day, but anyone who pays this fee hires experienced locals. Competing with the locals for this work could get you and the boat captain in trouble.

Restaurants that hire foreign staff are often shut down for immigration violations.

Volunteer Work

The **Asociación Nacional para la Conservación de la Naturaleza** (National Association for the Conservation of Nature, ANCON; ☎ 314-0061; www.ancon.org) offers opportunities for volunteering on projects in national parks and other beautiful natural areas. Volunteers might protect nesting turtles near Bocas del Toro, do environmental-education work in the Darién or assist park rangers. You can volunteer for any length of time from a week to several months; you won't get paid, but ANCON will supply your basic necessities, such as food and shelter. Contact ANCON for details.

Another excellent organization that takes volunteers from time to time is the **Fundación Pro-Niños de Darién** (☎ 254-4333; www

.darien.org.pa). This nonprofit organization started in 1990 and works on a variety of projects throughout the Darién. It's targeted at the improvement of the lives of *niños* (children), including educational and nutritional programs. The organization also works to help residents develop sustainable agriculture.

Transportation

CONTENTS

Getting There & Away	**306**
Entering the Country	306
Air	306
Land	308
Getting Around	**310**
Air	310
Bicycle	310
Boat	310
Bus	312
Car & Motorcycle	312
Hitchhiking	312
Local Transport	312
Tours	313
Train	315

GETTING THERE & AWAY

ENTERING THE COUNTRY

The proceedings for entering Panama by air are much less scrutinized than crossing by land. When you arrive at Tocúmen in Panama City or in David, depending on your nationality (see Visas, p303) you may have to fill out a tourist card (US$5) available near the passport checkpoint. It's a straightforward and painless procedure. The same cannot be said for the most popular overland crossing from Costa Rica at Paso Canoas. Many travelers have complained about this border crossing, and the Panamanian officials – who act as if their instructions were to keep people out – receive low marks for their officious attitude. At this crossing, you'll be asked to show an onward ticket and a credit card or US$500. The border post at Sixaola/Guabito is much more low-key. There's a third crossing at Río Sereno that's little used by travelers despite being a good option.

AIR
Airports & Airlines
Panama has two international airports. Panama City's **Tocumen International Airport**

THINGS CHANGE

The information in this chapter is particularly vulnerable to change. Check directly with the airline or a travel agent to make sure you understand how a fare (and ticket you may buy) works and be aware of the security requirements for international travel. Shop carefully. The details given in this chapter should be regarded as pointers and are not a substitute for your own careful, up-to-date research.

(☎ 238-4322; airport code PTY) lies 35km from downtown, and it's where most international flights to Panama arrive. **Aeropuerto Enrique Malek** (☎ 721-1072; airport code DAV), in David, which is 75km southeast of the Costa Rican border, frequently handles flights to and from San José.

COPA is Panama's national airline, offering flights to and from the USA, numerous Latin and South American countries, and the Caribbean. The US Federal Aviation Administration recently assessed COPA Airlines as Category 1, which means they are in full compliance with international aviation standards.

The following airlines fly in and out of Panama:

Aires (☎ 265-6044; www.aires.aero; airline code 4C; hub Cartagena, Colombia)

Aerolineas Argentinas (☎ 269-3815; www.aerolineas.com.ar; airline code AR; hub Buenos Aires)

AeroMexico (☎ 263-3033; www.aeromexico.com; airline code AM; hub Mexico City)

Air France (☎ 223-0204; www.airfrance.com; airline code AF; hub Paris)

Alitalia (☎ 269-2161; www.alitalia.com; airline code AZ; hub Rome)

America West (☎ 263-3033; www.americawest.com; airline code HP; hub Phoenix)

American Airlines (☎ 269-6022; www.aa.com; airline code AA; hub Dallas & Miami)

Avianca (☎ 223-5225; www.avianca.com; airline code AV; hub Bogotá)

Cathay Pacific (☎ 263-3033; www.cathaypacific.com; airline code CX; hub Hong Kong)

Continental Airlines (☎ 263-9177; www.continental.com; airline code CO; hub Houston & Newark)

COPA (☎ 227-2672; www.copaair.com; airline code CM; hub Panama City)

Cubana (☎ 227-2291; www.cubana.cu; airline code CU; hub Havana)

Cyprus Airways (☎ 226-5275; www.cyprusairways .com; airline code CY; hub Cyprus)

Delta Air Lines (☎ 214-8118; www.delta.com; airline code DL; hub Atlanta)

Grupo TACA (☎ 360-2093; www.taca.com; airline code TA; hub San Salvador)

Iberia (☎ 227-3966; www.iberia.com; airline code IB; hub Madrid)

Japan Airlines (☎ 223-1266; www.jal.com; airline code JL; hub Tokyo)

KLM (☎ 264-6395; www.klm.com; airline code KL; hub Amsterdam)

Korean Air (☎ 315-0356; www.koreanair.com; airline code KE; hub Seoul)

Lan Chile (☎ 226-7119; www.lanchile.com; airline code LA; hub Santiago)

LAB (☎ 264-1330; www.labairlines.com; airline code LB; hub La Paz, Bolivia)

Mexicana (☎ 264-9855; www.mexicana.com; airline code MX; hub Mexico City)

Singapore Airlines (☎ 264-2533; www.singaporeair .com; airline code SQ; hub Singapore)

United Airlines (☎ 225-6519; www.united.com; airline code UA; hub Los Angeles)

US Airways (☎ 263-3033; www.usairways.com; airline code US; hub Philadelphia)

Tickets

In addition to websites like **Travelocity** (www .travelocity.com), **Orbitz** (www.orbitz.com) and **Expedia** (www.expedia.com), all of the major carriers have their own website with online ticket sales, sometimes discounted for online customers. You can find a comprehensive list of all international airlines with links to their websites at http://airlinecontact.info/index.html.

From Panama

The best place to buy tickets out of Panama is Panama City, which has a number of travel agencies offering good fares (p80).

From Asia

In Asia, there's a proliferation of **STA Travel** Bangkok (☎ 02-236 0262; www.statravel.co.th); Singapore (☎ 6737 7188; www.statravel.com.sg); Hong Kong (☎ 2736-1618; www.statravel.com.hk); Japan (☎ 03 5391 2922; www.statravel.co.jp). Another resource in Japan is **No 1 Travel** (☎ 03 3205-6073; www .no1-travel.com); in Hong Kong try **Four Seas Tours** (☎ 2200-7760; www.fourseastravel.com/english).

> **DEPARTURE TAX**
>
> Panama levies a US$20 departure tax for outbound passengers on international flights.

From Australia & New Zealand

The cheapest routes usually go via the USA (often Los Angeles). If you're planning a longer trip through Latin America, an open-jaw (into one city, out of another) or even an around-the-world ticket will be your best bet. For online bookings try www.travel.com.au. The following are well-known agents for cheap fares with branches throughout Australia and New Zealand:

Flight Centre Australia (☎ 133-133; www.flightcentre .com.au); New Zealand (☎ 0800-243-544; www.flight centre.co.nz)

STA Travel Australia (☎ 1300 733 035; www.statravel .com.au); New Zealand (☎ 0508-782-872; www.statravel .co.nz)

From Canada

There were no direct flights from Canada to Panama at the time of writing; travelers needed to connect through one of the gateway cities in the USA. United Airlines, Continental Airlines and American Airlines all have good connections from major Canadian cities.

A recommended Canadian travel agency is **Travel Cuts** (☎ 800-667-243-544; www.travelcuts .com), Canada's national student travel agency. Websites such as www.expedia.ca and www.travelocity.ca are also good bets.

From Central America, Cuba & the Caribbean

Grupo TACA provides services between all the Central American capitals and Panama City. In addition, COPA (the Panamanian airline) offers flights between Panama City and Costa Rica, Cuba, the Dominican Republic, El Salvador, Guatemala, Haiti, Jamaica and Mexico. Cubana has the cheapest flights in the region between Panama City and Havana.

From Europe

At the time of writing Iberia was the only airline flying direct from Europe to Panama; the cheapest fares are usually via Madrid. Air France and Lufthansa also fly

TRANSPORTATION

from Europe, connecting in the USA. Recommended UK ticket agencies include the following:

Journey Latin America (☎ 020-8747-3108; www.journeylatinamerica.co.uk)

STA Travel (☎ 0870-160-0599; www.statravel.co.uk) For travelers under the age of 26.

Trailfinders (☎ 020-7937-1234; www.trailfinders.co.uk)

For online booking, try www.dialaflight.com or www.lastminute.com.

From South America

In South America you'll find that service to and from Panama is offered by Avianca and Aires in Colombia, LAB in Bolivia, Lan Chile in Chile and Aerolineas Argentinas in Argentina. American Airlines, Continental Airlines, Delta Air Lines and United Airlines all have connections from Panama City to several South American countries.

From the USA

The principal US gateways to and from Panama are Miami; Houston; Newark, NJ; New York; Washington, DC; Dallas; and Los Angeles. At the time of writing, sample round-trip economy fares for direct flights from Miami to Panama City ranged between US$375 and US$500. Fares from Los Angeles ranged between US$400 and US$675.

The following websites are recommended for online booking:

- www.cheaptickets.com
- www.expedia.com
- www.itn.net
- www.lowestfare.com
- www.orbitz.com
- www.sta.com
- www.ticotravel.com

LAND

Many travelers arrive in Panama by bus from Costa Rica. It's wise to get to the border early in order to ensure that you don't miss onward transportation on the other side. There are no roads into Colombia, and travelers are discouraged from crossing overland.

Border Crossings

There are three road border crossings between Costa Rica and Panama. The most frequently used (and least pleasant) crossing between the two countries is on the Interamericana, on the Pacific side. Border-crossers should note that Panama is always one hour ahead of Costa Rica.

To enter Panama from Costa Rica, you'll need a passport, an onward ticket and proof of solvency – US$500 or a credit card. At the border you'll fill out a US$5 tourist card (some nationalities are exempt, while others need a Visa to enter; see p303).

PASO CANOAS

This chaotic and heavily used border is on the Interamericana, not quite halfway between Panama City and San José. If you've been traveling overland through other countries, you're liable to find this one of the least pleasant crossings in Central America. The border hours here change frequently; at last check the border was open 7am to 11pm daily. Note that there are hotels on the Costa Rican side of Paso Canoas but none on the Panamanian side.

Make sure you get all of your stamps – proof of exiting from Costa Rica, proof of entry in Panama. None of the officials are very helpful and a few travelers in the past have gone through without the proper entry/exit stamps only to encounter problems later on.

If you don't have an onward ticket and are asked to show one, you'll have to buy a bus ticket from either Panaline or Tica Bus at the border. This will be a Panama City–San José ticket and will cost US$25.

Among the services here is a **Banco Nacional de Panamá** (☖ 8am-3pm Mon-Fri, 9am-noon Sat) just beyond the immigration window. At the bank you can use their ATM, cash traveler's checks and get cash advances against credit cards. However, it's not possible to change Costa Rican *colones* to US dollars. Men on the street will offer to change money if they see you standing in front of the bank looking perplexed. To lower the risk of being cheated, ask for their exchange rate and calculate how many US dollars you should receive for the amount of colones you intend to unload *before* reaching for your cash.

Once you have entered Panama, you will see taxis and buses stationed just past the border, on your left and ahead 50m. The nearest Panamanian city with a hotel is David. Buses depart Paso Canoas from this station (immediately to the left) for

David (US$1.50; 1½hr; every 10min, 5am-9:45pm); look for a bus with 'Frontera – David' on its windshield. Three buses depart daily for **Panama City** (adult/child US$12/6; 10hr; 8:30am, 11am & 4pm) making numerous stops along the way; a fourth bus departs at 10pm (adult/child US$17/$8.50; 8hr) making only a couple of brief food stops.

Fifty meters east of that bus station is an unmarked, often-overlooked bus station that features bus rides to **Panama City** (US$12; about 9hr ; 5:45am, 7am, 8:30am, 10am, 11:30am, 2pm, 4pm & 6:45pm), including two express services (US$17; about 7½hours; 9:45am and 10:45pm). These buses make stops at David and all the other major cities along the way (they'll even stop at a hamlet along the Interamericana or at a turnoff *if* you ask the driver to stop ahead of time).

There is a taxi stand near the first bus station. Taxis are available 24 hours a day. A taxi ride from the border to David will cost US$25 to US$30 per party, depending on the driver and the hour.

If you are entering Costa Rica, you may be required to show a ticket out of the country, although this is rarely requested.

SIXAOLA/GUABITO

This crossing is on the Caribbean coast. Sixaola is the last town on the Costa Rican side; Guabito is its Panamanian counterpart. There are no hotels or banks in Guabito, but stores there will accept your Costa Rican *colones,* Panamanian balboas or US dollars. *Colones* are not accepted south of Guabito.

The border is officially open from 7am to 11pm daily. However, immigration and customs officers often don't work past 7pm, which is when bus service on both sides also grinds to a halt. During the day, there are frequent minibuses from **Guabito to Changuinola** (US$1), 17km away. The minibuses can be found on the southern side of the elevated entrance road, just past the immigration office. Taxis are found on the northern side of the road; the fare to Changuinola is US$5.

A tourist card can be obtained for US$5 at the Panamanian Embassy in San José, Costa Rica (see p297). Or, in lieu of a tourist card, you can go to the **Banco Nacional de Panamá** (Av 17 de Abril) in Changuinola and for US$10 obtain a stamp, which you should then take to Changuinola's **immigration office** (☎ 758-8651; ☒ 8am-noon & 1-3pm Mon-Fri) across the street. The office will put the stamp in your passport along with an official signature; this will serve as your tourist card and entry stamp. If the immigration office is closed and you're on your way to Bocas, just return when you can and have the stamp and signature entered into your passport. Don't ignore the importance of the entry stamp; it's necessary to have one to be able to leave the country.

In Changuinola there are numerous hotels, several banks, some decent restaurants, and an airstrip with daily service to David and Panama City. You can catch a water taxi from here to Bocas del Toro (see p227 for details).

RÍO SERENO

This little town at the eastern terminus of the scenic Concepción–Volcán road sees so few tourists that locals often stare at those who pass through. If you arrive here from Costa Rica by small bus (as most people do), you'll be hard pressed to figure out where one country ends and the other begins. The Río Sereno crossing is open from 7:30 am to 5pm daily.

The little immigration office is near the base of a huge police communications tower. The office is identifiable by an orange-and-black 'Migracion' sign.

There's one hotel in this sleepy town nestled amid coffee plantations and patches of forest. The comfortable **Posada Los Andes** (s/d US$8/10; with bathroom US$15), above the pharmacy at the southeast corner of the town plaza, has 11 rooms with firm mattresses.

The **Banco Nacional de Panamá** has an ATM and provides services such as cashing traveler's checks and offering cash advances against major credit cards. However, foreign currency cannot be exchanged here.

There's a **bus terminal** two blocks northeast of the bank (ie, along the same street and away from the border). Buses depart from Río Sereno to **Volcán** (US$2.65, 40km, hourly) and continue on to **David** (US$4), with the first bus departing at 5am and the last at 5pm.

Bus

At all three border crossings, you can take a local bus up to the border on either side, cross over, board another local bus and continue on your way. Be aware that the last buses leave the border crossings at Guabito and Río Sereno at 7pm and 5pm, respectively; the last bus leaves Paso Canoas for Panama City at 10pm.

Two companies, **Panaline** (☎ 227-8648; fax 227-8647) and **Tica Bus** (☎ 262-2084; fax 262-6275), operate daily direct buses between San José, Costa Rica, and Panama City, departing from the Albrook bus terminal. Both recommend that you make reservations a few days in advance.

Car & Motorcycle

You can drive your own car, but the costs of insurance, fuel, border permits, food and accommodations will be much higher than the cost of an airline ticket. Many people opt for flying down and renting cars when they arrive in Panama City.

If you consider driving, factor in the following: driving Central American roads at night is not recommended – they are narrow, rarely painted with a center stripe, often potholed and subject to hazards such as cattle and pedestrians in rural areas. Traveling by day from the USA or Canada takes about a week, considerably more if you want to visit some of the fantastic sights en route.

If you decide to drive to Panama, get insurance, have your papers in order and never leave your car unattended (fortunately, guarded lots are common in Latin America). US license plates are attractive to some thieves, so you should display these from inside the car.

If you are bringing a car into Panama, you must pay US$5 for a vehicle control certificate *(tarjeta de circulación)* and another US$1 to have the car fumigated. You will also need to show a driver's license, proof of ownership and insurance papers. Your passport will be stamped to show that you paid the US$6 and followed procedures when you brought the vehicle into the country.

GETTING AROUND

AIR

Panama has one major domestic carrier, **Aeroperlas** (☎ 315-7500; www.aeroperlas.com; Calle 57, El Cangrejo), and two smaller ones, **Aero** (☎ 315-0888; www.aero.com.pa; Albrook terminal) and **Parsa** Parsa (☎ 315-0439; Albrook terminal). All domestic flights depart from **Aeropuerto Albrook** (Albrook Airport; ☎ 315-0403) in Panama City. For certain flights it's wise to book as far in advance as possible. This is particularly true of flights to the Comarca de Kuna Yala. At the time this was written, most islands had only one flight leaving per day, with flights booked weeks in advance. Fares run from US$38 to US$58 one way.

BICYCLE

The roads in Panama are the best in Central America, but that doesn't mean much once you leave the well-paved Interamericana. Roads in many provinces (Veraguas and Colón) are in bad shape. Plan accordingly. There's one professional outfitter in Panama City if you need gear, maintenance or to purchase a quality bicycle. See Bicicletas Rali on p62.

BOAT

Boats are the chief means of transportation in several areas of Panama, particularly in Darién Province, the Archipiélago de las Perlas, and the San Blás and Bocas del Toro island chains. Some of Panama's most fascinating destinations, such as Isla de Coiba, are only reachable by boat. And while at least one eccentric soul has swum the entire length of the Panama Canal, most people find that a boat simplifies the transit enormously.

The popular town of Bocas del Toro, on Isla Colón, is accessible from Changuinola and Almirante by speedy and inexpensive water taxis; see p227 for details.

To reach Coiba, local fishermen and expats living in Santa Catalina offer boat trips out to the islands in the marine park. Many boat trips are offered from Panama City, including ferry trips to offshore Isla Taboga, and full and partial transits of the Panama Canal. Trips are also offered to Isla Barro Colorado in the canal's Lago Gatún. See p119 for details.

There aren't many roads in eastern Darién Province, and, especially during the rainy season, boat travel is often the most feasible way to get from one town to another. The boat of choice here is a long canoe, or piragua, carved from the trunk of a giant *ceba* tree. Piraguas' shallow hulls allow them to ride the many rivers that comprise the traditional transport network of eastern Panama. Many such boats – including the

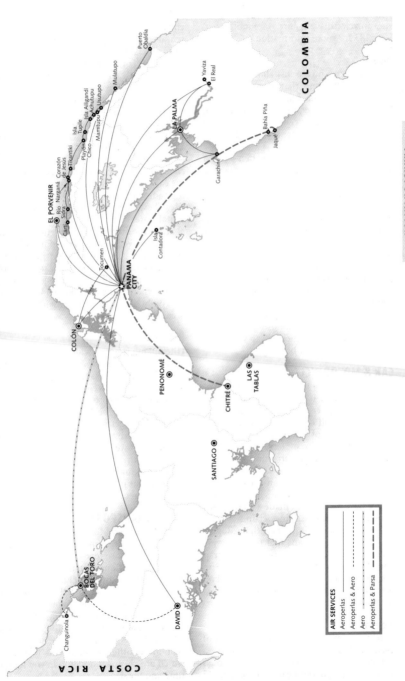

TRANSPORTATION

COLOMBIA

Puerto
Obaldia

Yaviza
El Real

Mulatupo

Usutupo
Achutupo
Isla Alligandi
Tupile
Isla

Mamitupu

LA PALMA

Bahía Piña

Jaqué

Playón
Chico
Tikantiki
Corazón
de Jesús

Garachiné

EL PORVENIR
Río Naranjá
Sidra
Carti

Isla
Contadora

Tocumen

PANAMA
CITY

COLÓN

PENONOMÉ

CHITRÉ

LAS
TABLAS

SANTIAGO

BOCAS
DEL TORO

Changuinola

DAVID

COSTA RICA

AIR SERVICES

Aeroperlas
Aeroperlas & Aero
Aero
Aeroperlas & Parsa

ones travelers usually hire – are motorized. See p283 for more information.

BUS

You can take a bus to just about any community in Panama that is reachable by road. Some of the buses are huge, new Mercedes Benzes equipped with air-con, movie screens and reclining seats. These top-of-the-line buses generally cruise long stretches of highway.

More frequently used – and often seen on the Carretera Interamericana – are Toyota Coaster buses that can seat 28 people. These are affectionately called *chivas*, and are not as comfortable as the Mercedes Benzes, but they aren't bad and they're less expensive. They are an excellent way to visit towns on the Península de Azuero and along the Interamericana.

Also seen on Panamanian roads – particularly within cities – are converted school buses. They are neither comfortable for most adults (they were designed for children) nor convenient (they stop every 10m, or so it seems), and they are usually crowded. Still, they are an extremely cheap way to get around and they beat hoofing it.

CAR & MOTORCYCLE

Few tourists drive to Panama in their own vehicles, though it is certainly possible to do so. Renting a car is also a possibility. Because of difficult driving conditions, there are speed limits of 80km/hr on all primary roads and 60km/hr or less on secondary roads. Drivers should carry their passports as well as driver's licenses.

If you are involved in an accident, you should not move the vehicles until after the police have arrived and made a report. This is essential for all insurance claims.

If you see oncoming cars with headlights flashing, it often means that there is some kind of road problem or a police speed trap ahead. Slow down immediately. Also be on the lookout for a pile of branches placed on the road near an edge; this often means that a vehicle is broken down just ahead.

Rental

Due to the low cost and ready availability of buses and taxis, it isn't necessary to rent a vehicle in Panama unless you intend to go to places far off the beaten track. Should you choose to rent, however, you'll find car-rental agencies in Panama City, David, Santiago and Chitré. Several agencies also have offices at Tocumen International Airport in the capital. To rent a vehicle in Panama, you must be 25 years of age or older and present a passport and driver's license (if you rent the vehicle using an American Express card, you need be only 23).

Prices for rentals in Panama run from US$45 per day for a tiny car to US$100 per day for a 4WD vehicle (or a *'cuatro por cuatro')*. When you rent, carefully inspect the car for minor dents and scratches, missing radio antennae, hubcaps and the spare tire. These damages *must* be noted on your rental agreement; otherwise you may be charged for them when you return the car.

There have been many reports of theft from rental cars. You should never leave valuables in an unattended car, and you should remove all your luggage from the trunk when you're checking into a hotel overnight. Many hotels provide parking areas for cars.

HITCHHIKING

Hitchhiking is not as widespread in Panama as elsewhere in Central America; most people travel by bus, and visitors would do best to follow suit. The exception is holiday weekends, when buses are full to overflowing and hitchhiking may be the only way out of a place. If you get a ride, offer to pay for it when you arrive; *'¿Cuánto le debo?'* ('How much do I owe you?') is the standard way of doing this.

Hitchhiking is never entirely safe in any country, but it's not uncommon as you arrive in rural areas.

LOCAL TRANSPORT

Local buses serve the urban and suburban areas, but services can be difficult to figure out and there are few roadside signs indicating destinations. Panamanians are usually friendly, and this includes bus drivers; they'll often be able to tell you where to wait for a particular bus, if you ask in Spanish (few bus drivers speak English). But in general, unless you've come to Panama specifically for its urban-bus experience, leave that for another lifetime and take taxis, which are cheap, and will save you a lot of time and hassle.

Taxis

Panamanian taxis don't have meters, but there are some set fares. Taxis are cheap and, most of the time, they are plentiful. However, they can be difficult to hail late at night and just before and during holidays. At times like these, it's best to call for a radio taxi. Listings for reliable radio taxis can be found in the yellow pages of phone directories throughout Panama, under the heading *Taxis*. In Panama City, see p114, for a list of radio taxis.

There is one group of taxis that do charge more than others. These 'sedan' taxis operate from particular upscale hotels (including the Hotel Caesar Park and the El Ejecutivo Hotel in Panama City). Taxi drivers generally mill about the front doors of the hotels and ask every exiting individual if he or she would like a cab. These drivers charge at least twice what you'd pay a hailed cab.

TOURS

Although Panama has much to offer the tourist, the country's tourism industry is young and the number of local tour operators quite small. In fact, Panama's tourism industry is so small that there's a list of the country's top guides further on in this section (below).

Most Panamanian tour companies specialize in nature tours, offering visits to the national parks and wilderness lodges. They can provide entire guided itineraries (with English-speaking guides) and private transportation to any part of the country. Most of these companies also specialize in adventure tourism, such as river running or jungle trekking. Almost all of them also provide services such as day trips to the Panama Canal, Panama City tours, hotel reservations and airport transfers.

Prices vary depending on the services you require. Two people wishing to travel with a private English-speaking guide and a private vehicle will obviously pay more than two people who are prepared to join a group or who can understand a Spanish-speaking guide. If you can afford it, consider hiring a guide for at least a portion of your travels. Good guides are like flying first class; they make the trip so much more enjoyable.

Tour Companies in Panama

All of the tour operators in Panama have their headquarters in Panama City. They offer the easiest way to explore Panama's natural wonders and all are reasonably priced. If you can afford it and want to get the most out of your time in Panama, we recommend that you use the services of one of the outfits listed here.

Ancon Expeditions of Panama (Map pp78-9; ☎ 269-9414/9415; www.anconexpeditions.com; El Dorado Bldg, Calle 49 A Este). Created by Panama's top private conservation organization, Ancon Expeditions employs most of the country's best nature guides, offers a variety of exciting tours, and the level of service the company provides is superlative. The majority of Ancon Expeditions' guides are avid birders; all speak flawless English and are enthusiastic about their work. In Panama, the standard for nature guides and tours is set by Ancon Expeditions. See p90 for sample tours.

Eco Circuitos (☎ 264-4821; www.ecocircuitos.com; inside the Country Inn & Suites, Causeway) This excellent outfit offers a wide variety of tours and activities from kayaking the Chagres River to caving at Lake Bayano. Horseback riding, hiking, mountain biking, snorkeling and overnight adventures round out their offerings. Check their website for the latest tours.

Panama's Top Guides

Many people in Panama refer to themselves as guides, but most couldn't distinguish a heron from an ibis or tell you which famous pirate's body lies at the bottom of the Bahía de Portobelo. Although the following list is not all-inclusive, those whose names appear on it are true guides.

HERNÁN 'HOWLER' ARAÚZ

A master naturalist, **Hernán** (home ☎ 268-0438, cellular ☎ 625-5755, office ☎ 269-9415; birder@sinfo.net; PO Box 3180, Panama 3, República de Panamá) specializes in bird watching, natural history, Panamanian history and jungle expeditions. He has vast experience in all of Panama's life zones and historical areas. He's also the foremost guide for the Darién region and the Panama Canal area, with 10 trans-Darién expeditions to his credit, as well as 350-plus tours to the Monumento Natural Barro Colorado and countless tours around the rest of Panama. Hernán is the official guide for several top US birding and natural-history tour operators. He is widely regarded as the best overall guide in Panama, a bit of a wild man who really knows his stuff. There's never a dull moment when this guy's around. He speaks

English and Spanish with dramatic precision and works for Ancon Expeditions. Contact him at home.

GUIDO BERGUIDO

Guido (☎ 676-2466; fax 228-6535; gcberguido@hotmail.com) is one of the country's most patient, qualified and enthusiastic all-around guides. Guiding seems to come naturally to him; indeed, you can't say his name without nearly saying 'guide' twice. A graduate of the University of Panama with a degree in biology, Guido is one of Panama's truly successful freelance nature guides in a country teeming with wannabes, working regularly with the Smithsonian Tropical Research Institute, Panama's top tour operators and numerous cruise lines. This very pleasant young man speaks English and Spanish, and his areas of expertise include the Panama Canal watershed, tropical ecology and bird watching. Some people will also be pleased to know that Guido is very prompt; there's never any waiting for him.

RICHARD JOHN 'CHICHARRON' CAHILL

One of Panama's top nature and expedition guides, **Richard** (home ☎ 315-1905, office ☎ 269-9415; rcahill@anconexpeditions.com) specializes in the former Panama Canal Zone, the Monumento Natural Barro Colorado, Isla de Coiba and trans-Darién expeditions (which he has led numerous times). He also has a lot of experience leading expeditions for yachts and small cruise ships. We've called upon Richard's expertise on many occasions – in the Darién, on the Península de Azuero, throughout the Archipiélago de las Perlas and the Archipiélago de San Blás, even into Colombia by small boat – he's always been extremely hard-working, thoughtful and patient. Richard has a can-do spirit and, as you might have guessed from his nickname, which means 'pork rinds' in English, he has a sense of humor. Educated in Panama and the United States, Richard speaks English and Spanish and works for Ancon Expeditions.

MARIA 'MARISIN' GRANADOS

Born in Puerto Armuelles in Chiriquí Province and educated in the USA and Panama, **Marisin** (☎ 269-9415; marising@anconexpeditions.com) was a nature guide at the prestigious Smithsonian Tropical Research Institute for seven years prior to joining the staff of Ancon Expeditions in late 2000. Her formal education includes instruction in bird watching and natural history from the American Training Institute in Panama. When not leading nature tours for AEP, Marisin devotes her time to teaching ecology at the Universidad Latina de Panama, where she holds the title of professor. Marisin, who is fluent in English and Spanish, is a fine nature guide and can speak intelligently about historical, cultural, ecological and social issues in Panama today. And she's as pleasant as she is knowledgeable.

IVAN HOYOS

An extremely enthusiastic, well-traveled and well-educated individual, **Ivan** (migratorio@hotmail.com) specializes in Panama's natural history and bird watching. Born and raised on the Península de Azuero, he spent much of the mid-1990s living in Changuinola and becoming the foremost wildlife expert of western Panama before moving to Panama City to work for Ancon Expeditions. Today, he is a freelance guide, working for himself when not on contract with AEP, Wildland Adventures or another leading tour operator. His experience also includes many tours to Barro Colorado Nature Monument and the national parks protecting the Panama Canal watershed. Ivan attended college in the United States and Germany and is fluent in English, Spanish and German.

WILBERTO 'WILLY' MARTINEZ

Willy (☎ 442-1340; panabird@cwpanama.net) is one of Panama's best birding guides, on an equal plane with Hernán Araúz (p313) in terms of his ability to spot and recognize birds, with many years of experience in this field. He leads tours for several US birding operators in all of Panama's life zones, and his talents are frequently sought after by private individuals as well. His areas of expertise include the Panama Canal watershed, and the Darién and the Chiriquí highlands. Willy's entertaining personality and natural ability to spot birds like few others make him an extremely popular guide. He owns and manages the Rancho Ecológico, on the Chiriquí Grande–David road, but birding tours generally prevent him from being there; see the Bocas del Toro Province chapter for details. Willy speaks English and Spanish.

RICHARD 'RICK' MORALES

Ask **Rick** (☎ 269-9415; rickm@anconexpeditions.com) to tell you the highlight of his life and you'll get a breathless story about the time he saw a mountain lion in Cana Valley near the jungly heart of Parque Nacional Darién. This Chiriquí Highlands native is the kind of nature guide that'll finish leading a group of birders on a long bird watching expedition only to return to the jungle to admire more birds and add new ones to his bird list. His enthusiasm for his country's wildlife is as addictive as it is appealing. You're more likely to find him without his wallet than without his binoculars. A linguist by training, Rick speaks English and Spanish flawlessly and was a great addition to Ancon Expeditions' staff when he joined the company in early 1999.

HECTOR SANCHEZ

Hector is Panama's most experienced white-water guide and outfitter. He owns and manages **Chiriquí River Rafting** (☎ 720-1505; www.panama-rafting.com; Av Central, Boquete), which runs the Ríos Chiriquí and Chiriquí Viejo. For many years Hector was the head tour coordinator for the US Armed Forces' recreational activities department in the canal area. He places great emphasis on safety. Although the rivers he runs contain lots of rapids, you always feel safe when accompanied by Hector and his team. Hector speaks English and Spanish.

IANN SANCHEZ

A native of the former Panama Canal Zone, **Iann** (☎ 231-1623, cellular ☎ 672-3534, czbirder@hotmail.com) left Panama for a university degree in geology in the US. His love of nature then led him to work for the US Forest Service as a ranger at several national parks. Thereafter, Iann worked as a rafting guide in Texas before returning to Panama to serve as a guide and operations manager for Chiriquí River Rafting, which is owned by his father. Most recently, Iann was a guide for a company that ran rafting trips down the Río Chagres near the Panama Canal, and as recently as 2001 he was the top nature guide at the Gamboa Rainforest Lodge on the northern bank of the Río Chagres. Today, he's cutting a trail all his own as a freelance nature guide, specializing in leading bird watchers in the canal area. A fluent English and Spanish speaker.

TRAIN

The country's only train line is the **Panama Railway Company**'s (☎ 317-6070 in Panama City) famous old passenger train that runs along the canal between Panama City and Colón. It has recently been restored and runs Monday to Friday, leaving in the morning and returning in the afternoon. It's a lovely ride, following along the canal, and at times the train is surrounded by nothing but thick jungle. See p254 for details.

Health Dr David Goldberg

CONTENTS

Before You Go	**316**
Internet Resources	317
Further Reading	317
In Transit	**317**
Deep Vein Thrombosis (DVT)	317
Jet Lag & Motion Sickness	318
In Panama	**318**
Availability of Health Care	318
Infectious Diseases	318
Traveler's Diarrhea	321
Environmental Hazards	321
Traveling with Children	322

Panama has a very high standard of hygiene and very few travelers get seriously sick during their stay. However, food-borne as well as mosquito-borne infections do exist, and though many of these illnesses are not life-threatening, they can certainly ruin your trip. Besides getting the proper vaccinations, it's important that you bring along a good insect repellent and exercise care in what you eat and drink.

BEFORE YOU GO

Since most vaccines don't produce immunity until at least two weeks after they're given, visit a physician four to eight weeks before departure. Ask your doctor for an International Certificate of Vaccination (otherwise known as the 'yellow booklet'), which will list all the vaccinations you've received. This is mandatory for countries that require proof of yellow-fever vaccination upon entry, but it's a good idea to carry it wherever you travel.

Bring medications in their original containers, clearly labeled. A signed, dated letter from your physician describing all medical conditions and medications, including generic names, is also a good idea. If carrying syringes or needles be sure to have a physician's letter documenting their medical necessity.

Most doctors and hospitals expect payment in cash, regardless of whether you have travel health insurance. If you develop a life-threatening medical problem, you'll probably want to be evacuated to a country with state-of-the-art medical care. Since this may cost tens of thousands of dollars, be sure you have insurance to cover this before you depart. You can find a list of medical-evacuation and travel-insurance companies on the **US State Department** (www.travel.state.gov /travel/abroad_health.html) website.

If your health insurance does not cover you for medical expenses abroad, consider supplemental insurance. (Check the Subway section of the Lonely Planet website at www.lonelyplanet.com/subwwway for

MEDICAL CHECKLIST

- Acetaminophen (Tylenol) or aspirin
- Adhesive or paper tape
- Antibacterial ointment (eg Bactroban) for cuts and abrasions
- Antibiotics
- Antidiarrheal drugs (eg loperamide)
- Antihistamines (for hay fever and allergic reactions)
- Anti-inflammatory drugs (eg ibuprofen)
- Bandages, gauze, gauze rolls
- DEET-containing insect repellent for the skin
- Iodine tablets (for water purification)
- Malaria pills (recommended if going to the Darién, see p320)
- Oral rehydration salts
- Permethrin-containing insect spray for clothing, tents and bed nets
- Pocket knife
- Scissors, safety pins, tweezers
- Steroid cream or cortisone (for poison ivy and other allergic rashes)
- Sun block
- Syringes and sterile needles
- Thermometer

RECOMMENDED VACCINATIONS

There are no required vaccines for Panama, but a number are recommended:

Vaccine	Recommended for	Dosage	Side effects
Hepatitis A	All travelers	One dose before trip; booster 6-12 months later	Soreness at injection site; headaches; body aches
Typhoid	All travelers	Four capsules by mouth, one taken every other day	Abdominal pain; nausea; rash
Yellow fever	All travelers	One dose lasts 10 years	Headaches; body aches; severe reactions are rare
Hepatitis B	Long-term travelers in close contact with the local population	Three doses over 6-month period	Soreness at injection site; low-grade fever
Rabies	Travelers who may have contact with animals and may not have access to medical care	Three doses over 3-4 week period	Soreness at injection site; headaches; body aches. Expensive.
Tetanus-diphtheria	All travelers who haven't had a booster within 10 years	One dose lasts 10 years	Soreness at injection site
Measles	Travelers born after 1956 who've had only one measles vaccination	One dose	Fever; rash; joint pains; allergic reactions
Chickenpox	Travelers who've never had chickenpox	Two doses one month apart	Fever; mild case of chickenpox

more information.) Find out in advance if your insurance plan will make payments directly to providers or reimburse you later for overseas health expenditures.

INTERNET RESOURCES

The Internet is a great source of travel-health advice. The **Lonely Planet** (www.lonelyplanet.com) website is a good place to start. A superb book called *International Travel and Health*, revised annually and available online at no cost is published by the **World Health Organization** (www.who.int/ith/). Another website of general interest is **MD Travel Health** (www.mdtravelhealth.com), which provides complete travel-health recommendations for every country, updated daily, also at no cost.

It's usually a good idea to consult your government's travel-health website before departure, if one is available:

Australia (www.dfat.gov.au/travel/)
Canada (www.hc-sc.gc.ca/pphb-dgspsp/tmp-pmv/pub_e.html)
United Kingdom (www.doh.gov.uk/traveladvice/index.htm)
United States (www.cdc.gov/travel/)

FURTHER READING

For further information, see *Healthy Travel Central & South America*, also from Lonely Planet. If you're traveling with children, Lonely Planet's *Travel with Children* may be useful. The *ABC of Healthy Travel*, by E Walker et al, is another valuable resource.

IN TRANSIT

DEEP VEIN THROMBOSIS (DVT)

Blood clots (deep vein thrombosis) may form in the legs during long-haul plane flights, chiefly because of prolonged immobility; the longer the flight, the greater the risk. Though most blood clots are reabsorbed uneventfully, some may break off and travel through the blood vessels

HEALTH

to the lungs, where they could cause life-threatening complications.

The chief symptom of deep vein thrombosis is swelling or pain of the foot, ankle, or calf, usually but not always on just one side. When a blood clot travels to the lungs, it may cause chest pain and difficulty breathing. Travelers with any of these symptoms should immediately seek medical attention.

To prevent the development of deep vein thrombosis on long flights you should walk about the cabin, perform isometric compressions of the leg muscles (ie contract the leg muscles while sitting), drink plenty of fluids, and avoid alcohol and tobacco.

JET LAG & MOTION SICKNESS

Jet lag is common when crossing more than five time zones resulting in insomnia, fatigue, malaise or nausea. To avoid jet lag try drinking plenty of fluids (nonalcoholic) and eating light meals. Upon arrival, get exposure to natural sunlight and readjust your schedule (for meals, sleep etc) as soon as possible.

Antihistamines such as dimenhydrinate (Dramamine) and meclizine (Antivert, Bonine) are usually the first choice for treating motion sickness. Their main side effect is drowsiness. A herbal alternative is ginger, which works like a charm for some people.

IN PANAMA

AVAILABILITY OF HEALTH CARE

Good medical care is widely available in Panama City. The following hospitals and clinics are generally reliable:

Centro Medico Paitilla (☎ 265-8800; cnr Av Balboa & Calle 53, Paitilla)

Clinica Hospital San Fernando (☎ 278-6300, emergency ☎ 278-6305; www.hospitalsanfernando.com; Vía España, Las Sabanas Apartado 363)

Clinica Hospital San Fernando Hospital Pediatrico (☎ 229-2299/229-2477; www.hospitalsanfernando.com; Vía España, Las Sabanas 363)

Hospital Nacional (☎ 207-8100 switchboard, 207-8110 emergency room; Av Cuba btwn Calle 38 and 39)

Medical facilities outside Panama City are limited. David has the best hospitals outside of the capital:

Hospital Centro Medico Mae Lewis (☎ 775-4616; Vía Panamericana, Apartado 333)

TRADITIONAL MEDICINE

The following are some traditional remedies for common travel-related conditions.

Problem	Treatment
jet lag	melatonin
motion sickness	ginger
mosquito-bite prevention	oil of eucalyptus; soybean oil

INFECTIOUS DISEASES

Chagas' Disease

Chagas' disease is a parasitic infection that is transmitted by triatomine insects (reduviid bugs), which inhabit crevices in the walls and roofs of substandard housing in South and Central America. In Panama, Chagas' disease occurs in rural areas. The triatomine insect lays its feces on human skin as it bites, usually at night. A person becomes infected when he or she unknowingly rubs the feces into the bite wound or any other open sore. Chagas' disease is extremely rare in travelers. However, if you sleep in a poorly constructed house, especially one made of mud, adobe, or thatch, you should be sure to protect yourself with a bed net and a good insecticide.

Cholera

Cholera has not been reported from Panama in recent years. Cholera vaccine is not recommended.

Dengue Fever (Breakbone Fever)

Dengue fever is a viral infection found throughout Central America. In Panama, most cases occur in San Miguelito and in the Panama City metropolitan area. Dengue is transmitted by aedes mosquitoes, which bite preferentially during the daytime and are usually found close to human habitations, often indoors. They breed primarily in artificial water containers, such as jars, barrels, cans, cisterns, metal drums, plastic containers and discarded tires. As a result, dengue is especially common in densely populated, urban environments.

Dengue usually causes flu-like symptoms, including fever, muscle aches, joint pains, headaches, nausea and vomiting, often followed by a rash. The body aches may be quite uncomfortable, but most cases resolve uneventfully in a few days. There is no treatment for dengue fever except to take analgesics such as acetaminophen/paracetamol (Tylenol) and drink plenty of fluids. Severe cases may require hospitalization for intravenous fluids and supportive care. There is no vaccine. The cornerstone of prevention is to avoid being bitten, see p321.

Hantavirus Pulmonary Syndrome

This is a rapidly progressive viral infection that typically leads to respiratory failure and is frequently fatal. The disease is acquired by exposure to the excretions of wild rodents. Most cases occur in those who live in rodent-infested dwellings in rural areas. An outbreak of hantavirus pulmonary syndrome was recently reported from Los Santos province.

Hepatitis A

Hepatitis A is the second most common travel-related infection (after traveler's diarrhea). It's a viral infection of the liver that is usually acquired by ingestion of contaminated water, food or ice, though it may also be acquired by direct contact with infected persons. The illness occurs throughout the world, but the incidence is higher in developing nations. Symptoms may include fever, malaise, jaundice, nausea, vomiting and abdominal pain. Most cases resolve without complications, though hepatitis A occasionally causes severe liver damage. There is no treatment.

The vaccine for hepatitis A is extremely safe and highly effective. If you get a booster six to twelve months later, it lasts for at least 10 years. You really should get it before you go to Panama or any other developing nation. Because the safety of hepatitis A vaccine has not been established for pregnant women or children under age two, they should instead be given a gammaglobulin injection.

Hepatitis B

Like hepatitis A, hepatitis B is a liver infection that occurs worldwide but is more common in developing nations. Unlike hepatitis A, the disease is usually acquired by sexual contact or by exposure to infected blood, generally through blood transfusions or contaminated needles. The vaccine is recommended only for long-term travelers (on the road more than six months) who

expect to live in rural areas or have close physical contact with the local population. Additionally, the vaccine is recommended for anyone who anticipates sexual contact with the local inhabitants or a possible need for medical, dental or other treatments while abroad, especially if a need for transfusions or injections is expected.

Hepatitis B vaccine is safe and highly effective. However, a total of three injections is necessary to establish full immunity. Several countries added hepatitis B vaccine to the list of routine childhood immunizations in the 1980s, so many young adults are already protected.

HIV/AIDS

This has been reported from all Central American countries. Be sure to use condoms for all sexual encounters. Reliable, American-made brands are available at most pharmacies.

Leishmaniasis

Leishmaniasis occurs in rural and forested areas throughout Panama, especially the eastern and south-central regions. The disease is generally limited to the skin, causing slow-growing ulcers over exposed parts of the body, but the infection may become generalized, especially in those with HIV. Leishmaniasis is transmitted by sandflies, which are about one-third the size of mosquitoes. There is no vaccine. To protect yourself from sandflies, follow the same precautions as for mosquitoes (p321), except that netting must be finer-size mesh (at least 18 holes to the linear inch).

Leptospirosis

Leptospirosis is acquired by exposure to water contaminated by the urine of infected animals. In Panama, leptospirosis is reported throughout the country. The greatest risk occurs at times of flooding, when sewage overflow may contaminate water sources. Outbreaks have been reported among military personnel performing jungle training exercises. The initial symptoms, which resemble a mild flu, usually subside uneventfully in a few days, with or without treatment, but a minority of cases are complicated by jaundice or meningitis. There is no vaccine. You can minimize your risk by staying out of bodies of fresh water that may be contaminated by animal urine. If you're engaging in high-risk activities in an area where an outbreak is in progress, you can take 200mg of doxycycline once weekly as a preventative measure. If you actually develop leptospirosis, the treatment is 100mg of doxycycline twice daily.

Malaria

Malaria is transmitted by mosquito bites, usually between dusk and dawn. The main symptom is high-spiking fevers, which may be accompanied by chills, sweats, headache, body aches, weakness, vomiting, or diarrhea. Severe cases may involve the central nervous system and lead to seizures, confusion, coma and death.

In Panama, malaria pills are recommended for rural areas in the provinces of Bocas del Toro, Darién and Kuna Yala. For Bocas del Toro, the first-choice malaria pill is chloroquine, taken once weekly in a dosage of 500mg, starting one to two weeks before arrival and continuing through the trip, and for four weeks after departure. Chloroquine is safe, inexpensive and highly effective. Side effects are typically mild and may include nausea, abdominal discomfort, headache, dizziness, blurred vision, or itching. Severe reactions are uncommon.

Protecting yourself against mosquito bites is just as important as taking malaria pills, since no pills are 100% effective.

If you may not have access to medical care while traveling, you should bring along additional pills for emergency self-treatment, which you should take if you can't reach a doctor and you develop symptoms that suggest malaria, such as high-spiking fevers. One option is to take four tablets of Malarone once daily for three days. If you start self-medication, you should try to see a doctor at the earliest possible opportunity.

In areas east of the Canal Zone, including the Darién and Kuna Yala, there are chloroquine-resistant mosquitoes. Your options there are mefloquine (which has severe side effects for some travelers), doxycycline (which is milder on the system, but makes you more susceptible to sunburn) or Malarone.

If you develop a fever after returning home, see a physician, as malaria symptoms may not occur for months.

Rabies

Rabies is a viral infection of the brain and spinal cord that is almost always fatal. The rabies virus is carried in the saliva of infected animals and is typically transmitted through an animal bite, though contamination of any break in the skin with infected saliva may result in rabies.

In Panama, rabies is transmitted mainly by vampire bats. All animal bites and scratches must be promptly and thoroughly cleansed with large amounts of soap and water, and local health authorities contacted to determine whether or not further treatment is necessary (see p321).

Tick-Borne Relapsing Fever

This fever, which may be transmitted by either ticks or lice, is caused by bacteria that are closely related to those which cause Lyme disease and syphilis. The illness is characterized by periods of fever, chills, headaches, body aches, muscle aches and cough, alternating with periods when the fever subsides and the person feels relatively well. To minimize the risk of relapsing fever, follow tick precautions as outlined below and practice good personal hygiene at all times.

Typhoid

Typhoid fever is caused by ingestion of food or water contaminated by a species of salmonella known as *Salmonella typhi*. Fever occurs in virtually all cases. Other symptoms may include headache, malaise, muscle aches, dizziness, loss of appetite, nausea and abdominal pain. Either diarrhea or constipation may occur. Possible complications include intestinal perforation, intestinal bleeding, confusion, delirium or (rarely) coma.

Unless you expect to take all your meals in major hotels and restaurants, typhoid vaccine is a good idea. It's usually given orally, but is also available as an injection. Neither vaccine is approved for use in children under the age of two.

The drug of choice for typhoid fever is usually a quinolone antibiotic such as ciprofloxacin (Cipro) or levofloxacin (Levaquin), which many travelers carry for treatment of traveler's diarrhea. However, if you self-treat for typhoid fever, you may also need to self-treat for malaria, since the symptoms of the two diseases may be indistinguishable.

Yellow Fever

Yellow fever is a life-threatening viral infection transmitted by mosquitoes in forested areas. The illness begins with flu-like symptoms, which may include fever, chills, headache, muscle aches, backache, loss of appetite, nausea and vomiting. These symptoms usually subside in a few days, but one person in six enters a second, toxic phase characterized by recurrent fever, vomiting, listlessness, jaundice, kidney failure and hemorrhage, leading to death in up to half of the cases. There is no treatment.

Yellow-fever vaccine is not required for travel to Panama, but is strongly recommended for all travelers greater than nine months of age, especially those visiting Chepo, Darién and Kuna Yala.

The vaccine is given only in approved yellow-fever vaccination centers, which provide validated International Certificates of Vaccination ('yellow booklets'). The vaccine should be given at least 10 days before any potential exposure to yellow fever and remains effective for approximately 10 years. Reactions to the vaccine are generally mild and may include headaches, muscle aches, low-grade fevers or discomfort at the injection site. Severe, life-threatening reactions have been described but are extremely rare. In general, the risk of becoming ill from the vaccine is far less than the risk of becoming ill from yellow fever, and you're strongly encouraged to get the vaccine.

Taking measures to protect yourself from mosquito bites, p321, is an essential part of preventing yellow fever.

TRAVELER'S DIARRHEA

To prevent diarrhea, avoid tap water unless it has been boiled, filtered, or chemically disinfected (iodine tablets); only eat fresh fruits or vegetables if cooked or peeled; be wary of dairy products that might contain unpasteurized milk; and be highly selective when eating food from street vendors.

If you develop diarrhea, be sure to drink plenty of fluids, preferably an oral rehydration solution containing lots of salt and sugar. A few loose stools don't require treatment but, if you start having more than four or five stools a day, you should start taking an antibiotic (usually a quinolone drug) and an antidiarrheal agent (such as loperamide). If diarrhea is bloody or persists for more than 72 hours, or is accompanied by fever, shaking chills or severe abdominal pain, you should seek medical attention.

ENVIRONMENTAL HAZARDS
Animal Bites

Do not attempt to pet, handle, or feed any animal, with the exception of domestic animals known to be free of any infectious disease. Most animal injuries are directly related to a person's attempt to touch or feed the animal.

Any bite or scratch by a mammal, including bats, should be promptly and thoroughly cleansed with large amounts of soap and water, followed by application of an antiseptic such as iodine or alcohol. The local health authorities should be contacted immediately for possible post-exposure rabies treatment, whether or not you've been immunized against rabies. It may also be advisable to start an antibiotic, since wounds caused by animal bites and scratches frequently become infected. One of the newer quinolones, such as levofloxacin (Levaquin), which many travelers carry in case of diarrhea, would be an appropriate choice.

Insect Bites

To prevent mosquito bites, wear long sleeves, long pants, hats and shoes (rather than sandals). Bring along a good insect repellent, preferably one containing DEET, which should be applied to exposed skin and clothing, but not to eyes, mouth, cuts, wounds, or irritated skin. Products containing lower concentrations of DEET are as effective, but for shorter periods of time. In general, adults and children over 12 should use preparations containing 25% to 35% DEET, which usually lasts about six hours. Children between two and 12 years of age should use preparations containing no more than 10% DEET, applied sparingly, which will usually last about three hours. Neurologic toxicity has been reported from DEET, especially in children, but appears to be extremely uncommon and generally related to overuse. DEET-containing compounds should not be used on children under the age of two.

Insect repellents containing certain botanical products, including oil of eucalyptus and soybean oil, are effective but last only

1½ to two hours. DEET-containing repellents are preferable for areas where there is a high risk of malaria or yellow fever. Products based on citronella are not effective.

For additional protection, you can apply permethrin to clothing, shoes, tents and bed nets. Permethrin treatments are safe and remain effective for at least two weeks, even when items are laundered. Permethrin should not be applied directly to skin.

Don't sleep with the window open unless there is a screen. If sleeping outdoors or in accommodations that allow entry of mosquitoes, use a bed net, preferably treated with permethrin, with edges tucked in under the mattress. The mesh size should be less than 1.5mm. If the sleeping area is not otherwise protected, use a mosquito coil, which will fill the room with insecticide through the night. Repellent-impregnated wristbands are not effective.

Snake Bites

Panama is home to several venomous snakes and any foray into forested areas will put you at (a very slight) risk of snake bite. The best prevention is to wear closed, heavy shoes or boots and to keep a watchful eye on the trail. Snakes like to come out to cleared paths for a nap, so watch where you step.

In the event of a venomous snake bite, place the victim at rest, keep the bitten area immobilized and move the victim immediately to the nearest medical facility. Avoid using a tourniquet, as they are no longer recommended.

Sun

To protect yourself from excessive sun exposure, you should stay out of the midday sun, wear sunglasses and a wide-brimmed sun hat, and apply sunscreen with SPF 15 or higher, with both UVA and UVB protection. Sunscreen should be generously applied to all exposed parts of the body approximately 30 minutes before sun exposure and should be reapplied after swimming or vigorous activity. Travelers should also drink plenty of fluids and avoid strenuous exercise when the temperature is high.

Water

Tap water in Panama City *is* safe to drink, as is the water in most other parts of the country. However, you're better off buying bottled water or purifying your own water in the provinces of Bocas del Toro and Kuna Yala.

If you have the means, vigorous boiling for one minute is the most effective way of water purification. Another option is to disinfect water with iodine pills; add 2% tincture of iodine to one quart or liter of water (five drops to clear water, 10 drops to cloudy water) and let stand for 30 minutes. If the water is cold, longer times may be required.

TRAVELING WITH CHILDREN

In general, pregnant women and children less than nine months of age should avoid going to Panama, since yellow-fever vaccine, which is strongly recommended for all parts of the country, may not be safe during pregnancy or the first few months of life.

Older children may be brought to Panama. However, you should be particularly careful not to let them consume any questionable food or beverage. Also, when traveling with children, make sure they're up-to-date on all routine immunizations. It's sometimes appropriate to give children some of their vaccines a little early before visiting a developing nation. You should discuss this with your pediatrician.

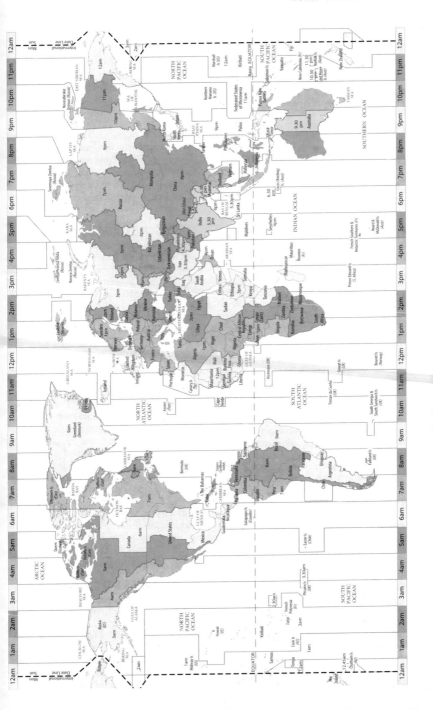

Language

CONTENTS

The Languages of Panama	324
Learn Some Lingo!	324
Phrasebooks & Dictionaries	324
Latin American Spanish	325
Pronunciation	325
Gender & Plurals	326
Accommodations	326
Conversation & Essentials	327
Directions	327
Health	328
Emergencies	328
Language Difficulties	328
Numbers	328
Paperwork	329
Shopping & Services	329
Time & Dates	330
Transport	330
Travel with Children	331

THE LANGUAGES OF PANAMA

Spanish is the official, and most widely spoken, language in Panama, but no fewer than 14 other languages can also be heard on the isthmus. Eight languages are spoken by Panama's seven Indian tribes (the Kuna living in the villages of Paya and Pucuro, in southeastern Panama, speak a language that is quite different from that of Kuna residing elsewhere). Two Chinese languages, Arabic, Hebrew, San Miguel Creole French and Western Caribbean Creole English are also spoken in the country.

San Miguel Creole French is spoken by scattered groups whose ancestors came from St Lucia during the mid-19th century as laborers. Western Caribbean Creole English is spoken by an estimated 14% of the population, whose ancestors came from Barbados and Jamaica in the 19th century to work in fruit plantations, and later to build the Panama Railroad and Canal. Creole English is commonly heard in Bocas del Toro Province and in Colón. Other Panamanians have learned English at school or from US soldiers and Panama Canal workers.

Many Chinese also came to Panama to work on the railway and the canal, and their descendants speak Cantonese or Hakka. During the 20th century, Chinese immigrants arrived as merchants. There is a hearty Chinatown in Panama City and a substantial Chinese community in Colón. Likewise, many Arabs and Jews came to these two cities to conduct business. Today Arabs from several Middle Eastern countries and Jews from Israel and the USA comprise two of the most powerful groups in Panama.

LEARN SOME LINGO!

Just as most Panamanian immigrants have learned to speak Spanish as a second language, any traveler to Panama would be wise to learn at least a little Spanish as a matter of courtesy and convenience. Basic Spanish is easily acquired (perhaps more so for speakers of English and Romance languages), and a month-long language course taken before departure can go a long way toward facilitating communication and comfort on the road. Language courses are available in Panama City (p90) for those interested in the added benefits of learning Spanish while in the country. Even if classes are impractical, you should make the effort to learn a few basic phrases and pleasantries. At the very least your Spanish should cover 'good morning,' 'good afternoon,' 'good evening,' 'goodbye,' 'thank you' and 'glad to meet you.' Don't hesitate to practice your language skills – in general, Latin Americans meet attempts to communicate in the vernacular, however halting, with enthusiasm and appreciation. If you try speaking Spanish in Panama and the person you are talking to speaks English, that person will usually respond in English.

PHRASEBOOKS & DICTIONARIES

Lonely Planet's *Latin American Spanish Phrasebook* will be extremely helpful during your trip. Another very useful resource is the University of Chicago *Spanish-English, English-Spanish Dictionary*. It's small, light and has thorough entries, making it ideal for travel. It also makes a great gift for any newfound friends upon your departure.

SPANISH IN PANAMA

Think you know enough Spanish? Here's a quick rundown on some of the local expressions and colorful colloquialisms you may hear while traveling in Panama:

salve – street slang for propina, or tip
tongo – street slang for cop
hota – street slang for police car
diablo rojo – 'red devil'; refers to public buses
mangajo/a (m/f) – someone who is filthy
buena leche – 'good milk'; means good luck
salado/a (m/f) – 'salty'; refers to someone who is having bad luck
Eso está bien pretty. – refers to something nice
¡Eso está pretty pretty! – refers to something super-nice
¡Entonces laopé! – Hey, dude!
¡Hey, gringo! – Hey, white person! (friendly)
¡Juega vivo! – Be alert, look out for your best interests!
Voy por fuera. – I'm leaving right now.
¡Ayala bestia! – Holy cow!
¡Chuleta! – common expression similar to 'Holy cow!'
pelao or pelaito – common expression for a child
Pa' lante. – Let's go now.
enantes – just now
Eres un comemierda. – refers to someone pretentious
¡Pifioso! – a showoff, or something that looks cool
Tas buena, mami. – You're looking good, mama.
Nos pillamos. – We'll see each other later.
una pinta or una fría – literally, 'one pint' or 'a cold one'; means a beer
Dame una fría. – Give me a cold one (a beer).
guaro – hard liquor

chupata – an all-out drinking party
¡Bien cuidado! – 'Well taken care of!'; often used by a street person when asking a tip for taking care of your car, normally in parking lots at restaurants, cinemas, bars, etc
Me estoy comiendo un cable. – 'I'm eating a cable'; I'm down on my luck.
rabiblanco/a (m/f) – 'white tipped'; pejorative reference to a member of the socioeconomic elite; the term comes from paloma rabíblano/a (white-tipped dove), a bird that walks with its head held out high and its chest thrust out in a seemingly pretentious way
racataca – also meña; both terms refer to women who wear lots of gold jewelry and are perceived as low class
chombo/a (m/f) – an acceptable reference to a black person of Antillean descent
ladilla – 'crab louse'; refers to an annoying person
nueve letras – 'nine letters'; refers to Seco Herrerano (the word 'Herrerano' has nine letters)
vuelve loco con vaca – 'makes crazy with cow'; refers to drinking seco and milk
vaina – common word that substitutes for 'thing,' as in Pasame esa vaina. (Pass me that thing.)
yeye – refers to kids and adults who wear fancy clothes and maybe drive a fancy car and who pretend to be rich but who in reality are living well beyond their means for as long as they can

LATIN AMERICAN SPANISH

The Spanish of the Americas comes in a bewildering array of varieties. Depending on the areas in which you travel, consonants may be glossed over, vowels squashed into each other, and syllables and even words dropped entirely. Slang and regional vocabulary, much of it derived from indigenous languages, can further add to your bewilderment.

Throughout Latin America, the Spanish language is referred to as *castellano* more often than *español*. Unlike in Spain, the plural of the familiar *tú* form is *ustedes* rather than *vosotros*; the latter term will sound quaint and archaic in the Americas. Another notable difference is that the letters **c** and **z** are never lisped in Latin America; attempts to do so could well provoke amusement.

PRONUNCIATION

Spanish spelling is phonetically consistent, meaning that there's a clear and consistent relationship between what you see in writing and how it's pronounced. In addition, most Spanish sounds have English equivalents, so English speakers shouldn't have too much trouble being understood.

Vowels

a	as in 'father'
e	as in 'met'
i	as in 'marine'
o	as in 'or' (without the 'r' sound)
u	as in 'rule'. Note that the 'u' is not pronounced after **q**, or in the letter combinations **gue** and **gui**, unless it's marked with a diaeresis (eg *argüir*), in which case it's pronounced as English 'w'

y at the end of a word or when it stands alone, it's pronounced as the Spanish **i** (eg *ley*); between vowels within a word it's as the 'y' in 'yonder'

Consonants

As a rule, Spanish consonants resemble their English counterparts. The exceptions are listed below.

While the consonants **ch**, **ll** and **ñ** are generally considered distinct letters, **ch** and **ll** are now often listed alphabetically under **c** and **l** respectively. The letter **ñ** is still treated as a separate letter and comes after **n** in dictionaries.

b similar to English 'b,' but softer; referred to as 'b larga'
c as in 'celery' before **e** and **i**; otherwise as English 'k'
ch as in 'church'
d as in 'dog,' but between vowels and after **l** or **n**, the sound is closer to the 'th' in 'this'
g as the 'ch' in the Scottish *loch* before **e** and **i** ('kh' in our guides to pronunciation); elsewhere, as in 'go'
h invariably silent. If your name begins with this letter, listen carefully if you're waiting for public officials to call you.
j as the 'ch' in the Scottish *loch* (written as 'kh' in our guides to pronunciation)
ll as the 'y' in 'yellow'
ñ as the 'ni' in 'onion'
r a short **r** except at the beginning of a word, and after **l**, **n** or **s**, when it's often rolled
rr very strongly rolled
v similar to English 'b,' but softer; referred to as 'b corta'
x usually pronounced as **j** above; in some indigenous place names **x** is pronounced as the 's' in 'sit'; in other instances, it's as in 'taxi'
z as the 's' in 'sun'

Word Stress

In general, words ending in vowels or the letters **n** or **s** have stress on the next-to-last syllable, while those with other endings have stress on the last syllable. Thus *vaca* (cow) and *caballos* (horses) both carry stress on the next-to-last syllable, while *ciudad* (city) and *infeliz* (unhappy) are both stressed on the last syllable.

Written accents will almost always appear in words that don't follow the rules above, eg *sótano* (basement), *América* and *porción* (portion).

GENDER & PLURALS

In Spanish, nouns are either masculine or feminine, and there are rules to help determine gender (there are of course some exceptions). Feminine nouns generally end with **-a** or with the groups **-ción**, **-sión** or **-dad**. Other endings typically signify a masculine noun. Endings for adjectives also change to agree with the gender of the noun they modify (masculine/feminine **-o/-a**). Where both masculine and feminine forms are included in this language guide, they are separated by a slash, with the masculine form first, eg *perdido/a*.

If a noun or adjective ends in a vowel, the plural is formed by adding **s** to the end. If it ends in a consonant, the plural is formed by adding **es** to the end.

ACCOMMODATIONS

I'm looking for ...	*Estoy buscando ...*	e·stoy boos·kan·do ...
Where is ...?	*¿Dónde hay ...?*	don·de ai ...
a cabin	*una cabina*	oo·na ca·bee·na
a camping ground	*un camping/ campamento*	oon kam·ping/ kam·pa·men·to
a guesthouse	*una casa de huespedes*	oo·na ka·sa de wes·pe·des
a hostel	*un hospedaje/ una residencia*	oon os·pe·da·khe/ oon·a re·see·den·sya
a hotel	*un hotel*	oon o·tel
a youth hostel	*un albergue juvenil*	oon al·ber·ge khoo·ve·neel

Are there any rooms available?

¿Hay habitaciones libres?	ay a·bee·ta·syon·es lee·bres

I'd like a ... room.	*Quisiera una habitación ...*	kee·sye·ra oo·na a·bee·ta·syon ...
double	*doble*	do·ble
single	*individual*	een·dee·vee·dwal
twin	*con dos camas*	kon dos ka·mas

How much is it per ...?	*¿Cuánto cuesta por ...?*	kwan·to kwes·ta por ...
night	*noche*	no·che
person	*persona*	per·so·na
week	*semana*	se·ma·na

MAKING A RESERVATION

(for phone or written requests)

To ...	*A ...*
From ...	*De ...*
Date	*Fecha*
I'd like to book ...	*Quisiera reservar ...* (see the list under 'Accommodations' for bed and room options)
in the name of ...	*en nombre de ...*
for the nights of ...	*para las noches del ...*
credit card ...	*tarjeta de crédito ...*
number	*número*
expiry date	*fecha de vencimiento*
Please confirm ...	*Puede confirmar ...*
availability	*la disponibilidad*
price	*el precio*

---

full board	*pensión completa*	pen·*syon* kom·*ple*·ta
private/shared bathroom	*baño privado/ compartido*	ba·nyo pree·*va*·do/ kom·par·*tee*·do
too expensive	*demasiado caro*	de·ma·*sya*·do *ka*·ro
cheaper	*más económico*	mas e·ko·*no*·mee·ko
discount	*descuento*	des·*kwen*·to

Does it include breakfast?

¿Incluye el desayuno?   een·*kloo*·ye el de·sa·*yoo*·no

May I see the room?

¿Puedo ver la habitación?   *pwe*·do ver la a·bee·ta·*syon*

I don't like it.

No me gusta.   no me *goos*·ta

It's fine. I'll take it.

Está bien. La tomo.   es·*ta* byen la *to*·mo

I'm leaving now.

Me voy ahora.   me *voy* a·o·ra

CONVERSATION & ESSENTIALS

In their public behavior, Latin Americans are very conscious of civilities. You should never approach a stranger for information without extending a greeting, such as *buenos días* or *buenas tardes*.

Central America is generally more formal than many of the South American countries, and the usage of the informal second-person singular *tú* and *vos* differs from country to country. When in doubt, use the more formal *usted*, which is used in all cases in this guide; where options are given, the form is indicated by the abbreviations 'pol' and 'inf.'

You should use only the polite form with the police and public officials.

Hi.	*Hola.*	*o*·la (inf)
Good morning.	*Buenos días.*	bwe·nos *dee*·as
Good afternoon.	*Buenas tardes.*	bwe·nas *tar*·des
Good evening/ night.	*Buenas noches.*	bwe·nas *no*·ches

The three most common greetings are often abbreviated to simply *buenos* (for *buenos días*) and *buenas* (for *buenas tardes* and *buenas noches*).

Bye/See you soon.	*Hasta luego.*	as·ta *lwe*·go
Goodbye.	*Adiós.*	a·*dyos*
Yes.	*Sí.*	see
No.	*No.*	no
Please.	*Por favor.*	por fa·*vor*
Thank you.	*Gracias.*	*gra*·syas
Many thanks.	*Muchas gracias.*	*moo*·chas *gra*·syas
You're welcome.	*De nada.*	de *na*·da
Apologies.	*Perdón.*	per·*don*
May I?	*Permiso.*	per·*mee*·so
(when asking permission)		
Excuse me.	*Disculpe.*	dees·*kool*·pe
(used before a request or when apologizing)		

How are things?

¿Qué tal?   ke tal

What's your name?

¿Cómo se llama usted?   *ko*·mo se *ya*·ma oo·*sted* (pol)

¿Cómo te llamas?   *ko*·mo te *ya*·mas (inf)

My name is ...

Me llamo ...   me *ya*·mo ...

It's a pleasure to meet you.

Mucho gusto.   *moo*·cho *goos*·to

The pleasure is mine.

El gusto es mío.   el *goos*·to es *mee*·o

Where are you from?

¿De dónde es/eres?   de *don*·de es/er·es (pol/inf)

I'm from ...

Soy de ...   soy de ...

Where are you staying?

¿Dónde está alojado?   *don*·de es·ta a·lo·*kha*·do (pol)

¿Dónde estás alojado?   *don*·de es·tas a·lo·*kha*·do (inf)

May I take a photo?

¿Puedo sacar una foto?   *pwe*·do sa·*kar* oo·na *fo*·to

DIRECTIONS

How do I get to ...?

¿Cómo llego a ...?   *ko*·mo *ye*·go a ...

Is it far?

¿Está lejos?   es·ta *le*·khos

Go straight ahead.

Siga/Vaya derecho.   *see*·ga/*va*·ya de·*re*·cho

LANGUAGE

Turn left.
  Voltée a la izquierda.   vol·*te*·e a la ees·*kyer*·da
Turn right.
  Voltée a la derecha.   vol·*te*·e a la de·*re*·cha
Can you show me (on the map)?
  ¿Me lo podría señalar   me lo po·*dree*·a se·nya·*lar*
  (en el mapa)?   (en el *ma*·pa)

SIGNS

Entrada	Entrance
Salida	Exit
Información	Information
Abierto	Open
Cerrado	Closed
Prohibido	Prohibited
Comisaria	Police Station
Servicios/Baños	Toilets
Hombres/Varones	Men
Mujeres/Damas	Women

---

north	*norte*	*nor*·te
south	*sur*	soor
east	*este*	*es*·te
west	*oeste*	o·*es*·te
here	*aquí*	a·*kee*
there	*ahí*	a·*ee*
avenue	*avenida*	a·ve·*nee*·da
block	*cuadra*	*kwa*·dra
street	*calle/paseo*	*ka*·lye/pa·*se*·o

HEALTH

I'm sick.
  Estoy enfermo/a.   es·*toy* en·*fer*·mo/a
I need a doctor.
  Necesito un médico.   ne·se·*see*·to oon *me*·dee·ko
Where's the hospital?
  ¿Dónde está el hospital?   *don*·de es·*ta* el os·pee·*tal*
I'm pregnant.
  Estoy embarazada.   es·*toy* em·ba·ra·*sa*·da
I've been vaccinated.
  Estoy vacunado/a.   es·*toy* va·koo·*na*·do/a

I'm allergic	*Soy alérgico/a*	soy a·*ler*·khee·ko/a
to ...	*a ...*	a ...
antibiotics	*los antibióticos*	los an·tee·*byo*·tee·kos
peanuts	*los maníes/*	los ma·*nee*·es/
	cacahuates	ka·ka·*wa*·tes
penicillin	*la penicilina*	la pe·nee·see·*lee*·na

I'm ...	*Soy ...*	soy ...
asthmatic	*asmático/a*	as·*ma*·tee·ko/a
diabetic	*diabético/a*	dya·*be*·tee·ko/a
epileptic	*epiléptico/a*	e·pee·*lep*·tee·ko/a

EMERGENCIES

Help!	*¡Socorro!*	so·*ko*·ro
Fire!	*¡Fuego!*	*fwe*·go
Go away!	*¡Déjeme!*	de·*khe*·me
Get lost!	*¡Váyase!*	va·ya·se

Call ...!	*¡Llame a ...!*	*ya*·me a
the police	*la policía*	la po·lee·*see*·a
a doctor	*un médico*	oon *me*·dee·ko
an ambulance	*una ambulancia*	oo·na am·boo·*lan*·sya

It's an emergency.
  Es una emergencia.   es oo·na e·mer·*khen*·sya
Could you help me, please?
  ¿Me puede ayudar,   me *pwe*·de a·yoo·*dar*
  por favor?   por fa·*vor*
I'm lost.
  Estoy perdido/a.   es·*toy* per·*dee*·do/a
Where are the toilets?
  ¿Dónde están los baños?   *don*·de es·*tan* los *ba*·nyos

I have ...	*Tengo ...*	*ten*·go ...
a cough	*tos*	tos
diarrhea	*diarrea*	dya·*re*·a
a headache	*un dolor de*	oon do·*lor* de
	cabeza	ka·*be*·sa
nausea	*náusea*	*now*·se·a

LANGUAGE DIFFICULTIES

Do you speak English?
  ¿Habla/Hablas inglés?   *a*·bla/*a*·blas een·*gles* (pol/inf)
Does anyone here speak English?
  ¿Hay alguien que hable   ai al·*gyen* ke *a*·ble
  inglés?   een·*gles*
I (don't) understand.
  (No) Entiendo.   (no) en·*tyen*·do
How do you say ...?
  ¿Cómo se dice ...?   *ko*·mo se *dee*·se ...
What does ... mean?
  ¿Qué significa ...?   ke seeg·*nee*·fee·ka ...

Could you	*¿Puede ..., por*	*pwe*·de ... por
please ...?	*favor?*	fa·*vor*
repeat that	*repetirlo*	re·pe·*teer*·lo
speak more	*hablar más*	a·*blar* mas
slowly	*despacio*	des·*pa*·syo
write it down	*escribirlo*	es·kree·*beer*·lo

NUMBERS

1	*uno*	*oo*·no
2	*dos*	dos
3	*tres*	tres

4	cuatro	kwa·tro
5	cinco	seen·ko
6	seis	says
7	siete	sye·te
8	ocho	o·cho
9	nueve	nwe·ve
10	diez	dyes
11	once	on·se
12	doce	do·se
13	trece	tre·se
14	catorce	ka·tor·se
15	quince	keen·se
16	dieciséis	dye·see·says
17	diecisiete	dye·see·sye·te
18	dieciocho	dye·see·o·cho
19	diecinueve	dye·see·nwe·ve
20	veinte	vayn·te
21	veintiuno	vayn·tee·oo·no
30	treinta	trayn·ta
31	treinta y uno	trayn·ta ee oo·no
40	cuarenta	kwa·ren·ta
50	cincuenta	seen·kwen·ta
60	sesenta	se·sen·ta
70	setenta	se·ten·ta
80	ochenta	o·chen·ta
90	noventa	no·ven·ta
100	cien	syen
101	ciento uno	syen·to oo·no
200	doscientos	do·syen·tos
1000	mil	meel
5000	cinco mil	seen·ko meel

PAPERWORK

birth certificate	certificado de nacimiento
border (frontier)	la frontera
car-owner's title	título de propiedad
car registration	registración
customs	aduana
driver's license	licencia de manejar
identification	identificación
immigration	migración
insurance	seguro
passport	pasaporte
temporary vehicle import permit	permiso de importación temporal de vehículo
tourist card	tarjeta de turista
visa	visado

SHOPPING & SERVICES

I'd like to buy ...
Quisiera comprar ...   kee·sye·ra kom·prar ...
I'm just looking.
Sólo estoy mirando.   so·lo es·toy mee·ran·do
May I look at it?
¿Puedo verlo/a?   pwe·do ver·lo/a

How much is it?
¿Cuánto cuesta?   kwan·to kwes·ta
That's too expensive for me.
Es demasiado caro   es de·ma·sya·do ka·ro
para mí.   pa·ra mee
Could you lower the price?
¿Podría bajar un poco   po·dree·a ba·khar oon po·ko
el precio?   el pre·syo
I don't like it.
No me gusta.   no me goos·ta
I'll take it.
Lo llevo.   lo ye·vo

Do you accept ...?	¿Aceptan ...?	a·sep·tan ...
American dollars	dólares americanos	do·la·res a·me·ree·ka·nos
credit cards	tarjetas de crédito	tar·khe·tas de kre·dee·to
traveler's checks	cheques de viajero	che·kes de vya·khe·ro

more	más	mas
less	menos	me·nos
small	pequeño/a	pe·ke·nyo/a
large	grande	gran·de

I'm looking for the ...	Estoy buscando ...	es·toy boos·kan·do
ATM	el cajero automático	el ka·khe·ro ow·to·ma·tee·ko
bank	el banco	el ban·ko
bookstore	la librería	la lee·bre·ree·a
exchange house	la casa de cambio	la ka·sa de kam·byo
general store	la tienda	la tyen·da
laundry	la lavandería	la la·van·de·ree·a
market	el mercado	el mer·ka·do
pharmacy/ chemist	la farmacia	la far·ma·sya
post office	la officina de correos	la o·fee·see·na de ko·re·os
supermarket	el supermercado	el soo·per·mer·ka·do
tourist office	la oficina de turismo	la o·fee·see·na de too·rees·mo

What time does it open/close?
¿A qué hora abre/cierra?
a ke o·ra a·bre/sye·ra
I want to change some money/traveler's checks.
Quisiera cambiar dinero/cheques de viajero.
kee·sye·ra kam·byar dee·ne·ro/che·kes de vya·khe·ro
What is the exchange rate?
¿Cuál es el tipo de cambio?
kwal es el tee·po de kam·byo

I want to call ...
Quisiera llamar a ...
kee-*sye*-ra lya-*mar* a ...

airmail	*correo aéreo*	ko-*re*-o a-*e*-re-o
letter	*carta*	*kar*-ta
registered (mail)	*certificado*	ser-tee-fee-*ka*-do
stamps	*timbres*	*teem*-bres

TIME & DATES

What time is it?	*¿Qué hora es?*	ke *o*-ra es
It's one o'clock.	*Es la una.*	es la *oo*-na
It's seven o'clock.	*Son las siete.*	son las *sye*-te
Half past two.	*Dos y media.*	dos ee *me*-dya
midnight	*medianoche*	me-dya-*no*-che
noon	*mediodía*	me-dyo-*dee*-a

now	*ahora*	a-*o*-ra
today	*hoy*	oy
tonight	*esta noche*	es-ta *no*-che
tomorrow	*mañana*	ma-*nya*-na
yesterday	*ayer*	a-*yer*

Monday	*lunes*	*loo*-nes
Tuesday	*martes*	*mar*-tes
Wednesday	*miércoles*	*myer*-ko-les
Thursday	*jueves*	*khwe*-ves
Friday	*viernes*	*vyer*-nes
Saturday	*sábado*	*sa*-ba-do
Sunday	*domingo*	do-*meen*-go

January	*enero*	e-*ne*-ro
February	*febrero*	fe-*bre*-ro
March	*marzo*	*mar*-so
April	*abril*	a-*breel*
May	*mayo*	*ma*-yo
June	*junio*	*khoo*-nyo
July	*julio*	*khoo*-lyo
August	*agosto*	a-*gos*-to
September	*septiembre*	sep-*tyem*-bre
October	*octubre*	ok-*too*-bre
November	*noviembre*	no-*vyem*-bre
December	*diciembre*	dee-*syem*-bre

TRANSPORT
Public Transport

What time does	*¿A qué hora ...*	a ke *o*-ra ...
... leave/arrive?	*sale/llega?*	*sa*-le/*ye*-ga
the bus	*el bus/autobús*	el bus/ow-to-*boos*
the ferry	*el barco*	el *bar*-ko
the minibus	*el colectivo/*	el ko-lek-*tee*-vo/
	la buseta/	la boo-*se*-ta/
	el microbus	el *mee*-kro-boos
the plane	*el avión*	el a-*vyon*
the train	*el tren*	el tren

the airport	*el aeropuerto*	el a-e-ro-*pwer*-to
the bus station	*la estación de*	la es-ta-*syon* de
	autobuses	ow-to-*boo*-ses
the bus stop	*la parada de*	la pa-*ra*-da de
	autobuses	ow-to-*boo*-ses
the train station	*la estación de*	la es-ta-*syon* de
	ferrocarril	fe-ro-ka-*reel*
the luggage locker	*la consigna para*	la kon-*see*-nya para
	el equipaje	el e-kee-*pa*-khe
the ticket office	*la boletería/*	la bo-le-te-*ree*-ya/
	ticketería	tee-ke-te-*ree*-ya

A ticket to ..., please.
Un boleto a ..., por favor.
oon bo-*le*-to a ... por fa-*vor*
What's the fare to ...?
¿Cuánto cuesta hasta ...?
kwan-to *kwes*-ta a-sta ...

student's	*de estudiante*	de es-too-*dyan*-te
1st class	*primera clase*	pree-*me*-ra *kla*-se
2nd class	*segunda clase*	se-*goon*-da *kla*-se
single/one-way	*de ida*	de *ee*-da
return/round trip	*de ida y vuelta*	de *ee*-da e *vwel*-ta
taxi	*taxi*	*tak*-see

Private Transport

I'd like to	*Quisiera*	kee-*sye*-ra
hire a ...	*alquilar ...*	al-kee-*lar* ...
4WD	*un todo terreno*	oon *to*-do te-*re*-no
car	*un auto/carro*	oon ow-to/*ka*-ro
motorcycle	*una motocicleta*	oo-na mo-to-see-*kle*-ta
bicycle	*una bicicleta*	oo-na bee-see-*kle*-ta

pickup (truck)	*camioneta*	ka-myo-*ne*-ta
truck	*camión*	ka-*myon*
hitchhike	*hacer dedo*	a-ser *de*-do

Where's a gas (petrol) station?
¿Dónde hay una gasolinera/bomba?
don-de ai oo-na ga-so-lee-*ne*-ra/*bom*-ba
How much is a liter of gasoline?
¿Cuánto cuesta el litro de gasolina?
kwan-to *kwes*-ta el *lee*-tro de ga-so-*lee*-na
Please fill it up.
Lleno, por favor.
ye-no por fa-*vor*
I'd like ... worth of gas (petrol).
Quiero ... en gasolina.
kye-ro ... en ga-so-*lee*-na

diesel	*diesel*	*dee*-sel
leaded (regular)	*gasolina con*	ga-so-*lee*-na kon
	plomo	*plo*-mo

ROAD SIGNS

Acceso	Entrance
Acceso Prohibido	No Entry
Acceso Permanente	24-Hour Access
Construcción de Carreteras	Roadworks
Ceda el Paso	Give Way
Curva Peligrosa	Dangerous Curve
Despacio	Slow
Desvío/Desviación	Detour
Mantenga Su Derecha	Keep to the Right
No Adelantar	No Passing
No Hay Paso	Road Closed
No Pase	No Overtaking
Pare/Stop	Stop
Peligro	Danger
Prohibido Estacionar	No Parking
Prohibido el Paso	No Entry
Salida (de Autopista)	Exit (Freeway)

petrol (gas)	*gasolina*	ga·so·*lee*·na
unleaded	*gasolina sin plomo*	ga·so·*lee*·na seen *plo*·mo
oil	*aceite*	a·*say*·te
tire	*llanta*	*yan*·ta
puncture	*agujero*	a·goo·*khe*·ro

Is this the road to ...?
  ¿Por acquí se va a ...?
  por a·*kee* se va a ...
(How long) Can I park here?
  ¿(Por cuánto tiempo) Puedo estacionar aquí?
  (por *kwan*·to *tyem*·po) *pwe*·do ess·ta·syo·*nar* a·*kee*
Where do I pay?
  ¿Dónde se paga?
  don·de se *pa*·ga
I need a mechanic/tow truck.
  Necesito un mecánico/remolque.
  ne·se·*see*·to oon me·*ka*·nee·ko/re·*mol*·ke
Is there a garage near here?
  ¿Hay un garaje cerca de aquí?
  ai oon ga·*ra*·khe ser·ka de a·*kee*
The car has broken down in ...
  El carro se ha averiado en ...
  el *ka*·ro se a a·ve·*rya*·do en ...
The motorbike won't start.
  La moto no arranca.
  la *mo*·to no a·*ran*·ka
I have a flat tire.
  Tengo una llanta desinflada.
  ten·go oo·na *yan*·ta des·een·*fla*·da
I've run out of petrol.
  Me quedé sin gasolina.
  me ke·*de* seen ga·so·*lee*·na

I've had an accident.
  Tuve un accidente.
  too·ve oon ak·see·*den*·te

TRAVEL WITH CHILDREN
I need .../Do you have ...?
Necesito .../¿Hay ...?
ne·se·*see*·to .../ai ...
  a car baby seat
  un asiento de seguridad para bebés
  oon a·*syen*·to de se·goo·ree·*da* pa·ra be·*bes*
  a child-minding service
  oon club para niños
  oon kloob pa·*ra* nee·*nyos*
  a creche
  una guardería
  oo·na gwar·de·*ree*·a
  (disposable) diapers/nappies
  pañales (de usar y tirar)
  pa·*nya*·les (de oo·*sar* ee tee·*rar*)
  an (English-speaking) babysitter
  una niñera (que habla inglesa)
  oo·na nee·*nye*·ra (ke *a*·bla een·*gle*·sa)
  formula (milk)
  leche en polvo
  le·che en *pol*·vo
  a highchair
  una silla para bebé
  oo·na *see*·ya *pa*·ra be·*be*
  a potty
  una bacinica
  oo·na ba·see·*nee*·ka
  a stroller
  una carreola
  oona ka·re·*o*·la

Are children allowed?
  ¿Se admiten niños?
  se ad·*mee*·ten *nee*·nyos

Also available from Lonely Planet:
Latin American Spanish Phrasebook

Glossary

For terms for food, drinks and other culinary vocabulary, see p63. For additional terms and information about the Spanish language, see the Language chapter on p324. This glossary contains some words of the language of the Kuna tribe (K).

ANAM – Autoridad Nacional de Ambiente; Panama's national environmental agency
ANCON – Asociación Nacional para la Conservación de la Naturaleza; National Association for the Conservation of Nature, Panama's leading private environmental organization
apartado – post office box
árbol – tree
artesanía – handicrafts

bahía – bay
balboa – the basic unit of Panamanian currency
baño(s) – restroom(s)
biblioteca – library
bohío – see *rancho*
boleto – ticket; for bus, museum etc
boroquera – blowgun once used by the *Emberá* and *Wounaan* Indians
bote – motorized canoe
buceo – diving

caballero(s) – gentleman (gentlemen)
cabaña – cabin
cacique – *Kuna* tribal leader
calle – street
campesino/a – rural resident; peasant
carretera – highway
casa de cambio – money-exchange house
cascada – see *chorro*
catedral – cathedral
cayuco – dugout canoe
centavos – cent(s); 100 *centavos* equal one US dollar (or one Panamanian *balboa*)
cerro – hill
certificación de vuelo – certification of entry date into Panama
cerveza – beer
chévere – cool (slang)
chitra – sand fly
chiva – a rural bus, often a 28-seat Toyota coaster bus
chocosano (K) – storm that comes from the east
chorro – waterfall
cielo – the sky; the heavens

cigarro – cigarette
cine – cinema
ciudad – city
cocina – kitchen
cocobolo – a handsome tropical hardwood; used for carving life-size images of snakes, parrots, toucans and other jungle wildlife
comarca – district
conejo pintado – raccoon-like animal abundant in Parque Nacional Volcán Barú
cordillera – mountain range
corredor de aduana – customs broker
cuatro por cuatro – 4WD vehicle
cuidado – caution
Cuna – See *Kuna*

dama(s) – lady (ladies)
día feriado (días feriados) – national holiday(s)

edificio – building
Emberá – indigenous group living in Darién Province

feria – festival
fiesta – party
finca – farm
floresta – forest
frontera – border
fuerte – fort

Gali-Gali – the distinct Creole language of Bocas del Toro Province; it combines English, Spanish and Guaymí
galón (galones) – gallon(s); fluid measure of 3.79L
gringo/a – tourist; especially a North American tourist
gruta – cave
guacamayo – macaw

habano – Havana cigar
haras – stable (for horses)
herida – injury
hombre – man
hormiga – ant
hospedaje – guesthouse
huaca(s) – golden object(s); made on the Panamanian isthmus in the pre-Columbian era and buried with Indians
huevo(s) – egg(s)

iglesia – church
INAC – Instituto Nacional de Cultura; Panama's National Institute of Culture

Interamericana – the Pan-American Hwy; the nearly continuous highway running from Alaska to Chile (it breaks at the Darién Gap)
invierno – winter
IPAT – Instituto Panameño de Turismo; the national tourism agency
isla – island

kilometraje – mileage
Kuna – the 70,000-strong indigenous tribe living in the Comarca de Kuna Yala

ladrón – thief
lago – lake
lancha – motorboat
lavamático/lavandería – laundromat
librería – bookstore
llanta – tire
llantería – tire repair shop
lleno – full
lluvia – rain
loro – parrot

manglar – mangrove
mariposa – butterfly
mercado – market
Merki (K) – American
mestizo/a – person of mixed indigenous and Spanish ancestry
metate – flat stone platform; used by Panama's pre-Columbian Indians to grind corn
migración – immigration
Migración y Naturalización – Immigration and Naturalization office
mirador – lookout point
molas (K) – colorful hand-stitched appliqué textiles made by Kuna women
mono – monkey
montaña – mountain
montuno – fine embroidered shirt; typically worn during festivals on the Península de Azuero
muelle – pier
mujer(es) – woman (women)
museo – museum

nadar – to swim
Naso – an indigenous group scattered throughout the Bocas del Toro Province; also called the Teribe
Ngöbe Buglé – an indigenous tribe located largely in Chiriquí Province

ola(s) – wave(s)

pájaro – bird
palapa – thatched, palm leaf–roofed shelter with open sides

panadería – bakery
parada (de autobús) – bus stop
Patois – a local dialect on the islands of Boca del Toro; a blend of English, Spanish and Gali-Gali
PDF – the Panama Defense Forces; the national army under Manuel Noriega
penca – palm tree leaves
permiso de salida – exit permit
pescador – fisherman
pescar – to fish
piragua – canoe carved from a tree trunk
playa – beach
polleras – the intricate, lacy, Spanish-influenced dresses of the Península de Azuero; the national dress of Panama for festive occasions
pozo(s) – spring(s)
preservativo(s) – condom(s)
prohibido – prohibited; forbidden
prórroga de turista – a permit that resembles a driver's license, complete with photo; it allows you to stay in Panama for longer than the 90 days permitted for tourists
propina – tip; gratuity
protector solar – sunscreen lotion
puente – bridge
puerto – port
punta – point
puro – cigar

quebrada – stream

rana – frog
rana dorada – golden frog
rancho – a thatched-roof hut
regalo – gift; present
río – river

seco – an 80- to 100-proof alcohol distilled from sugarcane
selva – jungle
Semana Santa – Holy Week; preceding Easter
sendero – trail
serpiente – snake
serranía – mountain range
sol – sun
supermercado – supermarket

tabla – surfboard
tagua – an ivory-colored nut that is carved into tiny figurines
taller – workshop
tarjeta(s) – plastic phonecard(s)
tarjeta de circulación – vehicle control certificate
taxi marino – water taxi
tigre – jaguar
típico – typical; traditional Panamanian folk music
tortuga – sea turtle

traje de baño – swimsuit
trucha – trout
urbano – local (as in buses)

valle – valley
verano – summer

viajero – traveler
viento – wind
volcán – volcano

waga (K) – tourist
Wounaan – indigenous group living in Darién Province

Behind the Scenes

THIS BOOK

This 3rd edition of Panama was written by Regis St. Louis. The 1st and 2nd editions were written by Scott Doggett. The Health chapter was written by Dr David Goldberg.

THANKS from the Author

This book is dedicated to the memory of my father, Ralph St. Louis.

I owe a big thanks to Scott Doggett for his excellent work on previous editions. The dozens of Peace Corps volunteers who helped me out deserve much credit; their dedication to sustainable development in Panama is truly admirable.

Many travelers and friends on the road also gave invaluable assistance: I thank KC, Claire, Ovidio Diaz-Espino, Rikke, Francis, Anne and Christian. I'd also like to thank Ancon Expeditions and Rick Morales, Richard Cahill, Julie Gomez, Ivan Hoyos and Marco Gandásegui.

As always, I'm grateful to my family for their support. Cassandra, you're the best.

CREDITS

Panama 3 was commissioned and developed in Lonely Planet's Oakland office by David Zingarelli, Kalya Ryan, Jeff Campbell, Erin Corrigan and Alex Hershey. Cartography for this guide was developed by Alison Lyall. This book was coordinated by Holly Alexander (editorial) and Owen Eszeki (cartography). Editing and proofing assistance was provided by Susannah Farfor, Brooke Lyons, Simone Egger, Suzannah Shwer, Samantha McCrow, Miriam Cannell, Jackey Coyle and Diana Saad. Michael Ruff

laid the book out. Gerilyn Atterbery designed the cover and James Hardy designed the cover artwork. Quentin Frayne prepared the language chapter. Overseeing production were Rachel Imeson (Project Manager), Chris Love (Acting Project Manager), Kerryn Burgess (Managing Editor) and Danielle North (Acting Managing Editor), with assistance from Gabbi Wilson.

THANKS from Lonely Planet

Many thanks to the hundreds of travelers who used the last edition and wrote to us with helpful hints, useful advice and interesting anecdotes:

A Stijn Aerts, Philip Alonzo, Scott Alperin, Jane Althorpe, Abigail Arauz, Pasquel Archibold, Daniel Arlotto, Andrea Aster, Serena Ayers, Sulun Aykurt, **B** Olaf Bahner, Amy Bann, Deborah Bansemer, Wilson Barton, Cynthia Berardocco, Tanya Bhalla, Sheila Bharat, Dimitri Blondel, David Blood, Jan Bohuslav, Bev Bourdin, Len Bourdin, David Bradley, Julika Breyer, Corina Browne, Martin Buehner, **C** Joshua Campbell, Laura Capinas, Bill Carleton, David Clayton, Stéphane Clément, Sybil Cline, Rachel Cohn, Chiara Conrado, Sarah Corkill, Paula Cormack, Cornelia Cotton, **D** Steven Davey, Alexandra de Sousa, John Deacon, María del Mar, John A Delong, Julian Dendy, Eliot Deutsch, Andrew Donohue, W Dorm, Chris & Sally Drysdale, Andy Dunbar, Varna Dutton, **E** Claus-Dieter Ellerbrock, Alastair England, Reinhard Enne, **F** Nicolas Fabbroni, Jess Falkenhagen, Mary Feldbruegge, Michelle Finkel, Brenda Fleming, Joseph Foss, Carl Frankel, **G** Angie Gammage, Carlo Gandolfi, Albert Garcia Muret, Alfred Geduldig, Beth Genovese, Lauren Giles, WJ Glass, Lisa Gough, Carl T Grimm, Kara Griswold, Susan Guberman-Garcia, **H** Carolyn Hall, Andrea Hamel, Mark Handel, Mulle Harbort, Bill Hassett, Brian Hatoff, Jerry Hedrick, Paul Hendel, Buck Hendrickson, Suzanne Heskin, Michael G Hinton, Sylvan Howells, Wu Ming Hsuan, Klothilde Hubner,

---

THE LONELY PLANET STORY

The story begins with a classic travel adventure: Tony and Maureen Wheeler's 1972 journey across Europe and Asia to Australia. There was no useful information about the overland trail then, so Tony and Maureen published the first Lonely Planet guidebook to meet a growing need.

From a kitchen table, Lonely Planet has grown to become the largest independent travel publisher in the world, with offices in Melbourne (Australia), Oakland (USA), London (UK) and Paris (France).

Today Lonely Planet guidebooks cover the globe. There is an ever-growing list of books and information in a variety of media. Some things haven't changed. The main aim is still to make it possible for adventurous travellers to get out there – to explore and better understand the world.

At Lonely Planet we believe travellers can make a positive contribution to the countries they visit – if they respect their host communities and spend their money wisely.

Adrian P Hull, Holly Hummel, **J** Ernesto Jonas, Esther Julier, Jae A Junkunc, Emily Keller, **K** David Kimball, Jos Koeleman, Mart Kok, Bart Konings, Benjamin Kroymann, Frank Kunc, **L** Robbin Lacy, Alexander Lang, Tom Larg, Hanne & Bruce Lawrence, Giselle Leung, Mervyn Lewis, Christian Liechti, Chris Little, Jordi Llorens Estape, Crystal Lorentzson, Gary Lowe, Steve Luce, Jason Maas-Baldwin, **M** Cinda MacKinnon, Eleanor Marquardt, Allegra Marshall, Alfred Martin, Jost Maurin, Edward McDonagh, Julie McGinn, Kristen McIvor, Phyllis McNaughton, Seán McNulty, Kirk Melcher, Debra Miersma, Belinda Minc, Rob Minc, David Miner, Mara Mlyn, Jonathan Moore, Tom Moore, P Moors, Jürg Mosimann, **N** Gregory Narizny, Lindsey Newbold, Nuno Nicolau, Charles Noirot, **O** Abdiel O'Callaghan, Carlos Olagüe, **P** Anne Parms, Fernando Pascal, Jerry Peters, Peter & Marian Phelan, John Phippen, Nicole Piscatelli, Becky Pledger, Sarah Porterfield, Michel Prevo, Andrea Puszkar, **R** Christy Rauch, Lisa Reeber, Linda Reynolds, Melissa Riccio, Mike Riley, Sioney Roach, Nathalie Robin, Philip Rodrigues, Amy Roleder, Hwa-Ling Russell, Casey Ryan, **S** Carl Salk, Melissa Santos, Laura Sawyer, David Schrier, Caroline Schwander Stolz, Brad Seevers, David Slobodin, David T Smith, Jennifer Smith, Jim Smith, Abbe Solomon, Randi Somers, Jakke St Clair, Robin Solomon Stevens, Ursula Strauss, Wolfram Strempfer, Dana & Diane Stringham, Barbara Strohbach, Amanda Sykes, **T** Lorenzo Taube, Marcel & Mara ten Cate, Anita Thewes, Chase Thompson, **V** Bart van Schie, Shalom & Vito Victor, Axel Vogt, **W** Wilfried Wagner, Pat & Al Wall, Peter Ward, Michael Washington, Kevin Waters, Will Wattles, Rachael Wellby, Sue Wentworth, Sandra Whiteley, Borre Wickstrom, Zita Wigger, Fiona Wilkinson, Gordon Williams, Merlin Williams, Carmen T Wong, Karen Wood, **Z** Tara Zagofsky, Jared Zaugg.

ACKNOWLEDGMENTS

Many thanks to the following for the use of their content:

Globe on back cover – Mountain High Maps® © 1993 Digital Wisdom, Inc

Index

A

accommodations 13, 14, 292-3
Achiote 256-7
activities 11, 53-62, 293, *see also
   individual activities*
Aguadulce 155-8, **156**
air travel 306-8
   airlines 306-7
   to/from Panama 307-8
   within Panama 13, 310, **311**
Almirante 243
ANAM 52
ANCON 52
animals 6, 21, 42-4
Antón 149
Araúz, Amado 285
Araúz, Hernán 285, 290, 313
Araúz, Reina 285
archeological sites 25, 154, 167
Archipiélago de Bocas del Toro
   227-42, **228**, 8
Archipiélago de las Perlas 8, 126-31,
   127
Arias, Arnulfo 30, 31
arts 38-40, *see also* handicrafts
ATMs 300
Ávila, Pedro Arias de 26

B

Balboa, Vasco Núñez de 15, 26
Bambito 219
banana industry 225
Bastidas, Rodrigo de 26
bathrooms 302
beaches 8, 22, **137**
   Boca del Drago 231
   Gorgona 137
   Playa Barqueta 205-6
   Playa Blanca 263
   Playa Cacique 128-9
   Playa Cambutal 183
   Playa Coronado 137-8
   Playa de las Suecas 128-9
   Playa de Muerto 291
   Playa Ejecutiva 128-9
   Playa El Aguillito 166
   Playa El Istmito 231
   Playa El Palmar 138
   Playa El Rompío 175-6
   Playa El Toro 180

Playa Galeón 128-9
Playa Guánico 183
Playa La Garita 180
Playa Larga 128-9
Playa Las Lajas 207-8
Playa Monagre 175-6
Playa Río Mar 138
Playa Santa Catalina 8
Playa Venao 8, 182
bicycling 62
bioprospecting 50
birds 42-3
   books 42, 49, 61
   migration 166
bird watching 46-7, 60-1,
   Alto de Piedra 192
   Archipiélago de Bocas del Toro 231
   Cana 286
   Cerro Tute 192
   Parque Nacional Soberanía 121
   Refugio de Vida Silvestre Isla
      Taboga 125
   San Lorenzo Protected Area 256
bird watching societies 89
Black Christ Festival 260
Blades, Rubén 15, 31, 32
boat travel 61-2, 310-12, *see also*
   kayaking, white-water rafting
Boca del Drago 231
Bocas del Toro (town) 8, 227-38, **230**
   accommodations 233-5
   drinking 236-7
   food 235-6
   travel to/from 237
Bocas del Toro Province 13, 223-47,
   224, 226
Bolívar, Simón 82
books, *see also* literature
   arts 34, 37
   biography 37
   birds 42, 49, 61
   environment 41, 50, 52, 60, 61
   fiction 33, 34, 35, 36, 38
   food 63, 64, 66, 67, 68
   health 317
   history 15, 25, 27, 30, 31, 54
   indigenous peoples 33, 34, 37
   Panama Canal 28, 61
   politics 31
   travel 14-16

wildlife 42, 44, 49, 51, 61
Boquete 208-16, **209**
   accommodations 212-14
   attractions 210-12
   food 214-15
   Internet access 208
   tourist information 209-10
   travel to/from/within 215-16
border crossings 308-9
Bosque Protector Palo Seco 242-3
Buena Vista 216-17
business hours 293-4
bus travel 309-10, 312

C

Camino Real 27
Cana 286-8
Cañita 132-3
Capira 135
car travel 310, 312
Carnaval
   Aguadulce 158
   Las Tablas 178
   Los Santos 175
   Panama City 14, 91-2
   Península de Azuero 14
   Penonomé 149
Cartí Suitupo 273-4
Casco Viejo 9, 81, **80, 82**, 9, 12
Causeway 86-7
caves 239
Cayos Holandéses 275
Cayos Los Grullos 275
Cayos Ordupuquip 275
Cerro Punta 219-20
Changuinola 244-6, **244-5**
Changuinola Canal 242
Chepo 132
children, traveling with 67, 90, 294,
   322
Chiriquí Province 198-222, **199, 200**
Chitré 161-5, **162**
cigars 151-2
climate 13-14, 294
Coclé Province 139-58, **140, 141**
Colón (town) 252-4, **253**
Colón Province 248-65, **249, 250-1**
colonization 25-7
Columbus, Christopher 15, 26, 187,
   225

Comarca de Kuna Yala 8, 13, 266-78, **267**, **268-9**, 8
consulates 297
Corazón de Jesús 276
Corpus Christi 298
costs 14, 16
courses 90, 232, 295
credit cards 300
crime 295, 296-7
Cruce de Ocú 169-70
culture 33-40
customs regulations 295
cycling 62

D

Darién Gap 53, 54, 131-132, 283-4, 285
Darién Province 279-91, **280**, **282**
David 202-5, **203**
  accomodations 202-4
  food 204
  Internet access 202
  tourist information 202
  travel to/from 204-5
  travel within 205
decompression chambers 54
deep vein thrombosis (DVT) 317
deforestation 45, 49-50, 166
  Darién Province 24, 49-50, 51
dengue fever 318-19
diarrhea 321
disabled travelers 297
diving & snorkeling 46-7, 54-5, 296
  Archipiélago de Bocas del Toro 231
  Isla Contadora 129
  Isla de Coiba 193-4, 197
  Isla Taboga 125
  Portobelo 259
Drake, Francis 15, 26, 250, 263
drinks 64-5
driving 310, 312
drug trafficking 271, 295

E

economy 24, 32
El Charcón 183
El Porvenir 272
El Real 285
El Valle 141-7, **143**
  accommodations 145-6
  attractions 142-4

food 146
  medical services 142
  tourist information 142
  tours 144-5
  travel to/from 146
  travel within 147
electricity 293
embassies 297
Emberá people 38, 281-3, 289, 10, see also indigenous peoples
emergencies, see inside front cover
Endara, Guillermo 24, 30, 31
environment 32, 41-52, see also deforestation
  conservation 45, 50, 51
  Internet resources 50, 52
  organizations 52, 304-5
Escobal 256
exchange rates, see inside front cover

F

Feria de Azuero 175
Feria de la Chorrera 135
Feria de la Mejorana 177
festivals 14, 15, 298, see also Carnaval
  Black Christ Festival 260
  Corpus Christi 298
  Feria de Azuero 175
  Feria de la Chorrera 135
  Feria de la Mejorana 177
  Fiesta de Corpus Christi 175
  Semana Santa 298
Fiesta de Corpus Christi 175
Finca La Suiza 221-2
fishing 62, 197
food 63, 65-9, 298
  customs 66, 67-8
  restaurants 14, 65-8
  vegetarian & vegan 66
  vocabulary 68-9, 327
Fuerte Davis 257
Fuerte Espinar 257
Fuerte San Lorenzo 255

G

Gamboa Rainforest Resort 32, 122
Gatún Dam 255
Gatún Locks 254-5
Gauguin, Paul 15, 40
gays & lesbians 298
Gehry, Frank 15, 87
geography 41, 42
gold 25, 27
Golfo de Chiriquí 206
Gorgona 137

Greene, Graham 15
Guabito 309
Guadalupe 220-1
Guararé 176-7

H

handicrafts 39, 281
  purchasing 110-11, 142, 193, 237, 301
harpy eagles 42, 48, 121, 286
health 316-23
  of children 322
  diarrhea 321
  infectious diseases 318-21
  insurance 316-17
  Internet resources 317
  vaccinations 316, 317
hepatitis A 319
hepatitis B 319
Herrera Province 159-70, **160**, **161**
Higueronal 134
hiking 46-7, 53-4, 211, 287
  safety 295
history 25-32, 33
  independence from Colombia 24, 28
  independence from Spain 27
  Scottish colonization 27
  US invasion 148
hitchhiking 312
holidays 298-9, see also festivals
hot springs 205, 208
huacas 111, 301
Humboldt Ecological Station 166

I

Iglesia San Francisco de Veraguas 189-90
Ikuptupu 273
immigration 35
indigenous peoples 10, 19, 25-6, 33, 34-5, 201, see also individual tribes
  women 38
insurance 299
  health 316-17
Interamericana 18, 131-2
Internet access 299
Internet resources 16, 317
Ipetí 133
Isla Ailigandí 277
Isla Barro Colorado 13
Isla Bastimentos 8, 239-41
Isla Carenero 238-9
Isla Colón 227-8
Isla Contadora 128-31, **130**

000 Map pages
000 Location of color photographs

Isla de Cañas 182-3
Isla de Coiba 51
Isla Grande 261-3
Isla Iskardup 277
Isla Pino 278
Isla San José 131
Isla Taboga 8, 123-6, **8**
Isla Tigre 276-7
Isla Tupile 277
Isla Uaguitupo 277
itineraries 17-22, **17-22**

J

jagua fruit 281, 289
Jaqué 291
Jimmy's Caribbean Dive Resort 265

K

kayaking 61, 147, 214, 231
King's Highway, *see* Camino Real
Kuanidup 274
Kuna people 35, 269-71, 273, **10**, *see also* indigenous peoples

L

Lago Bayano 133
Lagunas de Volcán 46-7, 218
language 227, 324-31
language courses 232, 295
La Arena 163
La Chorrera 134-5
La Palma 288
La Pintada 151-2
La Rica 153-4
Las Aguas Frías 283-4
Las Cruces Trail, *see* Sendero Las Cruces
Las Delicias 246-7
Las Palmas 193
Las Piscinas 157, **11**
Las Tablas 177-9, **178**
legal matters 299
leishmaniasis 319
leptospirosis 319-20
lesbians & gays 298
Lesseps, Ferdinand-Marie de 15
lifestyle 34
literature 16, 38, *see also* books
Los Santos Province 171-83, **172, 173**

M

Macaracas 183
malaria 320
Mamardup 274

maps 299
masks 168, 175, 301
medical services 318
Menchú, Rigoberto 16
Meseta Chorcha 207
Metetí 284
metric conversions, *see inside front cover*
molas 39, 111, 237, 301
money 14, 299-300, *see also inside front cover*
monkeys 43, 44, 60, 206
Monumento Nacional Isla Barro Colorado 46-7, 122
Morgan, Henry 27, 72, 84, 250
Moscoso, Mireya 24, 31, 32, 45
motorcycle travel 310, 312
Mulatupo Sasardí 278
museums 89
  Museo Belisario Porras 177-8
  Museo de Arte Religioso Colonial 82
  Museo de Herrera 163
  Museo del Canal Interoceánico 83
music 38-9

N

Nalunega 272
Naranjo Chico 274-5
Narganá 276
Natá 154-5
national parks & reserves 7, 21, 44-5, 46-7, **48-9**
  Parque Internacional La Amistad 45, 221, 247
  Parque Nacional Cerro Hoya 197
  Parque Nacional Coiba 7, 195-7, **196**
  Parque Nacional Darién 7, 13, 45, **7**
  Parque Nacional Marino Golfo de Chiriquí 7, 206
  Parque Nacional Marino Isla Bastimentos 242, **7**
  Parque Nacional Omar Torrijos 7, 141, 153-4
  Parque Nacional Sariguá 161, 166
  Parque Nacional Soberanía 7, 121, **11**
  Parque Nacional Volcán Barú 7, 216
  Parque Nacional y Reserva Biológica Altos de Campana 135-6
  Parque Natural Metropolitano 89-90
  Refugio de Vida Silvestre Cenegón del Mangle 161, 168
  Refugio de Vida Silvestre Isla de Cañas 46-7
  Refugio de Vida Silvestre Isla Iguana 181
  Reserva Natural Punta Patiño 288
New Edinburgh 27
newspapers 293
Nicuesa, Diego de 26
Nombre de Dios 26, 263-5
Noriega, Manuel 15, 24, 30-1
Nusagandi 132
Nusatupo 274

O

Ocú 168-9
Ogobsibu 272
orchids 191, 219, **6**
  books 44

P

Panama Canal 20, 45, 119-20, **120**
  history 29-30
  Internet resources 29
  locks 88, 119, 254-5
  murals 87-8
  museum 83
  tours 119-20
  treaties 24, 29-30
  US withdrawal 24, 32
Panama City 12, 70-114, **71, 72-3, 76-7, 78-9, 12**
  accommodations 92-8
  attractions 74, 81-90
  Carnaval 14, 91-2
  Casco Viejo 9, 81, **80, 82, 9, 12**
  Causeway 86-7
  courses 90
  drinking 106-8
  emergency services 75
  entertainment 108-10
  food 98-106
  history 26-9, 72-4, 81, 83-4
  Internet access 75
  medical services 79, 318
  Panamá Viejo 83, **85**
  safe travel 81
  shopping 87, 110-12
  tours 90-1
  tourist information 80
  travel to/from 112-13
  travel within 113-14
  walking tour 82, **82**
Panama hats 39, 151, 152, 169, 191
Panamá Province 115-38, **116, 118**
Panama Railroad 28

Panamá Viejo 9, 83, **85**
Parita 167-8
Parque Internacional La Amistad 45, 46-7, 221, 247
Parque Nacional Cerro Hoya 46-7, 197
Parque Nacional Coiba 7, 44, 46-7, 195-7, **196**
Parque Nacional Darién 7, 13, 45, 46-7, 7
Parque Nacional Marino Golfo de Chiriquí 7, 46-7
Parque Nacional Marino Isla Basti-mentos 46-7, 242, 7
Parque Nacional Omar Torrijos 7, 46-7, 141, 153-4
Parque Nacional Sariqua 46-7, 161, 166
Parque Nacional Soberanía 7, 46-7, 121, 11
Parque Nacional Volcán Barú 7, 46-7, 216
Parque Nacional y Reserva Biológica Altos de Campana 46-47, 135-6
Parque Natural Metropolitano 46-7, 89-90
Paso Ancho 219
Paso Canoas 308-9
passports 303-4, 306, see also visas
Pearl Islands, see Archipiélago de las Perlas
pearls 126-7
Pedasí 179-81
Pedrarias, see Ávila, Pedro Arias de
Penonomé 149-51, **150**
Pérez Balladares, Ernesto 31
Pesé 168
photography 40, 300-1
Pipeline Rd 121
pirates 84, 123-4, 128, 201, 225
Pirre Station 285-6
planning 13-16
    national holidays 298-9
plants 44
Playa Barqueta 205-6
Playa Blanca 263
Playa Cacique 128-9
Playa Cambutal 183
Playa Coronado 137-8
Playa de las Suecas 128-9
Playa de Muerto 291
Playa Ejecutiva 128-9
Playa El Aguillito 166

Playa El Istmito 231
Playa El Palmar 138
Playa El Rompío 175-6
Playa El Toro 180
Playa Galeón 128-9
Playa Guánico 183
Playa La Garita 180
Playa Larga 128-9
Playa Las Lajas 207-8
Playa Monagre 175-6
Playa Río Mar 138
Playa Santa Catalina 8
Playa Venao 8, 182
police corruption 295
politics 24, 33
polleras 39, 176-7, 179, 301
population 24, 34-5
Portobelo 257-61, **257**, 9
postal services 301
    stamps 33
Punta Burica 206-7
Punta Chame 136
Punulosa 284

Q
Quebrada Sal 239
quetzals 42, 43, 60

R
rabies 320
racism 36
radio 293
rafting, see white-water rafting
Refugio de Vida Silvestre Cenegón del Mangle 46-7, 161, 168
Refugio de Vida Silvestre Isla de Cañas 46-7
Refugio de Vida Silvestre Isla Iguana 46-7, 181
religion 37
    Baha'i 123
Reserva Natural Punta Patiño 46-7, 288
reserves, see national parks & reserves
Río Azúcar 275-6
Río Farallón 148-9
Río Hato 148-9
Río Sambú 289-90
Río Sereno 221, 309
Río Sidra 274
rock carvings 208

S
safe travel 81, 295-7
    crime 295, 296-7

diving safety 296
driving 310
drug trafficking 271, 295
hiking safety 295
hitchhiking 312
swimming safety 230-1, 296
Salt Creek, see Quebrada Sal
San José 169
San Lorenzo Project 45
San Lorenzo Protected Area 256-7
San-San Pond Sak Wetlands 46-47, 246
Santa Catalina 193-5
Santa Clara 147-8, 218-19
Santa Fé (Darién) 284
Santa Fé (Veraguas) 190-3, **190**
Santana, Valentín 15
Santiago 188-9, **188**
Santo Domingo 179
scuba diving, see diving & snorkeling
sea turtles 43-4, 242, 246
seco 64, 65
    factory 168
Semana Santa 298
Sendero Las Cruces 26, 121
shipwrecks 27
shopping 301
Smithsonian Tropical Research Institute 13, 41, 52, 89
snakes 322
snorkeling, see diving & snorkeling
solo travelers 301
Soná 193
special events 298, see also festivals
sports 35
surfing 55-60, 231, **56-7**, see also beaches
    surf lessons 194
Survivor 128
Swan Cay 242
swimming safety 230-1, 296

T
taxes 300, 307
taxis 313
telephone services 302
time 302, **323**
tipping 300
toilets 302
Tonosí 183
Torrijos, Martín 24, 32
Torrijos Herrera, Omar 24, 30, 34, 37
Tortí 133
tourism 24
tourist information 302-3

tours 313-15
traditional medicine 318
train travel 113, 254, 315
transportation 306-15
    to/from Panama 306-10
    vocabulary 330-1
    within Panama 310-15
traveler's checks 300
trekking, *see* hiking
Tropic Star Lodge 290
TV 293
typhoid 320

U
Union Club 36
US Army School of the Americas 257

Ustupo Ogobsucum 277-8

V
vaccinations 316, 317
vegetarian travelers 66
Veraguas Province 184-97, **185**, **186**
Villa de Los Santos 173-5, **174**
visas 303-4, *see also* passports
Volcán 217-18
Volcán Barú 41, 211, 216, 7

W
walking, *see* hiking
weights & measures 293, *see also*
    inside front cover
Wetso 247

whale-watching 6, 125
white-water rafting 61, 210-11, 214
Wichub-Walá 272-3
wildlife, *see* animals
women in Panama 36, 37-8
women travelers 304
work 304
Wounaan people 38, 281-283, *see also*
    indigenous peoples

Y
Yaviza 284
yellow fever 321

Z
Zona Libre 251, 252-4

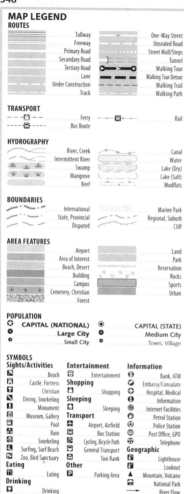

MAP LEGEND

ROUTES

Tollway	One-Way Street
Freeway	Unsealed Road
Primary Road	Street Mall/Steps
Secondary Road	Tunnel
Tertiary Road	Walking Tour
Lane	Walking Tour Detour
Under Construction	Walking Trail
Track	Walking Path

TRANSPORT

Ferry	Rail
Bus Route	

HYDROGRAPHY

River, Creek	Canal
Intermittent River	Water
Swamp	Lake (Dry)
Mangrove	Lake (Salt)
Reef	Mudflats

BOUNDARIES

International	Marine Park
State, Provincial	Regional, Suburb
Disputed	Cliff

AREA FEATURES

Airport	Land
Area of Interest	Park
Beach, Desert	Reservation
Building	Rocks
Campus	Sports
Cemetery, Christian	Urban
Forest	

POPULATION

CAPITAL (NATIONAL)	●	CAPITAL (STATE)	
	Large City	●	Medium City
	Small City	●	Town, Village

SYMBOLS

Sights/Activities	Entertainment	Information
Beach	Entertainment	Bank, ATM
Castle, Fortress	**Shopping**	Embassy/Consulate
Christian	Shopping	Hospital, Medical
Diving, Snorkeling	**Sleeping**	Information
Monument	Sleeping	Internet Facilities
Museum, Gallery	**Transport**	Petrol Station
Pool	Airport, Airfield	Police Station
Ruin	Bus Station	Post Office, GPO
Snorkeling	Cycling, Bicycle Path	Telephone
Surfing, Surf Beach	General Transport	**Geographic**
Zoo, Bird Sanctuary	Taxi Rank	Lighthouse
Eating	**Other**	Lookout
Eating	Parking Area	Mountain, Volcano
Drinking		National Park
Drinking		River Flow
		Waterfall

LONELY PLANET OFFICES

Australia
Head Office
Locked Bag 1, Footscray, Victoria 3011
☎ 03 8379 8000, fax 03 8379 8111
talk2us@lonelyplanet.com.au

USA
150 Linden St, Oakland, CA 94607
☎ 510 893 8555, toll free 800 275 8555
fax 510 893 8572, info@lonelyplanet.com

UK
72–82 Rosebery Ave,
Clerkenwell, London EC1R 4RW
☎ 020 7841 9000, fax 020 7841 9001
go@lonelyplanet.co.uk

France
1 rue du Dahomey, 75011 Paris
☎ 01 55 25 33 00, fax 01 55 25 33 01
bip@lonelyplanet.fr, www.lonelyplanet.fr

Published by Lonely Planet Publications Pty Ltd
ABN 36 005 607 983

© Lonely Planet 2004

© photographers as indicated 2004

Cover photographs: Kuna woman with traditional bead anklets, David Samuel Robbins/APL Corbis (front); The poisonous Strawberry Dart Frog, Alfredo Maiquez/Lonely Planet Images (back). Many of the images in this guide are available for licensing from Lonely Planet Images: www.lonelyplanetimages.com.

Printed through The Bookmaker International Ltd
Printed in China

Stevenson College Edinburgh
Bankhead Ave, EDIN EH11 4DE